FORGOTTEN HEROES
The Charge of the Heavy Brigade

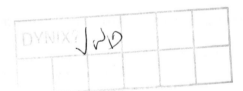

Roy Dutton BSc

Dedicated to my mother and father.

First published 25th October 2008 in Great Britain by InfoDial Ltd
Maritime House
14-16 Balls Road
Oxton, Wirral
CH43 5RE

www.infodial.co.uk

We are always interested in feedback from readers
email : feedback@infodial.co.uk

Contents

Acknowledgements

The highly successful Charge of the Heavy Brigade and the individuals who took part,has been ignored by most Historians, in favour of the disastrous Charge of the Light Brigade. Both events took place on the 25th October 1854.

To date no book has ever been written on the subject. My previous book Forgotten Heroes the Charge of the Light brigade, had the benefit of a wealth of material to research. Unfortunately this was not the case with The Heavy Brigade.

I would like to take this opportunity to thank the many friends and colleagues who have assisted my quest for information, their help and advice has been most helpful.

Doctor John Rumsby for putting the benefit of his wide knowledge at my disposal, and for checking the final draft.

Paul Burns for allowing me access to John Darwent's Achive, all the data was methodically stored on a manual card index system, which he very kindly photographed.

The Most Honourable The Marques of Anglesey, who has graciously allowed me to use extracts from his book Little Hodge, His Letters and Diaries of the Crimean War 1854-1856.

Special thanks are due to Captain (Retd) Alan Henshall Curator of The Regimental Museum of the Royal Dragoon Guards for access to the regimental archive, and for a most interesting personal tour of the Museum.

Roy Washington supplied some very useful information together with some original documents from The Canon Lummis Archive.

Mr Kevin Asplin and Sons for there help in photographing the various Scutari Musters and Discharge Books. Regrettably the Scutari Musters before January 1855 are "missing presumed lost"

My good friend Mr Chris Poole for his unwavering encouragement, and proof reading skills.

Jamie Hughes for his patience in helping me with the page layouts and graphic design. Plus numerous difficulties encountered on my climb to the heights of InDesign.

Mr Glenn Fisher for some spectacular portraits of officers of the 6th Inniskilling.

Miss Juliet McConnell, National Army Museum, for her help in locating some important documents.

Numerous individuals contributed information including, Derek Pardoe, Barney Mattingly,Michael Tweel, Peter Hill, John Lester, Helen and Ian Smith. Jennie McGregor-Smith, and Robert Cruse.

The work by Andrew Sewell entitled The Cavalry Division in the Crimea. An unpublished work can only be admired for its complete and accurate account of the Medal Rolls.

Newspaper reports play an important part in this work. With every issue of The Times published between 1785-1985, digitally scanned and fully searchable, it really helps to glue the fabric of history together. If only others were to follow their fine example while the records are still intact.

Finally without access to the National Archives at Kew none of my endeavours would have been possible. My only regret is to witness the disintegration of many of these fine records, missing pages. and musters falling apart from there bindings. Without intervention these records will not be available for future generations to enjoy and appreciate the endeavours of our forefathers.

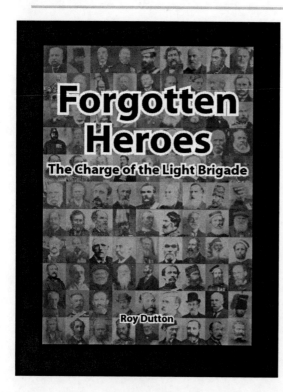

First in the series of Forgotten Heroes, The Charge of the Light Brigade. Contains first hand accounts of the men who took part in the heroic and tragic Charge at the Battle of Balaclava on the 25th October 1854.

Previously unpublished biographies of the men and photographs bring their stories to life. What became of our heroes? Some died penniless while others found fame and fortune.

Set within an unrelenting and cruel military campaign, where many would perish, unravelling the myths to find many of the missing Chargers was a massive undertaking.

With an a additional 47 Chargers identified, bringing the total number of known Chargers to 562 and 29 marked as "Possibily rode in the Charge"

This book is about the ordinary people that made an Empire and gave the World a Legacy.

(ISBN: 0955655404) 420 pages. Hardback.
(800 b/w photos, illustrations & tables)
First Edition

Introduction

The Charge of the Heavy Brigade at Balaclava on the 25th October 1854, is one of the most neglected events in the annals of British military history. On the day in question the Heavy Brigade were involved in two separate charges.

The first was the successful charge of the Brigade on the advancing Russian cavalry, who were intent on capturing the over crowded port of Balaclava, the main supply point for the British army.

The second was in support of the Light Brigade on their unsuccessful attack on the Russian artillery. Raglan's real intention was to prevent the Russians from removing the British guns situated in the redoubts along the Causeway heights, but the orders were confused. As the Light Brigade advanced down the valley the Heavies followed in support. Lord Lucan had sufficient foresight to halt the advance which had come under heavy bombardment, to prevent the brigade from being annihilated in the same fashion as the Light Brigade.

In character General Scarlett in command of the Heavy Brigade was brave, good-natured and unassuming; his men holding him in great regard. In contrast Lord Cardigan in command of the Light Brigade was wealthy, out spoken and full of his own self-importance. Both were involved in cavalry charges on the same day. The Heavy Brigade under the command of General Scarlett had assembled at the foot of the heights, organizing his troopers into a near perfect formation, he instructed his trumpeter to sound the charge. Then against all odds they attacked a Russian force which outnumbered them 5:1. The charge was made uphill against an oncoming force, the British taking few casualties the Russians were routed and annihilated and the British forces could claim another victory.

Lord Cardigan charged later as a direct result of a garbled message and a total misunderstanding. Riding straight at the Russian artillery located at the end of the valley, with enemy guns to the left and right of them. The result was the loss of the brigade with 118 men killed, and 127 wounded or taken prisoner.

Following on from the Charge of the Light Brigade William Russell was to write a poignant newspaper report which appeared in the Times some three weeks later. This in turn inspired Tennyson to write a poem, published on the 9th December 1854. The result was Cardigan landing to a hero's welcome at Dover the following January.

The poem was recited up and down the country in music halls. The scene was now set to immortalise the Charge of the Light Brigade who charged into the "jaws of death." The heroism of all the men involved in both of the charges along with their unwavering devotion to duty should have been equally recognised. As an after thought Tennyson wrote a poem about the Charge of the Heavy Brigade some 28 years after the event.

Various authors have put the total of Heavy Brigade troopers who charged at between 600 - 900. The number of men who were effective on the 25th October was 1311. There were 945 horses available taken from the musters. No allowance has been made for sick horses. To arrive at a meaningful number who could have participated, we would need to remove a quarter, approximately 327 men and horses from the total who were engaged on forage duties (see note 1). There would probably be pickets in position at various positions in the valley. We can add to this total 91 officers with their own horses, giving a grand total of 709.

Men and Horses effective on the 25th October 1854

Regiment	Effective men	Balaclava Clasp	No. Horses 1st Oct 1854	Horses Died 1-24th Oct	Horses available 25th Oct	Horses Lost in the Charge
Staff	13	13			13	
1st	253	239	182**		182**	22
2nd	300	270	156	3	153	22
4th	265	245	217	7	210	2
5th	245	230	220	7	213	17
6th	248	237	190*	3	187	35
Totals	1311	1234	965	20	945	76

* Includes 35 horses supplied by the Light Brigade on the 19th October
** Taken from Little Hodge p83 (Number of horses available on the 1st November)

Note 1 - A military board was assembled to discuss the findings of the Commissioners sent out to the Crimea in February 1855 to investigate the inefficiency of the supply chain with horses starving and men lacking basic necessities. Below are two extracts:

Because of the failings of the Commissariat, the Heavy Brigade was obliged to use its own horses to transport supplies from Balaclava. The duties included "carrying up of their own forage from Balaclava, and furnishing parties occasionally to bring down sick and carry up provisions to the front (which seems never to have occupied more than about a fifth of the whole)." This together with a stronger picket in the valley; and inlying pickets.

The next question to Lord Cardigan concerned the starvation of the horses of the Light Brigade, and why he did not seek assistance from the Heavy Brigade, when he found the Commissariat transport failing "What then was the state of the Heavy Brigade after the 21st November, which made it quite enough to forage for themselves" - a duty which usually occupied only one-fourth of the Force".

The Crimean Commission and the Chelsea Board by Colonel Tulloch 1857.

Format of Biographical Information

It has been the main object of the book to find the individuals that participated in the Charge of the Heavy Brigade at Balaclava on the 25th October 1854. Only individuals effective in the Crimea on the 25th October have been entered in the book. The obvious route was to use the Balaclava Medal Roll as the starting point but how this list was compiled can only be surmised. The Medal Roll was probably compiled from the entries in the musters for the period.

The musters were a monthly summary, compiled quarterly, of pay due to each man with comments in the margins if they were not effective, died, or were in hospital. Unfortunately it does not differentiate between individuals that rode in the Charge or were on other duties at the time.

On close examination of the musters there were others without the Balaclava clasp that were available for duty on the day of the Charge (Effective).

Also quite a few individuals were sent to Scutari Hospital on the day after the Charge, but were not on the official casualty list or issued with a Balaclava clasps. It is quite possible these troopers were victims of disease, both groups have been entered into the book.

The Queen sanctioned a medal with bars for Alma and Inkermann on 15th December 1854 followed by the Balaclava bar on the 23rd February 1855 and the Sebastopol bar on the 31st October 1855.

Title: Regimental number, Surname, Rank (taken from Medal Roll) and Christian name. As a mark of respect all the individuals who were killed on the 25th October are listed in a memorial black box.

Status: Categories are " Rode in the Charge","Killed in the Charge" with variations for the wounded (Slightly or Severely). We have accorded charger status to anyone:

> a) Killed or Wounded in the Charge and recorded in the casualty lists.
> b) Who has a citation for a medal award which indicates participation in the Charge.
> c) Where there is confirmation in letters or published accounts of the Charge.

The Heavy Brigade was involved in two actions on the 25th October 1854, the charge in the south valley at the Russian Cavalry under Major General Rijov and the charge in support of the Light Brigade in their attack on the Russian artillery in the north valley.

Also "Probably rode in the Charge" is used when the individual has been issued with a Balaclava clasp on his medal (as shown in the Medal Rolls at the National Archives) Individuals without the Balaclava clasp but who were effective on the 25th October 1854 are shown as "Effective during the period". Troopers sent to Scutari on the day after the Charge are shown as "To Scutari 26th October 1854".

Medals: WO100/24 Campaign Medal and Award Rolls (Crimea). These returns were prepared for the mint by each Cavalry regiment. No roll was available for the 5th Dragoon Guards Sebastopol clasp. But all present between 1st October 1854 and 9th September 1855 were entitled. Numerous auction catalogues have been examined and any details included.

Documents at the National Archives which have been examined include:
WO14/1 - Scutari musters January to March 1855, the preceding musters October to December 1854 are missing.
WO25 - Discharge books for the Heavy Brigade regiments
WO100/24 - Campaign Medal and Award Rolls (Crimea), WO102 - Long Service and Good Conduct Medal Rolls
Officers Casualty List from the London Gazette 12th November 1854, other ranks 16th December 1854.

1st Regiment of Dragoons (The Royals)
> WO 12/484 - Apr 1854-Mar 1855 Muster Books and Pay lists
> WO 12/485 - Apr 1855-Mar 1857 Muster Books and Pay lists

2nd Regiment Royal North British Dragoons (Scots Greys)
> WO 12/539 - Apr 1854-Mar 1855 Muster Books and Pay lists
> WO 12/541 - Apr 1855-Mar 1857 Muster Books and Pay lists

4th Regiment of Dragoon Guards (Royal Irish)
> WO 12/270 Apr 1854 to Mar 1857 Muster Books and Pay lists

5th Regiment of Dragoon Guards (Princess Charlotte of Wales)
> WO 12/324 Apr 1854 to Mar 1857 Muster Books and Pay lists*

6th Regiment of Dragoons (Inniskillings)
> WO 12/733 - Apr 1854- Mar 1855 Muster Books and Pay lists
> WO 12/734 - Apr 1855- Mar 1856 Muster Books and Pay lists
> WO 12/735 - Apr 1856- Mar 1857 Muster Books and Pay lists

*pages 21-22 are missing from the musters, the pages in the musters are loose after separating from the spine, luckily John Darwent's archive was found to contain the muster information for these pages. The Heavy Brigade regiments would normally be listed in order of precedence, 4th Dragoon Guards, 5th Dragoon Guards, 1st Royal Dragoons, 2nd Dragoons, 6th Dragoons. For ease of reference we have listed in numerical order.

Lord Lucan and Staff

BINGHAM, Lieutenant General George Charles (3rd Earl of Lucan)

Born : 16th April 1800
Died : 10th November 1888
Status : Slightly wounded in the Charge
Medals : Crimea (A.B.I.S) Commander (3rd Class) The French Legion of Honour, The Turkish or of the Medjidie (1st Class)

George Charles Bingham, came from a wealthy family and was educated at Westminster. At the age of sixteen he was Cornet in the 6th foot, exchanging into the 3rd Foot Guards as ensign, he later became lieutenant on 24th December 1818, he then went on to purchase a Lieutenancy in the 8th Foot on the 20th January 1820. On half pay before securing a Captaincy in the 1st Life Guards on the 20th June 1822, in December 1825 he bought his way into the 17th Lancers. At the age of 26 he was to become a Lieutenant-Colonel for the sum of £25,000 ousting an officer by the name of Bacon in the process. Using his own money he transformed the regiment by purchasing new horses and stylish uniforms. The debonair troopers now became known as "Bingham's Dandies". His quest for perfection resulted in endless parades, drills and inspections, if the results were not too his satisfaction reprimands would be handed out to his officers and floggings to his men. His meteoric rise up the military hierarchy was due to his wealth. The system of purchase was to ensure that only the wealthy and landed aristocracy would be in control of the army and be loyal to the monarch.

In 1828 he saw service in the Russo-Turkish War and was placed in command of a cavalry regiment where he was to show his indifference to all the perils and hardship encountered on this gruelling campaign. He was also to prove his valour and determination in getting things done. For his efforts he was awarded the Russian war medal and became a Knight of the Order of St Anne 2nd Class. On his return from the Balkans Lucan was to marry the youngest of the Brudenell sisters Anne on the 29th June 1829. His brother-in-law Lord Cardigan was also disliked by his officers and men, both men were arrogant, bad-tempered and full of their own self-importance. At the same time they both despised each other. The only training Cardigan had for war was fearlessly chasing foxes up and down the countryside, the only shots fired in anger were from his duelling pistols. When posted to India, his main preoccupation was hunting tigers and wreaking havoc with his officers and men. It was no wonder Lucan disliked Cardigan, his affluent life style was completely opposite to Lucan's. Cardigan was of the opinion his sister had been badly treated by Bingham, which was to be vindicated in 1842 when the couple parted. Later serving directly under Lucan it was inevitable there would be a clash of personalities.

With the money he received from his estates falling Lucan gave up the command of 17th Lancers, went on half pay, and returned to Castlebar in 1837 to personally supervise the running of his estates. He succeeded his father as 3rd Earl of Lucan on 30th June 1839 and was made Lord-Lieutenant of County Mayo in 1845. Lord Lucan, in his terse incisive style, asserted that he "would not breed paupers to pay priests" with the sort of military despotisms he had endeavoured personally to rule his estates (Finlay Dunn, Landlord and Tenants in Ireland, 1881). He was a ruthless landlord and earned the hatred of his tenants, by evictions and lawsuits, used to consolidate his estate and remove the uneconomic smallholdings. This was carried out during the potato famine, the result being starvation for many of his unfortunate tenants. Ironically many would later join the cavalry to escape from abject poverty, the very regiments that Lord Lucan was to command in the Crimea.

Lucan continued his meteoric rise through the ranks, on half-pay he was made a Colonel in 1841 and a Major-General in 1851.

When the Crimean War broke out in 1854 Lucan applied for a brigade and to the astonishment of more experienced officers he was appointed to the command of the Cavalry Division. This consisted of the Light Brigade, which his brother-in-law Lord Cardigan commanded, and the Heavy Brigade which was commanded by General Scarlett. Lord Lucan was determined that Lord Cardigan would do as ordered whilst Lord Cardigan was determined to do just as he liked. Lord Lucan relished the "hard life" which his unfortunate men had to endure. Lord Cardigan, however, lived on his private yacht in Balaclava harbour and seldom made an appearance before 10am.

On the morning of the 25th October the Russian attack led by Count Liprandi proceeded down the North Valley and turned left to capture the redoubts on the Causeway Heights. Scarlett responded in a heroic charge of the Heavy Brigade which drove the Russians back in total confusion Lord Raglan's staff, observed the Russians in the redoubts preparing to remove the captured cannons. Raglan issued an ambiguous order to Lord Lucan. "Lord Raglan wishes the cavalry to advance rapidly to the front, follow the enemy and try to prevent the enemy carrying away the guns, troop horse artillery may accompany. French cavalry is on your left. Immediate."

Lord Lucan instructed Lord Cardigan to charge at once. "Certainly, sir," said Cardigan, "but allow me to point out that the Russians have a battery in the valley on our front, and batteries and riflemen on both sides." Lucan replied, "I know it. But Lord Raglan will have it. We have no choice but to obey."

The Light Brigade charged down the north valley to their heroic place in history. As Lucan brought the heavy Brigade forward in support of the Light Brigade he was slightly wounded in the leg by a bullet, his horse also being hit in several places. With the brigade decimated, the sight of the wounded and shattered troopers returning had brought Raglan down from the heights. "What did you mean, sir, by attacking a battery in front, contrary to all the usages of warfare, and the customs of the service?" he demanded of Cardigan, but Cardigan had a cast-iron defence to that. Turning to Lucan, Raglan complained "You have lost the Light Brigade," but Lucan was having none of it and waved his own order at him. Raglan was deflated. "Lord Lucan, you were a Lieutenant-General and should therefore have exercised your discretion, and, not approving of the charge, should not have caused it to be made".

In Raglan's despatch of 28th October "from some misconception of the instruction to advance the Lieutenant-General considered that he was bound to attack at all hazards." Lucan complained against the censure but the government decided that he should be recalled. In March 1855 Lucan returned to England and applied for a court-martial, which was refused. He was later exonerated. On the 17th November he became Colonel of the 8th Hussars. He was promoted to Lieutenant-General on the 24th December 1858, to General on the 28th August 1865 and finally to Field-Marshal on the 21st June 1887. He died at 13 South Street, Park Lane on the 10th November 1888 and was buried at Laleham, Middlesex.

Lucan received the Crimean medal with four clasps, the Legion of Honour (3rd class), the Medjidie (1st class) and was made K.C.B. on the 5th July 1855.

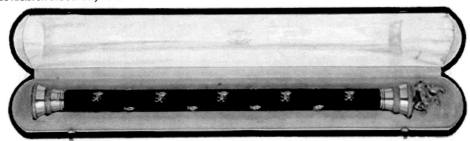

Spinks Auction 30th November 2004, Lot 83, The Highly Important Field Marshal's Baton to The Earl of Lucan for His Many Achievements, Including the Command of the Cavalry Division in the Crimea Where he Directed the Movements of the Heavy and Light Brigades at Balaclava. The Baton, overall length 55cm. including the 18ct gold top and bottom mounts (Hallmarks for London 1887), is covered in its original Imperial purple velvet and studded with eighteen gold lions; the base inscribed 'From Her Majesty Alexandrina Victoria Queen of the United Kingdom of Great Britain and Ireland to Field Marshal The Right Hon. 'The Earl of Lucan G.C.B.'; surmounted by a superbly modelled equestrian gold figure of St. George with the dragon, extremely fine in its original 'Garrard, London' Imperial purple velvet covered case of issue. Hammer Price £46,000

BINGHAM, Captain Charles George

Born : 8th May 1830

Died : 5th June 1914
Status : Rode in the Charge

Medals : Crimea (A.B.I.S)

Cornet by purchase 29th December 1848, Lieutenant by purchase 14th October 1851, Captain 22nd August 1854. After the success of the Charge of the Heavy Brigade, Captain Morris the acting Commanding officer of the 17th Lancers asked Cardigan on several occasions if they could charge the fleeing Russians. Cardigan's final remark in a voice toned with anger was "No, No, sir, we must not stir from here' Lucan watching from the escarpment sent his son with a message to Cardigan with what was effectively a reprimand. An opportunity had been lost to complete the victory.

Bingham was presented with his Crimean medal by the Queen at Horse Guards on the 16th May 1855. Charles George, the 4th Earl, was a total opposite of his father, he was a kind man even helping his tenants to buy their land.

The New York Times 6th June 1914:
The Earl of Lucan died today at the age of 84. He was aide-de-camp to his father, the third Earl of Lucan, when he was in command of the British cavalry during the Crimean War, and was largely responsible for the Charge of the Light Brigade at Balaclava. The estates consist of 63,000 acres in Ireland, and the heir to the title is his eldest son, Lord Bingham, who was born in 1860.

The Earl of Lucan was the son of the third Earl of Lucan and Mary, daughter of the sixth Earl of Cardigan, and succeeded his father to the title in 1888. He was educated at Rugby, and became A.D.C. to his father during the crimean War in 1854. In 1859 he married Lady Cecilia Catherine Gordon-Lennox, who died in 1910, the youngest daughter of the fifth Duke of Richmond. He was Lieutenant Colonel of the Coldstream Guards from 1859 to 1860, and then resigned. He was a member of Parliament for Mayo, Ireland, from 1865 until 1874, Vice Admiral for Connaught in 1889, and His Majesty's Lieutenant and Custos Rotulorum for County Mayo in 1901. He was created a Knight of the Order of Medjidie of the Fifth Class in 1857. Lord Bingham, the new Earl of Lucan, is 54 years old, and has been Colonel of the First London Infantry Brigade since 1912.

Lord Bingham on his Estate

The Lucan family left the family home at Laleham in 1922, the property changed hands many times, at one point becoming a Convent, it has now been developed into luxury apartments.

CHATERIS, Captain Hon. Walter

Born : 10th April 1828 - East Lothian, Scotland

Died : 25th October 1854
Status : Killed in the Charge

Medals : Crimea (B.I.S)

Walter Chateris was born on 10th April 1828 at Amisfield, Haddington, East Lothian, Scotland. He was the son of Francis Wemyss-Chateris, 9th Earl of Wemyss and Lady Louisa Bingham. Captain Hon. Walter Chateris was commissioned on 6 February 1846 with the rank of Ensign, in the service of the 92nd Regiment, The Gordon Highlanders. He gained the rank of Captain in 1854 in the service of the Gordon Highlanders. He was Aide-de-Camp to his uncle Lord Lucan in October 1854..

Chateris sailed to the Crimea on the Melita, arriving in Gibraltar on the 23rd April 1854. On the journey out the Captain shared a cabin with Lt-Colonel Walker and W.Pakenham, all suffering badly with sea sickness. Before the involvement of Lord Lucan in the support of Light Brigade, Captain Chateris was sent on a mission which is still surrounded in controversy to this day. Was Captain Chateris sent to speak to Sir George Cathcart to ask why he had not advanced, as Lord Lucan was to suggest later? Why did Captain Chateris engage in a discussion with Captain Shakespear on the heights, was it to tell him the cavalry were about to charge and his help would be appreciated? Captain Shakespear was commanding I Troop of the Royal Horse Artillery and they were to support the Light Brigade but did not fire a shot, not being able to get within the range of any useful target. Chateris galloped back down the north valley to rejoin Lucan and probably at the same time inform him of the Russian movements.

The Heavy Brigade for the second time had got their orders to advance, but as the Light Brigade moved off at speed, a gap opened up between the brigades. Lord Lucan could not keep up, it was then that they came under fire, Captain Chateris fell dead at his side and his other two ADCs were unhorsed or wounded. Lucan's horse was hit twice while he sustained a wound. He realised the seriousness of the situation, and arranged a tactical withdrawal. The whole Brigade were at the receiving end of the Russian artillery, bombarding them from the Fedioukine Heights.

HARDINGE, Captain Arthur Edward

Born : 2nd March 1828

Died : 15th July 1892 - Weymouth
Status : Rode in the Charge

Medals : Crimea (A.B.I.S), Turkish Crimea Medal, 2nd Class of the Turkish Order of the Mejedie (1876), (5th Class, 1858), Knight Commander of the Most Honourable Order of the Bath (c. 1886) (CB, 1856), Companion of the Most Eminent Order of the Indian Empire (c. 1886), Sutlej Medal for Moodkee, with clasps for Ferozeshah and Sobraon 5th Class (Chevalier) of the French Légion d'Honneur (1856)

RUSSELL & SONS   CHICHESTER

The son of Field Marshal Viscount Hardinge of Lahore and King's Newton. Educated at Eton, Ensign, 80th Regiment, by purchase, 7th June 1844, Lieutenant, without purchase, 22nd December 1845, Lieutenant & Captain, Coldstream Guards, by purchase, 1st June 1849, Brevet-Major, 12th December 1854, Captain & Lieutenant-Colonel, without purchase, 20th February 1855, Colonel, 25th May 1858, Major General, 6th March 1868, Lieutenant General, 1st October 1877, Colonel, 2nd Battalion, Royal Inniskilling Fusiliers, 20th November 1881, General, 1st April 1883, Colonel Commandant, King's Royal Rifle Corps, 13th March 1886, Colonel, Coldstream Guards, 26th February 1890.

General Hardinge served as Aide de Camp to Lord Hardinge throughout the campaign on the Sutlej in 1845-6, and was present at the Battles of Moodkee, Ferozeshah (horse shot), and Sobraon. Served in the Eastern Campaign of 1854-55, first as DAQMG to the 1st Division, and at Headquarters, and from the Spring of 1855 as AQMG at Headquarters, including the battles of the Alma, Balaklava, and Inkermann, and siege of Sebastopol. He married, on 30th December, 1858, Mary Georgiana Frances, woman of the bedchamber to HRH the Princess of Wales, eldest daughter of Col. A. F. Ellis, and had issue. He was Commander in Chief of the Bombay Army, 1881-85, and Governor of Gibraltar, he arrived to take up his post on the 2nd November 1886 and was governor until 1890.

"Times", Nov 14 1854:
After the charge, Captain the Hon. Arthur Hardingo came galloping up to Lord Reglan with the news of what the cavalry had done. He had sent orders to Lord Lucan, and at the moment of the charge he had joined the Grays and dashed with them into the Russian columns. He was an object of envy to all his friends on the staff while he sescribed in animated lauguage the glorious events of those brilliant five minutes.

Great War with Russia pp 148-149: 1895 Russell

"The first order was brought by Wetherall; the second was, I think, conveyed by General Sir Arthur - then Captain - Hardinge. I cannot be certain if he was the bearer of the second order, but I remember meeting him immediately after the charge, flushed and triumphant, his tunic in disorder, the straps of his overalls broken. "Did you see it all? Was it not glorious?" he exclaimed, as he pressed his horse up the slope which I was descending."

General The Viscount Hardinge G.C.B had asked Airey to keep an eye on his son Arthur, while Hardinge watched out for Mrs Airey and family at home. Arthur was now serving as a Captain in the Coldstream Guards. Cambridge University Library. References :- CUL Add.9554/x/xx

The Times Saturday, Jul 16, 1892;
General the Hon. Sir Arthur E. Hardinge. K.C.B., Equerry to the Queen, died at Weymouth yesterday afternoon from injuries received on Wednesday week. Sir Arthur was driving in the neighbourhood with one of his daughters when the horse took fright, and the occupants of the carriage were thrown out with great force on a heap of stones. Some passers-by proceeded to Weymouth for medical aid, and fortunately met Dr. Browning, who placed the sufferers in his carriage and brought them to Weymouth. The lady had sustained only a severe shaking and some slight cuts, but Sir Arthur had a fracture of the left collar-bone and of the eighth rib, with severe injuries to the head. He seemed to improve, but on Thursday a change for the worse took place, and the patient died yesterday afternoon in the presence of his wife and daughters and son-in-law.

He was buried at Fordrombe Church, near Penhurst, Kent. Photograph courtesy of Michael Hargreave

JOY, Trumpet Major Henry

Born : 1819 - Ripon, Yorkshire
Enlisted : 13th May 1833

Died : 17th August 1893
Status : Rode in the Charge

Medals : Crimea (B.I.S), Turkish Medal, Distinguished Conduct Medal, Long Service and Good Conduct Medal
Medals held in the National Army Museum, Crimea medal includes clasp for Alma.

Henry Joy was born in Ripon, Yorkshire in 1819. Soldering was a family tradition, his father James Joy had been a Private in the 1st Life Guards and had served under Wellington in the Peninsula and Waterloo campaigns. In 1825 at the age of only six Henry was to enter the Royal Military Asylum at Chelsea. In May 1833 he enlisted in the 17th Light Dragoons as a bandboy, becoming a trumpeter in 1838 and promoted to Trumpet-Major in 1847. The state funeral of Arthur Wellesley, 1st Duke of Wellington took place on the 12th November 1852, Trumpet-Major Henry Joy had the honour to be in charge of the regimental band.

At Balaclava Joy was Orderly Trumpeter to Lord Lucan and sounded the Charge of the Heavy Brigade on his bugle. He subsequently rode in the charge and had two horses shot from under him. Later, despite a wound, he carried a flag of truce into the Russian lines and appeared before General Liprandi. In The Pocket Hercules by M.J Trow Captain Morris describes the troop horses, three were grey (one was that of Henry Joy, the Trumpet Major, a typical colour for buglers' horses), one black, the others bay chestnut or brown. Virtually all were bought locally in Ireland.

On the regiment's return to Ireland the officers of the 17th were keen to display Joy's bugle in their mess. The plan was to make a copy in silver which they would present to Joy in exchange for his brass bugle. The exchange did not take place because Joy preferred to keep his own Bugle. In 1898 some 5 years after his death his family decided to sell the bugle at Auction by Messrs Debenham, Storr and Sons, the price realized was 750 guineas. The bugle along with Joy's medals was bought by Mr Middlebrook, the landlord of the Edinburgh Castle in Regent's Park. On the death of Mr Middlebrook in 1908 his executors once more put the bugle up for sale and it was bought by the Royal United Services Institute Whitehall and is now with his medals in the National Army Museum.

Private James Wightman of the 17th Lancers wrote an article in "Nineteenth Century Magazine" of May 1892 p 850: "Trumpet-Major Joy, of the 17th Lancers, was Lord Lucan's field-trumpeter, and we men of that corps envied him his good luck, for we made sure he had charged with the Heavies; but this was not so and, tied like he was to the divisional commander, he had the misfortune also not to share in the charge of the Light Brigade; wherefore we have been obliged to exclude him from our commemorative banquets ever since, as no man can take part in them who did not actually charge down the valley"

It is quite probable that Henry Joy accompanied Lord Lucan on their support of the Light Brigade. But it is debatable whether he charged with the Heavies, Wightman disagrees with Morris on this issue.

There is some controversy as to whether Joy sounded the Charge of the Light Brigade or indeed if the command charge was sounded at all.

In the 1861 census returns Henry Joy is living at No.4 Smarts Terrace, Addington Street, N.Lambeth London. Head of household age 42 Messenger and Chelsea pensioner, born Ripon, Yorks.

Jane	wife	age 31	born 1830 Hounslow
Amy	dau	age 10	born 1851 Dublin
Beatrice	dau	age 8	born 1853 Canterbury
Bertha	dau	age 6	born 1855 Hounslow
Emma	dau	age 2	born 1859 Canterbury
Jenny	dau	age 6 wks	born 1861 London.

In the 1881 census Henry Joy is shown living in the Commander-in-Chief's Office, London Middlesex, aged 62, occupation Messenger for the War Office, and married to Jane ten years his junior. Living with them are their three daughters and three sons, all born in London:

Emma	dau	age 20	born 1861 London
Marian	dau	age 19	born 1862 London
James	son	age 16	born 1865 London
Henry	son	age 15	born 1866 London
Grace	dau	age 13	born 1868 London
Herbert	son	age 8	born 1873 London

When comparing the previous census returns with the 1871

census it would appear that Emma born in 1859 died, the couple going on to name another daughter after her in 1861, another daughter named Amelia born in 1869 died in 1880 at the Strand aged 11 years. Henry and his wife had a total of twelve children.

Joy's son Henry Charles born in 1866 died whilst serving in the Royal Garrison Artillery at St. George's, Bermuda in 1894. His two other sons both joined the army and retired 1914.

In Spring of 1863 a libel action was taken out by Lord Cardigan with a large number of affidavits being sworn in. A letter from Joy to Cardigan is printed in "Statement and Remarks upon the Affidavits filed by Lt-Colonel Calthorpe", London, 1864. The letter was sent from 18 New Milman Street, Guilford Street, London, and dated the 4th September 1864. In the letter Joy confirms that Cardigan had reached the Russian guns.
Henry Joy was discharged from the army on the 24th April 1860. He attended the First Balaclava Banquet on the 25th October 1875. His portrait (below) can be seen in the "Illustrated London News" 30th October 1875.

Henry Joy died on the 17th August 1893. A service took place at the Parish Church of St Nicholas before he was buried in Chiswick Cemetery, London, a marble cross marks the grave. His obituary appears in "The Graphic" of 2nd September 1893. Henry took many unanswered questions to the grave with him.

TRUMPET-MAJOR HARRY JOY, 17TH LANCERS.

Portrait from the
Illustrated London News 1875

Henry, Jane and Son

Henry's grave at Chiswick
Parish Graveyard

From left to right:
J. Ireland, W.G. Cattermole, H. Joy, C. Aldous (standing), G. Weatherley, J. Scarfe, T. Dyer. This photograph was used to produce the sketches in the ILN 1875 Banquet issue.

In 1875 Joy attended the 1875 Balaclava Banquet, the photo above being taken at this event.

McMAHON, Assistant Quartermaster General Thomas Westropp

Born :   Died : 23rd January 1892

                                                          Status : Rode in the Charge

Medals : Crimea (A.B) The Turkish Order of the Medjidie (5th Class), Sutlej Medal for Sobraon (with 9th Lancers)
Army List shows Crimea medal as having a Sebastopol clasp, also CB, Sardinian Medal, Turkish Crimea.

Cornet 16th Lancers 24th December 1829, transferred to 6th Dragoons 25th June 1830, Lieutenant 2nd December 1831, Captain 9th June 1838. Transferred to the 9th Lancers 29th April 1842, Major (unattached) 13th July 1847, Lieutenant Colonel 12th December 1857, Colonel 12th December 1854, Major General 6th March 1868, Lieutenant General 1st October 1877, General 12th April 1880, Colonel 18th Hussars 6th January 1874 – 1885, Colonel 5th Dragoon Guards 16th March 1885 until his death. (*Hart, Army List 1885 Vol 1 p. 160, Vol2 p. 535; Jackson, Inniskilling Dragoons p. 288.*)

Paget states in "The Light Cavalry Brigade in the Crimea" that on the morning of the 25th "The division had as usual turned out an hour before daybreak…..We rode on….left of "Canrobert's Hill…"Holloa" said Lord William (Paulet), "there are two flags flying; what does that mean?" "Why that surely is the signal that the enemy is approaching," said Major McMahon. Hardly were the words out his mouth when bang went a cannon." This event was to mark the beginning of one of the most historic days in the annals of British military history.

During the support of the Light Brigade McMahon was hit in the in the leg by a musket ball while his horse was hit twice in the body from grape shot.

The Sardinian War Medal citation states "Served (in) the campaign of 1854-5, including the battles of the Alma, Balaclava, and Inkermann, and the siege of Sebastopol; served in 1854, as Assistant Quarter-Master-General of the Cavalry Division, and in 1855, as Lieutenant-Colonel commanding the 5th Dragoon Guards."

His fathers obituary from the Gentleman's Magazine January 1860 page 533:
April 10th 1860 In Great Cumberland Street, Hyde Park aged 80, General Sir Thomas McMahon, Bart., G.C.B., Col. 10th Regt of Foot….He was born in December 1779, and entered the army towards the close of the of the last century. He saw active service in almost every quarter of the globe, and held the post of Commander of the Forces at Bombay from 1839 till 1847. He was appointed Colonel of the 1st Foot in 1847, became K.C.B in 1827, and a G.C.B in 1859. He succeeded in 1817 to the baronetey, which had been conferred by the Prince Regent upon his brother, the late Right Hon. Sir J.McMahon, with a special remainder to himself. By his wife, Emily Anne,dau. of Michael Robert Westropp, esq., Sir Thomas had issue five daughters and four sons. He is succeeded in the title by his eldest son, Col.,of the 5th Dragoon Guards, who married and has issue. The present Baronet served in the Sutlej campaigns, and afterwards as Assistant-Quarter master-General to the Cavalry Division in the Crimea, and was made a Lieut-Col. for distinguished services in command of the 5th Dragoon Guards.

War Office 24th November 1854
5th Regiment of Dragoon Guards, Major Thomas Westropp McMahon, from half-pay Unattached, to be Major, vice Brevet-lieutenant Colonel Le Marchant, who exchanges, receiving the difference between cavalry and infantry only.

The Field of War, Temple Godman's letters, 24th December 1854, Camp Kadikoi "McMahon has been on Lord Lucan's staff as Adjutant and Quartermaster General, a very gentlemanly person, he has gone home ill, has been nearly all his life on the staff".

The Oxford English Dictionary definition of half-pay is: the allowance paid to an officer when neither retired nor in actual service.
During war, vacancies from death left open many commissions, and after a conflict when these vacancies were fewer, many went on half-pay.

Sir Thomas Mc Mahon.

late

5t Dr. Gds.

PAULET, Assistant Adjutant General Lord William

Born : 7th July 1804

Died : 9th May 1893
Status : Rode in the Charge

Medals . Crimea (D.I.5) , CB, Officier, Legion d'Honneur, Commander 1st Class, Order of St Maurice and St Lazarus, Order of Medjidie (3rd Class), Turkish Medal.
The medals are held in the Durham Light Infantry Museum

Lord William Paulet was born on the 7th July 1804 and was the fourth son of Charles Ingoldsby Paulet, 13th Marquess of Winchester. He was educated at Eton and on the 1st February 1821 was appointed an ensign in the 85th Light Infantry. On the 23rd August 1822 he became a Lieutenant in the 7th Royal Fusiliers. After purchasing an unattached company he exchanged to the 21st Royal Fusiliers on the 12th February 1825. In 1833 he joined the 68th Regiment as a major. During the long peace discipline and training in the regiment was allowed to slip and in 1842 the task of transforming the regiment was given to Lord William Paulet and he became Lieutenant Colonel on the 21st April 1843. Over the following five years, he brought the 68th to the peak of efficiency and, for the first time, made it a "fashionable" Regiment. When he retired his command in 1847, the 68th Light Infantry was inspected and the inspector's report ended - "I cannot say too much in praise of this beautiful Regiment".

After serving overseas he returned home until the 31st December 1848 when he was on half pay. The regiment would not see action again until the Crimea in 1854. He became Colonel of the Regiment in 1864. He was Assistant Adjutant-General in the Crimea, under Lord Lucan, and was present at Balaclava (see Kinglake's Invasion of the Crimea), Inkerman and Sevastopol. In November of 1854 he was appointed commander of British forces "on the Bosphorus, at Gallipoli, and the Dardanelles" where Florence Nightingale had earlier come with her nurses. Florence Nightingale opened a small reading room in Scutari and when she discovered how many soldier's were illiterate asked if she might, at her own expense, employ a school teacher. This idea was rejected vigorously by Lord William Paulet on the grounds that it would spoil "the brutes". From *"A Pictorial History of the Russian War" by George Dodd, p323*, "When it was found that Major Sillery, as military commandant at Scutari, was invested with insufficient power to infuse order into the chaos

at that spot, Lord William Paulet was appointed with increased power both to investigate and to execute; his Lordship, however, commissioned by Lord Raglan, found his authority too limited for the bewildering task entrusted to him. When Lord Paulet communicated to the home government the state of matters at Scutari, the Duke of Newcastle appointed Dr. Cummings, Dr. Spence, and Mr. Maxwell as Commissioners to enquire into the causes of the ill-treatment of the sick and wounded in the hospitals."

On the 25th October 1854 on seeing the Light Cavalry massacre unfold before him, Lord Lucan turned to Lord William Paulet and said, 'They have sacrificed the Light Brigade, they shall not have the Heavy, if I can help it.' He then ordered the halt to be sounded, withdrawing the brigade out of range of the Russian Artillery, but to a position where they could assist the light cavalry on its return.

Paulet returned to England in 1856 and became one of the first commanders at Aldershot. In 1858 he was appointed Major-General and from 1860 to 1865 was commander of the south-west district of Britain. In 1886 he became Field-Marshal and was Adjutant-General to the forces from 1865 to 1870. He was appointed to the Hon. Colonelcy of the 68th in 1864 and made a Field Marshal and G.C.B. On his death on the 9th May 1893 the whole of the 1st Battalion attended his funeral at Amport, near Andover, quite a remarkable tribute to a well respected Colonel. His life is described in detail in the Dictionary of National Biography.

There is a well-known painting of Paulet with a group of the 68th LI, illustrated on the cover of SGP Ward Faithful: The Story of the Durham Light Infantry (London, 1962).

WALKER, Lieutenant Colonel Charles Pyndar Beauchamp
Born : 7th October 1817 - Henbury, Gloucestershire   Died : January 1894
Status : Rode in the Charge (in support of the L.B)
Medals : Crimea (A.B.I.S), Order of Medjidie (5th Class), Turkish Crimea, Mutiny (no clasp), CB, 2nd China War (clasps), Austro-Prussian War 1886 (Prussia), Franco-Prussian War 1870-72 (Prussia), Iron Cross (Prussia). He was offered the Order of the Red Eagle with Swords (2nd Class) (Prussia), but was refused permission by the British Government to accept it.

The eldest son of Charles Ludlow Walker of Redland. Commissioned Ensign 27th February 1836 in the 33rd Foot, Lieutenant on 21st June 1839, in 1845 he married Georgiana, daughter of Captain Richard Armstrong of the 100th foot, she survived him. Became Captain 22nd December 1846, served in Gibraltar, West Indies, and North America. Exchanged into the 7th Dragoon Guards on the 16th November 1849.

On the onset of the war in the East Walker was appointed aide-de-camp to Lord Lucan, Commander of the Cavalry Division in the Crimea in March 1854. Arriving in the Crimea with Lord Lucan he was present at Alma, Balaclava, and Inkerman, and was later mentioned in dispatches, was awarded the Medjidie (5th class).

Walker left the Crimea when he was appointed Major of the regiment on 8th December 1854. On the 9th July 1855 he was appointed Assistant Quartermaster-General in Ireland and on the 9th November he was given an unattached Lieutenant-Colonelcy. On the 7th December 1858 he became Lieutenant-Colonel of the 2nd Dragoon Guards and was to proceed to India to join his regiment. In April 1859 he commanded a field force in Oudh and went on to defeat the rebels at Bungdon. A month later he served under Sir Hope Grant in the action at the Jirwah Pass and was again mentioned in dispatches.

On 14th May 1860 Walker was posted to China as assistant Quartermaster-General of cavalry in Sir Hope Grant's expedition. He was present at the actions of Sinho, Changkiawan (Zhangjiawan), and Palichiao (Baliqiao), was mentioned in dispatches and was made CB on 28th February 1861. He became a Colonel on the 14th December 1860. Returning to England on the 11th June 1861 he went on half pay and on the 1st July 1861 he was appointed assistant Quartermaster-General at Shorncliffe in Kent. He then joined the diplomatic service and on the 26th April 1865 he was made military attaché at Berlin. During the Austro-Prussian War of 1866 he was present at the battles of Nachod and Königgrätz as British military commissioner and held the post for eleven years. For his services he was awarded an Iron Cross. Promoted Major-General on the 29th December 1873, he resigned his post on the 31st March 1877 and became a Lieutenant-General on the 1st October. the same year. Appointed Inspector-General of military education from the 7th January 1878 to October 1884 he retired with the honorary rank of General. Made KCB on the 24th May 1881 and Colonel of the 2nd Dragoon Guards on the 22nd December 1881. He died at his London residence, 97 Onslow Square, South Kensington, and was buried in Brompton cemetery on the 19th January 1894. His wealth on his death was £58,179 9s. 1d., the probate granted 13 Feb 1894, CGPLA Eng. & Wales.

Below are extracts from *"Days of a Soldier's Life"* being letters written by the late General Sir C.P.Beauchamp Walker, K.C.B:
October 27th. No attack yesterday or this morning. I have just had my clothes off, for the first time since leaving the ship a great comfort. I was out an hour before sunrise this morning observing the Russian army. They are very strong, not much less than 25,000 men up the valley between Kamara and the Black River. I saw six or seven great masses of cavalry, seventeen or eighteen battalions of infantry, a number in the forts which they took from the Turks, and cavalry, artillery, and infantry on the hills this side of the Black River. I was sent up to Lord Raglan the moment I came in (half-past 8), hardly being allowed time to drink a cup of cocoa on horseback. However, Lord Raglan, after hearing my report, in the kindest manner pressed a good breakfast on me, even asking if fresh tea had been brought to me. I found myself a sort of lion there, as not having been killed on Wednesday, as they saw it all from the heights, and never expected to see any of us again. The return of killed, wounded, and missing is most fearful. In the Light Brigade are 10 officers killed and 10 wounded ; 135 men killed, 135 wounded, and 370 horses; this does not include the Heavy Brigade or Staff. The Greys lost 47 killed and wounded. I saw 30 struck down in the valley, without their even meeting the enemy, as they were in reserve. There was a most brilliant affair yesterday with Sir De Lacy Evans's division, who drove back the Russians with immense slaughter, only losing 12 or 15 killed, and about 40 or 50 wounded. Poor Connolly behaved like a hero, and was shot through the lungs. Oh, those brutes of Turks ! if it had not been for their cowardice we should never have been reduced to our fatal charge on Wednesday.

October 29th, before Sevastopol. Scene, a barren plain covered with stones and thistles, camps scattered over its whole extent, a tent which is occupied by a very cold old dog, thinking of home and a pair of warm gloves, foreground the sea, behind which Sevastopol is indicated by continual heavy firing, though only the smoke is visible, a black sky, north-east wind, and cold rain ; general characteristics, the reverse of cheerful. Notwithstanding all which, I am anything but cheerless, for if I am living like a dog in a canvas kennel, have we not great cause for thankfulness that I am not like poor Charteris lying in a bloody grave in an enemy's country ? I do most fervently hope I may never again see such a slaughter; 35 officers killed, wounded, and missing, 369 men, and 541 horses, out of one battery of Horse Artillery and our twenty weak squadrons. The first affair, which I did not see, was very brilliant. A large body of Russian cavalry, encouraged by the easy way their infantry had driven the Turks from the line of redoubts, came over the hill into our valley in two lines, and were received at the bottom by the Greys, 6th Dragoons, and 4th Dragoon Guards, assisted slightly by the 5th Dragoon Guards, and not at all by the Royal Dragoons, so that actually only eight squadrons were engaged. Five minutes sufficed for them, when they broke and fled in the greatest confusion, leaving a considerable number dead on the field, and taking with them marks of English prowess, which they will not easily forget, in the shape of a host of wounded men and officers. General Scarlett led most bravely, and sabred like a common soldier, cutting down a Russian lancer who was in the act of piercing a soldier of the Enniskillens. When the Greys and one squadron of the Enniskillens first charged, they were completely surrounded and even overlapped by the Russian line, but the other squadron of Enniskillens and the 4th Dragoon Guards by a skilful manoeuvre, brought up their shoulders, and fell on the enemy's flank, rolling up their line into one confused mass. Very few of our men were killed, though a good many, twenty -five or thirty were wounded, as the Russians were so thick that they could hardly use their weapons, and were single-handed, no match in skill, weight, or courage for our sturdy fellows.

This affair, had it been followed by a more prudent attempt to recover the guns taken from the Turks, would have made the 25th October for ever famous in the history of cavalry, as an instance of what pluck can do, against numbers and vantage ground, as our people actually charged uphill. Unfortunately, some little time afterwards an order was sent to Lord Lucan which led to the sad loss which we experienced, and was brought by an officer personally hostile to him, and received without the discretion fitting in an officer of high rank. Captain Nolan brought the order to advance rapidly, and endeavour to retake guns from the Russians. Lord Lucan, instead of taking the order, and exercising his own judgment as to how he carried it out, asked Captain Nolan what he was to attack, and was answered by his pointing to the Russians drawn up across the valley, with the words :"There, my lord, is your enemy, there are the guns." Lord Lucan immediately ordered the Light Cavalry to attack down the valley, a distance of a mile and a half, and as it proved into a terrain which was completely swept by the Russian artillery. As soon as we came within range, they opened on us from a line of guns formed right across the valley, from some more guns very well placed on their left, but which were partially occupied by the fire of our artillery, and on our left by a line of guns planted on the ridge of hills near the Black River. Before they opened fire I saw these guns or rather saw the horses pulled out my glass, and in a moment saw what they were, and how completely they swept the whole length of our advance. I would not live over that moment for a kingdom. My only consolation was seeing two squadrons of Chasseur d'Afrique stealing on them up the hill, and after they had pounded us for about ten minutes they did succeed in dislodging them, but were themselves repulsed with some loss by a body of Russian infantry which was in support. I thought the fire on the 17th was pretty heavy, but it was a joke to this, which certainly for eight or ten minutes exceeded my liveliest conception. I hope I shall not soon again get such a pelting. Luckily a great many of their shells burst too high, and though one or two burst within twenty yards of me, neither I nor Jemmy were hit. By the time I got with the head of the Heavy Brigade to the end of the valley, the Light Brigade, who, headed by Lord Cardigan, had charged the guns in front at full speed, were returning as best they could, from a field where they had left more than 213 of their numbers, and where they could do no possible good. They had ridden over the guns, sabred the gunners, and shot the horses, but were immediately attacked in front and flank, by such masses of cavalry, and received with such a fire of rifles from a fort and bushes on the right, that the only thing left was for each man to get out of the fray as he best could. Lord Lucan accordingly sounded the "recall," covered their retreat with the Heavy Brigade, and they ultimately formed to the number of 191 men and horses, besides officers, a little in the rear of the ground from which they started. Two divisions of infantry now came up, but nothing more was done. Had they supported the attack, it would probably have ended as disastrously to the enemy as it did to us. The front fire with which the Light Cavalry were received was tremendous, and the cause of our great loss in horses. The first man hit was Captain Nolan, who, led away by some mad desire of distinction, instead of returning to General Airey, joined the charge, and was killed at once by a cannon shot. I saw one shot knock over seven or eight men and horses of the Greys, and I saw a shell burst in the squadron interval of the 4th Dragoon Guards without hitting anybody. It was really a miracle that any of us who were at all in the front escaped unhurt ; but so it is under fire. I was very thankful when it was over, for though I believe I am not less brave than most of us, it was a great relief to find myself unhurt at the end of such a day. I believe the two charges of the 25th have convinced the Russians that we are devils, devils in red they call us and they have now found out that there are also devils in blue amongst us. The remark of the French on the Light Cavalry charge was :" C'est magnifique, mais ce n'est pas la guerre."

November 2nd. So cold, such frost; if I don't get two blankets I have applied for, I shall wake some day and find myself an icicle. Nothing can be duller than our present life, and to make it duller the Light Cavalry are going two miles away from us. We dine at 5, and go to bed at 7 to keep ourselves warm going to bed being putting on some more clothes and lying down. We have ascertained the Russians have fifty-six prisoners taken on the 25th, seventeen of whom are unwounded ; two of them are officers. Don't believe any bosh you hear about Lord Cardigan. He showed no head, and beyond riding with his brigade, no greater pluck than others. Old Scarlett is worth two of him.

The Heavy Brigade Charge

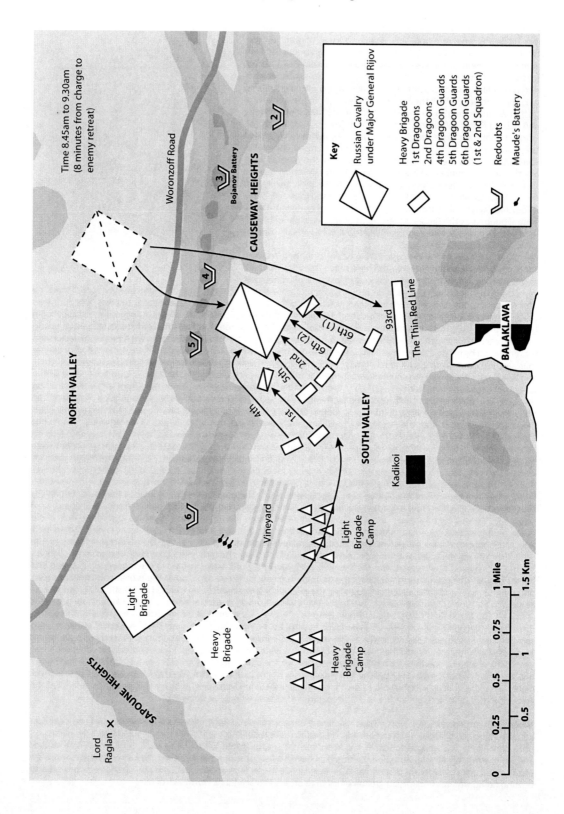

General Scarlett and Brigade Staff

SCARLETT, General Sir James York

Born : 1st February 1799

Died : 6th December 1871
Status : Led the Charge

Medals : Crimea (B.I.S)

The orders, decorations and medals of General Sir James Scarlett, which includes his miniatures and an officer's 'Albert' helmet of the 5th Dragoon Guards, had been kept in his family since his death in 1871. They have been passed to the state under the acceptance-in-lieu (AIL) scheme which enables taxpayers to transfer important works of art and other heritage objects into public ownership to the value of Inheritance Tax owed to the revenue. General Sir James Scarlett led the Charge of the Heavy Brigade at Balaclava in 1854. The helmet may have been worn during the charge although this has not been proved. The helmet also has a dent said to have been inflicted during the action. All of the artifacts are on display at the Regimental Museum of the Royal Dragoon Guards in York.

The anonymous donors settled tax worth £32,000. In 2004-5 this was one of 28 transactions reached under the AIL scheme which produced a total value of £13 million for the revenue.

General Scarlett's orders, decoration and medals consist of: Order of the Bath, sash badges and breast stars of both a Knight Grand Cross and a Companion; Crimea Medal with three clasps; Sardinian Al Valore Militare with the reverse inscribed 'Maj-Gen The Hon Sir James Scarlett KCB'; Turkish Crimea Medal (contemporary copy); French Legion d'Honneur, Commander's neck badge in gold and enamel; Turkish Order of the Medjidie, 2nd Class, neck badge and breast star. The Sardinian War Medal citation reads: "Commanded the Heavy cavalry brigade at the Alma, Balaclava and Inkermann; subsequently in 1855, the Cavalry Division."

James York Scarlett was born on the 1st February 1799 the second son of an eminent lawyer Sir James Scarlett who later was to become the 1st Lord Abinger. General Scarlett was educated at Trinity College Cambridge before being commissioned into the 18th Hussars on the 26th March 1818 as a Cornet, Lieutenant 24th October 1821, and Captain 9th June 1825. He was gazetted Major in the 5th Dragoon Guards on the 11th June 1830. On the 19th December 1835 he married Charlotte Anne, daughter and co-heir of Colonel Hargreaves of Burnley, Lancashire; they had no children, and Charlotte survived him.

From 1836 until 1841 he was Conservative member of Parliament for Guildford. In 1840 he was given command of his regiment, a post he was to hold for the next thirteen years, becoming Lieutenant Colonel on the 3rd July 1840 and Colonel on the 12th December 1851. He was on the point of retirement when the Crimean War commenced in 1854, up to this point he had seen no military action. He sailed for Turkey from Liverpool arriving at Varna on the 30th September 1854, only to find a large proportion of men had been suddenly struck down by cholera. Wanting to help he at once made his way to the hospitals, and went on a tour of inspection to help improve the lot of the men

and with his cheerful manner help reduce the panic that had seized them. Towards the end of September 1854 he sailed from Varna with the Heavy Brigade. The bulk of the army had already left and by the time the Heavies had arrived in the Crimea the opening battle of the Alma had already been fought. It was only later, before Sebastopol, as a Brigadier that he saw his first shot fired.

Early in the morning of the 25th October a large Russian force, including a strong force of cavalry under Liprandi, attacked and expelled the Turkish occupants of the redoubts and then went on to capture some of the earthworks which protected the allied rear. The Russians continued their advance towards the British base and harbour near Balaclava. The Heavy Brigade, consisting of 700-800 cavalrymen from the 1st, 2nd and 6th Dragoons and 4th and 5th Dragoon Guards, under the command of General Scarlett, advanced on the orders of Lord Raglan the British commander, to support the 93rd Highlanders, (Thin Red Line). On its way to meeting its objective it met an advancing force of Russian cavalry. The Russians halted at first, but began to advance at a rapid trot, with the intention of charging Scarlett's exposed flank. The threat was met with a cool and calculated response. Scarlett ordered 'left wheel into line' to the three squadrons nearest to him - Inniskilling and Scots Greys - organising them into a near perfect formation, then placing himself at the head of only 300 dragoons, drove straight uphill at the enemy, who could not believe their eyes and they gradually slowed to a

General Scarlett

trot, then a walk, and finally halted. Shortly after the impact of the initial force the remaining squadrons, about 400 men, attacked the unwieldy column of Russian cavalry. Then against all odds Scarlett, outnumbered 5:1, was able to rout the enemy. Scarlett was in the thick of the action and received five sabre cuts as well as the reputed dent to his helmet. Field Marshal Lord Raglan, commander of the British troops, sent a message 'Well done, Scarlett!' after the Charge of the Heavy Brigade. Became Major-General on the 12th December 1854.

The New York Times of the 21st May 1882 recounts how Lieutenant Elliot saved Scarlett's life during the charge: "Lieut. Elliot, of the Fifth Dragoon Guards, saved the life of Gen. Scarlett by his admirable devotedness. A tall Russian officer, perceiving that the officer leading the charge must be of high rank, placed himself so as to cut him down when he should reach the column. Gen. Scarlett, being extremely short sighted, was not prepared to guard his left. Elliot, who was riding close behind him as his aide-de-camp, gave his horse the spur, and dashing past him, just as the Russian had raised his arm to strike, ran the latter through the body with such force that the thrust went home to the hilt. The Russian was turned quite round in his saddle before the sabre could be disengaged, and then he fell dead to the ground."

The achievements of General Scarlett have been largely obscured by the heroic but disastrous Charge of the Light Brigade that occurred later that day. After the Heavy Brigade had offered support, coming under sustained artillery fire, Lucan ordered their halt and withdrawal. Later when the remnants of the Light Brigade came straggling back, with the Russian guns almost silenced, Scarlett attempted to capitalise on the tragic event. Positioning himself at the head of his dragoons, which were now in reserve, he began to make a second charge down 'the valley of death'. While advancing, Scarlett's aide-de-camp, Colonel Beatson, rode up alongside him and shouted that he was charging the Russians alone as his brigade had gone 'threes about'. Angry, Scarlett rode back to Lord Lucan, the cavalry commander, and was told that he had ordered the retreat. Scarlett afterwards maintained that if he had been allowed to continue he might have captured the Russian guns at the head of the valley, and would certainly have isolated a large number of enemy cavalry near the Traktir Bridge. For his services at Balaclava he was promoted to Major-General and in 1855 he was made a KCB.

In April 1855, after returning to England, Scarlett quickly succeeded Lord Lucan as commander of the British cavalry in the Crimea, with the local rank of Lieutenant-General. At first family matters made Scarlett reluctant to accept the post, however after assuming command and returning to the Crimea he found the original immaculate force of cavalry which had arrived in 1854 had been almost destroyed by active service, climate, and disease. To reinforce the regiments large numbers of new recruits had been sent out and by the spring of 1856, following training and drill Scarlett had brought them to fighting condition, however he said he would not have fought another Balaclava with them.

At the end of the war Scarlett was appointed to command the cavalry at Aldershot; from there he was transferred to Portsmouth, and in 1860 was gazetted Adjutant-General to the forces and Lieutenant-General in 1862. In 1865 he was selected for the prize of home appointments, command of the Aldershot camp. Towards the end of his tenure in office there was to be a revolution in the thinking of warfare. New tactics dictated a change in the ways of instruction, Scarlett felt he was too old for this and decided to leave the task to younger men.

In 1869 he was created a G.C.B, and on the 1st November 1870, on resigning the Aldershot command, he retired from active duty with the rank of General. He died suddenly on the 6th December 1871 at his residence, Bank Hall, near Burnley, Lancashire. He was buried in the churchyard at Holme-in-Cliviger, near Burnley. A simple stone cross marks his grave and there is a memorial to him in St.Peter's church, Burnley.

A room of the Towneley Hall Museum in Burnley is dedicated to him which has a model of the Heavy Brigade charge at Balaclava, and various artifacts, including his commissions, another dented helmet and a sword presented to him by Colonel Charles Towneley.

A life size memorial can be seen in the Royal Garrison Church, the statue also depicts troopers of his former regiment, the 18th Hussars and 5th Dragoon Guards.

BEATSON, Major General William Fergusson

Born : 25th June 1804 - Rossend Castle, Fife, Scotland   Died : 4th February 1872

Status : Rode in the Charge

Medals : Crimea (B.I.S)

Fourth and youngest son of Robert Beatson he joined the 2nd battalion 25th Bengal Native Infantry as an ensign in 1820. Lieutenant in 1823, Captain 1837, Major 1848, Lieutenant-Colonel 1853, Colonel 1864, and Major-General 1865. He was an accomplished horseman and he distinguished himself as a soldier throughout the campaigns in India. In 1832 on furlough from India he joined the British Legion in Spain during the fight against the Carlists. Beatson was severely wounded whilst in command of the 10th Infantry Regiment. For his gallant deeds on 28th May and 6th July 1836 he was awarded the cross of the Order of San Fernando, which he was allowed to wear. In 1837 Beatson returned to Central India and in 1840 formed the Bundelkhand Legion to help quell the disturbances in the area. Beatson married Margaret Marian Humphreys on the 12th February 1840. In 1844 the unit served under Napier in operations in the Bugti hills. In 1847 he travelled to Hyderabad to command the Nizam's cavalry, leaving in 1851 with the rank of Brigadier. Promoted Lieutenant-Colonel November 1853, returned to India in 1856 to command the Nizam's cavalry.

At the start of the Crimean war an agreement had been reached with Turkey to supply 20,000 men who would be trained and led by British and French officers. Beatson's knowledge and expertise as a leader of irregular cavalry was to play a part in this plan.

Camp at Devno, Saturday, The Times 8th July 1854
General Beatson passed up on Monday and pitched his tents about two miles beyond our outposts, on the road to Shumla. He is going on to that place to undertake the organization into cavalry of 4,000 Bashi-Bazouks, and he is accompanied by Captain Green.

The next reference to General Beatson is a communication in the Times dated 19th August 1854 Varna "At Silistria the party found the head-quarters of the Bashi-Bazouks (since disbanded) under General Beatson, who hospitably regaled them with English cheese and porter purchased from a man who had bought them from the Russians, looking on their taking the town as a settled thing". General Beatson was to organise a Turkish irregular Cavalry Brigade, however the first attempt failed. Beatson who was on furlough offered to join the staff of Scarlett.

General Scarlett used Major Beatson, who was an experienced officer, as an additional ADC. Below is an extract of a report from General Scarlet to Lord Lucan dated the 27th October, 1854:
'My best thanks are due to Brigade-Major Conolly, and to my aide-de-camp, Lieutenant Elliot, 5th Dragoon Guards, who afforded me every assistance, and to Colonel Beatson of the Honourable E.I.C. service, who as a volunteer, is attached to my Staff. Lieutenant Elliot, severely wounded in the head, was at my side in the charge, and previously displayed the greatest coolness and gallantry. Colonel Beatson also gave me all the assistance which his experience and well-known gallantry enabled him to do throughout the day."

Later the idea of an irregular Cavalry was to re-surface, Beatson was to offer his services to Omar Pasha, commander of the British Forces in the Crimea. Beatson became a Major-General in the Turkish Army. The force he raised consisted mainly of Albanians who lacked any form of discipline, would not obey orders, and were inclined to rape and pillage at any given opportunity. This unruly force soon came under the gaze of the British vice-Consul J.H.Skene, eventually Beatson and his marauding Bashi-Bazouks, who also became known as "Beatson's Horse", were to come under the control of Major General Robert Vivian, who was also attached to the Turkish army. The Bashi-Bazouks were notorious for their brutality and wore their own native dress.

April 15th 1855 Times correspondent
The Bashi-bazonka said they were starved, and they were obliged to plunder. This they did to such an extent, that the Commander-in-Chief earnestly wished them to operate as far as possible from the main body of the army. General Jougsouf gave up in disgust. General Beatson remained and received the appointment which he now holds.

September 10th 1855 Times Correspondent
"The Bashi-Bazouke have been attached to the command of General Vivian, under whose orders General Beatson will henceforward act. As regards the cavalry of the contingent, it is to be made up to between 3,000 and 4,000 sabres and lances. Its present strength is not above one-third of that number."

December 6th 1855 Times Correspondent
An interesting letter appeared in The Times entitled "A defence of the Bashi-Bazouks" In September, 1855 the Minister-at-War attached Beatson's Horse to the Turkish Contingent, thus degrading it from an independent to a secondary command, General Beatson resigned.
"The old and tried General who would see service, who was resolved at all hazards not to be shelved at Shumla or Magnesia, has lost his command. After the deadly campaigns on the Danube; after the bloody fields of Inkermann and Balaclava; after the weary labour of organizing and disciplining a force which Ibrahim Pasha, Omar Pasha and General

Yuenf found intractable, General Beatson has returned home unnoticed and unknown."

The Times 12th November 1856
Her Majesty's steam frigate Gladiator left Malta for Marseilles on the 31st of October, conveying, on their way to England, Mr Skeene, the British Consul at Aleppo, Major Mahomed Aga, Messrs. Girand, Malloaf, and Tabret, witnesses in the forthcoming court-martial which General Beatson, of Bashi-Bazouk fame, has demanded, in order to clear himself of the grave charges preferred against him by General Shirley.

In a letter to the Times 30th December 1856.
Various incidents which were taken from official correspondence are noted below. Beatson requested additional officers to control the "wild men, such as Albanians and others" and the power of summary executions to control the murderers. He also proposed that the remedy was to "send the whole of the men at once to the Crimea, where we can give them something to occupy them". The letter is signed "W.F. Beatson, Lieut.-General 5, Suffolk Place, Pall Mall"

The Times 28th February 1857.
The court of inquiry ordered by the General Commanding-in-chief on the charges preferred by Colonel Shirley against General Beatson at the urgent demand of the gallant General, has commenced proceedings.

The Times 20th April 1857.
The court decided that there are no grounds whatsoever to render it necessary to investigate the charges brought by Major General Beatson against Colonel Shirley by a court martial.

Controversy was to follow General Beaston, concerning his handling of the Bashi-Bazoukhs with numerous letters in the Times, Courts of inquiry, legal law suits.

In January 1860 another legal battle ensued Beatson vs Skene, the later suggesting that General Beatson was involved in an insurrection, "When General Smith arrived at the Dardanelles, General Beaston assembled the commanding officers of the regiments, and actually endeavoured to persuade them to make a mutiny in their regiments against General Smith and against the authority of Vivlan."

This was after Vivian had replaced him in September 1855 with Major-General Smith. Beatson denied the accusations and returned to England. The trial commenced in January 1860 and cost Beatson an estimated £3000. The jury found for Skene on purely legal technicalities, they went on to censure Skene for failing to withdraw his statements after he had discovered that they were unfounded.

Beatson was promoted Major-General on the 8th January 1865 to command the Allahabad division and travelled out to India shortly afterwards. He was a soldier of the old school, was used to living in rough conditions, led by example, handsome in appearance, and dignified in bearing, he was a soldier of the austere and earnest type. He commanded the Allahabad division from 1866 to 1869, and the Ambala division from 1869 until he returned home on leave in 1872. He died suddenly at the vicarage, New Swindon, Wiltshire, on 4th February 1872, aged sixty-eight.

Beatson's wife Margaret died on the 22nd December 1866 soon after Beatson had taken command Allahabad division. They had four daughters, only Mrs McMullen survived him.

Illustrated London News 10th February 1872
Obituary of Eminent Persons includes - General Beatson died at New Swindon Vicarage.
See "The Oxford Dictionary of National Biographies".

Engraved by D.J Pound from a photograph by Mayall

CONOLLY, Major James

Born : 1818

Died : 22nd June 1885 - Wiesbaden, Germany
Status : Rode in the Charge

Medals : Crimea (B.I.S)

Christie's 17th November 1987, Lot 111, Five: Lieutenant General James Connolly, Late 5th Dragoon Guards, Brigade Major to The Heavy Brigade: (a) Order of the Bath, Companion (C.B.), Military Division, 18ct. gold (Hallmarks for London) with its gold riband buckle. (b) Crimea, 1854-56, three clasps, Balaclava, Inkermann, Sebastopol (Major Cavy. Staff), engraved in large serif capitals. (c) France, Second Empire, Legion of Honour, Fifth Class, Badge, silver, gold centre and enamel; Third Republic, Legion of Honour, Commander, Badge. gold and enamel, some white enamel damage to both pieces, with two bestowal documents (1873, 1874) (d) Turkey, Order of the Medjidie, two Fifth Class Badges, silver, gold and enamel (e) Turkish Crimea, Sardinian issue, the group very fine and better unless otherwise stated, together with the licence to accept and wear the French award (7) Estimate £1,400-1,600

The following is extracted from Kinglake Vol. 4: Without orders, the trumpets sounded and, forming line on the move, the regiment leapt forward and plunged into the broken right wing of the enemy mass. On the other flank, Captain Connolly, Scarlett's Brigade Major, had ridden to the second squadron of the Inniskillings who charged the left flank of the Russians across good ground, free from the impediments of the cavalry camp. They smashed into the back of the inward-wheeling wing and so tightly did they become locked, Connolly found his arms held by the dead body of a Russian who had fallen across his saddle.

Harts annual Army List 1855, ensign 17th June 1836, Lieut 28th November 1837, Captain 14th March 1845, Major 12th December 1854, placed on half pay 30th March 1847. From Harts annual Army List 1860 : James Conolly, Major, unattached. Major 12th December 1854, Lt Col Conolly served the Eastern Campaign of 1854 as Brigade-Major to the Heavy Cavalry Brigade, including the battle of Balaclava, and siege of Sebastopol.

The Times, 27th June 1885, "General James Conolly, C.B.-Died at Wiesbaden on the 22nd inst. He was born in 1818, entered the army in 1836, became Captain in 1845, and served in the Eastern campaign of 1854-5, for which he obtained the medal with two clasps, the Legion of Honour, and 5th class of the Miejide, and the Turkish Medal. From 1867 to 1869 he acted as assistant Quartermaster-General at Aldershot, and he was also military attache at Frankfort, Vienna and Paris successively. He became a Lieutenant-Colonel in 1856, Colonel in 1862, Major-General in 1868, and a Lieutenant-General in 1880. He was nominated a Companion of the order of the Bath in 1875.

ELLIOT, Captain Alexander James Hardy

Born : Unknown

Died : 1st July 1909
Status : Slightly wounded in the Charge

Medals : Crimea (B.I.S) Knight (5th Class) The French Legion of Honour, Punniar Star, Sutlej (Ferozeshah, Sobraon)

A.J. Hardy Elliot, Cornet in 9th Lancers 18th July 1848, Lieutenant 5th Dragoon Guards 14th June 1850, Captain 22nd December 1854. Captain Elliot served five years in India . Served the Eastern campaign 1854 as Aid-de-Camp to General Scarlett and was wounded at the battle of Balaclava. He received his medal from the hand of the Queen on 18th May, 1855. Brevet Major 17th July 1855, Major 29th July 1856, Brevet Lieutenant Colonel 29th May 1863, Colonel 1st February 1871, Major General 1st July 1881, Colonel 6th Dragoon Guards 3rd January 1892, Colonel 21st Lancers 18th February 1902.

His recommendation states: "I beg to name Captain & Brevet Major Elliott of the Regt under my command as the person "whose distinguished prowess" at Balaclava most entitles him to the honour which it may be contemplated to confer. I hereto subjoin a short statement of Services in the Field of the Officer in Question: Captain & Brevet Major Elliott was present at the battle of " Punniar", as also the first Punjab Campaign, including the battle of "Ferozeshah." Served the Eastern Campaign of 1854 as Aide de Camp to General Scarlett, & was wounded at the battle of Balaclava. - T.W. McMahon. Lt Col Commg 5th Dn Gds."

Leaves from a Soldier's Note Book by Franks. page 70......He (Scarlett) was the first man into the ranks of the Russians. Accompanied by two others as brave as he, one was Lieutenant Elliott the Generals Aide-de-Camp and the other Sergeant James Shegog of the 5th Dragoon Guards, his orderly Sergeant. These two rode near the General, and I can affirm that they were the cause of three or four of the enemy "biting the dust".

The New York Times of the 21st May 1882 recounts "After the battle of his brother officers went into his tent and found him standing before a looking glass."Haloa, Elliot. Beautifying, are you?" "Yes," was the answer "I am sticking on my nose." It had been slashed nearly off his face in the melee."

Broad Arrow 10th July 1909 Major General Sir Alexander Elliot KCB Hon. Col. 21st Lancers Died on the 1st Inst. At 36 Ennismore Gardens. London, SW Aged 83....He took part in the Gwalior Campaign being present at the battle of Punniar, receiving the Bronze Star, two years later he was again on active service in the Sutlej campaign when he took part in the battles of Ferozeshah and Sobraon (wounded) Receiving the medal with three clasps. During the Crimean war he was A.D.C to Brigadier General Scarlett.

832 MONKS, Trumpeter Thomas

Born : Unknown

Enlisted :

Died : April 1902 - Shrewsbury

Status : Rode in the Charge

Medals : Crimea (B.I.S) French Medaille Militaire, Long Service and Good Conduct Medal

Scarlett's Brigade Trumpeter was Trumpeter Monks who came from Scarlett's old regiment. The musters show he was effective from the 1st October to the 31st December spending 3 days on board ship.

Monks accompanied Scarlett along with Elliot and Shegog at the front of the Charge. Before the Charge of the Heavy Brigade Lord Lucan lost patience and ordered his Trumpeter (Joy) to sound the Charge, this he did twice, but was totally ignored, the reason being was that the Inniskillings and Greys had to complete their formation, when this had been achieved the command was given "eyes front", then Scarlett turned to Monks and ordered him to sound the Charge. On this third signal the Brigade moved forward.

The French Medaille Militaire. (For) "gallantry in the field in the action of Balaclava on the 25th. of October, 1854; and served with uniform good conduct during the whole of the campaign." WO102 L.S & G.C awarded to Sgt. Thomas Monks, gratuity £5, recommended 6th March 1868, issued 20th April 1868.

Article right taken from *The Times* 5th January 1855.

French Medaille Militaire

LETTERS FROM THE CRIMEA.

The subjoined letter has just been received from a young man named Monks, a trumpeter in the 6th Enniskillen Dragoons :—

"Camp before Sebastopol, Dec. 4.

"My dear Father,—I now take the opportunity of writing to you, hoping to find you all well, as this leaves me quite well, thank God for it. I suppose you have been anxious about me because I did not write to you before, but the reason was, because I could not get any paper to write on. I was very glad to think that the little present came in so good time for you. I hope mother is better than she was. I was very ill myself for about six weeks with the bowel complaint. I was in hospital till we came to this country, and after we landed I got better every day. I thought it was all over with me, it made me so very weak.

"I suppose you have heard about the battle we had on the 25th of October. If you could see *The Times* of November the 12th, you will see a very good account of our regiment, and the old Scotch Greys, who made a grand charge against double their number. The heavy brigade got great credit for that day ; but I am sorry to say the light brigade got cut up. They lost about 600 men out of 800. It made me feel very much when we went out to cover them, to see them fall. It brought us under a very heavy cross fire from the enemy, the balls and shells bursting beside us. A ball would burst under a horse, and blow it to pieces, and never hurt the man. You would see men running back with arms off, and others bleeding from all parts of their bodies.

"Dear father, I never once thought that I should have seen such a sight as a battle. On the 5th of November we had another hard and bloody battle, but it did not come so near to us as we expected it would. It began near to Sebastopol. The Russians took our Foot Guards by surprise in their tents before they had got up. The poor fellows fought well, and only with their bayonets. There were about 4,000 of the Russians killed. What with ours, the French, and the Russians, the whole valley was full of the dead. We kept our lot back that we had had the fight with. Talk about the 5th of November being kept up for bonfires and firing of arms, it was a 5th, and no mistake. I thought of it often afterwards that that day of the battle was on a Sunday. I thought about you being at chapel, and how you could all be clean, while we were like navvies, all dirty and hungry, besides being in the rain. I can tell you, dear father, when one thinks about home, it is enough to make one cry ; but I hope we will have sunny days for these yet. It is now December, and we are in camp yet. We had a great storm about a week ago. I was on trumpeter's guard at the time the storm came across the plain, accompanied with hailstones and snow, and it blew all our tents down. The only way to keep still was to lie down. I had to do so for fear of being borne among the dirt. You may think in what sort of a state our tents were, as, after it was all over, we had to lay down that night on the wet ground without anything to eat, the cooks being unable to keep the fires in. We had our grog and a bit of biscuit at night. Ever since then it has been very wet and cold. Our poor horses are dying by sections every day, and Sebastopol is not taken yet, though we have had about seven weeks' hard firing at it. The Russians often make a sally out, but are driven back again. The Russian shipping is all that they can fire from, but we can't get at it yet. I was on picket the other day ; we have to stay out all night with our horses, and it was very wet and cold. I don't think we can stand this much longer, but still we all keep up our spirits well. I only hope we may get one more good charge at them and finish it. I must now conclude for the present, and I hope I have eased your mind about me. Accept of my kind love to yourself, and no more from your affectionate son,

"THOMAS MONKS,

"Trumpeter, 6th Enniskillen Dragoons.

"P.S. The guns are firing away now. We are about two miles off them, but we can see the flash and smoke.

"You may guess what sort of a state we are in when I tell you I have not had a chance of washing my face these four weeks, let alone having a clean shirt. We are, I am sorry to say, in a state of filth, but we do the best we can."

Monks' discharge papers stated he was born at Lancaster, his height being 5ft 3", with a fair complexion, blue eyes, light brown hair, and had "no trade" on enlistment. He served 28 years 3 months, of which 3 years 10 months were "under age", 8 years 7 months as Pte., 9 years 10 months as Trumpeter, 1 year 2 months as Cpl., and 8 years 8 months as Sgt. Served 2 years 1 month in the Crimea and 8 years 5 months in India. Conduct and character, "Exemplary". In possession of five G.C. badges. Discharged from the Army on the 9th April 1872.

Shrewsbury and Edowes Journal, 25th May 1902, The obituary of Thomas Monks: "Trumpet-Major Thomas Monks, a veteran with a remarkable military service who had for long been wont to entertain the younger members of the regiment with stories of the Crimean war, died this year. He had been Trumpeter to Sir James Yorke Scarlett... when he commanded the Heavy Brigade at Balaklava....Trumpeter Monks left the Inniskilling Dragoons after 28 years of service in 1872, and spent the following years with the Shropshire Militia Yeomanry (sic) at Shrewsbury. He joined the Shropshire Yeomanry Band in 1873 and became Trumpet-Major in 1882, serving regularly until the training at Ross, in 1900. There after, in view of his 25 years service with the Yeomanry, his pay was continued by Colonel Ormsby Gore until his death. He was given a military funeral with the band in attendance, the coffin being followed by his charger led by a Yeoman with his empty jack boots suspended from the saddle and reversed. He resided prior to his death at 28 Porthill Road, Shrewsbury, on May 2nd 1902 the funeral service was held at St. Georges Church, Alma Road, Shrewsbury." Trumpet-Major Monks' medals are housed in the Yeomanry section in the Shrewsbury Castle Military museum. He is buried in Shrewsbury general cemetery.

Trumpeter Thomas Monks. 6th Inniskilling Dragoons.

The 1st Dragoons
"The Royals"

The 1st Dragoons Strength

Departed Liverpool	Arrived Varna	Ship	Staff	Officers	Troopers	Horses
10th May	28th June	Gertrude	1	3	52	50
10th May	28th June	Pedestrian	1	3	51	52
20th May	14th July	Arabia	1	2	59	62
20th May	14th July	Rip Van Winkle	1	2	67	67
28th May	8th July	Coronetta	2	2	48	50
30th May	14th July	Conrad	0	2	17	15

1st Dragoons
294 troopers and 14 officers with 296 horses departed from England for the Crimea. From the musters it would appear the majority of men arrived in the Crimea on the 4th/5th October, with a few on the 9th October. 255 officers and men were effective on the 25th October 1854. Some 53 either died or were hospitalised or remained in Varna.

The Times, Friday, 12th May 1854, page 7
At Liverpool the preparations for despatching troopships are being prosecuted with unabated vigor. Yesterday the Gertrude (1,361 tons) and the Pedestrian went into the river, having on board upwards of 100 horses and a number of officers belonging to the 1st Royal Dragoons

Times dated Saturday 20th May 1854 page 12
The second squadron of the 1st Dragoons left Manchester yesterday morning for Liverpool, where they embark for Turkey this morning on board the Arabia and Rip van Winkle transports, now lying in the Mersey. Major Wardlow commanded, The squadron consists of 127 men, with 16 officers, and 113 troop horses.

The Times, 1st June 1854, page 9
The transport ship Conrad, belonging to Mr Edward Oliver of Liverpool, took her departure yesterday from Liverpool for Malta direct, with the 4th and last detachment of the 1st Royal Dragoons, from Hulme Barracks on board. The detachment consisted only of 15 men and horses, besides several officers. There being plenty of unoccupied space in the vessel, 50 tons of hay were place in her. on her arrival at Malta she will be placed at the service of the Admiralty agents if required.

The Times, 4th July 1854, page 9
The arrival of the Rip van Winkle at Malta on June 22nd number 82 from Liverpool 32 days, Captain Campbell, Cornet Hartopp, Vetinary Sergeant Poett, 67 troopers and 65 horses.

The Regiment on landing was placed under canvas, the tents being pitched about 50 yards from the southern margin of Varna Bay. Each bell-tent was occupied by 12 men. On the 19th July the Regiment marched from Varna to Devna, and pitched its camp to the west of the 5th Dragoon guards. On the 27th July, the Devna Camp moved on the outbrake of cholera, moving to Kara-Hassein. Cholera first appeared in the regiment, while it was camped at Kara-Hassein, the first case proved fatal on the 3rd August, with onother five cases reported in as many days. A new encampment was set up on the Adrianople Road, two more caught the disease and died. On the 17th, the regiment marched back from Kara-Hassein to the vicinity of Varna, and encamped to the southwest of that town, near the Adrinnople road. (They hoped to escape the desease by moving camp) On the 22nd, the Corps "moved its tents to the beach at Varna Bay, preparatory to embarking on the following day for the Crimea." Previous to the embarkation of the Regiment 10 men, who were unfit to accompany it were placed on board a sick transport, for conveyance to the General Hospital at Scutari. At the end of September the regiment embarked for the Crimea: and during the voyage across the Black Sea, the wind blew a heavy gale, "in which half the horses perished" The Regiment landed on the 4th October, at Balaklava, and the tents were pitched in the valley, outside the town. (*Medical and Surgical History of British Army in Turkey and Crimea during the Russian War, 1858 page 24*)

On the 26th September the regiment lost more horses than at Waterloo.... Total Loss 150 (Oct 1854, MS letter of Lieut-Col. John Yorke, 1st Royal Dragoons)

30th September 1854 Varna
We sailed at 4pm on the 26th........we towed a ship with the Royal Dragoons on board, we had not been long out when it blew a gale and we parted from the ship we towed (*The Fields of War, letters from Richard Templeman Goodman*)

On the 13th May 1856, the Corps embarked on board the "Orinoco" for England. It had proceeded on service with a strength of 19 officers and 294 men; and was reinforced by 10 officers and 279 men. Of the 29 officers and 573 who served in the East, four officers and seven men were wounded in action, one man died of wounds, one officer and 80 men died from disease, 14 officers and 46 men were "invalided to England," one man deserted, and 15 men were finally "discharged the service".

1260 ABBOTT, Private Charles

Born : Date unknown - Wellingborough
Enlisted :
Medals : Crimea (S)

Died : Unknown
Status : To Scutari 26th October 1854

A butcher prior to enlistment. The musters show he was effective from the 1st-25th October, 25 days ordinary pay, 3 days on board ship 22, days on shore. All three musters endorsed "Scutari". Marginal note reads "In payment of paymaster Genl. Depot Scutari from 26th Oct, 6th DN Guards No 626". WO14/1 Scutari Muster Roll January-March 1855 remarks indicates "Orderly Hospital Ship" 1st-31st January, no dates or remarks shown in the next two musters.

Medal Roll for Sebastopol clasp shows his entitlement to the clasp 1260 Pte Abbott, Charles. Marginal note reads "Dead" WO 100/24 Folio 144. Medal Roll - Class 2. Died, Retired from service, Discharged. Roll dated 10th February 1859, Royal Barracks, Dublin. - Entry No 19. 1260 Pte Abbott Charles -Dead- WO 100/24 page 151.

1195 ADAMS, Farrier Alexander

Born : Unknown
Enlisted :
Medals : Crimea (B.I.S)

Died : Unknown
Status : Probably rode in the Charge

The musters show he was effective from the 1st October to the 31st December, 92 days ordinary pay, 92 days at 2d Good conduct pay, 4 days on board ship, 88 days on shore. WO 100/24 page 138 Remarks: Promoted from Private since Crimean Medal Return went in.

Good Conduct pay was only paid to Corporals and below, those receiving it would wear a badge to signify the award.

764 ADAMS, Private George

Born : Unknown
Enlisted :
Medals : Crimea (B.I.S)

Died : Unknown
Status : Probably rode in the Charge

James Auction. 33 Timberhill, Norwich. Lot 65 on the 28th April 1987 £275. Crimea Medal 2 clasps Balaclava and Inkermann. Engraved naming large block capitals. VF

The musters show he was effective from the 1st October to the 31st December, 92 days ordinary pay, 92 days at 2d Good conduct pay, 9 days on board ship, 83 days on shore.

1114 ADAMSON, Private Henry

Born : Unknown
Enlisted :
Medals : Crimea (B.I.S)

Died : Unknown
Status : Probably rode in the Charge

The musters show he was effective from the 1st October to the 31st December, 92 days ordinary pay, 4 days on board ship, 88 days on shore. On Medal Roll for Sebastopol clasp WO100/24, page 144 Remarks: "H&R to replace lost 25/10/56". Medal Roll - Class 2. Died, Retired from service, Discharged. Roll dated 10th February 1859, Royal Barracks, Dublin. - Entry No 18. 1114 Pte Adamson Henry -Dead- WO 100-24 page 151.

The Royal Barracks Dublin (now the Colins Barracks Museum)

789 ALDERSON, Private Thomas

Born : 1820 - Newcastle-upon-Tyne
Enlisted : 26th February 1842
Medals : Crimea (B.I.S)

Died : 1892 - Birmingham
Status : Probably rode in the Charge

DNW 28th March 2002, Medals from the collection of Gordon Everson, Lot 40, A Heavy Brigade group of three to Private Thomas Alderson, 1st Royal Dragoons. Crimea 1854-56, 3 clasps, Balaclava, Inkermann, Sebastopol (T. Alderson, 1st Rl. Dragoons) officially impressed naming; Army L.S. & G.C., V.R., small letter reverse (789 Thos. Alderson, 1st Dragoons); Turkish Crimea 1855, Sardinian issue, unnamed, the first with heavy contact marks and repaired suspension at the claw, therefore fine, otherwise nearly very fine (3) Hammer Price £1400

Thomas Turnbull Alderson was born at Newcastle-upon-Tyne in 1820, and enlisted into the 1st Dragoons at Newcastle on 26th February 1842, aged 22. Height 5' 10 1/2", complexion dark, eyes grey hair brown. Trade cabinet maker.

The musters show he was effective from the 1st October to the 31st December., 92 days ordinary pay, 63 days Good conduct pay at 1d and 29 days at 2d good conduct pay, 3 days on board ship, 89 days on shore. Marginal note reads "Forfeited 1d per diem Good conduct pay - Oct".

When discharged on the 12th May 1866 he was in "possession of Five Good Conduct Badges, the Crimea Medal with 3 clasps, Turkish Medal, and Long Service and Good Conduct Medal with a Gratuity of £5." Discharged 11th May 1866 at Manchester where he intended to reside. Shown on the 1871 and 1881 census living in Birmingham. In 1891 he was resident at St. Josenlis Home in Smethwick, administered by "sisters of the poor", aged 76 and married.

1181 ALDRIDGE, Private John

Enlisted :
Medals : Crimea (B.I.S)

Died . Unknown
Status : Probably rode in the Charge

The musters show he was effective from the 1st October to the 20th December, 81 days ordinary pay, 4 days on board ship, 77 days on shore. 3rd Muster endorsed "Scutari". Marginal note reads "To payment of paymaster Scutari from 21st December". Medal Roll for Sebastopol clasp WO 100/24 page 145 Remarks: "H&R to replace lost 30/10/56".

1273 ALDRIDGE, Private Thomas

Born : Date unknown - Nottingham.
Enlisted : 29th November 1853
Medals : Crimea (B.I.S)

Died : 17th February 1855 - Camp Kadikoi
Status : Probably rode in the Charge

The musters show he was effective from the 1st October to the 31st December, 92 days ordinary pay, 9 days on board ship, 83 days on shore. A Farm Servant prior to enlistment. WO 100/24 page 138 Remarks : Died 17th. Feby. page 144 Remarks: Dead. Medal Roll - Class 2. Died, Retired from service, Discharged. Roll dated 10th February 1859, Royal Barracks, Dublin. - 1273 pte Aldridge Thomas -Dead- WO 100/24 page 151.

749 ALLEN, Private Robert

Born : Unknown
Enlisted :
Medals : Crimea (B.I.S)

Died : Unknown
Status : Probably rode in the Charge

The musters show he was effective from the 1st October to the 31st December, 92 days ordinary pay, 9 days on board ship, 83 days on shore.

1263 ANDREWS, Private William

Born : Unknown
Enlisted :
Medals : Crimea (B.I.S)

Died : Unknown
Status : Probably rode in the Charge

The musters show he was effective from the 1st October to the 31st December, 92 days ordinary pay, 4 days on board ship, 88 days on shore. No entry in the Sebastopol clasp Medal Roll, to which he is entitled.

1256 APPLEBY, Private John
Born : Unknown
Enlisted :
Medals : Crimea (B.I.S)

Died : Unknown
Status : Probably rode in the Charge

The musters show he was effective from the 1st October to the 31st December, 92 days ordinary pay, 9 days on board ship, 83 days on shore.

1208 ARNOLD, Private William
Born : Date Unknown - Hitchin
Enlisted : 5th June 1852
Medals : Crimea (B.S)

Died : 2nd March 1855 - Scutari
Status : Probably rode in the Charge

The musters show he was effective from the 1st October to the 20th December, 81 Days ordinary pay, 4 days on board ship, 77 days on shore. 3rd Muster endorsed "Scutari". Marginal note reads "To payment of paymaster Scutari 21st December". WO14/1 Scutari Muster Roll January-March 1855 remarks indicate Hospital 1st January to the 18th February. Died 18th February. Medal Roll for Sebastopol clasp. 1208 Pte Arnold William, marginal note reads "WO dead" WO 100-24 page 145.

1268 ASLETT, Private James Richard
Born : 1835
Enlisted :
Medals : Crimea (B.S), Distinguished Conduct Medal

Died : Unknown
Status : Severely wounded in the Charge

Spinks Auction 16th June 1987 Lot 353. Group of three to Pte Aslett 1st Dragoons. (a) DCM Victorian issue (James R. Aslett 1st RL. Drags (b) Crimea 2 Bars Balaclava, Sebastopol, (Pvte R. Aslett 1st RL DRS) Engraved, (c) Turkish Crimea Sardinian issue. Medals mounted on Bar and having attractive Silver Buckles on ribands VF (3) Hammer Price £1950.

The musters show he was effective from the 1st-25th October, 25 days ordinary pay, 4 days on board ship, 21 days on shore. 3rd Muster endorsed "Scutari". Marginal note reads "To payment of paymaster Scutari 26th Oct". Casualty roll lists Astlett as wounded severely at Balaclava. WO14/1 Scutari Muster Roll January-March 1855 remarks indicate "Hospital" 1st January to the 31st March, "Koulali" 1st-28th February, the March muster is endorsed with an un-readable word.

James Astlett aged 19, had his right humerus smashed by a round shot, it became necessary to remove the arm from the shoulder-joint, the amputation was done immediately after the injury. He was sent to Scutari, where the stump soon united without a bad sympton. (*Medical and Surgical History of British Army in Turkey and Crimea during the Russian War, 1858 page 25*)

The Distinguished Conduct Medal recommendation dated 9th January 1855, medal sent to Crimea 26th March 1855, returned, and sent to Chatham 14th May 1855. Medal Roll for Sebastopol clasp entitled. 1268. Pte. Aslett. James Richard. Marginal note reads "Discharged H&R 2/4." WO 100-24 Folio 144. Medal Roll - Class 2. Died, Retired from service, Discharged. Roll dated 10th February 1859, Royal Barracks, Dublin. - 1273 Pte Aslett. James -Dead- WO 100-24 p151.

914 AVERY, Private William
Born : Unknown
Enlisted :
Medals : Crimea (B.S), Long Service and Good Conduct Medal

Died : Unknown
Status : Probably rode in the Charge

The musters show he was effective from the 4th October to the 31st December, 89 days ordinary pay, 89 days at 1d good conduct pay, 3 days on board ship, 86 days on shore. Marginal note reads "from payment of paymaster Scutari 4th Oct". WO102 L.S & G.C awarded with a gratuity £5, recommended 25th March 1866.

582 AVES, Trumpeter Samuel
Born : 1824 - York
Enlisted :
Medals : Crimea (B.I.S)

Died : Unknown
Status : Probably rode in the Charge

The musters show he was effective from the 1st October to the 31st December, 92 days at 1s-7 1/2d per diem, 92 days at 1d Good Conduct pay, 3 days on board ship, 89 days on shore.

In the 1881 census Samuel Aves, age 57, army pensioner, living at 2 Demark Place, Blenheim Road, Deal, Kent, with his wife Mary age 50 and two sons Montagu aged 11 and William aged 6, both born in Kent.

649 BAILEY, Sergeant Matthew

Born : April 1810 - Edinburgh
Enlisted : 28th March 1839
Medals : Crimea (B.I.S), The French Medaille Militaire, L.S & G.C Medal

Died : Unknown
Status : Probably rode in the Charge

The musters show he was effective from the 5th October to the 31st December, 92 days at 2s-2d per diem, 4 days on board ship, 88 days on shore.

Troop Sergeant-Major Matthew Bailey. The citation for the French Medaille Militaire reads "Served as a Sergeant during the whole of the Eastern Campaign; distinguished himself on patrol duty when his party was attacked by some Cossacks. Never missed a day's duty and was always a valuable man on pickets".

Photograph by J.Cundall and R. Howlett (in the series Crimean Heroes) 1856, shown wearing British Crimea 3 clasp medal and French Medaille Militaire medal. Modern copy sold by the National Army Museum in 1983. Queen Victoria and Prince Albert commissioned Joseph Cundall and R.Howlett to photograph the veterans as they returned from the war in the east, most of the photographs being taken at Aldershot. Some 26 photographs were selected for the publication "Crimean Heroes", but many more were included in the Royal Collection which are still preserved at Windsor Castle.
A list of the photographs taken by J.Cundall & R.Howlett held in the National Army Museum can be seen at: http://groups.yahoo.com/group/CrimeanWar/files/

WO Form 83. Attested for the 1st Dragoons on the 28th March 1839 at the age of 19 years and 1 month. Service 24 years 11 day's, discharged the service on 27th day of AprIl 1863. LSGC Medal with £5 Gratuity.

751 BAILEY, Private James

Born : Unknown
Enlisted :
Medals : Crimea (B.I.S)

Died : Unknown
Status : Probably rode in the Charge

The musters show he was effective from the 1st October to the 31st December, 92 days ordinary pay, 92 days at 2d good conduct pay, 4 days on board ship, 88 days on shore. Medal Roll - Class 2. Died, Retired from service, Discharged. Roll dated 10th February 1859, Royal Barracks, Dublin. - Entry No 25. 751 Pte Bailey, James. Discharged. Entry crossed through. Endorsed "Sent 31/8/60" WO 100-24 page 151.

493 BAKER, Sergeant Robert

Born : Unknown - Huntingdon
Enlisted : 14th March 1855
Medals : Crimea (B.S)

Died : 28th March 1855 - Scutari
Status : Probably rode in the Charge

A Baker prior to enlistment. The musters show he was effective from the 1st October to the 31st December, 92 days at 2s-2d per diem, 9 days on board ship, 83 days on shore. Medal Roll - Class 2. Died, Retired from service, Discharged. Roll dated 10th February 1859, Royal Barracks, Dublin. - 493 SGT Baker. Robert -Dead - WO 100-24 page 151.

812 BALCOMB, Private James

Born : Unknown
Enlisted :
Medals : Crimea (B.I.S)

Died : Unknown
Status : Probably rode in the Charge

The musters show he was effective from the 1st October to the 31st December, 92 days ordinary pay, 88 days at 1d good conduct pay, 4 days on board ship, 88 days on shore. Marginal note reads "1st Dragoons restored to Good conduct pay at 1d per diem 5th Octr"
Medal Roll for Sebastopol clasp, Entitled 812 Pte Balcomb. James. Marginal note reads "H&R 19 6/56" WO 100-24 page 145. Medal Roll - Class 2. Died, Retired from service, Discharged. Roll dated 10th February 1859, Royal Barracks, Dublin. - Entry No 28. 812 Pte Balcomb, James. Discharged. Entry crossed through. "Sent ..." WO 100-24 page 151.

Russian Casualties

The Naval Brigade sent doctors down to attend to the wounded, and they described to us that evening the effect of some of the sword-cuts inflicted by our Heavy dragoons on the heads of the Russians as appalling; in some cases the head-dress and skull being divided down to the chin. The edge of the sword was used, for the greatcoats worn by the Russians were difficult to pierce with the point. A Russian officer who was present writes that they had between 300 and 400 casualties mainly from sword-cuts. (*The Crimea in 1854 and 1894 by General Sir Evelyn Wood, 1895 p113*)

1039 BALD, Corporal William

Born : Unknown
Enlisted :
Medals : Crimea (A.B.I.S)

Died : Unknown
Status : Probably rode in the Charge

The musters show he was effective from the 1st October to the 31st December. 92 days at 1s-7 1/2d per diem, 92 days on shore. WO100/24 page 120 Remarks: Clerk to the Asst. Adj. Genl.

1192 BALSHAW, Private John

Born : Unknown
Enlisted :
Medals : Crimea (B.I.S)

Died : Unknown
Status : Probably rode in the Charge

The musters show he was effective from the 1st October to the 31st December, 92 days ordinary pay, 92 days at 2d Good conduct pay, 4 days on board ship, 88 days on shore. Marginal note "6 Dgn Guards 762".

576 BARBER, Private Charles

Born : Unknown
Enlisted :
Medals : Crimea (B.I.S)

Died : Unknown
Status : Probably rode in the Charge

The musters show he was effective from the 1st October to the 31st December, 92 days ordinary pay. 92 days at 2d Good conduct pay, 3 days on board ship, 89 days on shore.

951 BARNFIELD, Private William

Born : Unknown
Enlisted :
Medals : Crimea (B.I.S)

Died : Unknown
Status : Probably rode in the Charge

A Crimea medal with clasps for Balaclava, Inkermann, and Sebastopol to "W.T.Bamfield" and Turkish Crimea to the same recipient were held in the Regimental museum in 1991.

The musters show he was effective from the 1st October to the 31st December, 92 days ordinary pay, 92 days at 1d good conduct pay, 9 days on board ship, 83 days on shore.

BASSET, Lieutenant Arthur

Born : Unknown
Enlisted :
Medals : Crimea (B.I.S)

Died : Unknown
Status : Probably in the Charge

Cornet 12th December 1851, Lieutenant 29th April 1853, Captain 15th February 1856, Half pay 6th June 1856 (*Harts Annual Army List 1857 page 424*) The musters show he was effective from the 4th October to the 14th November and from the 1st-31st December. Supplied with rations "on shore" for 43 days. On board ship 1st-3rd October. Two Horses foraged at public expense for 92 Days. Medal Roll for the Sebastopol clasp marginal note reads "England" WO 100-24 page 143. Roll dated 10th February 1859 Royal Barracks Dublin states "Retired from the service".

1161 BATES, Private William

Born : Unknown
Enlisted :
Medals : Crimea (B.S)

Died : Unknown
Status : Probably rode in the Charge

The musters show he was effective from the 1st October to the 31st December, 92 days ordinary pay, 4 days on board ship, 88 days on shore.

Ambulances

On the 25th October the battle of Balaclava was fought, on which occasion our ambulance wagons were first brought into operation for the transport of the wounded, and were found to answer well. All wounded men within reach were collected and their hurts dressed the same evening; but as considerable alarm existed about the safety of our position in Balaklava they were shipped for Scutari as speedily as possible for further treatment. (*Medical and Surgical History of British Army in Turkey and Crimea during the Russian War, 1858*)

1137 BATES, Private Thomas

Born : Unknown
Enlisted :
Medals : Crimea (S)

Died : Unknown
Status : To Scutari 26th October 1854

The musters show he was effective from the 1st-25th October, 25 days ordinary pay, 4 days on board ship, 21 days on shore. 1st and 2nd Musters endorsed "Scutari" third muster endorsed "Malta". Marginal note reads "In payment of paymaster Scutari from 26 Oct, to Malta 10 Dec." Medal Roll for Sebastopol Clasp 1137 Pte Bates, Thomas marginal note reads "England" WO 100-24 page 151.

1254 BATT, Private James

Born : Unknown
Enlisted :
Medals : Crimea (B.I.S), Maharajpoor Star?, Punjab (Clasps Chilianwala, Goojerat)

Died : Unknown
Status : Probably rode in the Charge

Originally in the 16th Lancers (No 1484). Forfeited pension rights due to conviction for desertion 1840. Sick at Loodiana in 1846 (No Sutlej Medal). Volunteered 3rd Light Dragoons 1st April 1846 (No 1691). Volunteered 1st Dragoons 30th June 1853 (WO 1279,593,598)

The musters show he was effective from the 1st October to the 4th December and from the 15th-31st December, 89 days ordinary pay, 4 days on board ship, 85 days on shore. Marginal note reads "Confined 12 Decr. tried and Sentd to 50 lashes. released 14 December". Medal Roll Sebastopol clasp 1254 Pte Batt. James Marginal note reads "England H&R 3/4." WO 100-24 Folio 145 Medal Roll - Class 2. Died, Retired from service, Discharged. Roll dated 10th February 1859, Royal Barracks, Dublin. Entry No 24 1254 Pt Batt James. Entry crossed through -Discharged- Endorsed S.O.P. Birmingham (?) WO 100-24 page 145.

924 BENGE, Private William

Born : Unknown
Enlisted :
Medals : Crimea (B.I.S)

Died : Unknown
Status : Probably rode in the Charge

The musters show he was effective from the 1st October to the 3rd December, 64 days ordinary pay, 64 days at 1d good conduct pay, 3 days on board ship, 61 days on shore. 3rd Muster endorsed "Scutari". Marginal note reads "To payment of paymaster Scutari 4th December"

1168 BETTLES, Private Thomas

Born : Unknown
Enlisted :
Medals : Crimea (B.I.S)

Died : Unknown
Status : Probably rode in the Charge

The musters show he was effective from the 1st October to the 31st December, 92 days ordinary pay, 4 days on board ship, 88 days on shore. Medal Roll - Class 2. Died, Retired from service, Discharged. Roll dated 10th February 1859, Royal Barracks, Dublin. - Entry No 29.1168 Pte Bettles Thomas. Discharged. Entry crossed through and endorsed "Sent 12/11/61" WO 100-24 page 151.

1150 BEXCON, Private George

Born : Unknown
Enlisted :
Medals : Crimea (B.I.S)

Died : Unknown
Status : Probably rode in the Charge

The musters show he was effective from the 1st October to the 31st December, 92 days ordinary pay, 4 days on board ship, 88 days on shore. Medal Roll Sebastopol clasp 1150 Pte Bexcin, George. Marginal note reads "Regt 5/9." WO 100-24 Page 145.

1224 BIRD, Private James

Born : Date unknown - Newport
Enlisted : 25th November 1852
Medals : Crimea (B.S)

Died : 7th February 1855 - Scutari
Status : Probably rode in the Charge

The musters show he was effective from the 1st October to the 31st December, 92 days ordinary pay, 9 days on board ship, 83 days on shore. Medal Roll Sebastopol clasp 1224 Pte Bird, James. Marginal note reads "Dead" WO 100-24 Folio 145. Medal Roll - Class 2. Died, Retired from service, Discharged. Roll dated 10th February 1859, Royal Barracks, Dublin. Entry No 40 1224 Pt Bird James -Dead- WO 100-24 page 151.

1098 BLACKSHAW, Private Robert

Born : Date unknown - Derby
Enlisted : 11th July 1849
Medals : Crimea (B.S)

Died : 2nd February 1855
Status : Probably rode in the Charge

A groom prior to enlistment. The musters show he was effective from the 1st October to the 15th December, 74 days ordinary pay, 74 days at 1d good conduct pay, 4 days on board ship, 70 days on shore. 3rd muster endorsed "Scutari". Marginal note reads "To payment of paymaster at Scutari 14 December". WO14/1 Scutari Muster Roll January-March 1855 remarks indicate he died on the 2nd January.

Medal Roll Sebastopol clasp 1224 Pte. Blackshaw Robert. Marginal note reads "Dead". Medal Roll - Class 2. Died, Retired from service, Discharged. Roll dated 10th February 1859, Royal Barracks, Dublin. Entry No 41 1224 Pte. Blackshaw Robert -Dead- WO 100/24 page 151.

745 BLAKE, Private James

Born : Unknown
Enlisted :
Medals : Crimea (B.S)

Died : Unknown
Status : Severely wounded in the Charge

The musters show he was effective from the 1st-25th October. 25 Days ordinary pay, 25 days at 1d good conduct pay, 3 days on board ship, 22 days on shore. All 3 musters endorsed "Scutari". Marginal note reads "To payment of paymaster at Scutari 26th October. 32 Regiment No 2556". Casualty roll shows Wounded Severely at Balaclava. WO14/1 Scutari Muster Roll January-March 1855 remarks indicate "Duty in Stables" 1st-31st January, "Hospital" 1st-28th February, "Sent Home" 29th March.

Medal Roll - Class 2. Died, Retired from service, Discharged. Roll dated 10th February 1859, Royal Barracks, Dublin. Entry No 31 745 Pte. Blake James - Discharged - WO 100-24 page 151.

915 BLOUNT, Private Henry

Born : Unknown
Enlisted :
Medals : Crimea (B.I.S)
Medal with three clasps Balaklava, Inkermann, Sebastopol in Regimental museum (June 1991)

Died : Unknown
Status : Probably rode in the Charge

The musters show he was effective from the 1st October to the 31st December, 92 days ordinary pay, 92 days at 1d good conduct pay, 4 days on board ship, 88 days on shore. Medal Roll - Class 2. Died, Retired from service, Discharged. Roll dated 10th February 1859, Royal Barracks, Dublin. Entry No 32 915 Pte. Blount Henry - Discharged - WO 100/24 page 151.

628 BOWERMAN, Private Thomas

Born : Unknown
Enlisted :
Medals : Crimea (B.I.S)

Died : Unknown
Status : Probably rode in the Charge

March Medals Spring 1982 list. A group of three medals - Crimea (Balaclava, inkermann, Sebastopol) Engraved. LS&GC (Victoria) 1st Dghs. and Turkish Crimea Sardinian version named. Pte Thomas Bowerman 1st Dragoons.

The musters show he was effective from the 1st October to the 31st December, 92 days ordinary pay, 92 days at 3d good conduct pay, 9 days on board ship, 83 days on shore. Medal Roll - Class 2. Died, Retired from service, Discharged. Roll dated 10th February 1859, Royal Barracks, Dublin. Entry No 32, 628 Pte. Boweman Thomas note reads "England. Regt 6/9" Discharged WO 100-24 page 145.

The Distinguished Conduct Medal

Eight Distinghished Conduct Medals were awarded to men of the 1st Dragoons:

1268 Pte Aslett, James Richard	958 Pte Taylor, Peter
1115 Cpl Jones, John Ball	626 Pte Thomas John
995 Sgt Noake, Maillard (invalided)	414 TSM Tripp, George
356 Cpl Swash, Robert	1042 Pte Wale, John

833 BRIDGE, Private Henry

Born : Unknown
Enlisted :
Medals : Crimea (B.I.S)

Died : Unknown
Status : Probably rode in the Charge

The musters show he was effective from the 1st October to the 31st December, 92 days ordinary, 3 days on board ship, 89 days on shore.

1048 BRIGGS, Private Richard

Born : Unknown
Enlisted :
Medals : Crimea (B.S)

Died : Unknown
Status : To Scutari 26th October 1854

Sotheby Auction 27th July 1979, Lot 37, Crimea clasp Balaclava (Pve Rd Briggs 1st Royal Dns) - Engraved naming VF £240. Reseach with the medal indicated that Briggs was sent to Scutari the day after the battle.

The musters show he was effective from the 1st-25th October, 25 days ordinary pay, 25 days at 1d Good conduct pay, 9 days on Board ship, 16 days on shore. All 3 musters endorsed "Scutari". Marginal note reads "82 Regiment No 2144. To paymaster Scutari 26 Oct". WO14/1 Scutari Muster Roll January-March 1855 remarks indicate he was sent to England 1st January.

Medal Roll Sebastopol clasp 1048 Pte. Briggs, Richard, marginal note reads "England" WO 100/24 page 145. Medal Roll - Class 2. Died, Retired from service, Discharged. Roll dated 10th February 1859, Royal Barracks, Dublin. Entry No 26 1048 Pte. Briggs, Richard - discharged. Entry crossed through. Endorsed "sent to HIM 19/3/61" WO 100/24 page 155.

1120 BRITTON, Private Richard

Born : Unknown
Enlisted :
Medals : Crimea (B.I.S)

Died : Unknown
Status : Probably rode in the Charge

The musters show he was effective from the 1st October to the 31st December, 92 days ordinary pay, 92 days at 2d good conduct pay, 3 days on board ship, 89 days on shore. Marginal note reads "6 Dgn. Guards No 727". Medal Roll Sebastopol clasp 1120 Pte. Britton Richard Henry, marginal note reads "Regt 5/9" WO 100-24 page 145. Medal Roll - Class 2. Died, Retired from service, Discharged. Roll dated 10th February 1859, Royal Barracks, Dublin. Entry No 31 1120 Pte. Britton Rich Henry, Discharged. Entry crossed through and medal signed for by recipient WO 100/24 page 151.

1197 BROPHY, Private Jeremiah

Born : Unknown
Enlisted :
Medals : Crimea (B.I.S), Long Service and Good Conduct Medal

Died : Unknown
Status : Probably rode in the Charge

Dixon's Gazette 51 (Autumn 2007) No 4267, 3 clasp (B.I.S) J.Brophy 1st Royal Dragoons, engraved in contemporary style. Top two rivets crudely affixed. V.F £480

The musters show he was effective from the 1st October to the 31st December, 92 days ordinary, 92 days at 2d good conduct pay, 4 days on board ship, 88 days on shore. WO102 L.S & G.C issued 30th June 1865, gratuity £5.

1281 BULL, Private William

Born : Unknown
Enlisted :
Medals : Crimea (B.I.S)

Died : Unknown
Status : Probably rode in the Charge

The musters show he was effective from the 1st October to the 31st December, 92 days ordinary pay, 9 days on board ship, 83 days on shore, 92 days at 2d good conduct pay.

CAMPBELL, Captain George

Born : Unknown
Enlisted :
Medals : Crimea (B.S), The Sardinian War Medal

Died : Unknown
Status : Severely wounded in the Charge

Ensign 25th February 1848, Lieutenant 4th September 1849, Captain 1st April 1853. Shot through the shoulder when present at the cavalry action of Balaklava. (*Harts Annual Army list 1855 Page 128*). The musters show he was effective from the 1st-25th October and from the 18th November to the 31st December. "On Board Ship" 1st-6th October. One Horse foraged at public expense for 78 days. Marginal note reads "Wounded in action in front of Balaclava on 25th October". Casualty roll shows Wounded Severely at Balaclava.

The citation for the Sardinian War medal states he "displayed gallant conduct under fire in the cavalry action at Balaklava, on the 25th. of October 1854, and continued in command of his troop, although severely wounded, until the regiment was out of fire".

Marginal note in Sebastopol Medal Roll reads "England Order sent to H&R 9/4". WO 100-24 page 143, Retired from the service. Discharged Roll dated Royal Barracks, Dublin 10th February 1859, Captain G. Campbell retired from the service.

George McCloud, a young Glasgow medical graduate, met the mother of Captain George Campbell, Mrs Campbell asked McCloud to go out and look after her son and to accompany him home when convalescent. McCloud travelled in November 1854 by the quickest route and found his patient in the Crimea (presumably a hospital at Balaclava) "In some straits" He eventually had him transferred to Scutari. On his return with his patient to London in January 1855 he was interviewed about the conditions in Scutari. (*The Crimean Doctors Page 413*)

1454 CARNEY, Private Edward

Born : Unknown
Enlisted :
Medals : Crimea (B.I.S)

Died : Unknown
Status : Probably rode in the Charge

The musters show he was effective from the 1st October to the 31st December, 92 days ordinary pay, 69 at 1d good conduct pay, 3 days on board ship, 89 days on shore. Marginal note reads "Forfeited good conduct pay at 1d per diem on 9th December".

1218 CHALLIS, Private Robert

Born : Unknown
Enlisted :
Medals : Crimea (B.I.S)

Died : May 1893
Status : Probably rode in the Charge

The musters show he was effective from the 1st October to the 31st December, 92 days ordinary pay, 9 days on board ship. His Obituary can be seen in the *Sheffield Independent dated 1st June 1893, page 6.*

CHARLTON, Captain St. John William Chiverton

Born : Unknown
Enlisted :
Medals : Crimea (B.I.S)

Died : Unknown
Status : Probably rode in the Charge

Cornet 14th February 181, Lieutenant 1st April 1853, Captain 18th May 1855, on Half Pay 10th November 1856. Captain Charlton served the Eastern campaign of 1854-55, including the battles of Balaclava, Tchernaya, and the siege of Sebastopol (*Harts Annual Army List 1857 page 419*)

The musters show he was effective from the 1st October to the 31st December. "Present all Musters, supplied with rations 5th-26th Oct, 8th Nov-31st Dec, 54 days on shore. 1st-4th Oct and 27th Oct-7th Nov "On Board Ship". One Horse foraged at public expense. Roll dated 10th February 1859 Royal Barracks Dublin states "Retired from the service"

The Times of 28th May 1856 reported that "Captain W.C Charlton arrived at Spithead yesterday on the steam transport Orinoco."

The French Médaille Militaire

Created by the emperor Napoléon III and first instituted in 1852 this medal was issued to non-commissioned officers or enlisted personnel who distinguished themselves by acts of bravery in action against an enemy force. The Médaille Militaire is one of rarest French decorations to be bestowed upon foreigners. Awarded to T.S.M John Norris, T.S.M Matthew Bailey and Pte John Savage of the the 1st Dragoons.

OBVERSE Head of the Prince-President Louis Napoleon (Emperor Napoleon III), within a blue enamelled border inscribed LOUIS - NAPOLEON. Above the medal the French eagle, head to right, with drooping wings touching the medal. In less than a year this was altered so that the wings did not touch the medal. REVERSE All types, VALEUR ET DISCIPLINE in the medallion. RIBBON 38mm, yellow with 5mm green edges.

1198 CLARK, Private James

Born : Date Unknown - Maryport
Enlisted : 5th October 1847
Medals : Crimea (B.I.S)

Died : 7th February 1855 - Scutari
Status : Probably rode in the Charge

Medal with three clasps Balaklava, Inkermann, Sebastopol in Regimental museum (June 1991)

The musters show he was effective from the 1st October to the 31st December, 92 days ordinary pay, 8 days on board ship, 84 days on shore. Marginal note reads "6 DN Guards No 998", 3rd muster states "on board ship Balaklava".

1182 CLAYDEN, Private William

Born : Unknown
Enlisted :
Medals : Crimea (B.I.S)

Died : Unknown
Status : Probably rode in the Charge

Crimea Medal with three clasps Balaklava, Inkermann, Sebastopol, LS & GC and Turkish medal in Regimental museum (June 1991)

The musters show he was effective from the 1st October to the 31st December, 92 days ordinary pay, 3 days on board ship, 89 days on shore.

990 CLEMENTS, Orderly Room Clerk George

Born : Unknown
Enlisted :
Medals : Crimea (A.B.I.S), Long Service and Good Conduct Medal

Died : Unknown
Status : Probably rode in the Charge

The musters show he was effective as a Sergeant 15th-16th October, 4 days at 2s-2d per diem, 3 days on board ship, 1 day on shore, the marginal note reads "In payment of paymaster Genl. Depot Scutari Sept 1st to 11th October - To Orderly Room Clerk 16th Oct vice Gordon." Effective as an Orderly Room Clerk from the 16th October to the 31st December, 77 days at 2s-2d per diem, 3 days on board ship 12 days on shore. Orderly to the Earl of Lucan.

Copies of his Diaries can be seen in the Household Cavalry Regimental Museum. He was a Clerk to a firm of land agents in Norwich, Norfolk, but found it boring, and enlisted in 1846. L/Cpl 1849. Orderly Sergeant to Lord Lucan at the Battle of the Alma.
Clements gave a description of the Charge: "The first line charged and rode straight into the Russian ranks, but they were so outnumbered that they were outflanked, and Colonel Yorke saw the mess they were in and gave us the order to charge. We inclined to the left and rode down on the right flank of the Russians. The charge broke through the enemy's lines and checked his advance and in a few minutes the whole column had retreated." (quoted in Horse Guards by Barney White-Spunner, page 378, others quotes can be seen on pages 367, 378, 372, 378)

WO102 L.S & G.C Sgt-Maj George Clements issued 10th July 1868, gratuity £5, states "Relinquished a promotion to a commission"

802 COATES, Private James

Born : Unknown
Enlisted :
Medals : Crimea (B.I.S)

Died : Unknown
Status : Probably rode in the Charge

The musters show he was effective from the 1st October to the 31st December, 92 days ordinary pay, 4 days on board ship, 88 days on shore.

CONEY, Captain Walter J.

Born : Unknown
Enlisted :
Medals : Crimea (B.I.S)

Died : 17th January 1888 - Maidenhead
Status : Probably rode in the Charge

The Orinoco

Cornet 18th January 1850. Lieutenant 25th February 1853.
Captain 22nd December 1854. (*Harts Annual Army List 1855 page 128*)

The musters show he was effective from the 1st October to the 21st December, 79 days, 1st-3rd October "On Board Ship". Two Horses foraged at public expense.

137 remarks: Promoted from Lieut. since Crimea medal Return went in. Medal Roll for the Sebastopol clasp WO 100-24 page 143 marginal note states "H&R 14/6"

The Times, 28th May 1856 stated "Captain Walter J Coney arrived at Spithead yesterday on the Steam transport Orinoco."
The London Gazette, 26th March 1872 stated "Major Walter Coney retires from the service receiving the value of his commissions".

Died at Braywich Grove, Maidenhead leaving an estate worth over £87,000. (*Leeds Mercury* 13th April 1888)

631 COOMBES, Private George

Born : Unknown
Enlisted :
Medals : Crimea (B.I.S)

Died : Unknown
Status : Probably rode in the Charge

The musters show he was effective from the 1st October to the 31st December, 92 days ordinary pay, 92 days at 2d Good conduct pay, 9 days on board ship. Medal Roll Sebastopol clasp .631 Pte Coombs, George Marginal note reads "Regt 6/9" WO 100-24 page 146. Medal Roll - Class 2. Died, Retired from service, Discharged. Roll dated 10th February 1859, Royal Barracks, Dublin. Entry No 42 631 Pte Coombs, George Discharged WO 100-24 page 151.

826 COOPER, Farrier William

Born : Unknown
Enlisted :
Medals : Crimea (B.I.S)

Died : Unknown
Status : Probably rode in the Charge

The musters show he was effective from the 1st October to the 31st December, 92 days ordinary pay, 92 days at 2d Good Conduct pay, 9 days on board ship. WO 100-24 page 144, 826 Pte Cooper William Marginal note reads "Regt 6/9"

941 COOPER, Private James

Born : Unknown
Enlisted :
Medals : Crimea (B.I.S), Long Service and Good Conduct Medal

Died : Unknown
Status : Probably rode in the Charge

The musters show he was effective from the 1st October to the 31st December, 92 days ordinary pay, 92 days at 1d Good Conduct pay, 3 days on board ship. WO 12-506 Discharges for the 1st Dragoons, up to June, 1876. from York 23rd May 1876. Sgt. 941 James Cooper born Edgbaston, A Butcher, enlisted 20 October 1845. Completed 30 years service. WO102 L.S & G.C Sgt Jas. Cooper issued 4th June 1870, gratuity £5, states under "previous appropriated" column "special list".

1174 COOPER, Private Henry

Born : Unknown
Enlisted :
Medals : Crimea (B.I.S)

Died : Unknown
Status : Probably rode in the Charge

The musters show he was effective from the 1st October to the 31st December, 92 days ordinary pay, 9 days on board ship, 83 days on shore. Medal Roll Sebastopol clasp .1174 Pte Cooper. Henry Marginal note reads "Regt 6/9" WO 100-24 page 146.

1271 COUP, Private Bernard

Born : Unknown
Enlisted :
Medals : Crimea (B.I.S)

Died : Unknown
Status : Probably rode in the Charge

The musters show he was effective from the 1st October to the 31st December, 92 days ordinary pay, 9 days on board ship, 83 days on shore. Medal Roll Sebastopol clasp . 1271 Pte Coup Bernard Marginal note reads "Regt 6/9" WO 100-24 page 146. Medal Roll - Class 2. Died, Retired from service, Discharged. Roll dated 10th February 1859, Royal Barracks, Dublin. Entry No 44 1271 Pte Coup Bernard Discharged entry crossed through and endorsed "Sent to HIM 20/10/.. WO 100-24 page 151.

900 CRANE, Farrier Evi

Born : Unknown
Enlisted :
Medals : Crimea (B.I.S), Long Service and Good Conduct Medal

Died : Unknown
Status : Probably rode in the Charge

Crimea Medal with three clasps Balaklava, Inkermann, Sebastopol, to Farrier E.Lane in Regimental museum (June 1991)

The musters show he was effective from the 1st October to the 31st December, 92 days ordinary pay, 37 days at 1d good conduct pay and 55 days at 2d good conduct pay, 3 days on board ship, 89 days on shore. Marginal note reads "Entitled to Good conduct pay at 2d per diem on 7 November." WO 100-24 page 144, 900 Pte Crane, Evi. Marginal note reads "Regt 6/9". WO102 L.S & G.C Farrier-Major Crane recommended 25th March 1866, gratuity £5.

CRUSE, Riding Master George

Born : 21st June 1818 - Somerset
Enlisted :
Medals : Crimea (B.I.S)

Died : 9th February 1878
Status : Probably rode in the Charge

George was the ninth of thirteen children born to Henry Cruse and Elizabeth Skinner. He was born on 21st June 1818 in Frome, Somerset, and baptised on 30th April 1819 in Frome. George became a career soldier at the age of 20 years joining the 1st Royal Regiment of Dragoons on 11th July 1838 as a private. He served as a private until 30th June 1840 when he was promoted to Corporal. He was promoted to Sergeant on 1st December 1842, and served as such for well over five years until 31st March 1848. On the 1st April 1848 George was promoted to Troop Sergeant Major on the retirement of Sam Woolley from the army. Sam Woolley was to become George's father-in-law as George married Eliza Woolley on 13th April 1848 at the Church of Cahir, County Tipperary. George and Eliza had a daughter named Mary Anna, who was born on 1st February 1849 and baptised at the Parish Church, Leeds.

On 21st May 1854 George sailed from Liverpool on the sailing ship Arabia for service in the Crimea. The sea journey lasted 42 days. In the Crimea, George served under Lord Raglan and General Simpson. He saw active service at the Battle of Balaclava, Inkerman, and Sebastapol. For his service he was awarded the Crimea Medal on 20th September 1855 with clasps for Inkerman, Balaclava and Sebastapol. Later, in March 1859, he was awarded the Turkish Medal.

George was promoted from Sergeant to Troop Sergeant Major on 1st April 1848 and he served as such for well over six years until 4th November 1854. While serving in the Crimea he was promoted to Regimental Sergeant Major on 5th November 1854. This promotion caused his Commanding Officer, Major Wardlaw, some anxiety as his letters seemed to get lost and he had to write on at least three occasions. (See below.) To qualify for promotion he had to have a medical which showed he was "in good health and fit for active service". There is no record of George sustaining an injury during his service in the Crimea.

During his service in the Crimea, from May 1854 to March 1855, George wrote 63 letters to his family. (The original letters are at the National Army Museum.) These letters show that George was posted to, Scutari and Buykdere in the Bosphorus (Istanbul, Turkey), Varna (Camp Adrianople Road), Devnya, Kanajusin/Kana Hussin, and Calasnya (Bulgaria), Balaclava and and a "Camp near Sebastapol" (now in the present-day Ukraine).

On 16th March 1855 George was promoted to Riding Master (without purchase) and served in this post until August 1871. (The promotion is recorded in the London Gazette.) On 9th August 1871 he was made an Honorary Captain and retired on half pay. A remarkable career – from Private to Captain, all on his own merit. George retired to Huntley House, 15, Elliston Road, Redland, Bristol and died on the 9th February 1878, wife Eliza receiving arrears of George's pay totalling £46. George was buried at Westbury-on-Trym Church, Bristol. George's daughter Mary Anna never married and died in 1936 in Bristol.

The following letter was sent by George Cruse to his father-in-law, Sam Woolley, from the Crimea. The letter is dated just eight days after the Charge of the Heavy and Light Brigade.

Camp before Sebastapol - Nov 2nd 1854

My Dear Father

I posted a letter yesterday for dear Lizzie, but I have just ascertained that the mail does not leave until tomorrow, so I have taken the opportunity of scribbling a few lines to you as I am quite certain you will all be anxious to get the latest intelligence from me, and knowing you to be fond of Military affairs and also able to comprehend any little tactic which I may be enabled to describe I have enclosed a rough sketch of the action before Balaklava on the 25th Oct and though it is a rough affair in every sense of the word ? as I said before, I think it will be rather interesting to all my dear friends at Peterborough. I will now endeavour to explain the movements of the troops on that day and describe the little sketch as well as my poor abilities will admit. You will see our encampment was nearly at the end of a large plain about 3 miles from the height – near the village of Kamara and between the two roads leading to Sebastapol.

The 93rd Highlanders were posted on our right front so as to protect the road leading to Balaklava, there was also a larger body of Turks on the right of the Highlanders. The heights round about Balaklava are well defended by Sailors and Marines so that the Russians will have a difficult job to retake that place. The Russian army was posted some few miles behind the height which were defended by the Turkish redoubt, and the whole of the heights round about that spot and near the village of Kamara had picquets and videttes(?) posted on them. We thought ourselves in a pretty decent position forgetting that our own Countrymen did not defend the Redoubts. As I mentioned in my former letter, we were always saddled and mounted by three o'clock in the morning; so on the morning of the 25th, about half past five we were roused by hearing the guns from all the redoubts open fire, and several of the picquets were sent in to give intelligence that the enemy was advancing in great force. Of course we were not long in advancing at a smart trot to the positions described in the sketch in rear of the redoubts defended by Turks and which the Russians were attacking in great force – our horse artillery was sent forward between the two large redoubts and opened a brisk fire but were soon obliged to retire as the Russian guns quite overpowered these and they lost several men and horses. The Russian guns began to advance and several round shot fell into ranks, breaking the legs of two horses and one large ball struck a man named 'M' right in the face, of course killing him instantly. I have marked the spot where he fell. The shot began to fall so thick around us that the men began to bob their heads which made 'L' and I pitch into them for being so foolish, just as if they could avoid a 32lb shot by moving their heads one side or another. Just about this time, the Turks fled in confusion down the hill towards us, abandoning the redoubts in a shameful manner.

The Russians came up in dense masses and bringing up their heavy guns with them, besides moving those the Turks had abandoned. They opened such a fire upon us that we could do nothing but retire, which we did about half a mile behind our encampment. Our tents had in the meantime been struck, but of course in the confusion they could not be packed up, and we had the pleasure of galloping over all our little property. We did not know at first whether the Russians would advance to us or not, but in about half an hour we saw an immense body of cavalry approaching, preceded by a cloud of Cossacks. One wing of them prepared to charge the 93rd, which you will see by the sketch, while the other wing prepared to charge us. It appears they had mistaken the 93rd for Turks, but when they came within 100 yards of them they were soon convinced of their error, for the highlanders (without forming a square), poured in such a volley upon them that they were glad to retire. Meanwhile, the other body came down in a very compact manner to attack us, but as we charged them, as you see by the sketch (Royals and Greys leading), they soon retired in great disorder leaving many on the field, but we did not follow them. They retired in great haste to the other side of the heights, and as our generals went to reconnoitre, they found the Russians strongly posted in the position which I have endeavoured to sketch. We remained at the edge of this height for some time, meanwhile a message had been sent to Lord Raglan, and reinforcements of infantry began to arrive. Some little time after, Captain 'N' rode up and gave the order to drive the enemy from their position.

We advanced over the heights to attack them, the Light Brigade leading the Greys, and we following, and the other heavy regt. in the rear; nothing could be more bold and daring than the advance of the Light Brigade who darted forward at a tremendous speed. They galloped right up to the position and cut down the gunners of the 30 guns in front, but the immense body of infantry in rear of the guns poured in such volleys upon them that as we advanced to the support, I could scarcely see a mounted man returning. Lord Cardigan saw that we had rushed upon an overwhelming force with a mere handful, and he ordered us to retire, but meanwhile we had been halted just between the fires of the cross batteries, which were also well filled with riflemen, and it was just at this spot that our officers and men were cut down. We retreated in a very orderly manner and our men did not bob their heads as they did in the morning, but it was the opinion of all the old officers present that in no previous battle on record was a body of cavalry exposed to such a murderous fire. How we escaped (a single man of us), God alone knows, and I am sure I have reason to remember his mercies as long as I live, for bringing me safely out of such a carnage. I could describe the affairs much better than I can write a description of it, but as I am denied the pleasures of a fire-side chat, I hope you will be able to understand the rough manner in which I have sketched it. We retired to the edge of the heights, which the Russians had been driven from, and after lighting fires to deceive them, we retired to our old ground, packed up our tents, and drew our picquet poles and ropes and retired about two miles nearer to Sebastapol. It was twelve o'clock before we lay down, having been out twenty-one hours that day, the men had scarcely any refreshment for that day, but I began to look out for number one. We have shifted camp twice since then but we are now pretty close to Sebastapol, which has been bombarded now seventeen days; there is a rumour of its being stormed tonight, but I cannot vouch for the truth of it, and as my paper is now pretty full, I must say good night and God bless you my dear father, and believe me your affectionate son,

George Cruse Letter and information supplied by Robert Cruse.

In another letter Sergeant-Major Cruse told his wife that 'I have not undressed or had my boots off for eight or nine days and God knows how much longer it will last. This is soldiering in real earnest.'

982 DALTON, Private Michael

Born : Unknown
Enlisted :
Medals : Crimea (S)

Died : Unknown
Status : To Scutari 26th October 1854

Crimea Medal with three clasps Balaklava, Inkermann, Sebastopol,in Regimental museum (June 1991)

The musters show he was effective from the 1st-25th October, 25 days ordinary pay, 4 days on board ship, 21 days on shore. 1st and 2nd musters endorsed "Scutari" third endorsed "Malta". Marginal note reads to payment of paymaster at Scutari 26 October - to Malta 15 December. The Malta Times February 1854 wrote "Orders were received here from England to prepare quarters for 10,000 men. Several localities are being fitted-up; among others, the Lazzaretto and adjoining Plague Hospital, where it is said there is room for 1000 men, and the Dockyard lofts where as many men can be housed. Convents will be used if absolutely required, but not otherwise." The first wounded soldier's arrived from the Crimea in November 1854.
Medal Roll Sebastopol clasp. Entitled 982 Pte Dalton Michael. Marginal note reads "Dead WO 8/1/57" 100-24 page 146 Medal Roll - Class 2. Died, Retired from service, Discharged. Roll dated 10th February 1859, Royal Barracks, Dublin. Entry No 53 982 Pte Dalton Michael -Dead- WO 100-24 page 151.

864 DAVIDSON, Private William

Born : Unknown
Enlisted :
Medals : Crimea (B.I.S)

Died : Unknown
Status : Probably rode in the Charge

The musters show he was effective from the 1st October to the 31st Decemberd 92 days ordinary pay, 4 days on board ship, 88 days on shore. Medal Roll Sebastopol Clasp marginal note reads "H+R 1/11/- WO100/24 page 146.
Medal Roll - Class 2. Died, Retired from service, Discharged. Roll dated 10th February 1859, Royal Barracks, Dublin. Entry No54, 864 Pte Davidson, William. Discharged. Medal signed for by recipient. WO100/24 page 151.

1020 DAVIES, Private Thomas

Born : Unknown
Enlisted :
Medals : Crimea (B.I.S), Long Service and Good Conduct Medal

Died : Unknown
Status : Probably rode in the Charge

The musters show he was effective from the 1st October to the 31st December. Good conduct pay 1d per diem for the period. WO102 L.S & G.C issued 7th July 1869.

1175 DAVIS, Sergeant Edward C.

Born : Unknown
Enlisted :
Medals : Crimea (B.I.S)

Died : Unknown
Status : Probably rode in the Charge

The musters show he was effective from the 1st October to the 31st December, 92 days at 1s-7 1/2d per diem, 3 days on board ship, 89 days on shore.

1205 DAVIS, Private William

Born : Unknown
Enlisted :
Medals : Crimea (B.I.S)

Died : Unknown
Status : Probably rode in the Charge

From a medal sales list: Crimea Medal (W. Davies, 1st Royal Dragoons). 4 clasps; Sebastopol, Inkermann, Balaklava and Alma (not entitled to this clasp on both rolls, the Regiment was not in the Crimea at the time of the battle of Alma. Medal officially impressed, GVF condition, with slight wear. Includes copy of discharge papers, certified copy of original Medal Roll for Balaclava, Inkermann and Sebastopol and photocopy of modern Sewell Medal Roll confirming his clasps. It appears the Alma bar has been on the medal for many years possibly attached by the recipient. The battle of Alma took place on the 20th September 1854, the 1st Dragoons landed on the 4th October 1854. In 2005 group with a collector in America.

The musters show he was effective from the 1st October to the 31st December, 92 days ordinary pay, 9 days on board ship, 83 days on shore.

1st Dragoons Uniform

Helmets made from brass with gilt decoration were worn by the 1st Royal Dragoons in 1854. The red coatee was single-breasted with eight buttons down the front. They wore blue overalls with scarlet stripes down the outside of each leg. His canteen strap was worn over his left shoulder, on top of his pouch-belt, and his haversack strap over his right shoulder; the canvas haversack contained his daily ration. Hung over the same shoulder was a blue painted heavy water canteen fitted with a leather strap. The sword was suspended on white leather slings, which in turn hung on a white leather waist belt with a square brass buckle in the front.

1125 DIPROSE, Private Henry

Born : Unknown
Enlisted :
Medals : Crimea (B.I.S)

Died : Unknown
Status : Probably rode in the Charge

The musters show he was effective from the 1st October to the 31st December. Medal Roll - Class 2. Died, Retired from service, Discharged. Roll dated 10th February 1859, Royal Barracks, Dublin. - Entry No 61.1121 Pte Diprose Henry. Discharged. WO 100-24 page 152.

777 DREW, Private John

Born : Date Unknown - Cradley, Staffordshire
Enlisted : 4th November 1841
Medals : Crimea (B.I.S)

Died : 23rd December 1854 - Scutari
Status : Probably rode in the Charge

A sword blade forger prior to enlistment. The musters show he was effective from the 1st October to the 31st December. Good conduct pay 1d per diem for the period. Medal Roll - Class 2. Died, Retired from service, Discharged. Roll dated 10th February 1859, Royal Barracks, Dublin. Entry No 62. 777 Pte Drew John. "Dead" WO 100-24 page 152.

1118 DUDLEY, Private John

Born : Unknown
Enlisted :
Medals : Crimea (B.I.S)

Died : Unknown
Status : Probably rode in the Charge

The musters show he was effective from the 1st October to the 31st December. Medal Roll - Class 2. Died, Retired from service, Discharged. Roll dated 10th February 1859, Royal Barracks, Dublin. Entry No 55 1082 Pte Duke Robert. "Discharged" Entry crossed through and endorsed sent to him 25/9/60. WO 100-24 page 152 Entry No 65.

1852 DUKE, Private Robert

Born : Unknown
Enlisted :
Medals : Crimea (B.I.S)

Died : Unknown
Status : Probably rode in the Charge

The musters show he was effective from the 1st October to the 31st December, 92 days ordinary pay, 4 days on board ship, 88 days on shore. Medal Roll - Class 2. Died, Retired from service, Discharged. Roll dated 10th February 1859, Royal Barracks, Dublin. Entry No55, 1082 Pte Duke, Robert. Discharged. Entry crossed through and endorsed sent to him 25/9/1860.

871 ELLIS, Private David

Born : Unknown
Enlisted :
Medals : Crimea (B.S)

Died : Unknown
Status : Probably rode in the Charge

The musters show he was effective from the 1st October to the 31st December. Medal Roll - Class 2. Died, Retired from service, Discharged. Roll dated 10th February 1859, Royal Barracks, Dublin. Entry No 74, 871 Pte Ellis David. "Discharged" WO 100-24 page 152

ELMSALL, Captain William de Cardonnel
Born : 25th December 1824   Died : Unknown
Enlisted :   Status : Severely wounded in the Charge
Medals : Crimea (B.S), The Knight (5th Class) The French Legion of Honour, The Turkish Order of the Medjidie (5th Class)

Son of Joseph Edward Greaves who assumed the name Elmsall in 1817 and served in the 1st Dragoons at Waterloo, obtaining the rank of Major. His mother was Hannah Mary Lawson the youngest daughter of Adam Mansfeldt de Cardonnel Lawson of Cramlington, Northumberland. The Queen held a formal reception (levee) at St James Palace on the 1st June 1842, Mr William de Cardonnel was accompanied by Lord Wharncliffe.

William de Cardonnel became Cornet 1st July 1842. Lieutenant 13th October 1843. Captain 4th September 1849. (*Harts Annual Army List 1855 page 128*) Appointed a Magistrate for the West Riding of Yorkshire 10th August 1858. Major in the 5th Regiment of West York Militia, resigned commission in 1860.

The musters show he was effective 1st-25th October, all three Musters endorsed "Scutari". Supplied with rations "on shore" 4th Oct to 25th Oct, 1st-3rd Oct "On Board Ship". Three Horses foraged at public expense 92 Days. Marginal note reads "Wounded in the action in front of Balaklava on the 25th October".
Listed on the Casualty Roll as wounded Severely at Balaclava. Returned home October 1854, The Times 12th December 1854 states he returned home on the "Cambria". He received his medal from the hand of the Queen on 18th May 1855 at Horse Guards.

The Medal Roll for the Sebastopol clasp reads "England order to H&R sent 12/3" WO 100-24 page 143. Medal Roll - Class 2. Died, Retired from service, Discharged. Roll dated 10th February 1859, Royal Barracks, Dublin. Major C.D. Elmsall retired from the service.

964 EMMS, Sergeant George
Born : Unknown   Died : Unknown
Enlisted :   Status : Probably rode in the Charge
Medals : Crimea (B.I.S)

The musters show he was effective from the 1st October to the 31st December, 92 days at 2s-2d per diem, 4 days on board ship, 83 days on shore. Medal Roll Sebastopol clasp, Entitled 964 Sgt Emms George WO 100-24 page 143, also shown on some records as Emans.

1231 FALCONBRIDGE, Private Edward
Born : Unknown   Died : Unknown
Enlisted :   Status : Probably rode in the Charge
Medals : Crimea (B.I.S)
Crimea medal with clasps Balaklava, Inkermann, Sebastopol, LS & GC and Turkish Crimea to T.S.M J Falconbridge in Regimental Museum (Household Cavalry) June 1991.

The musters show he was effective from the 1st October to the 31st December.

1073 FALCONER, Private William
Born : Unknown   Died : Unknown
Enlisted :   Status : Probably rode in the Charge
Medals : Crimea (B.I.S)

The musters show he was effective from the 1st October to the 31st December. Good conduct pay 1d per diem for the period.

762 FAWELL, Private John
Born : Date Unknown - Richmond   Died : 15th December 1854 - Scutari
Enlisted : 26th July 1841   Status : Probably rode in the Charge
Medals : Crimea (B.I.S)

The musters show he was effective from the 1st October to the 27th November, 58 days ordinary pay, 30 days at 1d good conduct pay, 4 days on board ship, 54 days on shore. First muster endorsed "Scutari" and second muster endorsed "Deceased". Marginal note reads "Forfeited Good conduct pay at 1d from 31 Oct. To payment of paymaster Scutari 28 Nov."

1004 FINN, Corporal Thomas
Born : Unknown
Enlisted :
Medals : Crimea (B.I.S)

Died : Unknown
Status : Probably rode in the Charge

The musters show he was effective from the 1st October to the 31st December.

985 FITZMAURICE, Private Lewis
Born : Unknown
Enlisted :
Medals : Crimea (B.S)

Died : Unknown
Status : Probably rode in the Charge

The musters show he was effective from the 1st October to the 31st December, 92 days ordinary pay, 3 days on board ship, 89 days on shore. Medal Roll Sebastopol clasp, Entitled 985 Pte Fitzmaurice, Lewis. Marginal note reads "England". WO 100-24 page 146. Medal Roll - Class 2. Died, Retired from service, Discharged. Roll dated 10th February 1859, Royal Barracks, Dublin. 985 Pte Fitzmaurice, Lewis. Discharged, WO 100-24 page 152.

732 FLITTON, Private David
Born : Unknown
Enlisted :
Medals : Crimea (B.I.S)

Died : Unknown
Status : Probably rode in the Charge

The musters show he was effective from the 1st October to the 31st December with Good conduct pay of 2d per diem.

581 FORSTER, Trumpet Major William
Born : Unknown
Enlisted :
Medals : Crimea (B.I.S)

Died : Unknown
Status : Probably rode in the Charge

The musters show he was effective from the 1st October to the 31st December, 92 days at 2s-2d per diem.

FORTEATH, Surgeon Alexander
Born : 26th October 1820 - Newton, Morayshire
Enlisted :
Medals : Crimea (A.B.I.S)

Died : 22nd May 1866 - Hastings
Status : Probably rode in the Charge

Educated at King's and Maris' Colleges, Aberdeen; MD Edinburgh 1842. The musters show he was effective from the 7th November to the 31st December. Marginal note reads "Joined from medical staff 7th November". The dates on the musters may be incorrect, it is possible Forteath joined on the 7th October (see below). The Medal Roll shows him as "Alfred Forteith" or "Alfred Forteath". Assistant Surgeon 10th Feb 1843, Staff Surgeon 28th Mar 1854. "Served with the troops engaged in surpressing the rebellion in Ceylon in 1848." (*Harts Annual Army List 1857*) To 1st Drgns 6th Oct 1854, Surgeon Major 1st Drgns 10th Feb 1863, Retired Half pay 20th Sept 1864 (Peterkin & Johnston, *Commissioned Officers in the Medical Services of the British Army 1660-1960* page 323)

605 FRANKLIN, Private Robert
Born : Unknown
Enlisted :
Medals : Crimea (B.I.S)
Glendinings Auction 27 May 1992, Lot 130 Crimea 3 clasp medal three bars, Balaklava, Inkermann, Sebastopol (Pte RT Franklin. RL Dgns). Contemporary engraved naming VF Est £200-£250 not sold.

Died : Unknown
Status : Probably rode in the Charge

The musters show he was effective from the 1st October to the 31st December. Good conduct pay 1d per diem for 7 days, and 2d Good conduct pay for 85 days (Forf). Marginal note reads forfeited 1d good conduct pay 25th December.

1009 FRENCH, Private Mark
Born : Unknown
Enlisted :
Medals : Crimea (B.I.S)

Died : Unknown
Status : Probably rode in the Charge

The musters show he was effective from the 1st October to the 31st December with Good conduct pay of 1d per diem.

1230 GEE, Private John

Born : Unknown
Enlisted :
Medals : Crimea (B.I.S)

Died : Unknown
Status : Probably rode in the Charge

The musters show he was effective from the 1st October to the 31st December.

932 GIBBS, Trumpeter John

Born : Unknown
Enlisted :
Medals : Crimea (B.I.S)

Died : Unknown
Status : Probably rode in the Charge

The musters show he was effective from the 1st October to the 31st December, 92 Days at 1s-5d per diem, 92 days at 1d Good Conduct pay, 4 days on board ship, 88 days on shore. WO25/3267 - Records show Discharged 25/1/1863

1242 GILL, Private Charles

Born : Unknown
Enlisted :
Medals : Crimea (B.I.S), Long Service and Good Conduct Medal
A Long Service and Good Conduct has appeared on the market.

Died : Unknown
Status : Probably rode in the Charge

The musters show he was effective from the 1st October to the 31st December. Good conduct pay 2d per diem for the period. WO102 L.S & G.C issued 30th June 1865, gratuity £5.

GLYN, Lieutenant Richard George

Born : Unknown
Enlisted :
Medals : Crimea (B.I.S), The Turkish Order of the Medjidie (5th Class)

Died : Unknown
Status : Rode in the Charge

A.H. Baldwin and Sons Ltd, September 1957, Lot 10634, Crimea Bal., Ink., Seb.; Turkish Crimea. R.G. Glyn, Lieut., Royal Dragoons. Original ribbons and buckle fitments. Engraved V.F. £8.10s

Cornet 22nd January 1853. Lieutenant 8th December 1854. Captain 3rd March 1857. (*Harts Annual Army List 1859 page 136*)
Lieutenant Gly was shot through the leg, present at the Cavalry action at Balaklava, also the siege of Sebastopol.(*Harts Annual Army List 1855 page 128*)

The musters show he was effective as a Cornet from the 1st October to the 7th December and as a Lieutenant from the 8th December to the 31st December, supplied with rations 24 days "on shore" Two Horses foraged at public expense. Marginal note "From Cornet 8th December". WO100/24 page 137 Remarks: Promoted from Cornet since Crimean Medal Return went in.

The Times, 28th May 1856, "Lieutenant Richard George Glyn arrived at Spithead yesterday on the Steam transport Orinoco. She left Scutari at 6pm on the 13th May and Malta on the 17th. The Orinoco went into Portsmouth yesterday afternoon to prepare for landing her troops this morning."

641 GOODWIN, Sergeant John

Born : Unknown
Enlisted :
Medals : Crimea (B.I.S), Long Service and Good Conduct Medal
Turkish Crimea Medal in the Regimental Museum (Household Cavalry) Named to Sgt J.Goodwin.

Died : Unknown
Status : Probably rode in the Charge

The musters show he was effective from the 1st October to the 31st December, 92 days at 1s-7 1/2d per diem, 92 days at 3d Good Conduct pay, 3 days on board ship, 89 days on shore. WO25/3267 - Records show Discharged 16/04/1867. WO102 L.S & G.C issued 30th June 1865, gratuity £5.

1170 GORDON, Sergeant Walter

Born : Unknown
Enlisted :
Medals : Crimea (B.I.S)

Died : Unknown
Status : Probably rode in the Charge

The musters show he was effective as an Orderly Room Clerk from the 1st-15th October, 15 days at 2s-2d per diem, 9 days on board ship 12 days on shore.
Effective as a Sergeant the from 16th October to the 31st December, 77 days at 2s-2d per diem. 77 days on shore. Marginal note reads "To Sergeant 16th October".
WO25/3267 - Records show to army staff corps 12/1859.
WO25/3267 - Records show to AHC 1/7/1873.

GORRINGE, Assistant Surgeon John

Born : 24th June 1824 - Calcutta, India
Enlisted :
Medals : Crimea (B)

Died : 4th August 1870 - Cambridge
Status : Probably rode in the Charge

Assistant Surgeon 59th Foot 8th June 1849 he exchanged into the 1st Dragoons on the 31st December 1852. The musters show he was effective from the 4th-24th October and from the 28th-31st December, 25 days on shore. 1st-3rd October and 30th October to the 11th November "On Board Ship". One Horse foraged at public expense. Marginal note reads "Messed on board the Arabia from the 30th October to the 11th November, in charge of the sick".

Staff Surgeon 2nd Class 29th June 1855. Half Pay 1st October 1856. To 4th Foot 15th May 1857, Staff Surgeon 17th November 1869, Surgeon Major 17th November 1869. (Peterkin & Johnston, *Commissioned Officers in the Medical Services of the British Army 1660-1960* page 346)

On the Medal Roll for Balaclava it states "Medal sent to H&R to be completed with 27/5". He is entitled to the S clasp but does not appear on his regiment's roll. Harts Army List of 1863 shows he was serving with the 4th Regiment of Foot.

1263 GRAY, Private William

Born : Date unknown - Cirencester
Enlisted : 29th August 1853
Medals : Crimea (B.I.S)

Died : 27th January 1855 - Scutari
Status : Probably rode in the Charge

Payne Collection 1911, Catalogue page 110. Crimea 2 clasps Balaklava, Inkermann. Wm. Gray, 1st Dragns. impressed naming. Also E.E.Needes Collection. Crimea medal in Regimental museum (Household Cavalry) June 1991.

The musters show he was effective from the 1st October to the 31st December.

912 GREENWOOD, Private Walter

Born : Unknown
Enlisted :
Medals : Crimea (B.S)

Died : Unknown
Status : Probably rode in the Charge

Sotheby 5th November 1986. lot 579. Crimea medal Clasps Balaklava, Sebastopol. (Pte. Jno. W. Greenwood 1st RL. DGS) suspension re-fixed. GVF sold with copies of attestation and discharge documents. naming not quoted. £180-£200 est.

The musters show he was effective from the 1st October to the 2nd November, 33 days ordinary pay, 33 days at 1d good coduct pay, 3 days on board ship, 30 days on shore. 2nd muster endorsed "Scutari", 3rd muster endorsed "Malta". Marginal note reads "to payment of paymaster at Scutari 3rd Nov. To Malta 10 December."

1017 GRIBBIN, Farrier Thomas

Born : Unknown
Enlisted :
Medals : Crimea (B.I.S), Long Service and Good Conduct Medal

Died : Unknown
Status : Probably rode in the Charge

The musters show he was effective from the 1st October to the 31st December. Good conduct pay 1d per diem for the period. WO 100-24 page 144, 1017 Farrier Gribbin, Thomas marginal note reads "Regt 6/9" WO25/3267 - Records show Discharged 28th September 1869. WO102 L.S & G.C Farrier Sergeant Gribbin issued 27th June 1868, gratuity £15.

1176 HALL, Corporal Edwin

Born : Date Unknown - Cheltenham
Enlisted : 27th June 1851
Medals : Crimea (B.I.S)

Died : 7th December 1854 - Scutari
Status : Probably rode in the Charge

The musters show he was effective from the 1st October to the 31st December, 92 days at 1s-7 1/2d per diem, 4 days on board ship, 88 days on shore. Trade on enlistment Clerk.

993 HALLETT, Private Charles

Born : Unknown
Enlisted :
Medals : Crimea (B.I.S)

Died : Unknown
Status : Probably rode in the Charge

DNW 30th June 1998, Lot 29, Crimea 3 clasps, Balaklava, Inkermann, Sebastopol (Pte. Chas. Hallett, Rl. Dgns.) contemporary engraved naming, contact marks and edge bruising, otherwise better than good fine. Hammer Price £380

The musters show he was effective from the 1st October to the 31st December.

1144 HARE, Private Richard

Born : Date Unknown - Codnor Park, Derbyshire
Enlisted :
Medals : Crimea (B.I.S)

Died : 25th August 1855 - Crimea
Status : Probably rode in the Charge

Medal Crimea medal with clasps Balaklava, Inkermann, Sebastopol, in Regimental museum (Household Cavalry) June 1991.

The musters show he was effective from the 1st October to the 31st December. 3rd muster endorsed "on board ship Balaclava". WO14/1 Scutari Muster Roll January-March 1855 remarks indicate "From 4th ... Hospital" 4th-31st January, "Abydos" 1st-28th February, "Sent Home" 31st March.
Trade on enlistment Collier.

882 HARKNESS, Private James

Born : Unknown
Enlisted :
Medals : Crimea (B.I.S)

Died : Unknown
Status : Probably rode in the Charge

Medal Crimea medal with clasps Balaklava, Inkermann, Sebastopol and Turkish Crimea in Regimental Museum (Household Cavalry) June 1991.

The musters show he was effective from the 1st October to the 31st December. 40 days Good conduct pay 1d per diem. Marginal note reads "Entitled to good conduct pay at 1d per diem from 22 November". WO25/3267 - Records show Discharged as a Corporal 19/5/1868.

1141 HARKNESS, Private David

Born : Unknown
Enlisted :
Medals : Crimea (B.I.S)

Died : Unknown
Status : Probably rode in the Charge

Medal Crimea medal with clasps Balaklava, Inkermann, Sebastopol and Turkish Crimea in Regimental Museum (Household Cavalry) June 1991.

The musters show he was effective from the 1st October to the 31st December.

557 HARLOCK, Private William

Born : Unknown
Enlisted :
Medals : Crimea (B.I.S)

Died : Unknown
Status : Probably rode in the Charge

Medal Crimea medal with clasps Balaklava, Inkermann, Sebastopol and Turkish Crimea in Regimental Museum (Household Cavalry) June 1991. A Long Service and Good Conduct has also appeared on the market.

The musters show he was effective from the 1st October to the 31st December. Good conduct pay 3d per diem for the period.

HARTOPP, Lieutenant William Wrey

Born : Unknown
Enlisted :
Medals : Crimea (B.S)

Died : 20th July 1870
Status : Severely wounded in the Charge

K.C. Lovell Medal list January 1984, item 2/25. Pair Crimea 3 clasps B.I.S engraved, nearly V.F, Turkish Crimea British version un-named.

Cornet 11th March 1853. Lieutenant 8th December 1854 (*Harts Annual Army List 1855 page 128*)

The musters show he was effective from the 1st-25th October, first and second musters endorsed Scutari, third muster blank and ruled though. Supplied with rations 1st-25th October, 19 days onshore, 1st-6th Oct "On Board Ship". One Horse foraged at public expense. Marginal note reads "Wounded in the action in front of Balaclava on the 25th October"

The Times, 23rd November 1854, reported from Scutari 10th November that Lieut Hartopp was in hospital. Shown on the Casualty Roll as a Cornet Severely wounded at Balaclava. Wounded in the leg at Balaclava. He received his medal from the hand of the Queen on 18th May 1855. On recovering from his wounds he returned to the Crimea where he served with the Royal Horse Guards from August to November 1855.

The will dated 5th October 1870 of Captain William Wrey Hartopp of the Royal Horse Guards Blue, late of Penorley-lodge, Beaulieu, Southampton, and of 8, Albert Terrace, Hyde Park, who died on the 20th of July last, was proved on the 5th inst, by Thomas Edward Howe, the acting executor, under £2,000. Testator leaves all his real and personal estate to his wife, Lina.

1128 HATCH, Private William

Born : Unknown
Enlisted :
Medals : Crimea (B.S)

Died : Unknown
Status : Probably rode in the Charge

Glendinings Auction 27th March 1983, Lot 74 Crimea medal with three bars, Balaklava, , Sebastopol, Inkermann (W. Hatch No 1128 1st Royal Dgns.), 6th Dragoons). regimental style engraved naming, bars fixed incorrectly. Nearly extremely fine. Glendining and co 27 April 1983. lot 74 same as above £130 Dixons Gazette, No 42, Summer 2005, Crimea 2 clasps, Balaklava and Sebastopol, contemporary engraved naming. 1128 W.Hatch, 1st Royal Dragoons. Confirmed on Crimea Medal Roll as present with the Heavy Brigade. NEF £680.

The musters show he was effective from the 4th October to the 31st December, 89 days ordinary pay, 3 days on board ship, 86 days on shore. Marginal note reads "from payment of paymaster at Scutari 4th Oct"

1130 HAWKER, Private George

Born : Unknown
Enlisted : 4th July 1850
Medals : Crimea (B.I.S)

Died : Unknown
Status : Probably rode in the Charge

Dixons Gazette, No 49, Spring 2007, Lot 594, Crimea 3 clasps, Balaklava, Inkermann, Sebastopol. Geo. Hawker, 7th Dragoon Guards. Officially impressed. Sold with photocopy Medal Roll pages. Ex Bonhams Lot 15 20.4.06. VF £750.00 Sold on Ebay July 2007 - Crimea Medal with bars for Balaclava, Inkermann and Sebastopol (GEO HAWKER 7TH DN GDS) officially impressed.

Saw service in the Crimea in the Heavy Brigade and on returning to Home Service with the Regiment he transferred to the 7th Dragoon Guards (No. 150) at Dublin on the 1st September 1857 as they were understrength and due to be shipped out to India for the Mutiny. He went with the Regiment to India, though did not see any action during the Mutiny (consequently no entitlement to the Indian Mutiny Medal). In 1863 he returned to England (noted as having had 114 days ships rations), being discharged at Canterbury on completion of service.

One can only assume George Hawker returned his medal for naming after he transferred to the 7th Dragoon Guards in 1857 and provided the Mint with those details. WO25/3267 - Records show transferred to the 7th Dragoon Guards together with 2 other troopers. (Name mispelt Hawket)

Officially impressed Crimea medal

847 HEBB, Private William W.

Born : Unknown
Enlisted :
Medals : Crimea (B.I.S)

Died : Unknown
Status : Probably rode in the Charge

The musters show he was effective from the 1st October to the 31st December. WO25/3267 - Records show transferred to the 1st Dragoon Guards.

1266 HEGARTY, Private Samuel

Born : Date unknown - Cawnpore, India
Enlisted :
Medals : Crimea (I.S), Punjab (clasps Chillianwallah, Goojerat)

Died : Unknown
Status : Effective during the period

He was one of three brothers who enlisted in the 16th Lancers as boys in the 1840s; almost certainly they were the sons of a soldier serving in the regiment. Enlisted in the 16th Lancers in Meerut 5th April 1845 aged 15. Volunteer 3rd Light Dragoons 1st April 1846, volunteer 1st Dragoons 1st September 1853. The musters show he was effective from the 1st October to the 31st December. Medal Roll Sebastopol clasp entitled 1266 Pte Hegarty, Samuel, marginal note reads "Regt 6/9. H&R to replace lost 30/10" WO-100-24 page 147. Volunteer 9th Lancers 1st May 1860, Discharged June 1869. (National Archives WO 97/1286; WO 12/1279, 598; WO 25/1458; WO 25/3251)

899 HENSHAW, Private William

Born : 1825- Hamilton, Lanark
Enlisted : 13th November 1844
Medals : Crimea (B.S)
An engraved Medal in the B.W Worthington collection October 1981.

Died : Unknown
Status : Probably rode in the Charge

The musters show he was effective from the 1st October to the 13th November and from the 24th November to the 31st December, 72 days ordinary pay, 10 days on board ship, 62 days on shore. Marginal note reads "In payment of paymaster at Scutari from 14th-23rd November". Medal Roll Sebastopol clasp Marginal note reads "England reset 6/9" Medal Roll - Class 2. Died, Retired from service, Discharged. Roll dated 10th February 1859, Royal Barracks, Dublin 899 Pte. Henshaw, William -Discharged- WO 100-24 page 152.

WO97 - 1287 Discharge documents: 899 William Henshaw. A labourer born Hamilton, Lanark. Enlisted in 1st Dragoons at Glasgow on 13th November 1844, aged 19 years. Total service 12 years 111 days. One year abroad, Turkey and Crimea. Discharged in consequence of a reduction in the army and not likely to become efficient. Character "Good", not in possession of any good conduct badges. Medical History "Has been repeatedly in hospital from debility and the effects of an impaired constitution infirmity", discharged at Newbridge on 5th March 1857, aged 31 years 5 months 5'10" fresh complexion, grey eyes, brown hair. Labourer. Scars nil. Intended residence Glasgow.

1089 HIBBS, Private Joseph

Born : Unknown
Enlisted :
Medals : Crimea (S), Long Service and Good Conduct Medal

Died : Unknown
Status : Effective during the period

The musters show he was effective from the 1st-25th October and from the 24th November to the 31st December. 63 Days ordinary pay, 10 days on board ship, 53 days on shore. Marginal note reads "To payment of paymaster at Scutari from 26 Oct - 23 Nov". WO 100-24 page 147 marginal note reads "Regt 6/9 H&R 30/10 to replace lost" . WO102 L.S & G.C issued 30th June 1868, gratuity £5.

976 HILL, Sergeant John

Born : Unknown
Enlisted :
Medals : Crimea (B.I.S), The Sardinian War Medal

Died : Unknown
Status : Rode in the Charge

The musters show he was effective from the 1st October to the 31st December, 92 days at 2s-2d per diem, 4 days on board ship, 88 days on shore. The citation for the Sardinian War Medal reads (He) " displayed coolness and intrepidity when on patrol and attacked by a party of Russians on the 10th of October, 1854; and again on the 25th. of October, when his horse was shot under him, on which occasion, having captured one belonging to the enemy, he immediately rejoined his regiment and did duty with it for the rest of the day". The King of Sardinian, followed the example of the Emperor of France and presented four hundred war medals for military valour to the British troops. The medal was distributed to both officers and men. (*Medals of the British Army by Thomas Carter, 1861, page 142*)

1164 HILL, Private Henry
Born : Unknown
Enlisted :
Medals : Crimea (B.I.S)

Died : Unknown
Status : Probably rode in the Charge

The musters show he was effective from the 1st October to the 31st December. Medal Roll - Class 2. Died, Retired from service, Discharged. Roll dated 10th February 1859, Royal Barracks, Dublin. 1164 Pte Hill, Henry. Roll endorsed "Dead" but also signed "H.Hill" WO 100-24 page 152. WO25/326 - Records show Discharged December 1856.

438 HILL, Private William
Born : Unknown
Enlisted :
Medals : Crimea (B.I.S)

Died : Unknown
Status : Probably rode in the Charge

Giuseppe Miceli, Northampton medal list May 1985 item 32. Pair to Pte William Hill - Crimea 3 clasps Balaclava, Inkermann, Sebastopol, engraved naming. Turkish Crimea Sardinian version un-named £325. Same vendor March 1986, list item 28, same pair reduced £295. Fred Walland Medal List April 1987 same pair £295. Giuseppe Miceli for sale again June 1990, item 11, GVF £300.

The musters show he was effective from the 1st October to the 31st December with Good Conduct pay at 2d per diem for the period. WO25/3267 - Records show Discharged 27th July 1857.

923 HOARE, Private Thomas
Born : Unknown
Enlisted :
Medals : Crimea (B.I.S)

Died : Unknown
Status : Probably rode in the Charge

A Long Service and Good Conduct has appeared on the market.

The musters show he was effective from the 1st October to the 31st December with Good Conduct pay at 1d per diem for the period. WO25/3267 - Records show Discharged 18th May 1869.

967 HODGE, Private John
Born : Unknown
Enlisted :
Medals : Crimea (B.I.S)

Died : Unknown
Status : Probably rode in the Charge

The musters show he was effective from the 1st October to the 31st December with Good Conduct pay at 1d per diem for the period. WO25/3267 - Records show Discharged 25th July 1866 (name spelt HODD)

1177 HOLLAND, Private James
Born : Unknown
Enlisted :
Medals : Crimea (B.I.S)

Died : Unknown
Status : Probably rode in the Charge

Crimea medal with clasps Balaclava, Inkermann, and Turkish Medal in Regimental museum (Household Cavalry) June 1991.

The musters show he was effective from the 1st October to the 31st December. WO25/3267 - Records show Discharged 11th July 1863.

1090 HOLMES, Private William
Born : Unknown
Enlisted :
Medals : Crimea (B.I.S)

Died : Unknown
Status : Probably rode in the Charge

The musters show he was effective from the 1st October to the 31st December, 18 days at 1d per diem Good Conduct pay. Marginal note reads "Forfeited good conduct pay at 1d per diem 19th October".

Medal Roll - Class 2. Died, Retired from service, Discharged. Roll dated 10th February 1859, Royal Barracks, Dublin. 1090 Pte Holmes William -Dead- WO 100-24 page 152.

790 HORNER, Private William
Born : Unknown
Enlisted :
Medals : Crimea (B.I.S)

Died : Unknown
Status : Probably rode in the Charge

1038 HOWELL, Private Charles
Born : Unknown
Enlisted :
Medals : Crimea (B.I.S)

Died : Unknown
Status : Probably rode in the Charge

The musters show he was effective from the 1st October to the 31st December. WO25/3267 - Records show Discharged June 1861.

The following is an extract of an account provided by Paul Patterson. The account was in the possession of Paul's father for nearly 70 years and purports to have been written by a Charles Howell who claimed to be Orderly to Scarlett from the 1st Dragoons. We know that it was Shegog who was the orderly to Scarlett, and that Shegog came from the 5th Dragoon Guards and not the 1st Royal Dragoons. The extract is printed as provided with original spelling mistakes:

"Mr. Chairman, Ladys and Gentlemen. The short time I aske your atension to night while I tell you some of my experiances of war. Do not let it be thought that I am in favour of that dreadful word war. I abore it. And I belive if they that are the cause of it had to fight, theire whould be much less of it than theire is at present. And in the next place do not expect to heare a lecture by a well lerned man, or you will be sadly deceived.

I wish to speake to you as an old soldier and in the langue of an old soldier. if I should put in any words as I go on that are not grammatical you will please to excuse it....Well, now comes the morning of the 25th October, earley in the morning the bugles began sounding the alarm to boot and saddal, orderlys galloping to and fro calling out, turn out as soon as posable the enemy is advancing. I must try heare for the benefit of those that have not read the acount of this battel to explain our posion, and why the Russians acted us heare. They knew all the suplies were taken from Balaclava to the army in front of sebastopol. So if they could drive us from that posion we should have been in rather an unpleasant fix. You remember I told you it was from this small place that all our food came, and if our suplys had been cut off we chould not fight long without food. So that is what theire plan was to take Balaclava, and surround us but thank God it did not succeeded. It is verry posable if it had I should not have been heare to give you this few rambling recollections.

Now in front of the cavelery encamped there were 4 redouts or batterys with 3 ships guns in each maned by, I was going to say Turkish soldier's but they hardly deserved that name. They fled from the guns and left them in the before the enemy got near them. I have read that they stood theire ground until driven out by the Russians baynots, that may be so but it was with the sight of it, and not the feel of it. Theire was none of them either killed or wounded, so that dose not speak much in theire favour for bravery. In those redouts with the Turks was stationed one Inglish artilery man in each battery, they remained and was killed and so the enemy captured the whole of the guns. And it was to retake them that the fatal charge was made, but more about that presently.

During the time that the Russian infentry ware taking those redouts, we saw two large bodies of cavelery to our left front coming over the low hills to actac us cavelery as we suposed. Now on our right and across the road that leads to Balaclava, Sir Collin Cambell with 3 company's of the 93rd Highlanders was form, and on that small body of British soldier's came at full gallop one of the large one of these bodies of cavelery, and as they passed in front of us a few hundred yards the thought was in my mind, oh the poor 93rd they will be all cut up theire is more than fifty to one against them. But the fine old Sir Collin and his men stood their ground as British soldier's. Two deep the front ranks kneeling to resist cavelery. As we sat on our horses we heard quite plain the sharp words, kneeling ranks ready present and in an instant many a Russian soldier's saddle was empty. They broke and fled across the plain. The other body came on with the intension of charging us on our flank but General Scar for us, General Scarlet gave the word for the heavy cavelery to charge at them. The General lead the charge with his two a.d.c.'s one on each side of him, and my self close behind them. We had not more than 300 yards to go before the crash came, the result was we broke theire lines and then the swords had to do its work. It was every man for him self and God for us all. paraps some one may In a verry short time the Russians was satesfied, so they broke and fled across the plain and left us masters of the field.

My friends it is a thing impossible for a person that is in a battel to give any thing like a true account of it, he knows scarsely any thing only what he happens to do himself not always then. All that I know is that I used my sword the best way I could. Someone may say was you wounded in that charge, my answer is thank God I was not and if you should want to know how I escaped, all that I know is that I did escape, but how that is a question I cannot answer. General Scarlett got a slight wound in the charge. Captain Eliot received a dreadful sword cut on the right side of the face and we never saw him after been taken from the field. Major Conley the other a.d.c. had a sword cut on the left arm.

Now verry soon after the charge of the heavy cavelery, the order was given to follow up the retreeting enemy and retake if posable the guns they had taken from the Turks. So we advance over the hills, the Light Brigade in front into the plain. Theire was some blunder some where but that we not speak of. The order was given for the light cavelery to charge and charge they did. They advanced down that valley in three lines They had quite a mile to go before they reached the enemy. And all the time they are going that distance, the Russians are poring shot and shell amongst them on their right and left and also in front. The heavy cavelery followed the light in suport some distance down. When we had got some for or five hundred yards down the valley a ball from a Russian cannon struck the horse I was on in the chest, and killed him on the spot. In falling he pitched me on my head, and the peak of my helmet left a marke here I shall carry about with me as long as I live. I thought when I saw the blood from my face that I had been hit as well as the horse. I pulled my self together as well as I could and began to look about me, and I soon got another horse belonging to some poor fellow that was less fortunate than I was. Just then the remenant of our poor light cavelery began to straddle back. They went down that valley 600 strong, half of them never got back. They were laid low by the Russian guns. We now begin after that fatal charge to retire towards our encampment for food and rest. We had not broke our fast as yet. When we got to our tents, those brave Turks that deserted the guns at the beginning of the day had plundered the camp and stole our days food. It was fully expected that the Russians would attack us again, but they did not. The next morning the 26th about eleven I whent with the General through the camp of the Light Breaged, and we heard the role call of differant regements. It was a sad sight to witness as the names of the men were called.

From the battel of Balaclava things whent pretty smoothly with us cavelery, until the 5th of November 54. It came on the Sunday that year. It was Guy Fawks day to perfection. I cannot tell you much about that great Battel, only that it began early in the morning and under cover of a very heavy fog. They almost caught our infentry soldier's of theire guard. As it was they got near enough to send shot and shell in the camp before they whare a ware of theire presence. The fighting lasted about 8 hours and a greate part of that time at quite close quarters. As the day advanced the fog cleared off, and we could see the fight from a distance. It was imposable for the cavelery to attempt to help our countrymen, as the country about Inkerman is so hilly and uneven, that it is imposable for cavelery to work in a body."

1126 HUGHES, Sergeant William
Born : Unknown
Enlisted :
Medals : Crimea (B.I.S)

Died : Unknown
Status : Probably rode in the Charge

The musters show he was effective as a Corporal from the 1st October to the 4th November, 35 days at 1s-71/2d per diem, and as a Sergeant from the 5th November to the 31st December, 57 Days at 2s-2d per diem. Marginal note reads "To Sergeant 5th November vice Pardoe promoted."

Medal Roll - Class 2. Died, Retired from service, Discharged. Roll dated 10th February 1859, Royal Barracks, Dublin. - 1126 SGT Hughes William entry crossed through "Discharged" endorsed "S.O.P. Gloucester". William discharged. WO 100-24 page 151. WO25/3267 - Records show Discharged 26/1/1857

1253 HULSE, Private Joseph
Born : Unknown
Enlisted :
Medals : Crimea (B.I.S)

Died : Unknown
Status : Probably rode in the Charge

The musters show he was effective from the 1st October to the 3rd December, 64 days ordinary pay, 9 days on board ship, 55 days on shore. 3rd muster endorsed "Scutari", marginal note reads "To payment of paymaster Scutari 4th December".

754 HUNT, Private George
Born : Date unknown - Clerkenwell, Middlesex
Enlisted :
Medals : Crimea (B.I.S)

Died : Unknown
Status : Probably rode in the Charge

Bonhams, 17th December 2002, lot 386. Pair, Crimea 3 clasps Balaclava, Inkermann, Sebastopol. (G. Hunt 1st Dragoons) offically impressed and Turkish Crimea Sardinian version (G.C.Hunt Royal Drags) engraved, fitted with silver buckle broach. Suspension claw on Crimea Medal loose, otherwise GVF. Est £1200-1500. Illustrated, sold with copy of discharge documents. A Long Service and Good Conduct has also appeared on the market.

The musters show he was effective from the 1st October to the 27th November, 58 days ordinary pay, 58 days at 2d good conduct pay, 9 days on board ship, 49 days on shore. 2nd and 3rd musters endorsed "Scutari" Marginal note reads "To Scutari on the 28th November". WO25/3267 - Records show Discharged 6/1862.

Died, Retired from service, Discharged. Roll dated 10th February 1859, Royal Barracks, Dublin. 754 Pte Hunt, George. Roll endorsed "Dead" WO 100-24 page 152.

The National Archives - Army Records

WO 100 - Medal Rolls (held on mircofilm) - Campaign Medal and Award Rolls (General Series) Subseries within WO 100 Crimea WO 100/24 refers to General and Line Cavalry 1854-1855.

WO 97 - Attestation and discharge papers - information such as age, place of birth, occupation, physical description, service history, punishments and court marshals. The line cavalry are all in one alphabetical run for this period.

WO12 - Muster and Pay lists up to 1878 - maintained by regiments/depots and shows pay and officers' expenses.

WO 25 - Casualty returns - cover the absentees, deserters, and discharges as well as dead and wounded. Index by pieces 2411-2755 and 3261-3471, also returns are in class 1359-2410 and 3251-3260.

WO 116 - Admission Books, Royal Hospital, Chelsea, 1715-1913.

Additional information can be found at http://nationalarchives.gov.uk/catalogue/

750 HUNT, Private George

Born : Date unknown - Thatcham, Berks
Enlisted :
Medals : Crimea (S)

Died : Unknown
Status : Effective during the period

The musters show he was effective from the 1st October to the 3rd November, 34 days ordinary pay, 34 days at 2d good conduct pay, 4 days on board ship, 30 days on shore. 2nd and 3rd musters endorsed "Scutari", marginal note reads "To Scutari on the 4th November".

WO14/1 Scutari Muster Roll January-March 1855 remarks indicate "Hospital Ship" 1st-31st January, "Sent Home" 23rd February. WO-100-24 page 147, 750 Pte Hunt, George. Marginal note reads "England".

879 HUNTER, Sergeant Peter

Born : Unknown
Enlisted :
Medals : Crimea (B.I.S), Long Service and Good Conduct Medal

Died : Unknown
Status : Probably rode in the Charge

The musters show he was effective from the 1st October to the 31st December, 92 days at 2s-2d per diem, 9 days on board ship, 83 days on shore. WO102 L.S & G.C T.S.M Peter Hunter recommended 12th July 1865 without gratuity.

1006 JACKSON, Private William

Born : Unknown
Enlisted :
Medals : Crimea (B.I.S)

Died : Unknown
Status : Probably rode in the Charge

The musters show he was effective from the 1st October to the 31st December.

1251 JACOB, Private Stephen

Born : Unknown
Enlisted :
Medals : Crimea (B.I.S)

Died : Unknown
Status : Probably rode in the Charge

The musters show he was effective from the 1st October to the 31st December, 1d per diem good conduct pay for the period.

1209 JAMES, Corporal John

Born : Unknown
Enlisted :
Medals : Crimea (B.I.S)

Died : Unknown
Status : Probably rode in the Charge

The musters show he was effective as a Private from the 1st October to the 9th November, 40 days at ordinary pay, 9 days on board ship, 31 days on shore. Marginal note reads " To Corpl 10th Nov vice Ridgeway promoted". Effective as a Corporal from the 10th November to the 13th December, 34 Days at 1s-7 1/2d per diem, marginal note reads "Promoted to ... Paymt of paymr Scutari 14th Decr".

WO14/1 Scutari Muster Roll January-March 1855 remarks indicate Hospital 1st January to the 2nd March. Sent Home 3rd March. Medal Roll Sebastopol clasp. Entitled. 1209. Cpl. James. John Marginal note reads "England Regt 6/9" WO 100-24 page 144.

1227 JAMES, Private John
Born : Unknown
Enlisted :
Medals : Crimea (B.I.S)

Died : Unknown
Status : Probably rode in the Charge

The musters show he was effective from the 1st October to the 31st December.

1066 JELLY, Private John
Born : Unknown
Enlisted :
Medals : Crimea (B.I.S)

Died : Unknown
Status : Probably rode in the Charge

Eugene G. Ursual, List No 129 Crimea 1854 bars Balaklava, Inkermann, Sebastopol (Pte J. Jelly, Royal Dragoons) regimentally engraved nicely toned. 1250 Canadian dollars £540.

The musters show he was effective from the 1st October to the 31st December.

472 JEWHURST, Sergeant Edward
Born : Unknown
Enlisted :
Medals : Crimea (B.S)

Died : Unknown
Status : Probably rode in the Charge

The musters show he was effective from the 1st October to the 31st December with 3d per diem good conduct pay, increased to 4d for 37 days. Marginal note reads "Entitled to Good conduct pay at 4d per diem on 25th November. Medal Roll Sebastopol clasp entitled 472 Sgt Jewhurst, Edward, WO-100-24 page 144. WO100/24 page 137 Remarks: Promoted from Private since Crimean Medal Return went in. WO25/3267 - Discharged 31/12/1860.

1190 JOHNSON, Corporal Thomas
Born : Unknown
Enlisted :
Medals : Crimea (B.I.S)

Died : Unknown
Status : Probably rode in the Charge

The musters show he was effective as a Private from the 1st October to the 4th November, 35 days ordinary pay, 3 days on board ship, 32 days on shore. Marginal note reads "to Corporal 5 Nov vice Hughes promoted." Effective as a Corporal from the 5th November to the 31st December, 57 days at 1s-71/2d per diem, 41 days on shore, 16 days in Regtl hospital. WO100/24 page 138 Remarks: Promoted from Private since Crimean Medal Return went in. Medal Roll - Class 2. Died, Retired from service, Discharged. Roll dated 10th February 1859, Royal Barracks, Dublin. 1190 Cpl Johnson, Thomas discharged. WO 100-24 page 151. WO25/3267 - Records show Discharged December 1856.

1238 JOHNSON, Private George
Born : Date Unknown - Monahan
Enlisted : 20th September 1833
Medals : Crimea (B.I.S)

Died : 10th March 1855 - Camp Kadikoi
Status : Probably rode in the Charge

The musters show he was effective from the 1st October to the 31 December with 2d per diem good conduct pay for the period. Trade on enlistment Shoemaker.

Two men died in the Field Hospital, both on the 10th of the month; one old soldier of 40 years of age and 21 years service, was "on the point of being invalided as completely worn out; he caught cold in camp and died from exhaustion on the 29th day of his illness." The duties, during the winter were severe. When not on picket, the men were engaged in carrying up provisions for the Infantry, through miles of mud ; bringing sick from the front to Balaklava; carrying forage and wood for stables and huts. (*Medical and Surgical History of the British Army during the War against Russia Vol 1 p 26*)

1212 JOHNSTONE, Private Thomas
Born : Unknown
Enlisted :
Medals : Crimea (B.I.S)

Died : Unknown
Status : Probably rode in the Charge

Crimea medal with clasps Balaklava, Inkermann, Sebastopol to Cpl T. Johnson in Regimental museum (Household Cavalry) June 1991.

The musters show he was effective from the 1st October to the 31st December. WO25/3267 - Records show Discharged unfit for further service 26/8/1861.

1115 JONES, Corporal John Ball
Born : Date Unknown - Birmingham
Enlisted : 3rd April 1850
Medals : Crimea (B.I.S), The Distinguished Conduct Medal

Died : 14th February 1855 - Camp Kadikoi
Status : Probably rode in the Charge

The musters show he was effective from the 1st October to the 31st December, 92 days at 1s-7 1/2d per diem, 88 days on shore, 4 days on board ship. The Distinguished Conduct Medal recommended 9th January 1855.
Medal Roll Sebastopol Clasp, Entitled. 1115 Cpl Jones, John Ball. Marginal note reads "Dead, over written WO 22/11/58" Wo 100-24 page 144. Medal Roll - Class 2. Died, Retired from service, Discharged. Roll dated 10th February 1859, Royal Barracks, Dublin. 1115 Cpl Jones, John Ball "Dead".

1143 JONES, Private John D.
Born : Unknown
Enlisted :
Medals : Crimea (B.I.S)

Died : Unknown
Status : Probably rode in the Charge

Crimea medal with only the Sebastopol clasp in Regimental museum (Household Cavalry) June 1991.

The musters show he was effective from the 1st October to the 31st December.

965 KENNEDY, Private Bryan
Born : Unknown
Enlisted :
Medals : Crimea (B.I.S)

Died : Unknown
Status : Slightly wounded in the Charge

Seaby December 1974, item No F12C4, Crimea medal with clasps Balaklava, Inkermann, Sebastopol, (Pte Bryan Kennedy. RL.Dgns) engraved VF £85

The musters show he was effective from the 1st October to the 31st December. Listed on the casualty roll as wounded slightly at Balaclava.

462 KENWARD, Private Henry
Born : Unknown
Enlisted :
Medals : Crimea (I.S)

Died : Unknown
Status : Effective during the period

The musters show he was effective from the 1st October to the 31st December with 6 days at 3d and 86 days at 4d per diem good conduct pay. Marginal note reads "Entitled to Good conduct pay at 4d per diem on 7th October". WO25/3267 - Records show Discharged 22/6/1859. Not shown by Sewell as entitled to a Balaclava clasp.

920 KEYTE, Sergeant William John
Born : 1824
Enlisted : April 1845
Medals : Crimea (B.I.S), The Knight (5th Class) The French Legion of Honour

Died : 15th February 1907
Status : Probably rode in the Charge

The musters show he was effective from the 1st October to the 31st December, 92 days at 2s-2d per diem, 3 days on board ship, 89 days on shore. WO25/3267 - Records show Discharged 26/4/1870.

His medal recommendation states:" I believe that in naming No. 920 Sergeant William J. Keyte of the Rgt. under my command, for your favourable consideration, I shall be acting in accordance with Lieut Colonel Wardlaw's wishes on the subject " Henry Davenport Capt. Commg Royal Drgs.
"I have the honor to enclose with my letter a short statement of the Services of Sergt. W.J. Keyte - recommended for the honour of the "Mark of Distinction for distinguished Service". No. 920 Sergt William John Keyte - enlisted for the Royal Dragoons April 1845. Corporal August 1852 Sergeant May 1854. He has been present with the Regt. during the whole time of its service in the East & on all occasion on which it has been called upon to perform its duties in the Campaign. In consequence of his good character as a a Non-Commissioned officer, he was selected by Lt. Col. Wardlaw Commg the Regt. to go to the Depot at Canterbury for the purpose of drilling the Recruits, with a draft of whom he will rejoin his Regt in the Spring." Henry Davenport. Capt. Commg Royal Drgs.

Buried in Northam cemetery, Devon, the inscription on the stone reads "In memory of Annie beloved wife of William John Keyte, who died August 22nd 1895, aged 62 years. Also of the above William John Keyte, Knight Legion of Honour Late Royal Dragoons, who died February 15th 1907, aged 83 years."

The Return of the 1st Dragoons

The Times 28th May 1856 - The steam ship Orinoco number 218 arrived at Spithead yesterday morning from the East with troops. She left Scutari at 6pm on the 13th May and Malta on the 17th.... The following officers and men, Liet.Col Robert Wardlaw; Captains Michael Stocks, John C.Davenport, James Ainslie, Walter J.Coney and St.John W.C.Charlton; Lieutenants T. Keane Fitzgerald, Richard George, Glyn, Gilbert M.Robertson, John G.Sandeman, Henry F.G Coleman, William Edmund Curtis and J.Gordon Graham; Paymaster Henry Dixon; Lieutenant-Adjutant John Lee; Assistant-Surgeon Henry Sherlock; Quartermaster William Scott; Veterinary-Surgeon Cherry, 411 men, and 241 horses. From dispatches by William Howard Russell (The Times correspondent)

594 KINNAIRD, Private William

Born : Unknown
Enlisted :
Medals : Crimea (I.S)

Died : Unknown
Status : Effective during the period

The musters show he was effective from the 1st October to the 17th November, 48 days ordinary pay, 19 days at 2d and 29 days at 3d good conduct pay, 3 days on board ship, 45 days on shore. 2nd and 3rd musters endorsed "Scutari", marginal note reads "Forfeited 1d per diem good conduct pay on 30th October. To payment of paymaster Scutari on 18th Nov." WO14/1 Scutari Muster Roll January-March 1855 remarks indicate Hospital 1st-31st January, "Sent Home" 9th February.
Medal Roll Sebastopol clasp entitled 594 Pte Hunt,Kinnaird, William. Marginal note reads "England so 1/8/56" WO100-24 page 148. WO100-24 page 152 Medal Roll - Class 2. Died, Retired from service, Discharged. Roll dated 10th February 1859, Royal Barracks, Dublin. 594 Pte Hunt,Kinnaird, Discharged. Name crossed through and signed by medal recipient.

682 LAMBERT, Sergeant Charles

Born : Unknown
Enlisted :
Medals : Crimea (B.I.S), Long Service and Good Conduct Medal

Died : Unknown
Status : Probably rode in the Charge

The musters show he was effective from the 1st October to the 31st December, 92 days at 2s-2d per diem, 4 days on board ship, 88 days on shore. WO25/3267 - Records show Discharged 12th January 1864. WO102 L.S & G.C issued 9th July 1861 without gratuity.

728 LAWS, Private William

Born : Unknown
Enlisted :
Medals : Crimea (S)

Died : Unknown
Status : Effective during the period

The musters show he was effective from the 1st October to the 2nd November, 33 days ordinary pay, 4 days on board ship, 29 days on shore. 2nd and 3rd musters endorsed "Scutari", marginal note reads "To payment of paymaster Scutari 3rd Nov." WO25/3267 - Records show Discharged December 1856.
WO-100-24 page 148, 728 Pte Laws,William. Marginal note reads "England Regt 6/9". WO 100-24 page 152 Medal Roll - Class 2. Died, Retired from service, Discharged. Roll dated 10th February 1859, Royal Barracks, Dublin. 728 Pte Laws,William discharged. Overwritten "sent 13/9/60".

787 LEE, Regimental Sergeant-Major John

Born : Unknown
Enlisted :
Medals : Crimea (B.I.S)
Medals held in the Regimental Museum (Household Cavalry)

Died : Unknown
Status : Rode in the Charge

The musters show he was effective as a Regimental Sergeant Major from the 1st October to the 4th November, 55 days at 3s 6d per diem, 9 days on board ship. Marginal note reads "Promoted Cornet 5th Nov." Effective as a Cornet from the 5th November to the 31st December, marginal note reads "Appointed Cornet from R.S.M 5th Nov". WO100/24 page 137 Remarks: Promoted from Regt. Serj. Major since Crimean Medal Return went in. Promoted Lieutenant 14th February 1856 (*Harts Army List 1860*)

From Private John Vahey, (Butcher Jack's) 17th Lancers account. "I galloped up to the Heavy Brigade, and formed up coolly on the left flank of the Royals. They laughed at me as if I had been a clown in a pantomime: and I had not been in position a couple of minutes when up came Johnny Lee, their adjutant, on his old bay mare, at a tearing gallop, and roared to me to "Go to Hell out of that!"

500 LEES, Hospital Sergeant-Major Dennis

Born : Unknown
Enlisted :
Medals : Crimea (B.I.S)

Died : Unknown
Status : Probably rode in the Charge

The musters show he was effective as a Sergeant from the 1st-8th October, 8 days at 2s-2d per diem, 3 days on board ship, 5 days on shore and as a Hospital Sergeant from the 9th October to the 31st December, 84 days at 2s-2d per diem, 84 days on shore. Marginal note reads "From Sergeant 9th October vice Scott". WO25/3267 - Records show Discharged March 1861.
"However short a time a battalion or a corps rested in one place, a regimental hospital was established" the purveying of a regimental hospital is for the most part a simple affair, and conducted successfully by the hospital sergeant, under the direction of the surgeon. (*The Monthly Journal of Medicine, 1855. Simpkin, Marshall and Co. page 481*)

1053 LEWIS, Private William

Born : Unknown
Enlisted :
Medals : Crimea (B.I.S)

Died : Unknown
Status : Probably rode in the Charge

The musters show he was effective from the 1st October to the 31st December with 1d per diem good conduct pay paid for the period. Medal Roll - Class 2. Died, Retired from service, Discharged. Roll dated 10th February 1859, Royal Barracks, Dublin. 1053 Lewis, William discharged. Overwritten "sent to S.O.P Bristol. WO 100-24 page 152. WO25/3267 - Records show Discharged 12/1858.

1172 LINCOLN, Private William

Born : Unknown
Enlisted :
Medals : Crimea (B.I.S)

Died : Unknown
Status : Probably rode in the Charge

The musters show he was effective from the 1st October to the 31st December. Medal Roll Sebastopol clasp entitled 1172 Pte Lincoln, William. Marginal note reads "England Regt 6/9" WO 100-24 page 148. Medal Roll - Class 2. Died, Retired from service, Discharged. Roll dated 10th february 1859, Royal Barracks, Dublin. 1172 Pte Lincoln, William. discharged. Overwritten "sent to Him 26/10/60 .WO 100-24 page 152. WO25/3267 - Records show Discharged 26/1/1857.

1007 LOCK, Private Alfred

Born : Unknown
Enlisted :
Medals : Crimea (B.I.S)

Died : Unknown
Status : Probably rode in the Charge

The musters show he was effective from the 1st October to the 31st December with 1d per diem good conduct pay paid for the period.

763 LOFTS, Private Henry

Born : Unknown
Enlisted :
Medals : Crimea (B.S)

Died : 29th August 1865 - Brighton
Status : Probably rode in the Charge

The musters show he was effective from the 1st October to the 31st December with 2d per diem good conduct pay paid for the period. WO25/3267 - Records show he died Brighton 29/8/1865.

1253 LOUCH, Private George

Born : Unknown
Enlisted :
Medals : Crimea (B.I.S), Sutley (for Aliwal, clasp Sobraon), Punjab (clasps Chillianwallah, Goojerat)

Died : Unknown
Status : Probably rode in the Charge

He went to India in 1843 with a draft for the 3rd Light Dragoons ("*The Radical Soldier's Tale: John Pearman, 1819-1908*" C. Steedman Ed 1988 page 247). The musters show he was effective from the 1st October to the 31 December with 56 days 1d per diem good conduct pay paid for the period. Marginal note reads "3rd Dragoons No 1540. Good conduct 1d per diem on 6th November". WO 100-24 page 152, Medal Roll - Class 2. Died, Retired from service, Discharged. Roll dated 10th february 1859, Royal Barracks, Dublin. 1253 Pte Louch, George. discharged.

System of Purchase Dragoon Guards and Dragoons circa 1854

Commission	Price	Difference	Annual Pay
Cornet	£840		£50
Lieutenant	£1190	£350	£70
Captain	£3225	£2035	£190
Major	£4575	£1350	£270
Lt-Colonel	£6175	£1600	£364

The granting of an officer's first commission was vested in the Colonel of the regiment. From 1849, the candidate for a commission was sent to Sandhurst to be examined. If accepted, he became eligible for a commission. He could then apply for a commission by purchase, and be appointed to the first vacancy which occurred from a regiment by sale. If he applied for a commission without purchase, he waited until a vacancy occurred by death, when his application was considered along with other applications. During Wars vacancies from death increased the number of commissions, in peacetime with fewer vacancies, many went on half-pay.

The Purchase system in the British Army, 1660-1871, Anthony Bruce, Royal Historical Society, London, 1980.

647 LUCAS, Private John

Born : Unknown
Enlisted :
Medals : Crimea (I.S)

Died : Unknown
Status : Effective during the period

The musters show he was effective from the 1st October to the 31st December.

872 LYNKSKEY, Farrier Patrick

Born : Unknown
Enlisted :
Medals : Crimea (B.S)

Died : Unknown
Status : Probably rode in the Charge

The musters show he was effective from the 1st October to the 31st December with 1d per diem good conduct pay paid for the period.

1240 MAGUIRE, Private Thomas

Born : Unknown
Enlisted :
Medals : Crimea (B.I.S)

Died : Unknown
Status : Probably rode in the Charge

The musters show he was effective from the 1st October to the 31st December.

856 MALE, Private John

Born : Unknown
Enlisted :
Medals : Crimea (B.I.S)

Died : Unknown
Status : Probably rode in the Charge

The musters show he was effective from the 1st October to the 31st December.

635 MANSELL, Private William

Born : Unknown
Enlisted :
Medals : Crimea (B.I.S)

Died : Unknown
Status : Probably rode in the Charge

The musters show he was effective from the 1st October to the 31st December. Marginal notes reads "3rd Dragoons No 2042". Medal Roll - Class 2. Died, Retired from service, Discharged. Roll dated 10th February 1859, Royal Barracks, Dublin. 635 Pte Mansell, William. Marginal note reads "Regt 6/9 x H&R to replace lost 30/10" WO 100-24 page 148.

1250 MARCHANT, Private Henry

Born : Unknown
Enlisted :
Medals : Crimea (B.I.S)

Died : Unknown
Status : Probably rode in the Charge

The musters show he was effective from the 1st October to the 31st December.

816 MARCHANT, Private Richard
Born : Unknown
Enlisted :
Medals : Crimea (B.I.S)

Died : Unknown
Status : Probably rode in the Charge

The musters show he was effective from the 1st October to the 31st December. WO25/3267 - Discharged 6/11/1866.

1069 MARSHALL, Private Edwin
Born : Unknown
Enlisted :
Medals : Crimea (B.I.S)

Died : Unknown
Status : Probably rode in the Charge

The musters show he was effective from the 1st October to the 3rd December, 64 days ordinary pay, 64 days at 1d Good conduct pay, 4 days on board ship, 60 days on shore. 3rd muster endorsed "Scutari", marginal note reads "To payment of paymaster at Scutari 4th December". WO14/1 Scutari Muster Roll January-March 1855 remarks indicate "48 hours Wife 13th" 1st-31st January, no dates or remarks shown in the next two musters.

947 MARTIN, Private William Henry
Born : Unknown
Enlisted :
Medals : Crimea (B.I.S)

Died : Unknown
Status : Probably rode in the Charge

The musters show he was effective from the 1st October to the 31st December with 1d per diem good conduct paid.

1157 MATTHEWMAN, Private Richard
Born : Unknown
Enlisted :
Medals : Crimea (I.S)

Died : Unknown
Status : Effective for the period

The musters show he was effective from the 1st October to the 31st December. Medal Roll Sebastopol clasp entitled 1157 Pte Matthewman, Richard. Marginal note reads "Regt 6/9 - H & R 30/10 to replace lost" WO 100-24 page 148.

572 MATTHEWS, Regimental Sergeant Major William
Born : Unknown
Enlisted :
Medals : Crimea (B.I.S)

Died : 1903
Status : Rode in the Charge

The musters show he was effective from the 1st October to the 31st December, 92 days at 3s-0d per diem, 9 days on board ship, 83 days on shore. WO25/3267 - Records show him becoming a Cornet in the Transport Corps.

Transferred as a Cornet into the Transport Corps 12th January 1856. Riding Master, Military train 10th March 1857. Riding Master 11th Hussars 18th May 1870. To half pay as Hon Captain 19th October 1872. Retired half pay 1st July 1881. His horse was shot from under him at Balaclava. Received the reward for Distinguished Services 27th Dec 1887.

1223 MAY, Private Frederick
Born : Unknown
Enlisted :
Medals : Crimea (B.S)

Died : Unknown
Status : Probably rode in the Charge

The musters show he was effective from the 1st October to the 31st December. WO14/1 Scutari Muster Roll Jan-Mar 1855 remarks indicate "From 4th ... Hospital" 4th-31st January, "Abydos" 1st-28th February, "Sent Home" 31st March.

825 MAYCOCK, Private Thomas

Born : Unknown
Enlisted :
Medals : Crimea (B.S)

Died : Unknown
Status : Probably rode in the Charge

Hayward Vol 2 No 4 July 1968, item 167. Family pair. Waterloo J.Maycock 1st Regt Lifeguards and Crimea medal with three clasps Balaclava, Inkermann, Sebastopol (T.Maycock 1st Royal Dragoons engraved naming F. Pair £36.

The musters show he was effective from the 1st October to the 3rd December, 64 days ordinary pay, 64 days at 2d Good conduct, 9 days on board ship, 55 days on shore. 3rd muster endorsed "Scutari", marginal note reads "To payment of paymaster ar Scutari 4th December". WO14/1 Scutari Muster Roll January-March 1855 remarks indicate "Hospital" 1st-31st January, no dates or remarks shown in the next two musters.
Medal Roll Sebastopol clasp entitled 825 Pte Maycock. Thomas. Marginal note reads "England Regt 26/9". WO 100-24 page 148. Medal Roll - Class 2. Died, Retired from service, Discharged. Roll dated 10th February 1859, Royal Barracks, Dublin. 825 Pte Maycock. Thomas Discharged Roll signed for by medal recipient.

1285 McMURRAY, Private Thomas

Born : Date Unknown - Portadown
Enlisted : 8th March 1854
Medals : Crimea (B.I.S)

Died : 22nd March 1855 - Scutari
Status : Probably rode in the Charge

The musters show he was effective from the 1st October to the 31st December. Marginal note reads "29 Reg 1482, 1 Dgs 1564 3 Dgs"

1044 MEEHAN, Private Terence

Born : Unknown
Enlisted :
Medals : Crimea (B.I.S)

Died : Unknown
Status : Probably rode in the Charge

Hamiltons, March 1974, item XS 2127. Crimea Medal with three clasps impressed naming, Balaclava, Inkermann, Sebastopol (T.Meehan 1st Royal Dragoons.Regt No 144) GVF £120.   Eugene G. Ursual, List No 139. Pair. Crimea 1854 bars Balaklava, Inkermann,Sebastopol (T. Meehan, 1st Royal Dragoons) impressed ; Turkish Crimea Sardinian issue, the 1st Royal Dragoons. Good VF. 1850 Canadian dollars £711.

The musters show he was effective from the 1st October to the 31st December. WO25/3267 - Records show transferred to Military Train December 1856 (writing difficult to read)
In 1855 the Land Transport Corps was established as there were insuffcient transport capabilities to move supplies between Balaclava harbour and the soldier's' encampments. In 1856 the L.T.C was organised as the military train.

1080 MERCER, Private Joshua

Born : Unknown
Enlisted :
Medals : Crimea (B.I.S)

Died : Unknown
Status : Probably rode in the Charge

The musters show he was effective from the 1st October to the 31st December.

1289 MEREDITH, Private Hugh

Born : Unknown
Enlisted :
Medals : Crimea (B.I.S)

Died : Unknown
Status : Probably rode in the Charge

The musters show he was effective from the 1st October to the 31st December. In 1881 Hugh Meredith is recorded as living in Birmingham, occupation a Cabman, widowed, living as a border with his three sons and a daughter.

1261 METCALF, Private Thomas

Born : Unknown
Enlisted :
Medals : Crimea (B.I.S)

Died : Unknown
Status : Probably rode in the Charge

Crimea medal with 3 clasps Balaklava, Inkermann, Sebastopol and Turkish Crimea in Regimental museum (Household Cavalry) June 1991.

The musters show he was effective from the 1st October to the 31st December.

1063 MIDDLETON, Private Charles
Born : Date Unknown - Thrandeston, Suffolk
Enlisted : 16th March 1848
Medals : Crimea (B.S)

Died : 25th October 1854 - Balaclava
Status : Killed in the Charge

The musters show he was effective from the 1st-25th October, 25 days ordinary pay, 25 days at 1p Good conduct, 3 days on board ship, 22 days on shore. All musters crossed through marginal note reads "Killed in Action at Balaclava on 25th October." Form 20 shows his mother as Daphne of Suffolk. Shown on the Casualty Roll as "Killed at Balaclava".

1204 MILLEN, Private Wilson
Born : Unknown
Enlisted :
Medals : Crimea (B.I.S)

Died : Unknown
Status : Probably rode in the Charge

The musters show he was effective from the 1st October to the 31st December. WO25/3267 - Records show Discharged June 1859.

1719 MITCHELL, Private Robert
Born : Unknown
Enlisted :
Medals : Crimea (B.I.S)

Died : Unknown
Status : Probably rode in the Charge

The musters show he was effective from the 1st October to the 31st December with 2d per diem good conduct pay for the period.

519 MOFFATT, Private George
Born : Unknown
Enlisted :
Medals : Crimea (B.I.S)
Crimea medal with 3 clasps Balaclava, Inkermann, Sebastopol and Turkish Crimea in Regimental museum (Household Cavalry) June 1991.

Died : Unknown
Status : Probably rode in the Charge

The musters show he was effective from the 1st October to the 31st December.

1034 MOORHOUSE, Sergeant John
Born : Unknown
Enlisted :
Medals : Crimea (B.S)

Died : Unknown
Status : Probably rode in the Charge

The musters show he was effective from the 1st October to the 31st December, 92 days at 1s-7 1/2d per diem, 92 days at 1d Good conduct pay, 3 days on board ship, 89 on shore. WO25/3267 - Records show transferred to the Military Train December 1856.

938 MURRAY, Sergeant Henry
Born : Unknown
Enlisted :
Medals : Crimea (B.I.S)

Died : Unknown
Status : Probably rode in the Charge

The musters show he was effective from the 1st October to the 31st December, 92 Days at 1s-7 1/2d per diem, 92 days at 1d Good conduct pay, 9 days on board ship, 83 days on shore.

973 NEALON, Private William
Born : Unknown
Enlisted :
Medals : Crimea (B.I.S)

Died : Unknown
Status : Probably rode in the Charge

The musters show he was effective from the 1st October to the 31st December. WO25/3267 - Records show Discharged 15th November 1870.

1140 NEWALL, Private John

Born : Unknown
Enlisted :
Medals : Crimea (D.I.S)

Died : Unknown
Status : Probably rode in the Charge

The musters show he was effective from the 1st October to the 31st December. WO25/3267 - Discharged March 1861.

1135 NICHOLLS, Corporal William

Born : Unknown
Enlisted :
Medals : Crimea (B.S)

Died : Unknown
Status : Probably rode in the Charge

The musters show he was effective from the 1st October to the 31st December, 92 Days at 1s-7 1/2d per diem, 4 days on board ship, 88 on shore. Medal Roll Sebastopol clasp. Entitled. 1135. Cpl. Nicholls. William. Marginal note reads "England SO 18/8/56" WO 100-24 page 144. Medal Roll - Class 2. Died, Retired from service, Discharged. Roll dated 10th February 1859, Royal Barracks, Dublin. - 1135 Cpl Nicholls Wm. "Discharged - sent 5/10/62" WO 100-24 page 151.

995 NOAKE, Sergeant Maillard

Born : 1828
Enlisted :
Medals : Crimea (B.S), The Distinguished Conduct Medal

Died : 1914
Status : Severely wounded in the Charge

The musters show he was effective from the 1st-25th October, 39 days at 2s-2d per diem, 9 days on board ship, 16 days on shore. First and second musters endorsed "Scutari", third muster "England", marginal note reads "To payment of paymaster GenL. Depot Scutari from 26th October. To England 20th December". Shown on the Casualty Roll as "Wounded Severely at Balaclava". WO100/24 page 144 Remarks: Discharged. Recommendation for the Distinguished Conduct Medal dated 9th January 1855.

"One very handsome intelligent, Active-Minded young man Sergeant N. of the 1st Royals asked me one day the meaning of my sleeves, which were certainly of a needless and rather in-convenient length and breath for nursing ....was nursed by Sarah Anne Terrot at Scutari...Had a severe wound in the thigh but he told me he had interest and hoped if his wound healed he might get a commission. To his great disappointment, however, he was discharged..." (*Nurse Sarah Anne by Robert G. Richardson, page 147*)

After his discharge Noake joined the Dumfries Militia before being appointed Riding master in the 15th (The King's) Regiment of Light Dragoons 20th February 1857 (Harts Army List 1860). Joined the mounted troops of New Zealand's Colonial Defence Force, commissioned Sub-Inspector 11th September 1863. "Another important example was Maillard Noake, a former British cavalryman and officer who had not only Crimean War service (serving in the Scots Greys), but in India in the latter stages of the Indian Mutiny. Whilst in India, Noake was invalided for the second time because of a re-occurring wound sustained back in the Crimea, and transferred into a home regiment, eventually leaving the service and deciding to settle in New Zealand in 1863. Finding the war in the Waikato was likely to continue, he applied for service and was appointed captain of militia and transferred to the Wellington Defence Force, which company as adjutant he materially assisted in organising. ... Noake afterwards commanded the force stationed in Rangitikei, which command he retained until it was disbanded. After this Noake was appointed Resident Magistrate in the Upper Wanganui District, but saw additional active service in the relief of Pipiriki in 1865, and then again during the campaigns of 1868-69." (*New Zealand"s Colonial Defence Force (Cavalry) and its Australian Context, 1863-66. by Jeff Hopkins-Weise, published in Sabretache 1st September 2002*)

The New Zealand National Register of Archives and Manuscripts holds various documents relating to Noake including commissions and letters of appointment. NOAKE, Maillard, 1828-1914 (B615) see below:

Major Noake was a former British Army officer who commanded the Rangitikei, Patea and Wanganui Military Districts in the 1860s and 1870s. He was Resident Magistrate for Rangitikei, Coroner for Patea and Inspector of the Colonial Defence Forces.

There are 24 commissions and letters of appointment from Noake's commission as ensign in the Dumfriesshire Regiment to his commission as Lieutenant-Colonel of the First Regiment (North Island) Cavalry in 1886.

Four items dealing with a land grant at Molyneux transferred to Noake from Robert Wilkin, 1866, and two letters acknowledging his reports of expeditions at Waitotara and Patea, 1869, are included.

Lord Raglan's Head Quarters, with Lord Raglan, Marshal Pélissier, Lord Burghersh, Spahi & A.D.C of Marshal Pélissier

803 NORRIS, Troop Sergeant-Major John

Born : Unknown   Died : Unknown
Enlisted :   Status : Rode in the Charge
Medals : Crimea (B.I.S), The French Medaille Militaire

The musters show he was effective from the 1st October to the 31st December, 92 days at 3s-0d per diem, 3 days on board ship, 89 days on shore. WO25/3267 - Records show Discharged as RSM 29/5/1866.

The citation for The French Medaille Militaire reads (He) "served as Troop Sergeant Major during the whole of the Eastern Campaign; was present at the action of Balaklava, where he distinguished himself by defending himself against four Russian Hussars, one of whom he killed, and whose horse he captured."

On the 16th November 1855, the Regiment gave over its huts to the 11th Hussars, and embarked from Balaklava; it arrived at Scutari on the 19th, and disembarked on the following day.

The men reached "their stables at 7 o'clock in the evening, and slept for the first three nights alongside their horses, as the ground was too damp for pitching the tents.

On the 28th, they got into wooden building appointed as barracks. The strength of the Regiment was increased by the addition of the depot at Scutari." (*Medical and Surgical History of British Army in Turkey and Crimea during the Russian War, 1858 page 30*)

Russian Swords

Few Russians had made any attempts to sharpen their swords. Many of our men survived after receiving an incredible number of cuts, and a Private of the Fourth Dragoon Guards had fifteen cuts on the head, none of which was more than skin deep. This and the faulty leading of the Russian officers account for the very slight loss incurred by the Heavy Brigade - seventy eight killed and wounded. (*Sir Evelyn Wood in The Fortnightly*)

846 OGDEN, Private James

Born : Unknown
Enlisted :
Medals : Crimea (B.I.S)

Died : 20th July 1857
Status : Probably rode in the Charge

The musters show he was effective from the 1st October to the 31st December. Medal Roll - Class 2. Died, Retired from service, Discharged. Roll dated 10th February 1859, Royal Barracks, Dublin. Entry 114 846 Pte Ogden James Dead 825 WO 100-24 page 152. WO25/3267 - Records show Died 20th July 1857.

989 OLIVER, Private Edward

Born : Unknown
Enlisted :
Medals : Crimea (B.I.S)

Died : Unknown
Status : Probably rode in the Charge

Crimea medal with 3 clasps Balaklava, Inkermann, Sebastopol held in Regimental museum (Household Cavalry) June 1991.

The musters show he was effective from the 1st October to the 31st December, 92 days ordinary day, 92 days at 1p Good conduct pay. WO25/3267 - Records show transferred to the Military Train December 1856.

1216 OVERTON, Private William John

Born : Unknown
Enlisted :
Medals : Crimea (S)

Died : Unknown
Status : To Scutari 26th October 1854

Glendinings 16th-18th July 1930, Lord Cheylesmore Collection, Lot 12, (With another medal) Crimea 2 Bars Balacklava and Sebastopol. J.Overton 1st Dragoons. Realised £4-5-0. Crimea medal with 2 clasps Balaklava, Sebastopol held in Regimental museum (Household Cavalry) June 1991.

The musters show he was effective from the 1st-25th October, 25 days ordinary day, 3 days on board ship, 22 days on shore. 1st and 2nd musters endorsed "Scutari" 3rd muster "England", marginal note reads "To payment of paymaster Gen Depot Scutari 26th Oct. To England 25th December". Medal Roll - Class 2. Died, Retired from service, Discharged. Roll dated 10th February 1859, Royal Barracks, Dublin. Entry No 115 1216 Pte Overton, William John. discharged. WO 100-24 page 152.

849 PACK, Private Joseph

Born : Unknown
Enlisted :
Medals : Crimea (B.I.S)

Died : Unknown
Status : Probably rode in the Charge

The musters show he was effective from the 1st October to the 20th December, 81 days ordinary day, 9 days on board ship, 72 days on shore. Third muster endorsed "Scutari", marginal note reads "To payment of paymaster Scutari on 21st December". WO14/1 Scutari Muster Roll January-March 1855 effective 1st -31st January, no dates or remarks shown in the next two musters.

Medal Roll - Class 2. Died, Retired from service, Discharged. Roll dated 10th February 1859, Royal Barracks, Dublin. Entry No 121 849 Pte Pack, Joseph. discharged. WO 100-24 page 152. WO25/3267 - Records show Discharged as unfit for further service 31st May 1858.

1165 PALMER, Private Joseph

Born : Unknown
Enlisted :
Medals : Crimea (B.I.S)

Died : Unknown
Status : Probably rode in the Charge

The musters show he was effective from the 1st October to the 31st December.

895 PARDOE, Troop Sergeant-Major Joseph

Born : 1821 - Worcestershire
Enlisted :
Medals : Crimea (B.I.S)

Died : 4th July 1889 - Manchester
Status : Probably rode in the Charge

The musters show he was effective as a Sergeant from the 1st October to the 4th November, 35 days, 3 days on board ship, 32 days on shore. Marginal note reads "To Troop Sergt. Major 5th Nov vice Cruse". Effective as a Troop Sergeant-Major from the 5th November to the 31st December, 57 days at 3s-0d per diem, 84 days on shore. Marginal note reads "From Corporal 9th Oct vice Lees".

Joseph's great-grandson, Derek Pardoe, has unearthed and researched family documents to compile his great grandfather's eye witness account of the Battle of Balaclava below:

"My name is Joseph James Pardoe, and I was born in Ribbesford near Bewdley in Worcestershire in 1821. My father, James, was a currier, that is he cured and coloured leather. I had little schooling, but did learn to read and write, and this stood me in good stead later, for when I was 23 years old, I fancied a soldier's life, and went to London to the Barracks of the 1st Royal Dragoons and there enlisted.

I was taught the regiment's history, especially their achievements in Flanders and their charge at Waterloo - why, that is why we have an eagle as a badge, for we captured one from the French 105th Infantry Regiment. I was proud to be part of an establishment with such a fine history, but any illusions I had of personal grandeur were soon swept away by the strict discipline maintained by the junior NCOs. Any disobedience or other offence was punished, and a soldier who struck a corporal would almost certainly be court-martialled and flogged for it. I was never flogged myself, but saw many men punished in this way, for the whole regiment would be paraded to witness it - the poor devil being tied to special fixings on the wall so he would not fall down whilst he was whipped on his bare back.

Shortly after I had been trained, the regiment moved to Ireland. After only one year and 234 days I was promoted to corporal, and a further 3 years and 132 days later I was made sergeant on 26th October 1849. In Ireland I met a girl called Elizabeth Farmer - her father was a gunmaker and sutler, a camp follower selling his wares. He and his family returned to England with the regiment when we moved to Nottingham, and as my pay as sergeant was now 3 shillings a day, Elizabeth and I were married on 24th February 1851 at the Parish Church, Lenton, Notts. My wife was then 'on the strength' of the regiment and so we obtained billets in the barracks at Nottingham. Slowly, living conditions for soldier's and their families were improving, savings banks and libraries were starting, and soldier's children were being educated. We started a family with our first son, Joseph, born in 1852, and then another, William, in 1854. Life was becoming very content for me and my little family.

Then there were rumblings of war, this time in a far away country as Russia threatened the Principalities on the Danube. A strange feeling came over the regiment, for none of us had experienced war. Some were elated, some full of foreboding. Only one in four wives would be able to accompany us, and Elizabeth was not chosen. So I left my dear family, not knowing if I would see them again, and embarked at Liverpool with the rest of the 1st Dragoons. Although we were only about two squadrons strong, we were spread over six old sailing ships, not the steamers which carried some regiments, and we sailed during May. A tedious journey through the 'Med' followed, but at last, after nearly two months sailing we reached Varna. After the main body of the British Army left to invade the Crimea, we remained until 26th September when we re-embarked, this time in three sailing vessels, and sailed direct to Balaklava. We had a terrible voyage, with violent gales and many horses lost, so the Light Brigade had to lend us 75 horses. Day patrols and night picquets followed, with the nights colder than anyone had ever experienced. Then came the fateful day, 25th October 1854. Aged nearly 70 I wrote the following words about the doings of that day.

It is now nearly 33 years since the memorable Battle of Balaklava, I have read many descriptions of the proceedings of our troops on that day, but none that give a perfectly true account. I will try to put together a few facts that came under my personal observation. We were, as was our general orders, on the plains of Balaklava an hour before sunrise on the 25th October 1854. We had not long to wait before the the report of a gun told us that the Russians were on the move and that an engagement had actually commenced. They were not long in driving the Turks from the redoubts, which they left without the guns or even spiking them, nor did they destroy the ammunition which the Russians used against us as soon as they could reverse our guns, but did not do us much harm, my old regiment the 1st Dragoons losing one man and two horses. After this they brought their cavalry forward, one mass against the Highlanders, and another against the Heavy Cavalry. I never saw at a field day a more splendid reception given to a pretended enemy than the Highlanders gave to a real one, they did not even form squares to receive them, they gave them a volley that sent them to the left about in quick time and another one to help them on, the runaway Turks taking refuge behind them and when the danger was past clapped them on the back and shouted 'Bono Johnny, Bono Johnny!'. Then came the Heavy Brigade charge. The Greys led followed by the 6th and 1st dragoons, the 4th and 5th Dragoon Guards taking them on left flank. It was a short but decisive struggle, there were some of their saddles empty, but only one of the heavies killed. The cavalry was soon got into order of battle again, when Captain Nolan arrived bringing an order from Lord Raglan to the Earl of Lucan to advance the cavalry and if possible prevent the Russians from carrying away the guns. The general had no support for his cavalry and asked where am I to advance, the Captain replied there are the guns and there is the enemy. The general then gave the order to bring up the Light Brigade. They formed in three lines, viz: first, 17th Lancers, 13th Light Dragoons; second 11th Hussars and 8th Hussars; third, 4th Light Dragoons. The Earl of Cardigan led them, Captain Nolan placed himself on the left in front of the 13th Light Dragoons. The 1st Dragoons and Scots Greys ordered to form the support. The Light Brigade advanced and the support followed them for some distance down the valley. I can at this point retell the true story of Butcher Jack,(*1)he came up between the two squadrons of the 1st Dragoons and joined us as we advanced, in fact he was on my right hand. Colonel Yorke looked round and said to me, Sergeant that man does not belong to my regiment, who is he? The man answered, I belong to the 17th Lancers, sir. Colonel Yorke replied, I admire your spirit my man, but you had better join your own regiment. He replied, all right sir, and galloped away. This was the last I saw of him that day. He was not mounted on a grey horse, nor had he an axe in his hand, he had no coat on and his shirt sleeves were turned up. He had one sword in his hand and one in a scabbard buckled round his waist. He had been made a prisoner the night before, having taken too much rum. I was told by one of the 17th that he was not seen or heard of for three days and it was thought he was killed but when he found out by some means he would be pardoned for breaking his arrest he turned up. Butcher Jack's story as told by Mr Archibald Forbes reads very well, but old soldier's have the name for throwing the hatchet and Jack threw his to perfection, when interviewed by Mr Forbes.

But to proceed to the charge. Poor Captain Nolan was the first to fall. The British Army lost a good officer and a brave man, one well qualified to fill the important post he held on the staff of Lord Raglan. It now became pretty warm work for us for we had advanced further than discretion should have led us, being a rallying support for the Light Brigade. A Russian battery was pouring shot and shell into us on the left and the rifles on the right and in front. Our colonel here was badly wounded, Captains Campbell and Elmsell and Lt. Hartopp wounded. A sergeant, trumpeter and one private wounded and one killed and several horses killed and wounded. We got the order to retire out of range and to reform and were waiting for the return of the Light Brigade or what remained of them. The first that came back was the Earl of Cardigan. He halted his horse about twenty yards in front of our left squadron, he draped his reins on the horse's neck lifted up his hands and exclaimed 'The whole of the Light Brigade is gone, gone, gone.' He then rode up to between our first and second squadrons, General Lucan and his staff being there. He addressed himself to Captain Walker, ADC to the General, in these words: 'Walker you never saw such a thing in your life, we charged them down to the muzzles of their guns, cut down their gunners, took their guns and when we got to the rear we were met by thousands of Cossacks'. Captain Walker then said, 'Are you wounded my lord', his reply was 'No, only a bit of a lance prod, that's all'. The thoughts that came into my mind were these, Old fellow, you must have a charmed life, you have fought a duel or two and now you have been where thousands of bullets were flying about. All are gone, and you the only one to return to tell the tale, but thank God it was not so bad as that but too many of our brave fellows did not return. Not the six hundred. I have never seen a correct return in print of the actual number of killed and missing. The return given below (D.P.Note - Tantalisingly, this is missing!) is from a copy of the official return sent to Lord Raglan from the Earl of Lucan, commander of the Cavalry Division, his orderly clerk being a Corporal belonging to my troop, therefore I can testify to the correctness of it. The enquiry into who was the cause of this mad charge being made never came to anything for this reason, those who could tell anything about it were never examined, but it had one good point in its favour for when the Russians saw the British Cavalry advance at the Battle of the Tchernaya it struck them with dismay and terror and they turned and fled - generals and officers lost all command. And so ended this campaign as far as the fighting was concerned. In conclusion I must say a word in praise of General Scarlett, then in command of the Heavy Cavalry for the splendid manner in which he brought his troops into the field.

Shortly after the battle, on 5th November I was promoted Troop Sergeant Major, and at the end of the war I was awarded the Crimean Medal, with three clasps, one each for Balaklava, Inkerman and Sevastopol, and also the Turkish Medal. When the war ended, we were sent home on the Steam Ship Himalaya, leaving on 27 April 1856. We rejoined our families in Nottingham. In 1857 our daughter, Emma, was born. I was Troop Sergeant Major until the end of 1860 but I was then reduced to Sergeant and posted to the barracks at Sheffield and our third son George was born there on 28 September 1861. After seven more years, including more service in Ireland, I was finally discharged in Dublin. I was still in good health, as the medical board found, and they recorded: Fair complexion, grey eyes, brown hair, 5' 9 3/4" tall. I was still only 47, and my good conduct was certified by a regimental board of officers which said: His conduct has been good and he was when promoted in possession of one good conduct badge and would have qualified for five if he had not been promoted. His name has never been entered in the regimental defaulters' book, nor has he ever been tried by court-martial. And so, after 24 years and 32 days' service I was a civilian again. We now had a fifth child, another son, Edward born in July 1868 in Castelbar, Co Mayo, so I sought employment in Manchester, as Hall Porter of a gentleman's club, and we settled in Hulme...What stories I could tell, of those days in faraway Crimea."

Joseph Pardoe lived in Manchester until his death at age 68 on the 4th July 1889. He is buried in Southern Cemetery, Chorlton, Manchester, in plot L1691. His great-grandson still lives near Manchester and he has a great-grand daughter, Mrs Rosa A Goodrich of Florida USA, without whose help with the family history this story could not have been reconstructed.

*Butcher Jack was Private John Vahey of the 17th Lancers, who broke free of a Guard tent having been arrested for drunkeness and rode in the Charge of the Light Brigade, later awarded the the D.C.M after Archibald Forbes published his story.

The Voyage to Scutari

Towards the end of the month (December 1854) there were nearly 8000 men in hospital. Wrapped in wet blankets they are taken from the muddy tents and placed on horseback, a dismal troop of mounted corpses, with closed eyes and lurid cheeks, some, fever stricken, glaring with wide eyes void of observations for whom the passers by, if they saw them at all, existed as phantoms which marked their delirium. Bound for the great hospital at Scutari the cavalcade would toil on, wading through and stepping past the dying horses, the half buried bullocks and skeletons and carcases in various stages of decay.... On, always on, to the place of embarkation.

Lying among crowds of other sick and wounded, on bare planks, in torture, lassitude and lethargy, without proper food, medicine or attendance, they were launched on the wintry sea. Their covering was scanty and the roll and plunge of the ship was agony to the fevered and the maimed. In place of the hush, cleanliness and quiet and the silent step which should be around the sick, were sounds such as the poets have feigned for the regions of the damned - groans, screams, entreaties, curses, the strain of the timbers, the trampling of the crews, and the weltering of the waves. The sick flocked in faster than the dead were carried out till the hospitals overflowed, while, still faster flowed the misery-laden ships down the Black Sea as they went on feeding the fishes with their dead.
(*quote from Army Doctor Cattell, The Crimean Doctors page 167*)

1278 PARTINGTON, Private Charles

Born : 1827
Enlisted :
Medals : Crimea (B.I.S)

Died : March 1902
Status : Probably rode in the Charge

The musters show he was effective from the 1st October to the 23rd December, 84 days ordinary day, 4 days on board ship, 44 days on shore, 36 days in Regimental hospital. Third muster endorsed "Scutari", marginal note reads "To Scutari on 24th December". WO25/3267 - Records show Discharged 21st February 1866. WO100/24 page 148a Remarks: H&R to replace lost 30th October 1856.

Absconded from college to enlist. Charged at Balaclava -'wounded by a Cossack' (sic) and nursed by Florence Nightingale. Killed in an accident at Sheffield when thrown from his horse and trap, March 1902. Buried with military Honours at Sheffield General Cemetery. His monument has lost its brass inscription, but retains the stone carving of his dragoon helmet. (*K.Horton, Into the Valley of Death. A military tour of the Sheffield General Cemetery*)

Photograph courtesy of John Rumsby.

1112 PATERSON, Private William

Born : 1828
Enlisted :
Medals : Crimea (B.I.S)

Died : 1873
Status : Probably rode in the Charge

Wallis and Wallis sale 452, 8th January 2002, Lot 1. Pair - Crimea Medal with three clasps impressed naming, Balaclava, Inkermann, Sebastopol (W.Patterson 1st Rl Dragoons). Turkish Crimea sardinian issue engraved (Priv WM. Paterson 1st Rl Dns) VF framed with early photograph on glass, mirror image sepia print of same, pair of spurs, some minor rusting. William Paterson was born in 1828 and died in 1873. Information supplied by an ancestor of William Paterson. See lot 2 for family medals Plate 2.

The musters show he was effective from the 1st October to the 23rd December, 84 days ordinary day, 9 days on board ship, 39 days on shore, 36 days in hospital. Third muster endorsed "Scutari", marginal note reads "To Scutari on 24th December". WO25/3267 - Records show Discharged 6/1862

911 PATTENDEN, Private George

Born : Unknown
Enlisted :
Medals : Crimea (B.I.S)

Died : Unknown
Status : Probably rode in the Charge

The musters show he was effective from the 1st-28th October, 28 days at 1s-7 1/2d per diem, 9 days on board ship, 19 days on shore. First muster endorsed "To Private", marginal note reads "Confined 29th Oct. Tried 29th sentd to reduction to Private on 31st October". An entry at the end of the roll shows he was effective from the 2nd November to the 31st December, 60 days ordinary pay, 60 days on shore, marginal note reads "From Corporal 31 Oct. Released 1 Nov. Forfeited good conduct pay at 1d per diem 29th Oct".

1191 PETERS, Private James

Born : Unknown
Enlisted :
Medals : Crimea (B.I.S)

Died : October 1899
Status : Probably rode in the Charge

London Stamp Exchange list Spring 1981 item 248. Pair J.Peters 1st Rl. Dragoons. Crimea medal three clasps officially impressed naming, Balaclava, Inkermann, Sebastopol. Turkish Crimea Sardinian version named. See photograph on back cover. VF £455. Photograph on the pack cover is a portrait of recipient wearing medal, in civilian clothes with a heavy moustache and beard. Photograph copied from original still in possession of the family. Sotheby 26th July 1995, Lot 649, Heavy Brigade pair. Crimea medal three clasps officially impressed naming. Balaklava, Inkermann, Sebastopol. Turkish Crimea Sardinian version engraved naming, but rank erased, E.K's and contact wear. Estimate £700-£900. Dixons Medals March 2008, Crimea War Medal 1854-1856 Officially impressed, 3 clasps, Balaklava, Inkermann, Sebastopol, (J. Peters. 1st Rl. Dragoons). J. Peters, 1st Royal Dragoons. For sale £2400.

The musters show he was effective from the 1st October to the 31st December. Marginal note reads "6 Dn Guards No 421". WO25/3267 - Records show Discharged 26th November 1863. According to a family source Private Peters "Cleft a Russian skull through to the breast bone with a single blow of his sabre during the Charge of the Heavy Brigade" no mean feat for a man of his size. He retired from Military service in 1858, but always wore his medals on "Crimean Sunday". The same source states that he died after sitting up in bed and saluting the day war was declared in South Africa in October 1899, perhaps not a surprising act from the man whose first born son was christened in the guidon of the 1st Royals carried at Balaclava. His death certificate lists his profession as "Gate Keeper at Gas Works." (*Sotheby's catalogue July 1995*)

1048 POLE, Armourer Sergeant James

Born : Unknown
Enlisted :
Medals : Crimea (B.I.S)

Died : Unknown
Status : Probably rode in the Charge

The musters show he was effective from the 1st October to the 31st December, 92 days at 2s-2d per diem, 4 days on board ship, 98 days on shore.

1193 POLLARD, Private Abraham

Born : Date Unknown - Warrington
Enlisted : 1st June 1833
Medals : Crimea (B.I.S)

Died : 26th September 1855 - Crimea
Status : Probably rode in the Charge

The musters show he was effective from the 1st October to the 31st December with an additional 2d per diem good conduct pay. Trade on enlistment Labourer.

988 POWELL, Private Thomas

Born : Unknown
Enlisted : 12th August 184
Medals : Crimea (B.I.S), Long Service and Good Conduct Medal

Died : Unknown
Status : Probably rode in the Charge

Glendining's 25th November 1987, Lot 177, Three: Crimea, three bar, Balaklava, Inkermann, Sebastopol (Thos. Powell, Royal Dns.), contemporary engraved naming; L.S. & G.C., Victoria (988 Thos.Powell, 1st Dragoons), impressed naming; Turkish Crimea 1855, Sardinian issue (Thos. Powell, 1st Royal Dragoons). Very fine. Hammer price £800. DNW 28th July 1993, Lot 338, Crimea 1854-55, 3 clasps, Balaklava, Inkermann, Sebastopol (Royal Dns.) contemporary engraved naming; Turkish Crimea, Sardinian issue, named, fitted with replacement ring suspension; Army L.S. & G.C., V.R., 3rd issue (988, 1st Dragoons) officially impressed naming, contact marks, otherwise nearly very fine (3). Sold with copy discharge papers and verification of all medals and clasps. Hammer Price £450. Neate Medals List March/April 1998, Item 529, three medals as above £795

Thomas Powell, a painter from London, enlisted for the 1st Dragoons at Westminster on the 12th August 1846, at the age of 17 years and 11 months.

The musters show he was effective from the 1st October to the 31st December with additional 1d per diem good conduct pay. WO25/3267 - Records show Deceased 22/8/1870 (Date is difficult to read, probably incorrect as he was discharged a year later)

On the 30th June 1868 (WO102) he was awarded the medal for long service and good conduct with a gratuity of £5 and was discharged on the 5th August 1871. Thomas Powell served as a Private throughout his 24 years in the regiment and earned five good conduct badges.

The Events on the 25th October 1854

Every morning an hour before dawn, Lord Lucan would call an early morning muster, the 25th October was no exception. Whilst the commanding officers checked their men and horses. Lucan and his staff set out towards Canrobert's hill. One of the party noted two flags were flying from redoubt No 1 on top of Canrobert's hill, a signal that the enemy was approaching. Lucan instructed Charteris to alert Raglan, at the same time Lord George Paget galloped back at speed to rally the Brigades.

The opening phase of the battle was a one sided duel of Artillery with the British being out gunned by the Russians. Lord Lucan had six light pieces of horse-artillery, which had been used without effect on the advancing Russian who were positioned on Canrobert's hill. The Russians returned the fire seriously wounding the commanding officer of 'I' troop Captain Maude. The shell entered the body of his horse and then exploded. The horse artillery quickly ran out of ammunition, which was limited to the rounds carried in the gun limbers. Lucan ordered that the troop should be withdrawn until re-supplied. At the same time 'W' Battery under Captain Barker were taking up a position west of No 3 Redoubt. It did not take long before Numbers 2, 3 and eventually 4 Redoubts fell into Russian hands. When the Turks in the redoubts saw how the Russians had overpowered Canrobert's hill they fled. The Russians were now able to fire their muskets from the captured redoubts. The Heavies now took up a position which lay opposite No 5 redoubt.

First Order 08:30 "Cavalry to take ground to the left of second line of redoubts occupied by Turks"
Lucan was now requested to withdraw his horsemen to ground on the left of Redoubt No 6 at the foot of the Chersonese upland. Sir Colin Campbell was left with a small body of men to defend the approach to Balaclava.
The 93rd Highlanders were drawn up in a line two deep in front of the village of Kadikoi. In support were Barker's field-pieces, together with a battery of two heavy guns under the command of lieutenant Wolfe. The main body of the Russian cavalry continued to advance up the North Valley until arriving at No 4 redoubt where they split into two, one group moving towards the ground that the 93rd Highlanders were defending.
Second Order 08:35 "Eight squadrons of Heavy Dragoons to be detached towards Balaclava to support the Turks who are wavering"
Hardinge rode off, it would take about 15 minutes for the message to be delivered. Requesting Lucan to detach eight squadrons towards Kadikoi. Lord Lucan told Cardigan that the Light Brigade were to remain north of No 6 Redoubt. He next instructed Sir James Scarlett, commanding the Heavy Brigade to move off with eight squadrons towards Kadikoi. It was at this time that the main body of Russian cavalry turned away from the North Valley and moved up over the summit of the Causeway ridge.
General Scarlett, with Elliot, his aide-de-camp was on the left of the column formed by the 2nd squadron of the Inniskillings and the Scots Greys marching in a parallel direction to the Causeway ridge some eight hundred yards from its summit. Elliot; chancing to turn his head towards the Causeway Heights, caught sight of the lance flags belonging to the Russian column. Lucan had also observed the Russians. Scarlett immediately gave the order "Left wheel into line," but the order was executed by only one squadron of Inniskillings and two squadrons of the Greys, the other five squadrons having passed on the Balaclava side of a vineyard. Having wheeled into line, the three squadrons moved a short distance to their right to give room for the 5th Dragoon Guards, which the General intended should come up on the left of the Greys.

By the time that the three leading squadrons of Scarlett's command had again wheeled into line, the Russians, were advancing at a walk. Both Lucan and Scarlett had become very impatient, an opportunity could be lost they had to get the three squadrons in motion before the Russians should increase their pace.. The advance was sounded repeatedly, but it was difficult to induce the commanding officers to move until the line had been dressed accurately. Captain Barker's Field battery had just come into action close to the 93rd Regiment, and fired about twenty rounds at the Russian column, when the squadron of Inniskilling Dragoons crossed the line of fire.

The 93rd Highlanders who were formed in line on rising ground out-side Kadikoi, were ready for the Russian onslaught. As the Russians advanced Campbell rode down the line, and said: "Remember there is no retreat from here, men! You must die where you stand" The Russians advanced closer . Breaking into a charge, the second volley fired by the 93rd seemed to slow the Russian attack. When the Russian cavalry came within range of the heavy guns on the Upland, several shots were fired, which caused the whole force to wheel to its left in confusion and return over the Causeway Heights.

At the same time Scarlett's "three hundred" pierced the centre of the Russian mass, the outside squadrons from either flank changed front inwards, in order to surround our dragoons. While this manoeuvre was being executed, the Russian flanks were ridden into by the remainder of the brigade, which in many cases struck the rear enemy; but our men gradually hacked their way through the Russian masses, and, considering the enormous disparity, of numbers, with successful. (Kinglake's *The Invasion of the Crimea Vol V* p109-126)

Third Order 09:40 "Cavalry to advance and take advantage of any opportunity to recover the Heights. They will be supported by infantry which have been ordered. Advance on two fronts"

The order was to say the least a little confusing. Lucan read the order, and decided to mount his cavalry, move his light brigade to the North valley, and leave the Heavy brigade in position and wait for the infantry to arrive.

Fourth Order 11:00 The fourth order was delivered by Captain Nolan it read; "Lord Raglan wishes the cavalry to advance rapidly to the front – follow the enemy and try to prevent the enemy carrying away the guns – Troop Horse artillery may accompany – French cavalry is on your left- R.Airey – Immediate.

Lord Cardigan's brigade stood, drawn up in two lines. Lucan rode over and informed Cardigan that the Light Brigade where to attack down the north Valley.

Lucan then decided that the formation was incorrect, and ordered the 11th Hussars back to support the 17th Lancers. After he was satisfied he rode back to the Heavy Brigade. The order firmly stated the whole division, so the Greys and the Royals were brought forward in advance of the other heavy Dragoons. The Heavy Brigade were to support the Light Brigade. It did not take long before the two brigades became separated. Lord Lucan had not long passed the Number Four Redoubt when he entered the firing range of the Russian Artillery. His aide-de-camp, Captain Charteris – fulfilling his premonition fell dead at his side. Lucan was to get as far as the Number three Redoubt, before looking back he saw the Royals and Greys under a destructive cross-fire, turning to Lord William Paulett "They have sacrificed the Light Brigade : they shall not the Heavy, if I can help it" The order was given to retire.

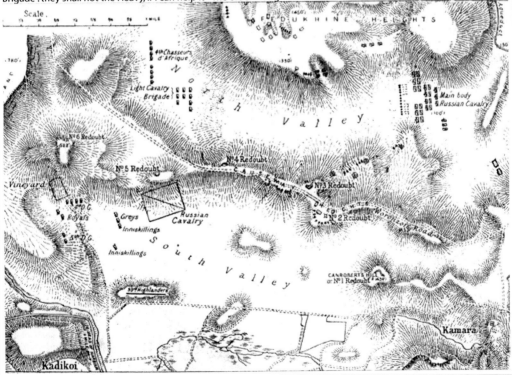

1290 RAMSDEN, Private Thomas

Born : Unknown   Died : Unknown
Enlisted :   Status : Probably rode in the Charge
Medals : Crimea (B.I.S)
Donald Hall List February 1977 Item 27, Crimea 3 clasp, Balaclava, Inkermann, Sebastopol, Thos. Ramsden No 1290 1st Royal Dgns engraved naming VF £190. Spinks circular February 1984 Item 661, same as above VF £350.

The musters show he was effective from the 1st October to the 7th December and from the 15th-31st December, 85 days ordinary pay, 9 days on board ship, 76 days on shore. Marginal note reads "confined 8th Dec tried and sentd 50 lashes. Released 14th December". WO 100-24 page 192 Medal Roll - Class 2. Died, Retired from service, Discharged. Roll dated 10th February 1859, Royal Barracks, Dublin. Entry No 122 1290 Pte Ramsden, Thomas - Dead.

896 READING, Private William

Born : Unknown   Died : Unknown
Enlisted :   Status : Probably rode in the Charge
Medals : Crimea (B.I.S), Long Service and Good Conduct Medal

The musters show he was effective from the 1st October to the 31st December, 92 days ordinary pay, 35 days at 1d and 57 days at 2d good conduct pay, 88 days on shore. Marginal note reads "entitled to good conduct pay at 2d from the 5th November". WO25/3267 - Records show Discharged 8th December 1868. WO102 L.S & G.C recommended 25th March 1866, gratuity £5.

361 REMLANCE, Farrier Major Charles

Born : Unknown   Died : Unknown
Enlisted :   Status : Probably rode in the Charge
Medals : Crimea (B.I.S)
Medal with clasps, B.I.S Together with LS & GC and Turkish crimea (Farrier Major C. Remnent) in regimental Museum.

The musters show he was effective as a Sergeant from the 1st October to the 31st December, 92 days at 2s-2d per diem, 4 days on board ship, 88 days on shore. WO100-24 page 151 Medal Roll - Class 2. Died, Retired from service, Discharged. Roll dated 16th Feb 1859, Royal Barracks, Dublin. - Discharged - Entry crossed and endorsed "Sent to him 29/9/60".

942 RICHARDSON, Corporal George

Born : Unknown   Died : Unknown
Enlisted :   Status : Probably rode in the Charge
Medals : Crimea (B.I.S)

The musters show he was effective from the 1st October to the 31st December with 1d per diem good conduct pay. WO25/3267 - Records show Died 27/2/1864

1083 RICHARDSON, Private Thomas

Born : Unknown   Died : Unknown
Enlisted :   Status : Probably rode in the Charge
Medals : Crimea (B.I.S)

The musters show he was effective from the 1st October to the 31st December with 1d per diem good conduct pay. WO25/3267 - Records show Discharged 28/12/1872.

1111 RIDGEWAY, Sergeant William

Born : Unknown   Died : Unknown
Enlisted :   Status : Probably rode in the Charge
Medals : Crimea (B.I.S)
Medal with clasps Balaclava, Inkermann, Sebastopol in Regimental Museum (Household Cavarly)

The musters show he was effective as a Corporal from the 1st-8th October, 8 days at 1s-7 1/2d per diem, 8 days on shore, marginal note reads "To Sergeant 9th October vice Lees appointed Hospital Sergeant". Effective as a Sergeant from the 9th October to the 31st December, 84 days at 2s-2d per diem.
Medal Roll Sebastopol clasp, entitled. 1111 Sgt Ridgway. William. Marginal note reads "H&R 30/10/56 to replace lost" WO100/24 page 144. Medal Roll - Class 2. Died, Retired from service, Discharged. Roll dated 10th February 1859, Royal Barracks, Dublin. - 111 SGT Rideway. William discharged. Entry crossed through endorsed "Sent to HIM 25/8/60" WO 100-24 page 152. WO25/3267 - Records show Discharged 30/4/1857

1097 ROBERTS, Private George

Born : Unknown
Enlisted :
Medals : Crimea (B.I.S)

Died : Unknown
Status : Probably rode in the Charge

The musters show he was effective from the 1st October to the 31st December, marginal note reads "3rd Dragoons No 964".

ROBERTSON, Lieutenant Gilbert Metcalf

Born : 1832
Enlisted :
Medals : Crimea (B.I.S)

Died : 4th June 1909 - London
Status : Probably rode in the Charge

The musters show he was effective as a Cornet from the 1st October to the 28th December, supplied with rations "on shore" 5th Oct to 28th Dec, 85 days, 1st-4th Oct "On Board Ship", one horse foraged at public expense. Effective as a Lieutenant from the 29th-31st December.

Cornet 12th May 1853. Lieutenant 29th December 1854 (*Harts Annual Army List 1855 page 128*) Medal Roll for the Sebastopol clasp WO 100-24 page 143 marginal note states "H&R 4/3"

The Times of Tuesday 29th January 1856, page 8 reported that "Lieutenant Robertson, 1st Dragoons" was "granted leave of absence,to the 21st March 1855, at the recommendation of the medical board. Head-quarters, Sebastopol, Feb 16th." The Times, 28th May 1856, reported Lieutenant Gilbert M. Robertson "arrived at Spithead yesterday on the Steam transport Orinoco."

The Broad Arrow 12th June 1909 reported "Captain Gilbert Metcalf Robertson, late of the 1st Dragoons, died on the 4th June 1909 at 47 Lennox Gardens, London, SW, aged 77. Educated at Eton and Oxford and joined the regiment in May 1853. Promoted Captain in 1857 and retired in 1865. Served throughout the Crimean campaign in 1854-55 and was present at Balaclava (where his horse was shot under him) and Inkerman and Sebastopol receiving a medal with three clasps and the Turkish Medal."

1138 ROBINSON, Private George

Born : Date Unknown - Sheffield
Enlisted : 12th November 1850
Medals : Crimea (B.I.S)

Died : 25th December 1854 - Scutari
Status : Probably rode in the Charge

Christie's 10th November 1992, Lot 21, Crimea medal to Private G.Robinson, two clasps, Balaklava, Inkermann, officially impressed, extremely fine.
John Darwent purchased the medal from B. Davies on 11th November 1992 for £525. Officially impressed naming. Lugs on Inkermann clasp have never been pierced. Sebastopol clasp has never been fitted.
DNW 2nd April 2004, The collection of medals formed by the late John Darwent, Lot 167, Crimea 1854-56, 2 clasps, Balaklava, Inkermann (G. Robinson, 1st Dragoons), officially impressed naming, edge nicks, good very fine. Hammer Price £1600

George Robinson enlisted in London on the 12th November 1850, aged 20 years. 5' 8 1/4" Born in Sheffield, prior occupation shown as a veterinary surgeon.

The musters show he was effective from the 1st October to the 3rd December, 64 days, 3 days on board ship, 44 days on shore, 17 days in hospital. 3rd muster endorsed "Deceased", marginal note reads "To payment of paymaster Genl. depot Scutari 4th Dec, died 25th December"

The Times of Wednesday 10th January, 1855; page 8 reported that "Private George Robinson 1st Royal Dragoons died at Scutari Hospital on the 25th December 1854 of dysentery."

1239 ROGERS, Private Robert

Born : Date Unknown - Faversham
Enlisted : 2nd September 1838
Medals : Crimea (B.I.S)

Died : 14th January 1855 - Camp Kadikoi
Status : Probably rode in the Charge

The musters show he was effective from the 1st October to the 31st December, paid 3d per diem good conduct pay for the period. Shown on the admissions into Hospital of the 1st Royal Dragoons as dying of pneumonia. (*Medical and Surgical History of the British Army during the War against Russia Vol 1 p 55*)

1255 ROOT, Private John
Born : Unknown
Enlisted :
Medals : Crimea (B.I.S), Sutlej (for Moodkee, clasps Ferozeshuhur and Sobraon), Punjab (clasps Chillianwallah, Goojerat)
A.H. Balwin and Sons Ltd. List June 1946. item 64. Pair - Crimea Medal with two clasps Balaklava, Sebastopol and Turkish
Crimea Engraved J.Root. £1.15.0

Died : Unknown
Status : Probably rode in the Charge

The musters show he was effective from the 1st October to the 31st December, marginal note reads "3rd Dragoons No
915". Served with 3rd Light Dragoons in Sutlej and Punjab campaigns (Medal Rolls).

1071 RUSSELL, Private George
Born : Unknown
Enlisted :
Medals : Crimea (B.I.S)

Died : Unknown
Status : Probably rode in the Charge

The musters show he was effective from the 1st October to the 31st December, paid 1d per diem good conduct pay for
the period. Medal Roll - Class 2. Died, Retired from service, Discharged. Roll dated 10th February 1859, Royal Barracks,
Dublin.Entry No 126 1071 Pte Russell,George - Dead - WO 100-24 page 152. WO25/3267 - Records show Dead.

916 RUSSELL, Private Thomas Connel
Born : Unknown
Enlisted :
Medals : Crimea (B.S)

Died : Unknown
Status : Probably rode in the Charge

The musters show he was effective from the 1st October to the 31st December. WO25/3267 - Records show Discharged
21/8/1856. Shown as "O'Connel" on some records

SANDEMAN, Lieutenant John Glas
Born : 18th August 1836
Enlisted :
Medals : Crimea (B.I.S)

Died : 1922
Status : Rode in the Charge

The second son of the late George Glas Sandeman (1793-1868) of Westfield, Hayling Island and Elizabeth Forster (1804-
1888). Married Eliza Victoire Cormick Lynch in 26th August 1862, two children Ella Sandeman and Florence Maud Lynch-
Staunton Sandeman. His family were the owners of the famous "Sandeman" Port beverage company.

Cornet 10th June 1853 (*Harts Annual Army List 1855 page 128*) The musters show he was effective from the 1st October
to the 31st December, supplied with rations "on shore" 5th Oct to 31st Dec, 88 days, 1st-4th Oct "On Board Ship", one
Horse foraged at public expense. Medal Roll for the Sebastopol clasp WO 100-24 page 143 marginal note states "H&R
10/6". The Times, 28th May 1856, reported Lieutenant John G. Sandeman "arrived at Spithead yesterday on the Steam
transport Orinoco." Captain by purchase, vice Stocks, 23rd October 1857 (Bulletins and Other State Intelligence). Harts
Army List of 1863 lists him as having sold his commission.

During the Heavy Brigade Charge at Balaclava his horse "Toby" was shot and killed by a bullet in the neck. The horse
was shipped back to Hayling Island where it was buried near the sea front, and a plaque placed on its grave. Sandeman
became a member of H.M. Bodyguard of Gentlemen at Arms and was later a Colonel in the Essex militia, he and his
family lived on Hayling Island at a fine residence called Whin-Hurst.

The obituary for John Glas Sandeman appeared in "*The Antiquaries Journal Vol. 2 1922 p.316*", it reads "Lt.-Col. John Glas
Sandeman was elected a Fellow in 1898. He was born in 1836 and after being educated at King's College, London,
entered the army as a subaltern in the Royal Dragoons at the age of seventeen. He served in the Crimea and was present
at the battles of Balaclava and Inkerman, and at the siege of Sebastopol. At his death he was the senior member of
H.M. Bodyguard of Gentlemen at Arms, in which corps he took a great interest, writing its history under the title of The
Spears of Honour and the Gentlemen Pensioners. He also collected Greek and Roman objects of art. He made but one
communication to the Society in which he corrected some errors as to the Gentlemen Pensioners occurring in the
edition of the Ordinaries of the Household published by the Society in 1790."

The Times, 20th April 1922 page 15, reported on the Will of J.G.Sandeman "SANDEMAN, Lieut.-Col. John Glas, M.V.O. (85)
of Whin Hurst, Hayling Island, Hants, late Sub-Officer and Senior Member of his Majesty's Bodyguard the Hon. Corps of
Gentlemen-at-Arms, who served throughout the Crimean war with the 1st Royal Dragoons, a member of the Royal St.
George's Yacht Club, Kingstown. Gross value of Estate: £68,304"

The Hospital at Karani

At the beginning of December 1854, the Regiment removed its encampment to the southern slope of the elevated valley, situated between the villages of Kadikoi and Karani, and distant rather more than a mile from Balaclava. Towards the end of January 1855 a wooden hut was erected for the Hospital, which was capable, on emergency, of containing 28 men, also boards and trestles, palliasses filled with straw, buffalo robes, blankets, etc, were supplied, which greatly added to the comfort of the sick, and afforded some chance for their successful treatment. (*Medical and Surgical History of the British Army during the War against Russia Vol 1 p 25*)

855 SAPWELL, Private George

Born : Date unknown - London
Enlisted : 14th July 1843
Medals : Crimea (I.S)

Died : 22nd December 1854 - Scutari
Status : Effective during the period

The musters show he was effective from the 1st October to the 3rd December, 64 days ordinary pay, 64 days at 1d good conduct pay, 4 days on board ship, 43 days on shore, 17 days in hospital. 3rd muster endorsed "Deceased", marginal note reads "To payment of paymaster Genl, depot Scutari 4th Dec, died 22nd December."

The Times of Saturday, 6th January 1855, page 8, reported from Scutari on the 25th December 1854 that "Private George Sapwell, 1st Dragoons" had died at Scutari Hospital on the 22nd December 1854 of rheumatism.

606 SAVAGE, Private John

Born : Unknown
Enlisted : 2nd June 1838
Medals : Crimea (B.I.S), The French Medaille Militaire

Died : Unknown
Status : Probably rode in the Charge

Glendinings Auction December 1969, Crimea medal with three bars, Balaclava, Inkermann, Sebastopol, J.Savage, 1st Dragoons. Impressed naming. Glendinings Auction 31th October 1979, Lot 172. Group of 3 Medals. Crimea medal with three bars, Balaklava, Inkermann, Sebastopol (J.Savage, 1st Dragoons). Impressed naming. French Medaille Militaire. Blue enamel on reverse damaged. Turkish Crimea Sardinian version. VF with photo copy of discharge papers £540. Spinks Auction 28th March 1995. Same group as above. With additional comments: Medaille Militaire 2nd Empire 2nd Type, enamel damage. With copied service papers.

The musters show he was effective from the 1st October to the 31st December, paid 3d per diem good conduct pay for the period. WO25/3267 - Records show Discharged 7/10/1862

The citation for the French Medaille Militaire reads (He) "served during the whole of the Eastern Campaign; distinguished himself on outpost duty, and by his care and attention to his horse during the severe winter. Never missed a tour of duty from sickness of any other cause".

1159 SAYER, Private William

Born : Date unknown - Folkstone
Enlisted : 7th April 1851
Medals : Crimea (B.I.S)

Died : 24th January 1855 - Scutari
Status : Probably rode in the Charge

The musters show he was effective from the 1st October to the 31st December, 3rd Muster endorsed "On Bd ship".

SCOTT, Quartermaster William

Born : 1806
Enlisted :
Medals : Crimea (B.I.S)

Died : 15th May 1894 - London
Status : Probably rode in the Charge

The Payne Collection 1911, catalogue pages 111 and 395. Crimea 3 clasps B.I.S, Turkish Crimea, also his minatures (p648) Captain W.M Scott late Quarter Master 1st Royal Dragoons. Now in the Regimental Museum (Household Cavalry)

Quartermaster 26th October 1849. The musters show he was effective from the 1st October to the 31st December, supplied with rations "on shore" 4th October to the 31st December, 89 days, 1st-3rd October "On Board Ship".

The Times, 28th May 1856, reported that Quartermaster William Scott "arrived at Spithead yesterday on the Steam transport Orinoco."

Captain 23rd March 1870. Retired pay 1st July 1881. The Broad Arrow 19th May 1894 reported "First Dragoons Captain William Scott died 15th May at number 58 Warwick Road, Maidavale, London in his 88th year."

1119 SEWELL, Private William

Born : Date unknown - Penrith
Enlisted : 27th April 1850
Medals : Crimea (B.I.S)

Died : 21st December 1854 - Scutari
Status : Probably rode in the Charge

Crimea medal with 2 clasps Balaclava, Inkermann, in Regimental museum (Household Cavalry) June 1991.

The musters show he was effective from the 1st October to the 27th November, 58 days ordinary day, 9 days on board ship, 49 days on shore. Second and third musters endorsed "Scutari", marginal note reads "To payment of paymaster Genl. dept Scutari 8th Nov. Died 21st December".

The Times of Saturday, 6th January 1855; page 8 reported from Scutari on the 25th December 1854 that "Private William Sewel, 1st Royal Dragoons" had died at Scutari Hospital on the 21st December 1854 of dysentery.

1166 SHANNON, Corporal Robert

Born : Unknown
Enlisted :
Medals : Crimea (B.I.S)

Died : Unknown
Status : Probably rode in the Charge

The musters show he was effective from the 1st October to the 31st December. WO25/3267 - Discharged 1/8/1863.

1339 SHERRY, Private Henry

Born : Unknown
Enlisted :
Medals : Crimea (B.I.S)

Died : Unknown
Status : Probably rode in the Charge

WO25/3267 - Records show Discharged December 1856.

1152 SHORE, Private Thomas

Born : Date unknown - Derby
Enlisted : 20th February 1851
Medals : Crimea (B.S)

Died : 25th October 1854 - Balaclava
Status : Killed in the Charge

The musters show he was effective from the 1st-25th October, 25 days ordinary pay, 4 days on board ship, 21 days on shore. All three musters crossed, marginal note reads "Killed in Action at Balaclava on the 25th October." Form 20 shows 1152 Pte Shore. Thomas, Born Derby, a labourer, enlisted 20th Feb 1851, Killed in action at Balaclava 25th October. 17s-4 1/2d in credit. Effects No 373442. Will None, next of kin Uncle Will Shore, Lockington. Leichester.

Listed on the Casualty Roll as killed at Balaclava. WO100/24 page 124 Remarks: Killed in Action in front of Balaclava 25th October 1854.

1188 SHREEVE, Private James

Born : Date unknown - London
Enlisted : 13th December 1851
Medals : Crimea (B.I.S)

Died : 10th March 1855 - Camp Kadikoi
Status : Probably rode in the Charge

The musters show he was effective from the 1st October to the 20th December, 81 days ordinary pay, 4 days on board ship, 77 days on shore. Third muster endorsed "Scutari", marginal note reads "To payment of paymaster Gnl Depot Scutari 21st December". WO14/1 Scutari Muster Roll January-March 1855 effective 1st-31st January, no dates or remarks shown in the next two musters.

James Shreeve had just returned from Scutari, where he had been under treatment for a long time for rheumatism, and on his re-admission into the field hospital, a metasiasis to the membranes of the brain took place which caused death on the 17th day. (*Medical and Surgical History of the British Army during the War against Russia Vol 1 p 26*)

1131 SLATER, Private Henry Frederick

Born : Unknown
Enlisted :
Medals : Crimea (B.I.S)

Died : Unknown
Status : Probably rode in the Charge

The musters show he was effective from the 1st October to the 31st December.

939 SMITH, Private George

Born : Unknown
Enlisted :
Medals : Crimea (B.I.S)

Died : Unknown
Status : Probably rode in the Charge

Glendinings Auction 25th September 1963, Ambrose Elson Collection Part 2 Lot 655. Crimea medal with three clasps, Balaclava, Inkermann, Sebastopol. G.Smith. 1st Royal Dragoons. Impressed. (Sold with nine other medals)

The musters show he was effective from the 1st October to the 31st December. Also in some records Reg No 937.

683 SMITH, Private William

Born : Unknown
Enlisted :
Medals : Crimea (B.I.S)

Died : Unknown
Status : Probably rode in the Charge

The musters show he was effective from the 1st October to the 31st December, paid 3d per diem good conduct pay for the period. WO25/3267 - Records show Discharged 6/1862.

1283 ST.CLAIR, Private Grant

Born : Unknown
Enlisted :
Medals : Crimea (B.I.S)

Died : Unknown
Status : Probably rode in the Charge

The musters show he was effective from the 1st October to the 31st December. Medal Roll - Class 2. Died, Retired from service, Discharged. Roll dated 10th February 1859, Royal Barracks, Dublin. Entry - Dead - WO 100-24 page 152.

1107 STACEY, Trumpeter George Andrew

Born : Unknown
Enlisted :
Medals : Crimea (B.S)

Died : Unknown
Status : Severely wounded in the Charge

Spink 19th July 2007, Lot 1263, Family Group: Three: Trumpeter G.A. Stacey, 1st Royal Dragoons, Crimea 1854-56, two clasps, Balaclava, Sebastopol, last clasp loose or riband (Trmptr. G. Stacey. 1st Rl. Dragoons), officially impressed, with contemporary silver foliate top riband bar; Volunteer Long Service & G.C., V.R., unnamed; Turkish Crimea, Sardinian die, contemporarily engraved in upright serif capitals, 'Trumr. George Stacey 1st Royal Dragoons', pierced for ring suspension, as issued, with contemporary silver riband buckle, 1st and last awards with edge bruising, nearly very fine, 2nd award good very fine. Pair: Aircraft Mechanician 1st Class G.H. Stacey, Royal Naval Air Service British War and Victory Medals (F.13077 G.H. Stacey A.M. 1 R.N.A.S.), extremely fine, in original named card box of issue (5) Hammer Price £3200. G.A. Stacey's Crimea Medal originally had the Inkermann clasp, to which he was not entitled, this was removed from the medal to leave his correct entitlement.

The musters show he was effective from the 1st-25th October and from the 14th-31st December, 43 days at 1s-5d per diem, 18 days on board ship, 25 days on shore. First and second musters endorsed "Scutari", marginal note reads "To payment of paymaster General Depot Scutari - 26 Oct to 13 Dec." Shown on the Casualty Roll as wound severely at Balaclava.

Cavalry trumpets were only used when dismounted and state trumpets were used for ceremonial occassions. When mounted all calls were played on a bugle.

885 STACEY, Trumpeter William S.

Born : Unknown
Enlisted :
Medals : Crimea (B.I.S)

Died : Unknown
Status : Probably rode in the Charge

The musters show he was effective from the 1st October to the 31st December, 92 days at 1s-5d per diem, 92 days at 1d Good Conduct pay, 9 days on board ship, 83 days on shore. Medal Roll for the Sebastopol clasp, 885. Pte. Stacy. William Samuel. Marginal note reads "Regt 26/9" WO 100-24 page 149. WO25/3267 - Records show Discharged 16/9/1873

1202 STAFFORD, Corporal William

Born : Unknown
Enlisted :
Medals : Crimea (B.I.S)

Died : Unknown
Status : Probably rode in the Charge

The musters show he was effective from the 1st October to the 31st December, 92 days at 1s-7 1/2d per diem, 9 days on board ship, 83 on shore. WO25/3267 - Records show Discharged 4/2/1864.

819 STAINBRIDGE, Private Stephen

Born : Unknown
Enlisted :
Medals : Crimea (B.I.S)

Died : Unknown
Status : Probably rode in the Charge

DNW Auction 13th December 2007, Lot 246, Crimea 3 clasps B.I.S (S.Stambridge, 1st Dragoons) officially impressed naming, minor edge bruising and contact marks. Hammer price £1200. Sold with copied service papers.

The musters show he was effective from the 1st October to the 31st December, paid 2d per diem good conduct pay for the period. Sebastopol roll spells his name Stanbridge. WO25/3267 - Records show Discharged 4/9/1856

STOCKS, Captain Michael

Born : 1825
Enlisted :
Medals : Crimea (B.I.S), The Turkish Order of the Medjidie (5th Class)

Died : 30th September 1895
Status : Probably rode in the Charge

Seaby Coin and Medal Bulletin May 1976 F5C11, Crimea 3 bars B.I.S, Capt M.Stocks 1st Royal Dragoons, impressed. V.F Sold £335.

The musters show he was effective from the 1st October to the 31st December, supplied with rations "on shore" 5th October to 31st December, 88 days on shore, 1st-4th Oct "On Board Ship", one horse foraged at public expense for 78 days.

Sailing on the 26th September 1854 the Royals ran into a terrible storm. Captain Stocks' memory of the event: no sooner were the poor beasts up than down they went again. The officers' chargers were thrown on top of the troop horses in the hold. Horses that had cost hundreds lying with broken backs and legs.. horses and saddles, carbines and swords, mixed up like as they had been shook up in a bag. I never saw such a wreck of as fine a troop of horses as ever in the service.'... Stocks's diary note dated 12th October 1854, 'out all night three miles from the camp. Had an awful cold night of it, the wind has changed to the north'....And on the 14th October 'the poorest fun I know of ....saw lots of Cossacks who retired when we approached and approached when we retired....They remind you of rabbits, only not quite so harmless'. Notes from the 18th October, 'after another night out, the Russians advanced with more serious intent, but no serious effect'. *History of the Royal Dragoons, 1661-1933*, C.T.Atkinson (University Press, Glasgow, 1934), p326-8.

The Times, 28th May 1856, reported Captain Michael Stocks "arrived at Spithead yesterday on the Steam transport Orinoco."

Cornet 11th December 1846. Lieutenant 20th July 1849. Captain 25th February 1853. Major 23rd October 1857. (*Harts Annual Army List 1860 page 136*). The *Aberdeen Weekly* 28th November 1895 states probate of the will was granted and duty paid on £336,453 of Major Michael Stocks of Upper Shibden Hall, Halifax, Brewer and of number 20 Rutland Gates of Woodhall Norfolk.

1180 STONEHILL, Private Henry

Born : Unknown
Enlisted :
Medals : Crimea (B.I.S)

Died : Unknown
Status : Probably rode in the Charge

The musters show he was effective from the 1st October to the 31st December. WO25/3267 - Discharged 3/6/1873.

1235 SUMNER, Private Thomas

Born : Date unknown - York
Enlisted : 10th March 1853
Medals : Crimea (B.I.S)

Died : 16th January 1855 - Scutari
Status : Probably rode in the Charge

The musters show he was effective from the 1st October to the 13th December, 74 days ordinary pay, 3 days on board ship, 71 days on shore. Third muster endorsed "Scutari", marginal note reads "To payment of paymaster Genl depot Scutari 14th December". WO14/1 Scutari Muster Roll January-March 1855 remarks indicate he died on the 16th January.

356 SWASH, Corporal Robert

Born : 1812 - Horsham St Faith, Norfolk
Enlisted : 10th December 1830
Medals : Crimea (B.I.S), The Distinguished Conduct Medal
Medal with clasps Balaclava, Inkermann, Sebastopol in Regimental Museum (Household Cavalry) 1991.

Died : Unknown
Status : Probably rode in the Charge

The musters show he was effective as a Private from the 1st October to the 1st November, 32 days ordinary pay, 32 days at 4d Good conduct pay, 3 days on board ship, 29 days on shore. Effective as a Corporal from the 2nd November to the 31st December, 60 days at 1s-7 1/2d per diem, 60 days on shore, marginal note reads "From Private 2nd Nov, vice Pattenden reduced". The Distinguished Conduct Medal recommendation is dated 9th January 1855.

Robert Swash was photographed by royal command when he returned from service in the Crimea in 1856. Queen Victoria commissioned the firm of Cundall ands Howlett to take the likenesses of some of the returning troops to capture their martial , heroic appearance. They were also commissioned to photograph some of the wounded at Chatham. Robert Swash and Matthew Bailey were selected from the 1st Royal Dragoons and Stewart and Michael MacNamara from the 5th Dragoon Guards.

Robert Swash was born in the parish of Horsham St Faith, just outside the city of Norwich around December 1812. He was attested into the 1st Royal Dragoons on 10th December 1830 in Norwich aged 18 years and was recorded as being a bricklayer by trade. The regiment had moved to Norwich and Ipswich in early June 1830 from Manchester. In the autumn of that year there was unrest among the agricultural labourers caused by the introduction of steam powered machines on some of the farms. With their livelihoods threatened some took to machine wrecking and incendiarism. The dragoons were deployed to suppress these activities.

Swash made his way carefully and was promoted to Corporal on 11th May 1845. By then he had married Elizabeth Phair, an Irish woman and was the father of two daughters (Elizabeth, born July 1841 and Julia born 1843). His fortunes took a negative turn in October 1846 when he was imprisoned and reduced to private with the loss of some of the good conduct pay he had accrued since enlisting. At some time before 1851 his wife died and he appears in the census as a widower and his daughters as visitors to the Nottingham Barracks.

"The Royal Collection © 2008, Her Majesty Queen Elizabeth II"

When war was declared against Russia on 27th March 1854, The regiment was in Manchester. They left for the East in detachments in May and June , arriving in July. When the regiment sailed for the Crimea from Varna on 24th September the ships carrying their horses were hit by a storm and most of the horses were killed. They received horses from other sources after the landing of officers and men at Balaclava on 4th October. On 25th October the 1st Royal Dragoons was part of the Heavy Brigade that charged and defeated a numerically superior Russian cavalry force in the early stages of the battle. Swash has the Balaclava clasp on his medal ribbon and it is likely that he participated in the charge of the Heavy Brigade. On 2nd November 1854 he was promoted to Corporal for a second time and on 9th January 1855 he was recommended for the Distinguished Conduct Medal. Swash survived the ravages of the Crimean winter and the Royals embarked for England on 13th May 1856. They arrived and landed at Portsmouth on 29th May and marched to Aldershot. Queen Victoria inspected them on 17th June. The regimental history states that she walked through the temporary stables and spoke to all the men who had been wounded and those who wore medals. It is possible she spoke to Swash for he was chosen to have his likeness taken.

He stands facing the camera wearing the new cavalry tunic, as per the order received from Horse Guards , 1st April 1855, 'the men to wear a scarlet tunic and white metal helmet with brass ornaments and black plume'. His Corporal's stripes are visible on his right sleeve and above the chevrons can be seen the spur which denotes he is a 'rough rider'. It is his job to break in unbroken horses and make them fit to be ridden in the regiment. He wears the Crimean Medal with clasps for Balaclava, Inkerman and Sebastopol, and his Distinguished Conduct Medal. He wears blancoed white cavalry gauntlets and a belt which is fasted by a buckle on which is displayed the early Victorian crown. Resting on his right shoulder is the heavy cavalry pattern sword.

On 26th June the regiment started its move to Dublin. Swash was promoted to Sergeant on 5th March 1861 and finally retired from the service on 21st March 1864 at Aldershot, having served 33 years and 89 days. His description on discharge stated that he was 51 years and 3 months old, 5'10" tall, of fresh complexion and with grey eyes. His hair was light brown. His intended place of residence was Birmingham and his trade a bricklayer. On his documents Swash has made his mark which has been verified by a witness.

Swash appears in the 1871 census in Aston, Birmingham and appears to have remarried. His wife, Hannah is from Worcestershire. Swash's occupation is recorded as a 'Pensioner (Army)'. Information supplied by Glenn Fisher

876 TAYLOR, Private George

Born : Date Unknown - Burton on Trent
Enlisted : 18th January 1844
Medals : Crimea (B.S)

Died : 14th November 1854 - Scutari
Status : Severely wounded in the Charge

Crimea medal with 1 clasp only Balaclava, in Regimental museum (Household Cavalry) June 1991.

The musters show he was effective from the 1st-25th October, 25 days ordinary pay, 9 days on board ship, 16 days on shore. First muster endorsed "Scutari", second "Deceased", third ruled through. Marginal note reads "To payment of paymaster Genl depot Scutari 26th October Died the 14th November". Form 20 shows 876 Pte Taylor. George. Born Burton on Trent, profession Butcher. Enlisted 18th Jan 1844. Died at Scutari 14th November.

On the 25th, the regiment was engaged at the battle of Balaclava, and lost two men, "who were struck by round shot and killed instantaneously" while four officers and ten men were wounded. George Taylor a ball lodged in the abdomen, and two passed through the fleshy part of the right arm. He was sent to Scutari, and died. In "all the others the injuries were flesh wounds from minie balls". A few days after the battle of Balaclava, the regiment proceded to the heights, on the south-east of Sebastopol, and while there the weather became wet, boisterous and cold. The horses soon cut up the ground, and the camp and roads became a sea of mud. The men were now much in want of boots, shoes and clothing, and in consequence of their feet becoming swollen from being constantly wet, and having no change, they never took off there boots until they were completely worn through. The interior of the hospital and tents were always wet and the clothes of the troopers were scarcely ever dry. The ration-meat consisted of salt pork and no vegtables. Not withstanding, however, theses adverse influences, the total admissions into hospital only amounted to 53. (*Medical and Surgical History of British Army in Turkey and Crimea during the Russian War, 1858 page 24*)

958 TAYLOR, Private Peter

Born : c. 1822 - Wigan
Enlisted : 6th May 1846
Medals : Crimea (B.I.S), The Distinguished Conduct Medal

Died : Unknown
Status : Probably rode in the Charge

On the 11th May 1979 Hayward's Gazette had a collection of 112 Distinguished Conduct Medals for sale ranging from the Crimean War to the Malayan Emergency. Included was a pair to Private P Taylor, 1st Dragoon Guards D.C.M. (Victoria) Crimea, three clasps Balaclava, Inkermann, Sebastopol (engraved). Good, Fine and better £625.00

The musters show he was effective from the 1st October to the 31st December, paid 1d per diem good conduct pay for the period. The Distinguished Conduct Medal recommendation is dated 9th January 1855. WO25/3267 - Records show Discharged 31st August 1869, served 23 years 119 days, all his service was as a private soldier. He was abroad for two years in Turkey and the Crimea. Conduct was very good. Discharged 31/8/1869 at Dublin as unfit for further service.

1226 THOMAS, Private Charles

Born : Unknown
Enlisted :
Medals : Crimea (B.I.S)

Died : Unknown
Status : Probably rode in the Charge

The musters show he was effective from the 1st October to the 31st December. WO25/3267 - Records show Discharged after 21 years service 30th December 1873.

626 THOMAS, Private John

Born : Unknown
Enlisted :
Medals : Crimea (B.I.S), The Distinguished Conduct Medal

Died : Unknown
Status : Probably rode in the Charge

The musters show he was effective from the 1st October to the 31st December, paid 3d per diem good conduct pay for the period. The Distinguished Conduct Medal recommendation is dated 9th January 1855. WO25/3267 - Records show Discharged 27th January 1863.

1248 THOMAS, Private William

Born : Unknown
Enlisted :
Medals : Crimea (B.I.S), Punjab Medal (clasps Chillianwallah, Goojerat)

Died : Unknown
Status : Probably rode in the Charge

The musters show he was effective from the 1st October to the 31st December. Marginal note reads "3 Dragoons No 1834". Attended a veteran's parade and dinner at the Empress Rink, Nottingham in 1911, his medals worn at the time being the Punjab, Crimea, and Turkish Medal. Name shown as "Thompson" on some records.

1103 THORNBACK, Private James

Born : Date unknown - London
Enlisted : 27th October 1849
Medals : Crimea (B.S)

Died : 22nd April 1855 - Scutari
Status : Probably rode in the Charge

The musters show he was effective from the 1st October to the 13th December, 74 days ordinary pay, 9 days on board ship, 65 days on shore. Third muster endorsed "Scutari", marginal note reads "To payment of paymaster Genl Depot Scutari 14th December." WO100/24 page 149 Remarks: Dead.

WO14/1 Scutari Muster Roll January-March 1855 remarks indicate "Hospital" 1st-31st January, no dates or remarks shown in the next two musters.

1221 THORNETT, Private John

Born : Unknown
Enlisted :
Medals : Crimea (B.I.S)

Died : Unknown
Status : Probably rode in the Charge

The musters show he was effective from the 1st October to the 31st December. WO100/24 page 149 Remarks: H&R 30/10 to replace lost. WO25/3267 - Records show Discharged 30th September 1856.

1199 TOBIN, Private Laurence

Born : Unknown
Enlisted :
Medals : Crimea (B.I.S)

Died : Unknown
Status : Probably rode in the Charge

The musters show he was effective from the 1st October to the 31st December. WO25/3267 - Records show deserted 1st September 1873.

790 TRESSLER, Private Joseph

Born : c. 1822 - Northampton
Enlisted : February 1842
Medals : Crimea (B.S)

Died : Unknown
Status : Probably rode in the Charge

Spinks 27th April 2000, Lot 570. Pair. Crimea Medal with two clasps Balaclava, Sebastopol engraved naming. Turkish Crimea Sardinian die un-named. edge bruising VF or better. Est £450-£550.

The musters show he was effective from the 1st October to the 31st December, 92 days ordinary pay, 92 days at 2d good conduct pay, 76 days on board ship, 16 days on shore. All three musters endorsed "On board ship Balaclava".

Medal Roll - Class 2. Died, Retired from service, Discharged. Roll dated 10th February 1859, Royal Barracks, Dublin. Entry crossed through and medal signed for by recipient WO 100-24 page 153. He was discharged in March 1857, his active service amounting to 10 months in Turkey and the Crimea.

414 TRIPP, Troop Sergeant-Major George

Born : 1811 - Alderby, Suffolk
Enlisted : 21st September 1831
Medals : Crimea (B.I.S), The Distinguished Conduct Medal

Died : Unknown
Status : Probably rode in the Charge

Christies 17th November 1987, Lot 81. Group of three to Troop Sergeant Major G.Tripp. 1st Royal Dragoons. D.C.M VR, Crimea three clasps, Balaclava, Inkermann, Sebastopol. Officially impressed. Turkish Crimea sardinian issued, engraved. Some edge brusing to Crimea otherwise VF. Includes copy of discharge papers. Hammer price £1320

The musters show he was effective from the 1st October to the 31st December, 92 days at 3s-0d per diem, 3 days on board ship, 89 days on shore.

The Distinguished Conduct Medal recommendation is dated 7th February 1855, medal ordered 9th February 1855 with an annuity of £20 per year.

Medal Roll - Class 2. Died, Retired from service, Discharged. Roll dated 10th February 1859, Royal Barracks, Dublin. - 414 T.S Major Tripp, George, - Discharged - Entry crossed through and endorsed "Sent to HIM 15/1/61". WO 100-24 page 151. He was discharged on medical grounds in 1857 after 25 years service.

1037 TUDOR, Private John
Born : Unknown   Died : Unknown
Enlisted :   Status : Probably rode in the Charge
Medals : Crimea (B.I.S), Long Service and Good Conduct Medal

The musters show he was effective from the 1st October to the 31st December, paid 1d per diem good conduct pay for the period. WO102 L.S & G.C issued 7th July 1869, gratuity £5.

1183 TURNER, Private Joseph
Born : Unknown   Died : Unknown
Enlisted :   Status : Probably rode in the Charge
Medals : Crimea (B.S)

The musters show he was effective from the 1st October to the 31st December. WO25/3267 - Deserted 3/6/1856.

1162 WAINWRIGHT, Private Joseph
Born : Unknown   Died : Unknown
Enlisted :   Status : Probably rode in the Charge
Medals : Crimea (B.I.S)

The musters show he was effective from the 1st October to the 31st December. Medal Roll - Class 2. Died, Retired from service, Discharged. Roll dated 10th February 1859, Royal Barracks, Dublin. Entry No 157 - Dead - WO 100-24 page 152. WO25/3267 - Records show Discharged 7th December 1858.

1042 WALE, Corporal John
Born : c. 1823 - Cambridge   Died : Unknown
Enlisted : May 1841   Status : Probably rode in the Charge
Medals : Crimea (B.I.S), The Distinguished Conduct Medal
Glendining's 30th June 1982, Lot 165, Three: D.C.M., Victoria (J. Wale, 1st Rl. Dgns.); Crimea, 1854, three bars, Balaclava, Inkermann, Sebastopol (Serjt. J. Wale, 1st Rl. Dgns.); Turkish Crimea. Slight wear on "Serjt.". Nearly very fine. DNW 19th April 1995, Lot 684, A Heavy Brigade D.C.M. group of three awarded to Sergeant John Wale, 1st Royal Dragoons. Distinguished Conduct Medal, V.R. (1st Rl. Drags.); Crimea 1854-55, 3 clasps, Balaclava, Inkermann, Sebastopol (Serjt., 1st Royal Dragoons) officially impressed naming; Turkish Crimea, Sardinian issue, unnamed, some heavy contact wear but better than good fine (3) Hammer Price £1500. Liverpool Medal Co. List July 1995 item 15, same group of medals for sale at £2400

Enlisted in the 6th Dragoon Guards at London in May 1841, transferred to the 1st Dragoons in April 1847. The musters show he was effective from the 1st October to the 31st December, paid 2d per diem good conduct pay for the period.

The Distinguished Conduct Medal recommendation is dated 9th January 1855. Promoted Corporal on the 15th February 1855 and Sergeant on the 1st December 1855. WO25/3267 - Records show Discharged 18th July 1865 at his own request aged 42.

689 WALES, Private Henry
Born : Unknown   Died : Unknown
Enlisted :   Status : Probably rode in the Charge
Medals : Crimea (B.I.S)
A Long Service and Good Conduct has appeared on the market.

The musters show he was effective from the 1st October to the 31st December, marginal note reads "From payment of paymaster Genl depot Scutari 3rd Oct".

956 WALSH, Private William
Born : Unknown   Died : Unknown
Enlisted :   Status : Probably rode in the Charge
Medals : Crimea (B.I.S)

The musters show he was effective from the 1st October to the 31st December. WO25/3267 - Records show Discharged 15th August 1865.

532 WANLACE, Private Lancelot
Born : Unknown
Enlisted :
Medals : Crimea (B.I.S)

Died : Unknown
Status : Probably rode in the Charge

The musters show he was effective from the 1st October to the 31st December, paid 1d per diem good conduct pay for the period. Marginal note reads "Restored to good conduct pay at 1d per diem on 12 Octr". WO25/3267 - Records show Discharged unfit for further duty 23rd July 1861.

1013 WARD, Private William
Born : Unknown
Enlisted :
Medals : Crimea (B.I.S), Long Service and Good Conduct Medal

Died : Unknown
Status : Probably rode in the Charge

The musters show he was effective from the 1st October to the 31st December, paid 1d per diem good conduct pay for the period. WO25/3267 - Records show Discharged 21st February 1871. WO102 L.S & G.C issued 15th August 1868.

1133 WARDEN, Private Edward
Born : Unknown
Enlisted :
Medals : Crimea (B.I.S)

Died : Unknown
Status : Probably rode in the Charge

The musters show he was effective from the 1st October to the 31st December. WO25/3267 - Records show Discharged March 1860.

WARDLAW, Lieutenant-Colonel Robert
Born : 11th June 1815
Enlisted :
Medals : Crimea (B.I.S), The Turkish Order of the Medjidie (5th Class)

Died : 1882
Status : Probably rode in the Charge

Cornet 5th June 1835, Lieutenant 28th July 1840, Captain 14th October 1842, Major 4th February 1853, Brevet Lieutenant Colonel 12th December 1854, Lieutenant Colonel 10th March 1857, Colonel 12th December 1857. (*Harts Annual Army list 1860 Page 136*)

The musters show he was effective from the 1st October to the 31st December, supplied with rations "on shore" 5th Oct to 13th Nov, 18th Nov-31st Dec, "On Board Ship" 1st-4th October. Two Horses foraged at public expense. Medal Roll Sebastopol Clasp. Entitled Lt Col Wardlaw, Robert signed the Roll as commanding officer - WO 100.24 page 143.

The Times, 28th May 1856, reported Lieutenant-Col Robert Wardlaw "arrived at Spithead yesterday on the Steam transport Orinoco".

On the 4th June 1841 Robert married Lady Louisa-Jane-Hay, second daughter of George, 7th Marquess of Tweedale and Lady Susan Montague, daughter of the Duke of Manchester. They went on to have one son, Robert George Wardlaw Ramsey, and eight daughters. The family is descended from the very ancient house of Warlaw, Baron of Torrie, which made a distinguished figure in Scotland, during the earliest times of authentic history. The Wardlaws suffered the loss of many of their possessions from their adherence to the cause of King John Balliol, but retained their estate of Torrie, in the county of Fife, which was handed down for ages in this family. (A Genealogical and Heraldic Dictionary of the Landed Gentry of Great Britain)

The Illustrated London News, 8th July 1882, p.50, Obituary - "Mr. Robert Balfour Wardlaw-Ramsay, of Whitehill, in the county of Edinburgh, and Tillicoultry, in the county of Clackmannan, J.P. and D.L., aged sixty-seven. He was son of the late Captain Robert Wardlaw-Ramsay, by Lady Anne Lindsay, his wife, daughter of Alexander, Earl of Balcarres, and grandson of Captain William Wardlaw, R.N. (a descendant of Wardlaw, of Torrie), by Elizabeth, his wife, daughter of Mr. Robert Balfour Ramsay, of Balbirnie and Whitehill. He married, 1841, Lady Louisa Jane Hay, daughter of the seventh Marquis of Tweeddale, and leaves one son and several daughters."

Roberts son 'Robert George Warlaw Ramsey' (1852-1921)

Presentation of Medals 18th May 1855

1st Dragoons: Captain William de Cardonnel Elmsall, Captain H. Sykes, Lieutenant (Riding Master) George Cruse, Lieutenant William Wray Hartopp, Veterinary Surgeon Matthew Poett, Pte Samuel Woodwards
2nd Dragoons: Captain Francis Sutherland, Lieutenant Lenox Prendergast, Pte Alexander Turner, Pte Charles Adam, Pte Robert Hunter
4th Dragoon Guards: Captain Arthur Masterson Robertson, Lieutenant Robert Gunter, Farrier John Innis, Pte James Parke, Corporal Henry Scholefleld
5th Dragoon Guards: Captain Alexander James Hardy Elliott, Captain Frederick Hay Swinfen, Surgeon George McCulloch, Corporal Edward Malone, Pte Michael Carney, Pte John Wilkins
6th Dragoons: Lt A. White*, Lt T.E. Anderson*, Pte John Brown, Pte Michael Rourke, T.S.M Alexander Shields, Pte James Watt*   *not effective

Her Majesty Queen Victoria presenting Crimea medals at the award ceremony at the Horse Guards, 18th May 1855. The Illustrated London News 6th January 1855

739 WARDROP, Private Thomas
Born : Unknown
Enlisted :
Medals : Crimea (B.I.S)

Died : Unknown
Status : Probably rode in the Charge

J.B Hayward list March 1970 item 206. pair Crimea Medal with three clasps, Balaclava, Inkermann, Sebastopol. Impressed (Pte.T.Wardrop, 1st Royal Dragoons) Turkish Crimea, Sardinian version. Fine £28.

The musters show he was effective from the 1st October to the 31st December, paid 1d per diem good conduct pay for the period.

1026 WATERS, Private Patrick
Born : Unknown
Enlisted :
Medals : Crimea (I.S), Long Service and Good Conduct Medal

Died : Unknown
Status : Effective during the period

The musters show he was effective from the 1st October to the 31st December, paid 1d per diem good conduct pay for the period. WO25/3267 - Records show Discharged 7th February 1871. WO102 L.S & G.C issued 7th July 1869.

643 WEAVER, Paymaster Clerk Edward Francis
Born : Unknown
Enlisted :
Medals : Crimea (B.I.S)

Died : Unknown
Status : Probably rode in the Charge

The musters show he was effective from the 1st October to the 31st December, 92 days at 2s-2d per diem, 4 days on board ship, 88 days on shore.

Edward Francis Weaver, appointed Lieutenant and Adjutant of the 5th Lancers on 17th March 1858, promoted Captain on 28th July 1863 and left with that rank in 1864.

986 WEST, Private Daniel

Born : Unknown
Enlisted :
Medals : Crimea (B.I.S)

Died : 6th March 1869 - Huddersfield, Yorkshire
Status : Probably rode in the Charge

The musters show he was effective from the 1st October to the 31st December. WO25 Discharge book shows he purchased his discharge on the 3rd September 1861.

Died on the 6th March 1869, aged 41, during a drunken quarrel in Huddersfield, Yorkshire. At the time of death he was employed as a coachman at Edgerton, Huddersfield. An article in a local newspaper described him as having "passed through the whole of the Crimean war with bravery, and been one of the heroes of the never-to-be-forgotten Balaclava charge, where he had two horses shot under him. At the time of his death he held several clasps and medals bestowed upon him in recognition of his valour and good conduct as a soldier." (*Huddersfield Observer 31st March 1869*)

1200 WHELAN, Private John

Born : Unknown
Enlisted :
Medals : Crimea (B.I.S)

Died : Unknown
Status : Probably rode in the Charge

The musters show he was effective from the 1st October to the 31st December, paid 1d per diem good conduct pay for 29 days. Marginal note reads "6 Dgn.Gds, forfeited good conduct pay at 1d on 30 October." WO25/3267 - Records show to 5th Lancers March 1858. WO100/24 page 150 Remarks: H&R 30/10 to replace lost.

1222 WHITE, Private Henry

Born : Unknown
Enlisted :
Medals : Crimea (B.I.S)

Died : Unknown
Status : Probably rode in the Charge

The musters show he was effective from the 1st October to the 13th December, 74 days ordinary pay, 4 days on board ship, 70 days on shore. Third muster endorsed "Scutari", marginal note reads "To payment of paymaster Genl. Depot Scutari 14th December".

Medal Roll - Class 2. Died, Retired from service, Discharged. Roll dated 10th February 1859, Royal Barracks, Dublin. Medal Roll Sebastopol clasp entitled 1232 Pte White Henry. Marginal note reads "England" WO 100-24 page 150.

1262 WHITMARSH, Private John

Born : Unknown
Enlisted :
Medals : Crimea (B.I.S)

Died : Unknown
Status : Probably rode in the Charge

The musters show he was effective from the 1st October to the 31st December. WO25/3267 - Records show died June 1859.

991 WHITTAKER, Private John

Born : Unknown
Enlisted :
Medals : Crimea (B.S)

Died : Unknown
Status : Probably rode in the Charge

The musters show he was effective from the 1st October to the 31st December. Medal Roll - Class 2. Died, Retired from service, Discharged. Roll dated 10th February 1859, Royal Barracks, Dublin. Entry No 151. 991 Pte Whittaker. James. Discharged WO 100-24 page 153. WO25/3267 - Records show Discharged December 1856.

1169 WICK, Private Charles

Born : Unknown
Enlisted :
Medals : Crimea (B.I.S)

Died : Unknown
Status : Probably rode in the Charge

The musters show he was effective from the 1st October to the 31st December.

1056 WICKHAM, Private William

Born : Unknown
Enlisted :
Medals : Crimea (B.S)

Died : Unknown
Status : Probably rode in the Charge

The musters show he was effective from the 1st October to the 31st December, 61 days ordinary pay, 61 days at 1d good conduct pay, 13 days on board ship, 48 days on shore. Third muster endorsed "Scutari", marginal note reads "To Scutari 1st December". Medal Roll Sebastopol clasp entitled 1232 Pte Whickham, William. Marginal note reads "England" sent to Gegt 27/8/57" WO 100-24 page 150.

WO14/1 Scutari Muster Roll January-March 1855 remarks indicate "Hospital" 1st-31st January, no dates or remarks shown in the next two musters.

1393 WILLIAMS, Private Henry

Born : Unknown
Enlisted : 2nd April 1831
Medals : Crimea (B.I.S)

Died : Unknown
Status : Probably rode in the Charge

For Sale at Spink 12th March 1996, Lot 703. Pair: Private H. Williams, 1st Royal Dragoons Crimea, three clasps, Balaklava, Inkermann, Sebastopol, officially impressed; Turkish Crimea, Sardinian die, this plugged and with Crimea style suspension, the pair very fine, with copied service papers (2) £300-350

Private Henry Williams, a glazier from Rye, Suffolk, enlisted in the 1st Royal Dragoons at Norwich and served 25 years, with the Colours and was discharged at Dublin January 1857 as unfit for further service due to "a varicose condition of the veins of the legs".

The musters show he was effective from the 1st October to the 31st December, paid 4d per diem good conduct pay for the period. Marginal note reads "3rd Dragoons No 1096", the only record of a 1096 in the 3rd Dragoons is a William Whyatt killed in action at the Battle of Mudki on the 18th Dec 1845, this entry is probably an error.

Medal Roll - Class 2. Died, Retired from service, Discharged. Roll dated 10th February 1859, Royal Barracks, Dublin. Entry No 153 1393 Pte Williams Henry. Discharged. Entry crossed through and endorsed "Sent to him. 11-10-60" WO 100-24 Page 153.

Through the 1800's up to 1500 troops of various regiments of foot and up to two troops of horse, were stationed at the Royal Barracks, however due to over crowding and disease the numbers had to be cut back dramatically.

1249 WILLIAMS, Private Samuel

Born : Unknown
Enlisted :
Medals : Crimea (B.I.S)

Died : Unknown
Status : Probably rode in the Charge

The musters show he was effective from the 1st October to the 31st December. Medal Roll - Class 2. Died, Retired from service, Discharged. Roll dated 10th February 1859, Royal Barracks, Dublin. Entry No 150 1249 Pte Williams Samuel. Discharged. WO 100-24 Page 153.

1178 WILSON, Private William

Born : Unknown
Enlisted :
Medals : Crimea (B.I.S)

Died : Unknown
Status : Probably rode in the Charge

The musters show he was effective from the 1st October to the 31st December.

1158 WOODHALL, Private William

Born : Unknown
Enlisted :
Medals : Crimea (S)

Died : Unknown
Status : To Scutari 26th October 1854

The musters show he was effective from the 1st-25th October, 25 days ordinary pay, 4 days on board ship, 16 days on shore, 5 days in hospital. All three musters endorsed "Scutari", marginal note reads "To Scutari 26th October".

Medal Roll Sebastopol clasp entitled 1158 Pte Woodall, William. Marginal note reads "Reg 6/9" WO 100-24 page 150.

1079 WOODWARD, Private Samuel

Born : Unknown
Enlisted :
Medals : Crimea (B.I.S)

Died : Unknown
Status : Slightly wounded in the Charge

The musters show he was effective from the 1st October to the 22nd November, 53 days ordinary pay, 3 days on board ship, 50 days on shore. Second and third musters endorsed "Scutari", marginal note reads "To Scutari 23rd November". Shown on the Casualty Roll as wounded Slightly at Balaclava.

He received his medal from the hand of the Queen on 18th May 1855. Medal Roll - Class 2. Died, Retired from service, Discharged. Roll dated 10th February 1859, Royal Barracks, Dublin. Entry No 152 1079 Pte Woodward Samuel. Discharged. WO 100-24 Page 153.

1167 WRIGHT, Private Andrew

Born : Unknown
Enlisted :
Medals : Crimea (B.S)

Died : Unknown
Status : Probably rode in the Charge

The musters show he was effective from the 1st October to the 31st December. Medal Roll - Class 2. Died, Retired from service, Discharged. Roll dated 10th February 1859, Royal Barracks, Dublin. Entry No 154 1167 Pte Wright Andrew. Entry crossed through and endorsed "sent to him 3/9/61" Discharged. WO 100-24 Page 153.

YORKE, Lieutenant-Colonel John

Born : 1813
Enlisted :
Medals : Crimea (B.S), The Turkish Order of the Medjidie (4th Class), The Sardinian War Medal, C.B
Medal with B.S clasps and other decorations in the Regimental Museum.

Died : 28th March 1890 - London
Status : Rode in the Charge

Ensign 21st December 1832. Lieutenant 5th December 1834. Captain 14th December 1841. Major 4th September 1849. Lieutenant-Colonel 4th February 1853. Colonel 23rd March 1856. (Harts Annual Army List 1857) Lieutenant-Colonel and Brevet-Colonel John Yorke, C.B., half pay unattached to be Commandant (London Gazette 1st April 1864)

The musters show he was effective from the 1st-25th October, supplied with rations "On Shore" 7th-25th October, 19 days at 2.1/2D per diem, on board ship 1st October to 6th Oct. First and second Musters endorsed "Scutari", third muster endorsed "On Board ship Balaklava". Medal Roll for Sebastopol Clasp entitled, Marginal note "England sent 8/3"

The citation for the Sardinian War Medal reads (He) "served in the Crimea until the action at Balaclava, when he was so severely wounded in command of his regiment, as to oblige him to retire from active service".

The Broad Arrow 5th April 1890 "General Sir John Yorke. Late of the 1st Royal Dragoons CB of Plas 'Newydd' Llangollen, died at No 39 St. Georges (London) on the 28th March in his 77th Year."

The Times, Monday 31st March 1890, "Obituary General John Yorke, General John Yorke C.B of Plas Newydd Langollen died on Friday after a short illness in his 77th year. He was grandson of the author of 'The Royal Tribes of Wales'. He entered the army in 1832, became Colonel in 1854, and commanded the 1st Dragoons through the Crimean campaign. He was severely wounded at the battle of Balaclava. On returning to England he received Her Majesty's medal with two clasps, also the Sardinian and Turkish Medals, the 4th class Medjidie and was create C.B and appainted General. He was presented with a sword of honour of the value of 120 guineas by the town and district of Wrexham on the termination of the war. He was Colonel of the 19th Hussars from 1872 until last year, when he was transferred to the command of his old regiment the 1st Dragoons."

The Oswestry Advertiser, dated 2nd April 1890 Obituary.
On Friday all the inhabitants of Llangollen received with profound regret the sad intelligence that at four o'clock that morning the gallant veteran General Yorke had breathed his last at his London residence, where as usual he had been spending the winter months. It appears that some time ago the General had been suffering from an acute attack of gout, from which he never seems to have entirely rallied. During the earlier part of last week telegrams and letters were being daily received in Llangollen intimating that dangerous symptoms were presenting themselves, and each succeeding communication intensified the fear that his life was gradually ebbing away, and when on Friday the news of his death was received, the expressions of regret and manifestations of sorrow to be observed on all hands showed the deep, sincere affection which was being entertained towards him by all classes of the community.
General Yorke, who died at the age of 76, was the youngest son of the late Mr Simon Yorke of Erddig, M.P. for Grantham from 1796 to 1802, by Margaret, daughter of Mr John Holland of Tydraw, and grandson of Mr Philip Yorke, author of the "Royal Tribes of Wales", and M.P. for Helston, Cornwall.

He first became acquainted with the "Ladies of Llangollen" when an Eton boy of eleven, in the year 1825, when in company with the late Dean Stanley he visited them at Plasnewydd. He used to relate how they "both were nearly frightened to death, powder and pomatum, old age, and the French decorations worn by Lady Eleanor Butler being very alarming to him." He entered the Army in 1832, became colonel in 1854, and commanded the 1stDragoons in the Crimea campaign in that year:he was severely wounded at Balaclava, a wound which necessitated amputation of one of his legs. He was created C.B. in 1855, and on his return to this country at the termination of the war with Russia in 1857, he received her Majesty's medal with two clasps, the Sardinian and Turkish medals, the 4th class Medjidieh, and was appointed General. He was presented by the town and district of Wrexham with a sword of honour, value 120 guineas, which now forms one of the most valuable relics among the thousand and one objects of interest to be seen at Plasnewydd. He was colonel of the 19th Hussars from 1872 until 1889, when he was transferred to the command of his old regiment, the 1st Dragoons. For upwards of 30 years carving in ivory was his principal recreation, and his wonderful productions in this art are also to be found among his collection of curiosities. Since he has become the owner of Plasnewydd, he has

expended an immense amount in beautifying the external and internal arrangements of this charming little mansion, and even to within a few days of his death was engaged in collecting in London fresh objects of interest to add to his museum. His death occurred within a week or two of that period of the year when it was his custom to take up his abode in the Hand Hotel for the summer season, and it is sad to reflect that his genial smile, portly and even handsome figure, a perfect type of an old "English gentleman." will never again be seen in our midst. General Yorke was a great employer of labour, and always held in high estimation a number of local handicraftsmen, who he maintained possessed marvellous skill in the production of carvings and antique work, with which he continually enriched his buildings. To the thousands of visitors who have frequented Plas Newydd he was well known, it being his pride to act as guide to them during their inspection of the house, while the free, easy, and unaffected manner in which he used to present an epitome of his life history was a thing never to be forgotten. Being natually kind-hearted and charitably disposed, the poor always found in him a constant and unfaltering friend. In politics the deceased General was a Conservative.

In accordance with the wish of the deceased gentleman his remains will be interred at 3.30, this afternoon, at Careby, Lincolnshire.

It is also currently reported, with a considerable degree of authority, that the will will contain stipulations for the preservation of Plas Newydd in its present form, and as without doubt it forms the principal object of attraction to Llangollen it is sincerely to be hoped that such will be the case.

Below are some excerpts from letters sent from John Yorke to his sister Etheldred Yorke. The letters form part of the Erddig manuscript collection held at the Flintshire Record Office. Ref NRA 18984 Erddig.

4th April 1854 - Reports on his preparation for embarkation at Liverpool aboard the Gertrude bound for the Crimea.

12th May 1854 - "Quarters on the Gertrude are comfortable, the troops well behaved and the horses settling well".

13th May 1854 - Aboard the Gertrude in Abergele Bay,. "Weather very calm and ship has to rely on a tug".

2nd August 1854 (Kara-Hussein) - "Many of the men are falling ill and recovery is difficult because of the heat, the flies and wild dogs trouble them a great deal". He also sends a sketch plan of the encampment (see opposite).

27th October 1854 (On board the Arabia, off Balaklava)
My dear Ethel,
More bad luck but do not make yourself unduly uneasy. I have been badly wounded in the last disastrous affair. A grape or canister shot caught one on the left thigh bone, and smashed my leg badly, but I continued to ride down nearly 4 miles with my leg swinging about. I suffered considerable pain but did not faint, and the doctors say I am all usually well.......

25th November 1854 -(Constantinople) "I have decided to stay on board the Arabia, as patients at the hospital have to cook their own

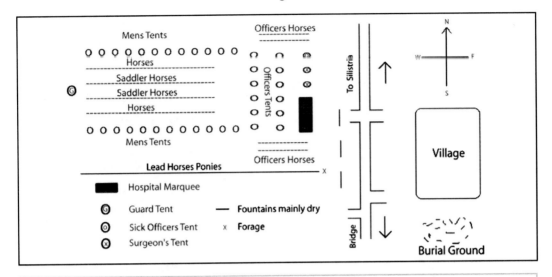

5th December 1854 Thanks for the letter of good wishes from the people of Wrexham. The letter also includes an account of the battle of Balaklava. Which infact was not such an extended or glorious affair as the papers made out and in which his regiment played only a supporting role at first, but later came under direct fire after the Light Brigade had been routed and he was wounded. "In answer to enquires relative to the Balaklava affair. I will give you an outline. Very early in the morning we advanced across the plain to one point where the Turks held the redoubts, and we had the mortification to see them all fall into the hands of the Russians. With very little resistance ....That means we were so placed directly in the line of fire, that all the very large shot (32 lbs) that overcrowned the heights naturally bowled like cricket balls into our ranks, we should have been equally useful if we had been just a few paces clear of the line of fire, but as it was not so, the large shot came down upon us. The officers could easily escape, we had only to move our horses a few yards to let the shot ---which movement I effected frequently, but when a shot came opposite the closely packed squadron it generally took a front & rear rank horse, and sometimes a man, or a single horse. In this foolish manner we lost 7 horses & two men."....... "The regiment were beautifully steady I never had a better line in a field day, the only swerving was to let through the ranks the wounded & dead men & horses of the Light Brigade which were even then thickly scattered over the plain. It was a fearful sight. I assure you, and the appearance of all who retired was as if they had passed through a heavy shower of blood, positively dripping and saturated, and shattered arms blowing back like empty sleeves, as the poor fellows ran to the rear, during all this time their was a constant squelching noise around me.... another moment and my horse was shot in the right flank."

15th December 1854 - 'The ship is loaded with supplies, charcoal, and wooden houses, and will leave port shortly'.

29th January 1855 - The Arabia has been ordered to go to Varna to pick up Turkish Cavalry, Yorke has to stay unfit to transfer to another ship.

19th February 1855 - Records a visit from Lord W. Paulet, who is doing all he can to help. Both are delighted that Lucan has been recalled. Lucan had few friends in the Brigade, Yorke observed that Lucan suffered from poor nerves. At the last alarm he was 'excited to madness' and abuses everybody.

25th February 1855 - A medical board has been to access the amount of compensation due to him.

28th February 1855 - Received orders on the 1st March to board the Cunard Steamer Alps, bound for England. Their was no suitable cabin so the Captain has given up his.

23rd March 1855 (George Hotel Portsmouth) has arrived safely.

1201 YOUNG, Corporal John

Born : Unknown
Enlisted :
Medals : Crimea (B.I.S)

Died : Unknown
Status : Probably rode in the Charge

Spinks Circular October 1985, item 7311, Crimea 3 Bars Balaclava, Inkermann, Sebastopol. Cpl.Jno Young Royal Drans. Engraved VF together with phot copies of Discharge documents £325.
Glendinings Auction 25th June 1986, Lot 58 Crimea medal with three bars, Balaclava, Inkermann, Sebastopol (Corpl.Jno. Young, Royal Dgns). Engraved, very fine. Hammer Price £220

The musters show he was effective from the 1st October to the 31st December, 92 Days at 1s-7 1/2d per diem, 92 days at 2d Good Conduct pay, 3 days on board ship, 89 days on shore. Marginal note reads "From Private 10 Nov, vice Rideway" Medal Roll - Class 2. Died, Retired from service, Discharged. Roll dated 10th February 1859, Royal Barracks, Dublin. - 1201 Cpl Young. John. discharged. Entry crossed through endorsed "S.O.P Brighton". WO25/3267 - Records show Discharged 30th March 1857.

RIFLES, GUNS, AND PISTOLS.

PARKER, FIELD, & SONS,

Invite attention to their Improved REVOLVING SIX-CHAMBERED PISTOLS, to which they have lately added their Patent SPRING RAMROD, rendering this Pistol the most effective and complete ever offered to the Public.

They manufacture all kinds of Guns, Pistols, and Rifles, particularly the LONG RANGE MINIE RIFLES, and supply Sporting Apparatus and Ammunition.

Contractors for Police-Truncheons, Rattles, Handcuffs, Cutlasses, &c. &c.

PARKER, FIELD, & SONS,

Manufacturers to Her Majesty, the Hon. East India Company, the Hudson's Bay Company, &c.,

233, HIGH HOLBORN, & 58, MANSELL STREET, MINORIES, LONDON.

HILL'S

REGISTERED CAMP BEDSTEAD,

WEIGHT, TEN POUNDS.

COMFORTS FOR THE CRIMEA.

No. 1 FULL COSTUME.

2 BOTTLE.	5 GLOVES.	8 BUCKET.
3 KNAPSACK.	6 BOOTS.	9 SHEET.
4 WASH BASIN.	7 BASIN.	10 REVOLVER POUCH.

OFFICERS proceeding to the East will find at this Establishment every requisite, at a moment's notice, STOUT WATERPROOF COATS, Woollen or Sheep Skin Lined, ditto ditto BOOTS. These Boots are made extra strong and stout, to stand the test of bogs or marshes. AIR BEDS AND PILLOWS, AND CAMP BEDSTEAD, in a compass of three feet by nine inches complete.

Waterproof Camp or Ground Sheets, regulation size; Haversacks and Knapsacks, Water Bottles and Cups, folding; Buckets, Baths, &c. Life Belts, to form a Pillow or Dry Seat, Canteens, &c.

EDMISTON and SONS, Siphonia Depot, 69, Strand, London.

THE CRIMEAN REQUIREMENTS are very WARM CLOTHING—namely, Waterproof Fur and Woollen-lined Coats, Wrappers, Leggings, Boots, Caps, Bivouacking Beds and Blankets, to resist ground-damp, which, with warm under clothing, camp kits, and every other article now so much needed, may be obtained at the Manufacturers',

S. W. SILVER & Co., 66 & 67, CORNHILL.

TO GENTLEMEN WITH TENDER FEET.

J. CHAPPELL, 388, Strand, corner of Southampton-street, Boot Maker, and Professor of Fitting, begs to call the attention of such to his method of Measuring, by which he guarantees, at the first trial, to produce a fit unprecedented for comfort, yet combined with the most fashionable shape. J. C., particularly solicits those gentlemen on whom bootmakers have practised unsuccessfully, and every day's experience proves there are plenty of such cases. He will undertake to fit them at once, however difficult.

A good pair of Wellington Boots, 25s. cash to order; ditto, fitted on from the stock, 21s. Established 1825.

HIGHLAND HAND-KNITTED HOSIERY.

SOFT, Warm, and very Durable. Officers in the Army and Navy are respectfully informed that their orders for Hosiery, & Hand-Woven Cloth will be thankfully received by the Royal Patriotic and Industrial Society of Scotland, at their Highland Depôt, 196, Piccadilly, on behalf of poor families in the Hebrides, again rendered destitute by the total failure of the potato crop, and a wet and bad harvest in 1854.

Subscriptions may be paid to Sir CHARLES FORBES, Bart., Broom Wood, Clapham; to GEORGE BAIN, Esq., 18 Parliament-street, & to Mr. CHARLES BOND, the Secretary, at 196, Piccadilly.

Military Hosiery, &c.

EVERY description of strong, serviceable HOSIERY, adapted for all seasons, in Stockings, Socks, Drawers, and Vests; also Shirts in coloured Flannels, Long Cloth, and Linen.

ELASTIC STOCKINGS, Leggings, and Knee Caps, for VARICOSE VEINS, Sprains, and Weakness, which yield a permanent and unvarying support under any temperature, without the trouble of lacing or bandaging. Instructions for measurement, with prices, on application, and the articles sent by post from the Manufacturers,

POPE & PLANTE, 4, Waterloo Place, Pall Mall, London.

MR. HOWARD, SURGEON-DENTIST, 52, FLEET STREET,

HAS introduced an entirely NEW DESCRIPTION of ARTIFICIAL TEETH, fixed without Springs, Wires, or Ligatures. They so perfectly resemble the natural Teeth as not to be distinguished from the original by the closest observer. They will NEVER CHANGE COLOUR OR DECAY, and will be found superior to any Teeth ever before used. This method does not require the extraction of roots, or any painful operation, and will support and preserve Teeth that are loose, and is guaranteed to restore articulation and mastication,

Decayed Teeth rendered sound and useful in mastication.

52, FLEET STREET.

At home from Ten till Five.

The 2nd Dragoons
"The Scots Greys"

The 2nd Dragoons Strength

After 38 years service at home, the 2nd Dragoons left Nottingham for service in the Crimea. 299 troopers and 14 officers with 294 horses departed from England. The Regiment sailed from Liverpool on the 25th July 1854 on the S.S.Himalaya and was the last regiment of the Heavy Cavalry Brigade to leave England for the Crimea and the first to arrive, its speed being ensured by travel direct from Istanbul (Constantinople) to the Crimea, not via Bulgaria. Whilst passing Malta on the 4th August a man drowned. The regiment arriving at Scutari on the 8th of August and on the following day it disembarked at Kullali. The Regiment were housed in the Turkish Cavalry Barracks and whilst there lost one trooper from Cholera. On the 22nd of September the Regiment embarked on board the Himalaya, and on the 24th landed at the river Katcha. The Battle of the Alma had been fought earlier before the Greys set foot on Russian soil. Victory at the Alma meant that the British and French Armies could advance on Sebastopol. The first encounter with the enemy occurred at Mackenzie's Farm. On the 26th September the 2nd Dragoons bivouacked on the plain in front of Balaklava. In September the admissions into Hospital numbered 120 mostly from Diarrhoea, with three men and one officer having Cholera, which proved fatal within the space of twenty-four hours. In October Dr. Brush observes "encamped in the valley of Balaklava, close to the town; the unhealthy site of this position, the noxious effluvia (arising from half-buried offal, dead horses lying exposed on the ground in the vicinity of the camp - filth accumulated from men and horses), and harassing duties which devolved upon the men, have contributed to render Diarrhoea and Fever the prevalent diseases. In many instances, however, the Diarrhoea was identical with Cholera in its early stage."

Once the siege of Sebastopol was under way a close supply port was required so the port of Balaklava was captured. The attempts by the Russians to retake Balaklava led to the battle on 25th October. The 2nd Dragoons defeated and routed a large body of Russian cavalry. The Corps was then ordered to support the Light Brigade. On this occasion it sustained many injuries, the wounds inflicted all being of a serious nature, and caused by round-shot, shell, grape, and rifle-balls. The loss to the Regiment in this action amounted to 4 officers wounded, and 2 men killed and 54 wounded several of whom subsequently died of their wounds. The first three men who fell were mortally wounded by rifle-balls, in covering the retreat of the Turks from the redoubts; and of the whole number, 48 passed through my hands and were attended to in the field Hospital, the remainder having been removed to the General Hospital at Balaklava. During the evening of the battle, and on the following, the wounded (with the exception of those whose wounds were dressed on the field and returned to their duty) were embarked on board ship, and sent down to the General Hospital at Scutari. In October 1854 the number of cases received into Hospital was still greater than in the preceding month, and amounted to 115; but while the proportion of cases of Diarrhoea subsided very considerably, 22 instances of Fever, 9 of dysentery, 54 of wounds, and 7 of Cholera, were presented. On the 16th August 1855, the Regiment was reinforced by a draft of 30 men, and on the 18th with an extra 29 men. Admissions into Hospital increased to 136 cases, "The large augmentation of the number of sick (observes the Surgeon) is to be attributed to the arrival of recent drafts from England, consisting of young boys, imperfectly drilled, and deficient in stamina, who were sent to this country during the intensity of the summer heats, and in my opinion unfit for the service. During the period the 2nd Dragoons served in the East, the number of cases admitted into Hospital amounted to 1,374, with only 145 from wounds and Injuries. The number of deaths numbered 86, 6 died from wounds. The strength of the Regiment on embarkation was 299, and the reinforcements received during the war amounted to 345, and it appears, that 86 deaths were recorded from disease and wounds, 2 men were killed in action, and 54 men invalided to England while the Regiment remained on active service, and that 40 men were discharged on account of disease or disability contracted during the war. (Extracts from *Medical and Surgical history of the British Army, during the War Against Russia 1854-56.p 33/36*)

The S.S. Himalaya

623 ADAM, Private Charles

Born : Unknown
Enlisted .
Medals : Crimea (B.I.S)

Died : Unknown
Status : Probably rode in the Charge

The musters show he was effective from the 1st October to the 31st December. Received his medal from the hand of the Queen, 18th May 1855. WO25 Discharge book shows he was discharged in 1857.

687 AITKEN, Private James

Born : Unknown
Enlisted :
Medals : Crimea (B.S)

Died : Unknown
Status : Slightly wounded in the Charge

The musters show he was effective from the 1st-25th October and from the 10th November to the 31st December. Remarks state sent to Scutari 26th October, returned to Camp 10th November. Regimental number shown as 684 on the musters. Listed on the Casualty Roll as slightly wounded at Balaclava.

1206 ALEXANDER, Private George

Born : Date unknown - Ayr, Scotland
Enlisted : 18th February 1853
Medals : Crimea (B.S), Distinguished Conduct Medal

Died : Unknown
Status : Slightly wounded in the Charge

Glendining's 28th September 1977, Lot 108, D.C.M Victoria, George Alexander 2nd Dragoons, Nearly V.F £170. Hayward's Gazette 11th May 1979, Collection of 112 Distinguished Conduct Medals, Item 2, Private G Alexander, 2nd Dragoons - D.C.M. (Victoria) - Nearly VF for sale at £420. Glendining's 24th June 1981 Lot 24 - £410.

Enlisted in the 2nd Dragoons at Edinburgh on the 18th February 1853 aged 18. The musters show he was effective from the 1st-25th October. Remarks state sent to Scutari Hospital 26th October. Listed on the Casualty Roll as slightly wounded at Balaclava. WO100/24 page 158 Remarks: Scutari. Sick. WO14/1 Scutari Muster Roll January-March 1855 remarks indicate he returned to his regiment on the 15th January 1855. Sentenced 7 Days ... Hard Labour.

The "London Gazette" 16th December 1854 reported he was wounded in the Charge of the Heavy Brigade on the 25th October 1854. His recommendation for the Distinguished Conduct Medal is dated 13th January 1855. His Discharge papers show he served 4 years 44 days, including 1 year 11 months with British Army in the East. Discharged at Dublin on the 11th June 1857 as unfit for further military service. Character good. Lost the two first joints of a forefinger of his left hand caused by a sabre cut at the Battle of Balaclava. Received a Royal Bounty in 1888 "For Gallant Conduct".

917 ALLEN, Private James

Born : Unknown
Enlisted :
Medals : Crimea (B.I.S)

Died : Unknown
Status : Slightly wounded in the Charge

The musters show he was effective from the 1st October to the 31st December. Listed on the Casualty Roll as slightly wounded at Balaclava.

1244 ALLEN, Private Robert

Born : Unknown
Enlisted :
Medals : Crimea (B.S)

Died : Unknown
Status : Probably rode in the Charge

The musters show he was effective from the 1st-25th October. Remarks state sent to Scutari Hospital 26th October. WO100/24 page 158 Remarks: Sick at Scutari. WO14/1 Scutari Muster Roll January-March 1855 remarks indicate he was on a Hospital Ship in January and February.

989 ALLIS, Private William J.

Born : Date unknown - Denain, Antrim
Enlisted : 4th January 1847
Medals : Crimea (B.S)

Died : 28th October 1854 - Aboard Ship
Status : Severely wounded in the Charge

A labourer prior to enlistment. The musters show he was effective from the 1st-25th October. Remarks state Died 28th October 1854. Listed on the Casualty Roll as severely wounded at Balaclava.

Russian Musket

One of weapons the Heavy Brigade had to face was the M1845 percussion smooth bore rifle, with a range of 150-200 yards it was capable of firing one round per minute.

745 ANGUS, Sergeant John
Born : Unknown
Enlisted :
Medals : Crimea (B.I.S)

Died : Unknown
Status : Probably rode in the Charge

The musters show he was effective from the 1st October to the 31st December. Discharged 21st August 1866.

1020 ARMOUR, Private James N.
Born : Unknown
Enlisted :
Medals : Crimea (B.I.S)

Died : Unknown
Status : Probably rode in the Charge

The musters show he was effective from the 1st October to the 31st December.

ARMSTRONG, Assistant-Surgeon James Jekell
Born : 13th July 1829 - Belturbet, Co Cavan
Enlisted :
Medals : Crimea (B.I.S)

Died : Unknown
Status : Probably rode in the Charge

The musters show he was effective from the 1st October to the 31st December. WO100/24 page 157 Remarks: Sent by Dr. Hall to the front on the day of that Battle (Inkermann). Assistant Surgeon 16th March 1852. Appointed to 2nd Dragoons 2nd April 1852. Resigned 8th June 1855.

445 ARNEILL, Private Matthew
Born : Unknown
Enlisted :
Medals : Crimea (B.I.S)

Died : Unknown
Status : Probably rode in the Charge

The musters show he was effective from the 1st October to the 31st December. Paid G.C.P 2nd Nov to the 31st Dec.

975 BAIN, Private James
Born : Unknown
Enlisted :
Medals : Crimea (B.I.S)

Died : Unknown
Status : Probably rode in the Charge

The musters show he was effective from the 1st October to the 31st December.

1073 BAIN, Private James
Born : Date unknown - Kirkaldy
Enlisted : 21st July 1849
Medals : Crimea (B.I.S)

Died : 28th January 1855 - Scutari
Status : Probably rode in the Charge

A labourer prior to enlistment. The musters show he was effective from the 1st October to the 30th December. Remarks state sent to Scutari Hospital 31st December. WO100/24 page 158 Remarks: Sick at Scutari. WO14/1 Scutari Muster Roll January-March 1855 remarks indicate he "joined on the 24th January" and died on the 28th January.

1137 BARNETT, Private Robert
Born : Unknown
Enlisted :
Medals : Crimea (B.I.S)

Died : Unknown
Status : Slightly wounded in the Charge

The musters show he was effective from the 1st October to the 31st December. Listed on the Casualty Roll as slightly wounded at Balaclava.

1196 BARRIE, Private William
Born : Unknown
Enlisted :
Medals : Crimea (B.I.S)
Died : 20th June 1859
Status : Probably rode in the Charge

The musters show he was effective from the 1st October to the 31st December. WO25 Discharge book reports that he died on the 20th June 1859.

966 BEESTON, Saddler Sergeant Thomas
Born : Unknown
Enlisted :
Medals : Crimea (B.I.S)
Died : Unknown
Status : Probably rode in the Charge

The musters show he was effective as a Saddler Sergeant from the 1st October to the 31st December. His entry under Sergeants is ruled through, the record for John Liddle shows he was promoted to Sergeant vice Beeston on the 26th November. WO14/1 Scutari Muster Roll January-March 1855 remarks indicate he joined on the 2nd March.

1176 BELL, Private James
Born : Unknown
Enlisted :
Medals : Crimea (B.I.S)
Died :
Status : Probably rode in the Charge

The musters show he was effective from the 1st October to the 31st December. Discharged 1857.

1207 BELL, Private James (1207)
Born : Date Unknown - Barony
Enlisted : 9th March 1853
Medals : Crimea (B.I.S)
Died : 8th January 1855 - Camp Crimea
Status : Probably rode in the Charge

The musters show he was effective from the 1st October to the 31st December. Trade on enlistment Labourer.

816 BENNETT, Private Charles
Born : Unknown
Enlisted : 30th December 1843 - Hitcham
Medals : Crimea (S)
Died : Date unknown - Scutari
Status : Effective during the period

The musters show he was effective from the 1st October to the 28th October. Remarks state sent to Scutari Hospital 29th October. Trade on enlistment Butcher.

1116 BISHOP, Private Charles
Born : Unknown
Enlisted :
Medals : Crimea (B.I.S)
Died : Unknown
Status : Probably rode in the Charge

The musters show he was effective from the 1st October to the 31st December. WO25 Discharge book shows he transferred to ....Corps June 1868.

1118 BLACKWOOD, Sergeant William
Born : Unknown
Enlisted :
Medals : Crimea (B.S)
Died : Unknown
Status : Probably rode in the Charge

The musters show he was effective from the 1st October to the 31st December. Discharged as "unfit" December 1858.

1011 BLACKWOOD, Private William
Born : Unknown
Enlisted :
Medals : Crimea (B.I.S)
Died : Unknown
Status : Probably rode in the Charge

The musters show he was effective from the 1st October to the 31st December.

1125 BLAIR, Private Thomas

Born : Unknown
Enlisted :
Medals : Crimea (B.I.S)

Died : Unknown
Status : Probably rode in the Charge

The musters show he was effective from the 1st October to the 31st December. To pension 22/4/1873.

1201 BLANDFORD, Private George

Born : Unknown
Enlisted :
Medals : Crimea (B.I.S)

Died : Unknown
Status : Probably rode in the Charge

The musters show he was effective from the 1st October to the 31st December, regimental number shown as 1210.

1091 BOOTH, Private James

Born : Unknown
Enlisted :
Medals : Crimea (B.I.S)

Died : Unknown
Status : Probably rode in the Charge

The musters show he was effective from the 1st October to the 31st December. WO25 Discharge book shows he was a Trumpeter when discharged in August 1865.

1108 BORLAND, Private John

Born : Unknown
Enlisted :
Medals : Crimea (B.S)

Died : Unknown
Status : Slightly wounded in the Charge

The musters show he was effective from the 1st-25th October and from the 29th December to the 31st December. Remarks state sent to Scutari 26th October, returned to Camp 29th December. Listed on the Casualty Roll as slightly wounded at Balaclava. Form 20 shows he was discharged on the 26th September 1865.

946 BORTHWICK, Private James

Born : Unknown
Enlisted :
Medals : Crimea (B.S)

Died : Unknown
Status : Slightly wounded in the Charge

The musters show he was effective from the 1st October to the 25th October. Remarks states sent to Scutari 26th October. Listed on the Casualty Roll as slightly wounded at Balaclava. WO100/24 page 158 Remarks: Sick at Scutari, page 79 Remarks: Gone to England. WO14/1 Scutari Muster Roll January-March 1855 remarks indicate he was in Hospital during January and February, sent home on the 27th February. WO25 shows he was discharged 9th November 1869.

1181 BOSWELL, Private Peter

Born : Unknown
Enlisted :
Medals : Crimea (B.I.S)

Died : Unknown
Status : Probably rode in the Charge

The musters show he was effective from the 1st October to the 31st December.

BOYD, Captain William

Born : Unknown
Enlisted :
Medals : Crimea (B.I.S)

Died : 12th September 1855 - Scutari
Status : Probably rode in the Charge

The musters show he was effective from the 1st October to the 31st December, 3 horses foraged at public expense for the period. WO100/24 page 176 Remarks: Died 12th. September 1855

William Boyd, 2nd Lieuteneant 87th Fusiliers 22nd February 1831, 1st Lieutenant 17th October 1834, Captain 26th April 1844. Scots Greys 1852. Major Army 31st August 1855. (*Illustrated Histories of the Scottish Regiments No2. 2nd Dragoons by Lt Col Percy Groves, page 28*) Boyd. W. Brevet Major 2nd Dragoons arrived 23 September 1854, Died 12th September 1855 of Disease at Scutari. (*Memorials of the Brave Appendix page 63*)

1104 BOYD, Private James
Born : Date unknown - Abbey, Renfrew
Enlisted : 24th April 1850
Medals : Crimea (I.S)

Died : 29th December 1854 - Scutari
Status : Effective during the period

The musters show he was effective from the 1st October to the 27th December. Remarks state sent to Scutari Hospital 27th December. Died 29th December. Trade on enlistment Labourer.

1078 BOYES, Private Richard
Born : Unknown
Enlisted :
Medals : Crimea (B.I.S)

Died : Unknown
Status : Probably rode in the Charge

Morton & Eden Ltd, Thursday 26th October 2006, Lot 864, Pair to the 2nd Dragoons: Crimea 1854, 3 clasps, Balaclava, Inkermann, Sebastopol, officially impressed (R. Boyce. 2nd Dragoons.); Turkish Crimea, Sardinian issue, depot impressed (R. Boycs [sic] 2nd Dragoons), some contact wear, good fine (2) Hammer Price £2,000

The musters show he was effective from the 1st October to the 31st December.

1220 BRASSINGTON, Corporal Joseph
Born : Unknown
Enlisted :
Medals : Crimea (B.I.S)

Died : Unknown
Status : Probably rode in the Charge

The musters show he was effective as a Private from the 1st-25th October and as a Corporal from the 26th October to the 31st December. Promoted to Corporal after Cpl Clifford was killed in the Charge.

457 BRODIE, Private James
Born : Unknown
Enlisted : 28th November 1834
Medals : Crimea (B.I.S)

Died : 18th January 1857 - Ireland
Status : Probably rode in the Charge

Hamiltons Vol 2 No1 1974, item SG 1569 Pair, Crimea, 3 clasps (Balaclava, Inkermann, Sebastopol) J. Brodie, impressed; LS & GC Medal Large Lettering (James Brodie, Royal Scotch Greys) , Engraved naming Rare VF £550
Glendining's 20th June 1991, Lot 879, Pair to Pte. J. Brodie, 2nd Dragoons; Crimea, 1854, three bars, Balaclava, Inkermann, Sebastopol, officially impressed; Army L.S. & G.C., Vic., type 2 (James Brodie, Royal Scotch Greys), engraved [but not renamed] in upright serifed caps. Good very fine or better. (£350-450)
Dixons Gazette, No 33, Spring 2003, item no 73, J. Brodie, 2nd Dragoons (The Scots Greys), Crimea War Medal 1854-1856, 3 clasps, Balaclava, Inkermann, Sebastopol (2nd Dragns.); Army Long Service and Good Conduct Medal, Victoria issue, 2nd type 1855-1874 with swivelling scroll suspension, large lettering reverse, naming not quoted, regiment misspelt "Scotch Greys". (2) VF/GVF £1850

A ploughman from Dalkeith prior to enlisting at Edinburgh. The musters show he was effective from the 1st October to the 31st December. WO25 Discharge book shows he died 18th January 1857.

1070 BRODIE, Private William
Born : Unknown
Enlisted :
Medals : Crimea (B.I.S)

Died : Unknown
Status : Probably rode in the Charge

The musters show he was effective from the 1st October to the 31st December.

1164 BROOMFIELD, Private Thomas
Born : Unknown
Enlisted :
Medals : Crimea (B.I.S)

Died : Unknown
Status : Probably rode in the Charge

Sotheby's 30th January 1974, lot 225, Crimea 1 clasp "Balaclava" T.Broomfield 2nd Dgns. Impressed. Contact Marks. Almost VF.

The musters show he was effective from the 3rd October to the 31st December. Remarks state in Scutari Hospital 1st to the 3rd October.

The Victoria Cross

Two Victoria Crosses were won during the famous Charge of the Heavy Brigade at the Battle of Balaklava. On the 26th June 1857 the first presentation of the Victoria Cross was made by Queen Victoria in Hyde Park when over 100,000 people gathered to see the event. The troops on parade formed up under the command of Sir Colin Campbell who had commanded the "Thin Red Line". The Royal party arrived at 10am with Queen Victoria accompanied by an impressive entourage escorted by the Royal Horse Guards. The Queen wore a suitably adapted Field-Marshal's uniform and took her position for the ceremony with Prince Alfred. The recipients of the Victoria Cross were drawn up in front of the troops. When all was ready, each man filed past the Queen. The Secretary of State for War handed a medal to the Queen who stooped from her saddle and fixed it on the man's chest. The 48 Army recipients were presented to the Queen in regimental order of precedence, Sergeant Major John Grieve of the 2nd Dragoons headed the Army group. Although not chronologically the first army recipient of the Victoria Cross, Sergeant Major John Grieve has the distinction of receiving the first Army Victoria Cross gazetted and the first Army Victoria Cross presented.

517 BROWN, Troop Sergeant-Major Matthew

Born : Unknown

Enlisted :

Medals : Crimea (B.I.S), Distinguished Conduct Medal

Died : Unknown

Status : Slightly wounded in the Charge

The musters show he was effective from the 1st October to the 31st December. Listed on the Casualty Roll as slightly wounded at Balaclava. The musters show he sent £3 home to a "Jessie Brown". Recommendation for the Distinguished Conduct Medal submitted 7th February 1855, medal ordered 9th February 1855.

875 BROWN, Private John

Born : Unknown

Enlisted :

Medals : Crimea (B.I.S)

Died : Unknown

Status : Probably rode in the Charge

In the Needes collection - Crimea 1 clasp "Balaklava" J.Brown 2nd Dragoons. Impressed.

The musters show he was effective from the 1st October to the 31st December. The Medal Rolls show 875 John Brown entitled to a Crimea medal with S. clasp only as a Corporal, either incorrectly numbered or entered twice.

1138 BROWN, Private Thomas

Born : Unknown

Enlisted :

Medals : Crimea (B.S)

Died : Unknown

Status : Probably rode in the Charge

The musters show he was effective from the 1st-28th October. Remarks state sent to Scutari Hospital 28th October. WO100/24 page 159 Remarks: Sick at Scutari. WO14/1 Scutari Muster Roll January-March 1855, present January.

709 BROWNLIE, Private Robert

Born : Unknown

Enlisted :

Medals : Crimea (I.S)

Died : Unknown

Status : Effective during the period

The musters show he was effective from the 1st October to the 2nd November and from the 29th December to the 31st December. Remarks state sent to Scutari 3rd November, returned 28th December. WO14/1 Scutari Muster Roll January-March 1855 remarks indicate he joined on the 2nd February and was in Koulali Hospital, sent home on the 31st March. WO25 Discharge book shows he was discharged 4th April 1865.

842 BRUCE, Private Peter

Born : Unknown

Enlisted :

Medals : Crimea (B.I.S)

Died : Unknown

Status : Probably rode in the Charge

The musters show he was effective from the 1st October to the 31st December.

BRUSH, Surgeon John Ramsay

Born : 27th February 1817
Enlisted :
Medals : Crimea (B.I.S). Knight of the Legion of Honour

Died : 18th November 1891 - Clifton
Status : Rode in the Charge

Apothecaries Hall, London - Names of gentlemen who passed their examinations, and were admitted Licentiates on Thursday, June 25th, 1840:- John Ramsay Brush. (The Medical Times March to September 1840)

Assistant Surgeon 26th Foot 8th June 1841. Scots Greys 13th Oct 1843. Surgeon 93rd foot 2nd April 1852. Scots Greys Oct 1854. Retired on half pay 16th August 1861. Dr Brush served with the 26th Foot on the China Expedition 1842 (Medal) and with the 93rd Highlanders and the Scots Greys in the Crimea 1854-55. (Medal with 3 clasps, Turkish Medal, and Knight of the Legion of Honour) *Harts Annual Army List* shows he was stationed in Limerick in 1861.

A letter by Brush was published in *The Times* on the 17th August 1868 in which he corrects an error in Kinglake's Invasion of the Crimea regarding Col. H. Darby Griffith. In the lettter he states that during the Charge "I seized the bridle of Col Griffith's Horse and endeavoured to reach my field hospital in the rear of the 93rd Highlanders" (see Colonel Henry Darby Griffith's biography on page 103 for the full letter)

The following excerpts are taken from *Crimea Doctors Vol 1* by John Shepherd - page 219: "John Brush, Staff-Surgeon to the 2nd Dragoons, went into the thick of the fighting to bring out his Colonel, stunned and bleeding from a head wound. But the Colonel objected strongly to being removed from the field and later managed to escape from hospital to rejoin the Heavy Brigade when it went to the support of the Light Brigade in the North Valley." Also page 225: "In some reception units the techniques employed were not exactly refined, Brush and Chapple of the Greys working with their sleeves turned up, arms bloody, faces the same, looking more like butchers than surgeons."

During the month of October 1854 John Brush described their camp "In the valley of Balaclava, close to the town; the unhealthy site of their position, the noxious effluvia (arising from half-burned offal, dead horses lying exposed on the ground in the vicinity of the camp – and filth accumulated from men and horses) and the harassing duties which devolved upon the men contributed to render Diarrhoea and Fever the prevalent diseases." (*Medical and Surgical History of the British Army 1854-56*, page 30)

BUCHANAN, Captain George

Born : Unknown
Enlisted :
Medals : Crimea (B.I.S), Sardinian War Medal

Died : Unknown
Status : Rode in the Charge

Glendinings and Co Auction 27 February 1963 Lot 388. Elson Collection, Three to Capt. George Buchanan 2nd DGNS. Crimea three clasps Balaklava, Inkermann, Sebastopol, impressed naming. Sardinian War Medal engraved, Turkish Crimea un-named. Very Fine Hammer Price £62.00
Coin and Medal Quarterly. A.D. Hamilton, Glasgow. June 1976. Item GS 734. Crimea Medal Captain G. Buchanan 2nd Dragoon's. Crimea three clasps Balaklava, Inkermann, Sebastopol, impressed naming. The same medal was offered for sale again in June 1986 item WS 4454, this time in was entered as a Fletcher, Davies Forgery VF £550.
Glendining and Co 27th February 1963 lot 388, Three to Capt George Buchanan. Crimea B.I.S impressed naming, Sardinian War Medal Engraved, Turkish Crimea un-named
Sotheby 5th November 1986, Group of 3 medals to Capt. C.Buchanan 2nd (R.N.B) Dragoons. Crimea three clasps Balaklava, Inkermann, Sebastopol, Turkish Crimea Sardinian Version. Both engraved in neat contemporary style. Sardinian Al Valore Militare. Rev. officially Engraved. Contained in a contemporary fitted leather case. The lid inscribed "Crimea/ Capt. George Buchanan Royal Scots Greys" Hinges damaged. illustrated....A similar trio of medals including an Officially impressed Crimea medal is known to exist. Estimate £800 - £1000
Christies 18th November 1986 Lot 161. "The original group of three" Awarded to Cap E. Buchanan Est £1400-£1600. A similar group is known to exist, which includes an un-officially engraved Crimea medal and a named copy Turkish Crimea. Ex Elson Collection 1963.

The musters show he was effective as a Lieutenant from the 1st October to 23rd December and as a Captain from the 24th-31st December. WO100/24 page 176 Remarks: Gone to England.

The citation for the Sardinian War Medal states "This officer's conduct in the heavy cavalry charge at the action of Balaklava was cool and gallant, and by his example great execution was done against the enemy; he afterwards commanded a squadron under fire in support of the light brigade charge."

Hart's Annual Army list 1855. George Buchanan Cornet by purchase 16th March 1849, Lieutenant by purchase 27th August 1852., Captain 8th December 1854. Photograph taken at Newbridge Barracks in 1859.

1089 BURLEY, Private Peter

Born : Unknown
Enlisted :
Medals : Crimea (B.I.S)

Died : Unknown
Status : Slightly wounded in the Charge

The musters show he was effective from the 12th October to the 27th November. Remarks state at Scutari Hospital until the 11th October, sent back 28th November. WO100/24 page 159 Remarks: Sick at Scutari. Listed on the Casualty Roll as slightly wounded at Balaclava. WO14/1 Scutari Muster Roll January-March 1855 remarks indicate he was in Hospital during all three musters.

651 BURNS, Private George

Born : Unknown
Enlisted :
Medals : Crimea (B.I.S)

Died : Unknown
Status : Slightly wounded in the Charge

The musters show he was effective from the 1st October to the 31st December. Listed on the Casualty Roll as slightly wounded at Balaclava. WO14/1 Scutari Muster Roll January-March 1855 remarks indicate he joined on the 2nd March.

589 CAIRNES, Private William

Born : Date unknown - Canongate, Edinburgh
Enlisted : 13th March 1838
Medals : Crimea (I.S)

Died : Date unknown - Scutari
Status : Effective during the period

The musters show he was effective from the 1st October to the 2nd November. Remarks state sent to Scutari Hospital 3rd November; Dead. MR 159 Remarks Died at Scutari date unknown. Trade on enlistment Printer.

591 CAMERON, Private Archibald

Born : Unknown
Enlisted :
Medals : Crimea (B.I.S)

Died : Unknown
Status : Probably rode in the Charge

The musters show he was effective from the 1st October to the 31st December. WO25 Discharge book shows he was discharged on the 15th April 1862.

1253 CAMERON, Private James

Born : Unknown
Enlisted :
Medals : Crimea (B.I.S)

Died : Unknown
Status : Probably rode in the Charge

DNW auction 4th July 2001, Lot 402; Crimea medal 1854-56, 3 clasps Balaclava, Inkerman, Sebastopol, (J.Cameron, 2nd Dragn.) officially impressed naming, Sebastopol clasp loose as issued, minor edge bruise. Nearly EF. Hammer Price £780. A Long Service and Good Conduct has also appeared on the market.

The musters show he was effective from the 1st October to the 31st December.

1225 CAMPBELL, Corporal Francis

Born : Unknown
Enlisted :
Medals : Crimea (B.S)

Died : 29th November 1854 - Scutari
Status : Severely wounded in the Charge

Enlisted as an ordinary trooper under the name Francis Campbell as he did not have the funds available to purchase a commission. See entry as a Cornet under real name Francis Beaufort Maconochie page 127.

789 CAMPBELL, Private James

Born : Unknown
Enlisted :
Medals : Crimea (B.I.S)

Died : Unknown
Status : Probably rode in the Charge

The musters show he was effective from the 1st October to the 31st December.

910 CAMPBELL, Private Henry

Born : Date Unknown - Lordship, Louth, Ireland
Enlisted : 4th April 1846
Medals : Crimea (B.I.S)

Died : 25th October 1854 - Balaclava
Status : Killed in the Charge

Glendining's 28th September 1977, lot 123, Crimea 1 clasp "Balaclava" H.Campbell 2nd Dragoons, naming style not stated. Plus two other medals £240.
DNW, 23rd September 2005, lot 382, Crimea 1 clasp, "Balaclava" (H. Campbell, 2nd Dragoons) officially impressed naming, lacquered and with minor edge bruises, otherwise good very fine and of the highest rarity. Hammer Price £5500. It is normal that medals issued after a trooper's death would be officially impressed.

The musters show he was effective from the 1st October to the 25th October. Remarks state killed in action 25th October. Form 20 shows he had £1.5s 11-1/2d of remaining pay upon his death but does not indicate any next of kin. Listed on the Casualty Roll as killed at Balaclava. WO100/24 page 159 Remarks: Killed in Action 25th October. Trade on enlistment Labourer.

985 CAMPBELL, Private William

Born : Unknown
Enlisted :
Medals : Crimea (B.I.S), Long Service and Good Conduct Medal

Died : Unknown
Status : Slightly wounded in the Charge

The musters show he was effective from the 1st October to the 31st December. Also states next to his surname "alias Caulfield". Listed on the Casualty Roll as "William Caulfield" slightly wounded at Balaclava. WO102 L.S & G.C issued 7th July 1869, gratuity £5.

924 CANNING, Private James

Born : Unknown
Enlisted :
Medals : Crimea (B.I.S)

Died : Unknown
Status : Probably rode in the Charge

Glendining's 28th October 1971, Crimea 3 clasps "Balaclava","Inkermann","Sepastobol". Impressed naming (J.Canning 2 Dragoons) £52.00.

The musters show he was effective from the 1st October to the 31st December.

CHAPPLE, Assistant-Surgeon Robert Augustus

Born : 12th May 1832 - Limerick
Enlisted :
Medals : Crimea (S), The Turkish Order of the Medjidie (5th Class)

Died : 3rd September 1888 - Bombay
Status : Rode in the Charge

No effective dates shown in the musters, a line being drawn through both columns, however pay for 36 days is shown. Remarks state sent to Medical Staff 6th November.

Assistant Surgeon Chappell 28th April 1854, Surgeon 20th June 1865, Surgeon Major 1st March 1873, Brigade Surgeon 27th November 1879. (*Illustrated Histories of the Scottish Regiments No2. 2nd Dragoons by Lt Col Percy Groves*) Darwent research indicates Chappell was attached to the Scots Greys on their proceeding to the Crimea and was present at the battles of Balaklava (horse wounded) and Inkermann, and during the siege of Sebastopol. Harts Annual Army List 1857 indicates Chapple became Assistant-Surgeon on the 1st August 1855.

In some reception units the techniques used were not exactly refined "Brush and Chapple of the Greys working with their sleeves turned up, arms bloody, faces the same, looking more like butchers than surgeons. Brush had some surgical experiences before the war, his assistant was the young Robert Chapple". (*Crimea Doctors Vol 1 John Shepherd p 225*)

1136 CHRISTIE, Private James

Born : Unknown
Enlisted :
Medals : Crimea (B.I.S)

Died : Unknown
Status : Probably rode in the Charge

The musters show he was effective from the 1st October to the 31st December. Attended a Crimean War and Indian Mutiny Veterans parade in honour of the Queen in Edinburgh, May 1903.

1273 CHRISTIE, Private James

Born : Unknown
Enlisted :
Medals : Crimea (I.S)

Died : Unknown
Status : Effective during the period

The musters show he was effective from the 1st October to the 31st December.

1065 CLAPPERTON, Private James

Born : 1838 - Galashiels, Scotland
Enlisted :
Medals : Crimea (B.I.S)

Died : Unknown
Status : Probably rode in the Charge

The musters show he was effective from the 1st October to the 31st December. In the 1881 census his occupation is shown as a Draper's porter/Chelsea pensioner, aged 43, married, living at 69 Little Clifton Street, Sidwell, Devon, with his three sons and other relatives.

CLARKE, Brevet Lieutenant-Colonel George Calvert

Born : 23rd July 1814 - London
Enlisted :
Medals : Crimea (B.I.S), The Knight (5th Class) The French Legion of Honour, Turkish Order of the Medjidie (5th Class)

Died : 1900
Status : Severely wounded in the Charge

The musters show he was effective from the 1st October to the 31st December, three horses foraged at public expense. Listed on the Casualty Roll as severely wounded at Balaclava.

George Calvert Clarke C.B. Appointed 23rd September 1891 (succession of Colonels) Ensign 89th Foot 30th May 1834. Lieut 7th October 1836. Captain 20th September 1839. Scotts Greys 28th March 1845. Major 26th Feb 1858. Brevet. Lt.Col 12th December 1854 Scots Greys 31st March 1866. Half pay 3rd Feb 1869. Brev.Colonel 23rd April 1860. Major General 6th March 1868. Lieut General 1st October 1877. Colonel 6th Dragoon Guards, Colonel Scots Greys 23rd September 1891. Honorary General 1st July 1881. General Clarke served with the Scots Greys in the Crimea 1854-1855, including the affair of M'Kenzie's Farm; Battles of Balaclava (wounded), Inkermann, Techernaya and Siege and fall of Sebastopol. (*Ilustrated Histories of the Scottish Regiments No2. 2nd Dragoons by Lt Col Percy Groves. Page 28. See Appendix 1 page 25*)

The Greys were led by Colonel Darby Griffith, and the two squadron leaders who followed him were Major Clarke on the right, and Captain Williams on the left. Clarke's charger, known as "Sultan", was liable to be un-nerved by galloping squadrons, the horse was spooked which resulted in the Majors bearskin being displaced, falling to the ground. The religious Russians, on seeing the bare-headed officer believed that he was probably gifted with satanic powers, which were being used against the acres upon acres of flashing swords. Clarke received a deep cut on the skull by the edge of a sabre and was covered by blood covering his face and neck. (Kinglake's *Invasion of the Crimea* Vol V page 118-135)

A photograph of Clarke with his horse "Sultan" that was wounded at Balaklava taken by Roger Fenton in the Crimea is shown right.

General Calvert Clarke's father, John Calvert Clarke was tenant of Kidbrooke Hall, Forest Row. Soon after the boy's 15th birthday his father wrote to Major General Lord Fitzroy Somerset requesting support for his son to enter military service. Calvert-Clarke was eventually admitted to Sandhurst and subsequently commissioned. On retirement in 1870 he came to live in Uckfield taking an active part in local affairs. He became Chairman of the Board of Guardians and the Grammar School Governors; he supported the Uckfield Institute and the Horticultural and Music Societies in a variety of ways. He served as a Churchwarden during Church restoration in the 1880s. Lived at Church House, Church Street, Uckfield. (*Uckfield & District Preservation Society Newsletter, Volume 6 Summer 2000 by Simon Wright*)

Buried at Holy Cross church Uckfield, Sussex. He has a simple stone cross erected to his memory in the church yard and a magnificent window in the Church, erected after he died in 1900.

1200 CLIFFORD, Corporal Andrew Paul
Born : Date unknown - Dumbarton, Kilpatrick
Enlisted : 7th January 1853
Medals : Crimea (B.S)

Died : 25th October 1854 - Balaclava
Status : Killed in the Charge

The musters show he was effective from the 1st October to the 25th October. Remarks state Killed in action 25th October. Form 20 shows debts of fifteen shillings, seven and a half pence. Listed on the Casualty Roll as killed at Balaclava.

965 COLTER, Private James
Born : Unknown
Enlisted :
Medals : Crimea (B.I.S)

Died : Unknown
Status : Slightly wounded in the Charge

The musters show he was effective from the 1st October to the 31st December. Listed on the Casualty Roll as slightly wounded at Balaclava. WO25 Discharge book shows "to pension" 13th May 1873.

1161 COLVIN, Private George
Born : Date unknown - Haddington
Enlisted : 23rd January 1852
Medals : Crimea (B.I.S)

Died : 6th January 1855 - Scutari
Status : Probably rode in the Charge

The musters show he was effective from the 4th October to the 13th December. Remarks state he was at Scutari until the 3rd October and was sent back on the 14th December. WO100/24 page 159 Remarks: Sick at Scutari. WO14/1 Scutari Muster Roll January-March 1855 remarks indicate he died in January. Trade on enlistment Farrier

865 COMITTIE, Private Alexander
Born : Unknown
Enlisted :
Medals : Crimea (B.I.S)

Died : Unknown
Status : Probably rode in the Charge

The musters show he was effective from the 1st October to the 31st December.

936 CONNELL, Private William
Born : Unknown
Enlisted :
Medals : Crimea (B.I.S), The Distinguished Conduct Medal

Died : Unknown
Status : Slightly wounded in the Charge

The musters show he was effective from the 1st October to the 25th October. Remarks state sent to Scutari 26th October. Listed on the Casualty Roll as slightly wounded at Balaclava. WO100/24 page 159 Remarks: Sick at Scutari, page 180 Remarks: Gone to England. WO14/1 Scutari Muster Roll January-March 1855 remarks indicate he was sent home on the 11th January.

The recommendation for the Distinguished Conduct Medal is dated 13th January 1855; the medal was sent to the Crimea on the 26th March 1855 but was returned and sent to Chatham on the 14th May 1855 as Connell had been invalided home.

The Distinguished Conduct Medal was created on December 4, 1854 for the Crimean War, and was conferred on NCO's and Soldier's who were recommended for "Distinguished Conduct in the Field". It is the second highest award for gallantry in action after the Victoria Cross awared to military ranks below commissioned officers.

791 COWAN, Private George
Born : Date unknown - Lasswade
Enlisted : 13th December 1842
Medals : Crimea (B.I.S)

Died : 8th February 1855 - Scutari
Status : Probably rode in the Charge

The musters show he was effective from the 1st October to the 31st December. WO14/1 Scutari Muster Roll January-March 1855 remarks indicate he joined on the 25th January and died on the 8th February. Cowan was one of eighteen troopers from the 2nd Dragoons who arrived at Scutari between the 19th-28th January 1855, in total 63 men were admitted during January of which five died from Typhus and Diahorrea.

574 CRAWFORD, Private George

Born : Date unknown - Stirling
Enlisted : 6th December 1837
Medals : Crimea (B.I.S)

Died : 21st January 1855 - Scutari
Status : Probably rode in the Charge

The musters show he was effective from the 1st October to the 13th December. Remarks state sent to Scutari 14th December. WO14/1 Scutari Muster Roll January-March 1855 remarks indicate he died on the 21st Janaury. WO100/24 page 180 Remarks: Died 21st January 1855.

1029 CREE, Private John T.

Born : Unknown
Enlisted :
Medals : Crimea (B.I.S)

Died : Unknown
Status : Probably rode in the Charge

The musters show he was effective from the 1st October to the 31st December. WO100/24 page 180 Remarks: Gone to England. WO14/1 Scutari Muster Roll January-March 1855 remarks indicate he joined on the 2nd February and was in Koulali Hospital in February, sent home 31st March.

1122 CULMER, Private George

Born : Date unknown - Stonemouth, Kent
Enlisted : 19th November 1850
Medals : Crimea (B.I.S)

Died : 29th December 1854 - Scutari
Status : Probably rode in the Charge

The musters show he was effective from the 1st October to the 20th December. Remarks state sent to Scutari Hospital, died 29th December. WO14/1 Scutari Muster Roll January-March 1855 remarks indicate he died.

1131 CURRIE, Private Charles

Born : Unknown
Enlisted :
Medals : Crimea (B.I.S)

Died : Unknown
Status : Slightly wounded in the Charge

The musters show he was effective from the 4th October to the 31st December. Remarks state at Scutari to the 3rd October. Listed on the Casualty Roll as slightly wounded at Balaclava. Transferred to the 5th Lancers 10/3/1858.

DARBY GRIFFITH, Colonel Henry

Born : Unknown
Enlisted :
Medals : Crimea (B.I.S), The Turkish Order of the Medjidie (4th Class), The Sardinian War Medal

Died : 17th November 1887
Status : Slightly wounded in the Charge

Christie's 17th November 1987, Lot 113, Five: Major General H. Darby Griffith, 2nd Dragoons, Royal Scots Greys, Order of the Bath, Companion (C.B.), 22ct., gold (Georgian hallmarks for London) with its gold riband buckle; Crimea, three clasps, Balaklava, Inkermann, Sebastopol (Col. Henry Darby Griffith, Scots Greys), engraved in large serif capitals; Sardinia, Al Valore Militaire, 1855-56, reverse re-inscribed, 'Colonel H. Darby Griffiths C.B. 2nd Dragoons'; Turkey, Order of the Medjidie, Fourth Class, Badge, gold centre, silver and enamel; Turkish Crimea, Sardinian issue, regimentally impressed (5) Hammer Price £3,300

Major General Henry Darby Griffith entered the army as a Cornet in 1828, Lieutenant 1831, Captain August 1834, Major 1846, Lieutenant Colonel 1852; served in the Crimea 1854-55 in command of the 2nd Dragoons, Scots Greys, was present at McKenzie's Farm, led his regiment in the Charge of the Heavy Brigade at Balaklava and also the Battles at Inkermann, Tchernaya and the siege of Sebastopol (C.B., Sardinian Medal and Order of the Medjidie); Major General 1866. The citation for the Sardinian War Medal states (He) "served in the campaign of 1854-5; commanded his regiment at the Battle of Balaklava". Listed on the Casualty Roll as slightly wounded at Balaclava.

Colonel 28th Nov 1854. Major General 31st March 1866. Lieut Gen 14th April 1874. General 1st October 1877. Colonel 5th Lancers 1st Jan 1872 until his death in 1887. Medal with 3 clasps. C.B, Sardinian and Turkish Medals 4th class of the Medjidie. A.D.C to the Queen. he died near Dover 17th November 1887. (*Illustrated Histories of the Scottish Regiments No2. 2nd Dragoons* by Lt Col Percy Groves, page 28)

He was wounded at Balaclava by a pistol ball in the head. Was the second son of General Matthew Chitty Darby, of Padworth, Warks. who assumed by Royal Licence the additional surname of Griffith in 1801, who served with the Grenadier Guards during the Peninsula War and was severely wounded at Corunna, losing a leg.

General Darby Griffith married a Miss Bainbridge and died without issue on 17th November 1887. See leaflet below concerning the alleged marriage of Henry Darby Griffith to Martha Bainbridge. (Falkirk Archive A72-4270)

A letter by J. Ramsay Brush was published in the Times on the 17th August 1868 in which he corrects an error in Kinglake's Invasion of the Crimea Vol. 4 regarding Col. H. Darby Griffith. The letter reads:

"Sir - In justice to Colonel, now Major-General, Griffith, who commanded the Scots Greys at the battle of Balaclava, I trust you will permit me to correct in your columns an erroneous statement made regarding him in Mr Kinglake's fourth volume of the Invasion of the Crimea.

Mr Kinglake says, at page 159, "Colonel Griffith, commanding the Greys, was so struck, it seems, by a shot in the head as to be prevented from continuing to lead on his regiment," and that Major Clarke had acceded to the command without knowing it. This is not the fact. I was present in this affair with my regiment, the Greys, and saw Colonel Griffith lead them into the dense mass of the Russian cavalry, go through them and into their supports, when the regiment went about and cut their way back again, Colonel Griffith being still in command. Observing that the colonel was bleeding from the head and suffering from the stunning effects of the blow he had received, I ordered his trumpeter to go in search of Major Clarke and tell him that he had succeeded to the command, and at the same time, perceiving that the Russian cavalry were again outflanking us, I seized the bridle of Colonel Griffith's horse and endeavoured to reach my field hospital in rear of the 93rd Highlanders. We had not gone many yards when the flank charge of the 4th and 5th Dragoon Guards was made, which, with a second charge of the Greys and Inniskillings, sent the Russian cavalry flying, a disorganized mass, up the hill and enabled us to reach our destination. When the report arrived that the Light Cavalry had been destroyed Colonel Griffith left the field hospital without my knowledge, rejoined his regiment, and resumed the command, which he continued to hold throughout the day. The above, Sir, is a brief statement of facts.

Mr Kinglake does not seem to be aware that there were two distinct and separate charges of "Scarlett's Dragoons." The first, in which the Greys and one squadron of the Inniskillings were alone engaged; and the second, in which those regiments were assisted by a flank attack of the 4th and 5th Dragoon Guards and the Royals. In the interval between these two charges the Russians retired a short way up the hill and reformed, the Greys and Inniskillings following suit. Colonel Griffith led the Greys in the first charge, which was by far the most formidable one, and brought them out of it; and it is the assertion on the part of Mr Kinglake that he was prevented from doing this that I must request you will permit me to contradict.

My sole object is to do justice to an officer who remained in command of his regiment during the whole period of the Crimean War, and from whom Mr Kinglake has - I would believe unintentionally - taken the credit due and given it to another.

I am, Sir, your most obedient servant, J Ramsay Brush, MD, late Surgeon Royal Scots Greys, Camden-crescent, Bath."

This prompted Kinglake to write to Henry Darby Griffith and a reply from Darby Griffth was printed in Kinglake's Invasion of the Crimea Vol. 6.

SHORTLY WILL BE PUBLISHED,
TO ALL WHOM THESE PRESENTS MAY CONCERN,
The POLLUTION of the Forms of the Sacred Altar
OF
THE ESTABLISHED CHURCH;
AND A MISREPRESENTATION IN THE MORNING POST, & OTHER NEWSPAPERS,
By HENRY DARBY GRIFFITH,
Youngest Son of the late Major-General Darby Griffith, of Padworth House, Berks,
AND
(Lieutenant of the 35th Regiment of Foot, lately promoted to be a Captain in the same Regiment, by the honorable means of Money,)
RELATIVE TO HIS ALLEGED MARRIAGE TO MARTHA,
YOUNGEST DAUGHTER OF THE LATE THOMAS BAINBRIDGE, Esq. of Croydon Lodge, Surrey,
ON THE 22nd DAY OF AUGUST, 1833,
By the Rev. Bryant Burgess, at the New Church in the Parish of St. Mary-la-Bonne,
Assumed to be witnessed by Henry Browning, Esq. 4, Gloucester Place, Portman Square, Thomas S. Waters, Esq. C. H. Gardiner, Esq. and Miss Emma Gardiner, of Whitchurch, near Reading, and C. Darby Griffith.

" They are all profane; yea, in my house have I found their wickedness, saith the Lord."
JEREMIAH, chap. 23, ver. 11.
" They have prepared a net for my steps, my soul is bowed down; they have digged a pit before me, into the midst whereof they are fallen *themselves.*"
PSALM 57, ver. 6.

770 DAVIDSON, Troop Sergeant-Major James

Born : Date unknown - Roxburgh
Enlisted : 9th August 1842
Medals : Crimea (B.S)

Died : 2nd January 1855 - Scutari
Status : Slightly wounded in the Charge

The musters show he was effective from the 1st-25th October and from the 10th November to the 3rd December. Remarks state he was sent to Scutari Hospital on the 26th October, returning on the 10th November but was sent back to Scutari Hospital on the 3rd December. Listed on the Casualty Roll as slightly wounded at Balaclava. WO14/1 Scutari Muster Roll January-March 1855 remarks indicate he died on the 2nd January. WO100/24 page 157 and 177 Remarks: Sick at Scutari. Died 2nd January 1855.

872 DAVIDSON, Corporal Donald
Born : Unknown
Enlisted :
Medals : Crimea (B.S)

Died : Unknown
Status : Slightly wounded in the Charge

DNW Auction 4th December 2001 Lot 73. Crimea 1854-56, 2 clasps, Balaklava, Sebastopol (Corpl. D. Davidson, 2nd Dragns.) officially impressed naming, suspension post repaired, contact marks and edge bruising, otherwise very fine Hammer Price £1200

The musters show he was effective from the 1st-25th October and from the 29th December to the 31st December. Remarks sent to Scutari 26th October returned 29th December. Listed Private on the Casualty Roll slightly wounded at Balaclava. WO25 Discharge book shows he discharged 23th November 1861.

1216 DAVIS, Private William
Born : Unknown
Enlisted :
Medals : Crimea (B.S)

Died : Unknown
Status : Severely wounded in the Charge

The musters show he was effective from the 1st October-25th October. Remarks state sent to Scutari 26th October. Listed on the Casualty Roll as severely wounded at Balaclava. WO100/24 page 159 Remarks: Sick at Scutari.

1240 DAWSON, Corporal Thomas
Born : Unknown
Enlisted :
Medals : Crimea (B.I.S)

Died : Unknown
Status : Probably rode in the Charge

The musters show he was effective from the 1st October to the 31st December.

1040 DEARDEN, Troop Sergeant-Major James
Born : 1823 - Edinburgh, Scotland
Enlisted : 23rd January 1841
Medals : Crimea (B.I.S)

Died : Unknown
Status : Slightly wounded in the Charge

Bought by John Darwent from Glendining's retail sale list in February 1996 item No 278, cost £950. Sold at DNW 17th September 2004: Crimea 1854-56, 3 clasps, Balaklava, Inkermann, Sebastopol (Serjt. J. Dearden, 2nd Dragoons) officially impresssed naming; Army L.S. & G.C., V.R., small letter reverse (1040 Tp. Sergt. Mjr. Jas. Dearden, 2nd Dragoons) officially impressed naming; Turkish Crimea, Sardinian issue (Troop Sergt. Major, 2nd Dragoons) engraved naming, all three fitted with contemporary silver ribbon buckles, light contact marks, otherwise nearly very fine or better (3) Sold with copy discharge papers. Hammer price £5000.

James Dearden was born in Edinburgh and enlisted into the 8th Hussars at Dublin on 23rd January 1841, aged 18 years 2 months. Promoted to Corporal in December 1845, he transferred as a Private to the 2nd Dragoons in September 1848. He was again promoted to Corporal in December 1849, to Sergeant in November 1852, and to Troop Sergeant Major in July 1854. In this rank he served in the Crimea where he was "wounded in the left thumb by Grape Shot received in action at Balaklava 25th October 1854." He reverted to Sergeant for a period of six months in July 1855 before regaining his senior rank, and was discharged at Aldershot on the 21st March 1865. His discharge papers carry a later notification of an increase in his pension "for 15 years service as Serjt. on Permt. Staff of Earl of Chester's Yeomy. Cav."

The musters show he was effective from the 1st October to the 25th October. Sent to Scutari Hospital 26th October. Listed on the Casualty Roll as slightly wounded at Balaclava. WO100/24 page 157 Remarks: Scutari sick. Shown on the musters as James Deardon. WO14/1 Scutari Muster Roll January-March 1855 remarks indicate he was on a Hospital Ship from the 1st-28th January and at Abydos during February and March.

Shown in the 1881 census as James Dearden, living with his wife Mary aged 48, at 29 Parkfield Terrace, Witton Cum Twambrooks, Cheshire, Occupation shown as "Troop Sergt Major From The Cavalry (Army Pensioner Unemployed)". Witton-Cum-Twambrooks is a parochial chapelry and township, which forms the populous, eastern suburb of the township of Northwich.

The Recruit

A room at the Hampshire Hog, Charles-Street, Westminster, is the place represented in the sketch. In the foreground is a light cavalry Sergeant about to give the shilling to a new recruit. In the background another sergeant is measuring the stature of a young military aspirant, who seems to have drawn himself to his full height for the occasion. The Hampshire Hog has long been a "a noted house" for cavalry recruits.

Many of the recruits came from rural backgrounds. The country recruit with his strong physique and what was considered a slower turn of mind was much preferred as a private soldier. Some Gaelic speaking Scotsmen and Irishmen could not even understand English before enlisting. So many Irishmen took the Shilling that a large proportion of the troopers came from Ireland. With a fearsome reputation for looting, drinking, brawling and desertion they were kept in check by flogging, and imprisonment.

The tale of a Kerry recruit is told in the song below.

Picture from The Illustrated London News 20th Jan 1855

The Kerry Recruit
At the age of nineteen, I was diggin' the land
With me brogues on me feet and me spade in me hand.
Says I to meself, "What a pity to see
Such a fine Kerry lad footing turf in Tralee."
Chorus:
To me Kerry-I-Ah, fa lal deral lay,
Kerry-I-Ah, fa lal deral lay.
So I buttered me brogues and shook hands with me spade
Went off to the fair like a dashing young blade.
A sergeant come up and said "Would ye enlist?"
"Sure, sergeant," says I, "Slip the bob in me fist".
Chorus:
The next place they took us was down to the sea,
Aboard a great warship, bound for the Crimee,
Three sticks in the middle, all covered with sheet
She walked on the water without any feet.

Chorus:
We whipped them at Alma and at Inkerman
But the Russians they foiled us along the Redan.
While scaling a rampart meself lost an eye
And a great Russian bullet ran away with me thigh.
Chorus:
All dyin' and bleedin' I lay on the ground,
With arms, legs and feet all scattered around.
Says I to meself, "If me father was nigh
He would bury me, sure, just for fear I might die."
Chorus:
But a surgeon come up and he soon staunched the blood,
And he gave me an elegant leg made of wood;
And they gave me a medal and tenpence a day
Contented with Sheelagh I live on half-pay.

1027 DEARDON, Trumpeter Robert

Born : Unknown
Enlisted :
Medals : Crimea (B.I.S)

Died : Unknown
Status : Probably rode in the Charge

The musters show he was effective from the 1st October to the 31st December.

731 DEER, Private George

Born : Unknown
Enlisted :
Medals : Crimea (B.I.S)

Died : 16th January 1864
Status : Probably rode in the Charge

The musters show he was effective from the 1st October to the 31st December. WO25 shows he died 16/1/1864.

892 DICKSON, Private David

Born : Unknown
Enlisted :
Medals : Crimea (B.I.S), Long Service and Good Conduct Medal

Died : Unknown
Status : Probably rode in the Charge

The musters show he was effective from the 1st October to the 31st December. WO102 L.S & G.C issued 24th July 1867, gratuity £5.

1189 DONALDSON, Private William

Born : Date unknown - Edinburgh
Enlisted :
Medals : Crimea (B.S)

Died : Unknown
Status : Severely wounded in the Charge

Glendining's Auction 28th October 1978 Lot 358. Pair to W.Donaldson. Crimea two Bars "Balaklava" "Sebastopol" Pte R.N.B, DGS. Engraved Naming. Turkish Crimea Sardinian issue Pte Scots Greys. VF £130

The musters show he was effective from the 1st-25th October. Remarks state sent to Scutari Hospital. Listed on the Casualty Roll as severely wounded at Balaclava. WO14/1 Scutari Muster Roll January-March 1855 remarks indicate he was sent home 21st January. WO100/24 page 180 Remarks: Gone to England.

Donaldson was nursed at Scutari by nurse Sarah Anne Terrot, one of the Sellonite Sisters of Mercy; "Another of the Scot's Greys lay on his other side....The younger named William Donaldson recovered more quickly and was sent home before his friend. Donaldson lost his leg in the second Balaclava Charge when the Greys and 1st Royals tried to cover the retreat of the Light Brigade. His horse was also disabled, so that it was with great difficulty he got away trying to crawl with his poor shattered leg. At first looking at his leg and seeing the flow of blood, he thought in twenty minutes it will all be over, and lay still. Trying to collect his thoughts and prepare for the great change. Then feeling the blood flowing less rapidly, he looked out for help and seeing the Duke of Cambridge riding called out "If noone is coming to help me will your Royal Highness shoot me through the head" Soon after some soldier's came and carried him, but his sorrows were not over, for some officers seeing so many carrying one man ordered them back to their regiments and he was left again. At last some turks came and lifted him so roughly he fainted and became unconscious. They took him to the Field Hospital, where his leg was taken off rather high up, and he was carried to the ship and taken to Scutari. On his way to the ship he waved his arm and cried "Huzza for auld reekie" he was only eighteen and seemed to have a robust constitution. He was also cheerful, patient, and sweet tempered which contributed to his recovery. The good Queen's letter was a great comfort to some of the poor men as well as to us. The assistance of her sympathy was deeply valued. Donaldson got a copy of it and put it over his head and on my noticing it he looked up with a sweet expression and said "Yes, it's very affecting and makes our suffering less to think she cares so for us." (*Nurse Sarah Anne by R.G Richardson page 146*)

The letter from the Queen which was so prized by Donaldson was written by Her Majesty in December 1854. In it she wrote, "no one takes a warmer interest, or feels more for their suffering, or admires their courage and heroism more than their Queen". The "Queen's Letter" as it became known, was written privately, but published in the press. It was well received and was copied and distributed among the sick and wounded in the hospital at Scutari on the Bosphorous, the main hospital for the British Army.

Queen Victoria also instituted the Patriotic Fund to co-ordinate the collection and distribution of money donated by the public for the widows and orphans of men killed during the Crimean War. Commissioners were appointed across the country for this purpose and the aid was distributed according to the needs of each family.

890 DORSETT, Private Edward

Born : Unknown
Enlisted :
Medals : Crimea (B.I.S)

Died : Unknown
Status : Probably rode in the Charge

The musters show he was effective from the 1st October to the 31st December. WO100/24 page 159 Remarks: Farrier.

1039 DOWNIE, Private Peter

Born : Unknown
Enlisted :
Medals : Crimea (B.I.S)

Died : Unknown
Status : Probably rode in the Charge

The musters show he was effective from the 1st October to the 31st December. WO100/24 page 180 Remarks: Gone to England.

1076 DRYSDALE, Private John

Born : Unknown
Enlisted :
Medals : Crimea (S)

Died : Unknown
Status : Effective during the period

The musters show he was effective from the 1st-26th October. Remarks state sent to Scutari Hospital 27th October. His entry on the Medal Rolls is hard to decipher. WO14/1 Scutari Muster Roll January-March 1855 remarks indicate he was in Hospital during January and February, sent home 31st March. WO25 Discharge book shows he discharged Sept 1861.

1173 FARRELL, Trumpeter Edward

Born : Unknown
Enlisted :
Medals : Crimea (B.I.S)

Died : Unknown
Status : Probably rode in the Charge

The musters show he was effective from the 1st October to the 31st December. Also shown as a Private.

1174 FAWKE, Private Walter

Born : Unknown
Enlisted :
Medals : Crimea (I.S)

Died : Unknown
Status : Slightly wounded in the Charge

The musters show he was effective from the 1st October to the 13th December. Remarks state sent to Scutari 14th Dec. Listed on the Casualty Roll as slightly wounded at Balaclava. WO14/1 Scutari Muster Roll January-March 1855 remarks indicate he was in Hospital during January. The casualty roll entry suggests that his ommision from the Balaclava clasp roll must be a mistake. WO25 Discharge book shows he was invalided out 9th February 1864. (See page 360)

1028 FERGUSON, Sergeant John

Born : Unknown
Enlisted :
Medals : Crimea (B.I.S)

Died : Unknown
Status : Probably rode in the Charge

The musters show he was effective from the 1st October to the 31st December. Promoted to Sergeant 1st October following the promotion of Tilsley to T.S.M.

661 FINDLATER, Private Gilbert

Born : Date unknown - Penport
Enlisted : 21st August 1839
Medals : Crimea (S)

Died : 4th January 1855 - Scutari
Status : Effective during the period

The musters show he was effective from the 1st October to the 18th December. Remarks state sent to Scutari 19th December. WO14/1 Scutari Muster Roll January-March 1855 remarks indicate he died on the 4th January.

1242 FISHER, Private Hugh

Born : Date unknown - Tacholton, Ayr
Enlisted :
Medals : Crimea (B.I.S)

Died : 16th June 1855 - Scutari
Status : Probably rode in the Charge

The musters show he was effective from the 1st October to the 31st December. WO14/1 Scutari Muster Roll January-March 1855 remarks indicate he joined on the 28th January and was in Koulali Hospital in January, Hospital February and March. WO100/24 page 180 Remarks: Died 16th June 1855.

691 FLANAGAN, Armourer Sergeant John

Born : Unknown
Enlisted :
Medals : Crimea (I.S)

Died : Unknown
Status : Probably rode in the Charge

The musters show he was effective from the 1st October to the 27th November. WO14/1 Scutari Muster Roll January-March 1855 remarks indicate he returned to his regiment on the 3rd February 1855. 157 remarks Sick at Scutari (Inkermann Medal Roll) 176 remarks gone to England.

1179 FLEMMING, Private James

Born : Unknown
Enlisted :
Medals : Crimea (B.I.S)

Died : Unknown
Status : Probably rode in the Charge

The musters show he was effective from the 1st October to the 13th December. Remarks state sent to Scutari 14th December. WO100/24 page 159 Remarks: Sick at Scutari. WO14/1 Scutari Muster Roll January-March 1855 remarks indicate he was in Hospital during January and February. WO25 Discharge book shows he was discharged in 1857.

1092 FLOCKHART, Sergeant James
Born : Unknown
Enlisted :
Medals : Crimea (B.S)

Died : Unknown
Status : Probably rode in the Charge

Christies 19th July 1983, Lot 196, Pair to Sergeant J. Flockhart, 2nd. Dragoons, Crimea 1854 - 56, three bars Balaklava, Inkermann, Sebastopol. (Serjt. 2nd Dragns), officially impressed; Turkish Crimea, Sardinian die (S.J.Flockhart, 2nd Dragoons) Good Fine and Better with Silver Riband Brooches. Spink 12th July 1994, Lot 256, Pair to Sergeant J.Flockhart, 2nd. Dragoons, Crimea 1854 - 56, three bars Balaklava, Inkermann, Sebastopol. (Serjt. 2nd Dragns), officially impressed; Turkish Crimea, Sardinian die (S.J.Flockhart, 2nd Dragoons), Very fine.

The musters show he was effective as a Corporal from the 1st October to the 2nd November. Remarks state sent to Scutari 2nd November. WO100/24 page 158 Remarks: At Scutari sick. WO14/1 Scutari Muster Roll January-March 1855 remarks indicate he was on a Hospital Ship in January and February. WO25 Discharge book shows he was invalided 26th October 1861.

1098 FOSTER, Private John
Born : Unknown
Enlisted :
Medals : Crimea (B.I.S)

Died : Unknown
Status : Probably rode in the Charge

The musters show he was effective from the 1st October to the 31st December. Discharged 17th December 1862.

647 FOSTER, Private Richard
Born : Date unknown - Abbylaer
Enlisted : 19th March 1839
Medals : Crimea (B.S)

Died : 2nd January 1855 - Scutari
Status : Severely wounded in the Charge

In February 1979 his medal was in Dr. W.A. Land's collection in Australia. London Stamp Exchange List "OMRS Convention" 1983 item 39. Crimea two clasps Balaklava, Sebastopol, R.Foster. 2nd Dragoons. Officially impressed. NEF £565. For sale on medal list of E.G Ursual Ontario, Canada 1984, No 51, item 82. Crimea 2 clasps Balaklava, Sebastopol, R.Foster. 2nd Dragoons. Officially impressed naming. EF $1150. Sotheby 7th November 1985, Lot 558 Crimea with 2 clasps Balaklava, Sebastopol, R.Foster 2 Dngns, offically impressed E.K's Otherwise VF and toned Est £250-£300.

The musters show he was effective from the 1st October to the 25th October and from the 10th November to the 13th December. Remarks state sent to Scutari Hospital 26th October, returned 10th November, sent back to Scutari 14th December. Listed on the Casualty Roll as severely wounded at Balaclava. WO100/24 page 159 Remarks: Sick at Scutari, page 180 Remarks: Died 2nd. January 1855. WO14/1 Scutari Muster Roll January-March 1855 remarks indicate he died 2nd January.

881 GALBRAITH, Private McAdam
Born : Date unknown - Dalmallington
Enlisted : 2nd December 1845
Medals : Crimea (B.S)

Died : Date unknown - Scutari
Status : Severely wounded in the Charge

The musters show he was effective from the 1st-25th October. Remarks state sent to Scutari Hospital 26th October. Listed on the Casualty Roll as severely wounded at Balaclava. WO100/24 page 160 Remarks: Died of wounds date unknown.

1035 GARDINER, Private Alexander Douglas
Born : c. 1826 - Norwich
Enlisted : 14th April 1848
Medals : Crimea (B.S)

Died : 14th May 1879 - Warrington
Status : Severely wounded in the Charge

Sotheby 5th November 1981. Lot 187 Family Group identical to the group sold by DNW below. Purchased by Imperial Medals, Clayton-le-Woods for £550. Later in the Greeson Collection. DNW 23rd September 2005, Lot 380, Gardiner Family Group to Sergeant-Major Alexander Gardiner, wounded with the Scots Greys at Waterloo, whose son lost a leg with the Greys at Balaklava and was plucked to safety by Private Ramage who thus won the Victoria Cross, and to his grandson who served with the Imperial Yeomanry in the Boer War. (a) Waterloo 1815 (Corp. Alexander Gardner, 2nd or R.N. Brit. Reg. Drag.) fitted with original steel clip and bar suspension (b) Crimea 1854-55, 2 clasps, Balaklava, Sebastopol (Pte. A. D. Gardiner, 2d Drgns.) contemporary engraved naming; Turkish Crimea, British issue, unnamed (c) Queen's South Africa 1899-1902, 2 clasps, Cape Colony, South Africa 1902 (38905 Pte. W. E. Gardiner, 32nd Bn. Imp. Yeo.) the first with edge bruising and contact marks, therefore good fine, otherwise good very fine (4) Accompanied by a comprehensive archive of research. Hammer Price £6,800

Alexander Gardiner, father of Alexander Douglas Gardiner, was born at New Kilpatrick, Dunbarton, Scotland, circa 1794, and enlisted for the 2nd Dragoons at Glasgow on 25 January 1809, aged 15 years. Promoted to Corporal in April 1815, he served at Waterloo in Captain Poole's Troop, and is noted in the various rolls as having been wounded. He was promoted to Sergeant in August 1818, and to Troop Sergeant-Major in January 1826. He was, however, reduced to Private from November 1829 until February 1830, when he was restored to the rank of Sergeant. He was discharged at Dalkeith on 5th May 1835, aged 41, intending to reside at Oswestry, Salop, where he died in June 1848. The local newspaper, Eddowes's Journal and General Advertiser for Shropshire, and the Principality of Wales, carried a lengthy report on Wednesday 28th June covering the 'Funeral of the late Sergeant-Major Gardiner, late of the Scots Greys.' He was buried with full military honours with an escort being provided by the North Shropshire Yeomanry. 'The late Sergeant-Major,' the report concluded, 'served in the Greys twenty five years, was with that fine regiment at Waterloo, and has now three sons in its ranks, the eldest of whom is a corporal, and all respected by their commanding officers.'

Alexander Douglas Gardiner was born at Norwich, circa 1826, second son of Troop Sergeant-Major Alexander Gardiner, who was then stationed in that town. He enlisted into the 2nd Dragoons at Athlone on 14th April 1848, being recruited by his brother, Private James Gardiner, of the same regiment. He was, in fact, one of three brothers to follow into their father's regiment, the now famous Scots Greys. Aged 22, he enlisted for a period of 12 years, but army life cannot have been to his immediate liking, if ever it was, as he had committed some misdemeanour before the year's end that landed him in prison for a week. He was in trouble again in August 1851, this time serving a sentence of three months. Gardiner was so severely wounded at Balaclava that he was discharged from the army at Chatham on 23rd October 1855, in consequence of being 'disabled by amputation of left thigh at its centre after cannon shot wound received at Balaklava.'

Gardiner's wound, which was reported in the London Gazette on 12th November 1854, and the circumstances of the occasion are of great interest in that his life was saved by Private Henry Ramage, who won the Victoria Cross on that day. His citation reads: "At the battle of Balaklava, Pte. McPherson, of the 2nd Dragoons, was severely wounded and surrounded by seven Russians. Pte. Ramage rode to his help, cut his way through the enemy and saved his comrade's life. On the same day, when the Heavy Brigade was covering the retreat of the Light Cavalry, Pte. Gardiner's leg was shattered by a round shot, and he lay on the ground exposed to a very heavy cross-fire. Ramage dashed to his rescue and carried him to the rear, the place where he had fallen being almost immediately covered by Russian cavalry." Alexander D. Gardiner died at Warrington on 14 May 1879, aged 52 years.

Wilfred Ernest Gardiner, the son of Alexander Douglas Gardiner, was born at St Paul's, near Warrington, Lancashire, on 10th May 1872, the fifth child and second son of Alexander Douglas Gardiner. He volunteered for service with the Imperial Yeomanry in South Africa at Worsley on 6th January 1902. He served in South Africa with the 144th Company, 32nd Battalion, Imperial Yeomanry, from 7th May until 18th October, 1902, just in time to witness the closing stages of the Boer War. He was discharged at Aldershot on 26th October 1902, at his own request after serving for only 294 days. He subsequently pursued a career as a Foreman Engineer, and died at Manchester on 29th April 1946, aged 73 years.

The musters show he was effective from the 1st-25th October. Remarks state sent to Scutari Hospital 26th October. Listed on the Casualty Roll as severely wounded at Balaclava. WO100/24 page 181 Remarks: Gone to England. WO14/1 Scutari Muster Roll January-March 1855 remarks indicate he was in Hospital in January and at Abydos until the 24th February.

The War Correspondent Vol 24, No 1, April 2006: Helen and Ian Smith forwarded to the Editor several snippets-the first, from the Osweslry Advertiser, March 1856, concerned a local 'Balaklava Hero', Private Douglas Alexander Gardiner, who lost a leg as a result of taking part in the Battle of Balaklava with the 2nd Royal North British Dragoons (The Scots Greys). His father, the late Sergeant-Major Gardiner of the North Shropshire Yeomanry, had also previously served with the 'Greys' and had taken part in the Charge at Waterloo. Three of his sons followed him into the regiment. A subscription to buy an artificial leg for Douglas was started, but failed to raise the required amount, resulting in Mr. Fox, a local bank manager, writing to the Queen. He received the following reply: "Windsor Castle, Feb. 5th, 1856. Sir- I have had the honour to lay before Her Majesty the Queen your letter of the 4th instant, and I have received Her Majesty's commands to desire that Douglas A. Gardiner may be supplied with a cork leg, and that you will send me the account of the expences (sic) incurred, beyond the subscriptions already collected, which I have received Her Majesty's commands to defray. It will give the Queen much pleasure thus to be able to alleviate the privations of a wounded soldier. I have the honour to be, Sir, your obedient humble servant, C.B. Phipps (Queen's Private Secretary)".

1243 GAUNT, Private Frederick R

Born : Date unknown - Worthley
Enlisted : 4th March 1854
Medals : Crimea (B.I.S)

Died : 30th January 1855 - Scutari
Status : Probably rode in the Charge

The musters show he was effective from the 1st October to the 31st December. WO14/1 Scutari Muster Roll January-March 1855 remarks indicate he joined on the 28th January and was in Koulali Hospital in January, died 30th January.

947 GIBSON, Cornet David

Born : Unknown
Enlisted :
Medals : Crimea (B.S)

Died : Unknown
Status : Severely wounded in the Charge

The musters show he was effective as a Sergeant from the 1st-25th October and as a Cornet from the 5th November to the 31st December. Second muster endorsed Scutari the third muster endorsed Mule Depot. Remarks state promoted from Sergeant 5th November. Listed on the Casualty Roll as severely wounded at Balaclava. WO100/24 page 195 Remarks: This Officer was retd. as a Sergt. in a former return since promoted.

1250 GIBSON, Private William

Born : Unknown
Enlisted :
Medals : Crimea (B.I.S), Long Service and Good Conduct Medal

Died : Unknown
Status : Probably rode in the Charge

The musters show he was effective from the 1st October to the 31st December. WO25 Discharge book shows he went to pension as a Sergeant 31st July 1877. Attended the War Veterans Dinner held at the Empress Rink, Nottingham, on Tuesday 20th June 1911. A publication by H.Seely Whitby, page 24 records - 2nd Dragoons. (Royal Scots Greys) 1250 William Gibson. 3 medals Crimean 3 clasps, Long Service & Good Conduct, Turkish.

1033 GILMOUR, Private William

Born : Unknown
Enlisted :
Medals : Crimea (B.I.S)

Died : Unknown
Status : Probably rode in the Charge

The musters show he was effective from the 1st October to the 31st December. Discharged 12th May 1857.

795 GLANCEY, Private Charles

Born : c. 1823 - Tradiston, Glasgow
Enlisted : 5th September 1843
Medals : Crimea (B.I.S)

Died : Unknown
Status : Slightly wounded in the Charge

A.H Baldwin & Sons, September 1934, item 8000 - Crimea 3 clasp medal "Balaclava", "Inkermann", "Sebastopol", C.Clancy, 2nd Dragoons. Fair State. Dixons Gazette, No 32, Winter 2002, item 4260, Private Charles Glancy, 2nd Dragoons. Crimea Medal 1854-56, 3 clasps, Balaclava, Inkermann, Sebastopol (2nd. Dragns.) Officially impressed with unofficial correction to "N" in name; Turkish Crimea Medal, British issue, Unnamed. Both with a superb, silver pin backed top buckle, which features the Scots Greys Eagle insignia, surmounted on a straight Laurel leaf bar. The reverse stamped; B. Bailey Coventry Regd Oct 10 1856 No.3888.(2) Sold with photocopy service record which details wounds and medal and clasp entitlement. Fine and a superb pair £1850

A joiner prior to enlistment at Glasgow aged 20. The musters show he was effective from the 1st October to the 31st December. Shown as sending £1 10s to Ellen Glancey. Listed on the Casualty Roll as slightly wounded at Balaclava. Received three wounds during the Charge; a lance wound to the head, a sabre cut to the forehead and a sabre cut to the left shoulder.

He is shown as being discharged on the 24th April 1866 at Newbridge after serving 22 years 170 days (one year 11 months in the Crimea). The reason for discharge states "In consequence of his being unfit for further military service, as a result of disease contracted from wounds received at Balaclava". His character and conduct described as very good and in possession of five good conduct badges. Three times entered in the Defaulters Book and never tried by court martial. Intended residence, Edinburgh.

565 GRAHAM, Private Alexander

Born : Date unknown - South Leith
Enlisted : 16th November 1837
Medals : Crimea (B.I.S)

Died : 11th January 1855 - Scutari
Status : Probably rode in the Charge

The musters show he was effective from the 1st October to the 13th December. Remarks state sent to Scutari Hospital 14th December. WO100/24 page 160 Remarks: Sick at Scutari. WO14/1 Scutari Muster Roll January-March 1855 remarks indicate he died on the 11th January.

The Times, 29th January 1855, reported that "Private Alexander Graham, 2nd Dragoons died at Scutari Hospital on the 11th January 1855 of diarrhoea". Trade on enlistment Boiler Builder.

538 GRAY, Farrier Major David

Born : Unknown
Enlisted :
Medals : Crimea (B.I.S)

Died : Unknown
Status : Probably rode in the Charge

Christies 20th November 1984, Lot 201 Three medals. Farrier Major D.Gray. Crimea 3 clasps B.I.S Scratch Engraved. MSM Victoria, Turkish Crimea Sardinian version. (Fm.D. Gray 2nd Dragoons) NVF and better £280.

The musters show he was effective from the 1st October to the 31st December. His regimental number shown as 530. WO25 Discharge book shows he was discharged 4th August 1863.

1099 GRAY, Private Francis

Born : Unknown
Enlisted :
Medals : Crimea (B.I.S)

Died : Unknown
Status : Probably rode in the Charge

Glendining's auction 26th September 1977. Lot 126, Pair to F.Gray, Crimea 3 bars Balaclava, Inkermann, Sebastopol, (F Gray 2nd Dragns.) Turkish Crimea Sardinian issue F Gray 2nd Dragoons VF £230.

The musters show he was effective from the 1st October to the 31st December. WO25 discharged 15th March 1862.

744 GRIEVE, Regimental Sergeant-Major John

Born : 3rd May 1822 - Musselburgh, Midlothian
Enlisted :
Medals : Crimea (B.I.S), The Victoria Cross, The French Medaille Militaire

Died : 1st December 1873 - Inveresk, Lothian
Status : Rode in the Charge

His medals are held by the Art Gallery of South Australia, Adelaide. The Gallery maintains a public access policy enabling you to view any objects in the collection (not on display) during normal office hours and this can be arranged by appointment."

The musters show he was effective from the 1st October to the 3rd December. Remarks state sent to Scutari Hospital. WO100/24 page 157 Remarks: Sick at Scutari. WO14/1 Scutari Muster Roll January-March 1855, shown present on the first muster.

The London Gazette 24th February 1857 states "John Grieve, No.774, Sergt--Major, 2nd Dragoons. Saved the life of an officer in the Heavy Cavalry Charge at Balaklava, who was surrounded by Russian Cavalry, by his gallant conduct of riding up to his rescue and cutting off the head of one Russian, disabling and dispersing the others." He was decorated by Queen Victoria on the 26th June 1857. His citation for the French Medaille Militaire states (For) "gallantry in the field at the battle of Balaklava on the 25th. of October 1854, and exemplary good conduct throughout the campaign, and during (his) period of service."
Charles Dickens wrote of John Grieve's heroic action in an early edition of his journal "All the Year Round": "It is not a thing that should be suffered to die away. When he cut off a soldier's head at a blow, and disabled and dispersed several others, he had no very exciting motives of self-devotion. Pay, promotion, or popularity could not well enter his head, for he knew the rules of the Service about rising from the ranks, and he knew too, that the British public rarely asks the names of the poor privates and non-commissioned officers who fall. What John Grieve did, then, was an act of the purest and most unselfish heroism; but I dare say, when the Queen pinned the Cross to his breast in Hyde Park that day, he felt he was more than rewarded for what to him was a very ordinary matter-of-fact bit of duty."

Grieve was held in such high respect by his fellow officers that they purchased him a commission. He is buried in his mother's grave at St. Michael's Churchyard, Inveresk, Lothian. A memorial stone was erected over the previously unmarked grave on the 4th September 2003 by the Royal Highland Fusiliers in conjunction with the Royal Scots Greys and the Black Watch.

In his article entitled *"A South Australian treasure: the VC to Sergeant Major John Grieve"*, Sabretache 1st September 2006, Anthony Staunton writes "John Grieve was born in Scotland on 3rd May 1822 at Musselburgh in what is now the eastern outskirts of Edinburgh. According to a nephew, Mr Charles Grieve, his uncle as a young man ran through a small fortune and then enlisted in the Scots Greys. He became Cornet without purchase on 4th December 1857, Adjutant on 15th February 1859 and Lieutenant on 30th January 1863....
John Grieve Oliver, the son of Catherine Oliver, a sister of John Grieve VC, arrived in Australia in 1880 and worked with the South Australian Railways until he retired in 1925. His mother sent the Victoria Cross to her son in Australia. In 1918 seeing an appeal by the Adelaide Museum for a Victoria Cross for its medal collection John Grieve Oliver loaned his uncle's medals to the museum. In 1936 he gifted the medals to the museum."

940 GROSSETT, Private John

Born : Unknown
Enlisted :
Medals : Crimea (B.I.S)

Died : Unknown
Status : Probably rode in the Charge

The musters show he was effective from the 1st October to the 31st December.

1170 HACKETT, Private James

Born : Date unknown - Longford
Enlisted : 27th June 1843
Medals : Crimea (B.I.S)

Died : 25th December 1854 - Scutari
Status : Slightly wounded in the Charge

The musters show he was effective from the 1st October to the 25th October and from the 10th November to the 13th December. Remarks state sent to Scutari Hospital 26th October, returned 9th November, sent back to Scutari 13th December. Listed on the Casualty Roll as slightly wounded at Balaclava.

The Times 6th January 1855, page 8, reported from Scutari on the 25th December 1854 that "1170 Haskett, 2nd Dragoons" had died on board the ship Sydney. Trade on enlistment Farmer

1213 HALL, Private Elijah

Born : Date unknown - Birmingham
Enlisted : 20th October 1845
Medals : Crimea (B.I.S)

Died : 17th June 1855 - Camp
Status : Probably rode in the Charge

The musters show he was effective from the 1st October to the 13th December. Remarks state sent to Scutari Hospital. WO14/1 Scutari Muster Roll January-March 1855 remarks indicate he was in Hospital during January. WO100/24 page 160 Remarks: Sick at Scutari, page 181 Remarks: Died 17 June 1855.

1123 HAMILTON, Private James

Born : Unknown
Enlisted :
Medals : Crimea (I.S)

Died : Unknown
Status : Effective during the period

The musters show he was effective from the 3rd October to the 26th October. Remarks state sent to Scutari 27th October. MR160.: Sick at Scutari, MR181.: Gone to England. Discharged 29th June 1857.

990 HAMILTON, Private Samuel

Born : Unknown
Enlisted : 4th January 1847
Medals : Crimea (B.S)

Died : 9th January 1855 - Scutari
Status : Probably rode in the Charge

The musters show he was effective from the 1st October to the 3rd December. Remarks state sent to Scutari Hospital. WO14/1 Scutari Muster Roll January-March 1855 remarks indicate he died on the 9th January. WO100/24 page 160 Remarks: Sick at Scutari, page 182 Remarks: Died 9th January 1855. Trade on enlistment Labourer

1079 HAMMOND, Private William

Born : Unknown
Enlisted :
Medals : Crimea (B.S)

Died : Unknown
Status : Severely wounded in the Charge

Donald Hall List 8th April 1974 item 61. Crimea 2 Bars Balaclava, Sebastopol. Pte Wm Hammond RNB DGS engraved in upright Serif capitals. With full documentation. Pte Hammond received a severe wound in the face at Balaclava. VF £120.

The musters show he was effective from the 1st October to the 25th October. Remarks state sent to Scutari 26th October. Listed on the Casualty Roll as severely wounded at Balaclava. WO100/24 page 160 Remarks: Sick at Scutari, page 181 Remarks: Gone to England.
Attended a Crimean War and Indian Mutiny Veterans parade in honour of the Queen in Edinburgh, May 1903. King Edward VII and Queen Alexandra rode through the decorated streets of Edinburgh to mark Edwards coronation in London the previous year.

HANDLEY, Lieutenant Henry Edwardes

Born : Unknown
Enlisted :
Medals : Crimea (B.I.S)

Died : Unknown
Status : Slightly wounded in the Charge

The musters show he was effective as a Cornet from the 1st October to the 28th December and as a Lieutenant from the 29th-31st December. Listed on the Casualty Roll as slightly wounded at Balaclava. WO100/24 page 176 Remarks: Gone to England.

Cornet Scots Greys 30th September 1853. Lieut 29th December 1854. Left the regiment in 1858. Lieut Handley served with the Scots Greys in the Crimea 1854-1855 including the Battles of Balaklava (Severely wounded by a lance thrust) and Inkermann and Siege of Sebastopol (*Illustrated Histories of the Scottish Regiments No2. 2nd Dragoons by Lt Col Percy Groves, page 28*)

"...the Colt and Adams revolvers used by many officers and NCO's were not issued by the army, and had to be purchased independently. They were five or six shot percussion revolvers and soon proved their value in hand to hand fighting. During the charge of the Heavy Brigade Cornet Handley having been stabbed by four Cossacks was able to shoot three with his revolver...." (*Crimea 1854-56 The war with Russia from contemporary photographs by Lawrence James, page 144*)

A double action, five shot pistol revolver by Deane, Adams and Deane, and shown by them at the Great Exhibition. The pistol was patented by Robert Adams in 1851. This was a formidable rival to the Colt pistol, the cylinder which resembles that of the Colt in so far as it is fitted with horizontal nipples of the "central-fire" type separated by partitions, is pivoted on a movable pin which can be withdrawn to free the cylinder for cleaning.

The Inverness Courier, 1st September 1914, page 5, "The Highland Brigade; Sir Colin Campbell's Farewell Address: London, 29th August 1914. Sir, -- At a dinner of Crimean veterans held at Auckland, New Zealand, in the early Eighties, Captain Handley, who was a Cornet in the Scots Greys, and wounded in the charge of the Heavy Brigade at Balaclava, took the chair, and Captain Macpherson, late of the 93rd Sutherland Highlanders, the vice chair. At this dinner Captain Macpherson recited Sir Colin Campbell's farewell address, which I now have the pleasure of enclosing. The Captain was my guest at the time, and the following morning was much annoyed because the local newspapers, while publishing all the speeches, omitted his recitation. I took it down from his dictation, but not for publication; the Captain remarking, 'No, no, the papers have neglected an opportunity of inserting a remarkable oration that has never been in print.'"

987 HARDY, Sergeant David

Born : Date unknown - St. Andrews's
Enlisted : 30th November 1846
Medals : Crimea (B.I.S)

Died : 4th October 1855 - Camp Crimea
Status : Probably rode in the Charge

The musters show he was effective from the 1st October to the 31st December. WO100/24 page 177 Remarks: Died on 4th October 1855. Trade on enlistment Labourer.

1172 HAWKINS, Private John

Born : Unknown
Enlisted :
Medals : Crimea (B.I.S)

Died : Unknown
Status : Probably rode in the Charge

The musters show he was effective from the 1st October to the 27th November. Remarks state sent to Hospital Scutari. WO100/24 page 160 Remarks: Sick at Scutari. WO14/1 Scutari Muster Roll January-March 1855 remarks indicate he was at Abydos during January, February and March.

1026 HECTOR, Private James

Born : Unknown
Enlisted :
Medals : Crimea (B.I.S)

Died : Unknown
Status : Probably rode in the Charge

The musters show he was effective from the 1st October to the 30th December. Remarks state sent to Hospital Scutari. WO100/24 page 160 Remarks: Sick at Scutari. WO14/1 Scutari Muster Roll January-March 1855 remarks indicate he joined on the 23rd January and returned to the regiment on the 25th February. Discharged December 1856.

825 HEPBURN, Private Thomas

Born : Unknown
Enlisted :
Medals : Crimea (B.I.S)

Died : Unknown
Status : Probably rode in the Charge

The musters show he was effective from the 1st October to the 31st December. WO100/24 page 181 Remarks: Gone to England. WO25 Discharge book shows he died on the 2nd February 1857.

723 HEPBURN, Private William

Born : Date unknown - Hamilton
Enlisted : 12th August 1841
Medals : Crimea (B.I.S)

Died : 17th June 1855 - Camp
Status : Probably rode in the Charge

The musters show he was effective from the 1st October to the 31st December receiving 92 days of Good Conduct pay at 3d per day. Shown on the Musters as sending £2 to Mary Hepburn. WO100/24 page 181 Remarks: Died 17th June 1855.

1038 HEYWOOD, Trumpeter William

Born : Unknown
Enlisted :
Medals : Crimea (B.S)

Died : Unknown
Status : Slightly wounded in the Charge

The musters show him effective as a Private from the 1st-23rd October and as a Trumpeter from 24th October to the 25th October. Promoted following the death of Trumpeter Mitchell. Listed on the Casualty Roll as slightly wounded at Balaclava. WO100/24 page 158 Remarks: Sick at Scutari, page 178 Remarks: Gone to England. WO14/1 Scutari Muster Roll January-March 1855 remarks indicate he was sent home 11th January.

Appeared before Queen Victoria in the Mess Room, Brompton Barracks on the 3rd March 1855. His age was stated to be 21 years, service 2 years 10 months. He had lost three fingers of his left hand at Balaclava, wounded by minie ball.

The Times, Monday 5th March 1855:"The Queen made the round of all the wards except those containing fever cases. Her Majesty addressed kind enquires to many of the wounded men, those who were well enough to be up to receiving her at the foot of the their respective cots with cards in their hands specifying the nature of their wound."

1219 HILL, Private George

Born : Unknown
Enlisted :
Medals : Crimea (B.I.S)

Died : Unknown
Status : Probably rode in the Charge

The musters show he was effective from the 1st October to the 27th December. Remarks state sent to Scutari Hospital. WO100/24 page 160 Remarks: Sick at Scutari. WO25 Discharge book shows he discharged 26th September 1865.

1134 HISLOP, Private James

Born : Date unknown - Selkirk
Enlisted : 9th June 1851
Medals : Crimea (B.I.S)

Died : 5th July 1855 - Camp
Status : Probably rode in the Charge

The musters show he was effective from the 1st October to the 31st December. WO100/24 page 181 Remarks: Died 5th July 1855. Trade on enlistment Draper.

1231 HOGG, Private Robert

Born : c.1833 - Harehope, Northumberland
Enlisted :
Medals : Crimea (S)

Died : Unknown
Status : Effective during the period

The musters show he was effective from the 1st October to the 27th October and from the 14th December to the 31st December. Remarks state sent to Scutari 28th October, returned 14th December. WO25 Discharge book shows he was discharged as unfit for further service December 1858. In the 1881 census Robert Hogg aged 48, married to Margaret, is living at Bolerow Street, Sheldon, Durham shown as a Chelsea Pensioner.

1135 HONE, Sergeant William. S. Jn

Born : Unknown
Enlisted :
Medals : Crimea (I.S)

Died : Unknown
Status : Effective during the period

E.E. Needes Collection, Crimea with 2 clasps (Inkermann, Sebastopol).

The musters show he was effective from the 1st October to the 31st December. Sebastopol Medal Roll 177 Remarks: Discharged 24th August 1855. Medal Roll shows his name as "W.S.J Stone", Mint 31/7/57.

446 HOOD, Private William

Born : c. 1812 - near Kilmarnock, Ayrshire
Enlisted :
Medals : Crimea (B.I.S)

Died : Unknown
Status : Probably rode in the Charge

Glendining's 28th September 1977, Lot 124. Same medals as per DNW Sold £240. DNW 4th December 2002, Lot 1014, A Heavy Brigade group of three to Farrier William Hood, 2nd Dragoons (Scots Greys) Crimea 1854-56, 3 clasps, Balaklava, Inkermann, Sebastopol (Farrier, 2nd Dns.) contemporary engraved naming; Army L.S. & G.C., V.R., large letter reverse (No. 446 Farrier, 2nd Dragoons) fitted with replacement Crimea suspension; Turkish Crimea 1855, British issue (Pt., 2nd Dgs.) contact wear and edge bruising, otherwise nearly very fine and better (3) Hammer Price £1300

Enlisted in the Royal Artillery at Dublin in August 1832, aged 20 years, he transferred to the 2nd Dragoons in November 1833. The musters show he was effective from the 1st October to the 27th December. Remarks state sent to Scutari 28th December. WO100/24 page 160 Remarks: (Farrier). Sick at Scutari, page 181 Remarks: Gone to England. WO14/1 Scutari Muster Roll January-March 1855 remarks indicate he was in Hospital during January and February, sent home 3rd March 1855. Discharged at Newbridge Barracks, Midlothian, in October 1856, as a result of "chronic rheumatism of long standing resulting from exposure to the cold."

HUNTER, Captain Robert Scott

Born : 1831 - Brechin, Angus
Enlisted :
Medals : Crimea (B.I.S), The Turkish Order of the Medjidie (5th Class)

Died : Unknown
Status : Probably rode in the Charge

Captain Robert Scott Hunter was a native of Brechin, Angus, Scotland, born 1831. He purchased his Cornetcy on the 17th June 1851, became a Lieutenant 17th February 1854. The musters show he was effective as a Lieutenant from the 1st October to the 31st December. Captain 13th September 1855. Transferred to the 6th Dragoon Guards 1860 and retired 1863. He married a Loughborough girl, Clara Maria Middleton in 1861 and was living with his in-laws in Ashley Road, Loughborough in 1871. By 1881 he was living in Alyth, Perthshire, Scotland.

During the Crimean war Robert Scott Hunter wrote a number of letters to his sister Helen Carnegy Hunter (1823-1884) the wife of Laurence Tuttiett (1825-1897) of Lea Marston Rectory, Colehill, Warwickshire. The letters were inherited by A.L.N. Russell, who was related to the Tuttiett family, and by him given to G.S. Dixon. The letters are now held by the Lincolnshire Archives (Archon Code : 57) In the letters he comments on camp life, the poor fighting quality of the French, mismanagement by ministers and generals, and Miss Nightingale's lady nurses. The following letters were transcribed by Dr. Douglas J. Austion
(Ref: DIXON 22/12/3/1)
H.M.S. Himalaya, At Sea, July 27th, 1854.

My dearest Molly,
        We got away all right yesterday & are having beautiful weather. This is a most splendid ship, & the best idea I can give of her size is that she is 80 feet longer than the Duke of Wellington. We are now getting near the Bay of Biscay, & the ship as you may see by my writing is rolling a few besides our screw makes such a thumping that it really is not easy to get the letters straight. We shipped all our horses in 12 minutes under the hour. They are all right as yet & none of them have been sea sick nor any of us but Miller the Adjutant. We had a very .... night & the decks this morning are very wet but now (11.40) the sun is coming out & the officers of the ship say that they think the afternoon will be fine. I don't suppose I shall get this finished today, in fact there is no use me doing so as we do not touch anywhere till we get to Malta where we are to be 12 hours. Andrew came out as far as the "Bell Buoy" with us where the Pilot left us. I was very glad as it gave me two hours more of his company. He dined with me on board the ship the day before & will be able to tell you how well we feel. We get breakfast at 9, lunch at 12, Dinner at 4. Tea at [blank] and grog at 9, & you never saw how we eat. I do so. I can tell you, for besides the fact of my being hungry, if I happened to be sick, I should be more comfortably so, than if I had an empty head basket. We have been allowed to take off uniform & go about the queerest figures imaginable, with all sorts of hats, wide-awakes, caps, boots, &c. &c. & enjoy the .... in the highest ... We expect to be at Malta this day week – July 31st.

Dearest Molly, We have just passed Gibraltar. The morning is lovely & the view perfect. The Rock is most curious & as we passed we cheered like anything & our band played Rule Britannia wh. was answered by the garrison lining the walls and returning the compliment. There never was anything like the beautiful weather we have had. The sea has been so smooth, & but for the heavy rolling of the ship with the enormous ground swell, you could have hardly told you were at sea. We made land last night about 10 o'clock after loosing it all day from Cape St. Vincent this morning.

Just before getting to Gib., we got a splendid view of Tangier on the African coast & Tariffa on the Spanish side. Both sides are very rocky especially the African, where the mountains enormous & their summits are lost in, or appearing above the clouds. We expect to be at Malta about Wednesday, where we are to anchor for the horses. I must write some more letters so will close this. Direct yr. letters to me thus. Name, Regiment, Army in Turkey
No more, that will find me. Kind regards to Ms.Mr.? Mittick? & love to the chicks. Excuse bad writing (& spelling, I'm afraid). This screw propeller goes thump thump so that it is next to impossible to write.
Ever Yr. Affect. R S H
This ship is 364 feet long! Her engines 700 horse power & they work up to 1200!!! Imagine her size. Her mainyard is 84 ft Long!!!!

(Ref : DIXON 22/12/3/5)

Balaklava, October 27th 1854

My dearest Holly
I don't know whether I have written to you since the seige commenced at any rate I'll give you a screed now. We began on the 17th, & are still at it, with no further effects that I can see, than having knocked their parapets about, & by all accounts from deserters, killed a good number inside. But now for my news. We have at last had a fight, & I have "fleshed my maiden sword". I was on picquet on the morning of the 24th, & all was quiet at 3 am & afterwards, till daybreak (about 5½) when an immense column of the enemy suddenly appeared, & our fire opened from our field works, wh: unfortunately, as you will see, were entirely manned with Turks. The Russians stormed, & took them, the Turks making a stand at one work, but bolting as soon as the bayonets crossed. The consequence of this was, that the Rs. soon got up a number of guns & turned our own Captured ones upon us, & commenced at 6 o'clock, to pepper us, with shot, shell, & rifle balls. We had no infantry, & stood their fire for some time loosing a few, but were obliged to retire, as the fire got hot. The Turks absolutely ran away from the other batteries, before the enemy got there, & we lost our position, & 9 guns, & retreated slowly towards our encampment. About 12½, their Cavalry came suddenly over the hill, with a cloud of Cossacks, who speared the unfortunate Turks, who were running away, & begging for mercy, in all directions. We came trotting up, wheeled into line, & our little regt. & one squadron of the Enniskillens charged, & broke 4 regiments of regular cavalry & about 100 Cossacks, they were 5 to 1, they were 2 regts. of blue hussars & 2 of Light Dragoons. The latter were fine fellows, & my squadron, the left (I commanded the left troop) was opposed to their right regt. & one squadron of the second. The scene was awful, we were so outnumbered, & there was nothing but to fight our way through them, cut & slash. I made a hack at one, & my sword bounded off his thick coat, so I gave him the point & knocked him off his horse. Another fellow just after made a slash at me, & just touched my bearskin, so I made a rush at him, & took him just on the back of his helmet. I didn't wait to see what became of him, as a lot of fellows were riding at me, but I only know that he fell forward on his horse, & if his head tingled like my wrist, he must have had it hard, & as I was riding out, another fellow came past me, whom I caught slap in the face. I'll be bound his own mother would'nt have known him.

They all by this time were broken, & running, our fellows gave some awful cuts & the 5th D.Gs. & Royals had now come up & finished what we began. Lord Raglan saw it from the heights & sent an A.D.C. to say 'he was delighted with the Greys'. The Light Brigade, viz. 8 & 11 Hussars, 17th Lancers, 4 & 13 Light Dgs went to the front, the Royals & Greys following, & pursued. The Lights went ahead, but were led too far by Capt. Nolan (15th Huss), an A.D.C., who suffered for his rashness with his life, & I am sorry to say were cut to pieces! Their loss is about 600!! We were following, & got into the cross fire, wh: cut them up, three batteries (two of them captured ones) turned on the Royals & us, & such a shower of round shot, shell, grape, canister & rifles for ages on us that we were obliged to retreat. Every officer of the 17th but 3 were killed or wounded & they only brought out about 45 men out of action. The 4th about the same, the 13 have only about 35, in short they are quite annihilated. Our loss was 4 officers wounded, but only one obliged to go to the ships, & 44 men wounded, 2 killed, our escape was miraculous. The round shot poured on us. Shells bursting before behind & above us & anything like the balls from cannister & rifles you cant imagine but by the awful results. A grape shot struck my cloak, & bounded off, it was just 2 inches above my knee. I have such cause to be & am thankful for my escape. It was an awful time & the men were falling, & horses on all sides. The din deafening & the poor fellows who were struck groaned awfully. A man riding beside me had his leg shattered just below the knee with grape shot, a fellow of the one I have no doubt that hit my cloak. The Russians were allowed to hold the position, as it is some miles to us, & we have fallen back upon the heights. There was a desperate sally made yesterday afternoon from the town but the 3rd division rec'd them & beat them back, I am told with immense loss. Their artillery is superb, & they fire magnificently as we (cavalry) can tell but I dont think so much of their other troops. The Turks are useless cowards & will need to ... , to wash off the stain they have put on their name here. There is a report that we are to leave Balaklava as our forces are not sufficient to hold such an extended position. This looks, it strikes me, very much as if we were getting the worst of it. From the door of my tent, I can see the Russians swarming like bees all over the place. They are intrenching themselves, but General Bosquet with a division of French went away I believe last night, & it is supposed is going to take them in rear, but his instructions were not made known- at any rate he has gone away among the hills, in front of our position, & that looks like it. But its very little use telling you all this, for you will get all the news in the papers. Do send me any that may have anything in them about us. But ... ... talking (There's a fellow speaking to me & I'm writing nonsense I see.) If you get a good Punch send him. The Carnegys always send the Ill News & they are the very best correspondts. I have. I heard from Tilly yesterday. She gives me better accounts of Mrs. C's health. I hope soon to be able to tell you that we have taken the town, & licked the Rs: again but I have not much time now to write as most days we are out all day & very often at night too. It is dreadful work & we have all a good many hardships to go through, but altogether we are jolly & look forward hopefully to go home some fine day. What on earth has become of Andrew? He has never written a word to me since I left England. I cannot understand it – I cannot have offended him. I'm sure we parted good friends. I hope & trust you are all well. How is Mrs. T? I was very sorry to hear of poor Mr. Knox's death. I would put a bit of crape on my arm if I had any but I have not. We are funny figures. Our red coats are crimson, & black stains all over them: Epaulettes no one wears, they are done away with, & we have to carry telescopes & havresacks, & pistols so that with our brown faces & patched clothes, we look queer figures I assure you. Especially when we have empty interiors wh: is sometimes the case, I suspect. When we do get home again, you will see a good deal of change. Write long & often. I assure you it's a charity. Begin a long letter, & just write 5 minutes every day. You cant think, however stupid, wh: home letters serve me, how welcome they are. I want you to subscr. to the United Services Gazette for me, & tell the Editor to send it by every mail, directed as you do your letters. You owe me some money so will be able to pay yourself. Like a good Holl, work me a pair of Mits[Mitts] that will cover hands & wrist high up, & send me them by post. Send two letters & a Mit[Mitt] in each. I am going, if I am spared, to send to England for things in wiater?, but want mits sadly. Now I have written a good long letter, so mind you follow my good example. With most affectionate love, I ever am

Your most attached brother

R S Hunter

How is that dear old Body? Give her my best & most affectionate love & tell her that I often think of her & her locket is on the paper now, there's the mark of it.

--

I have opened my letter again dearest Molly to tell you that I have just left Robert Methven, who now commands the Colombo, a magnificent steamer belonging to the Peninsular & Oriental Company. He has been so kind to me you cant imagine. Im sure you would like him much. He is such a particularly quiet gentlemanly fellow I like him very much. He has just left half a loaf of bread, the most acceptable present I could have had, as we get nothing but those hard ship biscuits & a pot of salt butter, also a great luxury. Good bye – God bless you   R.S.H.

360 HUNTER, Private James

Born : Unknown
Enlisted :
Medals : Crimea (B.S)

Died : Unknown
Status : Slightly wounded in the Charge

The musters show he was effective from the 1st October to the 25th October. Remarks state at Scutari 26th October to 31st December. Listed on the Casualty Roll as slightly wounded at Balaclava. WO100/24 page 160 Remarks: Sick at Scutari, page 182 Remarks: Gone to England. WO14/1 Scutari Muster Roll January-March 1855 remarks indicate he was in Hospital during January and February.

1198 HUNTER, Private John

Born : Unknown
Enlisted :
Medals : Crimea (S)

Died : Unknown
Status : Effective during the period

The musters show he was effective from the 1st October to the 26th October. Nothing is mentioned in the Remarks as to why he is not effective after the 26th October. WO14/1 Scutari Muster Roll January-March 1855 remarks indicate he was at Abydos in January. WO25 Discharge book shows he discharged 21st August 1866.

766 HUNTER, Private Robert

Born : Unknown
Enlisted :
Medals : Crimea (B.I.S)

Died : Unknown
Status : Probably rode in the Charge

Liverpool Coin and Medal List Sept 1986 item 107. Crimea 3 clasps Balaclava, Inkermann, Sebastopol R.Hunter 2nd Dragoons officially impressed Light Contacting VF £360

The musters show he was effective from the 1st October to the 31st December. WO100/24 page 182 Remarks: Gone to England. He received his medal from the hand of the Queen on 18th May 1855. Discharged 21/8/66. A Sergeant R. Hunter attended a Crimean War and Indian Mutiny Veterans parade in honour of the Queen in Edinburgh, May 1903.

1141 HUNTINGDON, Private John
Born : Unknown
Enlisted :
Medals : Crimea (B.I.S)

Died : Unknown
Status : Probably rode in the Charge

The musters show he was effective from the 1st October to the 31st December. Discharged December 1859.

954 IRVINE, Paymaster Sergeant Robert
Born : Unknown
Enlisted :
Medals : Crimea (B.I.S)

Died : Unknown
Status : Probably rode in the Charge

The musters show he was effective from the 1st October to the 31st December. Shown as sending £2 to Delilah Irvine.

1218 IRVINE, Private James
Born : Unknown
Enlisted :
Medals : Crimea (I.S)

Died : Unknown
Status : Effective during the period

The musters show he was effective from the 1st October to the 31st December.

1205 JACKSON, Private John
Born : Unknown
Enlisted :
Medals : Crimea (B.I.S)

Died : Unknown
Status : Probably rode in the Charge

The musters show he was effective from the 1st October to the 31st December. WO100/24 page 160 Remarks: Sick at Scutari. WO14/1 Scutari Muster Roll January-March 1855 remarks indicate he was in Hospital during January and February. Joined 19th January.

1249 JACKSON, Private William
Born : Unknown
Enlisted : 8th March 1854
Medals : Crimea (B.I.S)

Died : Unknown
Status : Severely wounded in the Charge

A.H.Baldwin & Sons Ltd June 1946, item 65. Pair Crimea 2 clasps Balaclava Sebastopol and Turkish Crimea. W.Jackson 2nd Dragoons impressed. Fine only, but scarce £3-5-0. The Gazette December 1987 (Richard Kirch) item 104. Crimea 2 clasps Balaklava, Sebastopol W.Jackson. Officially impressed. Bad edge bruises but naming is not affected. Good F/VF £875.

Enlisted at Edinburgh. The musters show he was effective from the 1st October to the 25th October and from the 3rd December to the 31st December. Remarks state sent to Scutari 26th October, returned 3rd December. Listed on the Casualty Roll as severely wounded at Balaclava. Discharged 19th March 1863 aged 29 years. Attended a Crimean War and Indian Mutiny Veterans parade in honour of the Queen in Edinburgh, May 1903.

998 JOHNSTONE, Private George
Born : Unknown
Enlisted :
Medals : Crimea (B.I.S)

Died : Unknown
Status : Probably rode in the Charge

The musters show he was effective from the 1st October to the 13th December. Remarks state sent to Scutari 14th December. WO100/24 page 160 Remarks: Sick at Scutari. WO14/1 Scutari Muster Roll January-March 1855 remarks indicate he was in hospital during January.

1157 JOHNSTONE, Private Thomas
Born : Unknown
Enlisted :
Medals : Crimea (I.S)

Died : Unknown
Status : Effective during the period

The musters show he was effective from the 1st October to the 31st December. WO14/1 Scutari Muster Roll January-March 1855 indicate he was in Hospital during January and February, joined 19th January. Invalided June 1861.

777 JOHNSTONE, Private James

Born : Date unknown - Berwick
Enlisted : 14th September 1842
Medals : Crimea (B.I.S)

Died : 16th April 1855 - Aboard Ship
Status : Probably rode in the Charge

The musters show he was effective from the 1st October to the 31st December. WO100/24 page 182 Remarks: Died 16th April 1855.

912 JOHNSTONE, Private William

Born : Unknown
Enlisted :
Medals : Crimea (B.I.S)

Died : Unknown
Status : Slightly wounded in the Charge

The musters show he was effective from the 1st October to the 25th October. Remarks state sent to Scutari 26th October. WO100/24 page 160 Remarks: Sick at Scutari, page 182 Remarks: Gone to England. Listed on the Casualty Roll as slightly wounded at Balaclava. WO14/1 Scutari Muster Roll January-March 1855 remarks indicate he was effective 1st-31 January, returned to the regiment 3rd February.

1063 JONES, Trumpeter David

Born : Unknown
Enlisted :
Medals : Crimea (B.I.S)

Died : Unknown
Status : Probably rode in the Charge

The musters show he was effective from the 1st October to the 31st December. Invalided 23rd August 1862.

697 JONES, Private Francis

Born : Unknown
Enlisted :
Medals : Crimea (B.I.S)

Died : January 1858
Status : Probably rode in the Charge

The musters show he was effective from the 1st October to the 20th December. Remarks state sent to Scutari 21st December. WO100/24 page 160 Remarks: B on C.O.Certif 9/9/57. Sick at Scutari, page 182 Remarks: Gone to England. WO14/1 Scutari Muster Roll January-March 1855 remarks indicate he was in Hospital during January and sent home 27th February. WO25 Discharge book shows he died January 1858.

874 KEALL, Private Robert

Born : Date unknown - Magby, Lincs.
Enlisted : 1st September 1845
Medals : Crimea (B.I.S)

Died : 15th August 1855 - Camp
Status : Probably rode in the Charge

The musters show he was effective from the 1st October to the 31st December. WO100/24 page 182 Remarks: Died 14th August 1855.

606 KELLY, Private Nathan

Born : Unknown
Enlisted :
Medals : Crimea (B.I.S)

Died : Unknown
Status : Probably rode in the Charge

The musters show he was effective from the 1st October to the 30th December. Remarks state sent to Scutari 31st December. WO100/24 page 160 Remarks: Sick at Scutari, page 182 Remarks: Gone to England. WO14/1 Scutari Muster Roll January-March 1855 remarks indicate he joined on the 23rd January and was in Hospital for February and March.

1060 KENNEDY, Private Robert

Born : Unknown
Enlisted :
Medals : Crimea (B.I.S), Long Service and Good Conduct Medal

Died : Unknown
Status : Probably rode in the Charge

The musters show he was effective from the 1st October to the 31st December. WO102 L.S & G.C recommended 3rd December 1867, issued 2nd March 1868, gratuity £5.

1236 KERR, Private Robert
Born : Unknown
Enlisted : 28th April 1848
Medals : Crimea (B.I.S)

Died : Unknown
Status : Slightly wounded in the Charge

The musters show he was effective from the 1st October to the 25th October and from the 14th December to the 31st December. Remarks state to Scutari 25th October returned 14th December. Listed on the Casualty Roll as slightly wounded at Balaclava. WO25 Discharge book shows he was a Sergeant, 21 years expired on the 2nd February 1875.

1061 KINLAY, Private James
Born : Date unknown - Camden Town
Enlisted : 28th April 1848
Medals : Crimea (B.I.S)

Died : 28th January 1855 - Scutari
Status : Probably rode in the Charge

The musters show he was effective from the 1st October to the 18th December. Remarks state to Scutari Hospital 19th December. WO100/24 page 160 Remarks: Sick at Scutari, page 182 Remarks: Died 28 January 1855. WO14/1 Scutari Muster Roll January-March 1855 remarks indicate he died 28th January.

1202 KIRK, Corporal James
Born : Unknown
Enlisted :
Medals : Crimea (B.I.S)

Died : Unknown
Status : Probably rode in the Charge

The musters show he was effective from the 1st October to the 31st December.

703 KIRK, Private George
Born : Date unknown - Kilpatrick
Enlisted : 12th January 1841
Medals : Crimea (B.I.S)

Died : 18th November 1854
Status : Probably rode in the Charge

The musters show he was effective from the 1st October to the 15th November. Remarks state to Scutari 16th November. Noted as "Dead" in the 3rd Muster. WO100/24 page 160 Remarks: Died of Cholera 18 Nov 1854, page 182 Remarks: Died 18th November 1854. Records also show he was a Farrier. Trade on enlistment Printer.

907 KNEATH, Sergeant Thomas
Born : Date unknown - Bath
Enlisted : 25th March 1846
Medals : Crimea (B.S)

Died : 17th July 1855 - Camp Crimea
Status : Severely wounded in the Charge

The musters show he was effective from the 1st October to the 25th October and from the 29th December to the 31st December. Remarks state he was sent to Scutari Hospital 26th October and returned to Camp on the 29th December. Listed on the Casualty Roll as severely wounded at Balaclava. Trade on enlistment Yeoman.

802 KNEVETT, Sergeant Henry
Born : Unknown
Enlisted :
Medals : Crimea (B.I.S)
A Long Service and Good Conduct has appeared on the market.

Died : Unknown
Status : Probably rode in the Charge

The musters show he was effective as a Private from the 1st October to the 31st December. (See 800 Pte T.Knevett)

803 KNEVETT, Private John
Born : c.1823 - Hoxne, Suffolk
Enlisted :
Medals : Crimea (B.I.S)

Died : Unknown
Status : Probably rode in the Charge

The musters show he was effective from the 1st October to the 31st December. Discharged 24th August 1869. Shown on the 1871 census as a Chelsea Pensioner, lodging with his mother Sarah Knevett in Ipswich. (See 800 Pte T.Knevett)

800 KNEVETT, Private Thomas

Born : c. 1819 - Hoxne, Suffolk
Enlisted : 30th October 1843
Medals : Crimea (B.I.S)

Died : Unknown
Status : Probably rode in the Charge

DNW 28th March 2002, Gordon Everson Collection, Lot 41, Crimea 1854-56, 3 clasps, Balaklava, Inkermann, Sebastopol (T. Knevett, 2nd Dragns.) officially impressed naming; Turkish Crimea 1855, Sardinian issue (T. Knevett, 2nd Dragoons); Army L.S. & G.C., V.R., small letter reverse (800 Thos. Knivett, 2nd Dragoons) light contact marks to the first, otherwise very fine or better (3) Hammer Price £2200. For sale at the Liverpool Medal Company September 2007: Crimea, 3 bars, Alma, Balaklava, Sebastopol, (officially impressed), L.S.G.C. (VR - impressed), Turkish Crimea Sardinian issue, (named), to T. Knevett, 2nd. Dragns. (Knivett on LSGC) , roll confirms. Heavy Brigade (R6149) V.F./G.V.F. £3000

Thomas Knevett was born at Hoxne, near Eye, Suffolk, and enlisted for the 2nd Dragoons (Scots Greys) at Ipswich on the 30th October 1843, aged 18 years 11 months, and given regimental number 800. Eight days later, his two brothers also joined up, John, aged 20, and Henry, aged 17 years 11 months. They were given numbers 803 and 802 respectively.

Thomas Knevitt served with the Scots Greys in the Crimea and Turkey for 1 year 11 months, the musters show he was effective from the 1st October to the 31st December. He received his Long Service and Good Conduct medal with a £5 Gratuity on the 1st May 1865 and was discharged at Dundalk on the 31st March 1868.

869 KNOWLES, Private John

Born : Unknown
Enlisted :
Medals : Crimea (B.I.S), Long Service and Good Conduct Medal

Died : 3rd December 1908 - Easton, Somerset
Status : Slightly wounded in the Charge

The musters show he was effective from the 1st October to the 31st December. Listed on the Casualty Roll as slightly wounded at Balaclava. WO102 L.S & G.C issued 24th July 1867, gratuity £5.

The Broad Arrow 12th December 1908, reported "2nd Dragoons. Mr John Knowles died on 3rd Inst at Easton, Somerset aged 83. He served in the army for 22 years and took part in the Crimean war, being present at the Battles of Balaklava and Inkermann and the siege of Sebastopol. He left the army on pension on 13th August 1867."

818 LACEY, Private James

Born : Date unknown - Charlton Kings, Gloucester
Enlisted : 20th December 1843
Medals : Crimea (B.I.S)

Died : 22nd December 1854 - Camp
Status : Probably rode in the Charge

Haywards medal Catalogue December 1975, item 134. Crimea 3 clasps. Balaklava, Inkermann, Sebastopol. J. Lacey 2nd Dragoons, (impressed) EF £250. DNW 23rd September 2005, Lot 384, Crimea 1854-56, 3 clasps, Balaklava, Inkermann, Sebastopol (J. Lacey, 2nd Drns.) officially impressed naming, good very fine. Hammer Price £1500

The musters show he was effective from the 1st October to the 22nd December. Remarks state died 22nd Dec. WO100/24 page 161 Remarks: Died 22nd Decr. 54. Catarrh, page 182 Remarks: Died 22nd December. 1854. Trade Labourer.

1224 LAIDLAW, Private Robert

Born : Date unknown - Dalkeith
Enlisted : 22nd September 1853
Medals : Crimea (B.I.S)

Died : 11th January 1855 - Scutari
Status : Probably rode in the Charge

The musters show he was effective from the 1st October to the 30th December. Remarks state To Scutari Hospital 30th December. WO100/24 page 161 Remarks: Sick at Scutari, page 182 Remarks: Died 11 January 1855. Trade Gardener.

633 LAING, Private Andrew Scott

Born : Unknown
Enlisted :
Medals : Crimea (B.S), The Distinguished Conduct Medal

Died : Unknown
Status : Severely wounded in the Charge

The musters show he was effective from the 1st October to the 25th October. Remarks state sent to Scutari 26th October. Listed on the Casualty Roll as severely wounded at Balaclava. Casualty Roll shows his name as "AS Long". The Distinguished Conduct Medal recommendation was dated 13th January 1855.

1150 LANGDON, Private Thomas
Born : Unknown
Enlisted :
Medals : Crimea (B.I.S)
Died : Unknown
Status : Slightly wounded in the Charge

Glendinings 7th June 1989 Lot 25, Crimea 3 clasps, Balaklava, Inkermann, Sebastopol (T.Langdon 2nd RNB DRGNS) Partly re-named. Turkish Crimea British issue, scroll suspender (T.Langdon 2nd Dragoons) and re-named M.M Geo V to another recipient TC. Good Fine others VF £110.

The musters show he was effective from the 1st October to the 31st December. Listed on the Casualty Roll as slightly wounded at Balaclava. WO25 Discharge book shows he was invalided as a Sergeant on the 22nd April 1873.

1193 LAUDER, Corporal John
Born : Unknown
Enlisted :
Medals : Crimea (I.S)
Died : Unknown
Status : Effective during the period

The musters show he was effective as a Private from the 1st October to the 31st December. WO14/1 Scutari Muster Roll January-March 1855 remarks indicate he was in Hospital during January and February, joined 19th January.

1194 LEISHMAN, Private Archibald
Born : Date unknown - Lasswade, Edinburgh
Enlisted : 27th November 1852
Medals : Crimea (B.I.S)
Died : Date unknown - Aboard Ship
Status : Probably rode in the Charge

The musters show he was effective from the 1st October to the 18th December. Remarks state sent to Scutari Hospital. WO100/24 page 161 Remarks: Sick at Scutari, page 182 Remarks: Dead. Trade on enlistment Forester.

LEX, Vetinary Surgeon T
Born : Unknown
Enlisted :
Medals : Crimea (S)
Died : Unknown
Status : Effective during the period

The musters show he was effective from the 1st October to the 31st December.

1121 LIDDLE, Sergeant John
Born : Unknown
Enlisted :
Medals : Crimea (B.I.S), The Distinguished Conduct Medal
Died : Unknown
Status : Probably rode in the Charge

The musters show he was effective as a Corporal from the 1st October to the 26th November and as a Sergeant from the 27th November to the 31st December. Remarks state he was promoted from Corporal following the promotion of Beeston. The Distinguished Conduct Medal recommendation dated 13th Janaury 1855.

1067 LINNAN, Private John
Born : Unknown
Enlisted :
Medals : Crimea (B.I.S)
Died : Unknown
Status : Probably rode in the Charge

The musters show he was effective from the 1st October to the 31st December. WO14/1 Scutari Muster Roll January-March 1855 remarks indicate he joined on the 2nd February and was in Koulali Hospital.
The Pay Lists name him "John Lennon".

666 LISTER, Private Thomas
Born : Unknown
Enlisted :
Medals : Crimea (B.I.S)
Died : Unknown
Status : Probably rode in the Charge

The musters show he was effective from the 1st October to the 31st December. WO25 Discharge book shows he discharged on the 20th October 1863.

Scots Greys depart for the Crimea.

1260 LITTLE, Private William

Born : Unknown
Enlisted :
Medals : Crimea (S)

Died : Unknown
Status : To Scutari 26th October 1854

The musters show he was effective from the 1st-25th October and from the 14th December to the 31st December. Remarks state to Scutari 26th October, returned 14th December. Transferred to the Military Train December 1856.

743 LIVINGSTONE, Private Richard

Born : Date unknown - West Kirk
Enlisted : 6th January 1842
Medals : Crimea (B.S)

Died : 3rd November 1854 - Scutari
Status : Severely wounded in the Charge

The musters show he was effective from the 1st October to the 25th October. Remarks state to Scutari Hospital 26th October. Listed on the Casualty Roll as severely wounded at Balaclava. Died of wounds at Scutari. Trade Corkcutter.

1022 LOCHRIE, Private Henry

Born : Unknown
Enlisted :
Medals : Crimea (B.I.S)

Died : Unknown
Status : Slightly wounded in the Charge

The musters show he was effective from the 1st October to the 25th October. Remarks state to Scutari Hospital 26th October. Listed on the Casualty Roll as slightly wounded at Balaclava. WO100/24 page 161 Remarks: Sick at Scutari, page 183 Remarks: Gone to England. WO14/1 Scutari Muster Roll January-March 1855 remarks indicate he was on a Hospital Ship during January, and in Hospital February 1855.

1148 LOCKHART, Private Robert

Born : Unknown
Enlisted :
Medals : Crimea (B.I.S)

Died : Unknown
Status : Probably rode in the Charge

The musters show he was effective from the 1st October to the 31st December.

1112 LOVE, Private Duncan

Born : Date unknown - Paisley
Enlisted : 21st August 1850
Medals : Crimea (B.I.S)

Died : 12th March 1855 - Camp Crimea
Status : Probably rode in the Charge

The musters show he was effective from the 1st October to the 31st December. WO100/24 page 183 Remarks: Died 12th March 1855.

930 LOUDEN, Sergeant John

Born : Unknown
Enlisted :
Medals : Crimea (B.I.S)

Died : Unknown
Status : Probably rode in the Charge

The musters show he was effective from the 1st October to the 31st December. Shown on the Musters as sending £2 to a person named just "Lowden". Name in Medal Rolls Lowden.

Vancouver News Advertiser (B.C., Canada) -Sept. 16 1892 NINEPENCE A DAY. A Balaclava Hero in the Work House:

New York, Sept. 10—The United States is not the only Government that sometimes forgets its heroes. John Loudon, who, with the gallant General Scarlett, was one of the first men to draw Russian blood in the memorable charge of the Heavy Brigade at Balaclava is an inmate of St. Pancras Workhouse, England. It was he who sounded the charge of the "Heavies" on that glorious morning when a mere handful of General Scarlett's men mowed down "the o'erlapping Russian lines" after the manner of a reaping machine. A London paper recently sent a representative to interview Loudon. He is 68 years of age, but is upright and active still, and very intelligent.

When the correspondent was introduced to him in his ward he was dressed in a blue serge suit, and was wearing a "Trilby" hat. But the clothes belonged to the rate-payers of St. Pancras. However, he looked as happy as any old warrior could under such circumstances. It was animating to find ourselves chatting with General Scarlett's trumpeter, and to hear how, when he was introduced to the Queen, in 1890, by Field-Marshal Sir Patrick Grant, who told her that it was Loudon who sounded the charge of the Heavy Brigade at Balaclava, she was greatly pleased to see one of the old brigade. "Yes," remarked Loudon, feelingly, "Her Majesty spoke to me so kindly and graciously—just like a mother would. She asked me several questions but I forget them for the moment. Not having a relative alive, it was so soothing and cheering—even to a hard-hearted old warrior— to be spoken to so kindly by the Queen." But to come to the awful collision between General Scarlett's Three Hundred and the Russian line of thousands?" "Well, I sounded the charge, and we then went for the Russians like tigers. I was stirrup to stirrup with the gallant General Scarlett when we plunged into the enemy's line."

"I suppose you had a good view of the charge?" "Oh, yes until the 'Lights' disappeared into a gulf of smoke from the Russian cannon. I was alongside General Scarlett when he gave the order, 'The Heavy Brigade will support the Lights.' These were, I believe, his exact words. The Lights had then broken into a gallop, and were close to 'The Valley of Death.' I sounded, and soon myself and General Scarlett were some 30 yards in front of the advancing squadrons. Suddenly he turned around in the saddle and exclaimed, 'Why! the Heavies are retiring! Have you sounded retire ?' He was very much excited. I replied, 'No, General.' We galloped back and met Lord Lucan. It was he who had stopped the Heavies. As near as I can recollect, Lord Lucan said to General Scarlett, 'We've lost the Light Brigade and we must save the Heavies.'" "Had the Heavies not been stopped by Lord Lucan, what do you think would have been the upshot?" "Oh, undoubtedly, we would have shared the same fate as the Lights; but we wouldn't have troubled about that. We were just in the humour for another charge." Loudon holds several letters from famous warriors. "Every 25th of October," said he proudly, "until the day of his death, I was always reminded of the charge by a letter from the gallant General Scarlett. When General Scarlett died I lost the best friend I ever had. I have not a friend left now, and here I am at last, in St. Pancras Workhouse!" sighed the old fellow. So he is ending his days with a pension of 9d. per day – or, at least, the St Pancras guardians get it instead.

1032 LOWDON, Corporal Charles

Born : Unknown
Enlisted :
Medals : Crimea (B.I.S)

Died : Unknown
Status : Probably rode in the Charge

The musters show he was effective as a Private from the 1st-5th October and as a Corporal from the 5th October to the 31st of December. Promoted after the death of 1248 Cpl John Wightman. WO25 Discharge book shows him as "1032 Charles London" discharged 17th July 1865.

MACONOCHIE, Cornet Francis Beaufort

Born : Unknown
Enlisted :
Medals : Crimea (B.S)

Died : 29th November 1854 - Scutari
Status : Severely wounded in the Charge

Francis was the son of Alexander Maconochie, a Naval Captain who saw service in the Napoleonic Wars and became famous as a reforming Superintendent of the penal settlement at Norfolk Island, Australia. An explaination for his two muster entries is revealed in a book about his father entitled *"Alexander Maconochie of Norfolk Island: A Study of a Pioneer in Penal Reform"*, it states "His youngest son, Francis Beaufort Maconochie, was a most attractive young man whose heart was set on being a soldier. The means were not available to purchase a commission for him, and he enlisted in the Scots Greys under the name of Francis Campbell."

The musters show he was effective as a Private (1225 Francis Campbell) from the 1st-25th October, remarks state sent to Scutari Hospital 26th October. Listed on the Casualty Roll as severely wounded at Balaclava. WO100/24 page 177 Remarks: Died 29th November 1854. Also listed as a Cornet (Francis Beaufort Maconochie) from the 28th-29th November, shown at Scutari during the second muster, remarks state promoted Cornet 28th November (without purchase) and died 29th November. Two horses foraged at public expense. Form 20 of the Musters states he died of wounds as Scutari on the 29th November.

Memorials of the Brave Appendix, page 63 states Maconochie. F. Cornet 2nd Dragoons arrived 23rd September 1854, died 29th November 1854 of wounds at Scutari (Promoted from Ranks). *The Gentlemans Magazine* 1855 - "Nov 8. At Scutari, of wounds received in the charge of the Scots Greys, at Balaklava, Francis-Beaufort, third son of Capt. Maconochie, R.N."

Captain
Alexander Maconochie

1149 MANSON, Private George

Born : Unknown
Enlisted :
Medals : Crimea (B.I.S)

Died : Unknown
Status : Probably rode in the Charge

The musters show he was effective from the 1st October to the 31st December. WO25 Discharge book shows he was discharged on the 11th September 1862.

1103 MARSHALL, Private William

Born : Unknown
Enlisted :
Medals : Crimea (B.I.S)

Died : Unknown
Status : Slightly wounded in the Charge

The musters show he was effective from the 1st October to the 31st December. Listed on the Casualty Roll as slightly wounded at Balaclava.

918 McARTHUR, Private Henry

Born : Date unknown - Aberdeen
Enlisted : 16th April 1846
Medals : Crimea (B.I.S)

Died : 25th January 1855 - Scutari
Status : Probably rode in the Charge

The musters show he was effective from the 1st October to the 31st December. WO100/24 page 161 Remarks: Sick at Scutari, page 183 Remarks: Died 25th. January/55. WO14/1 Scutari Muster Roll January-March 1855 remarks indicate he joined on the 22nd January and died on the 25th January. Trade on enlistment Printer.

McBEAN, Quartermaster Thomas

Born : Unknown
Enlisted :
Medals : Crimea (B.I.S)

Died : Unknown
Status : Probably rode in the Charge

The musters show he was effective from the 1st October to the 31st December however he was only paid for 50 days. *Illustrated Histories of the Scottish Regiments No2. 2nd Dragoons* by Lt Col Percy Groves, Edinburgh and London 1893 page 28 states "Quartermaster Scots Greys 16th August, 1850. Quartermaster McBean served with the Scots Greys in the Crimea 1854-1855 including the affair of McKenzie's Farm, battles of Balaklava, inkermann and Tchernaya, siege and fall of Sebastopol". (See page 131, Explosion of gunpowder at Birmingham)

1190 McCOMRIE, Private Archibald

Born : Unknown
Enlisted :
Medals : Crimea (B.I.S)

Died : Unknown
Status : Probably rode in the Charge

The musters show he was effective from the 1st October to the 31st December.

760 McCONNELL, Private Samuel

Born : Unknown
Enlisted :
Medals : Crimea (B.I.S)

Died : Unknown
Status : Probably rode in the Charge

The musters show he was effective from the 1st October to the 27th December. Remarks state sent to Scutari Hospital. WO100/24 page 161 Remarks: Sick at Scutari. WO14/1 Scutari Muster Roll January-March 1855 remarks indicate he was effective in January and February, written in the March remarks is "Sentenced to 7 Days Cells".

1204 McCOWAN, Private Robert

Born : 17th July 1835 - Paisley
Enlisted : 8th February 1853
Medals : Crimea (B.I.S)

Died : 27th February 1855 - Camp Crimea
Status : Probably rode in the Charge

Glendining's auction 30th November 1976, Lot 165, Crimea 2 clasps, Balaklava, Inkermann, Robert McCowan, 2nd Dragoons. Impressed naming in box of issue. Includes photograph with research letter from PRO. Almost EF toned £260. DNW 23rd September 2005: Crimea 1854-56, 2 clasps, Balaklava, Inkermann (Robt. McCowan, 2nd Dragns.) officially impressed naming, with original ribbon in its named card box of issue together with a portrait photograph by McKenzie, Paisley, of the recipient in a Volunteer uniform prior to joining the Greys, the box rather distressed, the medal with minor edge bruising, otherwise dark toned, good very fine Hammer price £2500.

The musters show he was effective from the 1st October to the 31st December. WO100/24 page 183 Remarks: Died 27th February 1855. The photograph cannot be of McCowan, since the rifle volunteers were only formed in 1859-60, after he had died.

1154 McDONALD, Private Alexander

Born : Date unknown - Carmichael
Enlisted :
Medals : Crimea (B.I.S)

Died : Unknown
Status : Rode in the Charge

The musters show he was effective from the 1st October to the 31st December. WO25 Discharge book shows he was discharged on the 12th December 1873. WO 117-21 Examination of invalid soldier's 2nd December 1873. 2nd Dragoons. Pte Alexander McDonald, 1154, Age 40 years. Total service 22 years. Disallowed 1/12. Rate of pension 81/4. Foreign service. Crimea and Turkey 1 yr 11 months character good. Disability or cause of discharge completed service. Wounded sabre cut on 2nd and 3rd finger of left hand at Balaclava 25th October 1854. Place of birth Carmichael. Ayr. A tailor 5ft 8 inches, fair hair, blur eyes. Fair complexion.

934 McDONALD, Private Henry

Born : Unknown
Enlisted :
Medals : Crimea (B.I.S)

Died : Unknown
Status : Probably rode in the Charge

The musters show he was effective from the 1st October to the 31st December. WO14/1 Scutari Muster Roll January-March 1855 remarks indicate he joined on the 2nd March. WO25 Discharge book shows he discharged 26/9/1865.

1115 McDONALD, Private Hugh

Born : Date unknown - Kilmarnock
Enlisted : 5th October 1850
Medals : Crimea (B.I.S)

Died : 8th March 1855 - Camp Crimea
Status : Probably rode in the Charge

The musters show he was effective from the 1st October to the 31st December. WO100/24 page 183 Remarks: Died 8th March 1855. Trade on enlistment Labourer.

595 McDOUGHALL, Private John

Born : Unknown
Enlisted :
Medals : Crimea (B.I.S)

Died : Unknown
Status : Probably rode in the Charge

The musters show he was effective from the 1st October to the 31st December. Discharged in 1857.

1113 McEWING, Corporal John

Born : Unknown
Enlisted :
Medals : Crimea (B.I.S)

Died : Unknown
Status : Probably rode in the Charge

The musters show he was effective as a Private from the 1st October to the 31st December. Discharged April 1859.

1156 McFADYAN, Private James

Born : Unknown
Enlisted :
Medals : Crimea (B.I.S)
Medal offered for sale privately in August 1993. Crimea 3 clasps Balaklava, Inkermann, Sebastopol officially impressed to J.McFadyan 2nd Dragoons £575. A Long Service and Good Conduct has also appeared on the market.

Died : Unknown
Status : Probably rode in the Charge

The musters show he was effective from the 1st October to the 31st December. Invalided 22nd April 1873.

993 McGREGOR, Sergeant Charles

Born : Unknown
Enlisted :
Medals : Crimea (B.I.S)
Seaby, May 1959 item F 5378 Crimea Bar Sebastopol, Turkish Crimea, both named P.McGregor 2nd Dragns, worn 25/-

Died : Unknown
Status : Probably rode in the Charge

The musters show he was effective from the 1st October to the 31st December. WO102 L.S & G.C - T.S.M Charles McGregor issued 7th July 1869, gratuity £15.

129

1152 McKAY, Private Daniel
Born : Unknown
Enlisted :
Medals : Crimea (B.I.S)

Died : Unknown
Status : Probably rode in the Charge

The musters show he was effective from the 1st October to the 31st December. WO25 Discharge book shows he was discharged as a Troop Sergeant Major on the 11th November 1873.

1197 McKAY, Private Donald
Born : Unknown
Enlisted :
Medals : Crimea (B.I.S)

Died : Unknown
Status : Probably rode in the Charge

The musters show he was effective from the 1st October to the 31st December. WO25 Discharge book shows he was discharged as a Sergeant in December 1859.

943 McKECHNIE, Private Hugh
Born : Date unknown - Barony, Lanark
Enlisted : 27th May 1846
Medals : Crimea (B.I.S)

Died : 14th June 1855 - Camp
Status : Probably rode in the Charge

The musters show he was effective from the 1st October to the 31st December.
WO100/24 page 183 Remarks: Died 14th June 1855. Trade on enlistment Dyer.

1185 McKIMNINGS, Private W.I.
Born : Unknown
Enlisted :
Medals : Crimea (B.I.S)

Died : Unknown
Status : Probably rode in the Charge

The musters show he was effective from the 1st October to the 31st December. WO100/24 page 183 Remarks: Gone to England. WO25 Discharge book shows he was discharged in 1857.

812 McKINNON, Private Donald
Born : Unknown
Enlisted :
Medals : Crimea (B.I.S)

Died : Unknown
Status : Probably rode in the Charge

The musters show he was effective from the 1st October to the 31st December.

1165 McLELLAN, Private John
Born : Unknown
Enlisted :
Medals : Crimea (B.I.S)

Died : Unknown
Status : Probably rode in the Charge

The musters show he was effective from the 1st October to the 31st December.

1117 McLEOD, Private Donald
Born : Unknown
Enlisted :
Medals : Crimea (B.I.S)

Died : Unknown
Status : Probably rode in the Charge

Glendining's auction 29th May 1980 Lot 165, Pair to C.P.McLeod Crimea three bars Balaklava, Inkermann, Sebastopol, McLeod initials erased by wear RL.Scots Greys Engraved. Turkish Crimea, Sardinian Version. Named 2nd Dragoons. First much contact wear, fine. Second slight wear, fine £110

The musters show he was effective from the 1st October to the 31st December. WO25 Discharge book shows he was disharged on the 18th October 1862.

686 McLEOD, Private John W.
Born : Date unknown - Ross
Enlisted : 18th August 1840
Medals : Crimea (B.I.S)

Died : 28th January 1855 - Scutari
Status : Probably rode in the Charge

Glendinings Auction 28th September 1972 Lot 110, Crimea three bars Balaklava, Inkermann, Sebastopol impressed naming J.W. McLeod 2nd Dragoons VF £110. E.E.NEEDES Collection Crimea 3 clasps Balaklava, Inkermann, Sebastopol J.W. McLeod. 2nd Dragoons.

The musters show he was effective from the 1st October to the 30th December. Remarks state sent to Scutari Hospital. Appears to have been sent to Scutari on the 31st December. WO14/1 Scutari Muster Roll January-March 1855 remarks indicate he joined on the 24th January and died on the 28th January. Trade on enlistment Labourer.

1047 McLUCKIE, Private Robert
Born : Date unknown - Stirling
Enlisted : 25th November 1848
Medals : Crimea (B.I.S)

Died : 20th January 1855 - Camp Crimea
Status : Probably rode in the Charge

The musters show he was effective from the 1st October to the 31st December.
WO100/24 page 183 Remarks: Died 20th January 1855. Trade on enlistment Printer.

657 McMILLAN, Private Alexander
Born : Date unknown - Paisley
Enlisted : 26th June 1839
Medals : Crimea (B.I.S)

Died : 5th January 1855 - Scutari
Status : Probably rode in the Charge

The musters show he was effective from the 1st October to the 20th December. Remarks state sent to Scutari Hospital. WO100/24 page 161 Remarks: Sick at Scutari, page 183 Remarks: Died 5th January 1855. WO14/1 Scutari Muster Roll January-March 1855 remarks indicate he died on the 5th January.

937 McMILLAN, Private James
Born : Unknown
Enlisted :
Medals : Crimea (B.I.S)

Died : Unknown
Status : Probably rode in the Charge

The musters show he was effective from the 1st October to the 31st December.

692 McMILLAN, Private John
Born : Date unknown - Kirkmaiden
Enlisted : 23rd September 1840
Medals : Crimea (B.I.S)

Died : 27th January 1855 - Scutari
Status : Probably rode in the Charge

The musters show he was effective from the 1st October to the 31st December. WO100/24 page 161 Remarks: Farrier, page 183 Remarks: Died 27 January 1855. Trade on enlistment Blacksmith.

A farrier in the Crimea would need the skills of a blacksmith to care for the horses in his regiment especially shoeing, coupled with a knowledge of veterinary medicine to address the care of a horse's hooves, feet & legs. After a battle it was the farriers' pistols that were brought into action to put down any poor beasts that were too mutilated for further service. It was also traditional for farriers to carry out the punishment of flogging on any gulity trooper using the cat o' nine tails.

1237 McNEE, Private Duncan
Born : Date unknown - Perth
Enlisted : 12th January 1854
Medals : Crimea (B.I.S)

Died : 16th February 1855 - Scutari
Status : Probably rode in the Charge

The musters show he was effective from the 1st October to the 31st December. WO100/24 page 183 Remarks: Died 16th February 1855. WO14/1 Scutari Muster Roll January-March 1855 remarks indicate he joined on the 28th January and was in Koulali Hospital during January, died 16th February. Probably brother of 1239 John McNee below.

1239 McNEE, Private John
Born : Unknown
Enlisted :
Medals : Crimea (B.I.S)
Died : October 1889 - near Ayre
Status : Slightly wounded in the Charge

The musters show he was effective from the 1st October to the 31st December. Listed on the Casualty Roll as slightly wounded at Balaclava. *The Broad Arrow* 12th October 1889 - "2nd Dragoons - there died at Drumshung Cottage Near Ayre, John McNee formerly of this Regiment, and survivor of Balaclava". Discharged 11th April 1866.

1229 McPHEDRON, Private John
Born : Date unknown - Cardross
Enlisted : 20th November 1853
Medals : Crimea (I.S)
Died : 2nd January 1855 - Scutari
Status : Effective during the period

The musters show he was effective from the 1st October to the 12th November. Remarks state sent to Scutari Hospital. WO14/1 Scutari Muster Roll January-March 1855 remarks indicate he died on the 2nd January 1855. Trade Labourer.

796 McPHERSON, Private James
Born : Unknown
Enlisted :
Medals : Crimea (B.I.S)
Died : Unknown
Status : Slightly wounded in the Charge

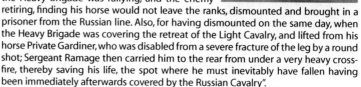

Sold on Ebay September 2007 for £700, the description stated: Crimea medal regimentally impressed to James McPherson 2nd Dragoons. Clasps Sebastopol, Inkermann, Balaklava. Comes with what could be the original box and photo of the man. The medal came with this box and photo when purchased some 10 years ago, at the time it was stated this was the original box and photograph of the recipient. Name erased (but still possible to read with a very good eye glass).

The musters show he was effective from the 1st October to the 31st December. Listed on the Casualty Roll as slightly wounded at Balaclava. WO25 Discharge book shows he discharged in 1857.

Sergeant Henry Ramage was awarded the Victoria Cross for assisting Private McPherson and saving the life of Private Gardiner during the Charge, his citation reads "For having, at the Battle of Balaklava, galloped out to the assistance of Private

McPherson, of the same regiment, on perceiving him surrounded by seven Russians, when by his gallantry he dispersed the enemy and saved his comrade's life. For having, on the same day, when the Heavy Brigade was rallying, and the enemy retiring, finding his horse would not leave the ranks, dismounted and brought in a prisoner from the Russian line. Also, for having dismounted on the same day, when the Heavy Brigade was covering the retreat of the Light Cavalry, and lifted from his horse Private Gardiner, who was disabled from a severe fracture of the leg by a round shot; Sergeant Ramage then carried him to the rear from under a very heavy cross-fire, thereby saving his life, the spot where he must inevitably have fallen having been immediately afterwards covered by the Russian Cavalry".

Medals were some times erased when they were pawned, also if an individual lost a medal they would often acquire a replacement from a pawn shop and remove the original name. It is sometimes possible to decipher the removed name because when a letter is stamped into a metal object the metal underneath is compressed and becomes harder, this makes it possible to read the erased name using a chemical process.

1130 McPHERSON, Private William
Born : Unknown
Enlisted :
Medals : Crimea (B.S)
Died : Unknown
Status : Probably rode in the Charge

The musters show he was effective from the 1st-25th October and from the 29th December to the 31st December. Remarks state sent to Scutari 26th October returned 29th December. WO25 Discharge book shows he discharged on the 27th March 1863.

The Times, Thursday March 10th 1864.
Quartermaster McBean's involvement in the mysterious gunpowder explosion at the Royal Scots Greys Barracks. at Birmingham

The Times, Friday September 10th 1869.
The tragic death of Quartermaster Samuel Seggie. (Please see page 142)

EXPLOSION OF GUNPOWDER AT BIRMINGHAM.—An explosion of gunpowder, the cause of which nobody seems at present to be able to fathom, took place at the barracks in Great Brook-street on Tuesday morning. The Royal Scots Greys, under Colonel Griffiths, are stationed there now. At a quarter to 11 o'clock Quartermaster M'Bean went to the magazine for the purpose of drawing some blank cartridge to be used in breaking young horses. The magazine is in the lower yard, apart from the other buildings. There was a very large quantity of gunpowder in it. It is used by the Volunteers and by the Pensioners, as well as by the Scots Greys. The Volunteers alone had 50,000 rounds in it. The quantity belonging to the Scots Greys and Pensioners was not so large, but was very considerable. The powder was contained in casks, each cask containing 700 rounds, and it consisted of both ball and blank cartridge. In a few moments after Quartermaster M'Bean had entered the magazine the report of an explosion was heard. The officers and men whose attention was attracted by it saw, that the magazine was smoking, that the roof had been blown off it, and that one of the end walls had fallen out, and was only prevented from coming to the ground by resting against a boundary wall that stood at the distance of about a foot behind it. It was evident that the shock previously felt would have been much more violent, and the report much louder, had more than a comparatively small portion of the powder in the magazine been exploded. To see the ruins on fire was therefore an indication of a coming danger far more terrible than that which had passed. It was known that the magazine was filled with blank and ball cartridge sufficient to blow almost the whole barracks to pieces. It was therefore an act of courage worthy of every acknowledgment when a number of officers and men approached it and climbed the walls, for the purpose of seeking the body of the quartermaster if he were dead, or of rescuing him should he be found still alive. Private Regan was the first to cross the ruined walls and endeavour to clear away the rubbish inside. He was followed by Lieutenant Philp, Cornet Sanderson, Sergeant Masterson, and several others. Quartermaster M'Bean was found among the rubbish in a state of insensibility. He was removed, and remained in that state for several hours. When this account was written no information could be obtained from him as to what he observed when he entered the magazine, or how the accident occurred. As soon as the quartermaster was removed the magazine was more closely examined than in had been before, and it was found that only one barrel of blank cartridge had exploded. Had the ball cartridge taken fire the consequences must have been fearful. An engine was brought, and water was poured upon the ammunition for about half-an-hour, to prevent the possibility of another explosion. Some of the men, in looking through the place, found a match-box containing unburnt matches lying on one of the casks. Nobody seems to know anything about how it came there. We were informed that the quartermaster did not smoke, and was, therefore, not likely to have matches in his possession. It is not safe to conclude, without some evidence upon the subject, that it was there before the explosion, because it is quite possible —although hardly probable—that it may have been brought there by some of the men who ran from the canteen to the magazine when they heard the explosion, or it may have been brought by the quartermaster himself. A very searching inquiry will of course be instituted by the authorities, and we may then learn who was in the magazine last before Quartermaster M'Bean, and the presence of the box of matches on a barrel of gunpowder may possibly be accounted for. On Tuesday evening Quartermaster M'Bean recovered consciousness, but by the direction of the surgeon no one has been allowed to enter into conversation with him as to his knowledge of the cause of the explosion.' —*Birmingham Daily Gazette.*

SUICIDE.—Dr. Diplock held an inquiry yesterday afternoon at the Duke of York, Hounslow, touching the death of Quartermaster Seggie, of the 9th Lancers, who committed suicide on the previous afternoon. From the evidence it appeared that the deceased had for some time past been in very low spirits, and on Wednesday he was found in a closet in the barracks with his throat dreadfully lacerated. The unfortunate man had been in the regiment for many years, and bore a high character. He formerly served with the Scots Greys, and had risen from the ranks. The instrument with which he took his life is a small pocket knife, with a blade about two inches long. The surgeon of the regiment said, on being called by the last witness he went to where the deceased was lying. He had him removed and tried to stop the bleeding, but he died almost immediately. He was a man of very active habits, and had been 24 years in the regiment. His accounts were perfectly correct. He had been confined to his room lately with a bad ankle, which might have induced temporary insanity. A verdict in accordance with the medical testimony was given—"That deceased destroyed himself while in a fit of temporary insanity."

The Association in Aid of Soldier's Wives and Families. Showing the number of women and children helped by the fund up to March 1856.

APPENDIX.

Regiment.	Women.	Children.	Regiment.	Women.	Children.
1st Dragoon Guards	37	57	28th ditto	97	150
4th Dragoon Guards	51	88	39th ditto	112	144
5th Dragoon Guards	60	92	41st ditto	106	132
6th ditto	34	58	42d ditto	114	112
1st Royal Dragoons	55	84	44th ditto	86	131
2d Dragoons	40	71	46th ditto	105	112
4th Light Dragoons	41	71	47th ditto	116	156
6th Dragoons	61	98	48th ditto	112	183
8th Hussars	46	53	49th ditto	114	160
10th ditto	56	94	50th ditto	88	111
11th ditto	29	34	51st ditto	72	102
12th Lancers	46	89	55th ditto	120	193
13th Light Dragoons	51	97	56th ditto	22	42
17th Lancers	42	71	57th ditto	137	163
3d.Bn. Gren. Guards	32	99	62d ditto	76	99
1st Bn. ditto	17	24	63d ditto	159	193
1st Bn. Coldstream Guards	78	105	66th ditto	52	70
			68th ditto	151	232
1st Bn. Scots Fusilier Guards	83	126	71st ditto	75	99
1st Bn. 1st Regimt.	116	154	72d ditto	71	82
2d Bn. 1st Regiment	53	77	77th ditto	123	165
3d Regiment	91	144	79th ditto	100	121
4th ditto	125	170	82d ditto	93	153
7th ditto	95	135	88th ditto	110	113
9th ditto	126	149	89th ditto	143	225
13th ditto	88	117	90th ditto	76	89
14th ditto	115	153	91st ditto	4	7
17th ditto	159	177	92d ditto	56	134
18th ditto	24	24	93d ditto	122	184
19th ditto	99	152	94th ditto	25	32
20th ditto	106	134	95th ditto	91	120
21st ditto	134	149	97th ditto	63	67
23d ditto	94	113	1st Bn. Rifle Brigade	54	63
28th ditto	146	199	2d Bn. ditto	70	101
30th ditto	57	76	Sappers and Miners	53	62
31st ditto	109	169	Royal Horse Artillery	26	31
33d ditto	110	167	Royal Artillery	715	1,007
34th ditto	65	88	Total	6,562	8,984

Relatives of Soldiers Relieved by the Central Association.

4	widows each with five sons in the Eastern Expedition.		
2	ditto	four	ditto
23	ditto	three	ditto
43	ditto	two	ditto
160	ditto	one	ditto

232 Total number of dependent relatives, not wives, of soldiers.

1106 MEIKLE, Private John

Born : Unknown
Enlisted :
Medals : Crimea (B.I.S)

Died : Unknown
Status : Probably rode in the Charge

The musters show he was effective from the 1st October to the 31st December. Regimental number shown as 1086. Shown on the Musters as sending £3 to Mary Ann Meikle.

Private John Meikle is shown on the photograph on page 160, serving the officers wine at Newbridge Barracks circa 1859.

1209 MELDRUM, Private William

Born : Unknown
Enlisted :
Medals : Crimea (B.I.S)

Died : Unknown
Status : Probably rode in the Charge

The musters show he was effective from the 1st October to the 31st December. WO25 Discharge book shows he deserted on the 16th May 1857.

MILLER, Captain William

Born : Unknown
Enlisted :
Medals : Crimea (B.I.S)

Died : Unknown
Status : Rode in the Charge

Glendining's auction 3rd March 1976, Lot 223. Pair: Captain W. Miller, Scots Greys, Crimea three clasps, Balaklava, Inkermann, Sebastopol, Turkish Crimea, Sardinian issue. Both engraved naming, with miniatures VF £190.
Christie's 17th November 1987, Lot 118, Pair: Captain W. Miller, Royal Scots Greys, Crimea three clasps, Balaklava, Inkermann, Sebastopol, (Captn. Wm. Miller, Scots Greys), engraved in small serif capitals; Turkish Crimea, Sardinian issue, engraved, with claw and foliate suspension, lacquered, very fine with contemporary decorative riband bars (2) Hammer price £1705

The musters show he was effective from the 1st October to the 31st December. Three horses foraged at public expense.
Miller entered the 2nd Dragoons in 1827 as a Private, his exemplary conduct during 19 years service included eight years as Regimental Sergeant Major; he earned the approbation of the Duke of Wellington when he was recommended by his commanding officer for an appointment as Adjutant in his regiment with the rank of Cornet on the 7th July 1846; became a Lieutenant on the 20th June 1850 and Captain on the 30th September 1854.

The following extract is taken from Kinglake's *The Invasion of the Crimea* Vol. 4 :"William Miller, the acting Adjutant of the Greys, was famous in his regiment for the mighty volume of sound which he drove through the air when he gave the word of command. Over all the clangour of arms, and all the multitudinous uproar, his single voice got dominion.
It thundered out, 'Rally!' Then, still louder, it thundered, 'The Greys!'. The Adjutant, as it chanced, was so mounted that his vast, superb form rose high over the men of even his own regiment, and rose higher still over the throng of the Russians.
Seized at once by the mighty sound, and turning to whence it came, numbers of the Scots saw their towering Adjutant with his reeking sword high in the air, and again they heard him cry, 'Rally!' - again hurl his voice at 'The Greys!'"

Illustrated histories of the Scottish Regiments No2. 2nd Dragoons, by Lt Col Percy Groves. Page 28. Captain Miller. Cornet and Adjutant Scots Greys 7th July 1846. Lieutenant 20th June 1850. Captain 30th September 1854. Adjutant Cavalry Depot, Maidstone 14th Nov 1856. Retired full pay 2nd September 1862. Honorary Major 2nd December 1862.
Captain Miller served with the Scots Greys in the Crimea 1854-1865 Including the affair of MacKenzie's farm. Battle of Balaklava and Inkermann and siege of Sebastopol.

The Times Nov 06 1861 "Desertion before the enemy". Staff Captain William Miller, from the Cavalry Dept, Maidstone was the prosecutor. For the trial of Henry Warner, 17th Lancers, No 1223 for having deserted from his regiment when in front of the enemy at Kadikoi, in the Crimea, on the 8th August, 1855.
The prisoner, who was dressed as a sailor and pleaded "Guilty" The prisoner then handed to the Court a written defence, throwing himself on the merciful consideration of the Court. he had concealed himself on board Her Majesty's ship Colossus, and subsequently served on board as a stoker up to 1856, when the ship was taken into dock at Portsmouth. He then gave himself up to to Sergeant Irish, Royal Marine Artillery. The first witness examined was Sergeant John Penn, followed by Sergeant William Pervis both of the 17th Lancers. The issue of this extraordinary trial will not be known until the proceedings have been laid before Her Majesty.

The photograph taken by Robertson shows Balaklava Harbour, which was the lifeline of the British Army. Through this narrow and congested harbour flowed food, ammunition, and all manner of supplies. No warehousing was available. Stores were kept on board ship, which made distribution difficult. To add to the confusion the operations were controlled by two totally separate departments, the Commissariat staffed by civilians and controlled by the Treasury, were responsible for land transport and non-military supplies such as food and forage for the horses. The Ordnance taking care of ammunition, and military supplies. Add to this the over-complicated rules and regulations, and we have a formula for failure.

1191 MILLS, Private William

Born : Date unknown - Shelton
Enlisted : 26th November 1852
Medals : Crimea (I.S)

Died : 6th February 1855 - Scutari
Status : Effective during the period

The musters show he was effective from the 1st October to the 31st December. WO14/1 Scutari Muster Roll January-March 1855 remarks indicate he joined on the 2nd February and was in Koulali Hospital during February and March. Pay List indicates he died on the 6th February 1855 at Scutari. Trade on enlistment Shoemaker.

On Form 8 of the musters entitled "Account of Soldier's under sentence of Forfeiture of Pay, or Additional Pay, during the Period of this Pay List" William Mills is shown as forfeiting 1d per day of his pay for 18 months from the 15th August 1853.

1147 MILNE, Private William

Born : Date unknown - Rathie May, Banff
Enlisted : 29th August 1851
Medals : Crimea (S)

Died : 17th November 1855 - Scutari
Status : Effective during the period

The musters show he was effective from the 1st October to the 26th October. Remarks state sent to Scutari 27th October. WO14/1 Scutari Muster Roll January-March 1855 remarks indicate he was on a Hospital Ship during January.

1005 MITCHELL, Corporal Alexander

Born : Unknown
Enlisted :
Medals : Crimea (B.I.S)

Died : Unknown
Status : Probably rode in the Charge

London Stamp Exchange Ltd List Summer 1985, item 271. Pair Crimea 3 clasps Balaklava, Inkermann, Sebastopol (Regimentally Engraved) Turkish Crimea British issue. Sold with orginal letter of recommendation from Col H. Parby Griffith dated 3rd October 1856. Nearly EF £225. Medal List from Capt Bob Baird, USA, December 1992, Medals as above but also states the letter from Col H. Parby recommended Mitchell for his skill with horses - $600.

The musters show he was effective as a Private from the 1st October to the 4th November and as a Corporal from the 4th November to the 31st December. Promoted to Corporal following the promotion of Stevenson.

MOODIE, Adjutant Daniel

Born : Unknown   Died : Unknown

Enlisted :   Status : Probably rode in the Charge

Medals : Crimea (B.I.S), The Turkish Order of the Medjidie (5th Class)

Sotheby 22nd November 1977, Lot 337, Four Lieutenant D. Moodie. 2nd Dragoons. Crimea 3 clasps Balaklava, Inkermann, Sebastopol (Lieut & Adjt. RL. Scots Greys 5th Novr 1856) Engraved L.S & G.C Victorian (No. 400 Regimental Serjeant Major Daniel Moodie 2nd Dragoons, 4th May, 1854) Order of the Medjidie 5th Class, Breast Badge, Silver, Gold and Enamel. Turkish Crimea, Sardinian issue (Naming similar to that of the British Crimea but dated 1859) Repair to suspension claw of L.S & G.C N.VF and better. Christie's 17th November 1987, Lot 119, Four: Lieutenant D. Moodie, 2nd Dragoons, Royal Scots Greys, Crimea, three clasps Balaklava, Inkermann, Sebastopol (D Moodie Lieutt & Adjt Rl. Scots Greys 5th Novr 1856), engraved in large serif capitals, date inscribed in running script; Army Long Service and G.C. (No. 400 Regimental Serjeant Major Daniel Moodie 2nd Dragoons, 4th May, 1854) large letter reverse, replacement scroll suspension; Turkey, Order of The Medjidie, Fifth Class, Badge, silver, gold and enamel; Turkish Crimea, Sardinian issue, named, contact marks to British Medals, reverse of Turkish order soldiered, otherwise nearly very fine (4) Ex Lovell Collection 1977 - £450-550 Hammer price £1045

Daniel Moodie was commissioned as Cornet from Regimental Sergeant Major on the 30th September 1854. Lieutenant 7th February 1856, Captain 60th Rifles 25th July 1865. Half Pay 25th July 1865. Served in the Eastern Campaign of 1854-55, including the affair at McKenzie's Farm, battles of Balaklava, Inkermann and Chernaya, Siege and Fall of Sebastopol. (*Harts Annual Army List*)

The musters show he was effective as Adjutant from the 1st October to the 31st December.
The Times Saturday 5th July 1856. The steam-transport Orinoco, No 218, arrived at Spithead yesterday morning, with the following troops:- 2d Royal North British Dragoons; Lieutenant-Colonel Sulivan, Captains Sir. G. Hampson, Prentis, and Hunter; Lieutenants McNeill and Brown; Cornets Parr and Armstrong; Adjutant Moodie, Surgeon Llewellyn, Assistant-Surgeon Rutherford, Veterinary-Surgeon Gudgin, Paymaster Lukin, Quartermaster McBean, 276 men and 191 horses.

616 MORRISON, Private William

Born : Unknown   Died : Unknown

Enlisted :   Status : Severely wounded in the Charge

Medals : Crimea (B.I.S)

The musters show he was effective from the 1st October to the 25th October. Remarks state to Scutari Hospital 26th October. WO100/24 page 162 Remarks: Wounded (at Scutari). Listed on the Casualty Roll as severely wounded at Balaclava. WO25 Discharge book shows he was invalided out on the 23rd August 1862.

1142 MOWAT, Private Alexander

Born : Unknown   Died : Unknown

Enlisted :   Status : Probably rode in the Charge

Medals : Crimea (B.I.S)

The musters show he was effective from the 1st October to the 13th December. Remarks state to Scutari Hospital 14th December. WO100/24 page 162 Remarks: Sick at Scutari. B on O.C. Certif 9/4/57. WO25 Discharge book shows he discharged 6th February 1864 as a Sergeant, name spelt "Mowatt".

1074 MUIR, Private John

Born : Date unknown - Dalghatty   Died : 10th March 1855 - Camp Crimea

Enlisted : 23rd July 1849   Status : Probably rode in the Charge

Medals : Crimea (B.I.S)

The musters show he was effective from the 1st October to the 31st December.
WO100/24 page 184 Remarks: Died 10th March 1855. Trade on enlistment Slater.

1252 NEILL, Private Thomas

Born : Date unknown - Kelso   Died : 29th January 1855 - Scutari

Enlisted : 15th March 1854   Status : Probably rode in the Charge

Medals : Crimea (B.I.S)

The musters show he was effective from the 1st October to the 31st December. WO100/24 page 184 Remarks: Died 29th January 1855. WO14/1 Scutari Muster Roll January-March 1855 remarks indicate he joined 21st January and died

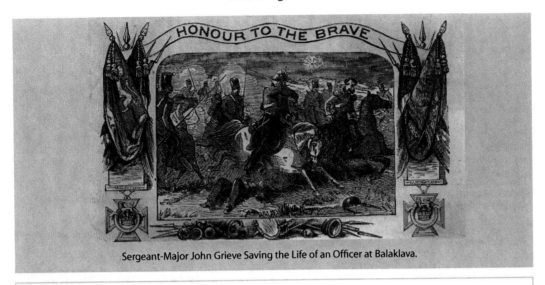

Sergeant-Major John Grieve Saving the Life of an Officer at Balaklava.

942 NEILSON, Private David

Born : Unknown
Enlisted :
Medals : Crimea (B.I.S)

Died : Unknown
Status : Probably rode in the Charge

The musters show he was effective from the 1st October to the 31st December.

1105 NEILSON, Private William

Born : Unknown
Enlisted :
Medals : Crimea (B.I.S)

Died : Unknown
Status : Probably rode in the Charge

The musters show he was effective from the 1st October to the 31st December. The Pay Lists spell this name Nelson.

841 NESBETT, Trumpeter Charles

Born : Unknown
Enlisted :
Medals : Crimea (B.I.S)

Died : Unknown
Status : Probably rode in the Charge

The musters show he was effective from the 1st October to the 31st December. WO25 Discharge book shows he was sent home on the 28th April 1856.

1025 NESBITT, Private William

Born : Unknown
Enlisted :
Medals : Crimea (B.I.S)

Died : Unknown
Status : Probably rode in the Charge

The musters show he was effective from the 1st October to the 31st December. WO25 Discharge book shows he was discharged in December 1859.

1093 NIMMO, Private Thomas

Born : Unknown
Enlisted :
Medals : Crimea (B.I.S)
For sale A.H Baldwin and Sons July 1948, One bar Balaklava. "Pte Thos. Nimmo" Engraved V.F. £1.15s

Died : Unknown
Status : Probably rode in the Charge

The musters show he was effective from the 1st October to the 2nd November. Remarks state sent to Scutari Hospital. WO100/24 page 162 Remarks: Sick at Scutari, page 184 Remarks: Gone to England. WO14/1 Scutari Muster Roll January-March 1855 remarks indicate he was at Abydos in January.

NUGENT, Lieutenant Andrew

Born : 30th March 1834
Enlisted :
Medals : Crimea (B.I.S)

Died : 10th July 1905
Status : Rode in the Charge

Andrew Nugent was a member of the Nugent family of Portaferry. The Public Record Office of Northern Ireland holds the family archive described as follows: The Nugent of Portaferry papers comprise c.8,650 documents and c.225 volumes, 1568-1962, deriving from the Portaferry House branch of the Anglo-Norman family of Savage of the Ards, Co. Down, which changed its name to Nugent in 1812 following the succession of Andrew Savage of Portaferry to the Dysart estate, baronies of Moyashel and Magheradernon, Co. Westmeath, of his kinsman, John Nugent of Dysart. This change of name gave rise to the famous remark of a disgruntled uncle of Andrew Savage/Nugent that he, for one, would "rather be an old savage than a new gent"!

The archive contains nine photograph albums and numerous photographs, c.1855-c.1920, some of them deriving from General Andrew Nugent of Portaferry, and including mainly commercial photographs of the Crimean War c.1854-1856, and the Afghan War 1878-1879.

The musters show he was effective as a Cornet from the 1st October to the 7th December and as a Lieutenant from the 8th-31st December.

Ilustrated Histories of the Scottish Regiments No2. - 2nd Dragoons by Lt Col Percy Groves, page 28, states Andrew Nugent became a Cornet in the Scots Greys on the 17th December 1852, a Lieutenant 8th December 1854, Captain 8th February 1856, Major 31st November 1866, Lieutenant-Colonel 3rd February 1869, Brevet Colonel 3rd February 1874, on Half pay 21st June 1880, Major General 19th February 1885, and retired as Honorary Lieutenant-General on the 13th November 1886. General Nugent Served with the Scots Greys in the Crimea 1854-1855. Battles of Balaclava, Inkermann and Tchernaya and siege and fall of Sebastopol.

The National Army Museum holds several letters written by Lieutenant Andrew Nugent from the Crimea in 1854-55 (Ref: 9601-22)

In a letter dated 9th Nov 1854.
Describing the scene after the battle of Inkermann that took place on the 5th November 1854:
"I rode on the field of battle about 2 hours after it had run it was a horrible sight the dead and dying lying in heaps all round, some of them giving out groans and cries"
After the battle he went in search of a Bernard Ward, after hearing his horse had been shot to pieces they had been school friends at Eaton.
I got a chance to ride over to see him after the battle and found him safe and well. We took a great number of prisoners, dirty miserable hungry wretches.
Later in the letter he describes the charge of the Heavy Brigade, the 93rd fired a volley into the Russians as they went past, the horse Artillery fired shots into them, and both times they ran away in a most dreadful manner.
I won't go through another campaign but if the war continues, they will not catch me out here a third year Tell Mamma I got her letter of the 12th.
He then goes on to ask for a copy of the Times concerning the action on the 25th, and a list of those killed and wounded to be sent to him.

The Times Obituary Wednesday July 12th 1905
Lieutenant-General Andrew Nugent, Colonel of the 2nd Dragoons (Royal Scots Greys), of Portaferry, county Down, Ireland, died at Bournemouth, on Monday, at the age of 71. He was the eldest son of Colonel Patrick J.Nugent, of Portaferry, by a daughter of the third Viscount de Vesci, and was born in 1834...
General Nugent became Colonel of the 7th Dragoon Guards, and so continued till 1900, when he was transferred to the colonelcy of his old regiment. He was a duputy lieutenant and justice of the peace for county Down, and in 1882 had been Sheriff.

Major Nugent, Dundalk 1868.

828 ORCHARD, Private William
Born : Unknown
Enlisted :
Medals : Crimea (B.I.S)

Died : Unknown
Status : Probably rode in the Charge

The musters show he was effective from the 1st October to the 31st December.

1043 PATERSON, Private Thomas
Born : Date unknown - Avondale
Enlisted : 13th October 1848
Medals : Crimea (B.I.S)

Died : 16th January 1855 - Scutari
Status : Probably rode in the Charge

The musters show he was effective from the 1st October to the 31st December. WO100/24 page 184 Remarks: Died 16th January 1855. *The Times*, Thursday 1st February 1855, page 8, reported that "Private W.Pattison 2nd Dragoons died on board the Colombo on the 16th January 1855."

1062 PATTON, Private Alexander
Born : Date unknown - Riecarton
Enlisted : 11th May 1849
Medals : Crimea (B.I.S)

Died : 20th February 1855 - Scutari
Status : Probably rode in the Charge

The musters show he was effective from the 1st October to the 30th December. Remarks state sent to Scutari Hosptial. WO100/24 page 162 Remarks: Sick at Scutari, page 184 Remarks: Died 20th February 1855. WO14/1 Scutari Muster Roll January-March 1855 remarks indicate he joined on the 23rd January and died on the 20th February.

1187 PENMAN, Private James
Born : Date unknown - Liberton, Edinburgh
Enlisted : 14th July 1849
Medals : Crimea (B.I.S)

Died : 29th April 1855 - Scutari
Status : Probably rode in the Charge

The musters show he was effective from the 1st October to the 31st December. WO100/24 page 162 Remarks: Sick at Scutari. WO14/1 Scutari Muster Roll January-March 1855 remarks indicate he joined on the 25th January and was in Hospital for February and March. Trade on enlistment Moulder.

1162 PIRNIE, Private John
Born : Unknown
Enlisted :
Medals : Crimea (B.I.S)

Died : Unknown
Status : Probably rode in the Charge

The musters show he was effective from the 1st October to the 31st December. WO14/1 Scutari Muster Roll January-March 1855 remarks indicate he joined on the 2nd February and was in Koulali Hospital in February and March. WO25 Discharge book shows he discharged on the 19th February 1864 as a Sergeant.

1097 POLSON, Private George
Born : Unknown
Enlisted :
Medals : Crimea (B.I.S)

Died : Unknown
Status : Probably rode in the Charge

In the Fitzpatrick collection, Crimea two Bars Balaklava,Sebastopol to Pte G. Polson 2nd Dragoons. Spinks Circular November 1954, item 9833, Crimea 2 Bars Balaklava,Sebastopol, G.Palson 2nd Dragoons Impressed, note different naming. First recorded at Sothebys in 1910.

The musters show he was effective from the 3rd October to the 31st December. Remarks state sent to Scutari Hospital 1st to the 3rd October. WO14/1 Scutari Muster Roll January-March 1855 remarks indicate he joined on the 2nd February and was in Koulali Hospital during February and March.

Describing Koulali Hospital and the fever epidemic, which was at its worst in March,"The fever is horrible in its virulence owing in great measure to the way they crowd the patients together - only 1 1/2 feet between beds" The hospital was visited during March 1855 and found to be grossly overcrowded, ill-ventilated, offensive and fever-stricken. Orders were given to correct these evils, although this involved, as with the other hospitals, extensive engineering and much rebuilding. (*The Crimean Doctors: A History of the British Medical Services in the Crimea* page 397)

1175 PREECE, Private William C.

Born : Unknown
Enlisted :
Medals : Crimea (B.I.S)

Died : Unknown
Status : Probably rode in the Charge

The musters show he was effective from the 1st October to the 31st December.

PRENDERGAST, Lieutenant Lennox

Born : 12th May 1830 - Hanover Square, London
Enlisted :
Medals : Crimea (B.S)

Died : Unknown
Status : Severely wounded in the Charge

Lennox Prendergast was the son of Guy Lennox Prendergast, formerly member of the Bombay council, and M.P for Lymington, and Eliza Emma Grieve. He married Marion Malcom, daughter of Neill Malcom and Harriet Clarke-Jervoise, on the 20th July 1860. They had four children, Pymold born 1864, Eleanor Mary born 1868, Anne Marguerite born 1870 and Edmund James born 1872. In 1881 he lived at 22 Grosvenor Gardens, St. George Hanover Square, London.

The musters show he was effective as a Lieutenant from the 1st October to the 31st December. However the first muster states "Hospital Wounded", the second "Sent to England" and the third "England". Two horses foraged at public expense for 25 days. Also shown as a Cornet during all three musters. Listed on the Casualty Roll as severely wounded at Balaclava. WO100/24 page 157 Remarks: On Sick Leave to England, page 176 Remarks: Gone to England. Balaklava Medal Roll marginal note reads "Received a pistol wound in sole of the left foot". He received his medal from the hand of the Queen on 18th May 1855.

Illustrated Histories of the Scottish Regiments No2 - 2nd Dragoons by Lt Col Percy Groves, page 28. A Cornet in the Scots Greys 11th March 1853. Lieutenant 3rd December 1854. Captain 13th June 1856. Major 3rd February 1869. On Half pay 30th June 1869. Brevet Lieutenant Colonel 1st October 1877. Retired pay (Honary Colonel) 1st July 1881. Colonel Prendigast served with the Scots Greys in the Crimea 1854-1855. Including the affair of M'Kenzie's Farm; Battles of Balaklava (severely wounded) and Siege and fall of Sebastopol.

852 RAMAGE, Sergeant Henry

Born : c. 1827
Enlisted :
Medals : Crimea (B.I.S)

Died : c.1859
Status : Rode in the Charge

Victoria Cross is displayed at The Royal Scots Dragoon Guards Museum (Edinburgh Castle, Edinburgh, Scotland).

The musters show he was effective as a Private from the 1st October to the 31st December. Ramage died in Newbridge, County Kildare, Ireland, at the age of 32 and was buried in an unmarked grave at Newbridge Cemetery.

Citation for the Victoria Cross *London Gazette* 2nd June 1858, reads "For having, at the Battle of Balaklava, galloped out to the assistance of Private McPherson, of the same regiment, on perceiving him surrounded by seven Russians, when by his gallantry he dispersed the enemy and saved his comrade's life. For having, on the same day, when the Heavy Brigade was rallying, and the enemy retiring, finding his horse would not leave the ranks, dismounted and brought in a prisoner from the Russian line. Also, for having dismounted on the same day, when the Heavy Brigade was covering the retreat of the Light Cavalry, and lifted from his horse Private Gardiner, who was disabled from a severe fracture of the leg by a round shot; Sergeant Ramage then carried him to the rear from under a very heavy cross-fire, thereby saving his life, the spot where he must inevitably have fallen having been immediately afterwards covered by the Russian Cavalry".

On the 2nd August 1858 at Portsmouth Sergeant Ramage of the Scots Greys was the 11th in line to receive his Victoria Cross. The recipients only 12 men in all, nine commissioned, two non-commissioned, and one private soldier formed in a line.Her Majesty stood upon the dais with the Prince Consort and Duke of Cambridge on her right, and immediately proceeded to confer the Crosses. Each recipient advanced in the order in which we have placed their names, saluted Her Majesty,and then stood while the Queen with her own hands affixed the Cross to their breasts. *The Times Tuesday Aug 3rd 1858.*

1188 RAMAGE, Private David

Born : Unknown
Enlisted :
Medals : Crimea (B.I.S)

Died : Unknown
Status : Probably rode in the Charge

The musters show he was effective from the 1st October to the 31st December. WO25 Discharge book shows he discharged on the 26th November 1878 as a Sergeant.

401 RAMAGE, Private George

Born : Unknown
Enlisted :
Medals : Crimea (B.I.S)

Died : Unknown
Status : Probably rode in the Charge

Wallis & Wallis 13th September 1967, Group of three, Crimea three bars Balaklava, Inkermann, Sebastopol engraved naming, Turkish Crimea, English Version, LS & GC Trophy type to Pte G. Ramage 2nd Royal North British Dragoons VF.

The musters show he was effective from the 1st October to the 31st December.

969 RAMSAY, Private James William

Born : Unknown
Enlisted :
Medals : Crimea (B.I.S)

Died : Unknown
Status : Probably rode in the Charge

The musters show he was effective from the 1st October to the 31st December. WO25 Discharge book shows he discharged on the 19th October 1870 as a Sergeant.

801 RANT, Sergeant William

Born : Unknown
Enlisted :
Medals : Crimea (B.I.S), The Knight (5th Class) The French Legion of Honour

Died : Unknown
Status : Rode in the Charge

The musters show he was effective from the 1st October to the 31st December. Shown on the Musters as sending £2 to Louisa Rant. Appointed Riding Master in the 5th Lancers on the 6th August 1858. Left the Regiment 1873.

His recommendation for the French Legion of Honour reads: "I have the honor to submit to the Brigadier General Commanding the Division the name of Troop Sergeant Major William Rant No. 801 of the Scots Greys, as a man, whom, from all I know of his general character and from what I have gathered from others of his gallant conduct at the Battle of Balaklava, I believe to be most deserving of any distinction that may be conferred upon him. Though not wounded in that action, he showed the greatest coolness and courage, and I know that he is looked upon among his comrades, as one of those who did most to maintain the honor of their country during the short charge of the Heavy Brigade on that day. He came out with the Regiment as a Sergeant when it first left England, and has hardly been absent for a day from his duty since that period. He has just been promoted to the rank of Troop Sergeant Major". Signed, George Calmont Clarke. Bt.Lt.Col. Commg. 2 Drgns.

952 RAVELY, Private John

Born : Unknown
Enlisted :
Medals : Crimea (B.I.S)

Died : Unknown
Status : Probably rode in the Charge

The musters show he was effective from the 1st October to the 31st December. WO25 Discharge book shows he died on the 15th June 1865.

646 ROBB, Private Charles

Born : Unknown
Enlisted :
Medals : Crimea (B.I.S)

Died : Unknown
Status : Probably rode in the Charge

The musters show he was effective from the 1st October to the 31st December.

1245 ROBERTSON, Private Adam
Born : Unknown
Enlisted :
Medals : Crimea (B.I.S)

Died : Unknown
Status : Probably rode in the Charge

The musters show he was effective from the 1st October to the 13th December. Remarks state sent to Scutari Hospital 14th December. WO100/24 page 162 Remarks: Sick at Scutari. WO14/1 Scutari Muster Roll January-March 1855 remarks indicate he was in Hospital during January, February and March.

1225 ROBERTSON, Private John
Born : Date unknown - Dundee
Enlisted :
Medals : Crimea (B.I.S)

Died : 22nd December 1854 - Aboard Ship
Status : Probably rode in the Charge

The musters show he was effective from the 1st October to the 20th December. Remarks state sent to Scutari Hospital 21st December. Noted as dead on the 3rd Muster. WO100/24 page 162 Remarks: Sick at Scutari. page 185 Remarks: Died 22nd. December 1854. *The Times*, Wednesday 10th January 1855, page 8, reported that "Private John Robinson, 2nd Dragoon Guards died on board the Brandon on the 22nd December 1854." Trade on enlistment Shoemaker.

736 RODGERS, Private James
Born : Unknown
Enlisted :
Medals : Crimea (B.I.S)

Died : Unknown
Status : Probably rode in the Charge

A.H. Baldwin and Sons March 1950, three bar Crimea B.I.S impressed medal, L.S & G.C Medal, and Turkish Medal, name "J.Rodger 2nd Dgns." From the Dr. Payne Collection. V.F £4.4s. Glendining's 24th June 1992, Lot 131, three bar Crimea B.I.S (J. Rodgers, 2nd Dragoons"), impressed naming, very fine. Ex Dr. Payne Collection. The same medal appeared in the Glendinings auction on the 27th June 1994, Lot 627, Hammer price £470.

The musters show he was effective from the 1st October to the 31st December. Later a Major in the Royal Artillery.

997 ROLLO, Private Peter
Born : Unknown
Enlisted :
Medals : Crimea (B.I.S), Long Service and Good Conduct Medal

Died : Unknown
Status : Probably rode in the Charge

The musters show he was effective from the 1st October to the 31st December. WO102 L.S & G.C issued 30th June 1868, gratuity £5.

1256 RUSS, Private James
Born : c.1834 - St.Giles, Reading
Enlisted : 30th March 1854
Medals : Crimea (B.I.S)

Died : Unknown
Status : Probably rode in the Charge

Glendining's auction 3rd July 1985, Lot 63, Crimea 3 clasps Balaklava, Inkermann, Sebastopol. (Pve. Jas. R.Russ 2D. DGNS) Contemporary engraved naming, Sebastopol clasp loose on ribbon VF £150. Glendining's auction September 1985. Crimea 3 clasps Balaklava, Inkermann, Sebastopol loose on ribbon.(Jas. R. Russ 2nd Dragoons) Contemporary engraved naming. Stockport Fair 8th October 1988, Crimea 3 clasps Balaklava, Inkermann, Sebastopol, naming as above engraved in large block capitals, large date obverse. Non-offical rivets on the Sebastopol clasp £325. DNW 2nd April 2004, The collection of medals formed by the late John Darwent, Lot 169, Crimea 1854-56, 3 clasps, Balaklava, Inkermann, Sebastopol (Pve. Jas. Russ, 2d Dgs.), contemporary engraved naming, neatly refixed suspension claw, contact marks and edge bruising, better than good fine. Ex E. E. Needes Collection. Hammer Price £500. Also appear at Sotheby's auction October 1971.

The musters show he was effective from the 1st October to the 31st December. WO100/24 page 185 Remarks: Gone to England.

WO 97/1298 Discharge documents state 1256 Pte James Russ born at St.Giles, Reading. Berks. Enlisted at Reading on 30th March 1854 aged 20 years. Served 2 years 234 days of which seven months were with the army in the Crimea. He appeared before a Regimental Board at Newbridge on 18th November 1856 and was discharged due to a reduction in the army and being unlikely to become an efficient dragoon. Description on discharge 22 years 9 months of age 5ft 7, Dark hair, Brown eyes, complexion fair. On the 1861 census he is shown as a Brewer's labourer living in Reading, Berkshire with his wife Mary. In 1871 he is shown as a Drayman, living in Reading with his wife Mary.

1254 RUTHERFORD, Private Peter

Born : Date unknown - Coldstream
Enlisted : 17th March 1854
Medals : Crimea (B.I.S)

Died : 27th January 1855 - Scutari
Status : Probably rode in the Charge

The musters show he was effective from the 1st October to the 31st December. WO100/24 page 162 Remarks: Sick at Scutari, page 185 Remarks: Died 27th. January 1855. WO14/1 Scutari Muster Roll January-March 1855 remarks indicate he joined on the 22nd January and died on the 27th January.

1045 RUXTON, Sergeant William

Born : Unknown
Enlisted :
Medals : Crimea (B.I.S)

Died : Unknown
Status : Probably rode in the Charge

Empire Medals and Militaria (Canada) sold a Crimea three clasp Balaklava, Inkermann, Sebastopol medal. Engraved to "Sergt.Wm.Ruxton 2nd DGs" sold on ebay in May 2008 for £620.

The musters show he was effective from the 1st October to the 3rd December. Remarks state sent to Scutari Hospital. WO100/24 page 158 Remarks: Sick at Scutari.

1048 SCOTT, Corporal Thomas

Born : Unknown
Enlisted :
Medals : Crimea (B.I.S)

Died : Unknown
Status : Probably rode in the Charge

The musters show he was effective from the 1st October to the 31st December. WO25 Discharge book shows he discharged on the 4th December 1860 as a Private.

758 SCURR, Private Robert

Born : Unknown
Enlisted :
Medals : Crimea (B.I.S)

Died : Unknown
Status : Probably rode in the Charge

Information from Darwent Archive. Glendining's 17th April 1964 Lot 288, R. Scurr 2nd Dragoons Crimea No Bar, Turkish Crimea Sardinian Version (Un-named) and eight other medals realised £34. Purchased by Baldwins.
Crimea three bars Balaklava, Inkermann, Sebastopol officially impressed naming "R.Scurr 2nd Drags" Large date obverse, Ribbon pin has been removed, non standard rivets Inkermann clasp broken and repaired at lugs on right hand side. GVF. Edge bruise 4 o clock on right hand side. Turkish Crimea Sardinian version. Additionally fitted with original suspender from British Crimean Medal., regimentally impressed "C.R. Scurr 2nd Dragoons" in possession of Andrew Gill 30th July 1985. Donald Hall Commission List No 47 June 1987 item 357. Medals as above. Both impressed VF £450. Toad Hall Medals List May/June 1988 item 255, Medals as above Pair GVF/NEF £425.

The musters show he was effective from the 1st October to the 31st December. WO25 Discharge book shows he died in December 1859.

458 SEGGIE, Corporal William

Born : Unknown
Enlisted :
Medals : Crimea (B.S), The Distinguished Conduct Medal

Died : Unknown
Status : Severely wounded in the Charge

The musters show him effective as a Private from the 1st-25th October. Remarks state sent to Scutari Hospital. Promoted Corporal 31st December following the death of Corporal Campbell who was also at Scutari. Listed on the Casualty Roll as severely wounded at Balaclava. WO14/1 Scutari Muster Roll January-March 1855 remarks indicate he was in Hospital during January and February. WO100/24 page 158 Remarks: Sick at Scutari, page 185 Remarks: Gone to England.

458 L/Sgt William Seggie. The Distinguished Conduct Medal. Recommendation dated 13:1:55; at Scutari 1:4:55 to 30:6:56 (non-effective date Scutari unknown); invalided to England; died; medal sent to Crimea and returned to War Office 30:6:55 for transmission to next-of-kin.
P.E. Abbott, Recipients of DCM 1855-1909, Page 19, 458 Lance Sergeant Seggie. William 2 Dragoons RD 13.1.1855 Died. The Naval and Military Gazette of 7th April 1855, page XIII, mentions the forwarding of DCM's to the Crimea and goes on to say "The relatives of those men who have died since their service will receive them". On 2 July 1855 DCM's for the next of kin of the following were sent to the Deputy Secretary-at-War for onward Transmission : Lance Sergeant W.Seggie 2nd Dragoons and three soldier's of the 95th Regiment.

1233 SEGGIE, Private William

Born : Unknown
Enlisted : 1845
Medals : Crimea (B.I.S)

Died : 8th September 1869, Hounslow.
Status : Probably rode in the Charge

The musters show he was effective from the 1st October to the 31st December.
An interesting possibility is that 458 William Seggie was a father with two sons, William and Samuel, who both joined the 2nd Dragoons. Samuel was awarded a commission in the 9th Lancers in 1855. The regimental number 458 suggests enlistment towards the end of 1834, and 1233 William Seggie early 1854. Newspaper cutting on page 131.

807 SELKRIG, Corporal John

Born : Date unknown - Wiskirk
Enlisted : 16th November 1843
Medals : Crimea (B.I)

Died : 3rd July 1855 - Camp Crimea
Status : Probably rode in the Charge

The musters show he was effective from the 1st October to the 31st December. Pay List remarks Died: Camp. Crimea. 3rd July 1855. WO25 Discharge book shows he was discharged in 1856.

1139 SHILLINGLAW, Private Walter

Born : Unknown
Enlisted :
Medals : Crimea (B.I.S)

Died : Unknown
Status : Probably rode in the Charge

The musters show he was effective from the 1st October to the 31st December.

891 SHORT, Corporal David

Born : Unknown
Enlisted :
Medals : Crimea (B.I.S)

Died : Unknown
Status : Probably rode in the Charge

The musters show him effective as a Private from the 1st October to the 27th November and as a Corporal from the 27th November to the 31st December. Promoted following the promotion of Liddle to Sergeant.

866 SIMMONDS, Corporal Thomas

Born : Unknown
Enlisted :
Medals : Crimea (B.I.S)

Died : Unknown
Status : Probably rode in the Charge

The musters show he was effective as a Private from the 1st October to the 31st December.

1251 SINCLAIR, Private James

Born : Unknown
Enlisted :
Medals : Crimea (S)

Died : Unknown
Status : Effective during the period

Sotheby and Co. 18th February 1970, Lot 61, Crimean War Medal, 2 bars, Balaclava, Sebastopol (Pve. Jas. Sinclair, 2d Dgs.), engraved in large caps, very fine and scarce. Hammer price £16.

The musters show he was effective from the 1st October to the 28th October. Remarks state to Scutari Hospital 29th October. WO100/24 page 162 Remarks: Sick at Scutari, page 185 Remarks: Gone to England. Discharged on the 15th December 1856 on reduction of the Army.

1264 SISSONS, Private George

Born : Unknown
Enlisted :
Medals : Crimea (B.I.S)

Died : Unknown
Status : Probably rode in the Charge

The musters show he was effective from the 1st October to the 3rd December. Remarks state sent to Scutari Hospital. WO100/24 page 162 Remarks: Sick at Scutari. WO14/1 Scutari Muster Roll January-March 1855 remarks indicate he was in Hospital during January and sent home 27th February.

1158 SKINNER, Private Thomas
Born : Date unknown - South Leith
Enlisted : 7th January 1852
Medals : Crimea (I.S)

Died : 13th December 1854 - Scutari
Status : Effective during the period

The musters show he was effective from the 1st October to the 15th November. Remarks state sent to Scutari Hospital. Noted as dead in the 3rd muster. WO100/24 page 162 Remarks Died Tetanus 13th December 1854.

1201 SMALL, Private James
Born : Unknown
Enlisted :
Medals : Crimea (B.I.S)

Died : Unknown
Status : Probably rode in the Charge

The musters show he was effective from the 1st October to the 31st December. WO25 Discharged in December 1856.

1143 SMART, Private William
Born : Unknown
Enlisted :
Medals : Crimea (B.I.S)

Died : Unknown
Status : Probably rode in the Charge

The musters show he was effective from the 1st October to the 31st December.

752 SMELLIE, Private George
Born : Date unknown - Glasgow
Enlisted : 11th April 1842
Medals : Crimea (B.I.S)

Died : 17th February 1855 - Camp Crimea
Status : Probably rode in the Charge

The musters show he was effective from the 1st October to the 31st December. WO100/24 page 185 Remarks: Died 17th February 1855. Trade on enlistment Calico Printer.

981 SMITH, Private Charles Edward
Born : Date unknown - Aberdeen
Enlisted : 28th November 1846
Medals : Crimea (B.I.S)

Died : 6th July 1855 - Scutari
Status : Probably rode in the Charge

The musters show he was effective from the 1st October to the 31st December. WO100/24 page 162 Remarks: Sick at Scutari, page 186 Remarks: Died 6th July 1855. WO14/1 Scutari Muster Roll January-March 1855 remarks indicate he joined on the 22nd January and died on the 6th February. Trade on enlistment Clerk

1263 SMITH, Private David
Born : Unknown
Enlisted :
Medals : Crimea (B.I.S)

Died : Unknown
Status : Probably rode in the Charge

The musters show he was effective from the 1st October to the 31st December. WO25 Discharge book shows he transferred to the 5th Lancers on the 10th March 1858. A letter from Robert Henderson,"Minister of Christ Church, and Chaplain to the Troops " Stirling Feb 22, 1856. Addressed to the Central Association in Aid of the wives and families of soldier's ordered on active service. "Sir,-The amount in my hands to pay the wives of soldier's here will be about exhausted by the payment for a fortnight on Wednesday next. I am glad to say that, with one exception, (a Mrs Smith, wife of D.Smith, Scots Greys they are now getting money from their husbands.

1257 SMITH, Private Edwin
Born : Unknown
Enlisted :
Medals : Crimea (S)

Died : Unknown
Status : Effective during the period

The musters show he was effective from the 1st-26th October and from the 24th November to the 31st December. Remarks state sent to Scutari 27th October, returned 24th November. WO14/1 Scutari Muster Roll January-March 1855 remarks indicate he joined on the 2nd February and was in Koulali Hospital during February and March.

1230 SMITH, Private George
Born : Unknown
Enlisted :
Medals : Crimea (I.S)

Died : Unknown
Status : Effective during the period

The musters show he was effective from the 1st October to the 31st December.

756 SMITH, Private James
Born : Date unknown - Westchurch
Enlisted : 4th May 1842
Medals : Crimea (B.I.S)

Died : 13th January 1855 - Scutari
Status : Probably rode in the Charge

Spinks auction 22nd June 1989, Lot 439, Crimea 3 clasps Balaklava, Inkermann, Sebastopol "J.Smith 2nd Dragoons" impressed VF £420

The musters show he was effective from the 1st October to the 31st December. WO100/24 page 162 Remarks: Sick at Scutari, page 186 Remarks: Died 13th January 1855. *The Times*, Thursday 1st February 1855, page 8, reported that "Private J.Smith 2nd Dragoons died on board the Colombo on the 13th January 1855." Trade on enlistment Baker.

827 SMITH, Private Joseph
Born : Date unknown - Cheltenham
Enlisted : 4th January 1844
Medals : Crimea (B.I.S)

Died : Date unknown - Scutari
Status : Probably rode in the Charge

The musters show he was effective from the 1st October to the 31st December. WO100/24 page 162 Remarks: Sick at Scutari. Pay List notes he died at Scutari.

913 SMITH, Private Robert
Born : Unknown
Enlisted :
Medals : Crimea (B.I.S)

Died : Unknown
Status : Probably rode in the Charge

The musters show he was effective from the 1st October to the 31st December. WO25 shows discharged 9/11/1869.

799 SMITH, Private Samuel
Born : Date unknown - Stoke
Enlisted : 25th October 1843
Medals : Crimea (B.I.S)

Died : 11th December 1854 - Camp
Status : Probably rode in the Charge

DNW 2nd May 1992, Lot 9, Crimea 1854-5, 2 clasps, Balaklava, Inkermann (S. Smith, 2nd Dragoons) officially impressed naming, fitted with silver ribbon buckle, edge knocks, otherwise very fine. Hammer Price £560

The musters show he was effective from the 1st October to the 11th December. Remarks state died 11th December. Form 20 shows he had £10 2s 8d of outstanding pay. Trade on enlistment Labourer.

1111 SMITH, Private William
Born : Unknown
Enlisted :
Medals : Crimea (B.I.S)

Died : Unknown
Status : Probably rode in the Charge

The musters show he was effective from the 1st October to the 31st December.

561 SOFTLEY, Private Thomas
Born : Date unknown - Edinburgh
Enlisted : 14th October 1837
Medals : Crimea (B.S)

Died : 3rd March 1855 - Scutari
Status : Slightly wounded in the Charge

The musters show he was effective from the 1st October to the 25th October and from the 10th November to the 31st December. Remarks state sent to Scutari Hospital 26th October, returned 10th November. Listed on the Casualty Roll as slightly wounded at Balaclava, name spelt "Thomas Gofley". WO100/24 page 186 Remarks: Died 3rd March 1855. WO14/1 Scutari Muster Roll January-March 1855 remarks indicate he joined on the 11th February and was in Koulali Hospital during February, died 3rd March. Trade on enlistment Gunmaker.

1145 SOUTAR, Private William
Born : Unknown
Enlisted :
Medals : Crimea (B.I.S)
Died : Unknown
Status : Probably rode in the Charge

The musters show he was effective from the 1st October to the 31st December. The Pay Lists name him "Soutter".

1155 STEVENS, Private George
Born : Unknown
Enlisted :
Medals : Crimea (B.I.S)
Died : Unknown
Status : Probably rode in the Charge

The musters show he was effective from the 1st October to the 31st December. WO100/24 page 186 Remarks: Gone to England. WO25 Discharge book shows he was invalided out on the 4th August 1863.

1050 STEVENSON, Sergeant Norman Sharp
Born : c.1832 - Scotland
Enlisted :
Medals : Crimea (B.I.S)
Died : Unknown
Status : Rode in the Charge

P. Burman Medal List 101, December 2002, Item 488. Pair Crimea 3 clasps B.I.S Norman Stevenson. Royal Scots Greys. Sold with original letter from the curator of the Dorset Regiment Museum dated 2nd December 1960. Both medals are named in contemporary gothic style lettering. They are heavily toned and have original ribbons and the British medal has a top wearing buckle (NVF) £1075

The musters show him effective as a Corporal from the 1st October to the 4th November and as a Sergeant from the 5th November to the 31st December. Remarks state he was promoted following the promotion of Gibson to Cornet. Riding Master in the 9th Lancers 12th March 1861, to half-pay 2nd November 1866 (*Harts Annual Army List 1869*).

An extract of a letter from the curator of the Dorset Regiment Museum to Stevenson's descendants reads "Norman Sharp Stevenson was Riding Master 9th Lancers he was commissioned as such on 12th March 1861 and placed on half pay on 2nd November 1866. These are the particulars relating to your uncle which I have traced in Harts Army Lists... ...His retirement in 1866 makes sense when considered against your information that he was invalided out fairly soon after Balaclava from the bang on his head he received in the action"

Shown on the 1861 census as unmarried, a Riding Master, aged 29, at the Divisional Staff Barracks at Aldershot.

Michael Hargreave Mawson purchased two miniatures in an eBay auction identified as being of "Lt. Stephenson and wife wearing Crimea medals - was in the charge of Heavy Brigade at Balaclava". The photograph shows him in the uniform of the 9th Lancers.

1129 STEVENSON, Private Thomas
Born : Unknown
Enlisted :
Medals : Crimea (B.I.S)
Died : Unknown
Status : Probably rode in the Charge

Stockport Fair 3rd May 1997, Crimea 2 clasps Balaklava, Inkermann, engraved naming "Pve. Thos. Stevenson 2 D." Price £365. Spinks auction 18th March 1997, lot 313, Pair. Pte. Thomas Stevenson 2nd Dragoons 2 clasps Balaklava, Inkermann Pte 2nd DNS. Engraved naming GVF and Turkish Crimea British die Un-named straight bar suspension, NVF Est £380.

The musters show he was effective from the 1st October to the 31st December.

1238 STEWART, Private John
Born : Unknown

Enlisted :

Medals : Crimea (I.S)

Died : Unknown

Status : Effective during the period

The musters show he was effective from the 1st October to the 31st December.

1241 STEWART, Private William
Born : Unknown

Enlisted :

Medals : Crimea (B.I.S)

Died : Unknown

Status : Probably rode in the Charge

The musters show he was effective from the 1st October to the 31st December. Probably brother of 1238 John Stewart. WO25 Discharge book shows he volunteered for the 7th Dragoons on the 14th September 1857.

1066 STOCKS, Private James
Born : Unknown

Enlisted :

Medals : Crimea (B.I.S)

Died : Unknown

Status : Probably rode in the Charge

The musters show he was effective from the 1st October to the 31st December. WO100/24 page 186 Remarks: Gone to England. The Pay List names him "Stokes".

702 STOCKTON, Private Charles
Born : Unknown

Enlisted :

Medals : Crimea (B.I.S)

Died : Unknown

Status : Probably rode in the Charge

The musters show he was effective from the 1st October to the 31st December. WO25 shows discahrged Dec 1856.

956 STREETER, Private James
Born : Unknown

Enlisted :

Medals : Crimea (B.I.S), Long Service and Good Conduct Medal

Died : Unknown

Status : Probably rode in the Charge

The musters show he was effective from the 1st October to the 31st December. WO102 L.S & G.C Sergeant James Streeter issued 30th June 1868, gratuity £10.

868 STURTEVANT, Troop Sergeant Major Richard L.
Born : 25th March 1825 - Bethnal Green, Middlesex

Enlisted :

Medals : Crimea (B.I.S), Long Service and Good Conduct Medal

Died : 25th October 1900 - Buxted, Sussex

Status : Probably rode in the Charge

The musters show he was effective from the 1st October to the 31st December. Also shown as an Orderly Room Clerk appointed 3rd January 1849 when he was a Private, his rank at the time of the muster being a Sergeant. Shown on the Musters as sending £2 to both Eliza and Charles Sturtevant. WO102 L.S & G.C T.S.M Sturtevant issued 1st December 1856, gratuity £15.

The following article was taken from http://www.sturtivant.org.uk. One of eleven children of Richard Lawrence and Hannah Sturtivant, he was the second son to receive his father's name, it being probable that his older sibling died young. The Richard Lawrence first names have continued in the family down to the present day.

This Richard Lawrence was born in the East End of London on 25th March 1825. He first married Mary Ann Sadler at Greenwich on 16th January 1844, and the following year he joined the Army. His wife died childless in April 1852. Eight months later he was remarried at Worcester to Elizabeth Buncle. He spent some years in the Army, serving in the Crimea and then Ireland. He had four children by his second wife, who died in Edinburgh in June 1867, and these included twins of whom one, John Buncle, founded the present Scottish line, some of whom are now living in southern England. After leaving the Army, he became Master of Bethnal Green Workhouse, and James King, his youngest son by Elizabeth, succeeded him in this post. He is reputed to have had about three illegitimate children before remarrying in 1882 to Elizabeth Sherman Arnold, though there is no evidence that any of these were registered in the Sturtevant name.

A newspaper cutting dated 3rd November 1900, found some time ago in an old soldier's trunk reads: "Death & Funeral of Sergt-Major Sturtevant, late Master of Waterloo Road Workhouse, an old Crimean veteran. On the 25th of October were laid to rest in the quiet of God's Acre, St.Mary's Churchyard, Buxted, Sussex, the mortal remains of one of England's old veteran soldiers, in the person of Sergt-Major Richard Lawrence Sturtevant, at the age of 75 years. Deceased served through the Crimean war, being present and taking part in the battles of the Alma, Balaclava and Inkerman, for which he received the medals and clasp. He also took part in that famous Charge of the Heavy Brigade at Balaclava, he being a sergeant in the Scots' Greys, the famous 'Second to None' cavalry regiment, and he again took part in routing the Russian army. It was when the battle of the Alma was nearly ended, and a lucky shot stopped a Russian convoy, that young Sergeant Sturtevant showed great pluck, determination, and presence of mind under very trying and difficult circumstances, for he rushed forward and raided the private carriage of the Russian Prince Menchikoff, seizing the official letters and documents, which, on being handed to Lord Raglan, disclosed the fact that they contained the particulars of the entire disposition of the Russian troops, and were therefore of the utmost value in directing subsequent activities. For this act he was promoted to Sergeant-Major. For the long term of 21 years Sergeant Major Sturtevant was Master of the Waterloo Road Workhouse, Bethnal Green, where he gained the respect of all who came in contact with him, and he retired from that position on a pension. He was a member of the Burdett-Coutts Lodge of Freemasons, No.1278, and only recently had been created an hon. member."

His discharge papers, now held in the Public Record Office at Kew, Surrey, show that he joined the Army on 25th August 1845, and was a Troop Sergeant Major in the 2nd Dragoons when he was discharged on 7th February 1867. By that time he had five good conduct badges, the Crimean and Turkish medals and a medal for Long Service and Good Conduct.

The newspaper article above is mistaken stating Sturtevant seized documents belonging to a Russian Prince during the battle of the Alma. The 2nd Dragoons did not arrive until the 24th September, some four days after the battle of Alma. The incident probably occured on the 27th September when the Regiment came into collision with the enemy at the affair of "Mackenzie's Farm," Menschikoff, and a large portion of his army where escaping from Sebastopol and were making their way out from the south side, when Lord Raglan just cut into the rear of that army. A number of baggage carts, ammunition and stores were captured including many personal items belonging to Prince Menschikoff.

SULIVAN, Lieutenant Colonel George Augustus Filmer
Born : 17th September 1819
Enlisted :
Medals : Crimea (B.I.S), The Turkish Order of the Medjidie (5th Class)
Died : Unknown
Status : Probably rode in the Charge

The musters show he was effective from the 1st October to the 31st December.

Illustrated Histories of the Scottish Regiments No2 - 2nd Dragoons by Lt Col Percy Groves, page 28, Major Sulivan. Cornet Scots Greys 29th July 1836. Lieutenant 26th February 1841. Captain 5th April 1844. Major 17th February 1854. Brevet. Lieutenant-Colonel 12th December 1854. Lieutenant-Colonel 5th Lancers 19th February 1858. Colonel 15th June 1861. Retired 15th June 1860. Colonel Sulivan served with the Scots Greys in the Crimea 1854-1855. Including the affair of M'Kenzie's Farm; Battles of Balaklava Inkermann and Tohernaya and Siege and fall of Sebastopol.

The son of Captain George James Sullivan formerly of the Royal Horse Guards, of Wilmington, Isle of Wight. He married Emily Anne Prince on the 12th of May 1842, daughter of Richard Prince of Walburton, Sussex, M.P for West Sussex.

War-Office, 3rd March, 1854. 2nd Dragoons, Captain George Augustus Filmer Sulivan to be Major, without purchase, vice Macleod, deceased.
Dated 17th February, 1854. Bulletins and other State Intelligence for the year 1854. Part One, p 253.

In the 1881 census, Colonel George Sulivan is aged 62, a retired Colonel, living at 47 Prince's Gardens, London, with his wife Eleanor born in Liverpool, aged 34 and some 28 years younger than him. It would appear that he has re-married. Living with the couple are 3 children, a daughter Constance aged 5 and two sons, Charles 3 and Robert 7 months. They also have nine servants, in the household.

Recorded in the *Plantagenet Roll of the Blood Royal being a complete table of all the descendants now living of Edward 111, King of England. London : T.C. & E.C. Jack, 1908*

An announcement appeared in the Times November 19th 1885. Arthur Sulivan deceased. That persons with claims against the estate of Arthur Sulivan late of number 47 Princess Gardens, Kensington and of Kurrachee in the East Indies, who died on the 5th of July inst at sea. Are required to send particulars to; Colonel George Augustus Filmer Sulivan the father of the deceased and one of the executors.

SUTHERLAND, Captain Francis

Born : 1828
Enlisted :
Medals : Crimea (B.I.S)

Died : Unknown
Status : Rode in the Charge

DNW 22nd September 2006, Lot 4. The Ron Penhall Collection.
Crimea 1854-56, 3 clasps, Balaklava, Inkermann, Sebastopol (Francis
Sutherland, Capt., 2nd Drags. Scots Greys), contemporary engraved
naming, with silver riband buckle for wearing, contained in its Hunt &
Roskell velvet lined fitted case, the lid with gilt title, 'Captn. Sutherland,
Royal Scots Greys'; Turkish Crimea 1855, Sardinian issue, unnamed,
polished, thus about very fine (2) Hammer Price £13,000

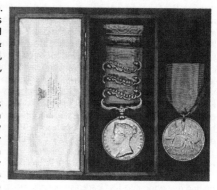

Third son of John Campbell Sutherland of Forse, County Caithness
and Margaret Munro. Educated at Eton. Purchased a Cornetcy in
the 2nd Dragoons on the 24th September 1847 and a Lieutenancy
on the 11th April 1851. His advancement to Captain in November
1854 was without purchase, possibly due to the part he played in
the action at Balaclava. During the Charge he served as one of four
Troop Leaders in the Scots Greys, and was memorably called upon to
"dress the ranks" as the Russian cavalry swept down on the Brigade
- this entailed turning his back on the enemy and facing the men in his Troop and no-one moved until the second-in-
command considered the regiment ready and brought them round.

The musters show he was effective as a Lieutenant from the 1st October to the 23rd November and as a Captain from
the 24th November to the 31st December. WO100/24 page 176 Remarks: Gone to England. Returned to England in
February 1855. He received his medal from the hand of the Queen on the 18th May 1855. Left the regiment in 1856.

Sutherland resigned his commission in February 1856, when he appears to have settled in Herefordshire, but
accompanying documentation suggests that he finally retired to Great Malvern, Worcestershire.

The auction of Sutherland's medals in 2006 included a quantity of original documentation and related artefacts,
including:

(i) A letter from the recipient to his mother, dated 5th January 1840.

(ii) His orders on appointment to a Cornetcy in the 2nd Dragoons, dated at Horse Guards, 30 September 1847 ('You will
join at Athlone on or before 20 November next'); a 'Leave of Absence' certificate, dated at Horse Guards, 26 November
1847, permitting Sutherland to be away 'from 24 September 1847 to the 31 December 1847'; his commission warrants
for the rank of Ensign, dated at St. James's 25 July 1848, Lieutenant, dated at St. James's, 17 April 1851 and Captain, dated
at Windsor, 12 February 1855, the reverse of this last with an illuminated armorial and text pertinent to his family's Grant
of Arms from the Lord Lyon, bearing an official 'VR' stamp, his name and military appointment, and the date January
1855 (the Arms appear to have originally been granted to an ancestor, John Sutherland of Forfar, in 1738).

(iii) His folded parchment passport, with additional interior pages
bearing numerous Consulate stamps for the Crimea period, in black
leather cover with gilt embossed title, 'Captn. F. Sutherland'.

(iv) Horse Guards letter inviting him to attend a ceremony 'for the
purpose of receiving the Medal from Her Majesty's hands', dated 11th
May 1855.

(v) A pair of watercolour sketches, presumably by the recipient,
one depicting a gentleman archer, no doubt a member of the
"Herefordshire Bowmen" (see ix); a pair of coloured prints depicting
officers of the 2nd Dragoons, one of them in action at Balaklava; and a
pair of cut-out military officer caricatures, mounted on cardboard.

(vii) A colour-printed membership certificate of The Clan Sutherland
Society, signed by the President and Secretary and with member's
name in ink, 'Captain Frank Sutherland'; Great Malvern 'Burial Board
for the Parish' certificate, dated 23 February 1871, in which Sutherland
is guaranteed 'the right of burial in grave space No. 1739'.

(viii) A pair of black leather gloves, with accompanying explanatory note in a contemporary hand, 'Worn at the Duke of Wellington's Funeral by Francis Sutherland, Esq., Lieutenant in Her Majesty's Royal Scots Greys, Nov. 1852'.

(ix) A bronze commemorative medallion, "England and France United to Defend the Oppressed", 1854, by Allens & Moore, the edge engraved, 'Presented to Francis Sutherland, Scots Greys, on Leaving for the Crimea, July 1854'; and a silver prize award, in the form of a maltese cross, with central circular wreath, this latter with embossed title, 'Herefordshire Bowmen', in fitted green leather case of issue.

(x) The recipient's cheroot case, a most attractive example with embroidered initials 'J.S.', family motto and 'the cat sejant proper' from his Arms; together with his pen-knife, with presentation inscription, 'F. Sutherland from H. W. Lyons, 2nd Life Guards', both of which may well have accompanied him to the Crimea.

(xi) Russian Campaign Medal for 1848, original silk riband, as undoubtedly brought back by Sutherland from the Crimea.

(xii) The recipient's bullion embroidered cross-belt pouch, 'VR' cypher, single battle honour "Waterloo", in its Andrews of Pall Mall leather cover, the former moth-eaten, particularly to reverse, and his gilt helmet plume holder.

(xiii) An old pottery ink-well / pen-stand, with transfer image of 'The Charge of the Scots Greys at Balaklava'.

1180 SWANSTONE, Private William

Born : c. 1835 - Edinburgh
Enlisted :
Medals : Crimea (B.I.S)

Died : Unknown
Status : Probably rode in the Charge

Sotheby 5th July 1974 Lot 61 3 Bars Balaklava, Inkermann, Sebastopol, "W Swanstone 2nd Dragns" impressed V.Good £65, purchased by Spinks. NW Collett January 1985 item 7629 3 Bars Balaklava, Inkermann, Sebastopol, "W Swanstone 2nd Dragoons" officially impressed naming. Obverse polished. Near VF £355.

A bookbinder prior to enlistment at Edinburgh aged 17. The musters show he was effective from the 1st October to the 31st December. Discharged 18th February 1865.

1146 TAYLOR, Private James

Born : Unknown
Enlisted :
Medals : Crimea (B.I.S)

Died : Unknown
Status : Slightly wounded in the Charge

The musters show he was effective from the 1st October to the 31st December. Listed on the Casualty Roll as slightly wounded at Balaclava.

909 THOMSON, Private David

Born : Unknown
Enlisted :
Medals : Crimea (no clasps)

Died : Unknown
Status : Effective during the period

The musters show he was effective from the 1st-26th October and from the 14th December to the 31st December. Remarks state sent to Scutari 27th October, returned 14th December. WO25 Discharge book shows he discharged December 1860.

1082 THOMSON, Private John

Born : Unknown
Enlisted :
Medals : Crimea (B.I.S)

Died : Unknown
Status : Probably rode in the Charge

Sotheby 21st March 1979 Lot 95 Turkish Crimea 1855 J.Thompson 2nd Dragoons Depot impressed VF £42.

The musters show he was effective from the 1st October to the 31st December.

1107 THOMSON, Private Robert
Born : Date unknown - Kilmarnock
Enlisted : 28th May 1850
Medals : Crimea (B.S)

Died : 26th October 1854 - Aboard Ship
Status : Severely wounded in the Charge

The musters show he was effective from the 1st October to the 25th October. Remarks state sent to Scutari Hospital. Noted as dead in the 3rd Muster. Listed on the Casualty Roll as severely wounded at Balaclava. The Pay Lists show he died aboard ship. WO100/24 page 186 Remarks: Died 26 Oct 1854.

898 TILSLEY, Troop Sergeant-Major George
Born : Unknown
Enlisted :
Medals : Crimea (B.I.S), The French Medaille Militaire

Died : Unknown
Status : Rode in the Charge

The musters show he was effective from the 1st October to the 31st December. The citation for the French Medaille Militaire reads (for) "gallantry in the field at the battle of Balaklava on the 25th. October, 1854, and exemplary good conduct throughout the campaign, and during (his) period of service".

Sergeant Fawke in his account of the Charge relates how Sergeant Major George Tidesley (Tilsley) ran a Russian through with his sword just as the enemy raised a sword to cut off Fawke's head. He subsequently gave the sword to Sergeant Fawke.

831 TODD, Hospital Sergeant William
Born : Unknown
Enlisted :
Medals : Crimea (B.I.S)

Died : Unknown
Status : Probably rode in the Charge

The musters show he was effective from the 1st October to the 31st December. Shown on the Musters as sending £2 and £4 to Maria Todd. WO25 Discharge book shows he was discharged 12th May 1868.

1159 TRAILL, Private Thomas
Born : Date unknown - South Leith
Enlisted : 7th January 1852
Medals : Crimea (B.S)

Died : 26th October 1854 - Camp
Status : Severely wounded in the Charge

The musters show he was effective from the 1st October to the 26th October. Remarks state died 26th October. Listed on the Casualty Roll as severely wounded at Balaclava. WO100/24 page 163 Remarks: Died of Wounds 26th October 1854. Trade on enlistment Moulder.

1167 TURNER, Private Alexander
Born : Unknown
Enlisted :
Medals : Crimea (B.I.S)

Died : Unknown
Status : Probably rode in the Charge

The musters show he was effective from the 1st October to the 3rd December. Remarks state sent to Scutari. WO14/1 Scutari Muster Roll January-March 1855 remarks indicate he was sent home 15th January. WO100/24 page 163 Remarks: Sick at Scutari, page 186 Remarks: Gone to England.

He received his medal from the hand of the Queen on 18th, May 1855. Received a gunshot wound in left wrist and had his horse shot under him during the Charge.

1208 VALENCE, Private Dixon
Born : Date unknown - Liberton
Enlisted : 10th March 1853
Medals : Crimea (B.S)

Died : 1st March 1855 - Scutari
Status : Probably rode in the Charge

The musters show he was effective from the 3rd October to the 28th October. Remarks state at Scutari Hospital 1st to the 3rd October, sent back 29th October. WO14/1 Scutari Muster Roll January-March 1855 remarks indicate he was in Hospital during January and February, died 1st March. Trade on enlistment Shepherd.

928 WARD, Private Owen

Born : Unknown
Enlisted :
Medals : Crimea (B.S), The Distinguished Conduct Medal

Died : Unknown
Status : Severely wounded in the Charge

The musters show he was effective from the 1st-25th October. Remarks state at Scutari Hospital 26th October to the 31st December. Listed on the Casualty Roll as severely wounded at Balaclava. WO14/1 Scutari Muster Roll January-March 1855 remarks indicate he was in Hospital during January and returned to his regiment 2nd February. The recommendation for the Distinguished Conduct Medal was dated 13th January 1855.

958 WARREN, Private John

Born : Unknown
Enlisted :
Medals : Crimea (B.I.S), Long Service and Good Conduct Medal

Died : Unknown
Status : Probably rode in the Charge

The musters show he was effective from the 1st October to the 31st December. WO102 L.S & G.C recommended 19th April 1868, issued 30th June 1868, gratuity £10. WO25 Discharge book shows he was discharged May 1871.

1096 WATSON, Private James

Born : Unknown
Enlisted :
Medals : Crimea (B.S)

Died : Unknown
Status : Severely wounded in the Charge

A.H. Baldwin and Sons September 1957 impressed Crimea 2 bar, Balaklava, Sebastopol. Jas. Watson, 2nd Dgns. rubbed edge, £7.10s

The musters show he was effective from the 1st October to the 25th October. Remarks state at Scutari Hospital 26th October to the 31st December. WO100/24 page 163 Remarks: Sick at Scutari, page 187 Remarks: Gone to England. Listed on the Casualty Roll as severely wounded at Balaclava.

955 WATT, Corporal George D.

Born : Unknown
Enlisted :
Medals : Crimea (B.I.S)

Died : Unknown
Status : Probably rode in the Charge

The musters show he was effective from the 1st October to the 31st December. Shown on the Musters as sending £2 10s to Margaret Watt.

1222 WATT, Private Peter

Born : Date unknown - Edinburgh
Enlisted : 27th September 1853
Medals : Crimea (I.S)

Died : 11th December 1854 - On Board Ship
Status : Effective during the period

DNW Auction 4th July 2001 Lot No 399, Crimea 1854-56, 2 clasps, Inkermann, Sebastopol (P. Watt, 2nd Dragoons) officially impressed, edge bruise, otherwise good very Hammer Price: £240

The musters show he was effective from the 1st October to the 11th December. Remarks state died 11th December. *The Times*, Thursday 1st February 1855, page 8 reported that "Private P. Watts, 2nd Dragoons died on board the Colombo on the 10th January 1855". Trade on enlistment Blacksmith.

1199 WATT, Private William

Born : Unknown
Enlisted :
Medals : Crimea (B.I.S)

Died : Unknown
Status : Probably rode in the Charge

The musters show he was effective from the 1st October to the 31st December.
WO14/1 Scutari Muster Roll January-March 1855 remarks indicate he joined on the 25th January and was in Hospital for January, February and at Koulali Hospital in March.
WO100/24 page 163 Remarks: Sick at Scutari, page 175 Remarks: Dead.

A view of Balaclava Harbour

835 WEIR, Private Alexander
Born : Unknown
Enlisted :
Medals : Crimea (B.I.S)

Died : Unknown
Status : Slightly wounded in the Charge

The musters show he was effective from the 1st October to the 31st December. Listed on the Casualty Roll as slightly wounded at Balaclava. WO25 Discharge book shows he transferred to the 5th Lancers 10th March 1858.

1258 WHITE, Private Cornelius
Born : Unknown
Enlisted :
Medals : Crimea (B.I.S)

Died : 27th April 1867
Status : Probably rode in the Charge

A.H. Baldwin & Sons Sales Catalogue July 1948: Crimea 3 Bars, Balaklava, Inkermann, Sebastopol. Pte.C.White Engraved, extremely fine and rare (Ex-Neede's collection) £3 3s Same medal sold Spinks Circular May 1984 item 3144 £330. Sotheby 1st March 1984 lot 45 £297 purchased by Spinks.

The musters show he was effective from the 1st October to the 31st December. WO25 Discharge book died 27/4/1867.

925 WHITE, Corporal William
Born : Unknown
Enlisted :
Medals : Crimea (B.I.S)

Died : Unknown
Status : Probably rode in the Charge

The musters show he was effective as a Private from the 1st October to the 27th December. Remarks state sent to Scutari Hospital. Shown on the Musters as sending £1 to Mary White. WO14/1 Scutari Muster Roll January-March 1855 remarks indicate he "Joined 4th January", no remarks in February or March. WO102 L.S & G.C recommended 14th May 1867, issued 24th July 1867, gratuity £10. WO25 Discharge book shows his "time expired" 18th August 1874.

861 WHITEHEAD, Private Joseph
Born : Unknown
Enlisted :
Medals : Crimea (B.I.S)

Died : Unknown
Status : Probably rode in the Charge

The musters show he was effective from the 1st October to the 31st December. WO102 L.S & G.C recommended 27th August 1866, issued 2nd October 1866, gratuity £5.

1144 WHYTE, Private Thomas
Born : Unknown
Enlisted :
Medals : Crimea (B.I.S)

Died : Unknown
Status : Probably rode in the Charge

The musters show he was effective from the 1st October to the 31st December. WO100/24 page 187 Remarks: Gone to England.

William Simpson

It was on the evening of the 26th October 1854 that William Simpson left for the crimea, he was to stay with the army until the fall of Sebastopol in September 1855. The battles of Alma,Balaklava and Inkerman had already taken place. He made sketches of the ground and trusted to those on the spot for a discription of events. When Simpson made the sketch of the Charge of the Light Brigade and submitted it for examination to Lord Cardigan, He gazed at it with a vacant stare, and said " its all wronge". Taking on board his comments, he returned with an updated sketch which was met with a simular reaction. On his third attempt and after making his lordship more conspicuous in the front of the brigade, it was finally accepted. With the advancement in printing techniques Simpson's watercolours were rapidly produced in London as realistic tinted lithographs. Two series were issued in 1855-6 under the title The Seat of War in the East. Several of his pictures have been reproduced in this publication. It was with his pencil and brush, that he was able to capture the drama and intrigue of war. Simpson's work together with other early War Correspondents such as William H Russell of The Times, and Roger Fenton, photographer, brought home to the public, the horrors and mismanagement of the conflict.

The Charge of the Heavy Brigade by Simpson

The Cavalry Camp in the Crimea near Kadikoi with portraits of General Scarlett and staff by Simpson 9th July 1855

WILLIAMS, Captain Samuel Toosey

Born : c. 1823
Enlisted :
Medals : Crimea (B.S)

Died : 23rd November 1854 - Pera, Constantinople
Status : Rode in the Charge

An engraved medal single clasp Balaklava , and a no clasp Punjab to brother Benjamin Rimmington Williams was purchased from Baldwins, together with photograph by John Darwent returned several years later, engraved medal should be impressed. Same medals sold in Christie's auction. Christie's 17th November 1987, Lot 126, Family Pair: Punjab, 1848-49, no clasp (2nd Lieut. B. R. Williams 3rd Troop 3rd Bde H.A.), extremely fine together with a fine cased daguerro type portrait of recipient in uniform. Crimea, 1854-56, two clasps, Balaklava, Sebastopol (Capt. S. T. Williams, 2nd Drgs.) engraved in serif capitals, last clasp loose on riband, extremely fine. £600-800. Hammer price £748

Captain Samuel Toosey Williams entered the army as a Cornet in 1840, Lieutenant 1842, Captain 1847. The musters show he was effective from the 1st October to the 23rd November, remarks state died 23rd November.

The following extract is taken from *Memoirs of the Brave*, page 128: WILLIAMS (Captain S. Toosey), Scotch Greys, died on the 23rd November, at Constantinople, where he had been conveyed from Balaklava. He was in the 32nd year of his age (half of which time he had passed in Her Majesty's service), and the eldest son of B.B. Williams, Esq, of Buscot Park, Faringdon, Berks. The letter conveying this sad intelligence to Captain Williams's afflicted family states, "The origin of his illness was low fever, the result of exposure, privation, and excessive fatigue, prior and subsequently to the battle of Balaklava, at which he gallantly led the second squadron of the Scots Greys, on the memorable 25th of October. Your gallant son has been taken from us amidst the universal sorrow of all who knew him. A more honourable and brave officer never existed."

Our Heroes of the Crimea: Biographical Sketches of our Military Officers by George Ryan (published 1855, available on Google Books) contains an entry on Williams, as well as the following extract it also quotes several letters of condolence sent to his family including one from the Emperor of France. The main entry on page 73 states: "Williams was educated at Rugby, under Dr. Arnold, and at the age of near seventeen he entered the 47th regiment of infantry as Ensign, by purchase, on the 26th of June, 1840, and on the 29th of April, 1842, he was promoted to a lieutenancy. Soon after joining his regiment he proceeded with it to Malta, and thence to the West Indies. While at Antigua, during the dreadful earthquakes, he was of essential service with his company on various arduous duties, and for which he received from the authorities the most nattering testimonials. Upon returning to England he was appointed extra aide-de-camp to Lord Besborough (the then Lord-Lieutenant of Ireland), and afterwards to Lord Clarendon, whose successor, Earl St. Germans, continued him in the honourable position.

In 1847, having obtained his company in the 47th, he exchanged into the Scots Greys on the 24th of December in the same year. Upon his regiment being ordered to the East, he resigned his staff appointment, and proceeded to Varna. When the army embarked for the Crimea, the Scots Greys followed ; but like the other cavalry regiments, it was from the very nature of the ground chosen by the enemy doomed to inaction save in reconnaissances. On the 25th of September, however, Captain Williams was with the handful of men that surprised several hundred Russians and put them to flight, and on which occasion he captured the Russian General, Cunija. In the following month, from excessive fatigue and privation, he was seized with fever, and was just out of his bed two days before the battle of Balaklava in which glorious affair his regiment was to play so distinguished a part. Against the most urgent entreaties of his medical advisers, he would go on duty. He knew of no illness as long as he could mount his charger, and he accordingly took his part in the labours of the camp at Balaklava. On the 25th of October, the day on which so many untried men were to win their spurs, the Scots Greys, to their great joy, were ordered to handle the enemy. They obeyed ! Captain Williams had the honour of leading the second squadron. How they speeded to meet the foe - how they slashed, cut, thrust, and pistolled the immense masses of Russian cavalry, who were as four to one to our heavy horsemen, has been told.

In this grand affair Captain Williams covered himself with glory. His swordsmanship stood him in good stead, for no less than four times was he beset, first by six, then three, two, and four of the enemy. Out of that bloody encounter he came without a scratch. How our heavy cavalry escaped is marvellous, for the enemy not only outnumbered it, as already stated, but fought most courageously. On two occasions during the Greys' cutting their way through the massive circle formed round them by the Russian horse, Captain Williams had near paid with his life his devotedness to two privates in his squadron. Out of this carnage came Williams without injury from the enemy. But there was death in him. He should have been in hospital, not in fight. The fever had not left him when he mounted, two days before this huge encounter. Excitement carried him through the fatigue, and a sort of miracle preserved him from the dangers of this fearful cavalry. The thrill of battle passed, Captain Williams was again attacked with fever, and was seriously

Williams' brother Benjamin Rimmington Williams

advised by the medical men of his regiment to leave the camp for Constantinople, but he refused. He looked upon his illness as momentary, and certain to wear off. His brave heart had deceived him. He could no longer mount the horse that so gloriously carried him through the Russians on the 25th of October ; and some five days after the battle of Inkermann his sickness was of so grave a character, that he was borne from the camp in a litter to the steamer for the purpose of being conveyed to Constantinople.

He was now so reduced by fever and dysentery, that the Duke of Cambridge, an old friend of Captain Williams, scarcely recognized the gallant officer. The Prince, and his old companion at the Castle in Dublin, embarked on board the Caradoc. His Royal Highness insisted on Captain Williams being conveyed to an hotel at Pera, where the best attention

could be paid him. Worn out, the brave fellow still hoped against hope that he would soon be back from Pera to the Crimea. He lingered on for some time, his high spirits leading his medical attendants to suppose him likely to get through the attack. His end was drawing to a close, not to be put aside by all that pluck and passion for war's grandeur could essay, to reanimate a body exhausted by war's privations. On the 23rd of November he died, and on the following day his body was conveyed to Scutari for interment. It was laid side by side with many of his late companions-in-arms. As many of his friends as were able joined the melancholy cortege ; among whom were Lord Guernsey, the Rev. S. G. Osborne, Captain Clifton, aide-de-camp to the Duke of Cambridge ; Mr. Grattan, formerly of his regiment; Mr. Lane, paymaster of the Himalaya ; Colonel Patton, of the 74th ; and many others, anxious to pay their last tribute to one who had in his maiden fight earned the laurels that brought his name first to their notice. A close friend, a gallant soldier, an unostentatious philanthropist-young, witty, and ingenuous in his nature, it will not be wondered that over the grave of such a man golden opinions from all to whom he was known should bear evidence of his worth as a friend, and of his devotion as a soldier to his country.

OUR HEROES OF THE CRIMEA.

There is a memorial at St. Mary's Church, Buscot, Oxfordshire, it reads "Sacred to the memory of Captain Samuel Toosey Williams, Royal Scots Greys, eldest son of B.B. Williams Esqre of Westbourne Terrace, Hyde Park Gardens now residing at Buscot Park in this parish who died aged 32 years in the service of his country, from fatigue and exposure prior and subsequently to the Battle of Balaklava in which he gallantly led the 2nd Squadn of his Regt. He was buried at Scutari Novr 24th 1854"

863 WILSON, Private Andrew

Born : Unknown
Enlisted :
Medals : Crimea (B.I.S), The French Medaille Militaire

Died : Unknown
Status : Rode in the Charge

The musters show he was effective from the 1st October to the 31st December. The citation for the French Medaille Militaire reads (For) "gallantry in the field at the battle of Balaklava on the 25th October, 1854, and exemplary good conduct throughout the campaign, and during the period of (his) service".

746 WILSON, Private James

Born : Unknown
Enlisted :
Medals : Crimea (B.I.S)

Died : Unknown
Status : Probably rode in the Charge

The musters show he was effective from the 1st October to the 31st December. Discharged 21st August 1866.

1052 WILSON, Troop Sergeant-Major John

Born : Unknown   Died : Unknown
Enlisted :   Status : Severely wounded in the Charge
Medals : Crimea (B.S), The Sardinian War Medal

The musters show him as a Sergeant effective from the 1st-25th October and from the 10th November to the 31st December. Remarks state sent to Scutari Hospital 26th October returning to Camp on the 10th November. Listed on the Casualty Roll as severely wounded at Balaclava.

The citation for the Sardinian War Medal reads (He) "was under arrest for a minor offence, but on finding the regiment was likely to be engaged, he made ready his horse, and coming up to the adjutant said, 'I have broken my arrest, sir, as I could not see my regiment going into action and remain quiet in camp; I have come to report myself, and wish to join and do my duty.' In the heavy cavalry charge at Balaklava he fought most gallantly, using his sword with great execution, and he was afterwards wounded by a round shot when his regiment went in support of the Light Brigade. He was promoted to troop sergeant-major for his gallant conduct".

405 WILSON, Private William

Born : Unknown   Died : Unknown
Enlisted :   Status : Probably rode in the Charge
Medals : Crimea (B.I.S)

The musters show he was effective from the 1st October to the 31st December. Sent home 31st March 1856.

1247 WINDOR, Corporal Robert

Born : Unknown   Died : Unknown
Enlisted :   Status : Probably rode in the Charge
Medals : Crimea (B.I.S)

The musters show he was effective as a Private from the 1st October to the 31st December.

1059 WOOD, Troop Sergeant-Major Archibald

Born : Unknown   Died : Unknown
Enlisted : 1849   Status : Probably rode in the Charge
Medals : Crimea (B.I.S)
Christies 25th July 1989, Lot 160, Crimea 3 clasps, B.I.S, "TSM ARCHD WOOD RL SCOTS GREYS" engraved in serif capitals, edge contact marks, otherwise good VF. Hammer Price £220.

Enlisted at Longford, Ireland in 1849, Corporal 1853, Sergeant 1854. Served on Lord Lucan's Staff at the battle of Inkermann. Troop Sergeant Major 1855. The musters show he was effective from the 1st October to the 31st December. WO100/24 page 158 Remarks: Attached to Lord Lucan's Staff. WO25 Discharge book shows he discharged June 1861.

1058 WYLIE, Private Joseph

Born : Unknown   Died : Unknown
Enlisted :   Status : Probably rode in the Charge
Medals : Crimea (B.I.S)

The musters show he was effective from the 1st October to the 31st December.

1221 YOUNG, Private David

Born : Unknown   Died : Unknown
Enlisted :   Status : Probably rode in the Charge
Medals : Crimea (B.I.S)
A.D.Hamilton Coin & Medal Quarterly, Glasgow, September 1976. Item HG 683. Family Group. Crimea 3 clasps Balaklava, Inkermann, Sebastopol D.Young. Royal Scots Greys Re-Named scratches on obv. VF. DCM Geo.V. 1647 CSM J.Young Royal Scots Fus. EF £115. Hamiltons Despatch Vol 3 No2 September 1980, XS 3010, 3 clasps Balaklava, Inkermann, Sebastopol D.Young. Royal Scots Greys Engraved NVF £120.

The musters show he was effective from the 1st October to the 31st December.

1259 YOUNG, Private John

Born : Date unknown - Regorton
Enlisted : 29th March 1854
Medals : Crimea (B.I.S)

Died : 8th February 1855 - Scutari
Status : Probably rode in the Charge

The musters show he was effective from the 1st October to the 31st December. WO100/24 page 187 Remarks: Died 8 February. 1855.

Photograph taken at Newbridge barracks 1859.

1. Capt Lenox Prendergast, Cornet by purchase 11th March 1853, Lieutenant 8th December 1854, Captain by purchase 13th June 1856. (See page 138)

2. Mr John Wallace Hozier, Cornet by purchase 17th December 1858, Lieutenant by purchase 17th November 1863.

3. Mr William Connel Black, Cornet by purchase 18th March 1859.

4. Mr John Lorn Stewart, Cornet by purchase 20th February 1855, Lieutenant by purchase 8th February 1856, Captain by purchase 2nd September 1862.

5. Assistant Surgeon Rutherford .

6. Mr James Brander Dunbar, Cornet 12th January 1855, Lieutenant by purchase 25th May 1855. Served in the Crimea 19th August - 1st September 1865.

7. Mr A.V.Nugent,Cornet by purchase 17th December 1852, Lieutenant 24th November 1854, Captain by purchase 8th February 1856. (See page 136)

8. Captain George Buchanan, Cornet by purchase 16th March 1849, Lieutenant by purchase 27th August 1852., Captain 8th December 1854.(See page 97)

"The garrison town of Newbridge, was chiefly occupied by public houses, and low kinds of music and singing halls, for the special recreation of the military. The barracks, occupied an enormous extent of ground, in fact, the whole side of the principal street of the town, and were surrounded by a high stone wall, loop holed for defence, and with a strong tower at each corner. Two sides of the barracks were flanked by the river Liffey, on the third side was the main street of Newbridge, on the fourth and open space of waste land, colonised by a number of unfortunate women, who were tolerated by the authorities, an lived in thatched straw huts known as 'wrens' nests." *Memoirs of Troop Sgt. Major Male (London 1893)*

1.Rutherford 2. Meikle 3.Nugent 4.Dunbar 5.Hozier 6.Uniacke (Newbridge Barracks 1859)

1.Dunbar 2. Rutherford 3.Buchanan 4.Browning 5.Nugent (Newbridge Barracks 1859)
Photographs on page 159/160. By permission of the Deputy Keeper of the Records, Public Record Office of
Northern Ireland PRONI reference D/552/B/3/5/12.

The 4th Dragoon Guards
"The Royal Irish"

The regiment had served continuously at home since its return from Portugal in 1813. The Regiment embarked at Kingstown, Ireland, for active service in the east. The Head-Quarters conveyed to the "Deva", and the total strength embarked 20 officers and 297 non-commissioned officers and privates.

Embarkation

(1) **Maori** 3 officers, 1 staff, 49 troopers, 50 horses. Embarked Kingstown (Capt Forster's Troop) 25th May 1854.

(2) **Burmah** 718 tons. 2 officers, 1 staff 47 troopers, 45 horses. Embarked Kingstown 27th May 1854.

(3) **Sir Robert Sale** 741 tons. 2 officers, 1 staff, 47 troopers, 47 horses. Embarked Kingstown 30th May 1854.

(4) **William Jackson** 956 tons. 3 officers, 2 staff, 53 troopers ,56 horses. Embarked Kingstown 1st June 1854.

(5) **Deva** 1033 tons. 3 officers, 2 staff, 58 troopers ,60 horses. Embarked Kingstown 2nd June 1854.

(6) **Palmyra** 749 tons. 1 officer , 4 staff, 43 troopers, 45 horses. Embarked Kingstown 3rd June 1854.

The first three sailed from London. The last three from Liverpool.

The Head-Quarter troops of the Regiment landed at Varna on the 10th July 1854. Towards the end of the month there were 49 cases of Diarrhoea and five of Cholera received into the Regimental Hospital, and four of the latter had proved fatal. In August eighteen deaths took place, of which 15 were from Cholera. September saw a marked improvement. Cholera had disappeared, and no deaths took place, except one due to a local cause, the sufferer having received a kick in the back from a horse.
On the 21st the Regiment embarked at Varna on board the "Simla" steam transport for the Crimea, having left its sick in Varna Bay, on board the hospital ship "Bombay". Both men and horses were much crowded on board; and for three days it blew a gale, with seventeen horses having to be put down. On the 1st October disembarkation commenced at Balaklava, owing to the crowded state of the harbour, the horses were landed in large lighters towed by a stream-tug. The men landed with only one suit of clothes, a cloak and a single blanket, the rest of their clothing was left on board the "Simla" in the valises, and sent to Scutari, whence it was not recovered till November. For the first week three tents only per troop were supplied, but the usual proportion of five per troop was then issued.
The rations consisted for about fifteen days of a pound of fresh meat and a pound of biscuit daily. Cholera reappeared among the men shortly after their landing, and in a very fatal form. Six cases were admitted during the month, of which five died; 64 cases of Diarrhoea, and 14 for Fevers, six from Jaundice, and two from gunshot wounds, one of which ultimately proved fatal at sea on the passage home, the lower jaw having been much comminuted. These two last-named cases, with two of sabre cuts, were the only instances of men of the Regiment wounded in action during the month who required hospital treatment. Many men were wounded on the day of Balaklava by sabres and lance, who did not come into Hospital, their cuts and probes being unimportant. A Serjeant was killed in the action by a round-shot.
(Extracts from *Medical and Surgical history of the British Army, during the War Against Russia 1854-56. p 5*)

Regiment transported from Varna to Crimea in the Simla. P & O Steamer of 2,400 tons . The whole of the 4th Dgn Guards and 26 of the 5th Dragoon Guards. Hodge had 5 horses on board, 230 Troop horses, 47 officers' horses and 17 baggage horses. (*Little Hodge* See page 28)

Staff remaining at Varna Depot. 1 Oct - 31st Dec 1854 . 868 Sgt John Clayton, 623 Pte Edward Ferrett, 414 Pte William Lotty, 1175 Pte Edward Rhodes, 667 Pte Clowes Ross, 1001 Pte Joseph Wheeler.

Camp of the 4th Dragoon Guards, near Karyni. Photograph by Fenton.

1150 ADAMS, Private John
Born : Unknown
Enlisted .
Medals : Crimea (B.I.S)

Died : Unknown
Status : Probably rode in the Charge

The musters show he was effective from the 1st October to the 31st December.

1049 ALBOT, Corporal George
Born : Unknown
Enlisted :
Medals : Crimea (B.I.S)

Died : Unknown
Status : Probably rode in the Charge

The musters show he was effective from the 1st October to the 31st December. Discharged 29th March 1860.

515 ALLEN, Private Thomas
Born : Unknown
Enlisted :
Medals : Crimea (B.I.S)

Died : Unknown
Status : Probably rode in the Charge

The musters show he was effective from the 1st October to the 31st December. Form 21 Soldier's' Remittances he sent £2.10s to Catherine Allen.

996 ANCHINCLASS, Private James
Born : Unknown
Enlisted :
Medals : Crimea (B.I.S)

Died : Unknown
Status : Slightly wounded in the Charge

The musters show he was effective from the 1st October to the 31st December. Listed on the Casualty Roll as slightly wounded at Balaclava. WO100/24 page 81 Remarks: Sent to England.

1017 ANDERSON, Private Thomas
Born : Unknown
Enlisted :
Medals : Crimea (B.I.S)

Died : Unknown
Status : Probably rode in the Charge

The musters show he was effective from the 1st October to the 31st December. Discharged 12th January 1861.

992 ARKELL, Private William
Born : Unknown
Enlisted :
Medals : Crimea (B.I.S)

Died : Unknown
Status : Probably rode in the Charge

The musters show he was effective from the 1st October to the 8th December. Remarks state to Scutari 9th December. WO14/1 Scutari Muster Roll January-March 1855 present 1st and 2nd Muster, no indication given of his whereabouts in March. WO25 Discharge book shows he was discharged as a Bandmaster on the 2nd March 1869.
Before the 20th century few cavalry regiments deigned to own a Quick March, regarding such infantry-style quicksteps as beneath the dignity of the mounted arm. It was not until 1881 that all regiments, cavalry and infantry, were instructed to submit details of their Regimental Marches to the War Office so that they could (for the first time) be officially approved. Only Slow Marches were submitted by the cavalry. Many had been in use for generations; some were based on traditional melodies; others had been specially written by long-forgotten Bandmasters.

322 ARMSTRONG, Sergeant Guy
Born : Unknown
Enlisted :
Medals : Crimea (B.I.S)

Died : Unknown
Status : Probably rode in the Charge

The musters show he was effective as a Paymaster's Clerk from the 1st October to the 31st December. Form 21 Soldier's' Remittances shows he sent £1 to a George Micklehurst. WO100/24 page 81 Remarks: Invalided. WO25 Discharge book shows he was discharged as a Paymaster Clerk on the 11th December 1860.

163

ARMSTRONG, Cornet William Bruce
Born : 8th December 1830 - Dublin
Enlisted :
Medals : Crimea (B.I.)

Died : 7th December 1906 - Pirbright, Surrey
Status : Probably rode in the Charge

The musters show he was effective as Assistant Surgeon from the 1st October to the 31st December. In the Regiment's Medal Roll there is no record of the Sebastopol clasp being issued, though clearly he was entitled to it. His diary is in the Regimental Museum, but lacks his account of the Charge.

Assistant Surgeon 4th Dragoon Guards 25th March 1854, resigned 11th May 1855. Cornet in 4th Dragoon Guards June 1855, Lieutenant September 1857, Captain 1861, Major March 1865. Resigned in 1869 selling his commission. Last known regiment was 7th Dragoon Guards. In 1878 Major William Bruce Armstrong privately published "An account of the Bruces of Newtoune" and in 1892 "The Bruces of Airth and Their Cadets". Also a member of the Society of Antiquaries of Scotland. Died at the Manor House, Pirbright, Surrey on the 7th December 1906 aged 75 years.

427 BAGNALL, Private James
Born : Unknown
Enlisted :
Medals : Crimea (I.S)

Died : Unknown
Status : Effective during the period

The musters show he was effective from the 1st October to the 31st December. Remarks state deprived of 1d good conduct pay 25th October. Form 21 Soldier's Remittances sent £2 to a Margaret Bagnall.

1022 BAKER, Private William
Born : Unknown
Enlisted :
Medals : Crimea (B.I.S)
A Long Service and Good Conduct has appeared on the market.

Died : 20th November 1872 - Dundalk
Status : Probably rode in the Charge

The musters show he was effective from the 1st October to the 31st December. WO25 Discharge book died at Dundalk on the 20th November 1872.

822 BARKER, Troop Sergeant-Major Charles
Born : Unknown
Enlisted :
Medals : Crimea (B.I.S)

Died : Unknown
Status : Probably rode in the Charge

The musters show he was effective from the 1st October to the 31st December. Form 21 Soldier's Remittances sent £4 to Peter Barker.

1071 BARTRAM, Private John
Born : Unknown
Enlisted :
Medals : Crimea (B.I.S)

Died : 20th December 1854 - On board ship
Status : Probably rode in the Charge

The musters show he was effective from the 1st October to the 17th December. Remarks state to Scutari 18th December. WO100/24 page 70 Remarks: Dead, page 75 Remarks: died 23rd Dec 1855. *The Times, Saturday 6th January 1855*, page 8 reported from Scutari on the 25th December 1854 that 1071, Private J. Bartram, 4th Dragoon Guards had died on board the ship Ottawa on the 20th December 1854.

1000 BELL, Private John
Born : Unknown
Enlisted :
Medals : Crimea (B.I.S)

Died : Unknown
Status : Probably rode in the Charge

Sotheby 1st July 1981, lot 144, Family Group. (a) John Bell 4th Dragoon Guards Crimea 3 clasps Balaklava, Inkermann, Sebastopol Engraved. Turkish Crimea French issue un-named. EF and toned. First with silver ribbon buckle brooch and contained in an old case, togther with contempoary newspaper cutting and two buttons. (b) 1914-15 trio and plaque A/Sgt J.Dovewis KRRC - with letter from records office at Dover to N/O/K £220.

The musters show he was effective from the 1st October to the 31st December.

164

1028 BENISON, Private John

Born : Date unknown - Rainhill, Lancashire
Enlisted : 9th November 1849
Medals : Crimea (B.I.S)

Died : 22nd January 1855 - Scutari
Status : Probably rode in the Charge

The musters show he was effective from the 1st October to the 31st December. WO100/24 page 70, Remarks Dead.
Page 76 Remarks: died 22nd Jan. 1855. Born in Rainhill, enlisted 9th November 1849 previous occupation a Tile Cutter.

1086 BENNETT, Private John

Born : Unknown
Enlisted :
Medals : Crimea (B.I.S)

Died : Unknown
Status : Probably rode in the Charge

The musters show he was effective from the 1st October to the 31st December. WO14/1 Scutari Muster Roll January-March 1855 1st Muster endorsed Joined 23rd Hospital, 2nd Muster endorsed To Regt 25th

661 BEVERLIN, Private Samuel

Born : Unknown
Enlisted :
Medals : Crimea (B.I.S)

Died : Unknown
Status : Probably rode in the Charge

A.H.Baldwin & Sons Ltd September 1934, item 7970, Crimea 3 clasps Balaklava, Inkermann, Sebastopol Cpl.S.Develin Impressed. Edge Knocks otherwise F 18/6. Neate Militaria and Medals List Sept/Oct 1996, item 34, Crimea 3 clasps Balaklava, Inkermann, Sebastopol ....Rpl . S. Beverlin 4th Dgn Gds Officially Impressed. Last Bar soldered on. E.K over first part of Rank F £550.
The musters show he was effective from the 1st October to the 31st December. Discharged as a Sergeant.

BIGGS, Paymaster John

Born : Unknown
Enlisted :
Medals : Crimea (B.S)

Died : Unknown
Status : Probably rode in the Charge

The musters show no effective dates. He is shown as receiving rations from 29th October to the 31st December. Remarks state Invalid on Board ship. In the returns relating to officers in the army Paymaster J.Biggs arrived in the Crimea October 1854 and his departure occured in December 1855 to the Bosphorus. Appointed Paymaster 16th Sept 1851.
Hart, *Army List* (1860) p132 Acting Chief Paymaster of the Osmanli Irregular Cavalry in the spring of 1856.

343 BLACKIE, Private Jasper

Born : Date unknown - Dalkieth, Midlothian
Enlisted :
Medals : Crimea (B.I.S)

Died : Unknown
Status : Probably rode in the Charge

Spinks 12th March 1996, Lot 699. Crimea, two clasps, Balaklava, Inkermann (Corpl. Jasper Blackie 4th Dn.Gds.), engraved, edge bruising, and contact marks, good fine, with copied service papers £240-260.
Eugene G. Ursual, Lists No 124. & 129 Crimea 1854 bars Balaklava, Inkermann. (Corpl. Jasper Blackie, 4th Royal Dragoons) regimentally named with service papers. 1250 Canadian dollars £540. Naming 4th Royal Dragoons very unusual.

The musters show he was effective from the 1st October to the 31st December.
Enlisted at Edinburgh. Form 21 Soldier's' Remittances sent £12 to Elizabeth Blackie. Invalided home from the Crimea 17th June 1855 suffering from "cronic rheumatism"; discharged at Dublin 19th November 1855 as unfit.

729 BLAKE, Sergeant Joseph

Born : Unknown
Enlisted :
Medals : Crimea (B.I.S)

Died : Unknown
Status : Probably rode in the Charge

The musters show he was effective from the 1st October to the 31st December.
Sergeant Joseph Blake was discharged on the 17th November 1862. After an eventful career in the Army Joseph was employed as a Coachman at the "Grove Hall Lunatic Asylum" Fairfield Rd London, Middlesex., which was situated in Grove Park together with St Catherine's Convent. Founded in 1866 the Church of Our Lady with St Catherine's built as a chapel would become the main Catholic church in the area. The nuns left during the War and the nunnery is now used by artists and includes a downstairs exhibition space. The park has a war memorial and is on part of the site of Grove Park Hall that was owned by the Byas family and run as a lunatic asylum in the nineteenth century.

574 BOTT, Private Thomas

Born : Unknown
Enlisted :
Medals : Crimea (I.S)

Died : Unknown
Status : Effective during the period

The musters show he was effective from the 1st October to the 14th November. Remarks state to Scutari 15th November. WO14/1 Scutari Muster Roll January-March 1855 1st Muster endorsed "Hospital", 2nd Muster endorsed "Sent home 23rd".

779 BRACKEN, Private Michael

Born : Unknown
Enlisted :
Medals : Crimea (B.I.S)

Died : Unknown
Status : Probably rode in the Charge

Glendining's 20th June 1991, Lot 546, four bars, Alma, Balaklava, Seb., Ink (M. Braken, 4th Drcs.), bars surmounted with a silver bar engraved "Balaklava Hero", crude engraved naming. Very fine £80-120

The musters show he was effective from the 1st October to the 31st December.

1024 BRADY, Corporal Thomas

Born : Unknown
Enlisted :
Medals : Crimea (B.I.S)

Died : Unknown
Status : Probably rode in the Charge

The musters show he was effective from the 1st October to the 31st December. Discharged 15th November 1867

1042 BRATTY, Private James

Born : Date unknown - Armagh
Enlisted : 10th April 1850
Medals : Crimea (B.I.S)

Died : Unknown
Status : Probably rode in the Charge

The musters show he was effective from the 1st October to the 31st December. Discharged by purchase 16th June 1860 at Aldershot. WO25 Discharged as a trumpeter in September 1860.

BRIGSTOCKE, Captain George Campbell Henville Player

Born : 13th May 1832
Enlisted :
Medals : Crimea (B.I.S)

Died : 13th October 1880
Status : Probably rode in the Charge

Little Hodge His letters and diaries of the Crimean War 1854-1856, edited by The Marquess of Anglesey. In a memorandum book which Hodge kept in 1855, there is no mention of Captain Brigstocke as being involved in Battle of Balaklava. (p46) Entry for 21st December 1855 page 66 Paddy Webb has got a turkey tied by the leg to his tent. "Briggy has got a couple of geese fastened up in the same fashion"
In Hodge's diary entry for 11th August 1855 on page 123, he mentions a sale in the camp of Brigstocke's things. He has deserted and has sent in his papers, and gone home today.
WO100/24 page 69 Remarks: Retired from the Service.

The musters show he was effective from the 1st October to the 31st December.

George Campbell Henville Player Brigstocke purchased a Cornetcy on the 16th February 1850. Lieutenant, by purchase 31st October 1851. Retired September 1855.

Large family grave with ornate railing surround and large granite obelisk can be found at Ryde Cemetery on the Isle of Wight

IN LOVING MEMORY OF GEORGE CAMPBELL HENVILLE PLAYER BRIGSTOCKE ESQUIRE
JOINT LORD OF THE MANOR OF ASHEY AND RYDE AND LATE CAPTAIN H.M. 4TH DRAGOON GUARDS
ELDEST SON OF THE LATE CAPTAIN T.R. BRIGSTOCKE, R.N., AND ELIZABETH LYDIA HIS WIFE
BORN MAY 13TH 1832 DIED OCTOBER 13TH 1880
"IN THE MIDST OF LIFE WE ARE IN DEATH"
"NOT LOST BUT GONE FOREVER"

865 BROWN, Private Josiah

Born : Unknown
Enllsted :
Medals : Crimea (B.I.S)

Died : Unknown
Status : Probably rode in the Charge

The musters show he was effective from the 1st October to the 8th December. Remarks Scutari 9th December. WO14/1 Scutari Muster Roll January-March 1855 January endorsed Hospital, and February Sent home 23rd. WO25 discharged 9th July 1859.

734 BROWN, Private William

Born : Date Unkown, Richmond
Enlisted : 8th September 1842
Medals : Crimea (I.S)

Died : 21st January 1855 - Scutari
Status : Effective during the period

The musters show he was effective from the 1st-26th October. Remarks note to Scutari 27th October. Servant upon enlistment. WO14/1 Scutari Muster Roll January-March 1855 effective 1st Muster endorsed Died 21st.

1055 BRYANT, Private William

Born : Unknown
Enlisted :
Medals : Crimea (B.I.S)

Died : Unknown
Status : Probably rode in the Charge

The musters show he was effective from the 1st October to the 31st December. Also shown as Bryan on the medal roll WO100/24 page 61. WO25 discharged 8th November 1857.

1167 BUCKNELL, Private George

Born : Unknown
Enlisted :
Medals : Crimea (B.I.S)

Died : Unknown
Status : Probably rode in the Charge

The musters show he was effective from the 1st October to the 14th November. Remarks to Scutari 15th November. Servant to Lt Col Hodge until 30.10.54 Musters read To Scutari 15th Nov. Deprived of 1p Good Conduct pay on the 27th October. Little Hodge. His letters and diaries of the Crimean War 1854-1856, Edited by The Marquess of Anglesey page 53. 30th October 1854...Sent Bucknall to his duty for being drunk and being in danger of losing our baggage. I have taken Little a young soldier in his place. This is probably the reason Bucknell lost his Good conduct pay. WO14/1 Scutari Muster Roll January-March 1855 effective 1st Muster endorsed Sent home 15th.

895 BUCKNELL, Private John

Born : Unknown
Enlisted :
Medals : Crimea (B.I.S)

Died : Unknown
Status : Probably rode in the Charge

The musters show he was effective from the 1st October to the 31st December. Form 21 Soldier's Remittances shows he sent £3 to a William Archer. WO25 discharged 1857

1169 BURBRIDGE, Private Frederick

Born : Date unknown - London
Enlisted : 12 December 1849
Medals : Crimea (B.I.S)
In E.E.Needes Collection Crimea 1 clasp Balaklava Fredk Burbridge 4th Dgn Gds. Muster roll

Died : 20th November 1854
Status : Probably rode in the Charge

The musters show he was effective from the 1st October to the 20th November. Remarks not readable?
Hodge's diary for the 20th November 1854 reads "Read the burial service over Private Burbridge by the light of a lamp. He died of cholera at 4pm. He was a terrible old drunkard". From Pay List Enlisted 12th December 1849 Previous occupation Waiter. WO100/24 page 70 Remarks: Dead. WO100/24 page 61 Remarks: Died 20th November

Shown in confinement 10th-11th November. Marginal note reads In Guard Room 18 November. Tried by C.M. Died 20 November. Form 20 1169 Pte Burbridge Frederick Born London, A waiter enlisted 12 December 1849. Died 20th November 1854 Crimea. 5s 1 3/4d in credit. Next of Kin Brother John County Middlesex Parish Cripplegate (London)

916 BURKE, Private Thomas
Born : Unknown
Enlisted :
Medals : Crimea (B.I.S)

Died : 12th April 1870 - Manchester
Status : Probably rode in the Charge

The musters show he was effective from the 1st October to the 31st December. WO25 died 12th April 1870 Manchester.

910 BURROWS, Private William
Born : Unknown
Enlisted :
Medals : Crimea (B.I.S)

Died : Unknown
Status : Probably rode in the Charge

The musters show he was effective from the 1st October to the 31st December.
L.S.G.C Medal date of recommendation 8.4.68 issued 27.6.68.

902 BYRNE, Private Patrick
Born : Unknown
Enlisted : 1846
Medals : Crimea (B.I.S)

Died : Unknown
Status : Probably rode in the Charge

Glendining 7 December 1988 Lot 182. Crimea 3 clasps Balaklava, Inkermann, Sebastopol. (Pte Patrick Byrne 4th DN. GDS) Contemporary engraved naming. One lug missing from Sebastopol Bar, NVF Est £250-£350. Not Sold
Toad Hall Medals List 2 1998, item 226. Now paired with Turkish Crimea. Crimea medal engraved. Sardinian issue un-named. Both suspened from Bailey of Coventry brooches. GVF £425

The musters show he was effective from the 1st October to the 31st December.
Patrick Byrne attested 4th D.G in 1846. Deserted 29th May 1848. Re-Joined imprisoned 2 months. Forfeited service. Deserted again on 18th September 1849, re-joined imprisoned 4 months forfeited service. Appointed shoeing smith in 1860. Previous service restored. resigned as a L/Cpl in October 1871 intending to be a smith at his home town of Portarlington. In 1904 he applied for an increase in pension aged 78 years.

872 CAMPBELL, Private Michael
Born : Unknown
Enlisted :
Medals : Crimea (B.I.S)

Died : Unknown
Status : Probably rode in the Charge

The musters show he was effective from the 1st October to the 31st December.
Form 21 Soldier's Remittances sent £1 to Maragret Shea. On the 2nd China War roll, transferred to the 1st Kings Dragoon Guards. To Depot, Canterbury,. Discharged 26th June 1862.

629 CAMPBELL, Farrier William
Born : Unknown
Enlisted :
Medals : Crimea (B.I.S)

Died : Unknown
Status : Probably rode in the Charge

The musters show he was effective from the 1st October to the 31st December. Form 21 Soldier's Remittances, sent £5 to Mary Campbell. WO25 discharged 1857.

A farrier is a specialist in horse care, especially shoeing. He uses many of the blacksmith's skills with a knowledge of veterinary medicine to address the care of a horse's hooves, feet & legs.

1164 CANTELL, Corporal William
Born : Unknown
Enlisted :
Medals : Crimea (B.I.S)

Died : Unknown
Status : Probably rode in the Charge

The musters show he was effective from the 1st October to the 31st December. W025 1164 Cantell William to pension 14th April 1865.

1100 CARLETON, Corporal Thomas
Born : Unknown
Enlisted :
Medals : Crimea (B.I.S)

Died : Unknown
Status : Probably rode in the Charge

The musters show he was effective from the 1st October to the 31st December. WO25 1164 Carleton Thomas to pension 29th April 1873.

820 CARROLL, Private Charles
Born : Unknown
Enlisted :
Medals : Crimea (B.I.S)

Died : Unknown
Status : Probably rode in the Charge

The musters show he was effective from the 1st October to the 31st December. WO25 discharged June 1862.

1037 CARSWELL, Private James
Born : Unknown
Enlisted : 30th January 1850
Medals : Crimea (B.I.S)

Died : Unknown
Status : Probably rode in the Charge

The musters show he was effective from the 1st October to the 31st December.
Muster Book January to March 1850 Form 7. Recruits. 1037 Carswell James. Enlisted 30th January 1850. Aged 21 years 5'10", at Manchester. Bounty paid to recruit £5-15-6. Paid to recruiting party £0-13-6. Total Levy money £6-9-0.
Reg No also shown as 1035

1025 CARTWRIGHT, Corporal William
Born : Unknown
Enlisted :
Medals : Crimea (B.I.S)

Died : Unknown
Status : Probably rode in the Charge

The musters show he was effective as a Private from the 1st October to the 31st December. WO25 discharged 31st October 1865 as a private.

988 CHADWICK, Corporal Thoams
Born : Unknown
Enlisted :
Medals : Crimea (B.I.S)

Died : Unknown
Status : Probably rode in the Charge

The musters show he was effective as a Private from the 1st October to the 31st December. WO25 discharged 24th February 1869 as a Sergeant.

958 CHAMBERS, Private Charles
Born : Unknown
Enlisted :
Medals : Crimea (I.S)

Died : Unknown
Status : Effective during the period

The musters show he was effective from the 1st October to the 31st December. WO25 discharged 20th March 1866 as a Sergeant.

1134 CHATTEN, Private Walter
Born : Unknown
Enlisted :
Medals : Crimea (S)

Died : Unknown
Status : Effective during the period

The musters show he was effective from the 1st-26th October. Remarks Scutari 27th October.
Medal Roll.: 70 Remarks Dead.

Dragoons Helmet

The Dragoon Guards and Dragoons wore the 'Albert' pattern spiked helmet introduced in 1849. The helmet worn by the Royals and the 6th Dragoons was made from white metal, with brass used for the other regiments. Helmets used by the officers were either silvered or gilt in appearance. The plume was not fitted during the Crimea campaign. The Scots Greys wore a black bearskin cap, with a white hackle on the left side. All the headdress had steel or brass chin chains, during the summer months the helmets were covered in a white quilted material. Officers favoured the undress peaked cap which had a small button and Russian braid on the flat top, with a gold band running around the circumference.

1142 CLARKE, Private Timothy

Born : Unknown
Enlisted :
Medals : Crimea (B.I.S)
His medal is held in the Royal Dragoon Guards Museum at York.

Died : Unknown
Status : Probably rode in the Charge

The musters show he was effective as a Private from the 1st October to the 31st December. WO25 discharged 18th October 1864.

1171 CLIPSHAM, Private Elijah

Born : Unknown
Enlisted :
Medals : Crimea (B.I.S)
His medals, Crimea and Turkish Crimea are held in the Royal Dragoon Guards Museum at York.

Died : Unknown
Status : Probably rode in the Charge

The musters show he was effective from the 1st October to the 31st December.
Little Hodge page 134 28 October 1855. My Cook, Clipsham, having taken himself off altogether, I am obliged to try a youth named Munro, a clean sort of lad, but utterly ignorant of cooking. Still by teaching him I hope we shall make something of him.
29th October1855 Our new cook managed very well today. We had two chickens very well roasted, and boiled ham. The lad is much cleverer than our late beast, who has this day been tried by a court martial for breaking his confinement to camp. This is the effect of drink. A disgraceful punishment: loss of a penny a day good conduct pay, and a quiet comfortable berth in which he had little to do. Now he will get worked.
Private Elijah Clipsham seems to have been the typical old soldier., hard drinking and hard fighting. He served in India, he held the Punjab Campaign Medal, 1848-9. On the Punjab medal roll 1852 Pte Elija Clipsham 3rd Light Dragoons, entitled to medal with clasps Chilianwala and Goojerat.

WO25 discharged 17th January 1866.

921 COFFEY, Private John

Born : 1827 Dublin
Enlisted :
Medals : Crimea (B.I.S)

Died : Unknown
Status : Probably rode in the Charge

The musters show he was effective from the 1st October to the 31st December.
Shown on the 2nd China War roll, transferred to the 1st Kings Dragoon Guards. On leaving the army John Coffey worked as a groom in Bristol.

897 COOKE, Corporal Henry

Born : Unknown
Enlisted :
Medals : Crimea (B.I.S)

Died : Unknown
Status : Probably rode in the Charge

The musters show he was effective as a Private from the 1st October to the 2nd December. Remarks read to Scutari 3rd December. WO14/1 Scutari Muster Roll January-March 1855 show he was there from the 1st-31st January, no indication given of his presence in February and March.

703 COOKE, Sergeant Michael

Born : April 1822 - Cork
Enlisted : April 1842
Medals : Crimea (B.I.S) LSGCM, MSM, French Medaille Militaire, Turkish Crimea.

Died : 26th February 1901
Status : Probably rode in the Charge

A.H.Baldwin & Sons, Ltd Sales Catalogue July 1948: Crimea. 3 Bars, Balaklava, Inkermann, Sebastopol; Long Service & G.C.; Meritorious Service Medal. Victorian head ; Medaille Militaire (Valeur et discipline); Turkish Crimea. Sgt. M. Cook, 4th Dgn. Gds. A rare and very fine group £10 10s (See Carter's "British War Medals," p 446)
Sotheby 22 November 1977. Lovell collection lot 338 Troop Sergeant Major Cooke 4th Dragoon Guards. Crimea 3 clasps Balaklava, Inkermann, Sebastopol (Sergt M.Cook 4th Dn Gds) LS & GC Victorian (TP. Sgt Major) Meritorious Service medal Victoria (Troop Sergent Major Late 4th DN. GDS.) Medaille Militaire France, with enamel damage. Turkish Crimea Sardinian type (named) Average condition VF.

The musters show he was effective from the 1st October to the 31st December. Form 21 Soldier's Remittances sent £3.10s to May Cooke. WO25 Pensioned off as a Troop Sergeant Major on the 2nd November 1875.
Sergeant Richard Cooke, incorrectly named on roll should read Michael. The French Medaille Militaire, for "exemplary and uniform good conduct during the campaign of 1854 and 1855."
A silver tankard presented to Sgt Michael Cooke from the officers of the regiment in appreciation of his valuable services, can be seen in the Royal Dragoon Guards Museum at York.

Born St Nicholas' parish, Cork, Co Cork, April 1822. Enlisted Cork April 1842. Cpl 3 March 1846. Forfeited rank 25 July 1847. Cpl 4 May 1849. Sgt 10 May 1854. TSM 26 Oct 1860. Medaille Militaire awarded 'for exemplary and uniform good conduct during the campaign of 1854 and 1855.' LSGCM awarded 22 Aug 1867. Served 33yrs 213 days, including 2yrs 6 months in Crimea. MSM and £10 gratuity awarded 14 Aug 1876. Discharged 2 Nov 1875, to live in Dublin. Died aged 79, 26 Feb 1901. Medal group formerly in Lovell Collection; later in Larimore Collection, USA. [McInnes, Annuity MSM, p. 9, and First Supplement, p. 7.]

Buried in St Michaels Churchyard, Camberley. Surrey. " In memory of Michael Cook, formerly troop Sergeant Major 4th Royal Irish Dragoon Guards, in which regiment he served for many years with great distinction. This cross is erected by some old officers of the regiment who knew and respected him. Died 26th February 1901 aged 78. Eternal rest, O Lord, and let perpetual light shine upon him. May he rest in peace. Amen"

821 COSTELLO, Troop Sergeant-Major Walter

Born : 1827 - Ireland
Enlisted : April 1842
Medals : Crimea (B.I.S)

Died : Unknown
Status : Probably rode in the Charge

The musters show he was effective as a Sergeant from the 1st October to the 4th November and a a Troop Sergeant Major from the 5th November to the 31st December. Form 21 "Soldier's Remittances" shows he sent £5 to a Anna Costello. He received 3s 1d per day pay.

In the 1881 Census shown living at 17 Gt Western Terrace, Fordington, Dorset. Chelsea Pensioner. With his wife Anna and seven daughters and one son. Anna 27 born in Ireland, Ellen 21 born in Brighton, Adelphine 19, Margaret 16, Georgina 14, all born in Ireland, Fanny 13 born in Aldershot, George 11 born in Sheffield and Emma 9 born in Evershot, Devon. WO25 to pension 11th April 1871.

653 COURD, Private Benjamin

Born : Unknown
Enlisted :
Medals : Crimea (B.I.S) The Distinguished Conduct Medal

Died : Unknown
Status : Probably rode in the Charge

The musters show he was effective from the 1st October to the 31st December. 653 Pte. Benjamin Courd (or Coward). The Distinguished Conduct Medal, recommendation dated 01/01/1855. WO25 Free Discharge June 1859.

970 COWHIG, Private Patrick

Born : Unknown
Enlisted :
Medals : Crimea (B.I.S)

Died : Unknown
Status : Probably rode in the Charge

The musters show he was effective from the 1st October to the 31st December.
WO14/1 Scutari Muster Roll January-March 1855 2nd Muster endorsed Joined 17th Hospital, no indication given of his whereabouts in the December muster. WO25 Discharged 3rd December 1858.

614 COX, Sergeant William

Born : Unknown
Enlisted :
Medals : Crimea (B.I.S)

Died : Unknown
Status : Probably rode in the Charge

The musters show he was effective from the 1st October to the 31st December. Form 21 Soldier's' Remittances shows he sent £3 to a Elizabeth Cox.

1184 CRAWLEY, Private James

Born : Unknown
Enlisted :
Medals : Crimea (B.I.S)

Died : Unknown
Status : Probably rode in the Charge

Glendining's 28th September 1988 Lot 86, Turkish Crimea, Sardinian issues (J.Crawley, 4 Dn. Gds.)On the Muster Roll of the Heavy Brigade.

The musters show he was effective from the 3rd November to the 31st December. Remarks from Varna 3rd November. First muster endorsed Varna pay from 22 September to 2 November 1854.
According to Medal Roll entry for Balaklava clasp states entitlement but musters appear to confirm he was at Varna from 22nd Sep to 2 Nov 1854, also gives Regimental number as 1148. WO25 Discharged December 1867. Regimental shown as 1184.

936 CROFTS, Sergeant George

Born : Unknown
Enlisted :
Medals : Crimea (B.I.S)

Died : Unknown
Status : Probably rode in the Charge

The musters show he was effective as a Corporal from the 1st October to the 31st December. Paid for 92 days, 3 days on board ship and 89 days on land. WO25 Discharged unfit 4th April 1868.

639 CROSHAW, Private Thomas

Born : Unknown
Enlisted :
Medals : Crimea (B.I.S)

Died : Unknown
Status : Probably rode in the Charge

The musters show he was effective from the 1st October to the 31st December. Paid for 92 days, 3 days on board ship and 89 days on land. WO25 Discharged 23rd November 1861.

509 CROSSLEY, Private John

Born : 1815 - Horton
Enlisted :
Medals : Crimea (I.S)

Died : Unknown
Status : Effective during the period

Spinks Numismatic Circular date unknown. J.Crossley 4th D.G's Crimea clasps for Balaklava, Inkermann, Sebastopol. Engraved naming, LS & GC medal, Turkish Crimea Sardinian type. Together with a coloured photograph of a painting of the charge of the heavy brigade. (Painted by General Elliot)
Liverpool Coin and Medal List March 1985 item 505. Same Group. Crimea now stated to have only two clasps Inkermann, Sebastopol, Engraved naming NVF/GVF £150. Also in Liverpool Coin and Medal List again March 1986 item 413 £135.
Dixons Gazette No 11 Autumn 1997 item 1842 Group of 3. Crimea Medal clasps for Inkermann, Sebastopol. Engraved 4 DN.Gds, Turkish Crimea Sardinian issue. LS & GC Medal Victorian 3rd type 1874-1901, 509 4th Dragn.gds impressed. With copy of discharge documents. F/GVF £250.

The musters show he was effective from the 1st October to the 14th November. Remarks Scutari 15th November.

John Crossley born and lived in Horton, Bradford. Trade a Hatter. Served 24 years 18 days. Discharged 25th March 1862, aged 47 years, 5'9 3/4" Grey eyes, light hair. Living in Everton, Liverpool. Discharged at own request. Good Character in possession of five good conduct badges.

WO14/1 Scutari Muster Roll January-March 1855 1st and 2nd Muster endorsed Hospital, 3rd Muster endorsed Sent home 3rd, WO25 Discharged June 1862.

685 CURREN, Private Henry

Born : Unknown
Enlisted :
Medals : Crimea (B.I.S)

Died : Unknown
Status : Probably rode in the Charge

The musters show he was effective from the 1st October to the 31st December Also spelt Curran on the medal Rolls.

748 DALTON, Private John

Born : Unknown
Enlisted :
Medals : Crimea (B.I.S)

Died : Unknown
Status : Probably rode in the Charge

The musters show he was effective from the 1st October to the 31st December.

619 DANIELS, Private John

Born : Unknown
Enlisted :
Medals : Crimea (B.I.S)

Died : Unknown
Status : Probably rode in the Charge

The musters show he was effective from the 1st October to the 31st December. WO25 Discharged 6th Sept. 1864.

DEANE, Lieutenant Hon M. Fitzmaurice

Born : Unknown
Enlisted :
Medals : Crimea (B.I.S)

Died : Unknown
Status : Rode in the Charge

The musters show he was effective from the 1st October to the 31st December .
Cornetcy 4th L.D 17th December 1852. To 10th Hussars almost immediately. To 2nd Dragoons 1853. To 4th D.G by 1854. Lieutenantcy 29th December 1854. He left the regiment in 1856.
Little Hodge his letters and diaries of the Crimean War 1854-1856, edited by The Marquess of Anglesey. In a memorandum book which Hodge kept in 1855, he states that Lt Deane on the 25th October, 1854, at the Battle of Balaklava was mounted in the Field. (p46)
WO100/24 page 69 Remarks: on sick leave in England. WO100/24 page 74 Remarks: Promoted from Cornet.

966 DELANY, Private David

Born : Unknown
Enlisted :
Medals : Crimea (B.I.S)

Died : Unknown
Status : Probably rode in the Charge

The musters show he was effective from the 1st October to the 31st December. WO25 to 5th Lancers 1st April 1858.

778 DELANY, Private Nicholas

Born : Unknown
Enlisted :
Medals : Crimea (B.I.S)

Died : Unknown
Status : Probably rode in the Charge

The musters show he was effective from the 1st October to the 2nd December. Remarks Scutari 3rd December. WO14/1 Scutari Muster Roll January-March 1855 1st and 2nd Muster endorsed Hospital, no indication given of his whereabouts in March. WO25 discharged June 1862.

890 DESMOND, Sergeant Denis

Born : Unknown
Enlisted :
Medals : Crimea (B.I.S)

Died : Unknown
Status : Probably rode in the Charge

The musters show he was effective as a Private from the 1st October to the 4th November and as a Corporal from the 5th November to the 31st December. WO102 awarded L.S.G.C Medal £10 Gratuity date of recommendation 17.5.69 issued 26.7.69. WO25 Discharged to pension September 1870.

1089 DONOVAN, Private John

Born : Unknown
Enlisted :
Medals : Crimea (B.I.S)

Died : Unknown
Status : Probably rode in the Charge

The musters show he was effective from the 1st October to the 31st December.
WO14/1 Scutari Muster Roll January-March 1855, 1st Muster endorsed joined 31st Hospital, present on 2nd Muster, no indication given of his whereabouts in the March muster.

845 DOOLEY, Sergeant John

Born : Manchester
Enlisted : 28th November 1845
Medals : Crimea (B.I.S)

Died : 7th December 1854 - Crimea
Status : Probably rode in the Charge

The musters show he was effective from the 1st October to the 7th December. WO100/24 page 60 Remarks: Died on 7th December. WO100/24 page 75 Remarks: Died on 7th Decr. 1854.
Form 20, 845 Sgt Dooley John. Born Manchester, A clerk enlisted 28th November 1845. Died 7th December 1854. Crimea 12s 8d in credit. Next of Kin. Father Martin Dooley, St Peters Manchester.

281 DOOLEY, Corporal Martin

Born : Unknown
Enlisted :
Medals : Crimea (B.I.S)

Died : Unknown
Status : Probably rode in the Charge

The musters show he was effective as a Corporal from the 1st October to the 26th November. Remarks Scutari 27th November. WO14/1 Scutari Muster Roll January-March 1855 show January endorsed Hospital, and February Sent home on the 17th March 1855.

486 DOOLEY, Private Maurice

Born : Unknown
Enlisted :
Medals : Crimea (B.I.S)

Died : Unknown
Status : Probably rode in the Charge

The musters show he was effective from the 25th October to the 31st December. Remarks record from Scutari 25th October.

DRAKE, Quarter Master John George

Born : Unknown
Enlisted :
Medals : Crimea (B.I.S)

Died : Unknown
Status : Probably rode in the Charge

The musters show he was effective as from the 1st October to the 31st December.
Appointed QM 6th June 1854. Still listed as QM in 1860, but gone by 1874.

McNeill/Tulloch Commission of Enquiry 1856,
QUARTERMASTER DRAKE examined, extracts below:

The men preferred salt pork to fresh beef; the beef being very indifferent - the salt pork good; but the Surgeon is of the opinion, that the substitution of salt for fresh meat would be injurious to their health. Besides the rations of meat and biscuit, the men have had about 2 ounces daily of rice, with onions and potatoes; the supplies of these articles have been irregular, the quantity of potatoes has not averaged more than ½ a-pound per man daily.
Whilst in stationary camp it would be an advantage to the men, that the alternations should be issued in the evening for the succeeding day; they would then have opportunities of soaking the beef.
The men are in the habit of buying soft bread off the hawkers at 1s. 6 d. and 2s. a loaf of 1½ pound weight...
Upon several occasions when the nosebags of the horses were worn out, notwithstanding repeated applications to Quartermaster-General's-Department they were not renewed for a considerable length of time during which the horses had to eat their grain off the ground: this caused great waste of grain and was injurious to the health of the horses.
The troop horses of the regiment were got under cover during the month of February 1855.

199 DRAKE, Hospital Sergeant-Major Joseph
Born : Unknown
Enlisted :
Medals : Crimea (B.I.S) The French Medaille Militaire, The Distinguished Conduct Medal

Died : Unknown
Status : Probably rode in the Charge

The musters show he was effective as a Hospital Sergeant from the 1st October to the 31st December. Form 21 Soldier's Remittances sent £5 to a Jane Drake.
WO100/24 page 81 Remarks: Invalided.

Little Hodge, His letters and diaries of the Crimean War 1854-1856. Edited by The Marquess of Anglesey. From Diary entry dated 5th October 1855 "My hospital sergeant, Sergeant-Major Joseph Drake, is going to England today. He has been 28 years in the Regiment with me, and is a truly excellent man. He will ,I hope, call and see you. I have given him your direction".
In a letter dated 30th January 1856 "I am most obliged to you for thinking about Segt-Major Drake. He is a thoroughly honest man, never drinks, and is most methodical and regular in his habits. He would make an excellent 'overlooker'.
The French Medaille Militaire, for "exemplary conduct in living in the same tents with, and unremitting attention to, numerous men when ill and dying of cholera in the Crimea in 1854 and 1855".
Eight other ranks of the regiment received Distinguished Conduct Medals. One of these, Hospital Sergeant-Major Joseph Drake, received a medal for distinguished conduct in the field, and an annuity of £20.
In August 1854 "It may be remarked that the Surgeon of the 4th Dragoon Guards in his monthly report, dated 31st August, stated :- "On the first days of the month admissions from Cholera were numerous and of a bad character, but on the 4th three extreme cases of the disease, of which no hope was entertained, began to improve, and all ultimately recovered in total eighteen deaths took place of which 15 were from 'Cholera'.

709 DRURY, Private Michael
Born : Date Unknown - Cork
Enlisted : 29th April 1842
Medals : Crimea (B.I.S)

Died : 24th November 1854 - Crimea
Status : Probably rode in the Charge

The musters show he was effective from the 1st October to the 24th November. Remarks record Died 24th November.
Form 20, 709 Pte Drury, Michael, Born Cork,.
A labourer, enlisted 29th April 1842. Died 24th November 1854 in the Crimea. £5-14-2 1/2 in credit, includes £1-1-4 1/2 savings bank deposit. WO100/24 page 62 Remarks: Died on 25th November. WO100/24 page 76 Remarks: died 25th November 1854.

1026 DUNNE, Private Robert
Born : Unknown
Enlisted :
Medals : Crimea (B.I.S)

Died : Unknown
Status : Probably rode in the Charge

The musters show he was effective from the 1st October to the 31st December. WO25 discharged 22nd Nov. 1857.

1111 DUNNE, Private Thomas
Born : Unknown
Enlisted :
Medals : Crimea (B.I.S)

Died : Unknown
Status : Probably rode in the Charge

The musters show he was effective as a Corporal from the 1st-29th October and as a Private from the 1st November to the 31st December. Remarks state reduced to Private 1st November. Shown in confinement 30th October to the 1st November. WO102 Sergeant Dunne awarded L.S.G.C medal ,date of recommendation 12.5.70 issued 21.7.70.
WO25 discharged 10th October. 1871.

1034 DUNNE, Private Thomas
Born : Unknown
Enlisted :
Medals : Crimea (B.I.S)

Died : Unknown
Status : Probably rode in the Charge

The musters show he was effective from the 1st October to the 31st December. WO25 discharged 27th Aug. 1867.

4th Dragoon Guards Mounted on the Field 25th October 1854

2 Field Officers. Lt Col Hodge, Major Forrest.   **4 Captains** Captain Forster, McCreath, Webb, Robertson.
4 Subaltern   Lt McDonnel, Fisher, Muttlebury, Deane.   **202 N.C.**   Officers and Men
1 Surgeon   Dr Pine.
Listed are 268 effective individuals. Of which 246 have Balaclava clasps. According to Hodge 213 men and officers were on the field on the 25th October 1854. (p46) *Little Hodge, His letters and diaries of the Crimean War 1854-1856.*

---

527 EGAN, Private Denis

Born : Unknown   Died : Unknown
Enlisted :   Status : Probably rode in the Charge
Medals : Crimea (B.I.S)

The musters show he was effective from the 1st October to the 31st December. WO25 discharged 16th Nov. 1859.

---

960 ENRIGHT, Private Patrick

Born : Date Unknown - Rathkeale Ireland   Died : 2nd March 1855 - Scutari
Enlisted : 27th November 1847   Status : Effective during the period
Medals : Crimea (I.S)

The musters show he was effective from the 1st October to the 31st December. WO14/1 Scutari Muster Roll January-March 1855 2nd Muster endorsed Joined 17th Hospital, 3rd Muster Died 2nd.
Entry records born Rathkeale, Trade on enlistment Labourer.

---

463 EVANS Troop Sergeant-Major John

Born : Date Unknown -   Died : 2nd March 1855 - Scutari
Enlisted :   Status : Slightly wounded in the Charge
Medals : Crimea (B.I.S)
Sotheby 22 November 1977. Lovell Collection Lot 440 "Al Valore Militare" Rev officially engraved "Troop Sergt Major John Evans 4 Drag'n Gds" GVF.
Spinks Auction 5th June 1986 Lot 155. Group of 3 to Troop Serjeant Major Evans 4th Dragoon Guards. Crimea 3 clasps Balaklava, Inkermann, Sebastopol TSM 4th Dragoon Gds. Impressed. Al Valore Militare silver TSM J. Evans 4th Dragoon Gds. Engraved. Turkish Crimea French issue un-named generally VF £700.

The musters show he was effective from the 1st October to the 31st December. 2nd and 3rd Musters record Scutari. Remarks state on duty to Scutari 22nd Nov.
Casualty Roll.: Listed wounded Slightly at Balaklava.
The Sardinian War Medal. "Displayed gallant conduct at the action of Balaklava, where he was wounded".

1154 FIELD Private Denis

Born : Unknown   Died : Unknown
Enlisted :   Status : Probably rode in the Charge
Medals : Crimea (B.I.S)

The musters show he was effective from the 1st October to the 31st December. WO25 discharged 14th May. 1872.

---

724 FIELD Private Patrick

Born : Unknown   Died : Unknown
Enlisted :   Status : Probably rode in the Charge
Medals : Crimea (B.I.S)

The musters show he was effective from the 1st October to the 31st December. WO25 discharged 3rd July. 1865.

---

963 FINUCANE Sergeant Edward

Born : Unknown   Died : Unknown
Enlisted :   Status : Probably rode in the Charge
Medals : Crimea (B.I.S)

The musters show he was effective as a Corporal from the 1st October to the 31st December. WO25 Deserted 12th August 1867. Records show he was a private in 1859.

FISHER Lieutenant Edward Rowe

Born : 1832
Enlisted :

Died : 8th November 1909
Status : Rode in the Charge

Medals : Crimea (B.I.S)

The musters show he was effective from the 1st October to the 31st December. Absent with leave 2nd-31st December.

Little Hodge, His letters and diaries of the Crimean War 1854 - 1856 ,Edited by The Marquess of Anglesey. In a memorandum book which Hodge kept in 1855, he states that Lt Fisher on the 25th October, 1854, at the Battle of Balaklava was mounted in the Field.(p46) Lieutenant Fisher did not have a high regard for Hodge (p22) the men "behaving very badly, and our Colonel is not fit to manage them. Privates and N.C.O's get drunk on escort duty, and the N.C.O's are not broken, or the privates flogged."

Below are quotes from *"Some Adventures of a Cornet of Horse in the Crimean War"*
By Kenneth Macrae Moir. Printed for private circulation 177 copies.

Moir writes "Edward Rowe Fisher-Rowe; he came down from Magdalene College, Cambridge, in 1852, at the age of twenty and shortly afterwards his father purchased him a commission as Cornet – or second Lieutenant as we should now call it – Her Majesty's 4th Regiment of Dragoon Guards. It is to his son, the late Colonel Herbert Fisher-Rowe, that I am indebted for leave to use his father's letters and diaries for the purpose of this paper."
Fisher-Rowe writes to his father on the 26th October 1854.
"I do not know when this may reach you as things are in great confusion just now. Yesterday, about 7 a.m., the Russians made their appearance at the Comora village on our extreme right, and in a very short space of time drove the Turkish force, who were in battery there, head over heels down into the plain. They abandoned their batteries; I believe, from what I now hear, that some, if not all, the guns were spiked. The Russians brought their own and turned them on the cavalry who were drawn up in the plain."
He then goes on say that after the attack on the Highlanders' by the Russian cavalry. "A second force of cavalry about the same size made for our camp and baggage, which were in great danger. The Heavy Brigade, however, were loosed at them, and rolled them over and over and cleared the plain."
Moir quotes from another letter "The Turks are found out at last; they are a blackguardly, cowardly race, without honour amongst the officers or honesty amongst the men. They are treated in a very different way since the action; instead of a nod and a "Bono Jonnie" from everyone, if one comes near a well when any soldier's are there he stands a good chance of a blow across the mouth from a Heavy Dragoon's fist and curses as long as he is in sight. I hear they get still rougher treatment with the French. The 93rd, who like all Highlanders can bear malice, swear, if they get a chance, to drive their bayonets through the whole lot. They stole all the Highlanders kits while they were actually defending them from the enemy. And when the work was over about half a regiment of Turks marched across the plain with their trumpets and drums sticking their weapons into the dead."
Moir concludes with " And as I began this paper by introducing our Cornet of Horse, perhaps I should close by reverting to him. He got his Captaincy soon after the end of the war, but unfortunately a very severe hunting accident caused his retirement from the Service at an early age. He lived on at his place at Thorncombe near Guildford to a ripe old age....., a country squire in the old tradition, a Justice of the Peace and a Deputy Lieutenant for his country".

Peerage.com. Edward Rowe Fisher-Rowe died 8th November 1909, married Lady Victoria Isabella Liddell his second wife on the 29th July 1874. Her married name became Fisher-Rowe. He was the only son of the late Thomas Fisher of Thorncombe.

Harts Cornet 17 June 1853, Lieutenant 29th December 1854.

Fisher Cornet Edward Rowe (later Edward Fisher-Rowe)
Crimea (BS). Cornet 17 June 1853. Lieut 29 Dec 1854. His Crimea letters were published by his son: L R Fisher-Rowe (ed), Extracts from Letters of E R Fisher-Rowe (late Captain 4th Dragoon Guards) During the Crimean War (Godalming, 1907). [Brereton, 4th/7th Dragoon Guards, pp. 222, 233.]

Broad Arrow 13th November 1909
Captain Edward Rowe Fisher-Row late 4th Dragoon Guards died on the 10th inst. aged 77. He was the only son of the late Thomas Fisher of Thorncombe.

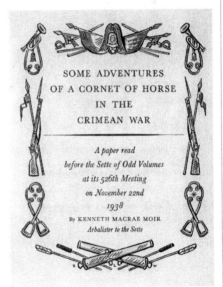

SOME ADVENTURES
OF A CORNET OF HORSE
IN THE
CRIMEAN WAR

A paper read
before the Sette of Odd Volumes
at its 526th Meeting
on November 22nd
1938

BY KENNETH MACRAE MOIR
Arbalister to the Sette

581 FISHER, Private William
Born : Unknown
Enlisted :
Medals : Crimea (B.I.S)

Died : Unknown
Status : Probably rode in the Charge

The musters show he was effective from the 1st October to the 31st December. WO25 to army hospital Corps 1/12/59.

695 FITZGERALD, Private Michael
Born : Unknown
Enlisted :
Medals : Crimea (B.I.S)

Died : Unknown
Status : Probably rode in the Charge

The musters show he was effective from the 1st October to the 31st December.
WO25 discharged 6th September 1864.

692 FITZPATRICK Private John
Born : Unknown
Enlisted :
Medals : Crimea (B.I.S)

Died : Unknown
Status : Probably rode in the Charge

The musters show he was effective from the 1st October to the 31st December.

942 FLEMMING, Sergeant Patrick
Born : Unknown
Enlisted :
Medals : Crimea (B.I.S) The Distinguished Conduct Medal.

Died : Unknown
Status : Probably rode in the Charge

The musters show he was effective as a Corporal from the 1st October to the 31st December.
The Distinguished Conduct Medal. Recommendation dated 01/01/1855. WO25 discharged 21st July 1868.

951 FLETCHER, Saddler Sergeant Robert
Born : Unknown
Enlisted :
Medals : Crimea (B.I.S) L.S.G.C Medal.

Died : Unknown
Status : Probably rode in the Charge

The musters show he was effective as a Saddler Sergeant from the 1st October to the 14th November. 2nd and 3rd musters note Scutari. Remarks reads To Scutari 15th November. Form 21 Soldier's' Remittances shows he sent £10 to his children. WO102 awarded L.S.G.C Medal £15 Gratuity date of recommendation 4.4.71 issued 5.10.71
WO14/1 Scutari Muster Roll January-March 1855 show January and February endorsed Hospital, no remarks in March.
WO25 to pension 18th November 1873.
WO25 Robert had a son Thomas Fletcher who retired as a Major in the 5th Lancers in 1893.

1155 FLETCHER, Private William
Born : Unknown
Enlisted :
Medals : Crimea (B.S)

Died : Unknown
Status : Probably rode in the Charge

The musters show he was effective from the 1st October to the 2nd November. Remarks Scutari 3rd November.

WO14/1 Scutari Muster Roll January-March 1855 1st and 2nd Muster endorsed Cook, 3rd Muster endorsed Hospital.

795 FLYNN, Private Bernard
Born : Unknown
Enlisted :
Medals : Crimea (B.I.S)

Died : September 1856
Status : Probably rode in the Charge

The musters show he was effective from the 1st October to the 31st December.
Form 21 Soldier's' Remittances shows he sent £1.10s to a Mary Anne Flynn. WO25 September 1856 died.

Eye witness accounts of the Charge of the Heavy Brigade

Captain Henry Clifford

The Scots Greys and the Enniskillen Dragoons advanced in a slow, steady trot towards them, the Russians looked at them as if fascinated, unable to move. The distance between the two cavalries at last decreased to about fifty yards, and the shrill sound of the trumpet, ordering the charge, first broke the awful silence.

William Henry Russell (Times War Correspondant)

The Greys rush on with a cheer that thrills to every heart - the wild shout of the Enniskilliners rises through the air at the same instant. As lightning flashes through a cloud, the Greys and the Enniskilliners pierced through the dark masses of Russians. The shock was for but a moment there was a clash of steel and a light play of sword blades in the air, then the Greys and the Redcoats disappear in the midst of the shaken and quivering columns...
It was a terrible moment. "God help them! They are lost!" Was the exclamation of more than one man, and the thought of many. With unabated fire the noble hearts dashed at their enemy. It was a fight of heroes.

773 FLYNN, Private James
Born : Unknown
Enlisted :
Medals : Crimea (B.I.S)

Died : Unknown
Status : Probably rode in the Charge

The musters show he was effective from the 1st October to the 31st December.

WO14/1 Scutari Muster Roll January-March 1855 1st Muster endorsed Joined 31st Hospital, 2nd Muster endorsed Hospital, 3rd Muster Sent home 3rd.

785 FLYNN, Private Lawrence
Born : Unknown
Enlisted :
Medals : Crimea (B.I.S) L.S.G.C Medal.

Died : Unknown
Status : Probably rode in the Charge

The musters show he was effective from the 1st October to the 31st December.
WO102 awarded L.S.G.C Medal £5 Gratuity date of recommendation 9.4.66 issued 16.6.66. WO25 pension 10.12.67.

FORREST, Major William Charles

Born : 1819 London, Middlesex
Enlisted :
Medals : Crimea (B.I.S) The Turkish Order of the Medjidie (5th Class), The Sardinian War Medal

Died : 1st April 1902
Status : Rode in the Charge

Eldest son of Lieut Col Forrest of the Hon East India Co's service.
Cornet 11th LD 11 March 1836. Lieut 5 Jan 1839. Capt 7 Sept 1841. Transfer to 4th DG 1 March 1844. Major 3 Oct 1848. Brevet Lieut Col 12 Dec 1854. Lieut Col 5 Aug 1859. Bvt Col 8 March 1860. Maj Gen 6 March 1868. Lieut Gen 1 Oct 1877. Col 8th Hsrs 14 March 1880. Col 11th Hsrs 8 Feb 1886. Retired as Hon Gen 1 July 1881. CB 29 May 1875. Died Winchester 1 April 1902 aged 82.
Forrest joined the 11th Hussars. and can be seen in this painting in the early style uniform . The dark brown fur busby is very tall with a white over crimon plume. Note the open front collar of the jacket the edges sloping back, this was to become a feature of the 11th's uniform.

The Sardinian War Medal "Served the campaign of 1854-5, including the battles of Balaklava and Inkermann, and siege of Sebastopol"
Major Forrest, was Hodge's second-in-command, and commented on the difficulty of the ground "First thro a vineyard, and over two fences, bank and ditch, then thro the Camp of the 17th and we were scarcely formed when we attacked."
William Charles Forrest was one of the officers that Cardigan quarrelled with. He was one of the best officers in the regiment but Cardigan regarded him as the leader of the 'Rebels'. When Forrest's wife suffered a difficult birth, he was refused compassionate leave and complained to Cardigan. The Duke of Wellington was drawn into the dispute, as he had been on numerous other occasions, and lost his temper with Cardigan, rebuking him for his 'foolish quarrels' with his officers.
His career progressed to the rank of General and he was Colonel of the 11th for 17 years until his death in 1902.

The Crimean War letters written by Major W.C Forrest are held in the National Army Museum, NAM 5804/32.
Varna 17 July 1854
Letter from Maj W.C Forrest, 4th Dragoon Guards to his brother.
I suppose you will have heard of Cardigan's reconnaissance a precious business it appears to have been and will cost about 50 horses to say nothing of about 150 very bad backs - Cardigan was away so long that they sent a Subaltern's party from here to look for him, they were out 6 days, marched 50 miles a day but saw nothing of My Lord, were two days without grub and have brought back horses that will not be fit for the field for a month, if ever, for the greater part of them have fever in the feet - Lord Lucan is here and a rum one he seems to be, I hear his staff all wish themselves off it, he is so uncertain and difficult to get on with, report says something disagreeable happened between him and Scarlett, the latter has gone ….and told me he found he was a nobody here, Lord Lucan had all reports made direct to himself.
Letter dated Balaclava 12th October 1854.
We have no faith in the generalship of my Lord Lucan, we all agree that two greater muffs than Lucan and Cardigan could not be, we call Lucan the cautious ass and Cardigan the dangerous ass, between the two they got us into two or three very awkward positions at Alma and also on the previous day and then began to dispute who commanded the brigade – Cardigan abused the officers of the 11th and called them a dead set of old women – the officers sent Douglas to remonstrate with him, when Lord Cardigan asked him what he meant by speaking to a Major General in that way - In the evening he sent for Douglas and Peel to his tent and said that under the excitement he had made use of some nasty expressions. He is now on board a ship with a touch of diarrhoea and we hope he will remain there!
There is one road upon which we sent a patrol every day at the same hour, the most dangerous for cavalry alone, it is out on the side of a mountain with thick wood on one side and a precipice on the other. I expect every day to hear of the Russians closing the road after our party have passed and then shooting them out of the wood.
Excerpts from a Letter dated 27th October 1854.
The Russians attacked our position in front of Balaklava at about 6am of the 25th, they first attacked our Field works on the heights occupied by the Turks who behaved very ill, deserting their guns and running away on the approach of the Russians and that before they came very near. The guns, 9 in number belonged to us but had been lent to the Turks, fortunately we had one of our Artillery men in each entrenchment who spiked the guns when the Turks began to run away. The Russians then brought up their artillery and pounded away at us, who were drawn up down in the plain, we had one troop of Horse Artillery, Maude's, but they were of no service against the Russian guns which were very much heavier and we had to retire, poor Maude being the first man wounded, a shell entered his horse, exploded and severely wounded him in the arm; upon our retiring the Russians advanced their Cavalry, they came on in great strength and with great boldness and one body charged our 93rd the only English Regiment we had on the ground. " Bedad, they must take them for Turks", said one of our men.

The 93rd gave them one volley and they immediately wheeled to their left and retired, another body of cavalry came down towards us, the Heavy Brigade and was charged by the Greys and I think the Inniskillings were in the first line, the Russians met them well and outflanking them, wrapped round both flanks and took them in front, flank and rear, our first line upon this retreated, at least we saw the greatest part of the men come back, upon which the 4th charged the Russians in flank, some other Regiment immediately afterwards charged them in front, the Russians stood a few minutes and then retired precipitously, but reformed in good order on the top of a hill, but on getting one shot from our Horse Artillery away they went.

Lord Raglan, who, by this time has arrived on the heights in our rear sent in aide-de-camp with this message, "Well done the Heavy Brigade", but for my part I think the Heavies might have done much better. The Greys charged at a trot and our pace was but very little better, but we had very bad ground to advance over, first this vineyard and over two fences, brush and ditch then through the camp of the 17th and we were scarcely formed when we attached and had but very little good ground to charge over still we did not go in at so good a pace as we might have done, once in we did better, but the confusion was worse than I had expected, the men of all regiments were mixed and we were a long time reforming. If we have to do it again I hope we shall do it better - I don't know what the loss of the Brigade was but we had only one man killed and 5 wounded and I did not see more than two or three English on the ground. We had one horse killed and 3 wounded, there were about 20 Russians on the ground or perhaps rather more, they were Hussars, well mounted, fought in great coats having their jackets in their valises, some of them were provided with spikes for guns which we have not got........(description of the charge of the light brigade)

We, the Heavies were taken down the valley as a support to the Light Brigade and we had batteries playing upon us, upon both flanks. We the 4th escaped in the most providential manner the round shot were flying over us and both in front and rear and occasionally through the ranks, however, we had but one man severely wounded since reported dead and 4 men and 3 horses slightly wounded. I saw the Greys drop to the number of about 12 or 15 but I think they were principally horses that suffered. I got a crack on the head in one charge but the Brass pot stood well and my head is only slightly bruised. I got a rap on the shoulder but the edge must have been very badly delivered for it has only cut my coat and slightly bruised my shoulder. We had three Turkish entrenchments in our front with a chain of Turkish sentries besides the 93rd Highlanders and our own Pickets and Patrols were not more than a quarter of a mile from our own camp and one Regiment would have been enough to have held our Picket. Lord Lucan blew up Scarlett as Lord Cardigan used to blow up a Captain and with about as much reason. No one can quite see the end of our work here and many believe we shall have to winter here. I was told this morning that all the transports now here had received orders to land the regimental baggage and go to Constantinople for stores. Lord Raglan sent down some of our infantry and a Regiment of French Cavalry after this mishap with the Light Brigade the French charged the battery in the flank and drove away the gunners and I have heard they took some of the guns. Our infantry were not called upon to do anything and were withdrawn the next day. The Russians are left on the heights which they took from the Turks and it is said Lord Raglan means to abandon Balaklava and make use of Chersonese thinking our present position too extended. The Russians attacked the Light Division yesterday but were repulsed with great loss and six officers taken prisoners. They made a sally on the French and spiked 7 guns but very few returned to Sebastopol and the French have extracted the spikes - the Siege is progressing but not rapidly, the Russians make a good defence and I think we shall see something more of the army outside - It is supposed that 1100 men were brought against us last Wednesday and that there are many more in the Neighbourhood – the Cavalry have been moved up nearer Sebastopol and had to shift our camp on our return - Hodge came out whilst we were engaged and joined the Regiment before we charged.

From a Letter dated 12 Dec 1854

I am glad that you did not accept old General Pigot's invitation, for I have heard that he is very troublesome about those two daughters (by different Mothers', I believe) and tries to thrust them upon people. You would probably at some future time have been asked to receive these two young ladies for a Birmingham or Coventry Ball. I may do the old man an injustice, but I would keep clear of his daughters.

From a letter dated 22 Dec 1854

It was very cold during the night and six of the unfortunate troop horses died in our regiment, 35 died in the brigade. I was quite rejoiced to hear the poor men most of whom had been out all day, and must have been wet through, singing in their tents last night, and was amused at hearing poor little Hodge say to himself with a huge sigh, "Ah I wish I was in spirits to sing like those fellows". He, Hodge, gets very much down in the mouth sometimes and he has a habit of thinking aloud, and my tent being next to his, I am made an involuntary deposit for all these thoughts. I frequently tell him of it and he says, "I believe I do always think aloud and talk to myself, I always used to do so in my barrack room, and living so much alone I have got into the habit of it."

In the 1881 Census Forrest is recorded as living at West Hill Place Winchester, Hampshire, Occupation Lieut Genl Active List and J.P. For Hants.Living with his wife Elizabeth.

The Annual Register 1902 (p. 122)
General William Charles Forrest, CB, the son of Lt.-Col. William Forrest, died 1st April (1902) at Winchester aged 82. He served with the 4th Dragoon Guards in the Crimean Campaign 1854-5, taking part in the heavy charge at Balaklava and the battle of Inkerman. In 1855 he was in command of the 4th Royal Irish Dragoons.

FORSTER, Captain Francis Rowland

Born : Unknown
Enlisted :
Medals : Crimea (B.I.S) The Turkish Order of the Medjidie (5th Class) Sardinian Medal

Died : Unknown
Status : Rode in the Charge

The musters show he was effective from the 1st October to the 31st December.

He commanded the right squadron at Balaclava. [Brereton, 4th/7th Dragoon Guards, p. 228; Hart, Army List.]

WO100/24 page 69 Remarks: Aide de Camp to Major General Chatterton. Commg. Limerick District.

Bt.Major Francis Rowland Forster. The Turkish Order of the Medjidie (5th Class)

The Sardinian War Medal."Commanded the first squadron of the regiment at the action of Balaklava, on the 25th October, 1854."

Cornet 7 Feb 1840. Lieut 11 March 1842. Capt 29 Jan 1847. Bvt Major 12 Dec 1854. Retired with rank of Lieut Col 20 April 1861.

From *Little Hodge His letters and diaries of the Crimean War 1854-1856.* Diary entry dated 5th November 1854, p54 (following the battle of Inkerman). Lord Lucan ordered a squadron of the 4th, and one of the Greys and the Royal Dragoons to the front in support of the Horse Artillery...Forster and myself rode to the field of battle. The sight was dreadful. The ground was covered with dead and wounded Russians.

11th May 1855. p107. I hope that you will receive the photographic views of my hut and camp. The man who did them has, I think, returned to England. He has taken with him the original plates, and he says he will give copies of them at five shillings each to any of our friends who wish for them.His address is as follows: Mr R.Fenton, Photographer to the British Museum, " Albert Terrace, Albert Road, Regent's Park. He did a very good thing of myself, Webb, Forster, sitting down at the door of his Marquee, and a white horse of Forster's being held by a servant. Then there is another of Webb, Forster and myself, with Mrs Rogers, and Webb's servant and pony. We are standing at the door of Webb's hut.

He also did some others of the officers in groups, which are extremely good. I hope he will keep his work and carry the plates back with him to England".

Writing to Hodge ten years later,Captain Forster remembered "when we moved down by the side of the vineyard to attack the Russians, we were in column of troops or squadrons left in front. At the bottom of the vineyard where we wheeled to the left, we were certainly in column of troops, as I remember perfectly your ordering me, when my squadron had passed through some broken ground at the end of the vineyard, to front-form my squadron, and charge immediately on the flank of the Russians, and that you would bring up the second squadron after me.

The Marquis of Londonderry has made the following appointment in his household :- Master of the House,Colonel F.R.Forster. *Times August 7th 1886*

Gravestone in Mount Jerome Cemetery, Dublin. -Plot C1135 - 13435. Lt Colonel Francis Rowland Forster, 4th Royal Irish Dragoon Guards. A Crimean Veteran died 16th August 1910, aged 88 years. Headstone is of limestone on a granite base and kerb.

"In memory of Lt. Colonel Francis Rowland Forster, formerly 4th Royal Irish Dragoon Guards, who died 10th of August 1910 at Parkgate House, Dublin, aged 88. He served in the Crimean war with his regiment including the battles of Balaclava, Inkerman and Sebastopol. He was Master of the House for many years at Dublin Castle to the Lord Lieutenants of Ireland and also Deputy Ranger of the Curragh.

1208 FOX, Corporal Samuel

Born : Unknown
Enlisted :
Medals : Crimea (B.I.S)

Died : 25th November 1886
Status : Probably rode in the Charge

The musters show he was effective as a Private from the 1st October to the 26th November. Remarks state to Scutari 27th November.
WO14/1 Scutari Muster Roll January-March 1855 show January and February endorsed Hospital, no remarks in March.
WO25 died 25th November 1886.

1124 FRANCOMB, Sergeant John

Born : Unknown
Enlisted :
Medals : Crimea (B.I.S)

Died : Unknown
Status : Probably rode in the Charge

Shown on medal roll as Cpl. Farncomb.

The musters show he was effective as a Private from the 1st-31st October and as a Corporal from the 1st November to the 31st December.

1138 FULLERTON, Private Robert

Born : Date unknown - Dublin
Enlisted :
Medals : Crimea (B.I.)

Died : Unknown
Status : Probably rode in the Charge

The musters show he was effective from the 1st October to the 2nd December. Remarks Scutari 3rd December.
WO14/1 Scutari Muster Roll January-March 1855 1st endorsed "Hospital", 2nd Muster "Cook", 3rd Muster "Hospital".
WO25 discharged on the 17th June 1858 rank Corporal.

From an Article in the *Liverpool Weekly Mercury* Saturday, February 29th 1908.
Robert FULLERTON, Late Corporal 4th Dragoon Guards, Seacombe, Cheshire served in Crimea and took part in the Charge of the Heavy Brigade at Balaclava.
For every photograph published one guinea will be contributed to the Liverpool Lord Mayors Fund .

Food and cooking was a big problem until the French-born chef Alexis Soyer travelled out to the Crimea . He volunteered his services following correspondence with Florence Nightingale.
When he arrived in Scutari in March 1855, the troops were malnourished, and suffering from cholera and scurvy. The soldier's main daily ration was 1 lb army biscuit, and 1 lb meat. With supply problems, no fuel to cook with, and each soldier having to fend for himself, cooking was a daily challenge
He immediately organised kitchens, arranged supplies of dried vegetables, and developed recipes using Army rations.
He trained and installed in every regiment the "Regimental cook" so that soldier's would get an adequate meal and not suffer from food poisoning or malnutrition. His biggest contribution was the mobile field oven.

1871 census: 57 Stitt Street, Everton, Robert Fullerton aged 37, Cotton Porter, born Dublin Ireland. Wife Margaret aged 38, son Robert aged 9 born Dublin Ireland, Thomas aged 2, William Edward aged 8 months and daughter Lizzy aged 6 all born in Everton.

1881 census: 57 Stitt Street, Everton, Robert Fullerton aged 47, Warehouseman, born Dublin Ireland. Wife Margaret aged 48, son Robert aged 19 born Dublin Ireland, William Edward aged 10, James aged 8 and daughter Lizzy aged 16 all born in Everton.

1891 census: 71 Brighton Street, Wallasey, Robert Fullerton aged 59, Freight Clerk, born Dublin Ireland. Wife Margaret aged 58, son James aged 18 and William Edward aged 20 both born in Everton.

1901 census: 4 Beatrice Street, Seacombe, Robert Fullerton aged 67, Cotton Porter, born Dublin Ireland. Wife Margaret aged 70, daughter Elizabeth aged 36 and son James aged 28 both born Liverpool.

586 GALLAGHER, Private Michael

Born : Unknown
Enlisted :
Medals : Crimea (B.I.S)

Died : Unknown
Status : Probably rode in the Charge

The musters show he was effective from the 1st October to the 31st December.
Form 21 Soldier's Remittances sent £2 to Rebecca Gallagher.

721 GALLAGHER, Private Michael

Born : Unknown
Enlisted :
Medals : Crimea (B.I.S)

Died : Unknown
Status : Probably rode in the Charge

The musters show he was effective from the 1st October to the 31st December.

On Form 8 of the musters entitled Account of Soldier's under sentence of Forfeiture of Pay, or Additional Pay, during the Period of this Pay List he is shown as forfeiting 1d per day of his pay for 30 days. WO25 discharged 3rd July 1866.

896 GANNAN, Private Martin

Born : Date unknown - Abbey
Enlisted : 7th August 1846
Medals : Crimea (B.I.S)

Died : 14th. February 1855
Status : Probably rode in the Charge

The musters show he was effective from the 1st October to the 31st December. Trade on enlistment Labourer.
WO100/24 page 77 Remarks: died 14th. February 1855. WO100/24 page 71 Remarks: Dead.
Form 21 Soldier's Remittances shows he sent £2 home.
WO14/1 Scutari Muster Roll January-March 1855 1st Muster endorsed Joined 28th Hospital, 2nd Muster endorsed Died 14th.

1066 GANNAN, Private Patrick

Born : Unknown
Enlisted :
Medals : Crimea (B.I.S)

Died : Unknown
Status : Probably rode in the Charge

The musters show he was effective from the 1st October to the 31st December.

From research carried out by Mr John Rumsby. The Fourth Dragoon Guards (The Royal Irish) in 1856 consisted of 55% English, 40% Irish and 5% Scots. Cavalry regiments were predominantly English reflecting the practice of recruiting in the manufacturing districts such as Birmingham and West Yorkshire.

1127 GASKIN, Private Johnson

Born : Unknown
Enlisted :
Medals : Crimea (B.I.S)

Died : Unknown
Status : Probably rode in the Charge

The musters show he was effective from the 1st October to the 31st December.

840 GILL, Private Thomas

Born : Unknown
Enlisted :
Medals : Crimea (B.I.S)

Died : Unknown
Status : Probably rode in the Charge

The musters show he was effective from the 1st October to the 8th December. Remarks state to Scutari 9th December.

WO14/1 Scutari Muster Roll January-March 1855 1st Muster endorsed Hospital Ship, no indication given of his whereabouts in the following two musters. WO25 discharged 13th August 1867

555 GILLETT, Private William
Born : Unknown
Enlisted :
Medals : Crimea (B.I.S)
Died : Unknown
Status : Probably rode in the Charge

Glendining's 27th May 1992, Lot 263, Three bars, Balaklava, Inkermann, Sebastopol (W. Gillett, 4th Dragoon Grds.), officially impressed. Surface nicks both sides and edge bruised at 5 o'clock, very fine. (£400-600)

The musters show he was effective from the 1st October to the 31st December.
Form 21 Soldier's' Remittances sent £2.10s to Elizabeth Gillet.
WO14/1 Scutari Muster Roll January-March 1855, 1st Muster endorsed joined 28th Hospital, 2nd Muster endorsed Died 14th.

780 GILLIGAN, Sergeant John
Born : Unknown
Enlisted :
Medals : Crimea (B.I.S) The Distinguished Conduct Medal
Died : Unknown
Status : Rode in the Charge

DNW 29th March 2000, Lot 905, Heavy Brigade D.C.M. group of three awarded to Sergeant John Gilligan, 4th (Royal Irish) Dragoon Guards. Distinguished Conduct Medal, V.R. (John Gilligan, 4th R. Irish Dn. Gds.) first two letters of christian name and 'G' of Gds. carefully re-tooled due to edge bruising; Crimea 1854-56, 3 clasps, Balaklava, Inkermann, Sebastopol (Serjt. John Gilligan, 4th Dragoon Guards) contemporary engraved naming, contemporary conversion to fixed suspension with reverse facing forwards; Turkish Crimea, Sardinian issue, with scroll suspension, unnamed as issued, edge bruising and contact wear, generally nearly very fine (3) Hammer Price £2900
Sold with four copied pages of service papers in which his character and conduct are described as 'very good, he was when promoted in possession of five good conduct badges. Also in possession of Crimea Medal with three clasps (for Balaklava, Inkermann and Sebastopol) and Turkish War Medal. He has also been granted a silver medal and gratuity of £5 for distinguished service in the field at the Battle of Balaklava.'
Dixons Gazette, No 22, Summer 2002, item no.1297, Group same as above, £4500.

The musters show he was effective as a Private from the 1st October to the 31st December.
780 Pte. John Gillingam. D.C.M. Recommendation dated 1 January 1855. Gratuity of £5. WO25 discharged unfit 30/6/68

442 GILLIGAN, Private Mark
Born : Date unknown - Ballington
Enlisted : 10th March 1836
Medals : Crimea (B.I.S)
Died : Unknown
Status : Probably rode in the Charge

Morton & Eden Ltd, Thursday 26 October 2006, Lot 737 *Crimea 1854-56, 3 clasps, Balaklava, Inkermann, Sebastopol, officially impressed (M. Gilligan. 4th Dragoon Grds.), some contact marks and wear on surface and rims, generally very fine £800-1,200. Hammer Price £1,600

The musters show he was effective from the 1st October to the 31st December.
Muster Book 1st July 1866 to 30th September 1860, form 29. 442 Pte Gilligan's mark. Born Ballington. A labourer, enlisted 10 March 1836. Form 21 Soldier's' Remittances shows he sent £1.1s to a Harriet Gilligan.
Discharged on completion of service at Aldershot on 28th September 1860.

The army descended on Aldershot in 1854. Close to London and Portsmouth it made an ideal location for a military base, The area around Aldershot was mainly heath land ideal for military manoeuvres. The effect of the massive influx of people was dramatic. Aldershot soon became a Wild West frontier town, with prostitutes and spivs on hand to help relieve the troops of their money. The soldier's were first housed in bell tents and later in wooden huts, which were in turn replaced by brick built barracks in the 1890s.

1168 GOLDSTONE, Corporal James
Born : Unknown
Enlisted :
Medals : Crimea (I.S)
Died : Unknown
Status : Effective during the period

The musters show he was effective from the 1st October to the 17th December. Remarks record to Scutari 18th December.

WO14/1 Scutari Muster Roll January-March 1855 shows he was there from the 1st January to the 24th February, Second muster endorsed Regiment 25th. WO25 discharged as T.S.M to pension 27th May 1873.

657 GOOD, Private William
Born : Unknown   Died : Unknown
Enlisted :   Status : Probably rode in the Charge
Medals : Crimea (B.I.S)
His medal is held in the Royal Dragoon Guards Museum at York.

The musters show he was effective from the 1st October to the 31st December. WO25 to 5th Lancers 1st March 1858.

990 GORDON, Private Robert
Born : Unknown   Died : Unknown
Enlisted :   Status : Probably rode in the Charge
Medals : Crimea (B.I.S)

The musters show he was effective from the 1st October to the 31st December. WO25 discharged June 1861.

1058 GRANT, Private John
Born : Unknown   Died : Unknown
Enlisted :   Status : Probably rode in the Charge
Medals : Crimea (B.I.S)

The musters show he was effective from the 1st October to the 31st December.

1093 GRIFFITHS Private Simon
Born : Unknown   Died : Unknown
Enlisted :   Status : Effective during the period
Medals : Crimea (I.S)

The musters show he was effective from the 1st October to the 31st December. In the remarks Hospital.
WO25 1093 Griffiths Simon discharged 1857, note different regimental number.

1114 HACKETT, Private Patrick
Born : Unknown   Died : Unknown
Enlisted :   Status : Probably rode in the Charge
Medals : Crimea (B.I.S)

The musters show he was effective from the 1st October to the 31st December.

584 HACKFORTH, Private John
Born : Unknown   Died : Unknown
Enlisted :   Status : Probably rode in the Charge
Medals : Crimea (B.I.S)

The musters show he was effective from the 1st October to the 31st December.

1144 HALL, Private Thomas
Born : Unknown   Died : Unknown
Enlisted :   Status : Probably rode in the Charge
Medals : Crimea (B.S)

The musters show he was effective from the 1st October to the 31st December.

913 HALL, Private Thomas
Born : Unknown
Enlisted .
Medals : Crimea (I.S)

Died : Unknown
Status : Effective during the period

The musters show he was effective from the 1st-26th October. Remarks state to Scutari 27th October.
WO14/1 Scutari Muster Roll January-March 1855 present in the 1st and 2nd muster, 2nd muster endorsed "Regt 3rd".

1068 HANCOX, Private William
Born : Date unknown - Buddenhall, Warwicks
Enlisted : 10th April 1851 - Coventry
Medals : Crimea (I.S)
A Crimea medal with B.I.S clasps is in the hands of a private collector.

Died : Unknown
Status : Effective during the period

The musters show he was effective from the 1st October to the 8th December. Remarks Scutari 9th December.
WO14/1 Scutari Muster Roll January-March 1855 1st Muster endorsed Sent home 15th.
WO97-1737 1068 William Handcox (Note different spelling on the medal roll) A labourer born in Buddenhall, Warwickshire. On the 10th April 1851 enlisted in 4th Dragoon Guards at Coventry, aged 19 years 6 months. Promoted corporal 24th August 1855, Sergeant 7th November 1857. On the 9th April 1863 Re-engaged at Dublin for 12 years. Promoted Troop Sergeant Major 25th December 1867.
Discharged at Belfast at his own request, free with pension after 21 years service. Character very good. No educational certificates. In possession of the Crimea medal and the Turkish medal. No entries in the regimental defaulters book. Never tried by court martial. No injuries or wounds recorded. On discharge was T.S.M and discribed as 41 6/12 years old 6 feet tall. Fresh complexion. Grey eyes. Light brown hair. A labourer. No marks or scars. His intended place of residence Dorchester. Final discharge 29 April 1873.
On the 1st May 1873 enlisted in Dorsetshire Yeomanry Cavalry as Sergeant Instructor on the permanent staff. Discharged character exemplary on completion of engagement on 30th April 1889. Chelsea No 18367 on 30th April 1873 awarded a pension of 2/- per day for service in the 4th Dragoon Guards. Final intended place of residence shown as Sherborne.
Surname is spelt Handcox on discharge papers, but as Hancox by the Yeomanry.
The soldier signed all documents in the name of Hancox. The medal roll does not credit this soldier with a Balaclava clasp but this clasp is specifically mentioned on the front sheet of the discharge documents.

863 HARPER, Private William
Born : Unknown
Enlisted :
Medals : Crimea (B.I.S)

Died : 12th February 1855 - Scutari
Status : Probably rode in the Charge

The musters show he was effective from the 1st October to the 31st December. WO100/24 page 71 Remarks: Dead.
WO100/24 page 77 Remarks: Died 12th February 1855.

HARRAN, Cornet Edward
Born : Unknown
Enlisted :
Medals : Crimea (B.S)

Died : Unknown
Status : Probably rode in the Charge

The musters show he was effective as a Troop Sergeant Major from the 1st October to the 4th November and as a Regimental Sergeant Major from the 5th November to the 31st December. Remarks state he was promoted.
He served as an Adjutant in the regiment.
WO100/24 page 74 Remarks: Promoted from T.S.Major Regt No 817

Appointed Cornet and Adjutant Sept 1855. [Brereton, 4th/7th Dragoon Guards, p. 240.]

From Little Hodge His letters and diaries of the Crimean War 1854-1856.
4th November 1854 page 54,. Recommended Troop Sergeant Major Harran to Lord Raglan for a cornetcy without purchase in the regiment with a view of getting him the Adjutancy, which Webb is quite unfit for, besides being absent in ill health. Captain John MacDonnell Webb retired on the 25th September 1855. Harran was to take on Webb's responsibilities and become Adjutant.
London Gazette. Friday 23 February 1855 page 703. 4th Regt of Dragoon Gds. Sgt Major Edward Harran to be Cornet without purchase.

967 HARRAN, Sergeant James

Born : Unknown

Enlisted :

Medals : Crimea (B.I.S)

Died : Unknown

Status : Probably rode in the Charge

The musters show he was effective as a Corporal from the 1st October to the 31st December.

488 HARRINGTON, Sergeant Jackson

Born : Unknown

Enlisted :

Medals : Crimea (B.I.S)

Died : Unknown

Status : Probably rode in the Charge

Wallis and Wallis 18th August 1981, Lot 12, Family Group of six, comprising Three: Crimea 3 bars Balaklava, Inkermann, Sebastopol (engraved naming), Meritorious Service, Vic issue without date, (impressed Farr Major Jackson Harrington, 4th Dragoon Guards), Turkish Crimea Sardinian issue, (impressed Farr Major Jackson, 4th Dn Gds), GVF or better, this regiment formed part of the Heavy Brigade, Three: 1914-15 star trio (Pte. A.S. Harrington A.S.C), VF. Hammer Price £350

The musters show he was effective as a Farrier Major from the 1st October to the 31st December. Form 21 Soldier's' Remittances records he sent £20 to a Eliza Harrington. WO25 records Farrier Major to pension 23rd April 1867.

849 HARRISON, Private George

Born : Unknown

Enlisted :

Medals : Crimea (B.I.S)

Died : Unknown

Status : Probably rode in the Charge

The musters show he was effective from the 1st October to the 31st December.

1135 HARROLD, Private William

Born : Unknown

Enlisted :

Medals : Crimea (B.I.S)

Died : Unknown

Status : Probably rode in the Charge

Sotheby Auction 5th March 1980 Lot 91. Turkish Crimea, Sardinian issue. W.Harrold 4th R.I Dragoon Guards depot impressed and two other medals VF and better.

Hamiltons Despatch 1980 Turkish as above. Steel ring suspender VF £36. Advertised again in the July 1981 Despatch VF £30.

The musters show he was effective from the 1st October to the 31st December. WO25 discharged 21st July 1868.

621 HARTLEY, Private John

Born : Date unknown - Wakefield

Enlisted : 8th September 1840

Medals : Crimea (B.S)

Died : 4th February 1855 - Scutari

Status : Probably rode in the Charge

The musters show he was effective from the 1st October to the 17th December. Remarks record to Scutari 18th December. WO100/24 page 77 Remarks: died 4th. Feby. 1855 WO100/24 page 71 Remarks: Dead. Trade on enlistment Cloth worker.

WO14/1 Scutari Muster Roll January-March 1855 1st Muster endorsed Hospital, 2nd Muster endorsed Died 4th.

1099 HEALY, Private James

Born : Unknown

Enlisted :

Medals : Crimea (B.I.S)

Died : Unknown

Status : Probably rode in the Charge

The musters show he was effective from the 1st October to the 31st December. Marginal note reads from corporal 1st October

Camp of the 4th Dragoons, convivial party, French & English Photograph by Roger Fenton 1855.
Men of the 4th Dragoon Guards, one smoking a pipe, two Zouaves, and one woman (Mrs. Rogers) in front of hut.

943 HEALY, Private William

Born : Unknown
Enlisted :
Medals : Crimea (B.I.S)

Died : Unknown
Status : Probably rode in the Charge

The musters show he was effective from the 1st October to the 31st December.
WO100/24 page 71 Remarks: Sent to England.

1162 HEELY, Private John

Born : Unknown
Enlisted :
Medals : Crimea (B.I.S)

Died : Unknown
Status : Probably rode in the Charge

The musters show he was effective from the 1st October to the 31st December.
Form 21 Soldier's' Remittances sent £2 to Michael Heely. WO25 to pension 28th July 1874.

1033 HIGGINBOTHAM, Private Samuel

Born : Unknown
Enlisted :
Medals : Crimea (I.S)

Died : Unknown
Status : Effective during the period

The musters show he was effective from the 1st October to the 31st December.

713 HOAGAN, Private Connor

Born : Unknown
Enlisted :
Medals : Crimea (B.I.S)

Died : 11th March 1860
Status : Probably rode in the Charge

The musters show he was effective from the 1st October to the 31st December. WO25 records he died on the 11th March 1860.

HODGE, Lieutenant-Colonel Edward Cooper

Born : 19 April 1810, Weymouth, Dorset   Died : 10 December 1894
Enlisted :   Status : Rode in the Charge
Medals : CB, Crimea (B.I.S), Officer of the Legion of Honour (France), Order of the Medjidie 3rd Class (Turkey), Turkish Crimea.

Edward Cooper Hodge was the only son of Major Edward Hodge of the 7th Hussars, who was killed on the day before the battle of Waterloo at Genappe aged 33. A popular and efficient officer, he was killed on the 17 June1815 during the rear guard action covering the withdrawal to Waterloo, his body was never found. His mother was the youngest daughter of Sir Edmund Bacon Bart of Raveningham Hall. Norfolk.

From the age of 5 Edward was without a father. Aged 7 Hodge started at Dr Pearson's School at East Sheen where he remained until July 1822. His education continued when he joined Eton college, his small stature made him into a rowing cox. Aged 16, Hodge measured only 5'1", the minimum height for a Heavy Dragoon soldier being 5'8". In 1826 Hodge left Eton and travelled to Paris to be with his mother and sisters. Family connections were to prove useful when the Commander-in Chief of the Army, the Duke of York gave Edward a Cornetcy in the 13th light Dragoons.

In August 1826 commissioned as a Cornet in the 13th Lt Dragoons. Four months later exchanged into 4th Dragoon Guards. Lieutenant by purchase 5th July 1828, Captain 19th December 1834. Major 3 December 1841. Lieutenant Colonel 3 Oct 1848. Colonel 28 Nov 1854. Half-pay 5 Aug 1859.
The musters show he was effective from the 1st October to the 31st December. Absent with Leave 1st-21st October 1854.
The Marquess of Anglesey, wrote a book entitled Little Hodge His letters and diaries of the Crimean War 1854-1856. Based on numerous letters written by Hodge to his mother, and two Lett's Diary volumes for the years 1854 and 1855.

3 October 1848 Musters WO 12 -270. 1st Oct to 31st Dec 1854. Absent 1 Oct -21 Oct 1854, invalid on board ship. 5 horses kept by officer and foraged at public Expense. 71 days rations on shore.
Entitled to Turkish order of the Medjidie 5th Class.

Lieutenant-Colonel Hodge's account of the charge 25th October 1854:
A large body of cavalry came into the plain and were charged by the Greys and the Inniskillings. We were in reserve and I brought forward our left and charged these cavalry in flank. The Greys were a little in confusion and retiring when our charge settled the business. We completely routed the Hussars and Cossacks and drove them back. (page 44)
The diary entry concludes:
"The Russians did not follow, or quit their strong position, and we remained on the ground till 8 pm, when we were ordered to return to our camp, and to go to the rear some two miles, which we did.
Both my servants got brutally drunk, and I found them lying on their backs, and with difficulty I was enabled to save my baggage. I got up my bed in Forrest's tent and slept there." Continues on to discribe casualties.

On the 20th September 1855 during a full dress parade the troops received in total 185 Crimean War Medals, described by Colonel Hodge as 'a vulgar looking thing, with clasps like gin labels', which were quickly dubbed 'port', 'sherry', and 'claret,' how odd it is that we cannot do things like people of taste'. He used the opportunity to deliver a speech to instil into the troops the "necessity of care of their horses and their appointments". (p130) His feelings towards the medal were later underlined when in his diary entry dated 21st September.1855 He suggests that the metal from the guns captured at Sebastopol, should be used to make a small Maltese Cross, and "given to those who were under fire in the trenches and to none other. These medals given to all the world are of no value. They are too common,"
A strange coincidence that the Victoria Cross was founded by Royal Warrant on January 29th 1856. The bronze from which all Victoria Crosses are made is supplied from the Central Ordnance Depot, and all the Crosses made have been made from the same source of metal. This was taken from captured enemy cannon.

11th November 1854. "Last night we had much drunkenness in the camp. The men have been paid some money and this is the only use they have for it. The following day "The state of our camp is beyond anything beastly. The mud is a foot deep all round the horses. The rain beats into our tents. How man or horse can stand this work much longer I know not. I was very unwell from diarrhoea all last night. I wish I had my £12,000 safe in my pocket, and that I was safe in a good lodging in foggy, murky London,. (£12,000 reference to the cost of his commissions)

In early February 1855 Lord Lucan was recalled to England, this followed the censure of Lucan by Raglan after the battle of Balaklava. On the 19th March Lord Lucan made a speech in the House of Lords. In which he took the credit for charge of the 4th Dragoons into the Russian flank, "that caused the Russian cavalry to turn and fly". Much to the annoyance of Hodge, from a letter dated 10th April "This I declare he never did. It was quite my own idea."

13th April 1855 "Parade under arms to inspect them, and to present medals for distinguished service". Eight medals were issued, Hospital Sergeant-Major Joseph Drake,, Sergts Patrick Flemming, John Gilligan, William Percy, and Frederick Wallace, Corporal Henry Preece, Privates Benjamin Courd and Thomas Marks.

On the 8th December 1855 the Oneida a modern screw ship moved majestically past the old Genoese towers which marked the entrance to Balaklava harbour. On board were 200 horses and 185 sick, dirty and miserable men. Hodge and his pitiful cargo, arrived in Scutari two days later. Hodge took up residence in the Palace of the Sultans. Christmas for the men was anything but merry, they to endure hastily erected buildings and were surrounded by mud, snow and sludge. On the 14th June Hodge embarked for England arriving at Portsmouth on the 29th June 1856. Three horses were lost on the voyage. On their arrival they were ordered to go to Aldershot. In a letter dated 30th June "I shall take the earliest opportunity of running up to see you, so if your servants see a ragged looking ruffian in a red jacket trying to get into No19, beg them not to call the police.

In the 1881 census shown Edward C Hodge aged 70 K.C.B. General Retd (Bart) living at 26 Cornwall Gdns London, Middlesex, with his wife Lucy Ann aged 51 and their 14 year old daughter Dorothy. (The child was probably adopted, see grave stone inscription below)

Hodge was to marry quite late on in life, he married at the age of 54, his bride was Lucy Anne the daughter of a Yorkshire squire.
The couple went on to have three sons and one daughter who died of scarlet fever when she was seven. All three sons were to join the military.
Hodge was to resume his military career, and after being on half-pay for the past three years. In December 1862 he accepted the command of the cavalry brigade at Aldershot, following in the foot steps of Lord George Paget. He took up residence in Anglesey House, and lived there with his family for the next five years. Promotions followed when in 1871 he was promoted to Lieutenant-General. In 1873 he became Sir Edward Hodge, KCB. In 1877 he was made a full General, followed by a GCB on the occasion of the Queen's Golden Jubilee in 1887. His wife died in 1885. He died at his London house, 26 Cornwall Gardens, South Kensington on the 10th December 1894.

Each year he would attended the annual Balaklava Dinner in London on the 25th October, often in the Chair.
In 1878 he became a committee member of the Royal Patriotic Fund, in later life he was to become involved in organisations concerned with the welfare of ex-soldier's. Including, Metropolitan Hospital Sunday Fund, The Royal School for Daughters of Officers of the Army, and Royal Cambridge Asylum for Soldier's Widows.

He was buried in the Brompton cemetery, in the same grave as his wife and daughter. The grave stone carries the following inscription:
Front:
Ethel Mary Hodge only daughter of General Sir Edward Hodge KCB - Born -- November 18-- Died 4th January 1878 Ethel Mary Hodge died of scarlet fever at the age of 7.
Right Side:
Also of General Sir Edward Cooper Hodge KCB Born 10th April 1810 - 10th December 1894.
Lucy Ann Hodge 1820-1885
The helmet worn at Balaklava by Lt-Col E.C.Hodge can be seen at the Royal Dragoon Guards Museum at York.

1112 HOGAN, Private Patrick

Born : Date unknown - Darley
Enlisted : 18th October 1848
Medals : Crimea (B.I.S) The French Medaille Militaire

Died : 21st January 1888
Status : Probably rode in the Charge

Sotheby's Auction 6th January 1903. Crimea Medal with clasps S.I and B, the French Military Medal, Turkish Crimea, and Long Service Good Conduct medal. Hammer price £10.

The musters show he was effective from the 1st October to the 31st December.
The French Medaille Militaire. "exemplary and uniform good conduct during the campaign of 1854 and 1855".

The Broad Arrow 28th January 1888. 4th Dragoon Guards. One of the survivors of this regiment who took part in the Balaclava charge. Mr Patrick Hogan, died on the 21st inst at Hamstead Road, London. Throughout the Crimean campaign he was allocated as the permanent orderly of Sir Edward Cooper Hodge and was one of the two men of the regiment who had the distinction of being awarded the French War medal. Mr Patrick Hogan served his second term of service in the Royal Horse Guards retiring from this regiment a few years since on a pension.
Muster Book 1st July to 30 September 1860 Form 29, 1112 Pte Hogan Patrick. Born Darley, A labourer. Enlisted 18 October 1848. Transfered to Royal Horse Guards at Aldershot on 31st August 1860.

Form 21 Soldier's' Remittances sent £3 to Margaret Hogan.

470 HORGAN, Private James

Born : Unknown
Enlisted :
Medals : Crimea (I.S)

Died : Unknown
Status : Effective during the period

The musters show he was effective from the 1st October to the 31st December.

819 HOULTON, Corporal Thomas

Born : Unknown
Enlisted :
Medals : Crimea (B.I.S)

Died : Unknown
Status : Probably rode in the Charge

The musters show he was effective as a Private from the 1st October to the 26th November and as a Corporal from the 27th November to the 31st December. Remarks promoted to Corporal.
WO102 awarded L.S.G.C Medal with £10 gratuity, date of recommendation 17.5.69 issued 26.7.69.

372 HYLAND, Private Richard

Born : Unknown
Enlisted :
Medals : Crimea (B.I.S)

Died : Unknown
Status : Probably rode in the Charge

Donald Hall Commission List 47 June 1987 item 120. Crimea 3 Bars Balaclava, Inkermann, Sebastopol, R.Hyland 4/Drgn Guards impressed VF £400. Same medal offered again List 48 Oct 1987 item 129 VF £350.
The musters show he was effective from the 1st October to the 31st December.

The musters show he was effective from the 1st October to the 31st December.

Form 21 Soldier's' Remittances sent £3 to Mary Hyland. WO25 discharged September 1861

1149 ILLSTON, Private Charles

Born : Unknown
Enlisted :
Medals : Crimea (B.I.S)

Died : Unknown
Status : Probably rode in the Charge

The musters show he was effective from the 1st October to the 2nd December. Remarks Scutari 3rd December.

WO14/1 Scutari Muster Roll January-March 1855 1st Muster endorsed Hospital, 2nd Muster endorsed to Regt 25th.
WO25 discharged 21 September 1865

The Turkish Crimea Medal 1855

Instituted by the Sultan of Turkey, this medal was conferred on troops of the three Allies who fought in the Crimea. The obverse shows the Ottoman Sultan's tughra with the Muslim calendar year of 1271 on all versions. The reverse depicts a cannon with four flags to its rear. The flag to the fore on the second from the left depicts the country to which the medal was intended.
Three types:
British "CRIMEA 1855" in exergue.
French "LA CRIMEE 1855" in exergue.
Sardinian "LA CRIMEA 1855" in exergue.

The orginal medal was fitted with a steel ring that fitted through a pierced hole in the disc. Most recipients replaced this with a more decorative suspension such as the Crimea medal suspender. All medals were issued unnamed. So various styles of engraving were used. Most of the consignment of British medals were lost at sea, hence the issue of all three types to British personnel. British officers had copies of superior quality made in higher grade silver with plain or scroll suspenders. These are thicker and heavier with clearer detail and are often seen in groups mounted by Messrs. Hunt and Roskill. Ribbon is crimson with green edges.

---

984 INGHAM, Farrier Joseph

Born : Unknown
Enlisted :
Medals : Crimea (B.I.S)

Died : Unknown
Status : Probably rode in the Charge

The musters show he was effective as a Private from the 1st October to the 31st December.

---

363 INNES, Farrier John

Born : Unknown
Enlisted :
Medals : Crimea (B.I.S)

Died : Unknown
Status : Probably rode in the Charge

The musters show he was effective as a Private from the 1st October to the 26th November. Remarks Scutari 27th November. Form 21 Soldier's' Remittances sent £6 to Margaret Innis.
WO14/1 Scutari Muster Roll January-March 1855 show he was there from the 1st-14th January, January muster endorsed sent home 15th.
He received his medal from the hand of the Queen on 18th May 1855.

1146 IRVING, Private William

Born : Unknown
Enlisted :
Medals : Crimea (B.I.S)

Died : Unknown
Status : Probably rode in the Charge

The musters show he was effective from the 1st October to the 31st December.

1015 JACKSON, Private James

Born : Unknown
Enlisted :
Medals : Crimea (B.I.S)

Died : Unknown
Status : Probably rode in the Charge

Wallis Wallis Sale 18th August 1981 Lot 12. Family Group of six Crimea 3 Bars Bal, Ink, Seb, (engraved naming), Meritorious Service, Vic issue without date, (impressed Farr Major Jackson Harrington, 4th Dragoon Guards), Turkish Crimea Sardinian issue, (impressed Farr Major Jackson, 4th Dn Gds), GVF or better, this regiment formed part of the Heavy Brigrade, Three: 1914-15 star trio (Pte A.S. Harrington A.S.C.) VF.
Spink Sale, 22 July 2004, Sale 4014 Lot 545, Crimea 1854-56, three clasps, Balaklava, Inkermann, Sebastopol (Corpl. J. Jackson. 4th Drgn. Gds.), officially impressed, edge harshly cleaned, contact marks, edge bruising, top clasp with unofficial rivets and with one lug missing, good fine, with contemporary silver riband buckle. Hammer Price £950.

The musters show he was effective from the 1st October to the 31st December.

1108 JACKSON, Private Robert

Born : Unknown
Enlisted :
Medals : Crimea (B.I.S)

Died : Unknown
Status : Probably rode in the Charge

The musters show he was effective from the 1st October to the 31st December.
Form 21 Soldier's Remittances sent £1.10s to Jane Jackson.

957 JACQUES, Private Joseph

Born : February 1827 - Leicester
Enlisted :
Medals : Crimea (B.I.S)

Died : 16th February 1885
Status : Probably rode in the Charge

The musters show he was effective from the 1st October to the
31st December. WO100/24 page 71 Remarks: to replace lost one.

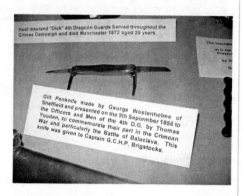

Joseph JACQUES was baptized on the 1 March 1827 in St.
Nicholas, Leicester. In 1841 he lived in Dunns Lane, St. Mary's
Parish, Leicester. In the 1871 census he is shown living at 5 Garden
Place, Hampstead. In 1881 Love Hill House, Langley Marish, Eton,
Bucks. He died on 16 February 1885 in Eton, Bucks. His occupation
in 1841 - tape weaver, 1856 - Pte in the 4th Dragoon Guards, 1861
- Servant, 1871 - Coachman, 1881 - Coachman.
The Regimental Museum of the Royal Dragoon Guards
3a Tower Street, York, has in its collection a Crimea six bladed Pen
Knife inscribed on one side " Private Joseph Jacques Balaklava,
Inkermann, Sebastopol "and on the reverse side "Presented to
the Crimean Heroes of the ?(?th)Dragoon Guards By Tho(s?)
Youdan, Sheffield "The inscription is not engraved but takes the
form of a metal print on a dull metal background. There is no regimental number shown on the knife. Pte Jacques was
promoted at a later date. The knives were presented to the officers and men of the 4th Dragoon Guards who served
in the Crimea. There were 225 pen knifes presented. Manufactured by the Wostenholm firm of Cutlers, the knives were
all six bladed and the inscription Fourth Dragoon Guards. Thomas Youdan was a local music hall proprietor who was
reported to have paid £100 for the presentation set.
The Adelphi began life as The Circus or the Adelphi Circus in 1837 and incorporated a ring for equestrian acts. In 1865
it was bought by Thomas Youdan and converted into the Alexandra Music Hall.

Parents: Joseph Jacques and Jane Walker. Spouse: Sarah Witham. Joseph Jacques and Sarah Witham were married on 4
November 1856 in Sutton In Ashfield. Children were: Thomas William Jacques John Joseph Jacques, Jane Jacques Joseph
Jacques, Frank Jacques, Anne Jacques, Frank Harvey Jacques, Sarah Ann Jacques.

754 JAMES, Trumpeter John

Born : Unknown
Enlisted :
Medals : Crimea (B.I.S)

Died : Unknown
Status : Probably rode in the Charge

Lord Cheylesmore Collection Gledining 16th -18th July 1930 Lot 9 with two other medals Hammer price 19/-
Medal List J.Hayward July 1969, item 46 Crimea 3 clasps Balaklava, Inkermann, Sebastopol Trumpeter J.James 4th
Dragoon Guards (engraved) VF £22-10-0
Crimea (BIS). [Eaton Collection p. 108.]

The musters show he was effective from the 1st October to the 31st December.

1031 JENNINGS, Private John

Born : Unknown
Enlisted :
Medals : Crimea (B.I.S)

Died : Unknown
Status : Probably rode in the Charge

The musters show he was effective from the 1st October to the 31st December. WO100/24 page 71 Remarks: Sent to
England. Form 21 Soldier's Remittances sent £4 to Margaret Jennings.

1036 JOHNSON, Private John

Born : Unknown
Enlisted : 29th January 1850
Medals : Crimea (B.I.S)

Died : Unknown
Status : Probably rode in the Charge

The musters show he was effective from the 1st October to the 31st December.
Muster Book January to March 1850 Form 7 recruits. 1036 Pte Johnson John, enlisted 29 January 1850, aged 18 years 5'8" at Manchester. HQ. Bounty £5-15-6, 13s-6d paid to recruiting party total levy money paid £6-9-0. WO25 discharged 19th August 1856

659 JOHNSTONE, Private Francis

Born : Date Unknown - Killalough
Enlisted : 14th June 1843
Medals : Crimea (B.S)

Died : 22nd November 1854 - Scutari
Status : Probably rode in the Charge

The musters show he was effective from the 1st October to the 27th October. Remarks to Scutari 28th October.
Died: Scutari 22nd November 1854.
WO100/24 page 71 Remarks: Dead. WO100/24 page 78 Remarks: died 22nd. November 1854.
Trade on enlistment Labourer.

801 JOICE, Regimental Sergeant-Major William

Born : Unknown
Enlisted : 16th January 1844
Medals : Crimea (B.I.S) The French Medaille Militaire

Died : Unknown
Status : Probably rode in the Charge

The musters show he was effective from the 1st October to the 31st December.
WO100/24 page 80 Remarks: Promoted from T.S.Major
The French Medaille Militaire, for exemplary and uniform good conduct during the campaign of 1854 and 1855.
Possibly shown standing at the back of the Fenton photo of the 4th DG camp. [Brereton, 4th/7th Dragoon Guards, pl. 31.] see page 187.
William Joice, Private 4th Dragoon Guards 16th January 1844, Corporal 13th December 1847, Sergeant 12th April 1852, Troop Sgt Major 10 March 1853, RMS 23 February 1855, Cornet 31st December 1857. Lieutenant and Adjutant 13 Light Dragoons 12th March 1861. Paymaster 13th Light Dragoons 8th May 1867. Exchanged to 7th Hussars on accepting Paymastership in 1871. Later attached to the 18th foot and did duty at Leicester Brigade Depot, finally retiring on the pension of a staff paymaster. Served in Crimean Campaign, Balaclava, Inkermann, Tchernya, Siege and capture of Sebastopol. Medal with 3 clasps, French War Medal and Turkish Medal. Served in Canada with the 13th Light Dragoons from September 1866 to July 1869
Form 21 Soldier's' Remittances sent £10 to James Joice.

1180 JONES, Private Benjamin

Born : Unknown
Enlisted :
Medals : Crimea (B.I.S)

Died : Unknown
Status : Probably rode in the Charge

The musters show he was effective from the 1st October to the 31st December.

1173 JONES, Private James

Born : Unknown
Enlisted :
Medals : Crimea (B.I.S)

Died : Unknown
Status : Probably rode in the Charge

Spinks Auction 14th September 1989. Lot 125. Group of Five. To James Jones 4th Dragoon Guards. (a) Cabul 1842 (James Jones 3rd K.O.L.D. No 1125) engraved (b) Sutlej for Moodkee 2 clasps Ferozeshuhur, Sobraon (3rd Lt DGNS) (c) Punjab 2 clasps Goojerat, Chilianwala (3rd Lt DGNS) (d) Crimea 3 clasps Balaklava, Inkermann, Sebastopol (4th DGN GDS) impressed (e) Turkish Crimea British issue. Drilled at 12 o clock un-named. Generally Fine and better (5) Estimate £600 Hammer Price £740.
Liverpool Medal Company. List May 1996. Lot 927 Same Group with copy service papers VF £2200. Listed again August 1996 same price.

The musters show he was effective from the 1st October to the 31st December. WO25 discharged 23rd June 1863

1038 JONES, Private Thomas

Born : 1829- Manchester
Enlisted : 19th February 1850
Medals : Crimea (B.I.S)

Died : Unknown
Status : Probably rode in the Charge

P.Burman Medal List March 1988 item 568. Pair Crimea 3 clasps Balaklava, Inkermann, Sebastopol. Engraved naming and Turkish Crimea. Engraved naming and Turkish Crimea. Engraved naming T.Jones 4th Dragoon Guards and original parchment discharged documents VF £375.

Crimea 3 Clasps Balaklava Inkermann Sebastopol Large date obverse. Engraved naming with reverse uppermost (1038 Pte T.Jones 4th Dns) in faint gothic style letters. Suspension damaged at swivel and badly repaired with new pin rivets for Sebastopol clasp slightly larger than those on Inkermann clasp. Turkish Crimea Sardinian version engraved naming neat block caps. "T. Jones 4th Dragoon Guards 1038" Medals purchased from P. Burman on 14th March 1988 by John Darwent.

DNW 2nd April 2004, The collection of medals formed by the late John Darwent, Lot 158, Pair: Private T. Jones, 4th Dragoon Guards. Crimea 1854-56, 3 clasps, Balaklava, Inkermann, Sebastopol (1038 Pte., 4th Dn.), rather crude but contemporary engraved naming; Turkish Crimea 1855, Sardinian issue (1038, 4th Dragoon Guards), contemporary engraved naming, the first with clipped upper clasp lugs and refixed suspension claw, contact marks and edge bruising, fine or better (2) Hammer Price £580

Sold with the recipient's original parchment certificate of discharge, dated 5 September 1860.

The musters show he was effective from the 1st October to the 31st December.
Parchment discharge Certificate. WO Form 64. 1038 Private Thomas Jones born at Manchester in county of Lancaster. Enlisted in 4th Dragoon Guards at Manchester on 19th February, 1850 aged 21 years. Served ten years 199 days. Discharged at his own request and on payment of £10. In possession of Crimean and Turkish medal. Conduct very good in possession of two good conduct badges.
Muster Search WO 12-127 to 275.
1038 Thomas Jones enlisted 4th dragoon Guards on the 18th February 1850 .A labourer from Manchester. At Manchester Feb-June 1850, Birmingham July 1859-Sept 1851. In hospital March 1851 and September 1851. Cahir Oct 1851, June 1852 in Hospital also Oct and Dec 1851. Dublin July -December 1852. Belfast Jan 1853-Oct 1853. Bembridge Dundalk Oct 1853-Jan 1854. Furlough 1-31 Dec 1853. Jan Re-Joined. January to June 1854 Dundalk Newbridge, Dublin at Sea. Crimea Oct 1854 to December 1855 Scutari. At Scutari until embarkation on 13th June 1856 on board "Simla", Leeds - Sheffield July 1856-June 1857. Manchester July 1857 to April 1858. Aldershot Apr 1858 to Sept 1859, Brighton Oct 1859 to Apr 1860. Aldershot June 1860. 5th September 1860 discharged by purchase at Birmingham.

Thomas Jones subsequently served out in the Crimea between October 1854 and June 1856, when he returned to the U.K. in the transport Simla, and would appear to have been present at Balaklava and Inkermann, in addition to the operations before Sebastopol.

1074 JONES, Private Thomas

Born : Unknown
Enlisted :
Medals : Crimea (B.I.S)

Died : Unknown
Status : Probably rode in the Charge

The musters show he was effective from the 1st October to the 31st December. WO25 discharged 27th May 1865.

961 KEATING, Private Jeremiah

Born : Unknown
Enlisted :
Medals : Crimea (B.I.S)

Died : Unknown
Status : Probably rode in the Charge

The musters show he was effective from the 1st October to the 31st December.

Form 21 Soldier's' Remittances shows he sent £2 to a Margaret Keating. WO25 discharged 8th December 1859.

701 KEEGAN, Private John

Born : Unknown
Enlisted :
Medals : Crimea (B.I.S)

Died : Unknown
Status : Probably rode in the Charge

The musters show he was effective from the 1st October to the 31st December.
WO25 discharged 17th November 1865.

835 KELLY, Private William

Born : Unknown
Enlisted :
Medals : Crimea (B.I.S)

Died : Unknown
Status . Probably rode in the Charge

A.H.Baldwin & Sons, Ltd Sales Catalogue February 1954: Crimea. 3 Bars, Balaklava, Inkermann, Sebastopol. M .Kelly Worn but scarce £1 15s

The musters show he was effective from the 1st October to the 31st December. WO25 to 7th Drags 1st July 1857.

1094 LANGTON, Private John

Born : Unknown
Enlisted :
Medals : Crimea (B.I.S)

Died : Unknown
Status : Probably rode in the Charge

Spink's Numismatic John Langton 4th D.G Crimea Clasps for Balaklava Inkermann Sebastopol. Engraved naming.

The musters show he was effective from the 1st October to the 8th December. Remarks state to Scutari 9th December. WO14/1 Scutari Muster Roll January-March 1855 show he was present in the 1st Muster, no indication given of his whereabouts in February and March. WO25 discharged 1856.

848 LAWDER, Private John

Born : Unknown
Enlisted :
Medals : Crimea (B.I.S)

Died : Unknown
Status : Probably rode in the Charge

Dlx Noonan Webb Auction 6 July 2004 Lot 63
Crimea 1854-56, 3 clasps, Balaklava, Inkermann, Sebastopol (J. Lauder, 4th Dragoon Grds.) officially impressed naming, edge bruising, otherwise better than very fine £800-1000 Hammer price £1200.

The musters show he was effective from the 1st October to the 31st December. WO25 discharged in Edinburgh November 1857.

458 LEARY, Private John

Born : Unknown
Enlisted :
Medals : Crimea (B.I.S)

Died : Unknown
Status : Probably rode in the Charge

The musters show he was effective from the 1st October to the 31st December.
On Form 8 of the musters entitled Account of Soldier's under sentence of Forfeiture of Pay, or Additional Pay, during the Period of this Pay List he is shown as forfeiting 1d per day of his pay for 2 years from the 29th April 1854.
WO14/1 Scutari Muster Roll January-March 1855 1st Muster endorsed Joined 19th Hospital, 2nd Muster endorsed Sent home 27th.

1095 LITTLE, Private John

Born : Unknown
Enlisted :
Medals : Crimea (B.I.S)

Died : Unknown
Status : Probably rode in the Charge

A.H.Baldwin & Sons List. July 1960 item 105. Crimea 3 Bars Balaklava Inkermann Sebastopol. J.Little 4th D.G Impressed F to VF £6-5-0

The musters show he was effective from the 1st October to the 31st December.
Servant to Lt Col Hodge from 30.10.1854
Little Hodge page 53. 30th October 1854...Sent Bucknall to his duty for being drunk and being in danger of losing our baggage. I have taken Little a young soldier in his place. WO25 discharged 9th November 1864.

414 LOTTY, Private William

Born : Unknown
Enlisted :
Medals : Crimea (B.I.S)

Died : Unknown
Status : Probably rode in the Charge

WO100/24 page 71 Remarks: Sent to England. WO12-270 Musters 1 Oct 1854 to 31st December 1854, all musters endorsed Depot Varna Marginal note reads Varna. (See page 162)

1007 LOWE, Sergeant John
Born : Unknown
Enlisted :
Medals : Crimea (B.I.S)

Died : 6th July 1864
Status : Probably rode in the Charge

The musters show he was effective as a Corporal from the 1st October to the 7th December and as a Sergeant from the 7th-31st December. Remarks promoted to Sergeant.
Form 21 Soldier's Remittances sent £2 to Emma Lowe. WO25 died rank T.S.M on the 6th July 1864.

1087 LYNCH, Private Michael
Born : Unknown
Enlisted :
Medals : Crimea (B.I.S)

Died : Unknown
Status : Probably rode in the Charge

The musters show he was effective from the 1st October to the 25th December. Remarks Scutari 26th December.

WO14/1 Scutari Muster Roll January-March 1855 1st Muster endorsed Joined 9th Hospital Ship, 2nd muster Hospital Ship, no indication given of his whereabouts in the following muster.

1019 MADDEN, Private John
Born : Unknown
Enlisted :
Medals : Crimea (B.I.S)

Died : Unknown
Status : Probably rode in the Charge

The musters show he was effective from the 1st October to the 31st December.
WO100/24 page 71 Remarks: Sent to England.

1023 MADDEN, Private Thomas
Born : Unknown
Enlisted :
Medals : Crimea (B.I.S)

Died : Unknown
Status : Probably rode in the Charge

The musters show he was effective from the 1st October to the 31st December.

886 MAGWICK, Private John
Born : Unknown
Enlisted :
Medals : Unknown

Died : Unknown
Status: Effective during the period

The musters show he was effective from the 1st October to the 31st December.
Appears at the end of the musters for the 4th under the heading Unattached 1st Dragoon Guards.

1122 MARKS, Private Thomas
Born : Unknown
Enlisted :
Medals : Crimea (B.I.S) The Distinguished Conduct Medal

Died : Unknown
Status : Probably rode in the Charge

The musters show he was effective as a Private from the 1st October to the 31st December.
The Distinguished Conduct Medal. Recommendation dated 1:1:55.
DCM, Crimea. [Abbot, Recipients of the DCM, p. 23.] Gratuity of £5. Discharged unfit on the 28th October 1872.

1123 MARKS, Corporal Timothy
Born : Unknown
Enlisted :
Medals : Crimea (B.I.S)

Died : Unknown
Status : Probably rode in the Charge

The musters show he was effective as a Private from the 1st October to the 31st December.

1205 MARLOW, Private James
Born : Unknown
Enlisted :
Medals : Crimea (B.I.S)

Died : Unknown
Status : Probably rode in the Charge

Donald Hall Medal List 3 Nov 1971, item 54. Crimea 3 clasps Balaklava Inkermann, Sebastopol Jas Marlow, 4th DN Gds. Very lightly engraved in an ornate contemporary style. Verified on PRO roll. Confirmed by Canon Lummis as being on the Heavy Brigade muster roll. The note with this medal states "was in action on 25th October 1854 per medal roll." £45.

The musters show he was effective from the 1st October to the 31st December.

In the 1881 census James Marlow Pensioner (Army) age 54, is shown living with his wife Elizabeth. Place of residence High Street, Desborough, Northampton. James was also born in Desborough. Sarah his 17 year old daughter is recorded on the census as being born in Montreal, Canada, occupation Pupil Teacher.

1177 MARSHALL, Private Edward
Born : Unknown
Enlisted :
Medals : Crimea (B.I.S)

Died : Unknown
Status : Probably rode in the Charge

The musters show he was effective from the 1st October to the 31st December.
Appears at the end of the musters for the 4th under the heading Unattached 1st Dragoon Guards. WO25 discharged 1st August 1865

891 MASON, Private Charles
Born : Date Unknown - Cork
Enlisted : 17th June 1846
Medals : Crimea (B.I.S)

Died : 30th August 1855 - Crimea
Status : Probably rode in the Charge

The musters show he was effective from the 1st October to the 31st December.
Trade on enlistment Slater. Died: Crimea. 30/Aug./55. WO100/24 page 72 Remarks: Dead.

McCREAGH, Captain Michael
Born : Unknown
Enlisted :
Medals : Crimea (B.I.S) ,The Knight (5th Class) The French Legion of Honour, The Turkish Order of the Medjidie (5th Class)

Died : 14th October 1902
Status : Probably rode in the Charge

The musters show he was effective from the 1st October to the 31st December. Absent with leave 17th-28th November.
The Knight (5th Class) The French Legion of Honour. His recommendation states: "In reply to the Confidential Memorandum dated 24th December 1855, I have the honor to submit to you the name of Captain Michael McCreagh of the Regiment under my command as that of the individual whom I consider best entitled to distinction. Captain McCreagh accompanied the Regiment on Service in 1854, he commanded the second Squadron at the Battle of Balaklava, and has been present on every occasion when the Cavalry have been engaged, he is still present with the Regiment, and has not received any accession of rank or honor. "Signed: Edward C. Hodge, Colonel Commg. 4th Dgn Guards.

Cornet 26 July 1844. Lieut 19 March 1847. Capt 18 July 1851. Retired with rank of Major 8 Feb 1863. [Hart, Army List.]

London Gazette Friday 17th 1896
Commission signed by the Lord Lieutenant of the County of Derby - Maj. McGreagh-Thornhill to be Deputy Lieutenant.

Midland Express Wednesday 15th October 1902, (Birmingham Newspaper) Major Michael McCreagh Thomhill, one of the few remaining survivors of "The gallant six hundred" died yesterday at his Derbyshire seat, Stanton Hall. He served in the fourth Dragoons and was the only son of the late Sir Michael McCreagh. He was in his seventy fourth year, and five years ago was High Sheriff of Derbyshire.
Stanton Hall, the seat of the Thornhill family, now occupied by Major McCreagh-Thornhill J.P. is a fine mansion, with several handsome terraces, and grounds are laid out with much taste ; the park contains about 130 acres, adorned with fine timber and stocked with deer: the carriage drive is 1 ¾ miles in length. Major McCreagh-Thornhill is lord of the manor and principal landowner. *Kelly's Directory of the Counties of Derby, Notts, Leicester and Rutland pub. London (May, 1891) - pp. 305-306*

McDONNEL, Lieutenant Christopher

Born : 1834 - Dublin
Enlisted :
Medals : Crimea (B.I.S)

Died : Unknown
Status : Rode in the Charge

The musters show he was effective from the 1st October to the 31st December.

In a memorandum book which Hodge kept in 1855, he states that Lt McDonnel on the 25th October, 1854, at the Battle of Balaklava was mounted in the Field.(p46)
Diary Entry 29th May 1854, just before departing for the East. "Sir Edward McDonnell, the Lord Mayor of Dublin, has kindly taken charge of all my baggage. He will put it into an empty room, and will have fires in it in winter". Sir Edward McDonnell (1806-1860) paper manufacturer, chairman of the Great Southern and Western Railway of Ireland. His son, Christopher, was in the 4th Dragoon Guards. (p10) *Little Hodge*.

In the returns relating to officers in the army Lieutenant C. McDonnell arrived in the Crimea October 1854 and his departure in December 1855 for the Bosphorus..
M'Donnel [McDonnel] Lieut Christopher Crimea (BIS), Turk Crim. Cornet 12 March 1852. Lieut 17 June 1853. Capt 14 March 1856. Retired with rank of Major 9 Dec 1871. [Hart, Army List (1885).]
1881 Census shown living with his wife Annie, two sons and one daughter at 24 Paulton Sq, London, Middlesex. Occupation Retired Army Officer,

1128 McGUIRE, Private John

Born : Unknown
Enlisted :
Medals : Crimea (B.I.S)

Died : Unknown
Status : Probably rode in the Charge

The musters show he was effective from the 1st October to the 31st December.
Form 21 Soldier's Remittances shows he sent £1 home.

1160 McKEE, Private James

Born : Unknown
Enlisted :
Medals : Crimea (B.I.S)

Died : Unknown
Status : Probably rode in the Charge

The musters show he was effective from the 1st October to the 31st December.
WO100/24 page 71 Remarks: Sent to England.

1120 McKENNA, Private Garrett

Born : Unknown
Enlisted :
Medals : Crimea (B.I.S)

Died : Unknown
Status : Probably rode in the Charge

B.Clark, Medal List Sept 1986, item 49 Turkish Crimea British Version (G.McKenna 4th D.Gds.) GVF £40
Christie 22 July 1986, Lot 59. British Crimea 2 clasps & un-named Turkish Crimea Sardinian version and Turkish Crimea British type (G.McKenna 4DN GDS) £108
Medal Crimea Clasps Balaklava Sebastopol named to G.McKenna Medal held in Royal Dragoon Guards Museum at York.

The musters show he was effective from the 1st October to the 31st December.
WO100/24 page 72 Remarks: to replace lost one 25/11/56. Form 21 Soldier's Remittances shows he sent £1.10s home.

711 McTRUSTRY, Private John

Born : Unknown
Enlisted :
Medals : Crimea (B.I.S)

Died : Unknown
Status : Probably rode in the Charge

Wellington Auctions April 2008 Postal Auction. Lot 47. Heavy Brigade Crimea Medal. Crimea Medal, three clasps, Balaklava, Inkermann, Sebastopol named in engraved style, to J. McTrustry, 4th Dragoon Guards. The 4th Dragoon Guards formed part of the heavy brigade at the Crimea along with the 5th Dragoon Guards, 1st or Royal Dragoon Guards, 2nd or Royal North British Dragoons and the 6th or Inniskilling Dragoons. 711 Private John McTrustry is confirmed on the roll for all three clasps, a copy of the roll is included with the medal. Good very fine Estimate £800-1,000

The musters show he was effective from the 1st October to the 31st December. WO25 discharged 30th Nov. 1865.

1193 MEADE, Private Robert

Born : Unknown
Enlisted :
Medals : Crimea (B.I.S)

Died : Unknown
Status : Probably rode in the Charge

The musters show he was effective from the 1st October to the 31st December.

1125 MEARES, Private Lewis

Born : Unknown
Enlisted :
Medals : Crimea (B.I.S)

Died : Unknown
Status : Probably rode in the Charge

The musters show he was effective from the 1st October to the 31st December.
WO100/24 page 72 Remarks: to replace lost one 25/11/56.

836 MERVYN, Trumpeter Henry

Born : Date unknown - Glasgow
Enlisted : 24th November 1845
Medals : Crimea (B.I.S)

Died : Unknown
Status : Probably rode in the Charge

Payne Collection 1911 Catalogue pages 111 and 394. Group of 3. Crimea 3 clasps Balaklava, Inkermann, Sebastopol, LS 7GC medal and Turkish Crimea Sgt. Henry Mervyn. (Trumpet Major)
For Sale at Spink 12th March 1996, Lot 700, Crimea, three clasps, Balaklava, Inkermann, Sebastopol, (H. Mervyn.T.M. 4.D.G.), engraved, light edge bruising and contact marks, very fine, with copied service papers.
Trumpet Major Henry Mervyn, from Glasgow, attested for the 4th Royal Irish Dragoon Guards at Edinburgh, 24 November 1845, at the age of 14 yean, appointed Trumpeter 1849; served with the Heavy Brigade in the Crimea and was promoted Corporal December 1855; Sergeant Mervyn was discharged 30 May 1865 as unfit due to epilepsy. £300-350

The musters show he was effective from the 1st October to the 31st December.
WO100/24 page 71 Remarks: Sent to England. WO25 discharged 30th May 1865 as a Sergeant.

802 MERVYN, Corporal Robert

Born : Date unknown - Dorchester
Enlisted : 12th January 1844
Medals : Crimea (B.I.S)

Died : 15 July 1855 - Crimea
Status : Probably rode in the Charge

Payne Collection (p 111). Crimea 3 clasps Balaklava Inkermann, Sebastopol H.Mervyn T.M., 4 D.G, Group of 3 listed on (p 394) 3 clasp Crimea, LS & GC and Turkish Crimea both named to Sgt Henry Mervyn. 4th (Royal Irish)
Glendining and Co. July 1946 R.Mervyn 4th D.G. Crimea clasps for Balaklava, Inkermann, Sebastopol. No description of naming. Ex Hamilton Smith and Dalrymple white collections.
Glendining and Co. 27 February 1963 Elson Collection Lot 239. Crimea clasps for Balaklava, Inkermann, Sebastopol R.Mervyn 4th D.G. impressed naming VF plus one other medal £9.0.0. Purchased by Spinks.

The musters show he was effective as a Private from the 1st October to the 7th December and as a Corporal from the 8th-31st December. Remarks state Promoted to Corporal.
Enlisted 12 January 1844, previous occupation Saddler WO100/24 page 81 Remarks: Dead

1101 MITCHELL, Sergeant Henry

Born : Unknown
Enlisted :
Medals : Crimea (I.S)

Died : Unknown
Status : Effective during the period

The musters show he was effective from the 1st October to the 31st December, rank private.
Not shown entitled to a B clasp *Sewell The Cavalry Division in the Crimea.* WO25 discharged 24th May 1864.

903 MOLONEY, Private James

Born : Unknown
Enlisted :
Medals : Crimea (B.I.S)

Died : Unknown
Status : Probably rode in the Charge

The musters show he was effective from the 1st October to the 31st December.

Ranks in the Cavalry
Sergeant-major Crown above four chevrons on forearm.
Troopsergeant-major Crown over four chevrons on upper arm,.
Sergeant Three chevrons point down.
Farriers A horseshoe in yellow worsted.
Roughriders A spur in yellow worsted.
Trumpeters Crossed trumpets in yellow worsted.

1185 MOORE, Private Daniel
Born : Date Unknown - Norwich
Enlisted : 12th December 1853
Medals : Crimea (B.I.S)

Died : 13th July 1855 - Crimea
Status : Probably rode in the Charge

The musters show he was effective from the 1st October to the 31st December. WO100/24 page 72 Remarks: Dead. Trade on enlistment Labourer.

1117 MOORE, Private John
Born : Date Unknown - London
Enlisted : 26th January 1852
Medals : Crimea (B.I.S)

Died : 31st July 1855 - Crimea
Status : Probably rode in the Charge

The musters show he was effective from the 1st October to the 31st December.WO100/24 page 72 Remarks: Dead. Trade on enlistment Clerk.

945 MORAN, Trumpeter Francis
Born : Unknown
Enlisted :
Medals : Crimea (B.I.S)

Died : Unknown
Status : Probably rode in the Charge

The musters show he was effective from the 1st October to the 31st December.

740 MORRIS, Private Edward
Born : Unknown
Enlisted :
Medals : Crimea (B.I.S)

Died : Unknown
Status : Probably rode in the Charge

The musters show he was effective from the 1st October to the 26th November. Remarks To Scutari 27th November. WO100/24 page 72 Remarks: Dead. WO14/1 Scutari Muster Roll January-March 1855 1st Muster endorsed "Sent home 11th".
Form 21 Soldier's' Remittances sent £1 to Mary Morris.

1188 MORRIS, Private Edward
Born : Unknown
Enlisted :
Medals : Crimea (B.I.S)

Died : Unknown
Status : Probably rode in the Charge

The musters show he was effective from the 1st October to the 31st December. Regimental number shown as 1088. WO14/1 Scutari Muster Roll January-March 1855. 2nd Muster endorsed Joined 11th Hospital, 3rd Muster endorsed Sent home 31st.

791 MORRISON, Private James
Born : Unknown
Enlisted :
Medals : Crimea (B.I.S)

Died : Unknown
Status : Probably rode in the Charge

A.H.Baldwin & Sons Ltd List. Sept 1934 item 7969. Crimea 3 clasps Balaklava, Inkermann, Sebastopol, Sgt Jas Morrison 4.D.G. Engraved F 18/6d

The musters show he was effective from the 1st October to the 31st December. WO102 awarded L.S.G.C Medal £5 Gratuity date of recommendation 18.6.67 issued 20.8.67.

Tents

Because of inadequate transport the tents had to be reloaded onto the ships because they could not be carried. The tents used in the Crimea had been made for the Peninsular War in 1811-12, and were full of holes and were not waterproof. Tents were also in short supply, when available the troopers were packed into them like sardines.

On the 28 November 1854 General Airey sent a requisition to England for 3,000 tents, 100 hospital marquees and 6,000 nosebags and various quantities of spades, shovels and pickaxes. On 4 April 1855 his request was still under discussion in Whitehall.

376 MOSSOP, Private Charles

Born : Unknown
Enlisted :
Medals : Crimea (B.I.S)

Died : Unknown
Status : Probably rode in the Charge

WO100/24 page 72 Remarks: Discharged.

The musters show he was effective from the 1st October to the 8th December. Remarks to Scutari 9th December. WO100/24 page 72 Remarks: Discharged.
WO14/1 Scutari Muster Roll January-March 1855 1st Muster endorsed Hospital, 2nd Muster Sent home 17th.

1159 MURRAY, Private John

Born : Unknown
Enlisted :
Medals : Crimea (B.I.S)

Died : Unknown
Status : Probably rode in the Charge

The musters show he was effective from the 1st October to the 31st December. WO25 died 17th March1866.

MUTTLEBURY, Lieutenant George Alexander

Born : 1831 Bath, Somerset,
Enlisted :
Medals : Crimea (B.I.S)

Died : Unknown
Status : Probably rode in the Charge

Spinks Circular November 1984 item 7671. Pair Crimea medals, 3 bars Balaklava, Inkermann, Sebastopol. Lieut. Muttlebury 4th D.G. Engraved. Turkish Crimea Sardinian version. Lieut Muttlebury charged with the Heavy Brigade VF £575.
Sotheby 27th June 1985 Lot 136, Pair to Lieutenant Muttlebury 4th Dragoon guards Crimea 3 clasps Balaklava, Inkermann, Sebastopol. Turkish Crimea Sardinian version some wear about VF Est £400-£450 Not Sold.
Spinks Circular July 1986 item 5627.3 clasps Balaklava, Inkermann, Sebastopol. No Turkish medal. Naming Engraved. Surface Scratches VF £600.
Same pair of medals appeared in Spinks Auction 27th March 1992 Lot 397. Pair. Est £500.

The musters show he was effective as a Cornet from the 1st October to the 31st December. Absent with Leave during the 2nd muster 17th-28th November.
The five transports destined to convey the 4th Dragoon Guards to the East have arrived in Kingstone harbour...The second detachment, consisting of ten men from each troop, left on Friday. The officers commanding are Lieutenant George M.Morgan and Cornet George Alexander Muttleburry. *The Times Saturday May 27th 1854*
In a memorandum book which Hodge kept in 1855, he states that Lt Muttlebury on the 25th October, 1854, at the Battle of Balaklava was mounted in the Field.(p46)
In the returns relating to officers in the army Lieutenant G.Muttlebury arrived in the Crimea October 1854 and his departure on the 15th December 1855 noted as Private Affairs.

Notice published in the *Times dated Wednesday June 12th 1861*
Widow deceased, any persons having claims against the estate Catherine Muttleburry, widow of Lieut.Colonel George Muttleburry C.B, and K.W, late of 184 Prospect Place, Mald Hill, Paddington and formerly of the city of Bath, who died on the 3d day of February 1861...

1881 Census living at 3 St James Crescent Bristol St Paul In, Gloucester. Occupation a Commission Agent . With Caroline his wife 25 years his younger, and their 4 year old son Albert.

866 NEESON, Private Daniel

Born : Date Unknown - Newry
Enlisted : 7th April 1846
Medals : Crimea (B.I.S)

Died : 7th July 1855 - Crimea
Status : Probably rode in the Charge

For sale at Spink 2005, A good Heavy Brigade Crimea medal to Private. D. Meeson, 4th Dragoon Guards. Crimea 1854-56 3 clasps, Balaklava, Inkermann, Sebastopol (D. Meeson. 4th. Dragoon. Guards.) officially impressed, minor edge nicks, otherwise extremely fine. Price £2400.

The musters show he was effective from the 1st October to the 31st December. Born: Newry. Trade on enlistment Shoemaker. Died: Crimea. 7/Jul./55. WO100/24 page 72 Remarks: Dead.
Musters WO12-270 Paid for 92 days. 3 days on board ship and 89 days on land.
Name shown on medal roll and musters as "Neeson" but medal shows "Meeson".

From Little Hodge His letters and diaries of the Crimean War 1854-1856., (p120) 11th July 1855. "Our sick list is very great. 49 today. Neeson of F Troop died of cholera".
The weather was oppressively hot. Disease was still rapidly on the increase, and during the month (July 1855) the admissions reached 50 per cent, of the strength present,while the deaths had increased to six in number. (Extracts from *Medical and Surgical history of the British Army, during the War Against Russia 1854-56. p 8*)

532 NEWMAN, Private John

Born : Date Unknown - Norwich
Enlisted : 9th April 1838
Medals : Crimea (B.I.S)

Died : 5th February 1855 - Scutari
Status : Probably rode in the Charge

E.E.Needes Collection Crimea 3 clasps Balaklava, Inkermann, Sebastopol H.J.Newman, 4th Dgn Gds
For sale The Liverpool Medal Company August 2007, Crimea three bar A.B.S "H.J.Newman. 4th. Dragn Gds." Officially impressed. Good V.F £2400

The musters show he was effective from the 1st October to the 31st December.
Trade: on enlistment Maltster WO100/24 page 72 Remarks: Dead. WO100/24 page 78 Remarks: Dead 5 February 1855.

979 NICHOL Trumpeter John

Born : 1834 - Montreal, Canada
Enlisted :
Medals : Crimea (B.I.S)

Died : 3rd November 1893
Status : Rode in the Charge

The musters show he was effective from the 1st October to the 31st December.
Coin and Medal News July 1984. An article by Brian Best :
"A trumpeter with the Heavy Brigade" A group of three medals and helmet and other artefacts had been purchased by him from an auction in Northumberland. The vendor John Nichol's Grand-Daughter. A Crimean Long Service and Good Conduct medal, Crimea Medal 3 clasps Balaklava, Inkermann, Sebastopol and a Turkish Crimea medal. John Nichol was born in 1834 in Montreal, Canada. His father was serving as an N.C.O with the 66th Regiment. In the winter of 1837 a revolt was started by colonists. It was during this revolt in early 1838 that Nichol's father was killed. His widow and four-year old child returned to England. Shortly after there return his mother died. As a military orphan he was eligible to enter the Duke of York's Military School. He was attested to the 4th Dragoon Guards on his fourteenth Birthday. In 1851 when he was 17 he was appointed Trumpeter. On the 3rd June 1854 he embarked at Dublin for service in the Crimea, the regiment was under the command of Colonel Edward Hodge. He was to charge with the Heavy Brigade on the 25th October 1854, the part played by the 4th Dragoons was to attack the right flank of the Russian force. At some 200 yards with swords drawn Hodge ordered Nichol to sound the charge. Men hacked, mauled, punched there way into the mass of Russians. When the Fourth at last emerged out of the Russian left flank he was ordered to sound the rally. This was to be the last time that the Brigade was to see action in the Crimea. Between 1859 to 1863 there followed a period of service in Ireland and England. He rose through the ranks to become Trumpet Major at the young age of 29. Discharged in 1875 after 23 years service. He was instrumental in bringing out an official manual of cavalry regulation calls. On discharge he sought a position of chief attendant at Durham County Asylum. His interest in music was to continue throughout his life, he organised a a band and choir at the Asylum. It was during a visit by an opera company that Nicol was to met his future bride, some twenty years his junior. It was a happy union which produced several children.
Also spelt Surname Nichole, Nicholl and Nicol.
John Nichol was for a time Supervisor of The County Lunatic Asylum .Located at Winterton, about one mile north from Sedgefield. Winterton Hospital was originally the Durham County Lunatic Asylum which started life in 1858. it had a cemetery attached where our Heavy brigade hero is buried. The head stone reads: John Nichole who died on

November 3rd 1893. he was -9 years old (figure missing) "for 18 years chief attendant at this institution" and "Formally a trumpet major in the 4th Dragoon Guards. He took part as trumpeter at the charge of the Heavy Brigade at Balaclava".

The trumpet, the gallop, the charge, and the might of the fight!
Thousands of horsemen had gather'd there on the height

John Nicol, 4 Dragoon Guards

The Broad Arrow 11th November 1893 - 4th Dragoon Guards- Mr John Nicholl, Late of this regiment died at the Durham County Asylum on the 3rd inst. After only an hour ot two's illness. Mr Nicholl joined the asylum staff upwards of 18 years ago as chief attendant and Bandmaster. He also acted as choir-Master during the past few years on the opening of St Luke's Chapel. He was a highly popular officer, esteemed and held in high regard by all the staff as well as the inmates of the Asylum and his loss is deeply felt. His funeral took place on the 8th in the Durham County Asylum Cemetery,. amidst every demonstration of regret and heartfelt sympathy for the widow and four children he has left behind. The following article appeared in a local daily newspaper. With that memorable day at Balaclava has been severed by the death of Mr John Nicholl for many years Trumpet-Major of the 4th Dragoon Guards and the last remaining trumpeter who rode with them in the famous and daring charge of the Heavy Brigade. He was the youngest boy in the regiment at that time. It was he who sounded the "Rally" for the commanding officer, now Sir Edward Hodge whose own trumpeter had been separate from him in the melee......

543 O'BRIEN, Private Edward
Born : Unknown
Enlisted :
Medals : Crimea (B.I.S)

Died : Unknown
Status : Probably rode in the Charge

The musters show he was effective from the 1st October to the 31st December.
An interesting letter sent to Hodge from J.W.O'Brien, late Band, 4th Dragoon Guards:
'I am not unknown to you,' it reads, 'having served in the 4th D.G. while under your command, as did my father for 25 years, including the whole of the Crimean campaign, as did my mother who accompanied the regiment there. My mother dead now some years, but my father is alive, and, I am sorry to say, married again, and in his 74th year of age has three young children, all now dependent on a private's pension. If you could kindly interest yourself with the Patriotic Fund to obtain him some increase of pension for the little remaining time he has to live, it would be a mercy for which I shall be ever grateful' (p150) Little Hodge edited by The Marquess of Anglesey. WO25 discharged 12th May 1863.

743 O'BRIEN, Private James
Born : Unknown
Enlisted :
Medals : Crimea (B.I.S)

Died : 23rd July 1894
Status : Probably rode in the Charge

The musters show he was effective from the 1st October to the 31st December.
The Broad Arrow 4th August 1894 - 4th Dragoon Guards. Another link with the past has been severed by the death of Mr James O'Brien. Formerly of the regiment, and one of the men who rode and fought in Scarlett's heavy Brigade. He died at Ennis Co Clare, Ireland on the 23rd July at the age of 74. He served 25 years in the regiment and being pensioned in 1878 was appointed as principal gate lodge keeper to the County Asylum where he again spent twenty years and from which he was recently pensioned. His wife, who died in 1887, was one of the four soldier's wives selected to accompany the regiment to the Crimea in the character of nurses and endured all the hardships of the campaign from first to close. She was the last survivor of the good women whose attentions were long remembered by the men of those days. Although an ungrateful country ignored their existence.....

873 O'CONNOR, Private John
Born : Unknown
Enlisted :
Medals : Crimea (B.I.S)

Died : Unknown
Status : Probably rode in the Charge

The musters show he was effective from the 1st October to the 31st December. WO25 discharged November 1857.

The Cavalry camp at Kadikoi, just outside Balaclava.

993 O'DONNELL, Private Henry
Born : Unknown
Enlisted :
Medals : Crimea (B.I.S)

Died : Unknown
Status : Probably rode in the Charge

The musters show he was effective from the 1st October to the 31st December.
WO14/1 Scutari Muster Roll January-March 1855 1st Muster endorsed Joined 31st Hospital, present during the 2nd Muster, no indication given of his whereabouts in the following muster. WO25 to 4th Lan. 1st October 1850.

1152 O'DONNELL, Private William
Born : Unknown
Enlisted :
Medals : Crimea (B.I.S)

Died : Unknown
Status : Probably rode in the Charge

The musters show he was effective from the 1st October to the 31st December.WO100/24 page 72 Remarks: Discharged.
WO14/1 Scutari Muster Roll January-March 1855. 1st Muster endorsed joined 26th Hospital, 2nd Muster Hospital, 3rd Muster Sent home 3rd.

514 O'HARA, Private John
Born : Unknown
Enlisted : 10th March 1838
Medals : Crimea (B.I.S)

Died : 21st June 1855
Status : Probably rode in the Charge

The musters show he was effective from the 1st October to the 31st December.
Trade: on enlistment Stonemason. WO100/24 page 72 Remarks: Dead.
National Army Museum, NAM 5804/32 Excerpts from Major W.C.Forrest Letters to his wife. There is a reference to John "J O'Hara has just brought me £3 and requested that I would ask you to send £3 to his wife".

786 O'KEEFE, Sergeant Joseph
Born : Unknown
Enlisted :
Medals : Crimea (B.I.S)

Died : Unknown
Status : Probably rode in the Charge

The musters show he was effective as a Corporal from the 25th October to the 31st December. Remarks state Promoted to Sergeant. Remarks also state from Scutari Hospital 25th October. Written through the 1st/2nd musters is "pay from 22nd Sept to 24th October charged".

422 O'LEARY, Private Timothy
Born : Unknown
Enlisted :
Medals : Crimea (B.I.S)

Died : Unknown
Status : Probably rode in the Charge

The musters show he was effective from the 1st October to the 31st December.

771 O'NEIL, Private Timothy

Born : 1825

Died : December 1908

Enlisted : 1843

Status : Probably rode in the Charge

Medals : Crimea (B.I.S), Long Service and Good Conduct Medal, Meritorious Service Medal

Sold by Capital Medals February 1986. Pte/Sgt Timothy O'Neill. 4th D.G. Pair. Crimea 4 clasps Engraved Capitals, MSM, Victoria as Sgt.

The musters show he was effective from the 1st October to the 31st December.

Heavy Brigade charger. Served 25 years with the regiment, and at least 17 years' pensioned service as a Superior Barrack Sergeant. MSM 1899. [McInnes, Annuity MSM First Supplement, p. 7.]

WO102 awarded L.S.G.C Medal £5 Gratuity date of recommendation 3.4.65 issued 30.6.65

The Broad Arrow 2nd January 1909 - 4th Dragoon Guards. Mr T.O'Neill died at Devonport on the 27th ult. At the age of 84. In 1854-1855 he served with the regiment at the battles of Balaklava and Inkermann and the fall of Sebastopol, receiving the medal with three clasps he possessed medals for Good conduct and Long and Meritorious service. He recently attended the dinner in London of old comrades of the regiment.

4th/7th Royal Dragoon Guards Regimental Magazine. December 1908 page 202. Obituary with photograph of O'Neill wearing medals. The late Timothy O'Neill, a Tipperary man, joined the 4th Royal Irish Dragoon Guards in 1843 and after serving with the regiment for 25 years was discharged to pension with the rank of Sergeant in 1868. In the same year he joined the Barrack Department at Devonport in which he served as 4th DG superior barrack Sergeant and another 18 years - Thus completing a total of 43 years in the service of his country. On discharge from the Barrack Department this worthy old veteran was given permission to wear its uniform. He took advantage of this privilege on every possible occasion until his death in 1908. Always remembering his first love. He discharged the badge of the Barrack Department and replaced it with the Harp and Crown of his old regiment, as the photograph here reproduced indicates. The late Sergt O'Neill had a distinguished career with the regiment and was one of that band of heroes who took part in the memorable charge of the Heavy Brigade....The veteran's medals which are in the possession of his son Lt. Col. T.T.O'Neill of Saltash, Devon, include the Crimean medal(with three clasps Balaklava, Inkermann, Sebastopol and the Turkish War medal. This old veteran, always inordinately proud of his regiment contributed to the press of his day many interesting items of his experiences.

At the age of 83 years he travelled from Devonport to London to attend the first annual dinner of its past and present members which took place in the throne room of the Holborn Restaurant on Saturday 28th March 1908. Colonel Philip. E.Pope presided and proposed a special toast in honour of Sergeant O'Neill who was the oldest member of the corps present. This fine old veteran died in December of the same year. Mr F.Summers, Grandson of the late Segt. O'Neill, is the present Chief Constable of Warrington. Lancashire.

1049 ORSON, Private John

Born : Unknown

Died : Unknown

Enlisted :

Status : Probably rode in the Charge

Medals : Crimea (B.I.S)

Glendining's 23rd September 1987 Lot 141, Crimea Medal three clasps, Alma, Balaklava, Sebastopol (J.Orson, 4th Dragoon Gds), impressed naming. On the Muster Roll of the Heavy Brigade. The same medal was sold again at Glendinings 7th June 1989 Lot 129. "N" of "Orson" has been re-engraved, otherwise very fine.

Dixons Gazette, No 29, Spring 2002, Lot 437, Crimea 3 clasp Alma, Balaklava, Sebastopol, Officially impressed. J.Orson, 4th Dragoon Guards.

224 Pte John Orson, 4th Drgn Gds. Clasps verified on Roll. 4th Dragoon Gds formed part of the Heavy Brigade which followed the Light Brigade at the famous Charge at Balaclava. No papers found. VF £1300

The musters show he was effective from the 1st October to the 31st December. Regimental number shown as 1090.

1147 PARKE, Private James

Born : Unknown
Enlisted :
Medals : Crimea (B.I.S)

Died : Unknown
Status : Probably rode in the Charge

James Auction, 25th April 1987 Lot 63. Est £350. Crimea Clasps Balaclava, Inkermann, Sebastopol. Pte Jas.Parks. 4th D.GDS. Engraved naming. Neat Capitals, contact marks, edge bruise. NVF
CJ and AJ Dixon List Summer 1988, item 122. Crimea 3 Bars same as above. NVF £295

The musters show he was effective from the 1st October to the 14th November. Remarks state to Scutari 15th November.
He received his medal from the hand of the Queen on 18th May, 1855.

597 PEDLEY Sergeant Henry

Born : Unknown
Enlisted :
Medals : Crimea (B.I.S)

Died : Unknown
Status : Probably rode in the Charge

The musters show he was effective as Armourer Sergeant from the 1st October to the 31st December.
Form 21 Soldier's Remittances records he sent £10 to a Anna Pedley. WO25 died 13th August 1863.

700 PERCY, Sergeant William

Born : 1828 - Doncaster
Enlisted :
Medals : Crimea (B.I.S) The Knight (5th Class) The French Legion of Honour, The Distinguished Conduct Medal

Died : Unknown
Status : Slightly wounded in the Charge

Medal List December 1992. Capt Bob Baird, California USA. Group of four medals Crimea B.I.S, contact marks, name partially obscured G.F. DCM engraved naming G.F contact marks and rubbing. Legion of Honour, France Gold coin replacing centre enamel. Chipping. Turkish Crimea VF. Hole drilled at 6 o clock for tie down. Price $4100.
DNW 20th october 1993, Lot 200, A fine Heavy Brigade D.C.M. group of four awarded to Lieutenant William Percy, 9th Lancers, late 4th Royal Irish Dragoon Guards. DISTINGUISHED CONDUCT MEDAL, V.R. (Serjt., 4th R. Irish Dn. Gds.); CRIMEA 1854-55, 3 clasps, Balaklava, Inkermann, Sebastopol (Serjt., 4th Dn. Guards) contemporary engraved naming; TURKISH CRIMEA, Sardinian issue (T.S.M. 4th Rl. Dragoon Guards) hole drilled at 6o'clock; France LEGION OF HONOUR, Knight, 5th class breast badge in silver and enamels, both centres replaced with French gold coins, enamel severely chipped, the medals with heavy edge bruising and contact wear, therefore fine or better but a rare group Hammer Price £2400

The musters show he was effective from the 1st October to the 31st December.
Form 21 Soldier's Remittances sent £3 to Catherine Percy. Casualty Roll, Listed as wounded slightly at Balaklava.
The Distinguished Conduct Medal. Recommendation dated 01/01/1855, Gratuity of £15.
D.C.M., London Gazette, 26 March 1855: 'Gallant Conduct in the Field 25th October 1854'

William Percy was wounded in the charge of the Heavy Brigade as a Sergeant in the 4th Royal Irish Dragoon Guards. For his distinguished conduct at Balaklava he was - awarded the D.C.M. with a gratuity of £15 and - the Legion of Honour, the only man in the regiment to receive these two decorations. 'Received an order to send in the name of the individual whom I conceived best entitled to distinction. I sent in that of Sergt. William Percy. It is I believe to receive a French Order.' (Ref 'Little Hodge - His Letters and Diaries of the Crimean War 1854-1856', General Sir Edward Hodge, G.C.B., Commanding 4th Dragoon Guards).

Percy was gazetted Ensign, 12th Lancers, in 1867 and transferred immediately to the 9th Lancers. He was appointed Adjutant in May, 1869, and promoted Lieutenant on 25 March, 1871. Born at Dorchester in 1828, Percy had begun his days as a Boy soldier, distinguished himself in battle and crowned his achievements with an officer's commission. He was placed on half pay in March 1876 after 34 years service in the cavalry.

Legion of Honour

The Légion d'honneur or Ordre national de la Légion d'honneur (National Order of the Legion of Honor) is a French order established by Napoléon Bonaparte, First Consul of the First Republic, on May 19, 1802.[1] This world-renowned Order is the highest decoration in France and is divided into five various degrees: Chevalier (Knight), Officier (Officer), Commandeur (Commander), Grand Officier (Grand Officer) and Grand-Croix (Grand Cross).

Roger Fenton

Many of the photographs reproduced in this publication were taken by Roger Fenton. He travelled out to the Crimea in February 1855. A wet plate was used to capture the image, exposure took between 5-20 seconds in the camera.
A dark-room had to be on hand to develop the plate, the process from start to finish could take no longer than ten minutes, being dependant on temperature, the hot summers in the Crimea presented added difficulties. Given the conditions he has to be congratulated on producing one of the first photographic records of war.

PINE, Surgeon Chilley

Born : 15th June 1810
Enlisted :
Medals : Crimea (B.S)

Died : 6th March 1855 - Balaklava
Status : Rode in the Charge

The musters show he was effective from the 1st October to the 4th November. 2nd Muster notes appointed Staff Surgeon 1st Class. WO100/24 page 69 Remarks: Appointed to Staff, since dead. WO100/24 page 74 Remarks: Promoted Staff Surgeon - since dead.
Surgeon Chilley Pine - Staff-Surgeon (first class) - died of typhus at Balaclava - 6 March 1855
The Times Friday June 17th 1853. Marrages:
On the 9th Inst at Handsworth, Staffordshire by the Rev Robert Gamson M.A of Normanton-on-Trent. Chilley Pine esq, 4th Dragoon Guards to Agnes, eldest daughter of the late James Gibson.

In a memorandum book which Hodge kept in 1855, he states that Dr Pine on the 25th October, 1854, at the Battle of Balaklava was mounted in the Field. (p46)
Extract from *Little Hodge, His letters and diaries of the Crimean War 1854-1856.* (p92)
"My poor friend Pine died 9-5 last night. I sincerely deplore his loss both as a private friend and as a public officer. He was one of the best and most active medical officers in the army. Now comes to me the melancholy task of writing to his poor 'wife.'
Assistant Surgeon (Staff) 2nd August 1833. To 26th Foot 30th August 1833, Surgeon 58th Foot 5th December 1843. To 4th Dragoon Guards 6th August 1847, Surgeon 1st Class 6th October 1854.

In a letter Lieut-Col Forrest wrote home on the 15th January he relates a conversation between Pine and Lord Raglan "How are you getting on with your sick in the Division, Mr Pine?" Reply "Nothing can possibly be worse, my Lord" What do you mean Sir?" Reply "I mean, my Lord, that it is merely a question of time as to the existence of this Division. More men come into hospital than we can either accommodate or find medicines for. The sickness is occasioned principally through exposure without sufficient clothing.
Dr Pine was a man who spoke his mind and was highly respected by his fellow officers. After several meeting with Lord Raglan, he requested" a written report of all the deficiencies which he conceived to exist" (p93) Little Hodge.

Active service: *Hart, Army list 1852 p.124.* "Mr Pine served with the 26th[Foot] on the China expedition, (medal) and was present at the first capture of Chusan, attack on Canton, attack and capture of Amoy, repulse of the night attack on Ningpo, attack and capture of Tacke, Chapoo, Shanghai Woosung and Chin Kiang Foo.
He acted as senior Medical officer [in the 58th Foot] in the campaigns in New Zealand, from April 1845 to May 1846, and was present at the destruction of Pomare's Pah, attack on Heki's Pah, destruction of the Waikadi Pah, storming of Kawiti's

953 POTTER, Private George

Born : Unknown
Enlisted : 10th March 1838
Medals : Crimea (I.S)

Died : Unknown
Status : Effective during the period

The musters show he was effective from the 1st October to the 31st December.
WO14/1 Scutari Muster Roll January-March 1855 3rd Muster endorsed "Joined 2nd".
WO25 discharged 22nd August 1864.

1045 PRATT, Private John

Born : Unknown
Enlisted : 10th March 1838
Medals : Crimea (B.I.S)

Died : Unknown
Status : Probably rode in the Charge

The musters show he was effective from the 1st October to the 31st December.

1061 PREECE, Corporal Henry

Born : 1816
Enlisted : 10th March 1838
Medals : Crimea (B.I.S) The Distinguished Conduct Medal

Died : 18th June 1907
Status : Slightly wounded in the Charge

Sotheby 10 November 1988 Lot 154. An extremely rare Heavy Brigade DCM Group to Corporal Henry Preece 4th Dragoon Guards. DCM Victorian 4th R.Irish Drg - Gds. Crimea 1854 3 clasps Balaklava Inkermann, Sebastopol Corpl 4th Dragoon Gds. Officially impressed. This with repaired suspension Turkish Crimea 1855, Sardinian issue. Corpl. 4 DN Gds Regt. Impressed. Mounted for wearing from contemporary riband bar woth edge knocks. contact wear and bruised. Generally fine. Together with 5th Class Badge of the Turkish order of the Medjidie. (4) Recommendation dated 1st January 1855. Recipient was slightly wounded during the famous charge of the heavy brigade 25th October 1854, est £800-£1200. Photograph of grave Cpl Henry Preece D.S.O (SIC) Died 18th June 1907, aged 77 years. Also wife Mary Ann. Died 7th February 1904 71 years and her sister Jane Hill who died 2 February 1929 aged 91 years.

The musters show he was effective as a Private from the 1st October to the 31st December.

Casualty Roll: Listed as Pte Wounded Slightly at Balaklava.
The Distinguished Conduct Medal. Recommendation dated 01/01/1855, Gratuity of £5

Shrewsbury Chronicle 3rd November 1893, Page 5 (Large Feature)...Wednesday last being the 39th Anniversary.... There was an interesting company at the London Apprentice Inn, Cotton Hill, on Wednesday night. Assembled to do honour to the two local survivors of the charge of the Heavy Brigade. Corporal H.Preece, late of the 4th (Royal Irish) Dragoon Guards and Trumpet-Major Monks who served in the 6th (Inniskilling) dragoons..... Cpl Preece was for 10 years in the 4th (Royal Irish) Dragoon Guards and although in his 64th year, he still looks "Hale and Hearty" He was in the Crimea and at Balaclava, Inkermann and Sebastopol. He wore his three medals on Wednesday evening. The medal for the Crimea has three clasps, he was awarded the "Distinguished Conduct Medal" for conspicuous gallantry in the charge of the Heavy Brigade under General Scarlett at Balaclava, during which Preece was hemmed in, with a cossack cavalryman on either side of him. The one on his left attempted to decapitate him by a heavy sabre cut, which nearly severed his nose. Preece's attention however, was directed to his opponent on the right, whom he cut down. Seeing this, the other cossack fled. Although he had lost a lot of blood Preece went in pursuit and served him in a similar manner to his companion returning afterwards through the Russian Cavalry to his own corps. His gallant conduct had been observed by his commanding officer, who paid him a high compliment. Corporal Preece claims

the honour of being the first British Dragoon to enter Sebastopol after its fall. Being at the time orderly to General Sir Edward Cooper Hodges......First occasion on which the famous charge had been celebrated in the town.......Henry Preece was the Landlord of the London Apprentice Hotel, Cotton Hill, Shrewsbury. He died at the age of 78 years.

554 PRICE, Cornet George

Born : Unknown
Enlisted :
Medals : Crimea (B.I.S)

Died : Unknown
Status : Probably rode in the Charge

The musters show he was effective from the 1st October to the 31st December. Remarks state he was commissioned on the 5th November, previously a Regimental Sergeant Major.
WO100/24 page 74 Remarks: Promoted from Regl.St.Major.
George Price's commission was backdated to 5th November 1854. He was appointed Regimental Riding Master, 13th April, 1855. Still listed as Riding Master in 1869, but gone by 1874.
Little Hodge, page 78, 18th January 1855. Regimental Sergeant Major Price obtained his Cornet's commission "I hope now I may have an adjutant that will do me something"

1107 PROUDFOOT, Private Adam

Born : Unknown
Enlisted :
Medals : Crimea (B.I.S)

Died : Unknown
Status : Probably rode in the Charge

His medal is held in the Royal Dragoon Guards Museum at York.

The musters show he was effective from the 1st October to the 8th December. Remarks state to Scutari 9th December. (Entry is ruled through, normally indicating a soldier's death) WO100/24 page 72 Remarks: 25/11/9 Clasp added.
WO14/1 Scutari Muster Roll January-March 1855 present in the 1st Muster, 2nd and 3rd muster endorsed "Hospital".

In 1881 the only Adam Proudfoot in the census is shown living at 19 Mackworth Street, Hulme. Lancashire. as a lodger. Age 49. Pensioner. The age and location close to Hulme Cavalry Barracks, makes him a possibility. So it is possible he survived the Crimean campaign and the paymaster's pen. WO25 to pension 21st October 1873.

1156 PURCELL, Private James

Born : Unknown
Enlisted : 10th March 1838
Medals : Crimea (I.S)

Died : Unknown
Status : Effective during the period

The musters show he was effective from the 1st October to the 31st December.

1050 RAE, Private John

Born : Unknown
Enlisted : 10th March 1838
Medals : Crimea (B.I.S)

Died : Unknown
Status : Probably rode in the Charge

For sale DNW 2nd March 2005: Crimea 1854-56, 3 clasps, Balaklava, Inkermann, Sebastopol (J. W. Rae, 4th D. Guards) crudely engraved regimental naming, suspension claw refixed, severe edge bruising and contact marks, otherwise good fine Hammer Price: £360 The 4th Dragoon Guards formed part of the Heavy Brigade; sold with Medal and clasp verification.
The musters show he was effective from the 1st October to the 31st December.

544 RANSOME, Farrier David

Born : Unknown
Enlisted :
Medals : Crimea (B.I.S)

Died : Unknown
Status : Probably rode in the Charge

The musters show he was effective as a Private from the 1st October to the 31st December.
Interestingly in the 1881 census we have a David Ranson, age 59, born 1822, living in the High Street Forge Cottage, Aldershot, occupation Blacksmith. His eldest son Henry born in Ireland in 1855. His low regimental number of 544, the similarity between Farrier and Blacksmith, locations and dates make it possible they are one and the same.

885 REID, Private Alexander

Born : Unknown
Enlisted :
Medals : Crimea (B.I.S)

Died : Unknown
Status : Probably rode in the Charge

The musters show he was effective from the 1st October to the 31st December.

854 RITCHIE, Private William

Born : Unknown
Enlisted :
Medals : Crimea (B.I.S)

Died : Unknown
Status : Probably rode in the Charge

The musters show he was effective as a Private from the 1st October to the 31st December. WO25 discharged 10th May 1864 rank Corporal.

ROBERTSON, Captain Arthur Masterson

Born : Unknown
Enlisted :
Medals : Crimea (B.I.S)

Died : Unknown
Status : Rode in the Charge

Robert Gottlieb of Historik Orders Ltd, private collection. Crimea Group named to: CAPTAIN. A.M. ROBERTSON. 4th DRAGOON GDS. Captain Robertson was a charger and formed part of the Heavy Brigade at Balaklava. The Crimea medal is Officially Impressed. Condition is GVF.

The musters show he was effective from the 1st October to the 31st December. Absent with leave 1st-23rd October and 3rd-31st December.
In a memorandum book which Hodge kept in 1855, he states that Captain Robertson on the 25th October, 1854, at the Battle of Balaklava was mounted in the Field.(p46) WO100/24 page 69 Remarks: Commg.Depot 4th Dn Gds.
In the returns relating to officers in the army Captain A. Robertson arrived in the Crimea October 1854 and his departure in November 1854 Medical Certificate.
Cornet by purchase 18th May 1846, Lieut by purchase 8th October 1847, Captain by purchase 25th June 1852. Harts Annual Army list 1855.

From the Times March 27th 1862.
A trial has just been concluded at Dublin, Captain Robertson of the 4th Dragoon Guards was brought before a Court-martial on charges affecting his character as an officer and a gentleman. Captain Robertson was an officer that was disliked in the regiment. He had been publicly insulted by Colonel Dickson, he had omitted to exact satisfaction for the offence, or, in other words, to send the offender a challenge. It will, of course, occur to the reader that the commission of such an act would have been more criminal than its omission. Colonel Bentinck the commanding officer, tried to induce him to leave the regiment. He was teased, bullied and persecuted till he can hold out no longer. The witnesses contradicted each other, the trial of an officer for not being a gentleman.
From the Times April 29th 1862.
The findings and the sentence in this case have appeared in the following General Order:
First charge for conduct unbecoming the character of an officer and a gentleman...in having, after being grossly and publicly insulted by Colonel Dickson, in London, at the Army and Navy Club, on the 17th of October, 1860, and after not succeeding in his endeavour to obtain an apology or redress for the same, and to have the difference adjusted between them, failed to comply with the provisions of the 17th Article of War, in not submitting the matter to be dealt with by superior military authority.
Second charge ....as above but failing to take proper lawful steps to vindicate his character.
Third charge. For having behaved in a scandalous manner, unbecoming an officer and a gentleman, in having stated, in a letter addressed by him to Major-General Forester, Military Secretary, and bearing date the 4th of October, 1861 that he had submitted his application to retire from the army by the sale of his commission 'entirely through intimidation' he, the said Captain Robertson, then well knowing the statement to be false.

"Sentence The court, having found the prisoner guilty of the second charge preferred against him, which being in breach of the Articles of War, do now sentence him, the prisoner, Captain Arthur Masterson Robertson, of the 4th Royal Irish Dragoon Guards, to be cashiered"

In consequence of the remarks as well as the recommendation of the Judge Advocate-General, the Queen has been pleased not to confirm the sentence of the Court. The prisoner is, therefore, released from arrest.

823 ROBERTSON, Private Thomas

Born : Unknown
Enlisted :
Medals : Crimea (B.I.S)

Died : Unknown
Status : Probably rode in the Charge

Christie 20th October 1981, Lot 10. Crimea Three clasps Balaklava, Inkermann, Sebastopol. T.Robertson 4th Dragoon Guards. Impressed VF £170.

The musters show he was effective from the 1st October to the 31st December. WO100/24 page 72 Remarks: to replace lost one 25/11/56.

Crimean War Trophies

In 1867 a pair of Russian Guns were brought to Burnley by Major James Legh Thursby, brother-in-law of General Sir James Yorke Scarlett. The wives of Major Thursby and Sir James were sisters, daughters of Colonel Hargreaves. The guns were located on the triangle of land at the corner of Colne Road and Bank Parade, in Burnley. They were melted down to aid the war effort in 1941. The picture was taken in 1900.

577 ROGERS, Private John
Born : Unknown
Enlisted :
Medals : Crimea (B.I.S)

Died : Unknown
Status : Probably rode in the Charge

The musters show he was effective from the 1st October to the 31st December. Marginal note reads "Entitled to 1p GC pay 20th Nov". WO25 discharged 8th March 1864.

1029 ROTHWELL, Corporal Thomas
Born : Unknown
Enlisted :
Medals : Crimea (B.I.S)

Died : Unknown
Status : Probably rode in the Charge

The musters show he was effective from the 1st October to the 31st December.

1040 RUTLEDGE, Private Robert
Born : 1829
Enlisted : 26th March 1850
Medals : Crimea (B.I.S)

Died : Unknown
Status : Probably rode in the Charge

The musters show he was effective from the 1st October to the 31st December.
Muster Books January to March 1850, form 7. Recruits. 1040 Pte Rutledge Robert. Enlisted 26th March 1850 at Manchester HQ. Aged 21 yrs, 5' 9 1/4", Bounty paid to recruit £5-15-6. Paid to Recruiting Party 13s-6d. Total Levy money paid £6-9-0. WO14/1 Scutari Muster Roll January-March 1855 1st Muster endorsed "Joined 19th Hospital", 2nd and 3rd Muster endorsed "Hospital". WO25 to 5th Lancers 1st April 1858.

1115 RYAN, Private Thomas
Born : Date Unknown - Clonmel, Co. Tipperary, Ireland
Enlisted : 17th January 1853
Medals : Crimea (B.S)

Died : 25th October 1854 - Balaclava
Status : Killed in the Charge

The musters show he was effective from the 1st October to the 25th October.
Remarks state Killed in action 25th October. Born Clonmel. Trade Carpenter, Enlisted 17/Jan/53.
Casualty Roll listed Killed at Balaklava.
WO100/24 page 72 Remarks: Killed in action 25 Oct. 54. WO100/24 page 79 Remarks: Killed in Action 25 Oct. 54.

"The dead soldier of the 4th Dragoon Guards had red or fair hair, which was cut as close as possible, and therefore well suited to show any wounds. His helmet had come off in the fight, and he had about fifteen cuts on his head, not one of which had more than parted the skin. His death wound was a thrust below the armpit, which had bled profusely."
The only man in his regiment to be killed in the Heavy Brigade attack - Lieutenant Fox Strangways RA, quoted by Colonel F.A. Whinyates in his book "From Coruna to Sevastopol", 1884.

Form 20 18s-11d in credit. Book not forthcoming.

Hodge's diary entry for the 25th October (p51) Concludes with:
Our loss today was 1 killed (Ryan), 1 severely (Scanlan) who died soon afterwards and 4 slightly wounded.
Many officers of the Light cavalry were killed, and a number slightly wounded. There were no infantry early in the morning, and when they did come they were not engaged. The light cavalry were murdered in doing work, when infantry should have been first engaged, and artillery were indispensable. A very fine, warm day.

770 SAVAGE, Private James
Born : Unknown
Enlisted :
Medals : Crimea (B.I.S)
His medal is held in the Royal Dragoon Guards Museum at York.

Died : Unknown
Status : Probably rode in the Charge

The musters show he was effective from the 1st October to the 31st December.

402 SCANLAN, Private William
Born : Unknown
Enlisted :
Medals : Crimea (B.I.S)

Died : 25th October 1854 - Balaclava
Status : Severely wounded in the Charge

The musters show he was effective from the 1st-24th October. Remarks state to Scutari 25th October. Entry ruled through indicating death.
C.R.: Listed W/D at Balaklava. He lived only a few hours after the Charge. WO100/24 page 73 Remarks: Dead.

On Form 8 of the musters entitled "Account of Soldier's under sentence of Forfeiture of Pay, or Additional Pay, during the Period of this Pay List" he is shown as forfeiting 1d per day of his pay for 6 months from the 5th September 1854.

1153, SCHOLEFIELD Private Henry
Born : Unknown
Enlisted :
Medals : Crimea (B.I.S)
His medal is held in the Royal Dragoon Guards Museum at York.

Died : Unknown
Status : Probably rode in the Charge

The musters show he was effective from the 1st October to the 14th November. Remarks state to Scutari 15th November.
He received his medal from the hand of the Queen on 18th May 1855. Casualty Roll, Listed as wounded slightly at Balaklava.

590 SELLICK, Private John
Born : Unknown
Enlisted :
Medals : Crimea (B.I.S)

Died : Unknown
Status : Probably rode in the Charge

The musters show he was effective from the 1st October to the 31st December. WO25 discharged March 1864 rank a Sergeant.

1163 SHAMBURG, Sergeant Bernard
Born : 1811
Enlisted : 25th September 1832
Medals : Crimea (B.I.S)

Died : Unknown
Status : Probably rode in the Charge

Sotheby 12th September 1989, lot 341. Group of 5 (a) Cabul 1842 (imp) with contemporary straight bar suspension 3rd Lt Dgns. (b) Sutlej Moodree reverse 2 clasps Ferozeshuhur, Sobraon. (c) Punjab 2 clasps Chilianwala, Goojerat (Cpl 3rd Lt Dgns) (d) Crimea 3 clasps Balaklava, Inkermann, Sebastopol (Sgt. contemporary eng) (e) Turkish Crimea British issue unnamed. Good fine or better. Contact wear and some EK's. A rare combination of awards est £600-800 Hammer Price £902.
Sotheby 28th June 1990, Lot 290 same group as above came up for Auction.

The musters show he was effective from the 1st October to the 26th November. Remarks state to Scutari 27th November.. Marginal note reads "Entitled to 1p GC pay 20th Nov". Sergeant Bernard Shamburg enlisted into the 4th Light Dragoons 25th September 1832. Volunteered to 3rd Light Dragoons 1st July 1837. (Regtl No 605), and subsequently saw service in the Sutlej and Punjab campaigns. Returning to the 4th Dragoon Guards 1st July 1853. He sailed with his regiment for the Crimea and was present in the famous charge. Transfered to Scutari Hospital just over a month later
Crimean War letters by Major W.C Forrest held in the National Army Museum, NAM 5804/32. Camp near Kadikoi Letter dated 7th December 1854. Poor old Schomberg (In the musters as Shamburg) is sick at Scutari, we have now only 150 men at their duty, and about 160 horses etc nominally at their duty, but scarcely able to carry their own provisions up from Balaclava. Discharged Chatham 28th October 1856 aged 45.

1183 SHAWE, Private Michael

Born : Unknown
Enlisted :
Medals : Crimea (B.I.S)

Died : Unknown
Status : Probably rode in the Charge

The musters show he was effective from the 1st October to the 31st December.

841 SHEA, Private James

Born : Unknown
Enlisted :
Medals : Crimea (B.I.S)

Died : Unknown
Status : Probably rode in the Charge

The musters show he was effective from the 1st October to the 31st December.

1157 SHERLOCK, Private James

Born : Unknown
Enlisted :
Medals : Crimea (S)

Died : Unknown
Status : Effective during the period

The musters show he was effective from the 1st-27th October and from the 14th-31st December. Remarks state to Scutari 28th October.

935 SHINE, Private Denis

Born : Unknown
Enlisted :
Medals : Crimea (B.I.S)

Died : Unknown
Status : Probably rode in the Charge

The musters show he was effective from the 1st October to the 31st December.
Little Hodge pages 138 and 143 Pte Denis Shine was servant to Mrs Forrest (Wife of Major Forrest)
(See 1018 Michael Whelan on page 224) WO25 to pension 2nd June 1874.

766 SHORT, Private Bartholemew

Born : Unknown
Enlisted :
Medals : Crimea (B.I.S)

Died : Unknown
Status : Probably rode in the Charge

The musters show he was effective from the 1st October to the 31st December.

938 SMITH, Private Thomas

Born : Unknown
Enlisted :
Medals : Crimea (B.I.S)

Died : Unknown
Status : Probably rode in the Charge

The musters show he was effective from the 1st October to the 31st December.

On Form 8 of the musters entitled "Account of Soldier's under sentence of Forfeiture of Pay, or Additional Pay, during the Period of this Pay List" he is shown as forfeiting 1d per day of his pay for 2 years from the 21st March 1853 and 1d per day for 6 months from the 12th August 1854. WO25 discharged June 18651

915 SMITH, Private William

Born : Unknown
Enlisted :
Medals : Crimea (B.I.S)

Died : Unknown
Status : Probably rode in the Charge

The musters show he was effective from the 1st October to the 31st December.
L.S.G.C Medal date of recommendation 8.4.68 issued 27.6.68. WO25 discharged 15th November 1868.

1096 SMITH, Private William
Born : Unknown
Enlisted :
Medals : Crimea (BIS)

Died : Unknown
Status : Probably Rode in the Charge

The musters show he was effective from the 1st-27th October and from the 14th-31st December.

1165 St. AUBERT, Sergeant Henri
Born : Date unknown - Stroud, Kent
Enlisted : 7th March 1842
Medals : Crimea (BIS), Maharajpoor Star, Sutlej (for Aliwal, clasp Sobraon), Punjab (clasps Chilianwala, Goojerat), LSGCM.

Died : April 1885. - Lewisham
Status : Probably Rode in the Charge

The musters show he was effective as a Corporal from the 1st October to the 4th November and as a Sergeant from the 5th November to the 31st December. Remarks state promoted to Sergeant. Marginal note reads to Scutari 27th November. Born Stroud, Kent. Trade: 'nil.' Enlisted 16th Lancers at Maidstone on the 7th March 1842 aged 18yr 4 months (No 1545). Volunteered to 3rd Light Dragoons Meerut 31 March 1846 (No 1707). Volunteered 4th DG 1 July 1853. Cpl 10 May 1854. Sgt 5th November 1854. TSM 12 Feb 1856. Served 26yr 158 days. Discharged 11 August 1868. Yeoman Warder until his death. Died Lewisham April 1885.
[Ref: WO 97/1300, WO 25/1458, WO 12/1276, 593; McInnes, Yeoman of the Guard p. 50.]
The stripes, Crown and medal ribbons of Troop Sergeant Major St Aubert, can be seen in the Royal Dragoon Guards Museum at York. (see page 200)

Stripes, Crown and Medal Ribbons of Troop Sergeant Major Henri St. Aubert 4th Dragoon Guards

877 STABLES, Private James
Born : Unknown
Enlisted :
Medals : Crimea (B.I.S)

Died : Unknown
Status : Probably Rode in the Charge

The musters show he was effective from the 1st October to the 31st December.
WO14/1 Scutari Muster Roll January-March 1855 1st Muster endorsed "Joined 31st Hospital", 2nd and 3rd Muster endorsed "Hospital".

1011 STEPHENSON, Private Isaac
Born : 1827 - Lancaster
Enlisted : 27th July 1849
Medals : Crimea (B.I.S)

Died : Unknown
Status : Probably Rode in the Charge

DNW 28th March 2002, Medals from the collection of Gordon Everson, Lot 37, Crimea 1854-56, 3 clasps, Balaklava, Inkermann, Sebastopol (I. Stephenson, 4th Dragoon Guards) officially impressed naming, good very fine. Hammer Price £980

The musters show he was effective from the 1st October to the 31st December. WO100/24 page 73 Remarks to replace lost one.
Isaac Stephenson was born at Lancaster in 1827, and enlisted at Manchester on 27 July 1849. He served in the Crimea from July 1854, and was present at Balaklava, Inkermann and Sebastopol. From July to December 1855 he is shown in hospital at Scutari, embarked for England February 1856. He was promoted to Corporal in December 1857, and purchased his discharge at Aldershot on the 11 March 1859.

1091 STEWART, Private James
Born : Unknown
Enlisted :
Medals : Crimea (B.I.S)

Died : Unknown
Status : Effective during the period

The musters show he was effective from the 1st-27th October and from the 14th-31st December.

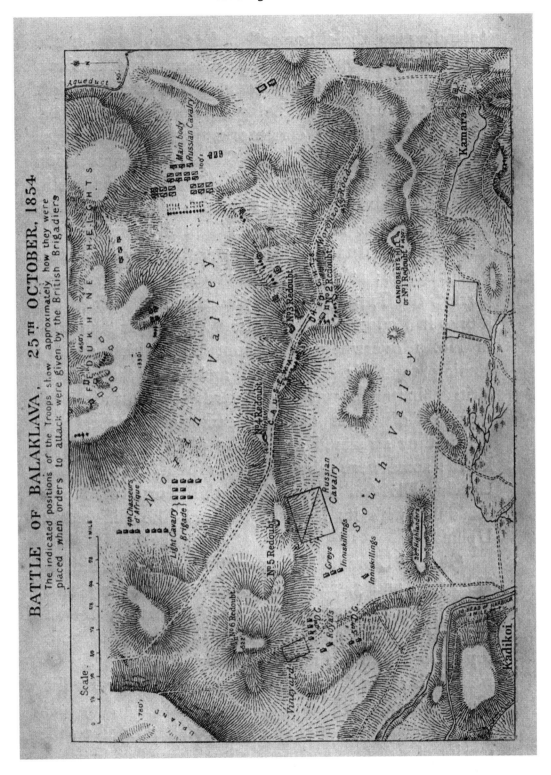

BATTLE OF BALAKLAVA, 25TH OCTOBER, 1854.

The indicated positions of the Troops show approximately how they were placed when orders to attack were given by the British Brigadiers

1076 STONE, Private Thomas
Born : Date Unknown - Hereford
Enlisted :
Medals : Crimea (B.I.S)

Died : 22nd December 1855 - Scutari
Status : Probably Rode in the Charge

The musters show he was effective from the 1st October to the 31st December. WO25 discharged 19th Sep. 1860.

1065 SUFF, Private Francis
Born : Unknown - Hereford
Enlisted : 24th February 1851
Medals : Crimea (B.I.S)
Dixons Medals July 2007. Crimea War Medal 1854-1856, 2 clasps, Balaklava, Inkermann, Officially impressed. Francis Suff, 4th Dragoon Guards £2,500.00

Died : 20th December 1854
Status : Probably Rode in the Charge

The musters show he was effective from the 1st October to the 17th December. Remarks state to Scutari 18th December. Occupation before enlistment Blacksmith WO100/24 page 79 Remarks: Died 22nd Decr. 1855. WO100/24 page 73 Remarks: Dead.

The Times of Saturday, 6th January, 1855; page. 8 reported from Scutari on the 25th December 1854 that "1065, private F.Luff, 4th Dragoon Guards" had died on board the ship Ottawa on the 20th December 1854.

830 TALBOT, Sergeant Edward
Born : Unknown
Enlisted :
Medals : Crimea (B.I.S)

Died : Unknown
Status : Probably Rode in the Charge

The musters show he was effective as a Corporal from the 1st October to the 26th November and as a Sergeant from the 27th November to the 31st December. Remarks state promoted to Sergeant.
Form 21 "Soldier's Remittances" shows he sent £1 to a Mary Talbot.

512 TALBOT, Troop Sergeant-Major William
Born : Unknown
Enlisted :
Medals : Crimea (B.I.S)

Died : Unknown
Status : Probably Rode in the Charge

The musters show he was effective from the 1st October to the 31st December.
Shown on the WO100/24 page 60 Inkermann medal roll as Talbott
He was appointed Cornet in the Land Transport Corps, 7th December 1855. Lieutenant 1st April 1857 - to Half-pay the same day. [Hart, *Army Lists]*

1047 TAYLOR, Farrier James
Born : Date unknown - High Ercall, Nr Wellington
Enlisted : 15th July 1850
Medals : Crimea (B.I.S)
Hayward Medal list Vol2 No7 Dec 1968. Lists a two clasp impressed medal, Balaklava and Inkermann to J.Taylor 4th Dragoon Guards EF £30 (Note Three J.Taylors on Roll) Wallis and Wallis 19th June 1968 Lot 422. Crimea 2 clasps Balaklava and Inkermann to James Taylor 4th Dragoon Guards, impressed naming EF.

Died : 13th June 1855 Crimea
Status : Probably Rode in the Charge

The musters show he was effective as a Private from the 1st October to the 31st December.
Enlisted 15 July 1850, previous occupation Farrier

1172 TAYLOR, Private James
Born : Unknown - Hereford
Enlisted :
Medals : Crimea (B.I.S)

Died : 22nd December 1855 - Scutari
Status : Probably Rode in the Charge

The musters show he was effective from the 1st October to the 26th November. Remarks state to Scutari 27th November. WO14/1 Scutari Muster Roll January-March 1855 present in all three musters, 1st and 2nd musters endorsed Hospital.

1016 TAYLOR, Private John
Born : Date : Unknown
Enlisted :
Medals : Crimea (I.S)
Please see 1047 Taylor for medal information.(Note Three J.Taylors on Roll)

Died : Unknown
Status : Effective during the period

The musters show he was effective from the 1st October to the 31st December. WO25 discharged 22nd Nov. 1860.

965 THOMPSON, Private Henry
Born : Unknown
Enlisted :
Medals : Crimea (B.I.S)

Died : Unknown
Status : Probably Rode in the Charge

The musters show he was effective from the 1st October to the 31st December.

1113 THOMPSON, Private James
Born : Unknown
Enlisted :
Medals : Crimea (B.I.S)

Died : Unknown
Status : Probably Rode in the Charge

The musters show he was effective from the 1st October to the 31st December. WO25 discharged 25th Aug 1868.

650 TOOLE, Private Arthur
Born : Unknown - Hereford
Enlisted :
Medals : Crimea (B.I.S)

Died : Unknown
Status : Probably Rode in the Charge

The musters show he was effective from the 1st October to the 31st December. WO25 Invalided 28th July 1863.

689 TURKE, Private Thomas
Born : Unknown
Enlisted :
Medals : Crimea (B.I.S)

Died : 20th January 1855
Status : Probably Rode in the Charge

The musters show he was effective from the 1st October to the 31st December. WO100/24 page 73 Remarks: Died. WO100/24 page 79 Remarks: died 20th January 1855.

1207 VAUGHAN, Private Thomas
Born : Unknown
Enlisted :
Medals : Crimea (B.I.S)

Died : Unknown
Status : Probably Rode in the Charge

The musters show he was effective from the 1st October to the 8th December. WO100/24 page 73 Remarks: Sent to England. Remarks state to Scutari 9th December.
WO14/1 Scutari Muster Roll January-March 1855 show all three musters endorsed Hospital.

604 WALFORD, Sergeant Thomas
Born : Unknown
Enlisted :
Medals : Crimea (B.I.S)

Died : 28th October 1857
Status : Probably Rode in the Charge

The musters show he was effective from the 1st October to the 31st December.
Thomas Walford is buried Saint George's Parish Church, Hulme, Manchester, It was the burial place of soldier's from the now demolished Hulme Cavalry Barracks. He died whilst stationed at Hulme, on the 28th October 1857, age 40. Cause of death not stated. The churchyard has now been cleared and made into a car park, and the graves no longer exist. Information supplied by John Lister. Copies of the burial registers are held in Manchester Central Library.

1126 WALLACE, Sergeant Frederick

Born : Unknown
Enlisted :
Died : Unknown
Status : Probably Rode in the Charge
Medals : Crimea (B.I.S) The Distinguished Conduct Medal.
Glendining 21 June 1967 Lot 95. Crimea 3 Bar Balaklava, Inkermann, Sebastopol. F.Wallace 4th Dragoon Guards imp (with 2 other medals) £13.
Spinks Auction 12th March 1996 Lot 701 Crimea 3 Bar Balaklava, Inkermann, Sebastopol. (....T.F.Wallis 4th Dragoons) officially impressed. Severe edge brusing and contact marks. Sergeant Fredrick Wallis was entitled to the Distinguished conduct medal est £200-£250

The musters show he was effective as a Private from the 1st-11th October and as a Corporal from the 11th October to the 31st December. Remarks state Promoted to Corporal.
The Distinguished Conduct Medal. Recommendation dated 01/01/1855, Gratuity of £10. WO25 discharged 24/4/1868

1106 WALLACE, Private Frederick

Born : Unknown
Enlisted : 16th December 1851
Medals : Crimea (I.S)
Died : 1st March 1855 - Scutari
Status : Effective during the period

The musters show he was effective from the 1st October to the 14th November. Remarks state Bat Man to Col Hodge to 21st Oct on B. Ship to Scutari 15th Nov.
WO14/1 Scutari Muster Roll January-March 1855 3rd Muster endorsed Died 1st. Trade on enlistment Servant.

981 WANGFORD, Private Richard

Born : Date unknown - Norwich
Enlisted : 16th September 1848
Medals : Crimea (I.S)
Died : Unknown
Status : Effective during the period

The musters show he was effective from the 1st October to the 31st December.
Muster Books 1 July to 30th September 1860. Form 29. 981 Pte Wangford Richard Born Norwich an Upholsterer, enlisted 26th September 1848. Transfered to ....at Birmingham 25 /09/1860

366 WARDROP, Private Henry

Born : Unknown
Enlisted :
Died : Unknown
Status : Probably Rode in the Charge
Medals : Crimea (B.I.S)
Donald Hall Commission List 40, November 1985 326. Pair Crimea 3 Bars B.I.S Pte Henry Wardrop 4th Dgn Gds. Engraved naming. Turkish Crimea Sardinian version N.VF £220.00 with service documents. James Auction, Northwich. Lot 44 25th April 1987 Est £200. Pair Crimea Clasps B.I.S, Turkish Crimea Sardinian Version. (Un-named) neatly engraved in capitals scratches in field. Reverse contact marks.

The musters show he was effective from the 1st October to the 31st December. Musters WO 12-270 Marginal note reads Entitled to 1d GC pay 10th Nov.

1148 WATSON, Corporal Richard

Born : Unknown
Enlisted :
Died : Unknown
Status : Probably Rode in the Charge
Medals : Crimea (B.I.S)

The musters show he was effective as a Private from the 1st October to the 31st December. WO25 discharged 28/10/57

883 WATSON, Private William

Born : Unknown
Enlisted :
Died : Unknown
Status : Probably Rode in the Charge
Medals : Crimea (B.I.S)

The musters show he was effective from the 1st October to the 31st December. Paid for 92 days 3 days on board ship 89 days on land. Regimental number has been altered from 978 to 883 note from John Darwent's Archive.

WEBB, Captain John MacDonnell

Born : Unknown
Enlisted :
Medals : Crimea (B.I.S)

Died : Unknown
Status : Probably Rode in the Charge

The musters show he was effective from the 1st October to the 31st December.
In Hodge's diary dated 17th February 1854 he remarks on the arrival of his new Adjutant Webb." How dreadfully bored and ignorant he was by being shown how to put his kit together."
2 September." Very weak and seedy. My Adjutant also ill. He has been drinking champagne - poisonous kind of liquid at best. It will not do to play these tricks out here".
A diary entry for the 30th October 1854 has Webb being in trouble once again, he had been before a Court of inquiry. "They acquit him, and say that he received orders to retire". Hodge did not agree with the findings. For a picket placed by a divisional general cannot receive orders from any inferior officer whatever. In a letter dated 31/10/1854 Cornet Rowe, 4th Dragoon Guards, wrote "... it was discovered that it was our duty pickets, commanded by Capt. Webb, who had run away in the most disgraceful manner and deserted their post, merely because they heard a shout from the camp of the enemy. Capt. Webb got fearfully abused by the Colonel and by Lord Lucan, and was ordered not to come back to camp, until relieved, what ever happened." *Fisher-Rowe, L. R. (Ed) (1907) Extracts From Letters of E. R. Fisher-Rowe. During the Crimean War 1854-55. Printed for private circulation by R. B. Stedman, Godalming. pp. 19:*

4th November 1854 "Recommended Troop Sergeant Major Harran to Lord Raglan for a cornetcy without purchase in the regiment with a view of getting him the Adjutancy, which Webb is quite unfit for, besides being absent in ill health".
11th August 1855 "A sale in the camp of Brigstocke's things. He has deserted and has sent in his papers, and has gone home today. I yesterday forwarded Webb's papers. He also wants to sell out. I do not approve of officers doing this".

In a memorandum book which Hodge kept in 1855, he states that Captain Webb on the 25th October, 1854, at the Battle of Balaklava was mounted in the Field.(p46)

Crimean War letters by Major W.C Forrest held in the National Army Museum, NAM 5804/32. Camp near Kadikoi Letter dated 7 Dec 1854.
"I believe that Paddy Webb (Capt John MacDonnell Webb, 4DG) acquitted himself as well as his neighbours, but he was in the right Squadron, the left was the first engaged."
Cornet by purchase 2nd April 1847, Lieutenant by purchase 2nd October 1849, Captain by purchase 20th April1852.
Retired 25 September 1855
WO100/24 page 69 Remarks: Retired from the Service.
3rd to 20th October 1854, 40 rations on shore. On board Simla. 21st-23th October on board Sea Nymph. 3rd to 6th December on board Sir R.Sale. 7th to 16th December 1854 on board Gertrude.
Three horses kept by officer and foraged at public expense.

Captain John MacDonnell Webb standing in the doorway of his hut looking at Colonel Hodge (standing in profile), Mrs. Rogers.

954 WEBB, Private Samuel

Born : Date Unknown - Chipping Norton
Enlisted : 8th October 1847
Medals : Crimea (B.I.S)

Died : 17th January 1855 - Scutari
Status : Probably Rode in the Charge

The musters show he was effective from the 1st October to the 17th December. Remarks state to Scutari 18th December.
WO100/24 page 73 Remarks: Dead. WO100/24 page 80 Remarks: died 17th. January 1855.
Born: Chipping Norton. Trade: Shoemaker. Died: Scutari. 17/Jan./55.

WO14/1 Scutari Muster Roll January-March 1855 1st Muster endorsed Died 17th.

1204 WELLS, Sergeant John

Born : 1834 - Witton, near Birmingham
Enlisted : 7th March 1848

Died : 30th November 1908 - Nottingham
Status : Rode in the Charge

Medals : Crimea (B.I.S), Long Service and Good Conduct Medal

Sotheby's 28th June 1990, lot 289, group of three medals and documentation (as below) Hammer Price £660. Purchased by John Darwent from S.Darlington in Accrington 4th November 2000, £1200. DNW 2nd April 2004, The collection of medals formed by the late John Darwent, Lot 159, Three: Permanent Staff Sergeant J. Wells, South Nottinghamshire Yeomanry, late 1st Dragoon Guards and Troop Sergeant-Major, 4th Dragoon Guards, who was twice wounded in the charge of the Heavy Brigade at Balaklava. Crimea 1854-56, 3 clasps, Balaklava, Inkermann, Sebastopol (Serjt., 4th R.I. Dragoon Guards), contemporary engraved naming; Army L.S. & G.C., V.R., 3rd issue, small letter reverse (1204 T.S. Major, 4th Dragoon Guards), officially impressed naming; Turkish Crimea 1855, Sardinian issue (Serjt. Major, 4 Dn. Gds.), regimentally impressed naming, mounted as worn from a contemporary wearing bar, the first with refixed suspension claw, contact marks, edge bruising and polished, good fine and better (3) Sold with an old photographic copy of a portrait and illuminated address presented to the recipient on his retirement from the South Nottinghamshire Yeomanry, together with an original copy of a Crimean and Indian Mutiny Veterans' Association printed obituary for him. Hammer Price £4,800

John Wells was born in the parish of Witton, near Birmingham and originally enlisted in the 1st Dragoon Guards in March 1848, aged 19 years, his occupation shown as a farmer. A tall man for the age, standing at 6ft., he served as a Private in the 1st until 31st March 1854 when he transferred to the 4th Dragoon Guards and was advanced to Corporal on the 13th August 1854 before serving with the regiment out in the Crimea.

The musters show he was effective as a Private from the 1st October to the 17th December 1854 and as a Corporal from 18th-31st December, marginal note reads "From private 18th Dec vice Grint Deceased". At Balaclava, according to his discharge papers, "he was wounded in the bridle hand by a sabre cut", and, according to an accompanying obituary notice, 'slightly in the face', Wells was duly advanced to Sergeant on the 23rd February 1855.

Back home, he gained further promotion to Troop Sergeant-Major on the 1st March 1858 and was re-engaged for a further 12 years with the Colours at Brighton on the 7th March 1860. He was, however, reduced to Sergeant on the 23rd March 1870, and, two months later he appeared in front of a Regimental Board at Manchester and was discharged as unfit for further service on the 21st June 1870. At the time of his discharge he was recovering from an attack of Typhoid and suffering from chronic Rheumatism. On the following day he was appointed a Permanent Staff Sergeant in the South Nottinghamshire Yeomanry and served in that capacity until he was finally discharged to pension on the 21st June 1886. Long Service and Good Conduct Medal issued 1st February 1872 (WO102). At discharge he was described as 57 years of age, 5ft 10" tall, light brown hair, grey eyes, fresh complexion, his intended address been given as Wilford, Notts. He was granted a pension of 1s 11d per day on the 29th September 1870 which was increased to 2s 7d per day on the 6th July 1886 in respect of his service in the Yeomanry. The gallant Wells died at 41 Dickenson Street, Nottingham on the 30th November 1908, aged 74 years. His death was registered by J.H. Wells (son) of 15 New Street, Selby, Yorkshire. He was interred in the Veterans Ground, General Cemetery Nottingham on the 4th December 1908 leaving a widow and one son. His grave can still be seen in the Waverley Street Cemetery, Nottingham.

Transcription of Sergeant Wells' testimonial shown right:
To Sergeant Major John Wells, We the Members of the Nottingham Troops of the South Notts Yeomanry Cavalry desire to place on record our regret at loosing your services as Drill Instructor.
Sixteen years ago to day you joined us from the 4th Dragoon Guards in which Regiment you had served upwards of twenty two years and during that time you have diligently exercised yourself for our benefit both on and off parade as the increased efficiancy of the Troops will testify.
We wish you good health and a long life to enjoy the pension you have so well earned and in presenting you with this testimonial and the accompanying token of our regard and esteem we on behalf of the Members of both Troops as well as several members of other Troops who also appreciate your services bid you a hearty farewell.
Nottingham 21st June 1886
Signed by four of his colleages

Wells' medals and rims

Crimean and Indian Mutiny Veterans Association.

Dear Sir, We regret to have to inform you that on Monday evening last Troop Sergt. Major John Wells who resided at 41 Dickinson Street, Nottm, passed away, after being confined to his sick room about six weeks.

On the 25th October 1854 this gallant soldier took part in the Heavy Cavalry Charge at Balaclava, under General Scarlett.

A French General who was present said it was "a truly magnificent charge," "the most glorious thing he ever saw" and when we take into consideration that 800 British Cavalry men completely routed 3,000 Russian Cavalry who turned and fled in great disorder from the field, we cannot but accept the opinion of the French general; what the fight was may be judged from the fact that General Scarlett received five wounds, and his aide-de-camp Alic Elliot received fourteen; the deceased was wounded slightly in the face and on the bridle hand.

After leaving the 4th Dragoons he became instructor to the South Notts. Hussars in which regiment he served sixteen years, and on his retirement in 1886 he received a beautiful illuminated address signed by J.T. Burnaby, A. Adams, Walter Clifton, and John Caddick, which he highly prized, his pension was increased on retirement from 1/11 to 2/7 per day.

The deceased was highly esteemed by all who knew him, and leaves behind to mourn his loss a widow and one son Mr J.H. Wells who resides at Selby in Yorkshire, his other son who served in the South African War and received medals for the same, died an heroic death on board a Petroleum Ship; he and three comrades were left on board whilst the Captain and 16 others went ashore and unfortunately owing to what expert evidence said "spontaneous combustion" caused the oil to take fire. Young Wells might have saved himself but he went back to rescue his comrades and in doing so was so badly burnt that in less than 14 days he passed away after great suffering, and as the old veteran said "Had my lad lived he would have been totally blind and badly scarred; I do know that he died in doing his duty."

The interment will take place in the Veterans Ground in the General Cemetery on Friday next at 1.15 by kind permission of the Officer Commanding, the Firing and Bugle Party will be furnished by the South Notts. Hussars.

The Rev. E.A. Sims will officiate.

The deceased is the last veteran belonging to the 4th Royal Irish Dragoons residing in Nottinghamshire who fought in the Crimea, and another link is severed from the chain of that historic campaign.

Yours very faithfully,

p.p. Crimean & Indian Mutiny Veterans' Association,

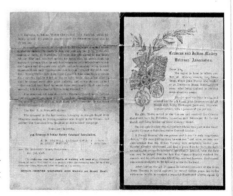

A.W. Brewill. Lt.-Colonel R.H.R   100, St. Stephens's Road,
H. Seely Whitby   Sneinton.
Joint Hon. Secs.   Dec 3rd 1908

P.S.- Veterans who feel capable of walking will meet at 41 Dickinson Street, St.Ann's Well Road at 12.45 prompt, while the remainder must fall in at the Cemetery Gates, Waverley Street entrance, at 1.15 prompt. Order- Winter uniforms with medals on great coat.

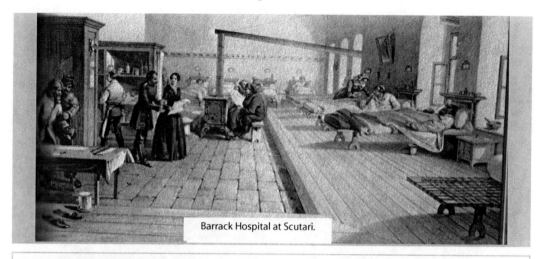

Barrack Hospital at Scutari.

1018 WHELAN, Private Michael

Born : Date unknown - Norwich
Enlisted : 16th September 1848
Medals : Crimea (B.I.S)

Died : 30th July 1859
Status : Probably Rode in the Charge

The musters show he was effective from the 1st October to the 31st December.
Crimean War letters by Major W.C Forrest held in the National Army Museum, NAM 5804/32. Camp near Kadikoi Letter dated 12 December 1854.
Whelan, Slime (probably 935 Denis Shine) and I have been very busy for the last three days, digging into the side of a hill in order to make a stable. I think it will be tolerably comfortable when finished. Sometimes when I express a doubt about one wall standing in case of rain followed by frost, Whelan by way of reassuring me says, "Oh there it, it will stand, Sir, never fear". Do you recollect now that expression of never fear used to provoke you".
Thank JH for me for the fur cloak and Canadian boots, I daresay that they will be the very things which I want and have been writing for. I should like to have had three of those common sailors waterproof coats and hats for O'Hare, Whelan and Slime, but I did not think of them when writing before. I think that they cost about 10 or 12 shillings each in England.
Letter dated 17th December
I bought a lot of bottled Porter for self, Whelan and Slime to drink whilst we are excavating the stable, and I fear that I do not work quite in proportion to the quantity of porter which I drink. WO25 died 30th July 1859.

1132 WHITEMAN, Farrier John

Born : Date Unknown
Enlisted :
Medals : Crimea (B.I.S)

Died : Unknown
Status : Probably Rode in the Charge

The musters show he was effective as a Private from the 1st October to the 31st December. Medal Rolls entered as a Farrier.
A member of a group of Crimean War and Indian Mutiny Veterans who paraded for the Queen in Edinburgh, May 1903.

880 WILKIE, Private Duncan

Born : Date Unknown
Enlisted :
Medals : Crimea (B.I.S)

Died : Unknown
Status : Probably Rode in the Charge

The musters show he was effective from the 1st October to the 31st December.
WO100/24 page 73 Remarks: Clasp added.
WO14/1 Scutari Muster Roll January-March 1855 3rd Muster endorsed joined Servant. WO25 discharged November 1857.

825 WILLIAMS, Troop Sergeant-Major Soloman

Born : 1828 - Ireland
Enlisted :
Medals : Crimea (B.I.S) Egypt medal (Clasp Tel-el-Kebir),Khedive's Star

Died : Unknown
Status : Probably Rode in the Charge

The musters show he was effective from the 1st October to the 31st December.
Form 21 "Soldier's' Remittances" shows he sent £5 to a Mary Williams.

Appointed Quartermaster 11th April 1868. Hon Captain 1st July 1881. Probably given Hon Majority on retirement.
According to Hart, *Army List* (1885) Vol 1 p.139, William's services included the Crimea, and also the Egyptian War 1882,
including the two actions at Kassasin, the Battle of Tel-el-kebir, and the capture of Cairo.
National Army Museum has a sketch he made of the Charge. 1983-12-52-1: Pencil sketch plan of the Charge of the Heavy
Brigade. (Battle of Balaklava, 25 Oct 1854) executed in later life by Hon Maj Solomon Williams, 4th Dragoon Guards, who
rode in the Charge as a Sergeant.
In the 1881 census Soloman Williams age 53 born Ireland occupation Quarter Master.Census Place, Aldershot, Hampshire,
4th Royal Irish Dragoon Guards.Living with his wife Mary Ann, age 49 born Dunstable, Bedford.Two Sons Arthur23 and
William 19, and four daughters, Elizabeth 18, Amy 16, Annie 12 and Mary Ann 8.

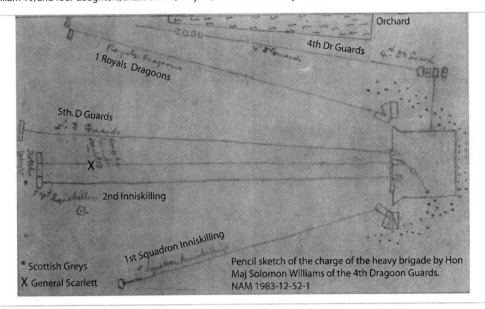

Pencil sketch of the charge of the heavy brigade by Hon
Maj Solomon Williams of the 4th Dragoon Guards.
NAM 1983-12-52-1

971 WILMOT, Farrier Jeremiah

Born : Date Unknown
Enlisted :
Medals : Crimea (B.I.S)

Died : Unknown
Status : Probably Rode in the Charge

The musters show he was effective as a Private from the 1st October to the 31st December. Medal Rolls entered as a
Farrier. WO25 discharged 7th November 1871
In 1881 census, shown living at the Cottage, Brandon and Bretford, Warwick.Age 54 Pensioner, With his wife Elizabeth
and daughter Mary.

978 WILSON, Private George

Born : Date Unknown - Kelso
Enlisted : 23rd August 1848
Medals : Crimea (B.I.S)

Died : 3rd January 1855 - Scutari
Status : Probably Rode in the Charge

The musters show he was effective from the 1st October to the 8th December. Remarks state to Scutari 9th December.
WO14/1 Scutari Muster Roll January-March 1855 1st Muster endorsed Died 3rd.
WO100/24 page 80 Remarks: died 3rd Jany.'55. WO100/24 page 73 Remarks: Dead.
Trade on enlistment Blacksmith. Enlisted 23/Aug./48. Died Scutari. 3/Jan./55.

606 WINTERBOURNE Corporal Frederick

Born : Unknown   Died : Unknown
Enlisted :   Status : Probably Rode in the Charge
Medals : Crimea (B.I.S)

Fitzpatrick Collection Crimea 3 clasps B.I.S to Cpl F Winterborne 4 Dragoon Guards.
F.S.Walland Medal List August 1985 item 017. Crimea 2 clasps Balaklava and Inkermann. Cpl Frederick Winterbourne 4th Dragoon Guards with service papers. Copy of medal roll details from Chelsea Pensioners Register and a print depicting the charge of the Heavy Brigade at Balaklava. Brooch Marks on obverse otherwise NVF £165.
Glendining 24th June 1987. Lot 88. Crimea two clasps Balaklava and Inkermann Corpl. Fredk. Winterborne 4th Dragoon Guards. Contemporary engraved naming in large upright serif Capitals. Brooch marks on obverse. Good Fine £95. with photocopies of relevant pages from medal roll and discharge docs from WO97 1760.

The musters show he was effective as a Private from the 1st October to the 31st December. Marginal note reads restored 1d Good Conduct pay 27 Nov.

1081 WYKES, Private Charles

Born : Unknown   Died : Unknown
Enlisted :   Status : Probably Rode in the Charge
Medals : Crimea (B.I.S)

The musters show he was effective from the 1st October to the 17th December. Remarks state to Scutari 18th December.
WO100/24 page 73 Remarks: Discharged. WO14/1 Scutari Muster Roll January-March 1855 1st Muster endorsed sent home 21st.

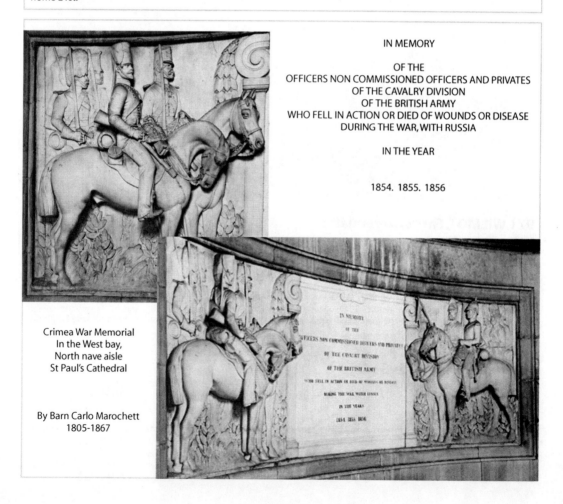

IN MEMORY

OF THE
OFFICERS NON COMMISSIONED OFFICERS AND PRIVATES
OF THE CAVALRY DIVISION
OF THE BRITISH ARMY
WHO FELL IN ACTION OR DIED OF WOUNDS OR DISEASE
DURING THE WAR, WITH RUSSIA

IN THE YEAR

1854. 1855. 1856

Crimea War Memorial
In the West bay,
North nave aisle
St Paul's Cathedral

By Barn Carlo Marochett
1805-1867

The 5th Dragoon Guards
"Princess Charlotte of Wales's"

In 1854 the Regiment was stationed at Ballincollig, 8 km west of Cork . The 5th (Princess Charlotte of Wales) Dragoon Guards received orders to deploy on March 17th 1854 but were short of full establishment. Four troops where to proceed on active service with two troops to form depot at home. To make up the numbers the 7th Dragoon Guards were ordered to provide volunteers for service with the 5th Dragoon Guards. Both the 5th & 7th were stationed in Ireland. The Hon. James Scarlett, commanded the Heavy Brigade while the regiment's Major was to command the Cavalry Depot at Maidstone. The 5th Dragoon Guards began their Crimea campaign without their two most senior officers. A very unpopular choice was the selection of Major T. le Marchant, late 7th Dragoon Guards, as Commanding Officer however an illness in August was to force his early departure a relief to many. Without a field officer the command devolved to Captain A.V.D. Burton.

The regiment embarked with its horses on 8th May 1854, in the screw transport "Himalaya" from Queenstown, for service in the East. Its strength was 295 men and 19 officers, and on board the same ship, a detachment of the 68th Regiment and a small body of Artillery. After a voyage of 14 days, unattended by any noticeable event, except the putting on shore at Malta of the Infantry detachment, the Regiment arrived at Varna Bay, on the southern beach of which it safely disembarked on the 13th June, 1854.

July 1854- At the end of July Cholera appeared in the regiment. The first case of Cholera occurred in the person of a healthy soldier who had just bathed in the river, and who admitted that he had had Diarrhoea for 12 hours previously. He died on the 25th, 15 hours after admission into hospital. One other case of Cholera, also fatal, occured in this camp, an officer's servant was seized with Cholera and died on the 27th. On the 29th July, two days after the arrival of the Regiment at Kotlubie, the third case of Cholera occurred, and proved fatal in 13 hours.

August- On the 5th the Regiment moved to a new encamping ground, on the opposite side of the village. Three days after taking up this ground, another case (also fatal) of Cholera occurred, plus another of Remittent Fever, which after a few days merged into Cholera, and the man died. Several cases admitted on the 9th, and another in the evening. Twenty-five cases were admitted on the 9th , and in the afternoon the ground was again suddenly changed. General Scarlett remaining behind with the hospital and sick. During the time the Regiment had occupied this camp from the 5th to the 10th of the month, upwards of 40 men had been admitted into hospital with Fever, Cholera, and Diarrhoea. The Regiment now on the 10th move, moved its camp back to the opposite side of the village. During the first day several men died, and in the night the Major commanding, and the Surgeon were taken ill with Diarrhoea, and the Senior Captain with Cholera. During the month of August, the Regiment had 195 men, or 76 per cent of strength under treatment in hospital. During the same period 35 deaths occurred. Of 18 officers present at the beginning, only 11 remained at the end of the month.

September- The Regiment remained in the neighbourhood of Varna until the middle of the month, when it embarked on board the screw steam ship "Jason" for the Crimea.

October- On the first of the month the Corps landed at Balaklava, leaving the baggage and men's kits on board ship. The site occupied by the tents was changed three times before the battle of Balaklava. In that battle two men were killed, and 31 wounded of whom 13 were dressed in the regimental Hospital, and sent immediately afterwards on board ship for conveyance to Scutari. Some of the wounds were severe - chiefly sabre, and lance wounds; many men were wounded on the head, and few escaped without wounds on the arms and hands. During the first 10 days in the Crimea, the sick were accommodated in a bell-tent, and the worst cases were sent into the General Hospital at Balaklava.

After that period, a house consisting of two small rooms and a kitchen, was set apart at Kadekoi. On the night after the battle of Balaklava, the sick were ordered within the lines, to their respective Regiments.

November- The Regiment presented a very great increase of sickness during this month. The admissions into hospital amounted to 133 or 54 per cent of the strength. In June 40 recruits, July a draft of 89 recruits, and August 64 recruits. The Regiment had left England with a strength of 295 men and 19 officers; 248 men and 11 officers joined it as reinforcements during the service in the East, making a total of 543 men and 30 officers. Of these 2 men were killed in action, and 31 men and 2 officers wounded. An officer died of wounds later; 79 men and 6 officers died of disease, one man deserted: and 72 men and 9 officers were invalided home.

The table below shows the disproportion between men and horses July-December 1854 :-

Month	Strength	Serjt.	Grds	R.G	Bat	Total	Sick	Total deduct from Stables	Remains at stables	Horses
July	274	18	7	20	24	51	14	83	52	242
August	256	20	7	18	24	49	24	93	51	237
September	253	20	7	18	20	45	39	95	59	224
October	249	20	10	14	17	41	35	96	67	198
November	243	27	9	14	17	40	48	135	48	165
December	237	27	8	14	17	39	72	138	17	140

Key:- Serjt - Serjeants, Grds - Guards, R.G - Regimental employ, Bat - Batmen.
Extracts from (*Medical and Surgical History of British Army in Turkey and Crimea during the Russian War, 1858 page 14-16*)

1053 ABBOTT, Private Charles

Born : Unknown
Enlisted :
Medals : Crimea (I.S)

Died : Unknown
Status : Effective during the period

The musters show he was effective from the 1st October to the 25th November. Second and third musters endorsed "Scutari". WO25 Discharged 11th November 1861.

1095 ABBOTT, Private John

Born : Unknown
Enlisted :
Medals : Crimea (B.I.S) The Distinguished Conduct Medal

Died : Unknown
Status : Rode in the Charge

The musters show he was effective from the 1st October to the 31st December.
The Distinguished Conduct Medal. Recommendation dated 21:1:55.

Leaves from a Soldier's Notebook by Henry Franks, p81, states "There was one thing that was, I think, very discreditable to the Russians, viz., two or three of them, and even four, would surround one of our men and attack him. This was the case when poor Mr. Neville was killed. His horse fell in the first Charge we made, and before the Officer could get on his feet again the horse had made off into the ranks of the Russians, and went away with them when they retreated. Mr. Neville was making his way on foot in the midst of the yelling and struggling men, when he was surrounded by four or five Cossacks, and before any one could get near to assist him, he had received two or three lance wounds, and had fallen to the ground. Two of our men rushed to his assistance, but he being on the ground there was the danger of the horses tramping him under their feet. One young fellow, with great presence of mind, saw the danger, and in a moment he dismounted, and stood across the prostrate Officer's body. With his left hand he held his horse's bridle, and with his sword he parried the assaults of the Cossacks for a few moments until two more men dashed in. Three of the Russians were killed. As soon as he could, Abbott, the young fellow who stood across the Officer's body, took him on his back and carried him to the doctors. His case was hopeless from the first; and he only lived a few minutes. His dying wish was that his father would take care of Abbott. Lord Braybrook afterwards made Abbott a grant of twenty pounds a year for his life, and he also received a medal for distinguished conduct." (See page 270 Hon. Grey Neville)
WO25 Discharged 22nd October 1855.

690 ADDY, Farrier Major John

Born : 1826
Enlisted :
Medals : Crimea (B.I.S)

Died : 25th November 1899
Status : Probably Rode in the Charge

Bonhams 11th July 2006, Lot 34 Crimea 1854-1856, three bars, Balaklava, Inkermann, Sebastopol, engraved (Lieutt John Addy. L.T.Corps.). Fitted with original riband and silver riband brooch. Light contact marks, otherwise very fine. (1) estimate £600-800

Christie's 17th November 1987, Lot 123 Pair: Lieutenant Colonel J. Addy, Land Transport Corps, Late 5th Dragoon Guards, Crimea, three clasps, Balaklava, Inkermann, Sebastopol (Lieut L.T. Corps), engraved in serif capitals; Turkish Crimea, Sardinian issue, very fine and better, with silver riband buckles, contained in velvet-lined fitted case (2) £300-400

Spinks Auction 11th May 2001. lot 375. Pair Lt. Col J. Addy, Land Transport Corps, Late 5th Dragoon Guards, Crimea, three clasps, Balaklava, Inkermann, Sebastopol (Lieut L.T. Corps), engraved in serif capitals; Turkish Crimea, Sardinian issue, very fine and better, with silver riband buckles, contained in velvet-lined fitted case (2) £300-400

The musters show he was effective from the 1st October to the 31st December.
Lieutenant Colonel John Addy was born circa 1826, he attested into the 5th Dragoon Guards in 1840 and became Farrier Major. He was appointed Sergeant in 1852 and was present at the Crimea. He was commissioned into the Land Transport Corps on 6th September 1855. to Captain 1856, Quartermaster to the newly reformed 5th Royal Irish Lancers. On 9th January 1858 The 5th Royal Irish Dragoons, were formed. The new commanding officer was Lt-Colonel G.A.F. Sullivan from the Scots Greys and second-in-command was Major Robert Portal from the 4th Light Dragoons. John Addy was placed on Half Pay in 1859 to become Recruiting Officer at Limerick. He attained the rank of Lieutenant Colonel in 1879. Colonel John Addy, late of the 5th Lancers, died at Brighton on the 25th of November 1899, aged 73 years.

970 ALDWELL, Sergeant William
Born : Unknown   Died : Unknown
Enlisted :   Status : Probably Rode in the Charge
Medals : Crimea (B.I.S)

The musters show he was effective from the 1st October to the 31st December. Paid as Orderly room clerk from 1st October 1854 to 31st December 1854. 92 days, 4 days on board ship, 88 on land. Note in margin states appointed Orderly Room Clerk 17th July 1854. Regtal rank when appointed Private. Medal Roll states H&R lost 21-8-56. WO25 discharged after 21 years service on the 13th November 1877.

1078 ALLEN, Corporal John
Born : Unknown   Died : Unknown
Enlisted :   Status : Probably Rode in the Charge
Medals : Crimea (B.I.S)

The musters show he was effective from the 1st October to the 31st December. WO25 discharged June 1862

866 ALLSOP, Private Henry
Born : Unknown   Died : Unknown
Enlisted :   Status : Probably Rode in the Charge
Medals : Crimea (B.I.S)

The musters show he was effective from the 1st October to the 31st December. WO102 L.S.G.C Medal awarded to Sergeant Allsop recommendation 16.4.1867, issued 24.7.1867 £10 Gratuity. WO25 discharged 11th January 1870

1134 ANDERSON, Private Isaac S.
Born : Unknown   Died : Unknown
Enlisted :   Status : Probably Rode in the Charge
Medals : Crimea (B.I.S)

The musters show he was effective from the 1st October to the 31st December. WO25 discharged 19th Nov. 1868

985 ARMSTRONG, Henry
Born : Unknown   Died : Unknown
Enlisted :   Status : Probably Rode in the Charge
Medals : Crimea (B.I.S)

The musters show he was effective from the 1st October to the 31st December. WO25 discharged 8th August 1856

734 BABBINGTON, Private Charles.
Born : Unknown   Died : Unknown
Enlisted : 1st April 1841   Status : Rode in the Charge
Medals : Crimea (B.S) The Knight (5th Class) The French Legion of Honour

The musters show he was effective from the 1st October to the 31st October. Written in the 3rd Muster is "To Scutari". Remarks state "wounded 25th October".
Knight (5th Class) The French Legion of Honour.
His recommendation stated: "I beg to name Private Charles Babbington late of the 5th Dragoon Guards as the individual "whose distinguished prowess" when serving with that Corps at Balaklava, entitles him to the intended mark of Honor. I have to add that the Man in question enlisted on the 1st of April 1841. He was sent to England on the 20th January 1855, & has since been discharged, in consequence I believe of more than one wound received in the action of Balaklava." Signed T.W. McMahon. Lt Col.Commg. 5th DnGds.

Also a mention in, Leaves from a Soldier's Notebook by Henry Franks, p81.

Listed in the 1881 census is a Charles Bebbington, Chelsea Pensioner, age 60. Living with his wife Alice age 35, and four children. Living at Market Street, Monks Coppenhall. Cheshire.

857 BAKER, Trumpeter Edward

Born : Unknown

Enlisted :

Medals : Crimea (B.I.S)

Died : Unknown

Status : Rode in the Charge

Sothebys 26th June 1997. Lot 430. Group of three. Crimea Medal 3 clasps B.I.S. Engraved naming in upright Serif Capitals. L.S & G.C Vict. Sergt. Mjr. Turkish Crimea, Sardinian version depot impressed. First with severe edge bruising, knocks and contact wear, thus fair, second VF. Third Good Fine. Est, £500-£700. Sgt Major Edward Baker after the Heavy Brigade's successful charge was riding with the "Heavies" in pursuit of the Light Brigade up the "Valley of Death" when the Russian Guns found their range.

The musters show he was effective from the 1st October to the 31st December.
Leaves from a Soldier's Notebook by Henry Franks, p76, records Baker was in support with Franks during the Light Brigade Charge. "Three of us were riding close together - Troop Sergeant Major Russel on the right, myself in the centre, and Trumpeter Baker on the left of the three. We were moving at a trot, when a shell from the Russians dropped and exploded close under the three horses.....The shock of the shell exploding actually lifted both my horse and Baker's off their feet, but that was all the injury we sustained." WO25 discharged as T.S.M on the 18th June 1872.

708 BAKER, Sergeant William C.

Born : Unknown

Enlisted :

Medals : Crimea (B.I.S)

Died : Unknown

Status : Probably Rode in the Charge

The musters show he was effective from the 1st October to the 31st December. WO25 discharged as Pte 31/3/1868.

1218 BARRETT, Private John

Born : Unknown

Enlisted :

Medals : Crimea (B.I.S)

Died : Unknown

Status : Probably Rode in the Charge

The musters show he was effective from the 1st October to the 31st December. WO25 discharged as Pte 31/12/1867.

1103 BARRINGTON, Private Richard

Born : Unknown

Enlisted :

Medals : Crimea (B.I.S)

Died : Unknown

Status : Probably Rode in the Charge

The musters show he was effective from the 1st October to the 31st December.

BEWLEY, Quarter Master George William

Born : Unknown

Enlisted :

Medals : Crimea (B.I.S)

Died : Unknown

Status : Probably Rode in the Charge

The musters show he was effective from the 1st October to the 31st December. Two horses foraged at public expense. *Leaves from a Soldier's note book*, page 46. Quartermaster Bewley issuing Green Coffee. Page 49 ...Mr Bewley ....managed to get tea instead of coffee for the use of the troops and he also succeeded in getting two barrels of porter and each man was allowed to purchase one pint daily but no more.... Previous mention of the officer on page 38. Concerning their visit to the Commissary Office in Varna, and an amusing incident concerning a fight between a Turk and a Frenchman.

Quartermaster Geo.Wm Bewley 5th Dragoon Guards. Commissioned 1853. Quartermaster, 5th Dragoon Guards, 8th July, 1853. Hon. Captain, 3rd June, 1864. Placed on Half-Pay, 3rd June, 1864
Served with 5DG in the Eastern Campaign of 1854-55, including the battles of Balaklava and Inkermann, and Siege of Sebastopol. Medal with two clasps, and Turkish medal. Still alive, 1893. No longer listed in 1906.

[Sources: Hart's Annual Army List for 1860, Official Monthly Army List for October, 1865, Hart's Annual Army List for 1869, Hart's Annual Army List for 1893, Hart's Annual Army List for 1906]

The medal roll states he was entitled to three clasps, but in Hart's it states two.

Camp of the 5th Dragoon Guards, by Roger Fenton

1170 BIRCH, Private Thomas
Born : Unknown
Enlisted :
Medals : Crimea (B.I.S)
Died : Unknown
Status : Probably Rode in the Charge

March Medals List 38 (August 1993) item 208. Group of 3 medals. Pte Thomas Birch, 5th Dragoon Guards Engraved, Indian Mutiny One clasp "Lucknow" (Cpl 7th Hussars) Turkish Crimea, Sardinian version (named) GVF £545.

The musters show he was effective from the 1st October to the 10th December.71 days. Third muster endorsed Scutari.

1184 BIRD, Private William
Born : Date Unknown - Leicester
Enlisted : 12th February 1853
Medals : Crimea (B.I.S)
Died : Date Unknown - Scutari
Status : Probably Rode in the Charge

The musters show he was effective from the 1st October to the 31st December. Trade on enlistment Labourer.

1201 BIRMINGHAM, Private Francis A.
Born : Unknown
Enlisted :
Medals : Crimea (B.I.S)
Died : Unknown
Status : Probably Rode in the Charge

The musters show he was effective from the 1st October to the 10th December. Remarks Scutari.
WO25 discharged as a sergeant 1st May 1863.

1235 BLACKBURN, Private John
Born : Date Unknown - Forfar
Enlisted : 17th September 1851
Medals : Crimea (B.I.S)
Died : 18th January 1855 - Scutari
Status : Probably Rode in the Charge

The musters show he was effective from the 1st October to the 31st December. Remarks state from Varna 3rd November. Third muster endorsed Scutari. Trade on enlistment Clerk.

735 BLEVINS, Sergeant William
Born : Unknown
Enlisted :
Medals : Crimea (B.I.S)
Died : Unknown
Status : Probably Rode in the Charge

The musters show he was effective from the 1st October to the 31st December. To 5th Lancers 20th February 1855.

1074 BLOOD, Private William

Born : 1834 - Astrey, Leicester,
Enlisted : 17th September 1851
Medals : Crimea (B.I.S)
Private W. Blood, 5th Dragoon, ebay Aug 2007

Died : Unknown
Status : Probably Rode in the Charge

A good Turkish Crimea Medal awarded to Private W. Blood, 5th Dragoon Guards, who took part in the charge of the Heavy Brigade at Balaklava on 25th October 1854.

Part of a collection of cavalry related Turkish Crimea medals that we are currently listing on Ebay.

Turkish Crimea Medal 1855, scarcer British flag to fore issue, named in correct regimentally impressed style to: (NO1074. PT. W. BLOOD. 5TH DRAGOON GDS.). With ornate suspension.

The musters show he was effective from the 1st October to the 31st December. Remarks state Servant.

William Blood was born in the parish of Astrey, Leicester, Leicestershire during 1834. He attested for the 5th Dragoon Guards at Birmingham, on 26th April 1850. He served as a Private (No.1074) from the 26th April 1851 through till 25th November 1871, 20 years in total. He was fives times awarded Good Conduct Pay, never being entered in the Defaulters Book, or tried by Court Martial. It appears he did not wish for promotion, but had exemplary service.

Blood served in the Crimean War, and was present with his regiment in the Charge of the Heavy Brigade at Balaklava on 25th October 1854. He received the Crimea Medal with 3 clasps for Inkermann, Balaklava, & Sebastopol, the Turkish Crimea Medal, and later on 4th July 1870, the Long Service & Good Conduct Medal.

On 16th January 1872 he was discharged as "his having been found unfit for further service" this being caused by "a fall racing upstairs to bed on the night of the 17th March 1871 when on leave with his Master, Captain Bourne of the 5th Dragoon Guards." He suffered a fracture, which resulted in permanent stiffening of the left leg and ankle joint, which was deemed to permanently affect his power of supporting himself.

It appears that Blood, when he incurred his injury, was serving as Groom or Orderly to Captain Bourne.

In the 1881 Census William Blood is shown as a Pensioner, age 47, however his birthplace which is given as Burton, Staffordshire, is different from the one he informed the Army on attestation. He is shown as married, to his wife Sophia, aged 33, and with one son, Charles, aged 18. His place of Census is shown as Alma Terr. Gate Fulford, York, Yorkshire.

1241 BOLTON, Private Robert

Born : Date Unknown - York
Enlisted : 10th February 1852
Medals : Crimea (B.I.S)

Died : 6th March 1855
Status : Probably Rode in the Charge

The musters show he was effective from the 1st October to the 31st December. Trade on enlistment Labourer.

1188 BONWELL, Private James

Born : Unknown
Enlisted :
Medals : Crimea (B.I.S)

Died : Unknown
Status : Probably Rode in the Charge

The musters show he was effective from the 1st October to the 31st December.

1085 BOYLE, Sergeant Richard Henry

Born : 25th March 1831
Enlisted : 1850
Medals : Crimea (B.I.S)

Died : 31st July 1895, Dolly Mount, Dublin
Status : Probably Rode in the Charge

The musters show he was effective from the 1st October to the 31st December. Marginal note reads from Cpl. 1st October 1854. Trade on enlistment Labourer.

Richard Henry Boyle, born 25th March 1831. Enlisted in the 5th Dragoon Guards 1850. Afterwards Sergeant Major Cavalry Depot Maidstone, Kent. Riding Master 15 Hussars 23rd April 1861. Riding Master 17th Lancers 1869-1879. Riding Master 16 Lancers 18th October 1879. Honorary Captain 1st July 1881. Retired pay 25th March 1889.

Died at Dolly Mount, Dublin 31st July 1895 aged 64 years 4 months. Served in Crimea 1854-55 rode in the charge of the heavy brigade at Balaclava. present at Inkermann, Tehernaya and siege and fall Sebastopol. Photograph of Sergeant Boyle in Hussar Uniform in the Mullen Archive. WO25 To riding establishment Maidstone 1st February 1860.

544 BREAKWELL, Farrier Andrew

Born : 1816
Enlisted : 6th November 1837
Medals : Crimea (B.I.S)

Died : Unknown
Status : Probably Rode in the Charge

Medal List Philip Burman Kings Lynn. List 5. April 1984. item 429. Group of three to Farrier Major A. Breakwell 5th Dragoon Guards. Crimea 3 clasps Balaklava, Inkermann, Sebastopol, Farr. Sgt. Officially impressed. L.S & G.C Victoria. Farrier Major. Turkish Crimea, Sardinian issue named. verified. VF £500
Listed again by Philip Burman List 6 July 1984. Price unchanged. States committed suicide 20th June 1862. Glendinings 12th November 1998 Lot 661. Same group as above, scratches to rim, generally almost VF or better. Est. £650-£750.

The musters show he was effective as a Private from the 1st October to the 31st December. Remarks state Farrier. WO12/315 date of enlistment 6th November 1837 at Birmingham, age 21, bounty paid to recruit £2.12.0. WO25 Rank shown as private committed suicide June 1862.

1146 BROWNRIGG, Private William Henry

Born : Unknown
Enlisted :
Medals : Crimea (B.I.S)

Died : Unknown
Status : Probably Rode in the Charge

The musters show he was effective from the 1st October to the 31st December.

637 BUCKLEY, Private James

Born : 1815- Kinderton
Enlisted : April 1839
Medals : Crimea (B.I.S)

Died : April 1882
Status : Probably Rode in the Charge

DNW 2nd April 2004, The collection of medals formed by the late John Darwent, Lot 163, Pair: Private J. Buckley, 5th Dragoon Guards. Crimea 1854-56, 3 clasps, Balaklava, Inkermann, Sebastopol (... James Buckley, 5th D...), contemporary engraved naming; Turkish Crimea 1855, British issue (No. 637 Pt., 5th Dragoon Gds.), regimentally impressed naming, last two clasps on the first loose on riband due to broken carriage, suspension refixed, severe edge bruising and contact marks, with resultant loss of some naming detail, fair to fine (2) Hammer Price £500

The musters show he was effective from the 1st October to the 27th December. Paid for 88 days, 11 days on board ship, 77 days on land. Third muster endorsed Scutari.

James Buckley was born at Kinderton, near Chester and enlisted in the 5th Dragoon Guards at Warrington in April 1839, aged 24 years. In his subsequent career of nearly 25 years with the Colours, he served for two years out in the Crimea and was entitled to the Medal with clasps for 'Balaklava','Inkermann' and 'Sebastopol', in addition to the Turkish Medal.
At the time of his discharge in January 1864, Buckley's conduct was assessed as 'Good', although his papers reveal a number of terms of imprisonment as a result of six appearances before a Court-Martial and 48 entries in the Regimental Defaulters Book. He was discharged at his own request Free with pension after 24 years service on the 24th January 1864, on discharge age 48 years 1 month, 5'10 1/2", Fresh complexion, blue eyes, light hair, no marks or scars. Intended residence Northwich, Cheshire.
He next appears in the 1881 census as an unmarried, 65 year old 'Government pensioner', resident at the Workhouse in London Road, Leftwich, Chester. And he was still an inmate there at the time of his death in April 1882.

1236 BUNTING, Private Thomas.

Born : Unknown
Enlisted :
Medals : Crimea (B.I.S)

Died : Unknown
Status : Probably Rode in the Charge

The musters show he was effective from the 1st October to the 31st December.
WO25 1236 Bunting, Joseph to 7th Hussars June 1857.

BURTON, Captain Adolphus William Desart

Born : 1827
Enlisted :
Medals : Crimea (B.I.S) The Turkish Order of the Medjidie (5th Class)

Died : 1882
Status : Rode in the Charge

Christie's 17th November 1987, Lot 112, Four: Lieutenant Colonel A. W. D. Burton, 7th Dragoon Guards, late 5th Dragoon Guards, Order of the Bath, Companion (C.B.), Military Division, 22ct., gold (Hallmarks for London 1815-16) with a silver-gilt riband buckle; Crimea, three clasps, Balaklava, Inkermann, Sebastopol (Bt. Major A. W. D. Burton C.B. 5th Dragoon Guards.), engraved in serif capitals; Turkey, Order of the Medjidie, Fifth Class, Badge, silver, gold and enamel; Turkish Crimea, Sardinian issue with swivel suspension, very fine and better (4) Estimate £1,800-2,200.

The musters show he was effective from the 1st October to the 31st December.
Lieutenant-Colonel Adolphus William Desart Burton, 1827-1882, entered the army 82nd Foot1845, Lieutenant, 1849, Captain, 1852, Major. 1854; exchanged into the 5th Dragoon Guards 1847, commanded the regiment at Balaklava, leading it during the Charge of the Heavy Brigade, 25th October, 1854 (Brevet Major, C.B.), and also the Battles at Inkermann, Tchernaya and the siege of Sebastopol.

Leaves from a Soldier's note book Franks, (p57) During the cholera outbreak at Varna ...."The command of the Regiment now devolved on Captain Burton who was a very young man, and as soon as General Scarlett was made aware of the facts, he moved his Head Quarters from where he was then stationed, and with his staff took up his Quarters with the 5th Dragoon Guards".
(p77) "It must be borne in mind that the 5th Dragoon Guards were still without a Colonel, and Colonel Hodge of the 4th Dragoon Guards, had still the supervision of the Regiment. That Order had never been cancelled, but that Officer could not be in two places at the same time; and Captain Burton was in charge of the 5th Dragoon Guards. The other Regiments that comprised the Brigade had each a Colonel in command, and two of them had a Major as well.

The Fields of War Edited by Philip Warner Letters of R.T.Godman. Letter dated 12th November 1854 (p85) "I am sure some officers would go, if it were not for leaving just now. Burton and Inglis both want to quit the service, but they wish to get their money and no one will pay a price beyond regulation out here".
In a letter dated 30th March 1855, Cavalry Camp, Kadikoi (p147) I have only just had a shine over Lord Lucan's evidence, there seem to be several inaccuracies in it. Burton has written to The Times to deny ever having made such a statement to Lord Lucan, he was very angry about it.

The Times Wednesday 28th May 1856.
Returned to England from Scutari and Malta with Brigadier-General Lord George Paget and Lady Paget on the steam transport Simla reaching Spithead on 27th May 1856.
Both photographs taken by Fenton in 1855.

Major Burton of the 5th Dragoon Guards.

Major Burton & Officers, 5th Dragoon Guards.

1073 BURTON, Private Thomas

Born : Date Unknown - Stourbridge
Enlisted : 25th April 1850
Medals : Crimea (B.I.S)

Died : 19th January 1855 - Scutari
Status : Probably Rode in the Charge

The musters show he was effective from the 1st October to the 31st December. Third muster endorsed "Scutari" 31st December. WO100/24 page 100 Remarks: Dead. Trade before enlistment Labourer.

1115 CALLERY, Private Bernard

Born : Date Unknown - Meath
Enlisted : 30th July1851
Medals : Crimea (B.S)

Died : 25th October 1854 - Balaclava
Status : Killed in the Charge

The musters show he was effective from the 1st-25th October. Written across the entry is Killed in action 25th October.
Form 20. 1115 Pte Callery. Bernard Born Meath. Trade a Hawker. Enlisted 30th July 1851. Killed in action 25th October 1854, 1s - 5d in credit. Reference number 354431. No will known
C.R.: Listed Killed at Balaklava. WO100/24 page 84 Remarks: Killed in Action 25th.Oct.1854. WO100/24 page 100 Remarks: Killed in the Action.

1130 CALVERT, Sergeant Edward

Born : Unknown
Enlisted :
Medals : Crimea (B.I.S)

Died : Unknown
Status : Probably Rode in the Charge

The musters show he was effective from the 1st October to the 31st December. Remarks read to Scutari 31st Dec.

917 CAMPBELL, Private James

Born : Unknown
Enlisted :
Medals : Crimea (B.I.S), Long Service and Good Conduct Medal
A Long Service and Good Conduct has appeared on the market.

Died : Unknown
Status : Probably Rode in the Charge

The musters show he was effective from the 1st October to the 31st December. Marginal note reads "1d GCP Servt."
WO102 L.S.G.C Medal recommendation 16.6.1868, issued 15.8.1868 with £5 Gratuity. WO25 pensioned 25/11/1870.

CAMPBELL, Captain William Richard Newport

Born :
Enlisted :
Medals : Punniar Star, Sutlej Medal (Sobraon), Punjab Medal (Chillianwallah, Goojerat), Crimea (B.I.S)

Died : 23rd December 1854
Status : Probably Rode in the Charge

The musters show he was effective from the 1st October to the 23rd December. Remarks record Died Scutari.
He died of dysentery in the hospital at Scutari. WO100/24 page 83 Remarks: Died 23rd. Decr. 1854.
Eldest son of Brigadier General Alexander Campbell CB KH of Blackburn House, Ayrshire.
Cornet by purchase 10th June 1836, Lieutenant 15th July 1841, To 9th Lancers c. 1843. Served in West Indies with 92nd Foot, India with the 9th Lancers. Captain 15th March 1853.

The British Army Garrison in Malta. 1828 - 1865. January1840 Ensign W.R.N. CAMPBELL

The Times, Tuesday, Mar 23, 1847 Bengal
Lieutenant W.R.N.Campbell appointed Aide-de-Camp to Brigadier Campbell.

The Fields of War Edited by Philip Warner Letters of R.T.Godman. Letter dated 22nd November 1854 "Campbell has been laid up for a month with a bad leg (an old affair) in a little tent... not a very lively state of existence as you may imagine, and no wonder he has made up his mind to go...He is engaged to be married, too, which is another reason. In a later letter dated 27th November." I fear Campbell has changed his mind and is not going yet."
Letter dated 7th December 1854 Camp near Balaklava. "Campbell is gone away very ill, I expect he will sell out, he says he will and I hope he may. 29th December 1854." My dear Father - We have lost another of our number , poor Campbell, who died a few days ago at Scutari - he owes his death entirely to the disgraceful mismanagement of our medical department."

"They would not let him go away till he was so ill he was nearly insensible, and in this state sometimes wet through in his bed, as the water comes through our tents.

He died of dysentery; a very sad thing indeed, a man who already gained three Indian medals and several clasps and had been all through this campaign to die like a dog through neglect.

He was a very clever and agreeable man, in fact very superior and had seen an immense deal of life. Unfortunately he was to be engaged to be married to Miss Mansel, daughter of the General at Cork.

We shall miss him much, he was so cheery (though not a first-rate officer) all through the cholera and bad times; he always cheered one up with his stories and anecdotes, he had served all over the world.

Seven months ago we sailed from Cork nineteen officers in all, out of which ten only are left, five being dead, and four gone home from ill health."

Letter dated 8th January 1855, Cavalry Camp, Kadikoi. "Today we are selling poor Campbell's kit and horses, which by the by only brought about £20 each, though costing about £100 or £150, while the cloths etc brought absurd prices. I was going to tell you in the middle of the bidding we heard a gun fired... everyone looked up and left off bidding".

Obituary: *Wigtownshire Free Press* 25th January 1855.

Marked on the Grave stone in the Crimea.

"Sacred to the memory of William Newport Campbell Captain 5th Dragoon Guards who died at Scutari on the 23rd December 1854 having served in the actions of Punniar, Sobraon, Chillianwalla, Goojerat and Balalclava. He fell a victim to the hardships and privations of the Crimean Campaign. This tablet is dedicated by his sorrowing mother."

(45.)	SACRED (*Marble.*)

TO THE MEMORY OF
WILLIAM RICHARD NEWPORT CAMPBELL
CAPTAIN 5TH DRAGOON GUARDS
WHO DIED AT SCUTARI
ON THE 23RD DECEMBER 1854
HAVING SERVED IN THE ACTIONS OF PUNNIAR
SOBRAON, CHILLIANWALLAH, GOOJERAT
AND BALACLAVA
HE FELL A V VICTIM TO
THE HARDSHIPS AND PRIVATIONS
OF THE CRIMEAN CAMPAIGN
———
THIS TABLET
IS ERECTED BY HIS SORROWING MOTHER
T. GAFFIN
REGENT ST. LONDON

The Barrack Hospital, Scutari. The cemetery lay in front of the timber building.

1164 CARNEY, Private Michael

Born : Unknown
Enlisted :
Medals : Crimea (B.I.S)

Died : Unknown
Status : Probably Rode in the Charge

The musters show he was effective from the 1st October to the 30th November. Third muster endorsed "Scutari"

He received his medal from the hand of the Queen on 18th May, 1855.

799 CARRIGAN, Trumpeter Charles

Born : Unknown
Enlisted :
Medals : Crimea (I.S)

Died : Unknown
Status : Effective during the period

The musters show he was effective from the 1st October to the 31st December. WO25 to 5th Lancers 31st August 1858.

1037 CARROLL, Corporal John

Born : Unknown
Enlisted :
Medals : Crimea (B.S)

Died : Unknown
Status : Effective during the period

The musters show he was effective from the 1st October to the 18th November. Remarks state to Scutari. WO25 Invalided 20th April 1868.

CATTELL, Assistant-Surgeon William

Born : 23rd November 1829 - Castle Bromwich, Warwickshire   Died : 20th March 1919
Enlisted :   Status : Probably Rode in the Charge
Medals : Crimea (B.I.S), The Sardinian War Medal, Afghanistan Medal (clasp Ali Musjid)

The musters show he was effective from the 1st October to the 31st December.

Assistant-Surgeon William Cattell. The Sardinian War Medal. (He) "was present during the whole of the campaign in the Crimea, and shewed great zeal during the time of the cholera, and during the action of Balaklava, and wherever his services were required under fire."
Franks' Leaves from a Soldier's note book, page 57. "Dr Cattell...was for three successive nights in the hospital tents and it was a miracle how he kept on his feet as during all that time he scarcely got any sleep. He was the kindest of men.....

William Cattell (1829-1919) was appointed Assistant-Surgeon on March 28th 1854, and soon thereafter took part in the Crimean War with the 5th Dragoon Guards, being present at the battles of Balaklava, Inkerman, Tchernaya, and Siege of Sebastopol (Medal with three Clasps, Sardinian and Turkish Medal).
He was promoted to Surgeon on July 12th, 1864, and left the 5th Dragoon Guards to be appointed Staff Surgeon at the Cape of Good Hope.
On November 16th 1866, he was appointed to the 20th Foot, the 2d Battalion of the Regiment was in the Cape Colony c. 1867, and then moved on to Mauritius. William Cattell was in Mauritius in 1870 with the 2nd Battalion of the 20th Foot. The Battalion returned to England in 1872, reaching Queenstown on board the Troopship Tamar on January 25th. William Cattell appointed from that Regiment to the 10th Hussars on December 10th, 1872.
He soon left with the Regiment for India, being on board the Jumna on the occasion of her departure from Portsmouth for Bombay on January 10th 1873. The Times reported among the 10th Hussars "Surgeon Callett" (sic), but also "Madame Callett and three children".
He held the relative rank of Lieutenant-Colonel from March 28th 1874.
William Cattell was also a botanist ; he was elected an F.L.S. (Fellow of the Linnaean Society) in 1878, and collected plants along his various postings.
Appointed Brigade Surgeon at Aldershot, on November 27th 1879. The appointment was mainly administrative, he did not reach England until 16th April 1880, arriving at Portsmouth on board the Indian Troopship Malabar.
Appointed principal medical officer of the forces in Canada in January 1882, following some service at Malta.
On April 18th 1882, gazetted Deputy Surgeon-General (dated 12th March).
Deputy Surgeon-General William Cattell retired pay on December 4th 1889 (dated November 23rd).
His memoirs are held within the Royal Army Medical Corps "Muniment Collection".

Officers of the 10th Hussars at Jallalabad, Afghanistan, 1879
http://www.hussards-photos.com/UK/UK_10_ALB_Jellalabad.htm
Picture courtesy of Djedj Lantz.

In the Afghan war, 1878-79, he served with the 10th Hussars, was present at the capture of Fort Ali Musjid and the action at Futchabad, and received the medal and clasp.

Assistant-Surgeon William Cattell with the Dragoon guards, describing the outbreak of cholera in the camp, records As cases were still recurring the O.C went to the Brigadier and in an excited manner urged that the camp should be changed. Brigadier Scarlett assented and was astonished to see the commanding officer of the regiment ride off to the lines and shouting to the men 'get on your horses and be damned and get off this accursed ground' there was panic, men rushing to mount and get away helter-skelter. This was because when ever there was an out break of disease they thought moving camp was the remedy.
Crimea Doctors Vol 1 John Shepherd p 78

966 CLARE, Sergeant Thomas

Born : Unknown
Enlisted :
Medals : Crimea (B.I.S)

Died : Unknown
Status : Probably Rode in the Charge

The musters show he was effective as a Private from the 1st October to the 31st December. Marginal note reads "Armourer". WO100/24 page 98 Remarks: From Private. He was the Armourer Sergeant.
WO25 discharged as a private on the 8th August 1856.

1104 CLARKSON, Private George

Born : Unknown
Enlisted :
Medals : Crimea (S)

Died : Unknown
Status : Effective during the period

The musters show he was effective from the 22nd October to the 31st December. Marginal note reads "joined from Depot". WO25 22/11/56 Factoryman Lancaster.

742 CLAY, Private David

Born : Unknown
Enlisted :
Medals : Crimea (B.I.S)

Died : Unknown
Status : Probably Rode in the Charge

The musters show he was effective from the 1st October to the 31st December. WO25 Corporal to 5th Lancers 28/2/58.

868 CLEAVER, Corporal John

Born : Unknown
Enlisted :
Medals : Crimea (B.I.S)

Died : Unknown
Status : Probably Rode in the Charge

Original Military Antiques and Collectibles. Feb 2008
British "Heavy Brigade" Crimea Medal: to Serjt. John Cleaver, 5th Dragoon Guards. Bars: Sebastopol/Inkermann/Balaklava. Confirmed on the Rolls as a "Heavy Brigade", 5th Dragoon Guards Cavalry Soldier. (Currently in Research)

He musters show he was effective from the 1st October to the 31st December.
WO14/1 Scutari Muster Roll January-March 1855 1st Muster endorsed "Abydos", 3rd Muster endorsed "To Regt 23rd".

British Crimea can be named in the following styles:

i. Officially impressed - In serif Roman capitals., similar to the Military General Service Medal 1793-1814.
ii. Depot impressed (regimental naming) - Comparison with known regimental styles is the only way to establish their authenticity which in the end can be a matter of opinion.
iii. Engraved naming - numerous styles and again it is a matter of comparison. and experience.

1055 COLLETT, Private Daniel

Born : Date Unknown - Oxfordshire
Enlisted : 29th November 1849
Medals : Crimea (B.I.S)

Died : 7th January 1855 - Scutari
Status : Probably Rode in the Charge

Trade: Labourer.
The musters show he was effective from the 1st October to the 31st December. WO100/24 page 100 Remarks: Dead.
Trade on enlistment Labourer.

CONSTANT, Veterinary Surgeon Stephen Price

Born : Unknown
Enlisted :
Medals : Crimea (A.B.S)

Died : Unknown
Status : Probably Rode in the Charge

He received the Alma and Balaklava Clasps whilst serving in the 17th. Lancers. Hart, *Army List (1874)* lists four clasps.
Appointed 27th October 1849. VS 1st class 26th November 1861. Still serving 1874.

1179 CONWAY, Private Francis

Born : Unknown
Enlisted :
Medals : Crimea (B.I.S)

Died : Unknown
Status : Probably Rode in the Charge

The musters show he was effective from the 1st October to the 31st December. WO25 discharged 8th March 1878.

1036 COWIE, Private John

Born : Unknown
Enlisted :
Medals : Crimea (I.S)

Died : Unknown
Status : Effective during the period

The musters show he was effective from the 1st October to the 31st December.

486 COWIE, Private William

Born : Unknown
Enlisted :
Medals : Crimea (B.I.S)

Died : Unknown
Status : Probably Rode in the Charge

The musters show he was effective from the 1st October to the 24th November. Marginal note reads "3 GCP to Scutari".
His wife was one of the unoffical nurses that travelled out to Scutari, other ladies from the 5th Dragoon Guards appear
to have travelled out in December 1854.
On the 23 Dec 1844 he married Margaret Chalmers at Manchester Cathedral, Lancashire, England.

02 Jan 1849 - Pvt. 5th. Dragoon Guards Residence: 2 Henry St., Aston, Warwickshire, England,
District and Sub District - Duddeston Nechells. This was at the time of his daughter's birth (Margaret Jane Cowie).
Family tradition said that he was an officer in the Crimean War, was wounded & later died of those wounds
also that his wife, Margaret Cowie went to the Crimea to nurse him.
He was awarded medals, which were distributed among the family. The Turkish Medal is in the possession of my family.
His occupation was given as "shoemaker" in 1874 (on daughter's marriage registration document).
Both William Cowie & his wife died shortly after their daughters marriage possibly in Scotland.
Information supplied by M.M. Sandness, Western Canada

1006 CROFTS, Private John

Born : Date Unknown - Leicester
Enlisted : 27th December 1847
Medals : Crimea (B.I.S)

Died : 12th December 1854
Status : Probably Rode in the Charge

The musters show he was effective from the 1st October to the 13th December. WO100/24 page 84 Remarks: Died 12th
Dec. 1854. WO100/24 page 100: Dead. Trade at enlistment Gardener.
Died: 13th December 1854 Crimea. 19s-10d in credit. Reference Number 358709. No will known. N.O.K Father, John.
Last known residence Leicester.

1178 DALLISON Private Mark Jas.

Born : Unknown
Enlisted :
Medals : Crimea (B.I.S)

Died : Unknown
Status : Probably Rode in the Charge

The musters show he was effective from the 1st October to the 10th December. Third muster endorsed Scutari.
WO25 discharged 7th June 1875.

1001 DARRELL, Corporal Mark

Born : Unknown
Enlisted :
Medals : Crimea (B.I.S) The Distinguished Conduct Medal

Died : Unknown
Status : Probably Rode in the Charge

The musters show he was effective from the 1st October to the 31st December. Regimental number shown as 1000.
The Distinguished Conduct Medal. Recommendation dated 21:1:55. WO25 discharged 31st March 1857.

1094 DAVERON, Private Michael

Born : Unknown
Enlisted :
Medals : Crimea (B.I.S)

Died : 2nd September 1859
Status : Probably Rode in the Charge

The musters show he was effective from the 1st October to the 31st December. WO25 died 2nd September 1859 .

863 DAVIDSON, Corporal Maxwell

Born : Unknown
Enlisted :
Medals : Crimea (B.I.S), The French Medaille Militaire

Died : Unknown
Status : Probably Rode in the Charge

Morton & Eden Ltd, Wednesday 24 May 2006, Lot 280. A Heavy Brigade Group of Four awarded to Sergeant-Major M. Davidson, 5th Dragoon Guards, comprising: Crimea, 3 clasps, Balaklava, Inkermann, Sebastopol, engraved (Sergt M.G. Davidson 5th Dn Gds); Army Long Service and Good Conduct, impressed (863. Regtl Sergt: Mjr. M. Davidson, 5th Dragoon Gds.); Turkish Crimea, Sardinian issue, depot impressed (No 863. T.S.M. M. Davidson. 5th Dragoon Gds.); and France, Médaille Militaire, in silver-gilt and blue enamel, unnamed as issued, British Crimea medal with soldered swivel and two replacement rivets and the Crimea period medals generally well-worn, LSGC very fine or better (4) £1,200-1,500
The roll confirms the award of four Médailles Militaires to the 5th Dragoon Guards – to the R.S.M., two T.S.M.s and to Sgt. M. Davidson. Hammer Price £3,200

The musters show he was effective from the 1st October to the 31st December. Marginal note reads 1 GCP from 31st October.

The French Medaille Militaire. (He) "served throughout the whole of the Eastern Campaign; was present at Inkermann, Balaklava, and the whole of the Siege of Sebastopol".and was always distinguished for his zeal and activity and irreproachable character in every respect. (Carter page 110). WO25 discharged 18th May 1875 .

1011 DAWSON, Private John

Born : Date Unknown - Yorkshire
Enlisted : 6th April 1848
Medals : Crimea (B.I.S)

Died : 19th January 1855 - Scutari
Status : Probably Rode in the Charge

The musters show he was effective from the 1st October to the 31st December. Third muster endorsed Scutari 31st December". WO100/24 page 100 Remarks: Dead. Trade on enlistment Farmer.

841 DEGUNAN, Private Patrick

Born : Unknown
Enlisted :
Medals : Crimea (B.I.S)

Died : Unknown
Status : Probably Rode in the Charge

The musters show he was effective from the 1st October to the 31st December. WO25 invalided 28th July 1863 .

1120 DELANEY, Private Peter

Born : Date Unknown - Wicklow
Enlisted : 7th January 1851
Medals : Crimea (B.I.S)

Died : 13th January 1855 - Scutari
Status : Probably Rode in the Charge

The musters show he was effective from the 1st October to the 31st December. Trade on enlistment Labourer.

1144 DEMPSEY, Private Martin

Born : Unknown
Enlisted :
Medals : Crimea (B.I.S)

Died : Unknown
Status : Probably Rode in the Charge

The musters show he was effective from the 1st-31st October. Written through the entry. Wounded 25th October sent to Scutari.
Casualty Roll for Crimea. Page 34. Pte Dickson G.H. 5DG, wounded slightly at Balaklava on 25th October 1854

1158 DICKSON, Private George Hy.

Born : Unknown
Enlisted :
Medals : Crimea (B.S)

Died : Unknown
Status : Slightly wounded in the Charge

The musters show he was effective from the 1st October to the 31st December. WO25 invalided 17th November 1862 .

610 DOHERTY, Private Thomas

Born : Unknown
Enlisted :
Medals : Crimea (B.I.S)

Died : Unknown
Status : Probably Rode in the Charge

The musters show he was effective from the 1st October to the 31st December. WO25 invalided 9th June 1863

1093 DONAHUE, Corporal Matthew

Born : Unknown
Enlisted :
Medals : Crimea (B.I.S)

Died : Unknown
Status : Probably Rode in the Charge

The musters show he was effective from the 1st October to the 31st December. WO25 T.S.M died 25th March 1868

1323 DONEGAN, Private William

Born : Unknown
Enlisted :
Medals : Crimea (B.I.S)

Died : Unknown
Status : Probably Rode in the Charge

Cannot locate name in Musters. WO25 discharged 6th November 1856

1028 DONNELLY, Private Malachy

Born : Unknown
Enlisted :
Medals : Crimea (B.I.S)

Died : Unknown
Status : Rode in the Charge

The musters show he was effective from the 1st October to the 31st December.
Shown at the bottom of the musters, not listed in correct place.
He is mentioned in 1020 T. Gough's account of the charge. Spelt Donnolly in the musters "The History of the Present War with Russia" pages 333 and 334.
The following letter is from a Corporal in the 5th Dragoon Guards, one of the regiments engaged in the battle of the 25th We had two men killed Corporal Taylor was one and Ealing was the other - fourteen wounded...The Donaly's are safe....I remain your . Affectionate Son, T.Gough 5th Light Dragoons. The T in Gough is probably a mistake possibly in the orginal transcription) for J. See Joseph Gough p250. WO25 discharged 27th August 1872.

Casualty List 5th Dragoon Guards

Rank	Name	Casualty	Rank	Name	Casualty
Corporal	James Taylor	Killed	Private	Henry Herbert	Severely Wounded
Private	Bernard Callery	Killed	Private	Joseph Jenkins	Severely Wounded
Lieutenant	F. H Swinfen	Slightly Wounded	Private	John McCabe	Severely Wounded
Cornet	Hon G. Neville	Severely Wounded	Private	Edward Malone	Severely Wounded
Corporal	Charles McKeegan	Severely Wounded	Private	William Morris	Slightly Wounded
Private	Charles Babbington	Severely Wounded	Private	William Willson	Severely Wounded
Private	G. H Dickson	Slightly Wounded			

Compiled from the London Gazette, 12th November 1854 & 16th December 1854.

756 DONNELLY, Private Michael

Born : Unknown
Enlisted :
Medals : Crimea (B.I.S)

Died : Unknown
Status : Rode in the Charge

Glendinings 20 November 1908. Lot 213 pair. Crimea Medal four bars. Alma, Balaklava, Inkermann, Sebastopol (M. Donolly 5th Dragoon Guards) and turkish medal to same recipient. both fine. Realised 12/-
A Long Service and Good Conduct has appeared on the market.

The musters show he was effective from the 1st October to the 31st December. He is mentioned in 1020 T. Gough's account of the charge. Spelt Donnolly in the musters "The History of the Present War with Russia" pages 333 and 334. The following letter is from a Corporal in the 5th Dragoon Guards, one of the regiments engaged in the battle of the 25th We had two men killed Corporal Taylor was one and Ealing was the other - fourteen wounded...The Donaly's are safe....I remain your . Affectionate Son, T. Gough 5th Light Dragoons.

1027 DONNELLY, Private Thomas

Born : Unknown
Enlisted :
Medals : Crimea (I.S)

Died : Unknown
Status : Effective during the period

Seaby July 1948 item F6. Crimea 3 Bars Balaklava, Inkermann, Sebastopol. T. Donnelly 5th Dragoon Guards. Impressed nearly VF 35/-. Same medal again Seaby August 1949 VF 35/-
Glendinings 24th June 1992, Lot 129, 3 Bar Crimea, B.I.S (T. Donnelly, 5th Dragn. Gds.), impressed naming, very fine. Estimate £300-£350. Hammer price £360.

Shown on the musters as being effective from the 1st October to the 30th November, 61 days. At Scutari during the third muster. WO102 L.S.G.C Medal recommendation 10.5.1869, issued 26.7.1869 with £5 Gratuity. Spelt Donnolly in the musters "The History of the Present War with Russia" pages 333 and 334. The following letter is from a Corporal in the 5th Dragoon Guards, one of the regiments engaged in the battle of the 25th We had two men killed Corporal Taylor was one and Ealing was the other - fourteen wounded...The Donaly's are safe....I remain your . Affectionate Son, T. Gough 5th Light Dragoons. It is quite probable that ' The Donaly's refer to 1027 Thomas and 1028 Malachy, their adjacent regimental numbers suggest that they joined together, and may have been brothers. WO25 to pension 23rd May 1871.

736 DUGDALE, Private Henry

Born : Date unknown - Marsdon, Lancashire
Enlisted :
Medals : Crimea (B.I.S)

Died : Unknown
Status : Probably Rode in the Charge

The musters show he was effective from the 1st October to the 31st December.
In the 1881 census Henry Dugdale aged 61 army pensioner, born Marsdon in Lancashire. Living in Byker, Northumberland, with his wife and family. WO25 discharged November 1857

466 EGAN, Private Patrick

Born : Unknown
Enlisted :
Medals : Crimea (B.I.S)

Died : Unknown
Status : Probably Rode in the Charge

The musters show he was effective from the 1st October to the 31st December. Marginal note reads "4 GCP"

1007 ELLISON, Sergeant William

Born : Unknown   Died : Unknown
Enlisted :   Status : Probably Rode in the Charge
Medals : Crimea (B.I.S)
Dixons Gazette, No 43, Autumn 2005, Lot 3228 Troop Sergeant Major W. Ellison, 5th Dragoon Guards.
Crimea War Medal 1854-1856, 3 clasps, Balaklava, Inkermann, Sebastopol, Officially impressed (Sjt.-Mr. W. Ellison 5th Dragn. Gds); Turkish Crimea Medal, Sardinian issue, Impressed naming (1007 Troop Serj. Mjr. W. Ellison 5th Dragn. Gds.). Edges a little rounded (2)
The Crimea War Medal roll shows William Ellison as serving as 1007 Sgt. 5th Dragoon Guards and entitled to medal and clasps. The 5th Dragoon Guards formed part of the Heavy Brigade at Balaclava and distinguished themselves in this famous charge along with the 4th Dragoon Guards and the Ist/2nd and 6th Dragoons.
Sold with photocopy roll pages. Fine £1350.00

The musters show he was effective from the 1st-16th October and from the 21st October to the 31st December. Remarks state Scutari 17th-20th October. He was the Paymaster Clerk.

1079 ELSTON, Sergeant William

Born : Unknown   Died : Unknown
Enlisted :   Status : Probably Rode in the Charge
Medals : Crimea (B.I.S)

The musters show he was effective from the 1st October to the 31st December. WO25 pte to 7th dragoons 3/11/1859

1107 EVANS, Private William

Born : Unknown   Died : Unknown
Enlisted :   Status : Probably Rode in the Charge
Medals : Crimea (B.I.S)

The musters show he was effective from the 1st October to the 31st December.

1008 FAILAM, Private Thomas

Born : Unknown   Died : Unknown
Enlisted :   Status : Probably Rode in the Charge
Medals : Crimea (B.I.S)
H.Baldwin & Son Ltd. List June 1946, item 43. Pair Crimea Three clasps Balaklava, Inkermann, Sebastopol.and Turkish Crimea. Pte. T. Failham (Sic) crudley engraved. Fine £1-1-0
Glendining's Auction December 1965 T.Failcram. 5th D.G clasps B.I.S engraved naming Ex Tinling collection.

The musters show he was effective from the 1st October to the 31st December. Written across the entry is With Staff Office full period. WO25 discharged 7th March 1860.

1207 FALLS, Private James

Born : 1836 Belfast, Co.Antrim   Died : 25th January 1891- Islington
Enlisted : 12th January 1854   Status : Probably Rode in the Charge
Medals : Crimea (B.I.S)
Sotheby and Co. 30th January 1974, Lot 229 J. Falls, 5th Dragoon Gds. (2), A pair, comprising: Crimea, 1854, 3 bars, Balaklava (acorn missing from bar), Inkerman, Sebastopol (impressed.), Turkish Crimea, 1855 (engraved.), contact marks but about very fine (2)
A 3 bar Crimea B,I & S engraved medal was sold on ebay for $925 dollars on the 1st June 2008. Medal engraved in contemporary style "J.Falls 5th Drag. Gds" clasps are loose on it's original sewed on ribbon. The Balakalva clasp looks like it has been adapted with a back strap, maybe for wearing. Contact marked. He was also entitled to a Turkish Crimea medal. A nice Heavy Brigade medal with full service papers, roll entries, muster page and later research. VF condition.

Enlisted age 18 in the 5th Dragoon Guards at Lancaster 12th January 1854, trade a Draper.
On 1st September 1857, transferred to the 7th Dragoon Guards with regimental No. 43 .He served a total of three years in the "Eastern Campaign" and 11 years in India. He held the rank of Serjeant for most of his service with the 7DG, being Troop Serjeant Major briefly on two occasions. Falls was finally discharged on the 20th April 1875, with 21 years, 100 days service having served the last year of his time as Drill Instructor with the Derbyshire Yeomanry Cavalry, with whom he carried on serving until 31st July 1880. In later years Falls was living at Mountgrove Road, Islington, N.London. He died on 25th January 1891 at Liverpool Road, Islington and in his will he is listed as a "Riding Master".

385 FARRELL, Private John

Born : Unknown
Enlisted :
Medals : Crimea (B.I.S)

Died : Unknown
Status : Probably Rode in the Charge

The musters show he was effective from the 1st October to the 31st December.

FERGUSON, Lieutenant John Stephenson

Born : 17th May 1834 - Belfast, Antrim, Ireland
Enlisted :
Medals : Crimea (B.I.S)

Died : 11th Jan 1885 - Eaton Sq, London
Status : Probably Rode in the Charge

The musters show he was effective as a Cornet from the 1st October to the 7th December and as a Lieutenant from the 8th-31st December. Supplied with rations 5th December-31st December 1854. 2 horses foraged at Public Expense. WO100/24 page 98 Remarks: from Cornet.
The Fields of War Edited by Philip Warner Letters of R.T.Godman. Letter dated 30th May 1854 .Describing the night of the 28th May the steamship Himalaya had just left Queenstown, (Cork Ireland) on its trip to the East. Before the horses had time to get used to the motion, the weather changed with torrents of rain a rough sea and a gale.
"Ferguson, the Major, and myself were the only ones not ill" The night was spent going around the horses "tieing them shorter, and putting those on their legs who had fallen from the rough sea and wet decks". The Himalaya was the biggest ship in the world when launched on 24 May 1853, 3,438 gross register ton
A letter dated 27th August 1854, Camp, Adrianople Road, near Varna. "McNeile, Burnand and Ferguson are ill, but not dangerously; they must go away for a time to recruit health"

Cornet by purchase 11th June 1852, Lieutenant 8th December1854, (Harts 1855) Captain 5th September 2nd Regiment of Life Guards 1856, (Harts 1864) Brevet Major 5th July 1872, Major and Lieutenant Colonel 10th April 1878.(reflecting the Guards' peculiar system of double ranks), Lietenant Colonel 1st July 1881, Colonel 10th April 1882.

Returned to England from Scutari and Malta with Brigadier-General Lord George Paget and Lady Paget on the steam transport Simla reaching Spithead on 27th May 1856. *The Times* ,Wednesday 28th May 1856.

1881 census records him as "Lt Col Qn Life Gds". Jno. S.Ferguson age 46 birthplace Ireland. Shown living at 92 Eaton Square, London, with his wife Sophia age 39, and J.A.B Ferguson son aged 7. With nine servants in attendance.

Born: Belfast, Antrim, Ireland 17th May 1834, Baptised: St. Anne's, Belfast, Antrim, Ireland 25th Jun 1834 Died: 92 Eaton sq, London, England 11th Jan 1885 .
Married at St. Paul's, Knightsbridge, London, England on the10th Jun 1863, Sophia Jane Holford(Ferguson) 1842 - 1928

973 FISHER, Sergeant James Amos

Born : Unknown
Enlisted :
Medals : Crimea (B.I.S)

Died : Unknown
Status : Probably Rode in the Charge

The musters show he was effective as a Sergeant from the 1st October to the 4th November and as a Hospital Sergeant Major from the 5th November to the 31st December. Remarks state from Sergeant 5th Nov vice Griffiths.

463 FISHER, Sergeant John

Born : Unknown
Enlisted :
Medals : Crimea (B.I.S)

Died : Unknown
Status : Probably Rode in the Charge

The musters show he was effective from the 1st October to the 31st December. WO25 invalided 12th Nov. 1859.
He was a Hospital Sergeant. *The Cavalry Division in the Crimea,* by Andrew Sewell.

597 FISHER, Private John

Born : Unknown
Enlisted :
Medals : Crimea (B.I.S)

Died : Unknown
Status : Probably Rode in the Charge

The musters show he was effective from the 1st October to the 21st December. Third muster endorsed "Scutari"

FITZGERALD, Lieutenant Hobart Evans

Born : Unknown   Died : Unknown
Enlisted :   Status : Probably Rode in the Charge
Medals : Crimea (B.I.S)

Spinks Numismatic Circular July/August 1971. Regtl. Sgt Major 5th D.Gds. Crimea clasps B.I.S engraved naming and Turkish crimea (British Issue) engraved naming

The musters show he was effective as a Regimental Sergeant Major from the 1st October to the 4th November and as a Cornet from the 5th November to the 31st December. Remarks state from RSM 5th November. Recorded on muster as H.E Fitzgerald. Cornet 5th November1854, Lieutenant 29th December 1854, Not in the Army List for 1858.
WO100/24 page 98 Remarks: Promoted from Serjt. Major since Last Return.
The Fields of War Edited by Philip Warner Letters of R.T.Godman. Letter dated 22nd January 1855. "Fitzgerald, our new cornet, does not wish to take the adjutancy, as he says he is not capable of performing its duties
Returned to England from Scutari and Malta with Brigadier-General Lord George Paget and Lady Paget on the steam transport Simla reaching Spithead on 27th May 1856. *The Times,* Wednesday 28th May 1856.

1177 FITZGERALD, Private James Evans

Born : Unknown   Died : Unknown
Enlisted :   Status : Probably Rode in the Charge
Medals : Crimea (S)

The musters show he was effective from the 1st October to the 31st December.

1110 FLYNN, Private James

Born : Unknown   Died : Unknown
Enlisted :   Status : Probably Rode in the Charge
Medals : Crimea (B.I.S)

The musters show he was effective from the 1st October to the 31st December. WO25 invalided 29th September 1863.

428 FOSTER, Private James

Born : Unknown   Died : Unknown
Enlisted :   Status : Probably Rode in the Charge
Medals : Crimea (B.I.S)

The musters show he was effective from the 1st October to the 31st December.

669 FRANKS, Troop Sergeant-Major Henry

Born : 2nd June 1818 - Little Abton   Died : 2nd June 1909
Enlisted : 1839   Status : Probably Rode in the Charge
Medals : Crimea (B.I.S)

The musters show he was effective as a Troop Sergeant Major from the 1st October to the 31st December.

These notes are taken from his autobiography *"Leaves from a soldier's note book",* privately printed for the author in 1904 and subsequently reprinted in a limited edition in 1979 by Mitre Publications of Brightlingsea, Essex.
Henry Franks was born at Newsham Mill, Little Abton, 2nd June, 1818.
The hamlet is 7 miles to the north west of Malton, along the B 1257.
The house is just to the north of the River Rye beyond Newsham Bridge Grid Reference: 747762 on the Landranger 100 map. His father was the mill tenant. Whilst he was still young his family moved to Tadcaster and later Thirsk. He joined the 5th Dragoon Guards at Nottingham in 1839 then under the command of Lieu-Col J M Wallace, the Hon J York Scarlett being the second in command.

He took part in the charge of the 'Heavy Brigade' in the Crimean War. *Leaves from a soldier's note book* Page 76 of Biography "Was with Light Brigade advance at Balaclava. Riding with Troop Sgt Major Russell and Trumpeter Baker when Russells horse was killed. This charge took place an hour before the ill-fated charge of the 'Light Brigade'. Franks witnessed this disastrous charge and described it in his book. At the end of the war he became ill and was nursed back to health by Florence Nightingale in Scutari.
WO25 11th March 1856 Franks, Henry Sergt. Brickmaker. PL. March 56 to England.

Served throughout the campaign, winter of 1855 regiment was at Scutari. Page 94 "Some time after we arrived at Scutari, I had a severe attack of illness and was sent to the General Hospital, where I was detained for eleven weeks then invalided home. Landed at Southampton, furlough for two months spent at Thirsk with relatives (May 1856)

In 1862 he went to Canada as a cavalry instructor. His discharge document held at the PRO at Kew makes reference to this. He retired whilst in Canada and went to live with relatives in the USA. In his book he says that, 'I lived in New York and Chicago for some time.' He returned to England in 1871, finally residing in Dalton, near Thirsk about 1893.

Dalton burials 1889 - 1985 1652 Parish register

Henry Franks retired to and was later buried at Dalton: June 2nd 1909 aged 90.

Some notes from Henry Franks' discharge document.

Conduct has been very good and he was when promoted in possession of one Good Conduct Badge and would had he not been promoted have been now in possession of Five Good Conduct Badges: he has the "Crimean Medal" with the clasps for Balaclava""Inkerman" and Sebastopol" and the Turkish Medal.

Has been once entered in the Defaulters Book. Has never been tried by Court Martial. Height : 5' 10 1/2", Complexion: Fresh, Hair Brown Trade: Brick & Tile Maker

Additional information supplied by Paul F. Brunyee Adv Dip Ed, MA. http://www.ryedale.co.uk/ryedale/misc/ryedalehistory/franks.html

Broad Arrow 5th June 1909. Sgt Major Franks died on the 30th May at Dalton near Thirsk. Born on 2nd June 1818 at Newsham Mill near Malton he joined the 5th D.G At Nottingham in 1839.....After about 27 years service he retired on pension and settled at Dalton nr Thirsk.

1005 GAMBLE, Private James

Born : Unknown

Enlisted :

Died : Unknown

Status : Rode in the Charge

Medals : Crimea (B.I.S) The Sardinian War Medal

Dixons Gazette, No 39, Autumn 2004, item 2863. Lance Sergeant J. Gamble, 5th Dragoon Guards.

A fine RARE Heavy Brigade Italian Al Valore Militaire Spedizione DOrient 1855-56 awarded to Lance-Sergeant James Gamble 5th Dragoon Guards who was under fire a considerable portion of the day on the 25th October as orderly to Major-General the Honourable Sir James Yorke Scarlett, K.C.B. Had his horse shot through the thigh but procured another, and returned to his duty immediately. James Gamble is also on the roll for the British Crimea Medal with four clasps. Alma, Balaclava, Inkerman and Sebastopol and also the Turkish Crimea Medal.

The musters show he was effective from the 1st October to the 31st December. Written across the entry is With Staff Office full period.

Lance-Sergeant James Gamble. The Sardinian War Medal. (He) "was under fire a considerable portion of the day on the 25th. October, as orderly to Major General the Honourable Sir James Yorke Scarlett, KCB.; had his horse shot through the thigh, but procured another, and returned to his duty immediately".

Leaves from a soldier's note book 1979 edition by Sgt Major H.Franks page 56 .....Accompanied by James Gamble (The Colonel's servant) ...Mentions the desertion by the commanding officer Colonel Le Marchant in a Turkish waggon covered with grass and driven by Gamble to Varna where Le Marchant embarked on board a ship. Gamble produced a pass signed by Le Marchant giving him 5 days leave of absence.

The 33rd Annivarsary of the Balaclava Charge - 25th October 1887

Last evening a number of officers, who had participated in the memorable engagement at Balaclava, celebrated the 33rd anniversary at Willis's Rooms, King-Street, St James's. Field Marshal the Earl of Lucan G.C.B., presided, and there were present Lord Tredegar, Lord Bingham, General Sir E.Cooper Hodge, G.C.B., General Shute, C.B., GeneralForrest, C.B., General Clarke, C.B., General Sir C.P.Beauchamp Walker, K.C.B., General Godman, Major-General Sir Roger Palmer, Major-General Sir George Wombwell, Surgeon-General Mouat, C.B, V.C., ColonelDuberly, Colonel Swinfen, Colonel Mussenden, Major M'Creagh Thornhill, Major Coney, Major Everard Hutton, Major Stocks, Captain Halford, Captain Fisher Rowe, Captain Teevan, Captain Clutterbuck, and Captain Frank Sutherland.
The Times, Wednesday October 26th 1887.

1112 GEARY, Private Daniel
Born : Unknown
Enlisted :
Medals : Crimea (B.I.S)

Died : Unknown
Status : Probably Rode in the Charge

The musters show he was effective from the 1st October to the 31st December. Remarks state Servant.

810 GEARY, Private John
Born : Unknown
Enlisted :
Medals : Crimea (B.I.S)

Died : Unknown
Status : Probably Rode in the Charge

The musters show he was effective as a Corporal from the 1st October to the 17th December and as a Private from the 18th-31st December. WO25 deserted December 1860.

1167 GILLEESE, Private John
Born : Unknown
Enlisted :
Medals : Crimea (B.I.S)

Died : Unknown
Status : Probably Rode in the Charge

The musters show he was effective from the 1st October to the 31st December.

1131 GLANVILLE, Private Samuel
Born : Unknown
Enlisted :
Medals : Crimea (B.I.S)

Died : Unknown
Status : Probably Rode in the Charge

The musters show he was effective from the 1st October to the 31st December. Third muster endorsed "Scutari"

963 GLEESON, Private Thomas
Born : Unknown
Enlisted :
Medals : Crimea (B.I.S)

Died : Unknown
Status : Probably Rode in the Charge

Spink Auction 22 November 2007 Lot 51 Crimea Medal three clasps, Balaklava, Inkermann, sebastopol (963. Thos. Gleeson. 5th D.G.) contemporarily engraved in upright serif capitals, unofficial rivets between 2nd and 3rd clasps, good very fine. Estimate £500-600. Provenance: Baldwins, 9.10.1934.

The musters show he was effective from the 1st October to the 31st December. WO25 31/8/57 to 7th D.G

778 GLYN, Private John
Born : Unknown
Enlisted :
Medals : Crimea (B.I.S)

Died : Unknown
Status : Probably Rode in the Charge

The musters show he was effective from the 1st October to the 31st December. Written across the entry is With Staff Office full period. WO25 discharged 29th January 1867.

GODMAN Lieutenant & Adjutant Richard Temple

Born : 1832 - Park Hatch, Surrey
Enlisted :
Medals : Crimea (B.I.S)

Died : 1912
Status : Probably Rode in the Charge

The musters show he was effective as a Lieutenant & Adjutant from the 1st October to the 31st December.

From *The Fields of War* p75, Godman observed the Greys going in..."Swords in the air in every direction, pistols going off, everyone hacking away right and left"

Franks Leaves from a soldier's note book, page 79. "We had re-formed in line after our first charge and were waiting for orders. Lieutenant and Adjutant Godman, who had led the Troop in the Charge, in a manner that proved he had true grit in him, did a little act that also proved a kind heart can beat beneath a soldier's coat. We were "sitting at ease", Mr Godman being in front of the Troop, when a Troop horse belonging to the Scots Greys came up with its hind leg broken by a cannon ball just below the hock. The foot was hanging by a piece of skin, and the poor animal came along it kept twisting round the other leg. The poor brute came up to Mr Godman's horse and stood for a few moments trembling, and rubbed its nose against the other horse. Lieutenant Godman took his pistol from the holster of his saddle, and placing the muzzle behind the horse's ear, shot him. An act like this needs no further comment by me".

Temple Godman in 1871

Richard Temple Godman's letter's were published under the title *"The Fields of War -A young cavalryman's Crimea campaign"* edited by Philip Warner published by John Murray, London 1977. The dispatches reveal his wide interests and give an insight into every day life, overcoming boredom, seeing friends die from battle and the lack of basic medicines. He arrived in the Crimea with three horses, and despite his adventures, both he and the horses managed to return unscathed. A photograph taken by Roger Fenton of Godman in uniform, together with his servant, Pte Kilburn, and his charger, "The Earl". Orginally taken in the Crimea in September 1855, can be seen below.

Bottom right a photograph of Godman in the uniform of a Major General, wearing his medals, 3 clasp Crimea and Turkish medal.

Godman was born in Park Hatch Surrey (Now Demolished). He was the second son of Joseph and Caroline Godman who had 12 other children. He was educated at Eaton. Commissioned as Cornet in 5th Dragoon Guards by purchase on 17th May 1851, Lieutenant 3rd March 1854, Captain 21st July 1855, Major 22nd June 1870, Colonel 1876. Retired in 1882 with honorary rank of Major General. Died in 1912.

In 1871 he married Eliza De Crespigny

Major-General Temple

1020 GOUGH Corporal Joseph

Born : Unknown
Enlisted :
Medals : Crimea (B.I.S)

Died : Unknown
Status : Probably Rode in the Charge

His medals are held in the Royal Dragoon Guards Museum at York.

The musters show he was effective from the 1st October to the 31st December.

Heroes of the Crimea by Michael Barthop, page 47: Corporal Gough had a narrow escape when his horse was shot "I fell and got up again and was entangled in the saddle. My head and one leg were on the ground, I tried to gallop on but fell and managed to get loose. A Russian Lancer was going to run me through, McNamara came up and nearly severed his head from his body, so thank god, I did not get a scratch" He grabbed a riderless horse and remounted. "A Russian rode up... I had seen a pistol in the holster pipe, so I shot him in the arm; he dropped his sword. I immediately ran him through the body".

"The History of the Present War with Russia" pages 333 and 334. The following letter is from a Corporal in the 5th Dragoon Guards, one of the regiments engaged in the battle of the 25th....The charge sounded and away we went into the midst of them ....my horse was shot he fell and got up again and I was entangled in the saddle....A Russian Lancer was going to run me through....MacNamara came up at the time and nearly severed his head from his body. So thank God I did not get a scratch.....We had two men killed Corporal Taylor was one and Ealing was the other - fourteen wounded...The Donaly's are safe....I remain your Affectionate Son, T.Gough 5th Light Dragoons (Sic)

Macnamara mentioned above was 743 Pte Michael McNamara, DCM. The Donaly's...were 756 Michael, 1027 Thomas, 1028 Malachy Donnelly. Corporal Taylor was James Taylor who was killed in action on the 25th October 1854, Ealing mentioned as killed, not identified, the other soldier killed was Pte Bernard Callery.   WO25 discharged as Fr Maj 29/10/73.

1066 GREATHOLDERS, Private John

Born : Date Unknown - Stafford
Enlisted : 19th March 1852
Medals : Crimea (B.S)

Died : 10th November 1854 - Crimea
Status : Probably Rode in the Charge

The musters show he was effective from the 1st October to the 10th November. Remarks state died Crimea 10th November. WO100/24 page 85 Remarks: Died 10 Nov. 1854. WO100/24 page 101 Remarks: Dead.
Trade: on enlistment Servant.

906 GREEN, Private Edward

Born : Unknown
Enlisted :
Medals : Crimea (B.I.S)

Died : Unknown
Status : Probably Rode in the Charge

The musters show he was effective from the 1st October to the 31st December.   WO25 discharged 18th July 1857

425 GREEN, Regimental Sergeant-Major Erasmus

Born : Date Unknown - Kilbegan, Co. Westmeath Ireland
Enlisted : 22nd August 1832
Medals : Crimea (B.I.S), The Distinguished Conduct Medal

Died : Unknown
Status : Probably Rode in the Charge

The musters show he was effective as a T.S.M from the 1st October to the 4th November and as a Regimental Sergeant Major from the 5th November to the 31st December. Remarks state from T.S.Major 5th Nov vice Fitzgerald.
WO100/24 page 98 Remarks: From Troop Serjt. Major.
The Distinguished Conduct Medal. Recommendation dated 21:1:55. Received 26th March 1855 gratuity £15.
Meritorious Service Medal submitted to the Queen 12:2:69.
Enlisted at Kildare aged 20, 5ft 9in, fresh complex, grey eyes, light brown hair. Private to Corporal 13th October 1836, Sergeant 29th October 1840, TSM 15th Sept 1848, RSM 5th November 1854.
Discharged from Chatham Invalid depot 2nd December 1856 being "medically unfit for further service. This man when in Turkey was attacked by fever induced by the climate which was followed by rheumatic pains for which he was sent to England. He at present suffers more or less from rheumatism, which renders him unfit for further service."
Awarded a pension of 2s 6d per day. Served 24 years 76 days. No record of being awarded the LS & GC medal.

758 GRIFFITHS, Troop Sergeant-Major George

Born : Unknown
Enlisted .
Medals : Crimea (B.I.S) The French Medaille Militaire

Died : 20th September 1893 - Eastbourne
Status : Probably Rode in the Charge

The musters show he was effective as a Hospital Sergeant Major from the 1st October to the 4th November and as a Troop Sergeant Major from the 5th November to the 31st December. Remarks record from H.S.Major vice Green.

The French Medaille Militaire. (He) "served throughout the whole Eastern Campaign, from May, 1854; whilst the regiment was in Bulgaria, and cholera raging to a fearful extent, he was most indefatigable in attending to the wants of the sick; and exerting himself to the utmost night and day, to rescue his comrades from the malady. He was present at the battles of Balaklava and Inkermann, and never absent from duty during the whole period of the war". Incessantly doing his best for the good of the men of his regiment (Carter page 110)

Appointed Quarter Master in the 5th Lancers on 3rd June 1859. Left the regiment in 1863. Could find no further trace of him in the army.

The Broad Arrow 23 September 1893. 5th Dragoon Guards Captain George Griffith Late 5th D.G. Whose death occurred at Eastbourne on the 20th September, and gained the rank of Honorary Captain in 1877. He became Quartermaster in the army (5th Lancers) in June 1859. He served with the 5th D.G During the Eastern Campaign of 1854-55 including the battle of Balaclava, Inkermann and the Tchernya. And the siege and fall of Sebastopol receiving the medal with three clasps, the Turkish Medal and the French Medal.

1148 GROVES, Corporal William

Born : Date Unknown - Wicklow
Enlisted : 22nd April 1852
Medals : Crimea (B.S)

Died : 8th February 1855
Status : Probably Rode in the Charge

The musters show he was effective as a Private from the 1st October to the 17th December and as a Corporal from the 18th December to the 31st December. Remarks state from Private 18th Dec vice Geary. WO100/24 page 99 Remarks: From Private. Trade on enlistment Servant.

GUDGIN, Vetinary Surgeon Thomas Parinder

Born : Unknown
Enlisted :
Medals : Crimea (B.S), Indian Mutiny medal, South African War Medal 1877-79, Meritorious Service Medal

Died : Unknown
Status : Probably Rode in the Charge

The musters show he was effective from the 13th October to the 31st December. WO100/24 page 195 Remarks: This Officer was attached to the 5th Dn Guards & has since been appd to the 2nd Dgs.
2nd Drag. musters show him as effective until the 12th Oct, this is when he transferred.

His Balaklava and Sebastopol Clasps were awarded whilst he served with the Scots Greys .
Gudgin served with the Scots Greys in the Crimea and with the 2nd Dragoon Guards during the Indian mutiny (Medal with clasp) He also served in the Zulu Campaign of 1879 (Mentioned in Despatches medal with clasp) and reward for Meritorious Service.

The London Gazette of Friday October 13th 1854
5th Regiment of Dragoon Guards - Tom Parinder Gudgin gent, to be Vet. Surg, vice Fisher deceased.
The London Gazette of Friday January 19th 1855
2nd Dragoons - Vet-Surg. Tom Parinder Gudgin from the 5th Dragoon Guards, to be Vet. Surg, vice Jex.
The London Gazette of Tuesday February 17th 1857
2nd Dragoon Guards - Vet-Surg. Tom Parinder Gudgin from the 2nd Dragoon, to be Vet. Surg, vice Opie Smith.
The London Gazette of Tuesday July 29th 1862
2nd Dragoon Guards - Vet-Surg. Tom Parinder Gudgin to be Vet. Surg, of the first class.
The London Gazette of Tuesday August 1st 1871
Tom Parinder Gudgin from 2nd Dragoon Guards, to be Staff Vet.Surg, vice R.J.G.Hurford, who retires upon halfpay.
The London Gazette of Tuesday July 1st 1859
Inspecting Veterinary Surgeon Tom Parinder Gudgin to have the local rank of Principle Veterinary Surgeon while serving during hostilities as the Senior Veterinary Surgeon at the Cape of Good Hope.
The London Gazette of Tuesday July 29th 1885
Inspecting Veterinary Surgeon Tom Parinder Gudgin has been placed on retired pay.

HALFORD, Captain Charles Augustus Drake

Born : Unknown
Died : 25th April 1907
Enlisted :
Status : Probably Rode in the Charge
Medals : Crimea (B.I.S) The Turkish Order of the Medjidie (5th Class)

The musters show he was effective as a Lieutenant from the 1st October to the 7th December and as a Captain from the 8th-31st December. Remarks state to Captain 8th December.

Cornet by purchase 30th March 1849, Lieutenant by purchase 5th April 1850, Captain 8th December 1854. *(Harts 1855)*

The Fields of War Edited by Philip Warner Letters of R.T.Godman.
From a letter dated 6th October 1854 Camp, Balaklava, near Sebastopol.
Halford writes again today to Grace to send his and my parcels, and I hope to get them soon; we are not very well off for food. (Grace was their agent)
From a letter dated 29th December 1854 Camp, Cavalry Camp, Kadikoi.
Did you see Halford has got one of the augmentation troops without purchase?
From a letter dated 23rd February1855 Camp, Cavalry Camp, Kadikoi.
Many of the men got their ears frozen. I fortunately discovered one of Halford's a quarter-frozen, the other beginning, Some snow brought them to life again, but frozen parts always burst afterwards. The ice hung from our eyebrows and lashes, and those who had beards and moustaches found them one solid lump of ice. (On the 19th all the cavalry were ordered to turn out at midnight, they remained on parade for two hours, they then moved off to surprise the enemy. At day break they found themselves near Kamara, when the enemy showed themselves on a hill, they then retired.)
From a letter dated March 27th 1856 Scutari,
Halford, myself, and an officer of the 1st D.G. have arranged that as soon as we know for certain of peace, to apply for six weeks' or two months' leave and start for Jerusalem.

An order to replace medal destroyed is dated 5/6/57.

Returned to England from Scutari and Malta with Brigadier-General Lord George Paget and Lady Paget on the Steam Transport Simla, No.118, Captain Thomas E.Russell(, reaching Spithead on May 27th 1856, along "Major Burton, C.B., Captain Halford, Lieutenants Ferguson and Fitzgerald , Cornet HIbbert, Assistant-Surgeon Cassel, 180men, 180 horses, and one woman of the 5th Dragoon Guards".
(*The Times, Wednesday, May 28th, 1856*)

Captain Charles Augustus Drake Halford married Geraldine Lee Frances Dillon, daughter of Charles Henry Dillon, 14th Viscount Dillon and Lydia Sophia Story, on 13 July 1859. He died on 25 April 1907. http://www.thepeerage.com/p3762.

Both photographs taken by Fenton in 1855.

HAMPTON, Lieutenant Thomas Lewis

Born : 9th August 1834   Died : 1912
Enlisted :   Status : Rode in the Charge
Medals : Crimea (B.S), The Turkish Order of the Medjidie (5th Class)
His medals are held in the Royal Dragoon Guards Museum at York.

The musters show he was effective as a Cornet from the 1st October to the 31st December.
Thomas Lewis Hampton Lewis was born and brought up in Henllys Hall, Llanfaes near Beaumaris on the Isle of Anglesey. He married Lettice Pritchard of Trescawen, and they had 6 children. It was their daughter, Mary Gwendoline, who eventually inherited Henllys Hall.

He is recorded as a Cornet, he commanded the Left Troop of the Line at the Battle of Balacklava' and that 'as a Lieutenant he commanded C Troop from formation in Crimea and brought the troop to England'. He was also proud to note that he was 'the only officer never on the sick list, never missed a days duty during the War'.
Cornet by purchase 21st January 1853. Lieutenant 24th December 1854. Captain 7th September 1858. (Harts 1860)

Camp Nr Varna, 4 August 1854, Monday morning

My Dear Papa,
I expected to hear from some of you by the post that came in today. Since I wrote to Mama, the orders for the attack on the Crimea have just come, we are all to land without tents, take 3 days bread and meat with us, and 3 days Forage for the Horses, we are only allowed to take 1 horse, our servants are to be mounted. They will not even allow us to take our Blankets, so it will be sharp work, the Light Infantry are to land first then the 1st, 2nd, 3rd and 4th Divisions then the Artillery and then we fellows will have hard work. I hope it may all turn out well – I have about £20 of my pay, and have no bills to pay, I have not drawn any money since we came out, I hope you paid Kinley for the money he gave me when I came out – I expect the next mail will come in before we start, I shall write again, if there is another post from Varna, before we are off. We can take about 200 men, and only 7 Officers all the others are ill and on the sick list, our 3rd Captain is to take us into action, we have no Major, he went away when the Cholera commenced, in such a fright that all the men, when dying in Hospital, said, the Cholera may catch the brute yet, as he goes through Varna, and since then the General Scarlett has written a strong letter, and even said, we do not want any home or wife, sick Officers out with the Regt so he is going to leave us, he never came back and we do not want to see his face again, if a man would run away, when the men were dying all round him, what would he do in action, the difference, the General used to go through the Hospital and speak to all the men. We are now all well, have had no further cases since we came here, our horses are getting all right again, I am very sorry Grey has not got is appointment, I hope he will get it soon, and keep to it. I am very glad you are getting on so will with the house. My horses are both very well, the cold nights are very trying for them, as I have no horse clothing for them, I had to send it on to store (just lost my gold pen in the ink bottle), when we left Varna for the Camp at Devna; the weather is not so hot as in England in September the winter sets in very soon, so we must do something at once for the winter quarters. I hope you are quite well, about time for the post to go.
I am dear Papa,
Your affect son   T Lewis Hampton

Balaclava 29 October 1854

My Dear Papa,
I was very glad to get your letter this morning, it was No. 3. I hope to have got the letter telling you all about the battle of Balaclava and how thankful I ought to be at having been spared. I said in my last letter the enemy had attacked our right flank and had been driven back. I have just heard from a wounded Officer that they killed, wounded, and made prisoners about 1100 Russians and we had only a few Regiments engaged; our loss was 30 men killed and wounded; our men let them come quite close, then let in at them, and shot them down like dogs, then the Horse Artillery came up and let into them as they were running away, and covered the ground with them, if we got so many of them, what a number must have been hit and gone away.
We expect an attack on Balaclava today, or very soon, they are supposed to have 30,000 men only 2 miles from this, it will be a dreadful struggle, as they cannot sent more than 10,000 French and 10,000 English from the front if that. We lost 17 horses and 2 men killed and 18 wounded last battle, and 4 Officers. The Generals Lts Swinfen, Neville and Elliott; Neville is not expected to recover. We lost 2 Officers, chargers, with everything on. I am very thankful to say I have never been in better health, than since I came here. I sent you the + I took, as well as the little image, that I sent in Mama's letter. I hop to write by the next post and hope we will have had good luck on our side; I am glad to hear you have had such a good crop of corn, I hope you may get something for it. I am glad you have got on so well with the house it was strange you were to use the Breakfast Room on your birthday; and it was the first time, I had a shot about me, you cannot imagine the way the shots were coming about us. I will try and make you a good sketch when I have time. They are not doing much at Sevastopol, I am afraid it will be a sad thing and take a great number of men to take it. I am rather badly off for things, only having what I can carry.
I am, my dear Papa
Your affect son   T Lewis Hampton

North Wales Chronicle, Saturday, 26th January 1856.
Mentions the return of Lieutenant Hampton from the Crimea. The townsfolk of Beaumaris presented him with a sword as a memento of his participation in the charge of the Heavy Brigade.

Thomas Lewis Hampton Lewis was born on the 9th August 1834, the eldest son, of Major John Lewis Hampton Lewis and his wife Frances Elizabeth I'Anson.
In 1849 he entered the Royal Military College, Sandhurst as a Gentleman Cadet

In the 1851 Census shown living at Cookham, Bray, Royal Military College.

In 1852 after a huge fire the house was again re-built.' TLHL refers to buying a carpet for the breakfast room in his letters home from Constantinople in 1854, on his way to the Crimea.

In 1866 Retired as Captain, from 5th Dragoon Guards

Chester Military Museum had at some time on display several trophies brought back from the Crimea.
A chair on display was marked with a plaque 'Thomas Lewis Hampton Lt 5th Dragoon Guards 8th Sep 1855 Sevastopol took chair from house'. Also a 'Bible taken from Sevastopol by the 5th Dragoon Guards'.

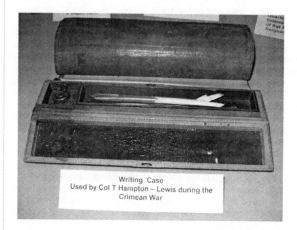

Writing Case
Used by Col T Hampton – Lewis during the
Crimean War

Medals of Col T Hampton – Lewis
Turkish Order of the Medjidie
Crimea Medal
Turkish Crimea Medal

The Fields of War Edited by Philip Warner Letters of R.T.Godman. Several referances to Hampton, letter 31st August 1855. " Yesterday I went out to shoot quail, which are just coming in. I and Hampton had a few shots and got some."

In a letter dated 2nd March 1856, "Halford and Hampton have come back, we expect the rest soon. Hampton was presented with a sword by his county, and made a great deal of, and so have several officers who went home."

1208 HANLON, Private Patrick
Born : Unknown
Enlisted :
Medals : Crimea (B.I.S)

Died : Unknown
Status : Probably Rode in the Charge

The musters show he was effective from the 1st October to the 20th November. Second and third musters endorsed "Scutari"

---

706 HARPER, Private Joseph
Born : Date Unknown - Halifax
Enlisted : 10th November 1846
Medals : Crimea (B.I.S)

Died : 17th November 1854
Status : Probably Rode in the Charge

The musters show he was effective from the 1st October to the 17th November. Remarks state Died 17th November Crimea. WO100/24 page 85 Remarks: Died 17th Nov. 1854. WO100/24 page 101 Remarks: Dead.
Trade on enlistment Woolcomber.

1105 HART, Private William
Born : Unknown
Enlisted :
Medals : Crimea (B.I.S)

Died : Unknown
Status : Probably Rode in the Charge

The musters show he was effective from the 1st October to the 24th November. Second and third musters endorsed "Scutari"

1099 HARTNELL, Sergeant Thomas Henry
Born : Unknown
Enlisted :
Medals : Crimea (B.I.S)
His medals are held in the Royal Dragoon Guards Museum at York.

Died : Unknown
Status : Probably Rode in the Charge

The musters show he was effective from the 1st October to the 31st December.
WO100/24 page 98 Remarks: On long loan to O/C 5 D. Gds.

838 HAVERON, Corporal John
Born : Unknown
Enlisted :
Medals : Crimea (B.I.S)

Died : Unknown
Status : Probably Rode in the Charge

The musters show he was effective from the 1st October to the 20th November. 2nd and 3rd Musters state Scutari. WO25 discharges rank Serjt 2nd September 1863.

1034 HAWKES, Private William
Born : Unknown
Enlisted :
Medals : Crimea (B.I.S)

Died : Unknown
Status : Probably Rode in the Charge

The musters show he was effective from the 1st October to the 31st December.

1129 HEALY, Private Patrick
Born : Unknown
Enlisted :
Medals : Crimea (B.I.S)

Died : Unknown
Status : Probably Rode in the Charge

The musters show he was effective from the 1st October to the 31st December.

1058 HERBERT, Private Henry
Born : Unknown
Enlisted :
Medals : Crimea (B.S) The Knight (5th Class) The French Legion of Honour

Died : Unknown
Status : Severely wounded in the Charge

The musters show he was effective from the 1st-31st October. Written through the entry is Wounded at Balaclava and sent to Scutari 31st October.

Casualty Roll.: Listed as W/Sv at Balaklava.

Leaves from a Soldier's Notebook by Henry Franks, p80-81, states "Private Harry Herbert was a fine dashing young fellow, and was attacked by three Cossack Lancers at the same time. He disabled one of them by a terrible cut across the back of the neck, and the second one scampered off. Herbert made a point at the third man's breast, but his sword blade broke off about three inches from the hilt, yet Harry was not to be foiled by this mishap. He threw the heavy sword hilt at the Russian, which hit him in the face, and the Cossack dropped to the ground; he was not dead, but it spoiled his visage. Herbert also spoiled the appearance of two or three more of them after that; and he escaped in the end with a nasty cut across his hand, but he was soon all right again. This plucky fellow was soon afterwards promoted to the rank of Sergeant, and he received the Cross of the French Legion of Honour."... There was one thing that was, I think, very discreditable to the Russians, viz., two or three of them, and even four, would surround one of our men and attack him.

731 HIGGINBOTTOM, Private Joseph

Born : Date Unknown - Hyde
Enlisted : 22nd March 1841
Medals : Crimea (B.I.S)

Died : 27th February 1855 - Scutari
Status : Probably Rode in the Charge

The musters show he was effective from the 1st October to the 31st December. Trade on enlistment Labourer.

923 HINDLE, Private John

Born : Unknown
Enlisted :
Medals : Crimea (B.I.S)

Died : Unknown
Status : Probably Rode in the Charge

The musters show he was effective from the 1st October to the 31st December. WO25 dischargee 22nd Nov. 1862.

1232 HORNE, Private George

Born : Unknown
Enlisted : September 1848
Medals : Crimea (B.I.S), L.S.G.C Medal

Died : 24th March 1870 - Leeds
Status : Probably Rode in the Charge

DNW 7th March 2007, Lot 728, Family group, An attractive Heavy Brigade group of three awarded to Sergeant George Horne, 5th Dragoon Guards. Crimea 1854-56, 3 clasps, Balaklava, Inkermann, Sebastopol (Geo. Horne, 5th Dn. Gds.), correctly engraved regimental naming; Turkish Crimea 1855, Sardinian issue, unnamed; Army L.S. & G.C., V.R., 3rd issue, small letters reverse (1232 Sergt. Geo. Horne, 5th Dragoon Gds.), this last with officially re-impressed naming, all with old riband brooch-bars for wearing, generally very fine. The Army L.S. & G.C. Medal awarded to George's brother, Sergeant William Horne, 16th Lancers Army L.S. & G.C., V.R., 3rd issue, small letters reverse (1622 Serjt. Willm. Horne, 16th Lancers) officially impressed naming, this with somewhat bent suspension post, otherwise good very fine (4) Hammer Price £3200

George Horne was born in Bristol and enlisted in the 5th Dragoon Guards in September 1848. In his subsequent career of 21 years with the Colours, he was present with his regiment in the actions at Balaklava and Inkermann, in addition to operations before Sebastopol. George died in service, at Leeds, in March 1870; sold with a pair of contemporary portrait images, one being a hand-coloured example on glass and the other in an old decorative copper frame, both depicting him in uniform.

William Horne was born in the parish of St. Michael's, Bristol and enlisted in the 16th Lancers in January 1844, aged 19 years. In his subsequent career of 24 years with the Colours, he served in the East Indies for two of them, but witnessed no active service, his L.S. & G.C. Medal being his only entitlement. William, who was advanced to Sergeant in May 1860, was discharged in February 1868.

The musters show he was effective from the 1st October to the 31st December.
WO102 L.S.G.C Medal awarded to Sergeant Horne recommendation 16th June 1868, issued 15th August 1868 with £5 Gratuity. WO25 died Leeds 24-3-1870

867 HOWARD, Private Charles

Born : Unknown
Enlisted :
Medals : Crimea (B.I.S)

Died : Unknown
Status : Probably Rode in the Charge

The musters show he was effective from the 1st October to the 31st December. WO25 to 7th D.G Nov 1857

905 HUGHES, Private John

Born : Unknown
Enlisted :
Medals : Crimea (B.I.S), L.S.G.C Medal

Died : Unknown
Status : Probably Rode in the Charge

The musters show he was effective from the 1st October to the 31st December.

1097 HUGHES, Private William

Born : Unknown
Enlisted :
Medals : Crimea (B.I.S)

Died : Unknown
Status : Probably Rode in the Charge

The musters show he was effective from the 1st October to the 31st December. WO25 Chester.

813 HUNTER, Private James

Born : Unknown
Enlisted :
Medals : Crimea (B.I.S)

Died : Unknown
Status : Probably Rode in the Charge

The musters show he was effective from the 1st October to the 31st December. Regimental number shown as 817.

824 HUTCHINSON, Private George

Born : Unknown
Enlisted :
Medals : Crimea (B.I.S), L.S.G.C Medal

Died : Unknown
Status : Probably Rode in the Charge

Sotheby's November 1984, Sgt G.Hutchinson. 5th D.Gds. Crimea - Medal clasps for B.I & S, last clasp unofficially joined. Cpl. surname spelt "Hutchison." Turkish Crimea British type to Sgt depot impressed and both with riband buckles, the last with a modified suspension.

The musters show he was effective from the 1st October to the 31st December. Written through his entry is "Trans shipped off Brasa Bombay to Himalaya"
WO102 L.S.G.C Medal recommendation 3.4.1866, with £15 Gratuity. he musters show he was effective from the 1st October to the 31st December. WO25 discharged 21st January 1868.

INGLIS, Captain William

Born : 1830
Enlisted :
Medals : Crimea (B.I.S), The Turkish Order of the Medjidie (5th Class)

Died : 8th June 1900
Status : Probably Rode in the Charge

The musters show he was effective from the 1st October to the 31st December. On board ship 1st-4th October 1854, 2 horses foraged at public expense.

The Fields of War Edited by Philip Warner - Letters of R.T.Godman page 108 " Halford will stay, he is a very good officer, but I forget Inglis, he will stay, a very bad officer does not care about it. (Discussion with his father concerning promotions within the regiment)
Inglis, William. Cornet, Feb. 2, 1849; Lieutenant, Feb. 22 1850; Captain, March 3, 1854' Brevet Major, Dec. 12, 1854; left regiment, Aug. 16, 1859; served in the Eastern campaigns, 1854-55, including the batlles of Balaklava, Inkerman, and the seige and capture of Sevastopol; afterwards a Lieut.-Colonel, and J.P., North Riding of Yorkshire; Inspector or Reformatory and Industrial Schools for Great Britain, 1875-95. Born 1830; son of William Inglis of Dulwich.
The Akbar training ship was last year ravaged by an epidemic of mutinous conduct, which leads Mr Inglis to question the utility of the employment of ships for reformatory boys. Extract from the 1887 Reformatory and Industrial Schools Report. The Times August 13th 1888.
Lieut-Colonel Inglis, of Haverholme, Appleby, Lincolnshire, died early yesterday, at the age of 70 years, after a long illness....He retired from the army with the rank of Major and was for several years H.M Inspector of Industrial Schools. The Leeds Mercury June 9th 1900.

520 JAMES, Private Robert

Born : 1819
Enlisted : 10th May 1837
Medals : Crimea (B.I.S)

Died : Unknown
Status : Probably Rode in the Charge

Medals first appeared in the Sotheby and Co Medal Auction Lot No 586 13th May 1926, from the late Colonel John Murray collection. For sale again Spink 12th March 1996, Lot 702. Three: Private R. James, 5th Dragoon Guards, Crimea, three clasps, Balaklava, Inkermann, Sebastopol, officially impressed, last clasp loose on riband; Turkish Crimea, British die, engraved No. 520. Pt. R. James. 5th Dragoon Gds., with swivel ring suspension; Long Service and Good Conduct, V.R., engraved No. 520 Private Robert James. 5th Dn. Gds. 1858, the group very fine, with copied service papers (3) £450-500

The musters show he was effective from the 1st October to the 31st December.
Private Robert James, a shoemaker from Minchinhampton, Gloucestershire, attested for the 5th Dragoon Guards at Egebaston 10 May 1837 at the age of 18 years; he served 24 years with the Colours, and was discharged, with a totally unblemished record at Brighton 10 May 1861; in 1874 he was refused a pension "as he has been in a lunatic asylum".

806 JAMIESON, Corporal Alexander

Born : Unknown
Enlisted :
Medals : Crimea (B.S), The Distinguished Conduct Medal, L.S.G.C Medal

Died : 3rd November 1866
Status : Probably Rode in the Charge

The musters show he was effective as a Private from the 1st October to the 31st December. WO100/24 page 99 Remarks: From Private.
The Distinguished Conduct Medal. Recommendation dated 21:1:55.
WO102 L.S.G.C Medal awarded to Sergeant Jamieson recommendation 3.5.1865, issued 22.6.1865 with £10 Gratuity.
WO25 Sergeant Jamieson died 3rd November 1866.

1174 JENKINS, Private Joseph

Born : Unknown
Enlisted :
Medals : Crimea (B.S)

Died : Unknown
Status : Severely wounded in the Charge

DNW 19th September 2003, The Collection of Medals Formed by The Late A. A. Mount, Lot 237, Crimea 1854-56, 2 clasps, Balaklava, Sebastopol (Private Josh. Jenkins, 5th Dn. Gds.) contemporary engraved naming, edge bruising, contact marks, nearly very fine. Hammer Price £700

The musters show he was effective from the 1st October to the 31st October. Written through the entry is Wounded at Balaclava 25th October and sent to Scutari 31st.

Casualty Roll.: Listed W/Sv at Balaklava.
Hit by shrapnel when in support of the Light Brigade.
Joseph Jenkins was born in the Parish of Walcott, near Bath in Somerset. A shoe maker by trade he attested for the 5th Dragoon Guards in 1852, aged 21 years. Serving in the Crimea War, he was discharged in July 1855 as being 'unfit for further service in consequence of persistant headache and vertigo the result of wd. of right side of head by fragments of shell received at Balaklava.' Sold with copied service papers and a letter from Canon Lummis confirming that Jenkins was 'Wounded at Balaklava, 25th October, sent to Scutari, 31st October.' Listed in British Battles and Medals 1988 as being one of the wounded from the 5th Dragoon Guards forming part of the Heavy Brigade at the battle of Balaklava.

1224 JENKINS, Private Thomas

Born : Unknown
Enlisted :
Medals : Crimea (B.S)

Died : Unknown
Status : Probably Rode in the Charge

The musters show he was effective from the 1st October to the 31st December. WO25 discharged 13th June 1866.

1162 JENKINSON, Corporal William

Born : Unknown
Enlisted :
Medals : Crimea (B.I.S)

Died : Unknown
Status : Probably Rode in the Charge

The musters show he was effective as a Private from the 1st October to the 24th November and as a Corporal from the 25th November to the 31st December. Remarks state from Private 25th Nov vice Owen.

929 JENNINGS, Private Richard

Born : Unknown
Enlisted :
Medals : Crimea (B.I.S)

Died : Unknown
Status : Probably Rode in the Charge

Spink's Numismatic Circular May 1977, Richard Jennings. 5th Dragoon Guards. Crimea clasps B.I & S engraved, and silver riband brooch.

The musters show he was effective from the 1st October to the 31st December. WO25 Lab. Hull PL Mar 56 to England.

1229 JENNINGS, Private Robert

Born : Unknown
Enlisted :
Medals : Crimea (B.I.S)

Died : Unknown
Status : Probably Rode in the Charge

The musters show he was effective from the 1st October to the 31st December. WO25 to 7 D.G June 1857.

1227 JOHNSON, Private John

Born : Unknown
Enlisted :
Medals : Crimea (B.I.S)

Died : Unknown
Status : Probably Rode in the Charge

The musters show he was effective from the 1st October to the 31st December. WO25 discharged 8th August 1856.

1199 JONES, Private John

Born : Unknown
Enlisted :
Medals : Crimea (B.I.S)

Died : Unknown
Status : Probably Rode in the Charge

The musters show he was effective from the 1st October to the 31st December. WO25 Salop discharged 17-11-1856

1143 KEATING, Private Patrick

Born : Unknown
Enlisted :
Medals : Crimea (B.I.S)

Died : Unknown
Status : Probably Rode in the Charge

Glendinings Monday 17th September 1990 Lot 177, Pair to Patrick Keating, 5th Dragoon Gds; Crimea 1854 - 56, three bars Balaklava, Inkermann, Sebastopol. Engraved contemporary script naming; Turkish Crimea, Sardinian issue (unnamed). First, heavy bruising on naming, worn; second nearly fine.

The musters show he was effective from the 1st October to the 31st December.
Pte Keating was sentenced to penal servitude for life in 1866 for being involved in an alleged mutiny.
John Boyle O'Reilly, the well known Irish poet was one of the principal characters in the plot, with fellow prisoners, where all held in an Irish jail. Colour Sergeant Charles McCarthy, Private Patrick Keating and James Wilson of the 5th Dragoon Guards, Private Michael Harrington of the 61st Foot, and Thomas Darragh of the 2nd Queens ? The testimony's of Private Foley and Rorreson? seem to indicate the soldiers, had taken part in a Fenian oath ceremony. All the mutineers were dealt with by the courts and O'Reilly, Keating and several others were deported to Fremantle in Australia on the last convict boat out of the UK. A small group of the ring leaders - Keating included kept good friends and a year later with the help of the Irish Republican Brotherhood managed to buy a boat and escape to America.

The Times February 5th 1867 from an American Correspondent. The Fenians have been remarkably quiet for some time, and no new defections, schisms, or contemplated raids are reported. At Buffalo they have established a weekly journal, to be called the Fenian Volunteer, but it promises to have only an ephemeral existence. The trials of Fenian prisoners at Toronto have continued with scarcely any delay, counsel employed by the United States in every case defending those claiming to be American citizens. On January 14, Thomas H. Maxwell and James Burk were found guilty, but their sentences were deferred. Patrick Norton pleaded guilty, and was sentenced to 20 years' imprisonment. On the 15th Patrick Keating was tried, and by instruction from the Judge, the jury acquitted him; John O'Connor was found guilty, but sentence was deferred. On the 16th Daniel Quinn and John Royan were found guilty, but sentence was deferred; James Spading was acquitted. On the 17th William Baker was acquitted. On the 18th James M'Donald was acquitted, and Peter Paul Ledwith found guilty, but sentence was deferred. Several of the above prisoners requested and were allowed to have juries composed one-half of aliens. The Court adjourned over on the 18th until yesterday (the 21st), but heavy storms of snow and wind interfering with the telegraph no report of the proceedings has yet been made.

259

1194 KELLY, Private Denis

Born : Unknown
Enlisted :
Medals : Crimea (B.I.S)

Died : Unknown
Status : Probably Rode in the Charge

The musters show he was effective from the 1st October to the 31st December.

1087 KELLY, Private Luke

Born : Unknown
Enlisted :
Medals : Crimea (B.I.S)

Died : Unknown
Status : Probably Rode in the Charge

The musters show he was effective from the 1st October to the 31st December.
Paid from 1st October 1854 to 31st December 1854, 92 days. 4 days on board ship 88 days on land.
Leaves from a Soldier's Notebook by Henry Franks, p77, states he was in support with Franks during the Light Brigade Charge. His horse was killed along with six others by a single shell, none of the riders being injured. Three of the six men were brothers, Luke, Thomas, and Martin Kelly.

1190 KELLY, Private Martin

Born : Unknown
Enlisted :
Medals : Crimea (B.I.S)

Died : Unknown
Status : Probably Rode in the Charge

Glendinings Auction November 1913. Martin Kelly 5th D.G. Crimea - clasps B.I & S, style of naming not shown.
A.H. Baldwin and Sons February 1954 Crimea 3 bar, worn but scarce £1.15s.

The musters show he was effective from the 1st October to the 10th December. Paid for 71 days, 11 days on board ship, 60 days on land. Shown at Scutari during the 3rd muster.
Leaves from a Soldier's Notebook by Henry Franks, p77, states he was in support with Franks during the Light Brigade Charge. His horse was killed along with six others by a single shell, none of the riders being injured. Three of the six men were brothers, Luke, Thomas, and Martin Kelly. WO25 discharged 20th September 1862.

1088 KELLY, Private Thomas

Born : Unknown
Enlisted :
Medals : Crimea (B.I.S)

Died : Unknown
Status : Probably Rode in the Charge

The musters show he was effective from the 1st October to the 31st December.
Paid from 1st October 1854 to 31st December 1854, 92 days. 4 days on board ship 88 days on land.
Leaves from a Soldier's Notebook by Henry Franks, p77, states he was in support with Franks during the Light Brigade Charge. His horse was killed along with six others by a single shell, none of the riders being injured. Three of the six men were brothers, Luke, Thomas, and Martin Kelly. WO25 discharged 6th May 1873.

988 KEMPSON, Private Thomas

Born : Unknown
Enlisted :
Medals : Crimea (B.I.S)

Died : Unknown
Status : Probably Rode in the Charge

The musters show he was effective from the 1st October to the 31st December. WO25 discharged November 1857.
The claim for the Inkermann clasp was supported by Lt. Col. McMahon 28th November 1855.

817 KENDALL, Private Charles

Born : Unknown
Enlisted :
Medals : Crimea (B.I.S)

Died : Unknown
Status : Probably Rode in the Charge

Spink's Numismatic Circular March 1976, Pte. Chris. Kendall. 5th D. G. Crimea clasps B.I & S engraved.

The musters show he was effective from the 1st October to the 10th December. Shown at Scutari during the 3rd muster.

1202 KERR, Private Peter

Born : Unknown
Enlisted :
Medals : Crimea (B.I.S)

Died : Unknown
Status : Probably Rode in the Charge

The musters show he was effective from the 1st October to the 31st December. WO25 to 7th D.G 31-8-1857.

998 KILBOURNE, Private Joseph

Born : Unknown
Enlisted :
Medals : Crimea (B.S)

Died : 1889
Status : Probably Rode in the Charge

Spink's Numismatic Circular February 19796 J.Kilburn 5th D. G. Crimea clasps B.I & S engraved naming.
DNW 22nd October 1997, Lot 20, Crimea 1854-55, 3 clasps, Balaklava, Inkermann, Sebastopol (Pte. J. Kilburn, 5th Dgn. Gds.) contemporary engraved naming, fitted with an attractive engraved ribbon buckle, very fine. Hammer Price £500

The musters show he was effective from the 1st October to the 31st December. Remarks state Servant.
Private Joseph Kilburn served throughout the Crimea as 'batman' to Lieutenant & Adjutant R. T. Godman, 5th Dragoon Guards, and is confirmed on the medal roll as a member of the Heavy Brigade at Balaklava. Kilburn is mentioned throughout Godman's Crimean letters which were published in 1977 under the title *The Fields of War*.
He features in a painting below by John Fearnley, at Newbridge Barracks, Ireland, 1852, holding Godman's charger 'The Earl' The horse served through the Crimea as Godman's charger, and after 19 years of faithful service was shot in 1869. Kilburn was photographed in the Crimea by Roger Fenton in April 1855, he is shown standing on the left see page 249. Godman's letters home do not even mention Fenton by name, with no recognition of the household name that he was destined to become:"The Photograph man has taken a picture of our camp, the officers and horses standing about, my hut does not come in well. He has also taken me and my horse (in fighting costume) and Kilburn, the latter likeness is excellent, when I can I will tell you where to go in London for copies, as many as you please at 5s each".Joseph Kilburn died in 1889 aged 61 years. Note Medal Roll spelt Kilbourne, musters spelt Kilburn.

1160 KIRKWOOD, Private Edward

Born : Unknown
Enlisted :
Medals : Crimea (B.S)

Died : Unknown
Status : Probably Rode in the Charge

The musters show he was effective from the 1st October to the 31st December.

633 LACEY, Private William

Born : Unknown
Enlisted :
Medals : Crimea (B.I.S)

Died : Unknown
Status : Probably Rode in the Charge

The musters show he was effective from the 1st October to the 31st December.

961 LAMB, Private James
Born : Unknown
Enlisted :
Medals : Crimea (B.I.S)

Died : Unknown
Status : Probably Rode in the Charge

The musters show he was effective from the 1st October to the 31st December. WO25 discharged 5th April1870

437 LAWRENCE, Private Robert
Born : Unknown
Enlisted :
Medals : Crimea (B.I.S)

Died : Unknown
Status : Probably Rode in the Charge

The musters show he was effective from the 1st October to the 31st December.

1111 LEAVERS, Private George Samuel
Born : Unknown
Enlisted :
Medals : Crimea (B.I.S)

Died : Unknown
Status : Probably Rode in the Charge

2004 Kaplan Auctions No B23, South Africa. Crimean Medal disk. Privately engraved in very neat serif capitals to "G. S. LAVERS 5th Dn. Gds." [for lower case read superscript] The rim of the medal is heavily contact-marked, and the naming is not entirely clear in some places. The hammer price was ZAR1120.00, cost £112.

The musters show he was effective from the 1st October to the 31st December.

Lavers appears on the medal roll as 1111 Private Leavers, Geo. Samuel, entitled to C/Bl (but obviously also S). There was a "George Samuel Leaver" who was Christened on 15th August, 1813, at St. Mary Magdalene, Woolwich, the son of William and Mary Leaver; he was born 26th July, 1813. If this is our man, he was getting on a bit for a Private in the Crimea.

Much more likely is the "George Samuel Lavers" who was Christened on 17th June, 1835, at The Higher Chapel (Independent/Congregational), Buckfastleigh, Devon, England, the son of George and Elizabeth Lavers. He was born 24th September, 1834. No WO97 papers seem to have survived.
Information supplied by Michael Hargreave Mawson.

746 LEE, Private John
Born : Date unknown - Kerry
Enlisted :
Medals : Crimea (S)

Died : 5th November 1854 - Balaclava
Status : Effective during the period

The musters show he was effective from the 1st October to the 5th November.

837 LEE, Private Patrick
Born : Unknown
Enlisted : 12th September 1841
Medals : Crimea (B.I.S)

Died : Unknown
Status : Probably Rode in the Charge

The musters show he was effective from the 1st October to the 31st December. Trade on enlistment Labourer.

976 LIVERSIDGE, Private James W.
Born : Yorkshire
Enlisted : 29th june 1847
Medals : Crimea (S)

Died : 30th April 1855 - Scutari
Status : Effective during the period

The musters show he was effective from the 1st October to the 20th December. Shown at Scutari during the 3rd muster.
An Iron Forger prior to enlistment. On the Musters surname spelt Liversedge.

777 MAGHER Private William

Born : 1821 - Limerick
Enlisted : 13th June 1842
Medals : Crimea (B.I.S)

Died : 5th February 1855 - Scutari
Status : Probably Rode in the Charge

DNW 28th March 2002, Medals from the collection of Gordon Everson, Lot 38, Crimea 1854-56, 3 clasps, Balaklava, Inkermann, Sebastopol (W. Magher, 5th Dn. Gds.) officially impressed naming, some edge bruising, therefore very fine. Hammer Price £1000

William Magher was born in Limerick in 1821, and enlisted for the 5th Dragoon Guards at Cahir on 13 June 1842, aged 21. He proceeded with the regiment to the Crimea in June 1854 and was present at Balaklava, Inkermann and Sebastopol. He died at Scutari on 5 February 1855.

The musters show he was effective from the 1st October to the 10th December. Shown at Scutari during the 3rd muster. Trade on enlistment Labourer.

757 MALONE, Private Edward

Born : 1826
Enlisted : January 1842
Medals : Crimea (B.S)

Died : 19th April 1901
Status : Severely wounded in the Charge

Sotheby's Auction July 1981. Edward Malone. 5th D.G. Crimea Clasp Balaclava only officially impressed naming. DNW 2nd April 2004, The collection of medals formed by the late John Darwent, Lot 161, Crimea 1854-56, 1 clasp, Balaklava (Edwd. Malone, 5th Dragn. Gds.), officially impressed naming, upper clasp lugs with remnants of old riveting, suspension claw slack, severe edge bruising and contact marks, otherwise about very fine. Hammer Price £1400

Edward Malone was born in Co. Clare and enlisted in the 5th Dragoon Guards at Limerick in January 1842, aged 18 years. According to his discharge papers, he was 'severely wounded at the Battle of Balaklava - lance and sabre wounds all over the body'. He received his Medal from Queen Victoria at Hyde Park on 15 May 1855, a 2 clasp award for 'Balaklava' and 'Sebastopol'. Malone was advanced to Corporal in September 1856 and was discharged at Dublin in May 1866. He died at Crewe in April 1901, aged 75 years.

The musters show he was effective from the 1st-31st October. Written across the entry is wounded 25th October sent to Scutari 31st October. WO100/24 page 102 Remarks: To England. Casualty Roll. Listed W/Sv at Balaklava.

Shrewsbury Chronicle June 15th 1855.
Edward Malone. 5th Dragoon Guards, with two good conduct stripes, standing 6 feet, 2 inches high, was on the memorable 25th Of October, 1854, in two charges, the first about 11 o clock in which a small body of dragoons charged through a large force of Russian cavalry, cutting their way back again. In this Malone escaped . Upon re-forming, the 1st, 2nd, 3rd, 4th, 5th and 6th Dragoons, charged several thousands of the enemy's cavalry. After this the men became a good deal scattered, and frequent instances of individual valour were conspicuous.

Gravestone reads: Of your charity pray for Corporal Edward Malone, Died April 19th 1901 aged 75 years.
Deceased soldier served for 25 years in the 5th Dragoon Guards went through the Crimean war and took part in the storming of Sebastapol and the famous "Balaklava Charge"

Extracts from the "Crewe Chronicle" dated the 27th April 1901:-
Death of a Balaclava Hero - A highly respected and old inhabitant of Crewe passed away on Friday evening, in the person of Mr Edward Malone, who resided at No 5 Castle Street, Crewe. The deceased was 75 years of age and came to Crewe to enter the employment of the L & N.W Railway Co. thirty years ago, remaining in their employ until within the last five years, when failing health necessitated his retirement from active duty. About a month ago the deceased was obliged to take to his bed, owing to an attack of paralysis, and he died as stated. Mr Malone was one of her Majesty's soldier's for 24 years and for nine years before leaving the service was a Corporal in the 5th Dragoon Guards.....where he took part in the famous Balaclava Charge, receiving no less than 17 wounds..... The remains of the deceased were interred in the cemetery on Monday afternoon and the service was conducted by the Revd. Canon Craig, vicar of St Mary's.
Information supplied by Paul Burns

1192 MARTIN, Corporal George
Born : Unknown
Enlisted :
Medals : Crimea (B.S)

Died : Unknown
Status : Probably Rode in the Charge

The musters show he was effective as a Private from the 1st October to the 4th November and as a Corporal from the 5th November to the 31st December. WO25 discharged as a sergeant 21st May 1857.

1185 MAY, Private Samuel
Born : Date Unknown - Nottingham
Enlisted : 18th February 1853
Medals : Crimea (B.I.S)

Died : 15th November 1854 - Crimea
Status : Probably Rode in the Charge

The musters show he was effective from the 1st October to the 15th November. Remarks state Died Crimea 15th November. WO100/24 page 86 Remarks: Died 15 Nov. 1854. WO100/24 page 102 Remarks: Dead. Trade on enlistment Labourer.

798 McANENY Private Philip
Born : Unknown
Enlisted :
Medals : Crimea (B.I.S)

Died : Unknown
Status : Probably Rode in the Charge

Christie's 24th April 1992, Lot 150, Crimea, 1854-55, three clasps, Balaklava, Inkermann, Sebastopol, lugs removed and acorn missing from last clasp (Pte. P. McEneny. 5th Dn Gds), contemporarily engraved, very fine. Private Philip McAneny clasp entitlement is confirmed-the 5th Dragoon Guards formed part of the Heavy Brigade. £200-250

The musters show he was effective from the 1st October to the 31st December. WO25 discharged 7th July 1868.

859 McCABE, Private John
Born : Unknown
Enlisted :
Medals : Crimea (B.S)

Died : Unknown
Status : Severely wounded in the Charge

The musters show he was effective from the 1st-31st October. Written across the entry is Wounded 25th October sent to Scutari 31st October.

C.R.: Listed W/Sv at Balaklava.
WO100/24 page 102 Remarks: To England.

In the portrait entitled "Queen Victoria's First Visit to her Wounded Soldier's" by Jerry Barret. McCabe can be seen sat down on the far left. In the Charge of the Heavy Brigade McCabe received ten lance wounds and three sabre cuts, besides having two horses shot from under him. The painting was sold at Christie's in March 1993, and can now be viewed at the National Portrait Gallery. The Queen visited Brompton Hospital, Chatham on March 3rd 1855.

794 McCABE, Private Mathew
Born : Unknown
Enlisted :
Medals : Crimea (B.I.S)

Died : Unknown
Status : Probably Rode in the Charge

The musters show he was effective from the 1st October to the 31st December. WO25 discharged 19th March 1867.

1239 McCREE, Private Edward
Born : Unknown
Enlisted :
Medals : Crimea (B.I.S)

Died : Unknown
Status : Probably Rode in the Charge

The musters show he was effective from the 1st October to the 10th December. At Scutari during the 3rd Muster.

McCULLOCH , Surgeon George
Born : 18th September 1819 - Glengarry House, Dublin
Enlisted :
Medals : Crimea (B.I.S)

Died : 31st October 1859
Status : Probably Rode in the Charge

The musters show he was effective from the 1st October to the 31st December. Musters WO 12-324. Supplied with rations from 17 Oct - 24 November 1854, 2nd and 3rd Musters marked "On Leave". 2 horses foraged at public expense. MD Glasgow 1843, Assistant Surgeon 54th Foot 6th June 1845. To 2nd Life Guards 4th July 1845, Surgeon 5th Dragoon Guards 15th August 1854, Staff Surgeon 2nd Class 17th August 1855. Half pay 10th September 1856.
He received his medal from the hand of the Queen on 18th May, 1855.

1125 McDONALD, Private James
Born : Unknown
Enlisted :
Medals : Crimea (B.I.S)

Died : Unknown
Status : Probably Rode in the Charge

The musters show he was effective from the 1st October to the 31st December.

1058 McGALL, Trumpeter John
Born : Unknown
Enlisted :
Medals : Crimea (B.I.S)

Died : Unknown
Status : Probably Rode in the Charge

The musters show he was effective from the 1st October to the 31st December. Regimental number shown as 1038.
Marginal note reads "From private 1st Oct vice Davidson"

617 McGREGOR, Sergeant James
Born : 1820
Enlisted :
Medals : Crimea (I.S)

Died : 8th February 1865
Status : Effective during the period

The musters show he was effective from the 1st October to the 30th November. At Scutari 25th Nov and 7th Dec 1854 Troop Sergeant Major J.McGregor 5th Dragoon Guards died at the Tower of London. (Yeoman Warder) on the 8th of February 1865. WO25 discharged 25th November 1862.'He wore the Crimea Medal with four clasps and the Turkish Crimea Medal, however, research suggests he was entitled only to Inkermann and Sebastopol...He was not awarded the Long Service and Good Conduct Medal as he was court martialled twice and had four other entries in the Defaulter's Book.[Ref McInnes, *The Yeoman of the Guard*, p. 37] He was a Yeoman Warder from 1862 until his death.

833 McILROY, Private John
Born : Unknown
Enlisted :
Medals : Crimea (B.I.S)

Died : Unknown
Status : Probably Rode in the Charge

The musters show he was effective from the 1st October to the 31st December.

924 McKEEGAN, Corporal Charles

Born : Unknown   Died : Unknown
Enlisted :   Status : Severely wounded in the Charge
Medals : Crimea (B.I.S), The Distinguished Conduct Medal

The musters show he was effective from the 1st October to the 31st December. Written across his entry is Wounded Balaclava 25th October. Remarks to Scutari. Casualty Roll: Listed W/Sv at Balaklava.
Crimean War Research Society Published a letter in "The War Correspondent, Volume 7, issue No1. April 1989, page 7. Written by "A Cpl Charles McKeggan" No regiment quoted. Letter in archives of Chester Military Museum and copy submitted by Helen Smith. C.R.: Listed W/Sv at Balaklava.
The Distinguished Conduct Medal. Recommended dated 21:1:55.

598 McLEAN, Private William

Born : Unknown   Died : Unknown
Enlisted :   Status : Effective during the period
Medals : Crimea (S)

The musters show he was effective from the 1st-31st October. Shown at Scutari during the 2nd and 3rd muster.

1021 McLUSKY Sergeant William

Born : Unknown   Died : 8th January 1882.
Enlisted : July 1829   Status : Probably Rode in the Charge
Medals : Crimea (B.I.S)

The musters show he was effective from the 1st October to the 31st December. WO100/24 page 99 Remarks: S on O/C Certificate.
History of the King's Body Guard of the Yeoman of the Guard by Hennell 1904. Page 251. Trumpet Major John McLuskey 5th Dragoon Guards. Enlisted July 1829. Served 24 years. Appointed Yeoman of the Guard 1859. Died 8th January 1882.
It is possible that John McCusky did not serve overseas.[Ref McInnes, *The Yeoman of the Guard*, p.135..]

743 McNAMARA, Private Michael

Born : Unknown   Died : Unknown
Enlisted :   Status : Rode in the Charge
Medals : Crimea (B.I.S) Distinguished Conduct Medal.

The musters show he was effective from the 1st October to the 31st December. He is mentioned in 1020 T.Gough's account of the charge.

The Distinguished Conduct Medal. Recommendation dated 21:1:55. Replacement ordered 9:12:57.

The History of the Present War with Russia by Henry Tyrell ,pages 333 and 334. The following letter is from a Corporal in the 5th Dragoon Guards, one of the regiments engaged in the battle of the 25th....The charge sounded and away we went into the midst of them ....my horse was shot he fell and got up again and I was entangled in the saddle....A Russian Lancer was going to run me through....MacNamara came up at the time and nearly severed his head from his body. So thank God I did not get a scratch.
Queen Victoria and Prince Albert met with the returning troops, and it was after one such visit to Woolwich Arsenal that the soldier's shown on the stamps were photographed.

"The Royal Collection © 2008, Her Majesty Queen Elizabeth II"

1065 MEAKIN, Private John
Born : Unknown
Enlisted :
Medals : Crimea (B.I.S)

Died : Unknown
Status : Probably Rode in the Charge

The musters show he was effective from the 1st October to the 31st December. WO25 invalided 8th November 1860.

818 MEALIAGH, Private John
Born : Unknown
Enlisted :
Medals : Crimea (B.S)

Died : Unknown
Status : Probably Rode in the Charge

The musters show he was effective from the 1st October to the 31st December.
There is no record of the medal awarded by this regiment's roll. *The Cavalry Division in the Crimea*, Andrew Sewell p65

613 MILLER, Private William
Born : Unknown
Enlisted :
Medals : Crimea (B.I.S)

Died : Unknown
Status : Probably Rode in the Charge

The musters show he was effective from the 1st October to the 31st December.

MONTGOMERY, Lieutenant Robert James
Born : Unknown
Enlisted :
Medals : Crimea (B.I.S)

Died : Unknown
Status : Probably Rode in the Charge

The musters show he was effective as a Lieutenant from the 1st October to the 31st December. Remarks state from Cornet 25th August 1854.
WO100/24 page 98 Remarks: from Cornet. Supplied with rations from 4th October 1854 to 30th December 1854 on board ship 1st - 3rd October 1854. Two horse's foraged at public expense.
From The Fields of War letter dated 7th December 1854, Camp near Balaklava, p103, Godman records that Montgomery is ill on board ship. FRom a letter dated 18th May 1855 "Montgomery and I had just arranged to try and get leave for ten days to go to Constantinople; he knows Lord Stratford very well, which is an advantage".
From a letter dated 29th July 1855 Cavalry Camp, Kadikoi. "Montgomery leaves today for England, having been sent home by a medical board".
Cornet by purchase 14th June 1850, Lieutenant 8th December 1854, Captain 29th July 1856.

1142 MOODIE, Private Walter
Born : Unknown
Enlisted :
Medals : Crimea (B.I.S), L.S.G.C Medal
DNW 18th September 1998, Lot 501, Three: Farrier Sergeant W. Moodie, 5th Dragoon Guards
Crimea 1854-56, 3 clasps, Inkermann, Balaklava, Sebastopol, unnamed, clasps mounted in this order; Army Long Service and Good Conduct, V.R., small letter reverse (1142 Far'r. Serjt. Wal'r. Moodie, 5th Dragoon Guards); Turkish Crimea 1855, Sardinian issue, contact marks and edge bruising, otherwise very fine (3) Hammer Price £410
Sold with 3 copied pages of Service Papers confirming medal and clasp entitlement.
The 5th Dragoon Guards charged with the Heavy Brigade at Balaclava. The same group of medals for sale: Eugene G.Ursual, Catalogue No 137, item No 9913 £580.
Spink Auction 22 November 2007 Lot 55 Turkish Crimea, Sardinian die (No1142. Pt.W. Moodie. 5th Dragoon Gds) Regimentally impressed.

Died : Unknown
Status : Probably Rode in the Charge

The musters show he was effective from the 1st October to the 31st December.
Medal information shows his rank as Farrier Sergeant.

The musters show he was effective from the 1st October to the 31st December.
WO102 L.S.G.C Medal awarded to Farrier Sergeant Moodie recommendation 13.4.1865, issued 30.6.1865 with £5 Gratuity.

816 MOORE, Farrier George
Born : Unknown
Enlisted :
Medals : Crimea (B.I.S)

Died : Unknown
Status : Probably Rode in the Charge

The musters show he was effective as a Private from the 1st October to the 31st December. WO25 invalided 9-6-1868

815 MOORE, Farrier Joseph
Born : Unknown
Enlisted :
Medals : Crimea (B.I.S)

Died : Unknown
Status : Probably Rode in the Charge

The musters show he was effective as a Private from the 1st October to the 31st December. WO25 F.Major died 4-9-74.

1041 MORLEY, Private Alfred
Born : Unknown
Enlisted :
Medals : Crimea (B.I.S)

Died : Unknown
Status : Probably Rode in the Charge

The musters show he was effective from the 1st October to the 31st December. WO25 discharged 13th February 1860.

641 MORLEY, Private Thomas
Born : Unknown
Enlisted :
Medals : Crimea (S)

Died : Unknown
Status : Effective during the period

The musters show he was effective from the 1st-31st October. Shown at Scutari during the 2nd and 3rd muster.

1039 MORRIS, Private William
Born : Unknown
Enlisted :
Medals : Crimea (B.S)

Died : Unknown
Status : Slightly wounded in the Charge

The musters show he was effective from the 1st-31st October. Remarks state wounded and sent to Scutari 31st October. Casualty List: W/Sl at Balaklava.

848 MORTON, Private Edward
Born : Unknown
Enlisted :
Medals : Crimea (B.I.S)

Died : Unknown
Status : Probably Rode in the Charge

The musters show he was effective from the 1st October to the 31st December. WO25 Chester J57.

1083 MULHOLLAND, Corporal Samuel
Born : Unknown
Enlisted :
Medals : Crimea (B.S)

Died : Unknown
Status : Probably Rode in the Charge

The musters show he was effective from the 1st October to the 31st December. WO25 discharged 28th June 1873.

1168 MURPHY, Private George
Born : Unknown
Enlisted :
Medals : Crimea (B.I.S)

Died : Unknown
Status : Probably Rode in the Charge

The musters show he was effective from the 1st October to the 31st December.

1116 MURPHY, Private Henry

Born : Unknown
Enlisted :
Medals : Crimea (B.I.S)

Died : Unknown
Status : Probably Rode in the Charge

The musters show he was effective from the 1st October to the 31st December. Something written across musters "Scutari See Cert 18th Dec 54" WO25 discharged 6th May 1873.

912 NAYLOR, Private Joseph

Born : 1824
Enlisted : 14th July 1846
Medals : Crimea (B.I.S),.L.S.G.C Medal

Died : 1901
Status : Probably Rode in the Charge

John Hayward's list July 1978. Corp. Joseph Naylor 5th D.G Turkish Crimea depot impressed.
For sale Ebay 4th June 2007: Victorian Turkish Crimea Medal, Sardinian issue with ring suspender, regimentally impressed to "No 912. Corp.Jos.Naylor 5th Dragoon Gds". VF. With complete service papers and census entries etc. Sold for £233.

The musters show he was effective from the 1st October to the 31st December.

Joseph Naylor, 5th Dragoon Guards was born at Hipperholme, Halifax and enlisted in the 5th Dragoon Guards at Leeds on 14th July 1846 and served a total of 24 years 294 days with the regiment, being discharged back in Leeds on 2 May 1871. He was present throughout the Crimea, being awarded the Crimea medal with clasps "Balaklava" "Inkermann" and "Sebastopol", in additon to the Long Service and Good Conduct medal. WO25 discharged 6th May 1873. Photograph courtesy of RDG Museum, York.

Private Joseph Naylor (1824-1901)
5th Dragoon Guards
who took part in the Heavy Brigade Actions at
the Battle of Balaclava in October 1854

NEVILLE, Cornet Hon. Grey

Born : Unknown
Enlisted :
Medals : Crimea (B.S)

Died : 11th November 1854 - Scutari.
Status : Severely wounded in the Charge

WO100/24 page 83 Remarks: Died of Wounds received in the Action of Balaklava 11 Nov. 54. WO100/24 page 98 Remarks: Died of Wounds rec'd in the Action.

Casualty Roll: Listed W/Sv at Balaklava.

Memoirs of the Brave p85:
NEVILLE (The Hon. Grey), of the 5th Dragoon Guards, Severely wounded at Balaklava, has since died. He was youngest son of the present Lord Braybrooke; grandson, maternally, of the second Marquis Cornwallis; and brother of the Hon. Captain Henry Aldworth Neville, who fell at Inkerman. These two gallant brothers, who have thus sacrificed their lives in their country's cause, were direct descendants of Sir Edward Neville, Lord Bergavenny, uncle of Richard Neville, Earl of Warwick, "The King Maker." (Sad to note he died on the same day that his brother was killed.)

Heroes of the Crimea by Michael Barthop, page 47: Among the 5th, Grey Neville went into the charge with a presentiment of his own death which had haunted him since the outbreak of war. He became separated from his troop and saw several Russian cavalrymen ride towards him. According to a friend, "he thought it was better to attempt to ride through them and rode with all his might against the centre of the party." The concussion knocked him off his horse and knocked his antagonist, horse and all, down, and, he thought, killed him. He was then on the ground and was wounded while there. He had one large wound and three others in his back. He lay still, with his face to the ground. He heard them moving away, and, thinking they were gone, raised his head to look, when a Russian dragoon [sic] dismounted and cut him with his sword over his head. His helmet saved his scalp but his right ear was cut into. Some cavalry rode over him and he felt dreadfully hurt by the horses' hooves.
Private Abbott, hearing his calls for help, dismounted and "lifted him from the ground and made him stand for a moment. He tried to walk but was so weak he could not and wanted to lie down again. The soldier would not leave him and ended finally by dragging him by bodily strength to a place of safety."
Neville's worst wound had broken a rib which pierced his chest, and his foreboding was realized 19 days later.

The Field of War page 76...."Neville being a bad rider, and too weak to use his sword well, was soon dismounted and had it not been for one of our men who stood over him, private Abbot, he would have been killed. He was wounded in the head and in three places in his back, and they fear that his liver is injured, in which case he cannot recover....
Franks Leaves from a Soldier's note book, page 71. Our regiment had one officer killed and two wounded.....the officer killed was the Hon. Grey Neville, a son of Lord Braybrook. He was a very promising young officer and was very popular in the 5th Dragoon Guards....see page 81 for further details.
Memorials of the Brave Appendix page 63. Neville. Hon. G. Cornet. 5th Dragoon guards. Date of arrival October 1854. Date of Death 11th November 1854. Remarks died of wounds at Scutari.

689 NICKLESS, Private John

Born : Unknown
Enlisted :
Medals : Crimea (S)

Died : Unknown
Status : Effective during the period

The musters show he was effective from the 1st-31st October. Shown at Scutari during the 2nd and 3rd muster.

1119 O'LEARY, Private David

Born : Unknown
Enlisted :
Medals : Crimea (B.I.S), L.S.G.C Medal

Died : Unknown
Status : Probably Rode in the Charge

The musters show he was effective from the 1st October to the 31st December.
WO102 L.S.G.C Medal awarded to Corporal O'Leary recommendation 7.7.1869, issued 10.9.1869 with £5 Gratuity.

773 O'TOOLE, Private Peter

Born : Unknown
Enlisted :
Medals : Crimea (B.I.S)

Died : Unknown
Status : Probably Rode in the Charge

The musters show he was effective from the 1st October to the 31st December.

493 ORR, Private James
Born : Unknown
Enlisted :
Medals : Crimea (B.S)

Died : Unknown
Status : Probably Rode in the Charge

The musters show he was effective from the 1st October to the 31st December. WO25 invalided 23rd August 1860.

1077 OWEN, Private James
Born : Unknown
Enlisted :
Medals : Crimea (B.I.S)

Died : Unknown
Status : Probably Rode in the Charge

The musters show he was effective as a Corporal from the 1st October to the 24th November and as a Private from the 25th November to the 31st December. Remarks state to Private 25th November. WO25 Discharged in 1856.

909 PARTRIDGE, Sergeant Samuel
Born : Unknown
Enlisted :
Medals : Crimea (B.I.S)

Died : Unknown
Status : Probably Rode in the Charge

Midlands Medals Catalogue 1977. 5th Dragoon Guards Partridge, C.S Engraved naming. Rank and name almost obliterated due to contact wear. The medal has heavy contact marks on the obverse and reverse. Three bars B.I.S Fine £125.
Romsey Medals 1986 item 90. Crimea 3 clasps Balaklava, Inkermann, Sebastopol. Impressed Samuel Partridge 5th Dragoons and 5th Lancers. Photocopies of documents. Name is clear, but rank and Regiment worn. Fine only £220.

The musters show he was effective from the 1st October to the 31st December. Marginal note reads: from pte 1st October 1854.

1113 PENKEYMAN, Private William
Born : Unknown
Enlisted :
Medals : Crimea (B.I.S)

Died : Unknown
Status : Probably Rode in the Charge

The musters show he was effective from the 1st October to the 31st December.

In the 1881 census the only Penkyman listed in the age range is William Penkyman, cab driver. living at 36 Rothwell Street. Everton, Liverpool. Born 1830. Married to Ann age 45. Living with them Thomas there 12 year old son, and a lodger. WO25 Cabdriver, Liverpool discharged 1856.

525 PERRY, Corporal William
Born : Date Unknown - Birmingham
Enlisted : 24th May 1837
Medals : Crimea (B.I.S)

Died : 10th November 1854 - Crimea
Status : Probably Rode in the Charge

The musters show he was effective from the 1st October to the 10th November.
Remarks state Died Crimea 10th November. WO100/24 page 83 Remarks: Died 10th. November 1854.
WO100/24 page 99 Remarks: Dead.
Trade on enlistment Brass Caster.

962 PLANT, Sergeant Edward
Born : Unknown
Enlisted :
Medals : Crimea (B.I.S)

Died : Unknown
Status : Probably Rode in the Charge

The musters show he was effective from the 1st October to the 31st December. Marginal note reads"From Corp 1st October 1854"

1152 PLUMPTON, Private Moses

Born : Unknown
Enlisted :
Medals : Crimea (B.I.S)

Died : Unknown
Status : Rode in the Charge

The musters show he was effective from the 1st October to the 31st December.

Leaves from a Soldier's Notebook by Henry Franks, p77, states he was in support with Franks during the Light Brigade Charge. His horse was killed along with six others by a single shell, none of the riders being injured, Plumpton being covered by the dead horses had to be released by other soldier's.

808 POLE, Private John

Born : Unknown
Enlisted :
Medals : Crimea (B.I.S)

Died : Unknown
Status : Probably Rode in the Charge

The musters show he was effective from the 1st October to the 31st December.

640 PORTER, Private Robert

Born : Unknown
Enlisted : 29th April 1839
Medals : Crimea (S)

Died : Unknown
Status : Effective during the period

Glendenings 24th June 1992, Lot 132, a 4 bar Crimea medal, Alma, Balaklava, Inkermann, Sebastopol, (R. Porter, 5th Dragoon Gds.) impressed naming, very fine.
The medal roll does not list bar entitlement and has "W.O" entered alongside the column headed "Medal". In the "Remarks" column the following is noted: "Died 7th Nov. 1854. On 361692/8 the date of birth does not agree with that given on the slip". The 5th Dragoon Gds were not present at Alma.

Form 20 of the musters states Porter was killed in action, does not state any date. The musters show that he was effective from the 1st October to the 31st October. It would appear from this he met his demise after the the 31st October.

Shown on the Inkermann medal roll (86) as having died on the 1st November, however other dates have been recorded. A Frame Wool Knitter prior to enlistment.

1069 PRICE, Private James

Born : Unknown
Enlisted :
Medals : Crimea (B.I.S)

Died : Unknown
Status : Probably Rode in the Charge

The musters show he was effective from the 1st October to the 31st December.
WO102 L.S.G.C Medal recommendation Corporal Price 2.11.1869, issued 26.1.1870. WO25 discharged 29th Oct. 1873.

1133 PRINCE, Private James

Born : Unknown
Enlisted :
Medals : Crimea (B.I.S)

Died : Unknown
Status : Probably Rode in the Charge

The musters show he was effective from the 1st October to the 31st December. WO25 Chester D/56.

1004 RAMSBOTTOM, Private Thomas

Born : Unknown
Enlisted :
Medals : Crimea (B.I.S)

Died : Unknown
Status : Probably Rode in the Charge

Spink's Numismatic Circular March 1979, T. Ramsbottom. 5th Dragoon Guards. Crimea clasps B.I & S engraved.

The musters show he was effective from the 1st October to the 31st December. Regimental number shown as 1005. WO25 Regimental No 1004, shwn discharged 28th February 1860.

1080 REAZLER, Private John
Born : Unknown
Enlisted :
Medals . Crimea (B.I.S)
Died : Unknown
Status : Probably Rode in the Charge

The musters show he was effective from the 1st October to the 31st December. WO25 to 7 D.G P57.

487 REID, Private James
Born : Unknown
Enlisted :
Medals : Crimea (B.I.S), The Distinguished Conduct Medal, L.S.G.C Medal
Died : Unknown
Status : Probably Rode in the Charge

The musters show he was effective from the 1st October to the 31st December.
The Distinguished Conduct Medal. Recommendation dated 21:1:55.
WO102 L.S.G.C Medal awarded to Sergeant Reid recommendation 10.5.1869, issued 26.7.1869 with £5 Gratuity.

903 REID, Private Mark
Born : Date Unknown - Malta
Enlisted : 1st June 184?
Medals : Crimea (B.I.S)
Died : 12th November 1854 - Crimea
Status : Probably Rode in the Charge

The musters show he was effective from the 1st October to the 12th November. Remarks state died Crimea 12th November.
WO100/24 page 86 Remarks: Died 12 Nov:1854. WO100/24 page 103 Remarks: Dead.
Trade on enlistment Joiner.

1118 REILLY, Private Mathew
Born : Unknown
Enlisted :
Medals : Crimea (B.I.S)
Died : Unknown
Status : Probably Rode in the Charge

The musters show he was effective from the 1st October to the 31st December. Written across his entry is the following
"Transferred?? off board Bombay to Himalaya 21st October.

1015 REYNER, Corporal Henry
Born : Unknown
Enlisted :
Medals : Crimea (B.I.S)
Died : Unknown
Status : Probably Rode in the Charge

The musters show he was effective from the 1st October to the 31st December.
WO102 L.S.G.C Medal recommendation 16.10.1869, issued 6.11.1869. WO25 Discharged 30th November 1869.

944 RICHARDS, Private Hiram
Born : Unknown
Enlisted :
Medals : Crimea (B.I.S)
For sale A.H Baldwin and Sons Ltd July 1948. A three bar impressed Crimea B.I.S in a fair state £1.15s
Died : Unknown
Status : Probably Rode in the Charge

The musters show he was effective from the 1st October to the 31st December.

989 RINGER, Private Benjamin
Born : Unknown
Enlisted :
Medals : Crimea (B.I.S)
Died : Unknown
Status : Probably Rode in the Charge

The musters show he was effective from the 1st October to the 31st December.

1071 ROBERTS, Private George
Born : Unknown
Enlisted :
Medals : Crimea (B.I.S)

Died : Unknown
Status : Probably Rode in the Charge

Spink's Numismatic Circular May 1978, G. Roberts. 5th D G. Crimea clasps B.I & S impressed naming.

The musters show he was effective from the 1st October to the 31st December.

1145 ROBERTSON, Private William
Born : Unknown
Enlisted :
Medals : Crimea (B.I.S), L.S.G.C Medal

Died : Unknown
Status : Probably Rode in the Charge

The musters show he was effective from the 1st October to the 31st December.
WO102 L.S.G.C Medal recommendation 14.3.1868, issued 20.4.1868.

992 ROWAN, Private Charles
Born : Unknown
Enlisted :
Medals : Crimea (B.I.S)

Died : Unknown
Status : Probably Rode in the Charge

The musters show he was effective from the 1st October to the 31st December. WO25 Discharged 2nd August 1856.

553 RUSSELL, Troop Sergeant-Major James
Born : 1819
Enlisted : 30th October 1837
Medals : Crimea (B.I.S), The French Medaille Militaire.

Died : Unknown
Status : Rode in the Charge

The musters show he was effective from the 1st October to the 31st December.
Acting Regimental Sergeant-Major J. Russell. The French Medaille Militaire. (He) served during the whole Eastern Campaign from May, 1854, until the end of the war, and was never absent from his duty a single day; he was present at the Battle of Balaklava, on which occasion he had his horse killed under him, but procured for himself a second horse, and immediately rejoined the regiment; he was also present at Inkermann".

Leaves from a Soldier's Notebook by Henry Franks, p76. (Heavy Brigade Advance with Light Brigade) Three of us were riding close together - Troop Sgt Major Russell on the right, myself in the centre, and Trumpeter Baker on the left of the three. We were moving at a trot, when a shell from the Russians dropped and exploded close under the three Horses. The whole of the contents of the shell seemed to have entered into the body of Russells horse and literally shattered him to pieces. Russel was shot over the Horse's head and was on his feet again in a moment none the worse for his sudden flight. The shock of the shell exploding actually lifted both my horse (Franks) and Baker's off their feet, but that was all the injury we sustained. Russell caught hold of my right foot stirrup and ran along for a few yards, until he caught a horse that had lost its rider, and then joined us again.....
WO12/315 date of enlistment 30th October 1837 at Glasgow, age 18, Bounty paid to recruit £2.2.0
WO25 R.S.M to 2nd Dragoon Guards September 1858. Appointed Riding Master 24th September 1858.

880 RUSSELL, Private James
Born : Unknown
Enlisted :
Medals : Crimea (B.S)

Died : Unknown
Status : Probably Rode in the Charge

There is no entry for the award of the medal on this regiment's roll. Also unable to find on the musters.
WO25 discharged June 1861

675 SANDHAM, Private George
Born : Unknown
Enlisted :
Medals : Crimea (B.I.S)

Died : Unknown
Status : Probably Rode in the Charge

The musters show he was effective from the 1st October to the 31st December.

Koulali and Abydos Hospitals

Scutari was not the only hospital in use. In January 1855 the Turkish Cavalry Barracks at Koulali was turned into a hospital. On the arrival of a team of nurses under the supervision of Mary Stanley, they found no beds or food. Shortly after their arrival three hundred wounded were bought in, sacks were hastily found and filled with straw. Also Abydos was used as a small convalescent hospital and "was most probably used in the main as a staging post for invalided patients awaiting transport home." (*The Crimean Doctors: A History of the British Medical Services in the Crimea*)

From *Eastern Hospitals and English Nurses* : "Koulali is about five miles north of Scutari... built on the banks of the Bosphorus, a few yards from the quay; the depth of water allows steamers to come alongside, therefore its facility for landing the sick is very great. The hospital is a square red building, three stories high in front, very much smaller than Scutari, but a large building nevertheless...

In the hospitals of Koulali there were then very few wounded. The wounded of Alma and Inkermann had either recovered or died. It was the sick from the trenches who poured down upon us. Fever, dysentery, diarrhoea, and frost-bite, were our four principal diseases... The wards of Koulali hospital were classified: No.2 surgical, No.3 fever, No.4 dysentery, No.5 diarrhoea, No.6 dysentery. Every ward was full."

At Koulali, the worst of all the hospitals, in February 1855, the mortality was 52 per cent, on all the cases treated in Hospital during the month!

In other words, had the rate of mortality at Koulali continued,- in two months, the troops in Hospital there would have been swept away. *(Florence Nightingale: Measuring Hospital Care Outcomes)*

Koulali Hospital

1680 SANDS, Private Richard

Born : Unknown
Enlisted :
Medals : Crimea (B.I.S)

Died : 1906 - Bristol
Status : Probably Rode in the Charge

Sotheby's June 1970. Pte Richard Sands. 5th D.G. Crimea clasps B.I.S (impressed naming) L.S &G.C Medal "680, 5th Dn. Gds." Also a letter signed on behalf of Florence Nightingale dated at Scutari Barracks, 23 November 1854 and referring to Sand's illness and the plight of his wife. Sands was at one time servant to Ass. Sgn Cattrell 5th Dragoons, and is mentioned in his memoirs.

The musters show he was effective from the 1st October to the 31st December.
The Crimea and Indian Mutiny Veterans Association 1892-1912, p79. Records Richard Sands of 5th Dragoon Guards as a member and states that he died at Bristol in 1906.

927 SCOTT, Private Arthur

Born : Unknown
Enlisted :
Medals : Crimea (B.I.S)

Died : Unknown
Status : Probably Rode in the Charge

The musters show he was effective from the 1st October to the 31st December. WO25 discharged 13th August 1867.

931 SCOTT, Private William

Born : Unknown
Enlisted : 23rd September 1846
Medals : Crimea (B.I.S), L.S.G.C Medal

Died : 21 January 1905
Status : Rode in the Charge

Group of three medals. Crimea Medal B.I.S , Turkish Crimea & Long Service Good Conduct Medal named to 931 William Scott-5th Dragoon Guards. Medals in the collection of John T.M.Reilly.

The musters show he was effective from the 1st October to the 31st December. Third muster endorsed Scutari.
WO102 L.S.G.C Medal recommendation 16.6.1868, issued 15.8.1868 with £5 Gratuity.

Mr John T.M.Reilly from Douglaston, New York sent a letter dated 31 Jan 1978 to Canon Lummis. Asking for information on William Scott. Reply :"I have a photo-copy of Pte Scott's service record and this shows that he enlisted 23 Sept 1846, discharged 11 July 1871. The service record also lists under wounds that he received a sabre cut on the right side of his nose at the Battle of Balaclava.....I do know that Pte Scott died on 21 Jan 1905. WO25 discharged 11th July 1871.

409 SHEGOG Sergeant James
Born : 1811 - County Monaghan, North of Ireland
Enlisted : 21st December 1834
Medals : Crimea (B.I.S), Distinguished Conduct Medal

Died : 24th April 1896 - Tasmania
Status : Rode in the Charge

The musters show he was effective from the 1st October to the 24th November and from 8th-31st December. Remarks state Scutari 25th November - 7th December.

Obituary in *'The Launceston Examiner'* (Monday 27th April 1896)
"On Friday last there passed away at the ripe old age of 85 a Crimea veteran of no mean distinction in the person of Sergeant-Major James Shegog, late of the 5th Dragoon Guards, whose death took place at Glen, near Lefroy, where he had lived since his arrival in this colony. It is not given to many men to hold such a record for distinguished service in the field as was possessed by the late Sergeant-Major. Born in County Monaghan, North of Ireland, in the year 1811, he served five years in the Royal Irish Constabulary, after which he enlisted in the 5th Dragoon Guards on December 21, 1834 and served in that celebrated regiment 21 years and 103 days, securing his discharge on March 22, 1856. At the outbreak of the Crimean war in 1854 Mr. Shegog had completed service sufficient to entitle him to his discharge, but he volunteered to go out with his regiment to the Crimea, being at that time the rough riding sergeant-major. On arrival at the seat of war he was appointed orderly to General Sir Yorke Scarlett and is several times referred to by Mr. A. W. Kinglake in his 'Invasion of the Crimea.' This writer says that he "had attained to high skill as a swordsman and was a valorous, faithful soldier". At the charge of the Heavy Brigade on that ever to be remembered 25th October, 1854, which took place just prior to that of the Light Brigade Sergeant-Major Shegog was at the head of the brigade in attendance on Sir James Yorke Scarlett, who, accompanied by his aide-de-camp, Lieutenant Elliott, and Bugler Baker, rode in front of his troops and, having in the excitement of the charge outpaced the brigade, these four men rode at a mass of cavalry many thousands strong, and were completely engulfed in the Russian columns. "Of course," says Kinglake," the incursion of the brigadier and the three horsemen with him had more of the 'forlorn hope' that could belong to the enterprise of the squadrons which followed him into the columns; but, upon the whole, these combats of Scarlett's and his aide-de-camp were more or less samples of that war of the one against several which each of the 'three hundred' waged. They cut their way in and they cut their way out." As mentioned previously Sergt.-Major Shegog secured his discharge at the close of the war, and became troop sergt.-major of the Staffordshire yeomanry cavalry, which position he held for 11 years, when he retired from the service altogether. In 1880 he came to Tasmania where he has resided since; it certainly seems strange that a man who has made himself so famous in history should have resided here so long and yet so few knew it. The deceased was recommended for the Victoria Cross by Sir Yorke Scarlett, but was not fortunate enough to receive it. He, however, obtained the medal 'for distinguished conduct in the field' which carried with it an annuity of £20; the Crimean Medal, with clasps for Sebastopol, Inkermann and Balaclava; and also the Turkish Medal. After retiring from active service he made application to be appointed a Yeoman of the Guard but was regretfully refused on account of having exceeded the stipulated age. It has been suggested that a military funeral should be tendered the deceased. Strictly speaking, this is an honour he is not entitled to, but seeing it is so seldom that the members of the Tasmania Defence Force have an opportunity of paying this tribute of respect to so distinguished a soldier it would have been a graceful act to have availed themselves of it when one was offered them." Information supplied by Derek Pardoe.

1205 SIMPSON, Private James
Born : Unknown
Enlisted :
Medals : Crimea (B.I.S)

Died : Unknown
Status : Probably Rode in the Charge

The musters show he was effective from the 1st October to the 31st December.

754 SKIFFINGTON, Private Hugh
Born : Unknown
Enlisted :
Medals : Crimea (B.I.S)

Died : Unknown
Status : Probably Rode in the Charge

The musters show he was effective from the 1st October to the 31st December. WO25 discharged May 1857.

913 SMITH, Private William
Born : Unknown
Enlisted :
Medals : Crimea (B.I.S)

Died : Unknown
Status : Probably Rode in the Charge

The musters show he was effective from the 1st October to the 31st December. WO25 discharged 9th February 1869.

Lieutenant Elliot

"A particularly vicious-looking Russian trooper with a large blue nose and savage glittering eye managed to strike Lieutenant Elliot on the forehead, while at the same time another divided his face with a deep slashing wound. Hacked at and struck at again and again, and by this time completely dazed, he nevertheless managed miraculously to leave the melee still in the saddle. It is strange that although wounded fourteen times, he was returned in despatches later as only "slightly wounded"
Kinglake, A.W. The invasion of the Crimea, 8 vols. (London 1868)
For addition information on Lieutenant Elliot please see page 24

932 SMOUT, Private Richard

Born : Unknown
Enlisted :
Medals : Crimea (B.I.S)

Died : Unknown
Status : Probably Rode in the Charge

The musters show he was effective from the 1st October to the 31st December. WO25 discharged 6th May 1873.

956 SPIRIT, Private Isaac

Born : Unknown
Enlisted :
Medals : Crimea (B.I.S)

Died : Unknown
Status : Probably Rode in the Charge

Sotheby 7th November 1985, Lot 560. Crimea Medal 3 clasps. Balaklava, Inkermann, Sebastopol. Isaac Spirit 5th D.G Engraved in a contemporary style. Some contact wear and polished. Good Fine or better. Sold with confirmation. Est £180-£220.
Capital Medals February 1986. Isaac Spirit 5th D.G Crimea 3 clasps, A.B. and S Upright engraved capitals. Said to be confirmed Heavy Brigade Charger.

The musters show he was effective from the 1st October to the 31st December.

1230 STATHER, Private Joel

Born : Unknown
Enlisted :
Medals : Crimea (B.I.S)

Died : Unknown
Status : Probably Rode in the Charge

The musters show he was effective from the 1st October to the 31st December.

878 STEAD, Private Michael

Born : Unknown
Enlisted :
Medals : Crimea (B.I.S)

Died : Unknown
Status : Probably Rode in the Charge

The musters show he was effective from the 1st October to the 31st December. WO25 to 7th D.G June1857.

1000 STEPHENSON, Private John

Born : Unknown
Enlisted :
Medals : Crimea (B.I.S)

Died : Unknown
Status : Probably Rode in the Charge

The musters show he was effective from the 1st October to the 31st December. WO25 discharged 2nd February 1860

1124 STERRETT, Private Joseph

Born : Unknown
Enlisted :
Medals : Crimea (B.I.S)

Died : Unknown
Status : Probably Rode in the Charge

The musters show he was effective from the 1st October to the 10th December. Paid from 1st October 1854 to 10th December 1854. 71 days, 11 days on board ship, 60 on land 3rd Muster endorsed Scutari. WO25 Desert 26th April 1860.

555 STEWART, Troop Sergeant-Major William

Born : 1814 - Perthshire   Died : 28th July 1859
Enlisted : 16th November 1837   Status : Rode in the Charge
Medals : Crimea (B.I.S) French Medaille Militaire, L.S. G.C Medal

An extremely rare Heavy Brigade French Medaille Militaire group of four awarded to Troop Sergeant-Major W. F. Stewart, 5th Dragoon Guards, who had three horses killed under him in the famous engagement at Balaklava.
The collection of medals formed by the late John Darwent

DNW Auction 2nd April 2004. Lot No 165 Crimea 1854-56, 3 clasps, Balaklava, Inkermann, Sebastopol (Troop S.M. W. F. Stewart, 5th Dn. Gds.), contemporary engraved naming, with attractive Royal Coat of Arms riband device; Army L.S. & G.C., V.R., large letter reverse (5555 Tp.-Sjt.-Mjr. W. Steward, 5th Dragn. Gds.), officially impressed naming; France, Medaille Militaire, silver, gilt and enamel, fitted with hinge-bar suspension and attractive French Eagle riband device; Turkish Crimea 1855, Sardinian issue (No. 555 T.S.M. W. Stewart, 5th Dragoon Gds.), regimentally impressed naming, with attractive Royal Coat of Arms riband device, note slight variations in name, number and initials, the third with badly chipped enamel, edge bruising, otherwise generally very fine (4) Hammer Price: £8800

William Fife Stewart was born in Perthshire and enlisted in the 5th Dragoon Guards at Glasgow in November 1837. Aged 23 years, he stood at over 6ft., an impressive height for the age. Advanced to Corporal in September 1847 and to Sergeant in June 1852, he embarked at Queenstown in the S.S. Himilaya in May 1854, arriving at Varna, Turkey a week or two later. And in September of the same year, shortly before the Battle of Balaklava, he was advanced to Troop Sergeant-Major. Carter gives the following citation in respect of Stewart's award of the French Medaille Militaire:

'Troop Sergeant-Major William Stewart served in the Eastern Campaign from May 1854 until the end of the War and was present at the Battle of Balaklava, on which occasion he had two horses killed under him but still continued to act, procuring a third horse and remaining in the action with his Regiment. He was present at Inkermann and never absent from his duty a single day throughout the War.'

In point of fact, or certainly according to an eye-witness in the form of Troop Sergeant-Major Franks, also of the 5th, Stewart actually had three horses killed under him that fateful day:

' ... We had a Troop Sergeant-Major named William Stewart, who had no less than three horses shot that day. The first one was by a rifle bullet. Stewart caught another horse belonging to the 4th Dragoon Guards, and he had hardly got mounted when a shell burst under him and blew him up. Stewart escaped without a scratch and managed to catch another loose horse which he rode for a while, until a cannon ball broke one of the horse's legs. Stewart, who was still without a scratch, took pity on the poor dumb brute and shot him. He then procured yet another horse, which made the fourth he had ridden that day. Very few men, I should say, have had such an experience as this and all within an hour ...' (Leaves from a Soldier's Note Book refers)

Undoubtedly it was just such accounts of his bravery that resulted in Stewart being among those Crimea veterans to have their photographs taken at the request of Queen Victoria - probably in his case at Aldershot in May 1856. Sadly, Stewart died at Brighton in July 1859, while on sick furlough, and - as would prove to be the case with his French decoration - his Army L.S. & G.C. was awarded posthumously in the following month.

Sold with original French Medaille Militaire certificate and letter of notification, both dated March 1861, together with two old handwritten translations, the former erroneously inscribed to the 6th Dragoons, and fragments of original ribbons.

Photograph "The Royal Collection © 2008,
Her Majesty Queen Elizabeth II"

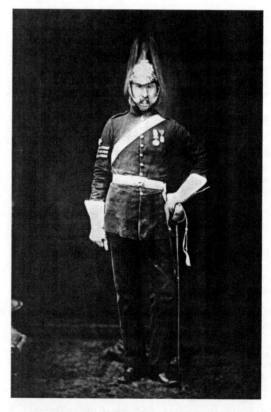

S-M William Stewart taken at Aldershot in July 1856.

The French Medaille Militaire. (He) served in the Eastern Campaign from May, 1854, until the end of the war; was present at the battle of Balaklava, on which occasion he had two horses killed under him, but still continued to act, procuring a third horse, and remaining in action with his regiment; was present at Inkermann, and never absent from his duty a single day throughout the war".

United Services Gazette 5th August 1859 - TSM William Stewart of the 5th Dragoons who lately came on sick furlo, died on Thursday last from the effects of illness contracted by his service in the Crimea, he belonged to the Heavy Brigade and at the battle of Balaclava had two horses shot from under him.

French   Empire

Military medal

Mr William Stewart Sergeant Major in the 5th Regiment of Dragoon Guards, is informed that by a decree of the 6th of March 1861, issued on the proposal of the Secretary of State. Minister of the War Department The Emperor has conferred upon him the Military Medal Communication of this decree has been sent to His Excellence The Great Chancellor of the Legion of Honor, for him to insure the execution of it in as far as he is concerned.

1228 STEWART, Sergeant William

Born : Unknown
Enlisted :
Medals : Crimea (B.I.S)

Died : Unknown
Status : Probably Rode in the Charge

The musters show he was effective as a Private from the 1st October to the 26th November and as a Saddler Sergeant from the 27th November to the 31st December. Remarks state from Private 27th November. WO100/24 page 99 Remarks: From Private. WO25 Saddle Sergt. Comp 5th November 1876.

SWINFEN, Captain Frederick Hay

Born : Unknown
Enlisted :
Medals : Crimea (B.S)

Died : 22nd June 1914
Status : Slightly wounded in the Charge

A fraudulently impressed Crimea medal, named to this officer was produced by Messrs Fletcher and Davies in 1976. In 1984 the medal was in possession of G. Taylor Manchester. (Darwent Archive)

Christie's 24th July 1990, Lot 208, A family group - A Heavy Brigade Group of Three To Lieutenant Colonel F. H. Swinfen, 5th. Dragoon Guards, Crimea, two clasps, Balaklava, Sebastopol (Captn.), engraved, one top lug lacking, severe edge bruise, contact marks, fine; Jubilee 1897; Turkish Crimea, a "fine quality" contemporary copy of the Sardinian Issue, nearly very fine, together with an original copy of The Times, 13th., November, 1854, detailing "The attack on Balaklava"; newspaper cutting relating to recipient's funeral.

WATERLOO, 1815, a fine quality silver miniature, edge inscribed "Captn Swinfen/Queen's Lancers"; two St. Helena Medal miniatures by Kretly, Palais Royal, good very fine, and an original copy of The Times, 22nd. June, 1815, with details of the Battle of Waterloo (6).

Lieutenant Colonel Frederick Hay Swinfen, entered the 5th. Regiment of Dragoon Guards as a Cornet, 1849; Lieutenant 1850; Captain 1854; served in the Eastern Campaign and was present at the Battle of Balaklava, 25th. October, 1854 (wounded; Casualty Roll for the Crimea-Hayward refers). Former Commanding Officer of the 5th Dragoon Guards, wounded during the Charge of the Heavy Brigade at Balaklava.

Served at the siege of Sebastopol; was presented with his Crimea Medal by Queen Victoria at the Horse Guards (original cutting from The London Illustrated News, 26th. May, 1855, sold with the group refers); Lieutenant Colonel 1869; placed on half pay, 1871; Colonel Swinfen later became the senior Military Knight of Windsor.

Lieutenant Francis Swinfen served with the 16th. Light Dragoons at the Battle of Waterloo, 18th. June, 1815; died, 1839. estimate £400-450 Hammer price £715

A group of four to Col. F.H. Swinfen, are held in the Barney Mattingly collection (USA).
1897 Jubilee Medal, 1902 Coronation Medal, Crimea Medal, 2 clasps, Balaklava, Sebastopol, (engraved Captn. Swinfen, 5 Dragn. Gds.), Turkish Crimea Medal, British issue (engraved Captn. Swinfen. 5th Dragn. Gds.). Swing mounted. Photograph on page 281.

The musters show he was effective from the 1st October to the 31st December. Remarks state Wounded 25th October. Shown on leave 2nd and 3rd Musters 1st November to the 31st December. Casualty Roll: Listed W/Sl at Balaklava. He received his medal from the hand of the Queen on 18th May, 1855.

The Fields of War, edited by Philip Warner. Letter dated the 7th December 1854. Swinfen had recovered from his wounds, (Cut in the hand, and a lance wound in the chest) but was now very ill at Scutari.
2nd January 1855 - also comments on the fact that Swinfen would sell out if given the opportunity,
6th January 1855 - reported that he was sick in Malta.

Frederick Hay Swinfen was born on 15 January 1830 and purchased his commission into the 5th Dragoon Guards on 10 April 1849. He served with the regiment during the Charge of the Heavy Brigade. Swinfen was shipped home to England early and received his Crimea Medal from Queen Victoria during a special parade on 18 May 1855.

Swinfen remained with the regiment throughout his entire service, eventually commanding the regiment from 1869 to 1871. Swinfen was prematurely forced to sell his commission in 1871 due to the financial hardships resulting from a lawsuit described in the book, The Great Swinfen Case. As a result, Swinfen lost the entire family estate.

In Swinfen v Swinfen an action to establish whether the late Samuel Swinfen was of sound mind and capable of making his will. The plaintiff, Patience Swinfen, was the widow of Henry Swinfen, only son of the testator, who died a short time before his father. The defendant Frederick Hay Swinfen was the eldest son of the testator's half brother, and he also claimed the estate.

The final straw, seems to have been a court case involving Mrs Swinfen and a disputed will. Mr Kennedy a barrister had become her advisor from May 1850. The case had been protracted but he carried the litigation to a successful conclusion.

On the 26th March 1862 he brought an action against her for £20,000 for the services rendered. Complications arose because a barrister could not sue for his fees, but he did hold the deed to the Swinfen Hall estates in Staffordshire.

Eventually the estate was sold to pay off all the debts.

Appointed a Military Knight of Windsor in 1893. The Military Knights of Windsor claim to be the oldest military establishment in the Army List. Known as the Alms Knights, they formed part of the College of St George which was created to support the establishment of the Most Honourable and Noble Order of the Garter. He remained in residence at Windsor until his death on 22 June 1914.

1st DRAGOONS : Pte Charles Middleton, Pte Thomas Shore
2nd NORTH BRITISH DRAGOONS : Pte Henry Campbell, Corporal A.P. Clifford
4th DRAGOON GUARDS : Pte Thomas Ryan
5th DRAGOON GUARDS : Pte Bernard Callery, Corporal James Taylor
6th DRAGOONS : Pte Robert Elliot, Pte Alexander Latimer

1234 SYKES, Private James
Born : Unknown
Enlisted :
Medals : Crimea (B.I.S)

Died : Unknown
Status : Probably Rode in the Charge

The musters show he was effective from the 1st October to the 31st December.

654 TAGG, Private Joseph
Born : Unknown
Enlisted : 15th June 1839
Medals : Crimea (B.I.S), L.S.G.C Medal

Died : Unknown
Status : Probably Rode in the Charge

DNW 2nd April 2004, The collection of medals formed by the late John Darwent, Lot 164, Three: Private J. Tagg, 5th Dragoon Guards. Crimea 1854-56, 3 clasps, Balaklava, Inkermann, Sebastopol (5th Dragoon Guards), contemporary engraved naming; Army L.S. & G.C., V.R., 3rd issue, small letter reverse (654, 5th Dragn. Gds.), officially impressed naming; Turkish Crimea 1855, British issue (No. 654 Pt., 5th Dragoon Gds.), regimentally impressed naming, edge bruising and contact marks, otherwise generally about very fine (3) Hammer Price £1200

The musters show he was effective from the 1st October to the 31st December.
Joseph Tagg was born near Nottingham and enlisted in the 5th Dragoon Guards in June 1839, aged 17 years. In his subsequent career of nearly 25 years with the Colours, he served for two years out in the Crimea and was entitled to the Medal with clasps for 'Balaklava', 'Inkermann' and 'Sebastopol', in addition to the Turkish Medal.

WO97-1301. He gave his intended place of residence as Burton Joyce, Nottingham, and he turns up there in an abode at Martin's Yard in the 1881 census, being described as an unmarried 58 year old 'Army pensioner'.   In possession of five good conduct badges, LS & GC, with Gratuity. Been entered in the Regimental defaulters book 19 times, never tried by court martial. Appeared before a Regimental Board at Cahir, Ireland on the 7th September 1863 for discharge purposes, was at the time illiterate signing documents with a cross. His statement of service notes that on the 31st October 1859, he transferred to the Army Hospital Corps, but was re-transferred the following day.
Discharged to pension on the 29th September 1863, after 24 years service.
WO25 Invalided 29th September 1863.

1086 TAYLOR, Corporal James
Born : Date Unknown - Lancaster
Enlisted : 15th August 1850
Medals : Crimea (B.S)

Died : 25th October 1854 - Balaclava
Status : Killed in the Charge

The musters show he was effective from the 1st-25th October. Written across his entry is Killed in Action 25th October Balaclava. Shown with 5s-10d in credit. Reference Number 354065. No Will Known. Brother Samuel residence, Liverpool. Co Lancaster. WO100/24 page 84&89 Remark: Killed in Action 25 Oct. 1854.
Casualty Roll: Listed Killed at Balaklava. Trade on enlistment Butcher.
The Fields of War edited by Philip Warner Letters of R.T.Godman page 102 From a letter dated 7th December 1854....."Our Corporal who was killed was nearly cut to pieces, his left arm nearly severed in four places. I suppose there must have been a good many at him at once, as he was very strong and a good swordsman. All the Russians seem to cut at the left wrist, so many men lost fingers, and got their hands cut....."

984 THOMAS, Private David
Born : Date Unknown - Wicklow
Enlisted : 27th August 1847
Medals : Crimea (B.I.S)

Died : 6th January 1855 - Scutari
Status : Probably Rode in the Charge

The musters show he was effective from the 1st October to the 27th December. 3rd muster states Scutari.
Trade on enlistment Clerk.

THOMPSON, Captain Richard
Born : Date Unknown - Wicklow
Enlisted : 27th August 1847
Medals : Crimea (B.I.S) The Turkish Order of the Medjidie (5th Class)

Died : 6th January 1855 - Scutari
Status : Probably Rode in the Charge

The musters show he was effective as a Captain from the 15th October to the 11th December and as a Major from the 12th-31st December. Remarks state "Joined Y depot 18th Nov. To Major 12th Dec."

Franks Leaves from a Soldier's note book page 87. Major Thompson was sent out from the depot troops and took command of the Regiment, up to this time we had been under the nominal command of Colonel Hodge of the 4th Dragoon Guards.
The Fields of War Edited by Philip Warner. Letters of R.T.Godman.
In a letter dated 22nd November 1854. Godman notes that Captain Thompson "has joined us - he is as great an ass as ever, and perhaps more consequential; as to consulting him on matters connected with the regiment, I might as well talk to a post. He always says 'yes' or, if he does not, 'I don't mind'; in fact I do pretty much as I like with the direction of affairs….. Letter dated 31st December 1855, Scutari. "Thompson has ordered his horses to be sold, they are not worth much, he seldom has a good horse, but perhaps he intends leaving. I should not be surprised if he does not come out again." Another letter dated 27th March 1856. "Thompson is most anxious to go on half-pay. I hope he will be able to do so, he is kept at home by the commission now sitting; he is sure to make a mess of it, pretending to know more than he does, and he will contradict himself often enough. They will have some fun examining him, but for all the information they get he might as well be here."

Richard Thompson, Cornet by purchase 25th February 1842, Lieutenant by purchase 17th November 1843, Captain by purchase 23rd May 1848, and Major 22nd December 1854. (Harts 1855) Retired on Half pay 2nd December 1859.

1237 TOPHAM, Corporal William
Born : Date Unknown - Wicklow
Enlisted : 27th August 1847
Medals : Crimea (I.S)

Died : 1882
Status : Effective during the period

Toad Hall Medal List Autumn 1991 HCM 76. Turkish Crimea British issue regimentally impressed "No 1237 TSM W.D Lemmon 5th Dgn. Gds. GVF £45
Philip Burman List 97 January 2002 item 20. Crimea 3 Bars Balaclava, Inkermann, Sebastopol. Sgt.Wm.Topham. 5th Dragoon Guards. Regimentally engraved. Complete with orginal ribbon and top pin buckle NVF £635.

The musters show he was effective from the 1st October to the 15th November. 3rd muster states Scutari.

Excerpts taken from A Heavy Brigade Charger? by Barney Mattingly.

William Denis Lemmon was born on September 8, 1833 and enlisted in the 7th (Princess Royal) Dragoon Guards, then stationed in Ireland, on March 21, 1851 under the name 'William Topham'. It's unclear why Lemmon chose to enlist under a pseudo-name but he also faked his birth date, giving this as August 29, 1832. At the time, soldiering in the ranks was considered a less than honorable profession and one could surmise that Lemmon's decision to enlist was not approved by his family. Given his underage status, it seems possible that Lemmon was concealing his enlistment from his parents.

The 5th (Princess Charlotte of Wales) Dragoon Guards received orders to deploy on March 17th but were short of full establishment. The 5th, like the 7th, were stationed in Ireland and; as a result, the 7th Dragoon Guards were ordered to provide volunteers for service with the 5th Dragoon Guards. Lemmon (alias Topham) was one of 15 volunteers from the 7th who were selected, transferring to the 5th Dragoon Guards (regimental number 1237) on April 1, 1854. The 5th Dragoon Guards left Queenstown on the 27th of May with a strength of 19 officers, 295 other ranks, and 295 horses. His 1870 officer's papers confirm that Lemmon departed with his regiment.

The muster rolls indicate that Lemmon (alias 'Topham') was sent to Scutari on November 15, 1854, arriving back in England on February 28, 1855. Like many of his compatriots, Lemmon probably was suffering from Cholera.

The regiment's primary medal roll lists 'Topham' as qualifying for the Inkermann clasp but not for the Balaklava clasp. In addition, the name 'Topham' does not appear on the supplemental Balaklava roll. According to the muster rolls, Lemmon (alias 'Topham') was in the Crimea; however, they do not specify if he was on duty on October 25th. Given the considerable number of 5th Dragoon Guards who contracted Cholera during the first few months of the war, Lemmon might have missed the battle due to illness. Alternatively, it's possible that the rolls are incorrect. Since Lemmon left the Crimea a few weeks after the battle, he might have been overlooked when the Balaklava roll was compiled. The Balaklava clasp is listed on his 1870 officer's papers.

In addition, The Story of a Regiment of Horse (the regimental history of the 5th Dragoon Guards) states that Lemmon was present at the battle of Balaklava. Unfortunately, neither source is particularly reliable. The first source represents what Lemmon believed he was entitled to but not necessarily what he actually earned. The second source frequently has shown itself to be inaccurate when relating the services of individual soldier's. Since he was present in the Crimea on October 25th, Lemmon could have thought himself entitled to the clasp even if his claim was not justified by the regulations. Without an indisputable source available, it might never be known with any certainty whether Lemmon participated in the 'Charge of the Heavy Brigade'.

After the war, the 5th Dragoon Guards landed in Portsmouth on June 24, 1856, proceeding to Aldershot, and it was on this date that Lemmon rejoined his regiment from depot service. Queen Victoria reviewed the troops at Aldershot on July 8th, thanking them for their efforts. Lemmon was promoted to Sergeant on June 8, 1855 and Troop Sergeant Major on August 9, 1857. He married Caroline Reilly on November 18, 1856 and they had eight children. It was at this time that Lemmon abandoned his alias. The April-June 1857 muster rolls (WO 12/327) list him as "1237 Topham William" but then there is a note immediately under this identifying him as "alias W. Dennis Lemmon". Although no reason is recorded, it could be theorized that Lemmon had achieved a considerable level of success in the Army and no longer felt the need to hide his identity. Perhaps his recent marriage or pending birth of his first child (born September 28, 1857) forced him to admit his true identify. Whatever the case, he appears as 'Lemmon' on the muster rolls after this date. It is interesting to note that 'Topham' had the same regimental number as 'Lemmon' (1237) as this lends credence to the two being the same man.

The 5th Dragoon Guards would not be again deployed overseas until 1893 and the remainder of Lemmon's service was spent in England, Ireland, and Scotland. He was appointed Regimental Sergeant Major on August 13, 1862 and commissioned as Quartermaster on June 3, 1864. The Quartermaster almost inevitably was selected from a senior non-commissioned officer and, as RSM, it is not surprising that Lemmon was appointed. What is unusual is that Lemmon was appointed after only 13 years of service. No doubt, the Crimean War presented Lemmon with opportunities for rapid promotion and the poor educational background of recruits in the mid Nineteenth Century meant that relatively few soldier's could aspire to senior NCO status. Regardless, to become RSM after only 11 years and Quartermaster after only 13 years suggests that Lemmon was a man of exceptional abilities.

Lemmon was promoted Honorary Captain on June 25, 1881 and Honorary Major upon his retirement on August 24, 1881, having served an impressive 17 years as Quartermaster. Despite 30 years in the British Army, Lemmon did not qualify for the Long Service & Good Conduct Medal. Lemmon served for only 13 years in the ranks, while the LS&GC Medal required 18 years. Sadly, Lemmon did not have the opportunity to enjoy his retirement as he died in the spring of 1882. He was only 49 years of age.

Lemmon's Medals

A Crimea Medal engraved to "SEJT WM TOPHAM 5TH DN GDS" with clasps for Balaklava, Inkermann, and Sebastopol has appeared on the market several times. Published sources (including The Fields of War, which contains an eyewitness account written by an officer in the regiment) indicate that unnamed Crimea Medals were issued to the 5th Dragoon Guards on September 20, 1855. Officially impressed medals were issued later but these were to replacement soldier's who arrived later or to those who had died before receiving their medals. Lemmon returned to England in February 1855 and; therefore, did not receive his medal while in the Crimea.

After the war, the Crimea Medals to the 5th Dragoon Guards frequently were engraved with a soldier's current rank and not the rank as it appeared on the Medal Rolls. Accordingly, the Crimea Medal to 'Topham' is named to a Sergeant, a rank Lemmon held from June 8, 1855 to August 8, 1857 (and which he never held while actually serving in the Crimea), and not to a Corporal, which is how 'Topham' is listed on the Crimea Medal Rolls. Still, Lemmon's Crimea Medal is engraved and one can never be sure about these, especially when named to the Light and Heavy Brigades. Given his status as Quartermaster and the number of unnamed Crimea Medals issued, it would have been relatively easy for Lemmon to obtain a replacement and the possibility exists of there being a second Crimea Medal named to 'Lemmon'.

A Turkish Crimea Medal impressed to "NO 1237. T.S.M. W.D. LEMMON. 5TH DRAGOON GDS." was sold at the November 1997 Glendining's auction. In the late 1850's, the Turkish Crimea Medals to all officers and other ranks still serving with the regiment were depot impressed using the rank at that time, not the rank as found on the medal rolls. In Lemmon's case, it is compelling to note that not only is his Turkish Crimea Medal depot impressed to a Troop Sergeant Major (a rank he held from August 9, 1857 to August 12, 1862) but that it also is named to 'Lemmon', not 'Topham'. Since the name 'Lemmon' does not appear on the Crimea Medal Roll and since his medal entitlement is obscured by his alias, this lends some credence to Lemmon's Turkish Crimea Medal being genuine.

These two medals currently are in the hands of different collectors. Given the different surnames, it could be surmised that they were separated by someone who was unfamiliar with their unusual story. However, the amount of wear and edge bruising on these medals is inconsistent, suggesting that they were not worn together. It is possible that either one or both medals are replacements or forgeries.

900 TURNBULL, Private John

Born : Date Unknown - Leeds
Enlisted : 24th May 1848
Medals : Crimea (B.I.S)

Died : 10th November 1854
Status : Probably Rode in the Charge

Sotheby's Auction 5th March 1980 lot 94.Crimea 3 clasps Balaklava, Inkermann, Sebastopol. J.Turnbull 5th. Drogoon Guards. Officially impressed with the final "L" of surname inverted.Some scratches, otherwise Good VF £240.
Sotheby's Auction 1st November 1984.lot 39 as above VF £508.
Q & C Militaria July 2007 J. TURNBULL. 5TH DN. GDS Crimea Medal   Balaclava / Inkermann / Sebastopol J. TURNBULL. 5TH DN. GDS. Turkish Crimea Medal Unnamed
Copy muster and medal roll. John Turnbull enlisted 24 May 1846 as 900 Private, 5th Dragoon Guards. Sailed for the Crimea July 1854.
Died in the Crimea 10 November 1854. He was on duty and there was no reason why he did not charge with the Heavy Brigade at Balaclava. Have not found what killed him, but this may be hidden in the casualty lists published in The Times newspaper. The last L of his surname has been impressed upside down. Pair: £2200

The musters show he was effective from the 1st October to the 10th November. Musters endorsed transhipped off board Bombay to Himalaya. WO100/24 page 87 Remarks: Died 10th Nov. 1854. WO100/24 page 104 Remarks: Dead.

Form 20. 900 Pte Turnbull, John. Born Leeds.18s-6 1/2d in credit. Reference No 363607. No will Known. NOK Father Benjamin, Last residence Yorkshire, Leeds. Trade on enlistment Coach Smith.

1172 VENTON, Private John

Born : Unknown
Enlisted :
Medals : Crimea (B.I.S)

Died : Unknown
Status : Probably Rode in the Charge

Spink's Numismatic Circular November 1979, Thomas Venton. 5th Dragoon Guards. Turkish Crimea (British Type) Impressed naming and straight bar suspension. Note different Christain name.
Christies 21st November 1989. Lot 23 Crimea 3 clasps Balaklava, Inkermann, Sebastopol. J.Venton 5th Dragoon Gds. Officially impressed. Contact marks. Fine Est. £150-£180. Hammer Price £242.

The musters show he was effective from the 1st October to the 31st December.
WO25 Comp. 21 yrs 3rd January 1877.

768 WALCH, Private Edmond

Born : Unknown
Enlisted :
Medals : Crimea (B.I.S)

Died : Unknown
Status : Probably Rode in the Charge

The musters show he was effective from the 1st October to the 31st December. The Pay Lists show various spellings for this trooper's surname: Welch, Walsh, and Welsh.

1061 WALCH, Private William

Born : Unknown
Enlisted :
Medals : Crimea (B.I.S) ,L.S.G.C Medal

Died : Unknown
Status : Probably Rode in the Charge

The musters show he was effective from the 1st October to the 31st December. The Pay Lists show various spellings for this trooper's surname: Welch, Walsh, and Welsh.
WO102 L.S.G.C Medal recommendation 18.6.1868, issued 15.8.1868.

1101 WALSH, Sergeant David

Born : Unknown
Enlisted :
Medals : Crimea (B.I.S) ,L.S.G.C Medal

Died : Unknown
Status : Probably Rode in the Charge

The musters show he was effective as a Corporal from the 1st October to the 4th November and as a Sergeant from the 5th November to the 31st December. WO100/24 page 99 Remarks From Corporal. WO25 to casualty depot March 1868.

1092 WALSH, Corporal Thomas
Born : Unknown
Enlisted :
Medals : Crimea (B.I.S)

Died : Unknown
Status : Probably Rode in the Charge

The musters show he was effective from the 1st October to the 31st December. WO25 Compl. 21 years 2nd July 1874.

1173 WARDEN, Private William
Born : Date Unknown - Leicester
Enlisted : 4th December 1852
Medals : Crimea (B.I.S) ,L.S.G.C Medal

Died : 25th January 1855 - Scutari
Status : Probably Rode in the Charge

The musters show he was effective from the 1st October to the 31st December. WO100/24 page 104 Remarks: Dead. Trade on enlistment Labourer.

1090 WEYMES, Private James
Born : Unknown
Enlisted :
Medals : Crimea (B.I.S) ,L.S.G.C Medal

Died : Unknown
Status : Probably Rode in the Charge

The musters show he was effective from the 1st October to the 31st December. WO25 to 5th Lancers 28th Feb. 1858.

1231 WILKINS,Private John
Born : Unknown
Enlisted :
Medals : Crimea (A.B.I.S)

Died : Unknown
Status : Probably Rode in the Charge

The musters show he was effective from the 1st October to the 31st December. Written across his entry is "Servant to Lord Lucan full period" WO100/24 page 105 Remarks: To England with Lord Lucan.

He holds the Alma clasp - the only one in the Regiment - because he was Lord Lucan's orderly, and was present at that action which took place before the Regiment had landed. As Lucan's orderly, it seems unlikely that he would have taken part in the Charge, although he would of course have been present on the field of battle.

573 WILLIAMS, Private John
Born : Unknown
Enlisted :
Medals : Crimea (B.I.S) ,L.S.G.C Medal

Died : Unknown
Status : Probably Rode in the Charge

The musters show he was effective from the 1st October to the 30th November. Paid from 1st October 1854 to 30th November 1854. 61 days, 10 days on board ship, 51 days on land. 3rd Muster endorsed Scutari . Marginal note reads 2d G.C.P

655 WILLIAMS, Private Joseph
Born : Unknown
Enlisted :
Medals : Crimea (B.I.S) ,L.S.G.C Medal

Died : Unknown
Status : Probably Rode in the Charge

The musters show he was effective from the 1st October to the 31st December. Musters endorsed With Staff Officers Full Period Marginal note reads 3d G.C.P

1081 WILLIS, Private Richard
Born : Unknown
Enlisted :
Medals : Crimea (B.I.S) ,L.S.G.C Medal

Died : Unknown
Status : Probably Rode in the Charge

The musters show he was effective from the 1st October to the 31st December.

287

804 WILSON, Private Robert

Born : Unknown
Enlisted :
Medals : Crimea (B.I.S)

Died : Unknown
Status : Probably Rode in the Charge

The musters show he was effective from the 1st October to the 31st December. WO25 discharged March 1857.

1182 WILSON, Private William

Born : Unknown
Enlisted :
Medals : Crimea (B.S)

Died : Unknown
Status : Severely wounded in the Charge

The musters show he was effective from the 1st October to the 31st December. Casualty Roll for Crimea, page 34. Pte Willson, William 5D.G. Wounded Severely at Balaklava 25th October 1854

891 WINDRAM, Sergeant William

Born : Unknown
Enlisted :
Medals : Crimea (I.S)

Died : Unknown
Status : Effective during the period

The musters show he was effective from the 1st October to the 31st December.

1155 WINTERBOURNE, Private George

Born : 1834
Enlisted : 23rd June 1852
Medals : Crimea (B.I.S)

Died : Unknown
Status : Probably Rode in the Charge

The musters show he was effective from the 1st October to the 31st December.
WO25 To 7th D.G June 1857
George Winterbourne was born about 1834 at Aberford, near Leeds. He was one of a large family but just how large is uncertain. The nature of his early employment is not known, though he seems to have left it without notice or permission. Various hints in his letters suggest that it was probably horticultural. Certainly he became a professional gardener after leaving the army. He left home in June, 1852 (not for the first time, apparently) to go to sea but, that ambition having been thwarted, he joined the army. He served in the 5th Dragoon Guards during the Crimean war. After a brief return to the United Kingdom he transferred to the 7th Dragoon Guards to seize an opportunity of service in India, part of his service there having been during the Indian Mutiny.
He left the army late in 1864 and married some time after that, possibly in mid-1866, and became the father of five children, three girls and two boys. He was awarded a pension by the Governors of the Royal Hospital, Chelsea in 1898 but seems to have ended his days in somewhat straitened circumstances about 1905 (surviving press cuttings reporting his death are, unfortunately, not dated.) his collection comprises twenty two letters, all but one of them to his parents, written between June, 1852 when he joined the army and November, 1862, about two years before his discharge. The single surviving letter to a sibling is interesting for the changes in attitude it seems to disclose. After ten years service his attitude to soldiering seems to have cooled a little ["I hope you will never wear (the uniform)"]. It is probable that in writing to a brother he felt able to disclose a little more of his real self than to his parents; he comes across as more human and less moralistic than in his letters to them (though his sense of having caused them pain seems to have been genuine enough). He often mentions having written to his sisters; it is a pity more of those letters have not survived.
The originals of his letters from his army days, with a single exception, have not survived. They seem to have been used, many years later, as copy-book material by one or more of his children; possibly by or under guidance of his elder daughter, Alice, sometime pupil-teacher at St Chad's School. It is these copies that, in part at least, have survived, thanks to that same daughter who preserved them during her lifetime – until the early 1950's. There is some evidence to suggest the she might have had them from her Uncle Charlie, the sibling referred to above. However that may be, they are subject to copyist's errors; here and there words seem to have been omitted and is not clear whether mis-spelling is original or not. The dates The dates of some of the copy letters are almost certainly inaccurate, the content being clearly anachronistic or the time-scale impossible.

He was employed as a gardener by a Mr William Lomas Joy JP, probably in the Weetwood area, for ten years. Mr Joy later lived at Beverley and provided a reference to support his application for a Chelsea pension.
Opposite are two examples of George Winterbournes letters.

He seems to have continued a prolific writer for the rest of his life, utilising any scrap of paper which came to hand. The stroke(s) he suffered in 1898 do not seem seriously to have inconvenienced him in that regard at least, though he did on one occasion (not included here) complain of the frustration of muddled thinking. He left many scraps of newspaper on which he had written in pencil; a few letters in verse and some "social comment", both published and unpublished. As they have no direct bearing on his military service their transcriptions are not included here.
Shurdington,
Gloucestershire.

Information supplied by George Winterbourne. (January, 1992)

FROM ENLISTMENT TO EMBARKATION
1. Liverpool June 25th 1852
Dear Father and Mother,
By the time that you receive this letter I shall be in Ireland. My purpose of going to sea having failed, it being difficult to obtain a berth in either the Navy or the Merchant Service and, being resolved to see the world in one capacity or another, on the 23rd I enlisted into the 5th Heavy Dragoon Gds now lying at Newbridge in the County of Kildare in Ireland. I know too well the severity of the stroke it will give you but do not yield to unnecessary and useless anxiety for me for it will avail nothing. If I follow the track of Virtue and of honour it will be not matter where or what situation I may be placed in the world.
I did not enter the army for want nor was I intoxicated when I enlisted. When I left my home I was resolved that a sailor or a soldier I should be and when Fortune denied me the former I took the latter. The chances of war are many and hazardous but Providence is kind and watches over all. The decrees of Fate cannot be avoided and if it was my lot to be a soldier, as most assuredly it was, I could not evade it.
My old companion Francis McCarter inlisted at the same time and place and we shall be companions in the same Regiment. If we had waited another day we could have shipped on board the Navy as next day we heard that orders had come to ship some boys. But it was too late; the die was cast.
In a few days you will have another letter from me and then I shall tell you where to direct to. Till then compose yourselves as best you may. My love to all my brothers and sisters.

So now farewell,
Your loving son,

Dear Parents,
I am very sorry that you have been troubled with reports which, than God, I am able to contradict. No doubt you have heard many tidings all disagreeing from each other and all far from the truth. No person knows about the army but a soldier and even a Foot soldier knows little about the Cavalry regiments regulations.
You say you have heard that we have but two meals a day. It is false, we have three. In the morning we have one pound of bread and three gills of good coffee and at noon we have each 1/3rd of a pound of beef and three pounds of potatoes and in the evening we have the same as in the morning with the exception of tea for coffee. The provisions are all of the best quality and supplied to the army by contract.
You have heard that my bounty would not procure me the necessaries requisite. When I had got all settled I had a balance of £3.2s.5d. You say we have our clothes to find; our jackets, dress coats and trousers with our helmets and decoutriments are served to us from Regimental stores at the Governments expense.
Some may say that the bounty will be deducted from our pay, which is 1s.4d per day, but it is not so; it is free. A soldier's pay in Cavalry regiments is sufficient for his wants to spend moderately. 8d each day is paid for our victuals and washing. 2 shirts each week, a pr of draws, stockings and flannel shirts, and the other 8d for ourselves. The victuals cost more than we pay but it is an allowance made. You have heard that we have to sleep without shirts. It is all false.
We have, it is true, straw instead of feathers but it is necessary for the health of the army where there is so many together. The bedding is good and remarkably clean; 2 sheets, 2 blankets and one rug to each man, all having a separate bed. We have no plate or dish or pot of any kind to find. Do not think I have stated things uncorrect on purpose to soothe and lull your mind; everything is in its true statement. Some people talk of severity in the army. There is no such thing, at least in our regiment. I am perfectly content and healthy, so is my comrade.

Your loving son,
G. Winterbourne 5th Dr Gds

1197 WINTLE, Private Charles

Born : Unknown
Enlisted :
Medals : Crimea (B.I.S)

Died : Unknown
Status : Probably Rode in the Charge

The musters show he was effective from the 1st October to the 31st December.
WO25 Discharged 2nd December 1874, rank T.S.M after 21 years service.

660 WIXTED, Trumpeter Joseph

Born : Unknown
Enlisted :
Medals : Crimea (B.I.S)

Died : Unknown
Status : Probably Rode in the Charge

The musters show he was effective from the 1st October to the 31st December. WO25 To 5th Lancers 21st March 1858.

960 WOOD, Private David

Born : Unknown
Enlisted :
Medals : Crimea (B.I.S)

Died : Unknown
Status : Probably Rode in the Charge

A.H.Baldwin & Sons, Ltd Sales Catalogue February 1954: Crimea. 3 Bars, Balaklava, Inkermann, Sebastopol. Cpl. Wood Rather worn, Engraved name £1 15s

The musters show he was effective from the 1st October to the 31st December. WO25 Invalided 8th November 1860.

936 WOOD, Private Henry

Born : Unknown
Enlisted :
Medals : Crimea (B.I.S)

Died : Unknown
Status : Probably Rode in the Charge

The musters show he was effective from the 1st October to the 31st December.

882 WOOD, Private William

Born : Unknown
Enlisted :
Medals : Crimea (B.I.S)

Died : Unknown
Status : Probably Rode in the Charge

Spink's Numismatic Circular March 1974, Corporal W.Wood. 5th D. G. Crimea clasps B.I & S engraved naming. Top rivets unofficial.

The musters show he was effective as a Corporal from the 1st October to the 17th November and as a Private from the 18th November to the 31st December. WO25 Invalided 22nd October 1857.

1102 YATES, Private Richard

Born : Unknown
Enlisted :
Medals : Crimea (B.I.S)

Died : Unknown
Status : Probably Rode in the Charge

The musters show he was effective from the 1st October to the 31st December. WO25 discharged 7th March 1863.

995 YORKE, Farrier James

Born : Unknown
Enlisted : 5th December 1847
Medals : Crimea (B.I.S)

Died : Unknown
Status : Probably Rode in the Charge

In January 1975 the medals listed below were in the collection of Richard Walsh, a letter to Cannon Lummis dated the 8th January 1975 confirms this fact. Crimea 3 clasps 995 Far. Jas Yorke 5 Dgn Gds. Turkish Crimea named to "York"
DNW 2nd July 2003, Lot 973, A Heavy Brigade Pair to Farrier Sergeant J. Yorke, 5th Dragoon Guards. Crimea 1854-56, 3 clasps, Balaklava, Inkermann, Sebastopol (... J. Yorke, 5th Dra ....), engraved naming, part of naming illegible ; Turkish Crimea 1855, British issue (No.995 Far. Jas. York (sic) 5th Dragoon Dgs.), privately impressed naming, pierced with ring and straight bar suspension, severe edge bruising, possibly sometime brooch mounted, contact marks, good fine (2) Hammer Price £500

The musters show he was effective from the 1st October to the 31st December. Remarks state Farrier.
James Yorke, a Shoeing Smith by trade, enlisted into the Army at Malton, York on 5th December 1847, aged 30 years. As a Private in the 5th Dragoon Guards he served in the Crimea and gained the medal with clasps for Balaklava, Inkermann and Sebastopol.
In 1859 he re-enlisted and in the following year was promoted Farrier Sergeant, a rank he held until his discharge in 1871. WO25 discharged 26th December 1871.

The 6th Dragoons
"Inniskilling"

567 AINSWORTH, Private William

Born : Unknown
Enlisted :
Medals : Crimea (B.I.S)

Died : Unknown
Status : Probably Rode in the Charge

The musters show he was effective from the 1st October to the 31st December. Saved from the wreck of the "Europa".

553 ALMOND, Private John

Born : Date Unknown - Darwin
Enlisted : 21st April 1838
Medals : Crimea (B.S)

Died : 11th February 1855 - Aboard Ship
Status : Probably Rode in the Charge

The musters show he was effective from the 1st October to the 31st December. WO100/24 page 245 Remarks: Died passage to Scutari 11th February 1855. WO100/24 page 261 Remarks: Died. 11/2/55. On bd. Ship. Born: Darwin. Trade at enlistment Weaver.

788 APPLEBY, Private James

Born : Unknown
Enlisted :
Medals : Crimea (B.I.S)

Died : Unknown
Status : Probably Rode in the Charge

The musters show he was effective from the 1st October to the 31st December.

1208 ARCHER, Private William

Born : Date Unknown - St. John's.
Enlisted : 15th February 1853
Medals : Crimea (B.I.S)

Died : 17th January 1855 - Aboard Ship
Status : Probably Rode in the Charge

The musters show he was effective from the 1st October to the 31st December. WO100/24 page 245 Remarks: Died passage to Scutari 17/1/55. WO100/24 page 256 Remarks: Died 17 Jan:55. Disease. WO100/24 page 261 Remarks: Died 17/1/55, On bd. Ship.
Trade on enlistment Groom.

830 ATKIN, Private John

Born : Unknown
Enlisted :
Medals : Crimea (B.I.S)

Died : Unknown
Status : Probably Rode in the Charge

The musters show he was effective from the 1st October to the 31st December.
WO25 Atkin, J. 831 To pension 08/12/1868.

1140 BACKLER, Private James

Born : Unknown
Enlisted :
Medals : Crimea (B.I.S)

Died : Unknown
Status : Probably Rode in the Charge

The musters show he was effective from the 1st-25th October. All three musters endorsed Scutari. Remarks state to Scutari 26th October. C.R.: Listed W/SI at Balaklava. WO100/24 page 256 Remarks: Invalided, sent to England. WO100/24 page 245 Remarks: Invalided, sent home 2/6/56. WO100/24 page 260 Remarks: Discharged 5th. July 1855.

908 BALLARD, Private William

Born : Unknown
Enlisted :
Medals : Crimea (B.I.S)

Died : Unknown
Status : Probably Rode in the Charge

The musters show he was effective from the 1st October to the 31st December. WO25 To 18th Hussars June 1858.

1088 BARNETT, Private Charles

Born : Date Unknown - Bedwin
Enlisted : 8th February 1850
Medals : Crimea (B.S)

Died : 20th February 1855 - Scutari
Status : Probably Rode in the Charge

Seaby December 1972. item F12G1. Pair "Balaklava" plus Turkish Crimea British version un-named, C.Barnett 6th Dragoons. Impressed naming. Heavy Brigade. Good VF £65.

The musters show he was effective from the 1st October to the 14th November. 2nd and 3rd musters endorsed Scutari. Remarks state to Scutari 15th November. WO100/24 page 256 Remarks: Died 20th. Febuary 1855. Disease. WO100/24 page 245 Remarks: Died at Scutari 20 Febuary 1855. Trade on enlistment Labourer.

1107 BARR, Private James

Born : Unknown
Enlisted :
Medals : Crimea (B.I.S)

Died : Unknown
Status : Probably Rode in the Charge

The musters show he was effective from the 1st October to the 31st December.
WO25 Discharged as Sergeant 29th of March 1870.

833 BIGGS, Private William

Born : May 1826
Enlisted : January 1844 - Nottingham
Medals : Crimea (B.I.S)

Died : 4th January 1859 - Kirkee
Status : Probably Rode in the Charge

Glendining's 25th November 1987 Lot 71, Crimea Medal three clasps, Alma, Balaklava, Sebastopol (W.Biggs, 6th Dragns), impressed naming. Very Fine. Sold again at Glendinings on the 2nd March 1988 Lot 116.
DNW 2nd April 2004, The collection of medals formed by the late John Darwent, Lot 171, Crimea 1854-56, 3 clasps, Balaklava, Inkermann, Sebastopol (W. Biggs, 6th Dragns.), officially impressed naming, with additional regimentally engraved 'No. 833' and '6th D.', edge bruising, very fine Hammer Price £1450

The musters show he was effective from the 1st October to the 14th December. Remarks state to Scutari 15th December.
WO100/24 page 261 Remarks: Died 4 Jany. 1859 at Kirkee. William Biggs enlisted in the 6th Dragoons at Nottingham in January 1844, aged 17 years 9 months.
He was actively employed out in the Crimea and is verified as having received the Medal and 'Balaklava', 'Inkermann' and 'Sebastopol' clasps. Sadly, he died whilst serving in India in January 1859, while stationed at Kirkee, the cause of his death being given as 'concussion of the brain'. Biggs was 32 years old and does not appear to have qualified for an Indian Mutiny Medal.

1348 BLACKWELL, Private William

Born : Date Unknown - Farringdon
Enlisted : 8th October 1852
Medals : Crimea (B.I.S)

Died : 16th January 1855 - Crimea
Status : Probably Rode in the Charge

The musters show he was effective from the 1st October to the 31st December. Name shown as James.
Died: Camp Kadikoi. 16/Jan./55. WO100/24 page 256 Remarks:
Died 16th. Jan:55. WO100/24 page 246 Remarks: Died in Crimea 16th. Jan:55.
Trade: on enlistment a Grocer.

BOATE, Assistant Surgeon Henry Charles

Born : 3rd August 1828 - Dungarvan, Co Waterford
Enlisted :
Medals : Crimea (B.I.S)

Died : Unknown
Status : Probably Rode in the Charge

The musters show he was effective from the 1st October to the 31st December. WO100/24 page 243 Remarks: Order given as he is in possession of the Clasp for B. WO100/24 page 254 Remarks: Placed under arrest for leaving the Field without permission & for not returning. WO100/24 page 260 Remarks: Retired 21 May 1855.
Acting Assistant 22nd October 1852. Assistant Surgeon 6th Dragoons 26th November 1852. Resigned 30th April 1855.
He became a Captain in the Osmanli Cavalry, Major General Beatson's Irregular Turkish Cavalry.

1129 BOLTON, Sergeant Frederick

Born : Date Unknown - Stockton
Enlisted : 13th February 1851
Medals : Crimea (B.S)

Died : 26th October 1854 - Aboard Ship
Status : Severely wounded in the Charge

The musters show he was effective from the 1st-25th October. Remarks state to Scutari 26th October died of wounds the same day as subsequently notifed. WO100/24 page 232&255 Remarks: Died 26 Oct. 1854 of wounds rec'd in Action at Balaklava on 25th. Oct.54.
WO100/24 page 244 Remarks: Died 26 Octr. 1854, of wounds rec'd in action at Balaklava.
WO100/24 page 261 Remarks: Died, 26 Octr. 1854 on board Ship of wounds received in action at Balaklava.C.R.
Heroes of the Crimea by Michael Barthrop p41 - Sergt Maughan of the Inniskillings saw how Sergt Bolton had his leg knocked off "The shot hit my horse first, came between us and doubled up my sword like a hook and grazed my leg".
This stone is erected by his friends in memory of Frederick Hardwicke Bolton. Aged 21 years Sergeant in the Inniskilling Dragoons who fell in the Memorable charge Heavy cavalry at Balaclava on the 25th of October MDDCCCLIV. Beloved by all who knew him. The monument is located in St. Edmund's Churchyard, Sedgefield.

1272 BOTTERILL, Private Matthew

Born : Date unknown - Scumpston
Enlisted : 11th January 1853
Medals : Crimea (I.S)

Died : 17th January 1855 - Crimea
Status : Effective during the period

The musters show he was effective from the 1st October to the 31st December.

909 BOULT, Private Charles

Born : Unknown
Enlisted :
Medals : Crimea (B.I.S)

Died : Unknown
Status : Probably Rode in the Charge

The musters show he was effective from the 1st October to the 31st December.

1152 BRACKLEY, Sergeant David

Born : Unknown
Enlisted :
Medals : Crimea (B.I.S)

Died : Unknown
Status : Probably Rode in the Charge

Glendinings Auction 7th December 1988, Lot 183 Crimea medal with three bars, Balaklava, inkermann, Sebastopol (Sergt. D. Brackley, 6th Dragoons), Impressed naming . Nearly Very Fine.

The musters show he was effective from the 1st October to the 31st December. Corporal Brackley served at the battles of Balaklava and Inkermann and was promoted to Sergeant, on the 29th September 1855. Soon after this promotion he was "Left in Genl. Hospital, Crimea, attached to the 11th Hussars, and subsequently Invalided", and his name disappears from the musters of the service battalion. He re-appears on the musters of the Depot at Canterbury from the 16th January 1856, until March 1857. On the return of the service battalion from overseas service, the two were merged together at Shorncliffe.WO100/24 page 261 Remarks: Discharged 31st. March 1857.

1167 BRADY, Private James

Born : Unknown
Enlisted :
Medals : Crimea (B.I.S)

Died : Unknown
Status : Probably Rode in the Charge

The musters show he was effective from the 1st October to the 31st December.

1163 BREADON, Private William

Born : Unknown
Enlisted :
Medals : Crimea (B.I.S)

Died : Unknown
Status : Probably Rode in the Charge

The musters show he was effective from the 1st-25th October. All three musters endorsed Scutari. Remarks state to Scutari 26th October. WO100/24 page 246 Remarks: Invalided, sent home 25th December1854. Casualty Roll: Listed Breadins W/SI at Balaklava. WO100/24 page 261 Remarks: Discharged 1st January 1857.

1252 BRIDGES, Private James

Born : Date unknown - Tillington
Enlisted : 10th October 1853
Medals . Crimea (B.I.S)

Died : 12th January 1855 - Aboard Ship
Status : Probably Rode in the Charge

The musters show he was effective from the 1st October to the 31st December. WO100/24 page 256 Remarks: Died 12th. Jan:55. WO100/24 page 246 Remarks: Died passage to Scutari 12/1/55.
The Times of Thursday 1st February, 1855; page 8 reported that "Private J. Bridger, 6th Dragoons" died on board the Colombo on the 10th January 1855.
Trade on enlistment Carpenter. The Pay Lists name him Bridger.

1003 BRIDGES, Saddler Sergeant John

Born : Unknown
Enlisted :
Medals : Crimea (B.I.S)

Died : Unknown
Status : Probably Rode in the Charge

The musters show he was effective from the 13th November to the 31st December. Remarks state from Scutari 13th November.

1136 BROOKS, Private Isaac

Born : Unknown
Enlisted :
Medals : Crimea (B.I.S)

Died : Unknown
Status : Probably Rode in the Charge

The musters show he was effective from the 8th October to the 31st December. Remarks state from Scutari 8th October.
Extract from the Broad Arrow dated 3rd November 1895:
6th Dragoons - A complimentary dinner was held on the 25th October at Newtown in honour of Isaac Brooks late Inniskilling Dragoons, who was in the Charge of the Heavy Brigade at Balaclava and is the only survivor in Bristol.
The Crimea and Indian Mutiny Veterans Association 1892-1912. P16 records Pte I Brooks 6th Inniskilling Dragoons and Pte W.H.Midwinter as members of the Society at Bristol. Page 14 records Pte I.Brookes as in possession of 2 medals Crimea 3 clasp B.I.S, and Turkish Medal. And still alive in 1912.

1282 BROWN Private Alfred

Born : Unknown
Enlisted :
Medals : Crimea (I.S)

Died : Unknown
Status : Probably Rode in the Charge

The musters show he was effective from the 1st October to the 31st December.

1023 BROWN, Trumpeter Edward

Born : Unknown
Enlisted :
Medals : Crimea (B.I.S)

Died : Unknown
Status : Probably Rode in the Charge

The musters show he was effective from the 1st October to the 31st December.
WO25 Died rank Sergeant 7th of April 1873.

954 BROWN, Private John

Born : Unknown
Enlisted :
Medals : Crimea (B.I.S)

Died : Unknown
Status : Probably Rode in the Charge

The musters show he was effective from the 1st October to the 28th December. Remarks state to Scutari 29th December. WO100/24 page 246 Remarks: Invalided-sent home 2nd March 1855. WO100/24 page 261 Remarks: Corporal. Discharged 25th March 1857.
He received his medal from the hand of the Queen 18th May 1855.

1119 BROWN, Private William
Born : Unknown
Enlisted :
Medals : Crimea (B.I.S)

Died : Unknown
Status : Probably Rode in the Charge

The musters show he was effective from the 1st October to the 31st December.
WO100/24 page 261 Remarks: Discharged 31st March 1857.

1257 BUDD, Private John Thomas
Born : Date unknown - Worcester
Enlisted : 8th November 1853
Medals : Crimea (B.I.S)

Died : 2nd April 1855 - Crimea
Status : Probably Rode in the Charge

The musters show he was effective from the 1st October to the 31st December.
WO100/24 page 246 Remarks: Died Crimea 2nd April 1855.
Trade on enlistment Clerk.

1095 BURKE, Private Thomas
Born : Date unknown -Tuam, Ireland
Enlisted : April 1850
Medals : Crimea (B.I.S)

Died : Unknown
Status : Probably Rode in the Charge

Medal List Dec 1992, Capt Bob Baird, California, medal as below 600 dollars
DNW 2nd April 2004, The collection of medals formed by the late John Darwent, Lot 170, Crimea 1854-56, 3 clasps, Balaklava, Inkermann, Sebastopol (T. Burke, 6th Dragns.) officially impressed naming, with additional regimentally engraved 'No. 1095' and '6th D.', fitted with Hunt and Roskell silver riband buckle with gold pin, contact marks and edge nicks, very fine Hammer Price £1450

The musters show he was effective from the 1st October to the 31st December.
Thomas Burke was born at Tuam, Ireland and enlisted in the 6th Dragoons at Westminster in April 1850, aged 20 years. He was actively employed out in the Crimea and is verified as having received the Medal and 'Balaklava', 'Inkermann' and 'Sebastopol' clasps. Burke transferred to the 7th Dragoon Guards in September 1857, served out in India between 1858-62 and was advanced to Corporal. He does not appear to have been awarded an Indian Mutiny Medal and was discharged on his return to England in October 1862.

638 BURKITT, Corporal Edward Webber
Born : Unknown
Enlisted :
Medals : Crimea (B.S)

Died : Unknown
Status : Probably Rode in the Charge

The musters show he was effective from the 1st October to the 31st December.
WO100/24 page 261 Remarks: Private. Discharged 3rd. September 1856.

990 BURNS, Private Charles
Born : Unknown
Enlisted :
Medals : Crimea (B.I.S) L.S. G.C Medal

Died : Unknown
Status : Probably Rode in the Charge

The musters show he was effective from the 1st October to the 31st December. WO102 L.S.G.C medal recommendation 13th November1868, issued 8th February1869 with £5 Gratuity. WO25 to pension 11th of July 1871.

1047 BURNS, Private Thomas
Born : Date Unknown - Devenish
Enlisted : 18th January 1849
Medals : Crimea (B.I.S)

Died : 9th March 1855 - Scutari
Status : Probably Rode in the Charge

The musters show he was effective from the 1st October to the 14th December. Remarks state to Scutari 15th December.
WO100/24 page 246 Remarks: Died at Scutari 9th March 1855. Trade on enlistment Labourer.

530 BUSH, Private Jeremiah
Born : Date unknown - Warminster
Enlisted : 28th February 1838
Medals : Crimea (B.I.S)

Died : 23rd June 1855 - Crimea
Status : Probably Rode in the Charge

The musters show he was effective from the 1st October to the 31st December.
WO100/24 page 246 Remarks: Died in Crimea 23 June 1855.
Trade: on enlistment Labourer.

393 BUTLER, Private Peter
Born : Unknown
Enlisted :
Medals : Crimea (B.I.S), L.S.G.C Medal

Died : Unknown
Status : Probably Rode in the Charge

The musters show he was effective from the 1st October to the 31st December.
WO102 L.S.G.C recommendation 13th November1868, issued 8th February 1869 with £5 Gratuity.

1278 CAMPELL, Private William
Born : Unknown
Enlisted :
Medals : Crimea (B.I.S)

Died : Unknown
Status : Probably Rode in the Charge

The musters show he was effective from the 1st October to the 31st December.

807 CARTER, Private James
Born : Unknown
Enlisted :
Medals : Crimea (B.I.S)

Died : Unknown
Status : Probably Rode in the Charge

The musters show he was effective from the 1st October to the 31st December.

750 CAUGHIE, Private Thomas
Born : Unknown
Enlisted :
Medals : Crimea (B.I.S)

Died : Unknown
Status : Probably Rode in the Charge

The musters show he was effective from the 1st October to the 31st December.
WO100/24 page 246 Remarks: Invalided, sent home 30th November 1855.

1079 CLARKE, Private Charles
Born : Date Unknown - Swallowsfield
Enlisted : 3rd November 1849
Medals : Crimea (B.I.S)

Died : 1st February 1855 - Camp Kadikoi - Crimea
Status : Severely wounded in the Charge

The musters show he was effective from the 1st-25th October. Remarks state to Scutari 26th October.
WO100/24 page 246 Remarks: Died in Crimea 1st February 1855.
WO100/24 page 256 Remarks: Died 1st Febuary 1855, Disease. Died: Camp Kadikoi. 1st Febuary 1855.
Casualty Roll: Listed W/Sv at Balaklava. Trade on enlistment Labourer.

1259 COATES, Private John T.R.
Born : Date Unknown - Worksop
Enlisted : 21st November 1853
Medals : Crimea (B.I.S)

Died : 3rd January 1855 - Aboard Ship
Status : Probably Rode in the Charge

The musters show he was effective from the 1st October to the 30th December. Remarks state to Scutari 31st December.
WO100/24 page 246 Remarks: Died passage to Scutari 3rd January 1855.
WO100/24 page 256 Remarks: Died 3rd. January 1855 Disease.

COLLINS, Veterinary Surgeon James

Born : Unknown
Enlisted :
Medals : Crimea (I.S)

Died : Unknown
Status : Effective during the period

The musters show he was effective from the 1st October to the 31st December.
Veterinary Surgeon - James Collins, 23rd June 1854. Harts Annual Army List 1855.

1172 COOK, Corporal Henry

Born : Unknown
Enlisted :
Medals : Crimea (B.I.S)

Died : Unknown
Status : Probably Rode in the Charge

The musters show he was effective from the 1st October to the 31st December.

1198 CORPS, Private William

Born : Date Unknown - Foxfield
Enlisted : 7th December 1852
Medals : Crimea (B.I.S)

Died : 9th April 1855
Status : Probably Rode in the Charge

Toad Hall Medals January 1988, item 59. Crimea two clasps Balaklava, Inkermann to Corporal Wm. Corps 6th Dragoons.
Died Crimea 7th April 1855. Scarce officially impressed medal to NCO of the Heavy Brigade, GVF £425.
Dixons Gazette, No 39, Autumn 2004, item 2857, Crimea 3 clasps, Balaclava, Inkermann, Sebastopol, officially impressed.
Private W. Corps, 6th Dragoons. Sebastopol medal roll shows his date of death as the 7th April 1855. VF/GVF £1250
The musters show he was effective from the 1st October to the 31st December.
Adm1/5631 Saved from the wreck of the "Europa". Trade on enlistment Servant.

1045 CORRIE, Private John

Born : Unknown
Enlisted :
Medals : Crimea (B.I.S)

Died : Unknown
Status : Probably Rode in the Charge

The musters show he was effective from the 1st October to the 31st December. WO25 shows Corrie transferred to the
7th Dragoon Guards on the 12th of August 1857.

1292 CORSTON, Private Edward

Born : Date unknown - Marham
Enlisted :
Medals : Crimea (I.S)

Died : Unknown
Status : Effective during the period

The musters show he was effective from the 1st October to the 27th November. Remarks state to Scutari 28th
November.
Medal rolls 247 and 262 offer contradictory dates of death, Dec 54 or Dec 55, however both agree he died at Scutari.

973 COWAN, Private James

Born : Unknown
Enlisted :
Medals : Crimea (B.I.S), L.S.G.C Medal

Died : Unknown
Status : Probably Rode in the Charge

The musters show he was effective from the 1st October to the 31st December. WO102 L.S.G.C Medal awarded to
Corporal Cowan recommendation 19.6.1868, issued 20.9.1868 with £5 Gratuity. WO25 Discharged 12th of March 1870.

518 CRIDGE, Private John

Born : Unknown
Enlisted :
Medals : Crimea (B.I.S)

Died : Unknown
Status : Probably Rode in the Charge

The musters show he was effective from the 1st October to the 31st December. WO100/24 page 247 Remarks: Invalided,
sent home 30th June 1855. WO100/24 page 262 Remarks: Discharged 14 August 1856.

1032 DALE, Private William

Born : Unknown
Enlisted :
Medals : Crimea (B.I.S)

Died : Unknown
Status : Probably Rode in the Charge

The musters show he was effective from the 1st October to the 31st December.

999 DALY, Private Charles

Born : Unknown
Enlisted :
Medals : Crimea (B.I.S)

Died : Unknown
Status : Probably Rode in the Charge

The musters show he was effective from the 1st October to the 31st December. WO25 Discharged 12/03/1870.

1230 DAVIES, Private John

Born : Unknown
Enlisted :
Medals : Crimea (B)

Died : Unknown
Status : Slightly wounded in the Charge

The musters show he was effective from the 1st-25th October. All three musters endorsed Scutari. Remarks state to Scutari 26th October. Casualty Roll: Listed J.Davies W/Sl at Balaklava.

879 DeCARLE, Corporal Benjamin E.

Born : Unknown
Enlisted :
Medals : Crimea (B.I.S)

Died : Unknown
Status : Probably Rode in the Charge

The musters show he was effective from the 1st October to the 31st December.
WO25 shows DeCarle transferred to the 7th Dragoon Guards on the 12th of August 1857.

1059 DELANEY, Private Charles

Born : Unknown
Enlisted :
Medals : Crimea (B.I.S), L.S.G.C Medal

Died : Unknown
Status : Probably Rode in the Charge

The musters show he was effective from the 1st October to the 31st December.
WO100/24 page 247 Remarks: Invalided, home 15th April 1855. Adm1/5631 Saved from the wreck of the "Europa"
WO102 L.S.G.C Medal awarded to Corporal Delaney recommendation 29.8.1867, issued 9.11.1867 with £5 Gratuity.

928 DEVENPORT, Private Henry

Born : Unknown
Enlisted :
Medals : Crimea (B.I.S)

Died : Unknown
Status : Probably Rode in the Charge

The musters show he was effective from the 1st October to the 31st December. WO25, To 7th Dragoons 14/09/1857.

1120 DIBBLE, Sergeant William

Born : Unknown
Enlisted :
Medals : Crimea (B.I.S), L.S.G.C Medal

Died : 27th April 1884 - Broadlands, Newport
Status : Probably Rode in the Charge

The musters show he was effective as a Corporal from the 1st-10th October and as a Sergeant from the 11th October to the 31st December. Remarks state Promoted from Corpl vice McKee reduced.
WO102 L.S.G.C Medal awarded to Troop Sergeant Major Dibble recommendation 8.9.1868, issued 12.12.1868 with £15 Gratuity. Naval and Military Gazette, May, 1884. QSM William Dibble, late Inniskilling Dragoons died on the 27th of April 1884 at Broadlands, Newport on the I.O.M. The deceased served with his Regiment for 24 years and was present during the Crimean Campaign.....He held the rank of Troop Sergeant Major for some years and afterwards as Troop Quarter-Master Sgt and after long and arduous service retiring with a pension of 2/3d per day. WO25 To pension 12/08/1873.

1029 DOBSON, Private John
Born : Unknown
Enlisted :
Medals : Crimea (B.I.S), L.S.G.C Medal

Died : Unknown
Status : Probably Rode in the Charge

The musters show he was effective from the 1st October to the 31st December.
WO102 L.S.G.C medal recommendation 24th April 1869, issued 7th July 1869 with £5 Gratuity.

945 DONES, Trumpeter Joseph
Born : Unknown
Enlisted :
Medals : Crimea (B.I.S)
E.E.Needes Collection. Crimea 3 clasp B,I,S Trumpeter Jos. Dones 6th Innis. Dgns.

Died : Unknown
Status : Probably Rode in the Charge

The musters show he was effective from the 1st October to the 31st December. WO100/24 page 245 Remarks: Invalided, sent home 19th June 55. WO12-742 Musters 31st July to 30th Sept 1863. 945 Trumpet Major Dones, Joseph (India).

779 DOOBY, Private John
Born : Unknown
Enlisted :
Medals : Crimea (B.I.S)

Died : Unknown
Status : Probably Rode in the Charge

The musters show he was effective from the 1st October to the 31st December. WO25 Deserted March 1857.

1207 DOUBLE, Private John
Born : Date unknown - St.James
Enlisted : 27th January 1853
Medals : Crimea (I.S)

Died : 19th December 1854 - Scutari
Status : Effective during the period

The musters show he was effective from the 1st October to the 27th November. 2nd and 3rd musters endorsed Scutari. Remarks state to Scutari 28th November.
The Times of Saturday, 6th January, 1855; page 8 reported from Scutari on the 25th December 1854 that "Private Johnson Doubler, 6th Dragoons had died at Scutari Hospital on the 19th December 1854 of "Febris". Trade on enlistment Smith.

994 DOULAN, Private Peter
Born : Unknown
Enlisted :
Medals : Crimea (B.I.S) ,The Distinguished Conduct Medal

Died : Unknown
Status : Probably Rode in the Charge

The musters show he was effective from the 1st October to the 31st December. Regimental number shown as 1120.
The Distinguished Conduct Medal. Recommendation dated 3rd January 1855.
The Times of Tuesday 15th January, 1856; page 5 reported that "Private P.Donlon, 6th Dragoons" had been appointed assistant to the Deputy Provost-Marshal of the Cavalry Division receiving 1s a day from the 20th December.

437 EASEY, Private Robert
Born : Unknown
Enlisted :
Medals : Crimea (B.I.S)

Died : Unknown
Status : Probably Rode in the Charge

The musters show he was effective from the 1st October to the 31st December.

919 ELLIOT, Private Robert
Born : Date Unknown - Clougher
Enlisted : 21st April 1846
Medals : Crimea (B.S)

Died : 25th October 1854 - Balaclava
Status : Killed in the Charge

The musters show he was effective from the 1st October to the 25th October. Remarks state killed in action 25th October. Listed on the Casualty Roll as killed at Balaclava. WO100/24 page 234 Remarks: Killed in Action 25th October. WO100/24 page 257 Remarks: Killed in Action - 25th. Oct:54. Trade on enlistment Farmer.

885 ELMES, Private Henry
Born : Date Unknown - Bagshot
Enlisted : 12th February 1846
Medals : Crimea (B.I.S)

Died : 19th March 1855 - Camp Kadikoi
Status : Probably Rode in the Charge

The musters show he was effective from the 1st October to the 31st December. Trade on enlistment Groom.

1170 ELMES, Private John
Born : Date Unknown - Clougher
Enlisted :
Medals : Crimea (B.I.S)

Died : 25th October 1854 - Balaklava
Status : Probably Rode in the Charge

The musters show he was effective from the 1st October to the 31st December.
WO100/24 page 234 Remarks: I cl. upon List. WO100/24 page 247 Remarks: Invalided, 15 April 1855 sent home.

1251 FAIRBURN, Private John
Born : Date Unknown - Darlington
Enlisted : 29th September 1853
Medals : Crimea (B.I.S)

Died : 15th November 1854 - Crimea
Status : Probably Rode in the Charge

The musters show he was effective from the 1st October to the 15th November. Remarks state died 15th November in Camp Hospital. WO100/24 page 234 Remarks: Died 15th November 1854 of disease.
WO100/24 page 247 Remarks: Died in Crimea, 15th November 54. Trade on enlistment Draper.

1265 FALL, Private William
Born : Date unknown - Oldbury, Birmingham
Enlisted : 16th December 1853
Medals : Crimea (B.I)

Died : Unknown
Status : Probably Rode in the Charge

The musters show he was effective from the 12th October to the 31st December. Remarks state from Scutari 10th October. Deserted 20th May 1855
Struck off for desertion, he is not on the Sebastopol clasp Roll, he was entitled to the clasp.

1074 FARNES, Farrier Major Charles
Born : Unknown
Enlisted :
Medals : Crimea (B.I.S)

Died : Unknown
Status : Probably Rode in the Charge

The musters show he was effective from the 1st October to the 31st December.

709 FELLOWS, Private William
Born : Unknown
Enlisted :
Medals : Crimea (S)

Died : Unknown
Status : Probably Rode in the Charge

The musters show he was effective from the 1st October to the 3rd November. 2nd and 3rd musters endorsed Scutari. Remarks state to Scutari 4th November. Medal roll 247 remarks: Invalided, sent home 21st August 1855.
WO25 Discharged 3rd of April 1866.

753 FERGUSON, Private Andrew
Born : Unknown
Enlisted :
Medals : Crimea (B.S)

Died : Unknown
Status : Probably Rode in the Charge

The musters show he was effective from the 1st October to the 31st December.
WO100/24 page 247 Remarks: Invalided, sent home 11 July 1855. WO25 to England 14th of January 1863.

992 FERRIS, Private John
Born : Unknown
Enlisted :
Medals : Crimea (B.I.S)

Died : Unknown
Status : Probably Rode in the Charge

The musters show he was effective from the 1st October to the 31st December.
WO100/24 page 262 Remarks: Discharged 25th. Decr. 1856.

1334 FLANNERY, Private John
Born : Date unknown - Manchester
Enlisted :
Medals : Crimea (B.I)

Died : 28th January 1855 - On board ship
Status : Probably Rode in the Charge

The musters show he was effective from the 1st October to the 31st December. Medal Roll 257 remarks: Died 28th January 1855 - Disease. 263 remarks: Died 28th January 1855 - on bd. ship

864 FLETCHER, Trumpeter Charles
Born : Unknown
Enlisted :
Medals : Crimea (B.I.S),D.C.M

Died : Unknown
Status : Probably Rode in the Charge

The musters show he was effective from the 1st October to the 31st December. The Distinguished Conduct Medal. Recommendation dated 3:1:55. The following Non-commissioned Officer has been granted medals with gratuity for distinguished conduct in the field under the provisions of the Royal Warrant of 4 December 1854, vis: Charles W. Fletcher £5. WO25 To pension, Corporal Fletcher 11th of January 1873.

948 FORSYTHE, Private Samuel
Born : Unknown
Enlisted :
Medals : Crimea (B.I.S)

Died : Unknown
Status : Probably Rode in the Charge

The musters show he was effective from the 1st October to the 31st December.

837 FOSTER, Troop Sergeant-Major George
Born : Unknown
Enlisted :
Medals : Crimea (B.I.S)

Died : Unknown
Status : Probably Rode in the Charge

The musters show he was effective from the 1st October to the 31st December.
WO100/24 page 263 Remarks: Discharged 25/12/56.

1269 FRENCH, Private George R.
Born : Date unknown - Wardley
Enlisted : 19th December 1853
Medals : Crimea (I.S)

Died : 19th January 1855 - Scutari
Status : Effective during the period

The musters show he was effective from the 1st October to the 14th December.
Remarks record to Scutari 15th December. Trade on enlistment Carpenter.

852 FROST, Armourer Sergeant George
Born : Unknown
Enlisted :
Medals : Crimea (B.I.S)

Died : 10th February 1855
Status : Probably Rode in the Charge

The musters show he was effective from the 1st October to the 31st December. WO100/24 page 244 Remarks: Died passage to Eng. Feb:55.
WO100/24 page 263 Remarks: Died. 10th. Feb. 1855.

1768 GEORGE, Private Charles
Born : Unknown
Enlisted :
Medals : Crimea (B.I.S)

Died : Unknown
Status : Probably Rode in the Charge

The musters show he was effective from the 1st October to the 31st December.
WO100/24 page 248 Remarks: Invalided-sent home 2nd June 1856. WO25 Deserted March 1867.

1133 GIBB, Private William
Born : Unknown
Enlisted :
Medals : Crimea (B.I.S)

Died : Unknown
Status : Probably Rode in the Charge

The musters show he was effective from the 1st October to the 31st December.

829 GIBSON, Sergeant James
Born : Unknown
Enlisted :
Medals : Crimea (B.I.S)

Died : Unknown
Status : Probably Rode in the Charge

The musters show he was effective as a Private from the 1st October to the 7th November and as a Corporal from the 8th November to the 31st December. Paid 54 days on shore at 1s-7 1/2d per diem, 54 days at 1d G.C pay. 9 days on board ship. Marginal note reads promoted on augmentation.
Two regimental numbers shown, 1594 and 829. He served in two regiments.
WO100/24 page 244 Remarks: Sent home 29 Sep:55.

When Colonel Crawley took over the command of the 6th Inniskilling Dragoons at Ahmednugger (India) in April 1861. Thus began a chain of events which led to the tragic death of the Regimental Sergeant Major Lilley.
Sergeant James Gibson's wife spoke to the wife of one of the conspirators a R.S.M Lilley who was under arrest. This resulted in the arrest of Pte Little for allowing Mrs Gibson to talk to Mrs Lilley. Major Swindley much to the annoyance of Crawley who intervened and "let him off"
This confrontation between an unpopular C.O. and his junior officers, ended up in a Court Martial at Aldershot, in the full glare of Victorian publicity, and came to be known as "The Crawley Affair".

628 GIBSON, Corporal John
Born : Unknown
Enlisted :
Medals : Crimea (B.I.S)

Died : Unknown
Status : Probably Rode in the Charge

The musters show he was effective as a Private from the 1st-26th October and as a Corporal from the 27th October to the 31st December.
Remarks state Promoted Corporal 27th October vice Parker.

1162 GIBSON, Private William
Born : Unknown
Enlisted :
Medals : Crimea (B.I.S)

Died : Unknown
Status : Probably Rode in the Charge

September 2007, An impressed 3 clasp medal for sale with a registered medal business on the internet called Our Heritage War Medals.

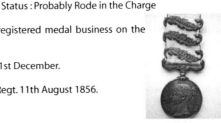

The musters show he was effective from the 1st October to the 31st December.
Paid 92 days on shore at odinary pay. 9 days on board ship.
WO100/24 page 248 entitled to clasp Sebastopol Roll endorsed Regt. 11th August 1856.
263 remarks: Discharged 26th March 1857.

443 GILLICE, Private James

Born : Unknown
Enlisted :
Medals : Crimea (B.S)

Died : Unknown
Status : Probably Rode in the Charge

The musters show he was effective from the 1st October to the 31st December.
WO100/24 page 263 Remarks: Discharged 14 Augt. 1856. The Pay Lists name him Gilleece.

968 GOBLE, Private Charles

Born : Unknown
Enlisted :
Medals : Crimea (B.I.S)

Died : 1st March 1858 - Brighton
Status : Probably Rode in the Charge

The musters show he was effective from the 1st October to the 31st December.
WO100/24 page 263 Remarks: Died 1/3/58, at Brighton.

1016 GOLDINGAY, Private William

Born : Date Unknown - Kinsale
Enlisted : 20th December 1847
Medals : Crimea (B.I.S)

Died : 5th June 1855 - Aboard Ship
Status : Probably Rode in the Charge

The musters show he was effective from the 1st October to the 30th December.
Remarks state to Scutari 31st December. Died: 5/Jan./55.
WO100/24 page 248 Remarks: Died passage to Scutari 6/6/55.
WO100/24 page 263 Remarks: Died. 5/6/55. On bd. Ship.
The Pay Lists and the Medal Rolls do not agree on his date of death.

401 GOODING, Corporal David

Born : Unknown
Enlisted :
Medals : Crimea (B.I.S)

Died : Unknown
Status : Probably Rode in the Charge

Dix Noonan Webb Auction 6 July 2004.
Crimea 1854-56, 3 clasps, Balaklava, Inkermann, Sebastopol (D. Gooding, 6th Drag.) impressed naming, has been brooch mounted and much restored, fitted with replacement suspension claw, fine £200-300. Hammer price £310.

The musters show he was effective as a Private from the 1st October to the 31st December.
Regimental number shown as 461.

667 GORDON, Private Joseph

Born : Unknown
Enlisted :
Medals : Crimea (B.I.S)

Died : Unknown
Status : Probably Rode in the Charge

The musters show he was effective from the 1st October to the 31st December.

1351 GRAINGE, Private George

Born : Unknown
Enlisted :
Medals : Crimea (B.I.S)

Died : Unknown
Status : Probably Rode in the Charge

The musters show he was effective from the 1st October to the 31st December. Two regimental numbers shown, 585 and 1351, he served in two regiments. Pay Lists record surname Grange.

1141 GRAY, Private Daniel

Born : Unknown
Enlisted :
Medals : Crimea (5)

Died : Unknown
Status : Effective during the period

The musters show he was effective from the 1st-27th October. All three musters endorsed Scutari. Remarks state sent to Scutari 28th October.
Medal roll 248 remarks: Invalided-sent home 23rd March 1855
Medal roll 263 remarks: Discharged 4th October 1855

1250 GRAY, Corporal John

Born : Unknown
Enlisted :
Medals : Crimea (I.S)

Died : Unknown
Status : Probably Rode in the Charge

The musters show he was effective from the 1st October to the 31st December.
WO25 To England, Corporal Gray, J. 14th of January 1863.

1234 GREEN, Private Albert

Born : 1835 Totteridge
Enlisted : 8th August 1853
Medals : Crimea (B.I.S)

Died : Unknown
Status : Probably Rode in the Charge

Medals appeared on Ebay 9th July 2006, Group of three medals to a Heavy Brigade Charger; 1) Crimea Medal with 3 clasps Balaclava/Sebastopol/Inkerman. Engraved naming to Private Albert Green, 6th Dragoons (PVT ALBT GREEN 6th D). Edge knock at 7 o clock, original ribbon, Balaclava clasp loose on left hand rivet (which is still intact). 2) Indian Mutiny Medal with clasp Lucknow. Officially impressed to Corporal A Green, 2nd Dragoon Guards (CORPL A.GREEN. 2nd DRAGOON GDs). Medal has been plugged at 12 oclock, original ribbon. 3) Turkish Crimea Medal-unamed as issued. Sold with 4 pages of photocopy service papers (WO 97/1736) which confirm all medal entitlements and his transfer from 6th Dragoons to 2nd Dragoon Guards on 1st December 1855. Muster Roll of 6th Dragoons WO12/733 p15 (Oct-Dec 1854)confirms that Green was present at the Charge of the Heavy Brigade on 25th October 1854 ie not in hospital or out foraging! Albert Green was born in Totteridge, near Barnet in 1835. He attested on 8th August 1853 aged 18 years. Served 1 year in the Crimea and 8.5 years in East Indies. Discharged on 16th December 1874 as Sergeant, after 21 years service. No LSGC as he had been a bad lad early on in his career. Albert Green aged 47, born Totteridge, is shown on the 1881 census residing in the Middlesex Lunatic Asylum as a Vestry Keeper. An excellent trio of medals to a cavalryman in the rather more "successful" charge. Sold for £1220.

The musters show he was effective from the 1st October to the 31st December.
WO100/24 page 248 Remarks: 2nd. Drgn. Gds.

876 GREEN, Farrier Henry

Born : Date Unknown - Paisley
Enlisted : 21st January 1846
Medals : Crimea (B.I.S)

Died : 28th December 1854
Status : Probably Rode in the Charge

The musters show he was effective as a Private from the 1st October to the 28th December. Remarks state died 28th December in Camp Hospital. WO100/24 page 232 Remarks: Died 28/12/54 of disease.
WO100/24 page 245 Remarks: Died in Crimea 28/12/54.
Trade on enlistment Smith.

1342 GROVER, Private William
Born : Date Unknown - Oxford
Enlisted : 19th September 1853
Medals : Crimea (B.I.S)

Died : 20th March 1855 - Scutari
Status : Probably Rode in the Charge

The musters show he was effective from the 1st October to the 31st December.
WO100/24 page 248 Remarks: Died at Scutari 20 Mar:55.
WO100/24 page 263 Remarks: Died 20 Mar 55, Scutari.
Trade on enlistment Servant.

1093 GROVES, Sergeant Jacob
Born : Unknown
Enlisted :
Medals : Crimea (B.I.S)

Died : Unknown
Status : Probably Rode in the Charge

The musters show he was effective from the 1st October to the 31st December. Regimental number shown as 1098.

GRYLLS, Assistant Surgeon William Richard
Born : Unknown
Enlisted :
Medals : Crimea (B.I.S)

Died : Unknown
Status : Probably Rode in the Charge

WO100/24 page 239 Remarks: Returned on Lists of 19th. Regt.
WO100/24 page 260 Remarks: Retired 17 Octr. 1856. WO25 To 5th Lancers March 1858.
Assistant Surgeon Staff 7th April 1854. To 19th Foot 28th April 1854. To 6th Dragoons 1st May 1855.
Resigned 17th Oct 1856

1031 HAINES, Private George
Born : Date Unknown - Ripley
Enlisted : 18th June 1848
Medals : Crimea (B.I.S)

Died : 17th March 1855 - Scutari
Status : Probably Rode in the Charge

A.H.Baldwin & Sons, Ltd Sales Catalogue February 1954: Crimea. 3 Bars, Balaklava, Inkermann, Sebastopol. G .Haines.
Impressed and V.F £1 15s
The musters show he was effective from the 1st October to the 31st December. WO100/24 page 248 & 263 Remark: Died
at Scutari 17 March 1855.
Trade on enlistment Labourer.

HALL, Cornet William
Born : Unknown
Enlisted :
Medals : Crimea (B.I.S)

Died : Unknown
Status : Probably Rode in the Charge

The musters show he was effective as a Troop Sergeant Major from the 1st October to the 4th November and as a Cornet
from the 5th November to the 31st December. Remarks state "Promoted to a Cornetcy in 6th Dragoons 5th November
but not notified till 18th January 1855."

WO100/24 page 238 Remarks: Promoted from Troop S. Major 5th. Novr. 1854. WO100/24 page 243 Remarks: Proceeded
to England 18th June 1855. WO100/24 page 254 Remarks: Promoted from Troop S. Major G.O. dated 17th January 1855.
Commission dated 5th November 1854. Regimental number 812.

1196 HAMBROOK, Private George J.
Born : Date Unknown - Greenwich
Enlisted : 3rd December 1852
Medals : Crimea (B.I.S)

Died : 6th January 1855 - Aboard Ship
Status : Probably Rode in the Charge

The musters show he was effective from the 1st October to the 30th December.
To Scutari 31st December. WO100/24 page 248 Remarks: Died passage to Scutari 6th January 1855.
WO100/24 page 257 Remarks: Died 6th January 1855. Disease.
WO100/24 page 263 Remarks: Died 6th January 1855. On bd. Ship. Trade on enlistment Servant.

Bounty *illustrated London News June 24th 1854 p605*
The nominal bounty given to a cavalry recruit is £5 15s 6d., and is dispensed as follws:- On being attested, 2s 6d; on intermediate approval, 7s 6d; on final approval, in cash and necessaries, when reaching his regiment, £5 5s 6d making the before-named total. But from this sum the soldier is furnished, at his own expence, with certain articles. After paying for these items, not much can remain for the individual's benefit.

988 HAND, Private Charles

Born : Unknown
Enlisted :
Medals : Crimea (B.I.S)

Died : Unknown
Status : Probably Rode in the Charge

The musters show he was effective from the 1st October to the 31st December.
WO25 Shows regimental number as 998. To England January 1862.

1261 HANSON, Private William

Born : Unknown
Enlisted :
Medals : Crimea (B.I.S)

Died : Unknown
Status : Probably Rode in the Charge

The musters show he was effective from the 1st October to the 31st December.
WO25 Discharged 9th of July 1866.

602 HARDY, Trumpeter John

Born : Unknown
Enlisted :
Medals : Crimea (B.I.S), The Sardinian War Medal

Died : Unknown
Status : Rode in the Charge

Sotheby and Co. 9th July 1975, Lot 39, ITALY, SARDINIA, "Al Valore Militare", 1855-56, in silver (Trumpeter J. Hardy, 6th Drags.), very fine and rare, sold again November 1977.
The Sardinian War Medal. "Trumpeter John Hardy acted as field trumpeter to Lieutenant-Colonel White, C.B., during the action of Balaclava, and was consequently more exposed during the whole of that day than any other man in the regiment, more particularly during the Charge of the Heavy Brigade, on which occasion he behaved very gallantly".- Carter, page 147. Only two 'Al Valore medals' were awarded to the 6th Dragoons, the other recipient being Captain D'Arcy Hunt.
The musters show he was effective from the 1st October to the 31st December.

1144 HARTE, Private John

Born : Unknown
Enlisted :
Medals : Crimea (B.I.S)

Died : Unknown
Status : Probably Rode in the Charge

The musters show he was effective from the 1st October to the 31st December.

951 HASLER, Private Thomas

Born : Unknown
Enlisted :
Medals : Crimea (B.I.S)

Died : Unknown
Status : Probably Rode in the Charge

The musters show he was effective from the 1st October to the 31st December.

861 HERRIN, Private George

Born : Unknown
Enlisted :
Medals : Crimea (B.I.S)

Died : Unknown
Status : Probably Rode in the Charge

The musters show he was effective from the 1st October to the 31st December. WO25 Discharged January 1862.

307

Officer Hut in Balaklava.

666 HICKMOTT, Sergeant Henry

Born : Unknown
Enlisted :
Medals : Crimea (I.S)

Died : 28th January 1897
Status : Effective during the period

The musters show he was effective from the 1st October to the 31st December. Promoted to Sergeant before Sebastopol.
February 6th 1897. Extract from the "Broad Arrow"
Sgt. William Hicknett - late of the 6th Inniskillings, died at Cardiff on the 28th of January, aged 73. He had served in the Crimea, taking part in the Charge of the Heavy Brigade, and had also served during the Mutiny. He had lived in Cardiff since 1867. The funeral took place on the 1st. inst. with full military honours. The coffin was covered with the Union Jack, on which rested his sword an helmet, and a wreath sent by the 6th Inniskillings from Edinburgh. The funeral expenses were sent by the Adjutant of the Inniskillings through Sgt. Major Robinson, who kindly wrote a letter to Sgt Foster of the 41st Regiment who had arranged the funeral, containing expressions of regret at losing an old comrade....
Discharged on the 31st of December 1867, with a pension of 2/- per day.

893 HIGGS, Private George

Born : Unknown
Enlisted :
Medals : Crimea (B.I.S)

Died : Unknown
Status : Probably Rode in the Charge

The musters show he was effective from the 1st October to the 31st December.

1240 HILSON, Private Henry

Born : Unknown
Enlisted :
Medals : Crimea (B.I.S)

Died : Unknown
Status : Probably Rode in the Charge

The musters show he was effective from the 1st October to the 31st December. WO25 Discharged 26/06/1867.

1151 HUGHES, Private Richard

Born : Unknown
Enlisted :
Medals : Crimea (B.I.S)

Died : Unknown
Status : Probably Rode in the Charge

John Hayward's list December 1967. R.Hughes. 6th Dragoons. Crimea clasps B.I & S impressed naming Stated as "Verified on Heavy Brigade Roll" Fine £24-0-0 .
John Hayward's list January 1974 item 102. same medal now described as "repaired at suspension claw, Good Fine £60.

The musters show he was effective from the 1st October to the 31st December. WO25 Discharged November 1860.

HUNT, Captain Edward D'Arcy

Born : Unknown
Enlisted :
Medals : Crimea (B.I.S) The Turkish Order of the Medjidie (5th Class), The Sardinian War Medal

Died : Unknown
Status : Rode in the Charge

The musters show he was effective from the 1st October to the 31st December. Disembarked from the "Trent" 1st October. 3 horses foraged at public expense.

WO100/24 page 243 Remarks: Brigade Major 1st. Cav. Bde.
The Sardinian War Medal. "Captain Hunt was squadron leader of the second squadron of the 6th Dragoons, which was detached under the command of Lieutenant-Colonel Shute, during the action of Balaklava, and lead the squadron with great steadiness and gallantry".

Turkish Medal Roll WO100-24 Folio 269 entitled.

Medals of the British Army: And how They Were Won By Thomas Carter

Captain EDWARD D'ARCY HUNT.-Captain Hunt was squadron leader of the second squadron of the 6th. Dragoons, which was detached under the command of Lieutenant-Colonel Shute, during the action of Balaklava, and led the squadron with great steadiness and gallantry, particularly in a flank attack made by Lieutenant-Colonel Shute on the squadrons of the enemy, when threatening to surround that portion of the regiment which was under the immediate command of Lieutenant-Colonel White.

In August 1860 Colonel Shute disillusioned with India wanted to sell out and retire on half-pay and return to England. The opportunity arrived for Hunt to purchase the commission, but he was only to hold the new rank for a year before he too retired from the Army.

Cornet by purchase 29th October 1847, Lieutenant by purchase 19th October 1849, Captain by purchase 15th September 1854. *Harts Annual Army list 1855.*
Captain Hunt served with the 9th Lancers in the last Punjab campaign and was present at the battles of Chillianwallah and Goojerat (Medal and clasps)....*Harts Army List 1856 note 8 page 140*
To 6th Dragoons 18th January 1850. Major July 1858. Retired (Lieut Col) 15th February 1861.

Battles of Chillianwallah were against the Sikhs of the Khalsa The seven battles of the war and the siege of the city of Multan were hard fought. British and Indian soldier's who took part in the Second Sikh War received the silver medal entitled "Punjab Campaign, 1848-9".
Clasps were issued for the battles (or in the case of Mooltan the siege) which were described as:"Mooltan","Chilllianwalah", and "Goojerat".

Photograph courtesy of Glenn Fisher

---

982 HUNTER, Private Henry

Born : Date unknown - Lisbellaw, Co Fermanagh
Enlisted : 28th January 1847
Medals : Crimea (B.I.S)

Died : Unknown
Status : Probably Rode in the Charge

Mark Carter Medal list Spring 1985 item 39. Turkish Crimea, Sardinian issue medal Henry Hunter 6th Dragoons. with photocopies of service papers. Henry Hunter was born at Lisbellaw, Co Fermanagh and enlisted on the 28th January 1847 at Enniskillin. Twice tried by Regimental Court martial. First occasion imprisoned, 2nd offence sentenced to 25 lashes. discharged 8th April 1862 at Mauritius. A probable Heavy Brigade Charger, medal fitted with silver wire suspension. VF £40. WO25 Discharged February 1862.

The musters show he was effective from the 1st October to the 31st December.

898, INSOLE Troop Sergeant-Major Joseph

Born : Unknown   Died : 17th October 1856
Enlisted :   Status : Probably Rode in the Charge
Medals : Crimea (B.I.S)
Andrew Bostock list 178B January 2001.Item CX07 Crimea 2 Clasps Balaklava,Inkermann. Troop Sergt Major Jos.Insole 6th Dgns. Verified with correct rivets. Contemporary upright engraved as seen to the Regiment GVF £1400. (You would normally expect an officially impressed medal)
For sale at DNW 23rd June 2005: Crimea 1854-56, 2 clasps, Balaklava, Inkermann (Troop Sejt. Major Jos. Insole, 6th Dgs.), contemporary engraved naming, minor edge bruising, very fine £600-700 - Unsold.
898 Troop Serjeant-Major Joseph Insole, 6th Dragoons, confirmed on roll for the two clasps. The 6th Dragoons formed part of the 'Heavy Brigade' at the Battle of Balaklava.

The musters show he was effective from the 1st October to the 31st December. WO100/24 page 244 Remarks: Sent Home 25/6/55. WO100/24 page 263 Remarks: Shot himself 17/10/56.

A letter dated 3rd September 1855 addressed to 645 Alexander Shields Ref 102/545 Reproduced below courtesy of the Museum of The Royal Dragoon Guards, York.

Canterbury
3rd September 1855

Dear Shields
       Your kind lines, for which I heartily thank you have reached me a few days ago and it has given me great pleasure to hear that by your arrival in old England you found Mrs Shields and the little ones in perfect health and that they continue to enjoy so, is a great blessing. Concerning myself I am happy to say that I have quite recovered from what you very properly call horror's of field Pestilence, filth & famine.
I need not say how much I wish soon to see you in order to have a chat together.
Captain Tower has taken Command of B. Troop here and I have therefore every reason to hope that I will get leave for some time for the purpose of visiting old friends, - as it is my intention to stay for some time in Leeds, I have no doubt that I will see you then and tell you a good deal about our old Corps, - I left it as well as can be expected under circumstances in the Crimea, previous to any departure from there I was with Captain Tower witness of the grand affair of the 18th of June. - I volunteered for the purpose how painful that the result of so grand an undertaking was not a successful one. Let us hope for the future-

This being a very busy time here prevents me from writing more to you to day. I will do my best when I persenally see you, - till then I hope you will remain with your family in the best health and if you see old friends of mine, give them all my best aspects and believe me always to remain.

Yours Truly
J.Insole
S Major 6th Dns

946 JACKSON, Private John

Born : Unknown   Died : Unknown
Enlisted :   Status : Probably Rode in the Charge
Medals : Crimea (B.I.S)
Payne Collection 1911. Catalogue page 111 Crimea Medal 3 clasps Balaklava,Inkermann,Sebastopal. J.Jackson. 6th Dragoons impressed naming.
John Haywards list January 1967. J.Jackson 6th Dragoons Crimea 3 clasps B,I and S impressed naming and turkish medal.

The musters show he was effective from the 1st October to the 31st December.
Adm1/5631 Saved from the wreck of the "Europa"

1091 JAMES, Sergeant Edward

Born : Unknown   Died : Unknown
Enlisted :   Status : Probably Rode in the Charge
Medals : Crimea (B.I.S)

The musters show he was effective from the 1st October to the 31st December. WO25 Discharged June 1857.

802 JEFFREYS, Sergeant Richard

Born : Unknown   Died : Unknown
Enlisted :   Status : Severely wounded in the Charge
Medals : Crimea (B.S) The Knight (5th Class) The French Legion of Honour

The musters show he was effective from the 1st-25th October. Remarks state to Scuatari 26th October. All three musters endorsed Scutari. Regimental number shown as 608. Casualty Roll.: Listed Jeffries W/Sv at Balaklava.
WO100/24 page 244 Remarks: Invalided, Sent home 25th Dec:ember 1854.
WO100/24 page 255 Remarks: Invalided, sent to England.
WO100/24 page 264 Remarks: Discharged 14th. Augt. 1856.

The French Legion of Honour recommendation states: "Scutari. December 31 1855. With reference to your Circular of the 24th December, I beg to recommend the name of No 802 Sergeant Richard Jeffreys of the 6th Dragoons. This Non Commissioned Officer came on service with the Regiment, and he was severely wounded at Balaklava, and he behaved very gallantly in that action.

He is now at home on account of his wounds". (Signed) H.D. White, Lt. Colonel Commanding 6 Dragoons".

1165 JENKINSON, Private Robert

Born : Date Unknown - Durdeston   Died : 23rd February 1855 - Crimea
Enlisted : 10th December 1851   Status : Probably Rode in the Charge
Medals : Crimea (B.I.S)

The musters show he was effective from the 1st October to the 31st December.
WO100/24 page 249 Remarks: Died in Crimea 23/2/55.
WO100/24 page 257 Remarks: Died 23rd. Feb:55. Disease.
Trade on enlistment Labourer.

881 JENNINGS, Private Robert

Born : Unknown   Died : Unknown
Enlisted :   Status : Probably Rode in the Charge
Medals : Crimea (B.I.S)
Glendining's 25th November 1992, Lot 496, Two: Crimea 1854- 1856, three bars, Balakiava, Inkermann, Sebastopol (R. Jennings, 6th Dragoons), impressed naming; Turkish Crimea, 1855, Sardiman issue, double ring suspender. Very fine. (£400-500)

The musters show he was effective from the 1st October to the 31st December.
Adm1/5631 Saved from the wreck of the "Europa"

1155 JOHNSTON, Private Arthur

Born : Unknown   Died : Unknown
Enlisted :   Status : Probably Rode in the Charge
Medals : Crimea (B.I.S)
Spink's Numismatic Circular October 1974, Arthur Johnston. 6th Dragoons. Crimea clasps B.I & S engraved.
Toad Hall Medals Summer 1994 item No 80 Crimea clasps B.I. and S contemporarily engraved "No 1155 Artur Johnston. 6th D." GVF £295
Toad Hall Summer 1995, List item 98 same medal £295

The musters show he was effective from the 1st October to the 31st December.

1184 JOHNSTON, Private James

Born : Unknown   Died : Unknown
Enlisted :   Status : Probably Rode in the Charge
Medals : Crimea (B.I.S)

The musters show he was effective from the 1st October to the 31st December.
1184 Pte Johnston, James Paid 92 days on shore at ordinary pay. 9 days on board ship.
WO25 Discharged 19th of August 1865.

927 JONES, Private Thomas

Born : Unknown   Died : Unknown
Enlisted :   Status : Probably Rode in the Charge
Medals : Crimea (B.I.S)

The musters show he was effective from the 1st October to the 31st December.

1058 KEANE, Private Robert

Born : Date Unknown - Kern. Glenallen   Died : 15th February 1855 - Scutari
Enlisted : 28th April 1849   Status : Slightly wounded in the Charge
Medals : Crimea (B.S)

The musters show he was effective from the 1st October to the 31st December. WO100/24 page 249&264 Remark: Died at Scutari 15/2/55.
Casualty Roll :Listed W/Sl at Balaklava.
Trade: on enlistment Labourer.

986 KELLY, Private James

Born : Unknown   Died : Unknown
Enlisted :   Status : Probably Rode in the Charge
Medals : Crimea (B.S), L.S.G.C medal
Glendinings 25th September, 1963. Lot 759. Elson Collection Part 2. Pair to J.Kelly 6th Dreagoons. Crimea 3 clasps B.I.S impressed. L.S.G.C Victorian medal V.F. Purchased by Baldwins.

The musters show he was effective from the 1st October to the 31st December. WO100/24 page 249 Remarks: Invalided-sent home 26 Mar:55.

The Army Long Service and Good Conduct Medal was instituted in 1830. Orginally awarded for exemplary conduct to soldier's with 21 years service in the infantry or 24 years in the cavalry. In 1870 the period was reduced to 18 years. In 1837 with the accession of Queen Victoria to the throne the Hanoverian emblem was removed from the coat of arms. In 1855 the fixed type suspension was replaced by a swivelling scroll suspension, with small lettering introduced on the reverse in 1874 . The ribbon plain crimson until 1917, when a pair of white stripes where added to the edges.

WO25 To pension 30th of June 1860.

446 KELLY, Private James

Born : Unknown   Died : Unknown
Enlisted :   Status : Probably Rode in the Charge
Medals : Crimea (B.I.S)
Glendinings and Co Auction 5th July, 1978. Lot 52. Crimea clasp Balaklava. J.Kelly 6th Dragoons. Impressed naming N.VF £185
The musters show he was effective from the 1st October to the 31st December. WO25 To England April 1860.

1007 KENNARD, Corporal John

Born : Unknown   Died : Unknown
Enlisted :   Status : Probably Rode in the Charge
Medals : Crimea (B.I.S)

The musters show he was effective from the 1st October to the 31st December.

1105 KENNEDY, Private William

Born : Unknown   Died : Unknown
Enlisted :   Status : Probably Rode in the Charge
Medals : Crimea (B.I.S)

The musters show he was effective from the 1st October to the 31st December.
WO25 Discharged 19th of March 1862.

944 KIDNEY, Sergeant John
Born : Unknown
Enlisted :
Medals : Crimea (B.I.S)

Died : Unknown
Status : Slightly wounded in the Charge

Eugene Ursual of Ottowa Catalogue 131, No 6531 March 1998. Crimea 1854 medal, clasps Balaklava, Inkermann, and Sebastopol contemporary engraving "Serjt. John Kidne....dns" naming obscured by contact wear and clasps loose, price £364.
The musters show he was effective as a Corporal from the 1st October to the 15th November and as a Sergeant from the 16th November to the 31st December. Remarks state Promoted from Corpl vice Thompson reduced.
Casualty Roll: Listed Corporal W/Sl at Balaklava.

895 KING, Private William
Born : Unknown
Enlisted :
Medals : Crimea (B.I.S)

Died : Unknown
Status : Probably Rode in the Charge

The musters show he was effective from the 1st October to the 31st December.

933 KISBIE, Trumpeter Franklin
Born : Unknown
Enlisted :
Medals : Crimea (B.S)

Died : Unknown
Status : Probably Rode in the Charge

Donald Hall Medal Catalogue November 1975. Crimea Medal 3 bars, B.I.S (No.933 Trmr. Franklin Kisbie, 6th Dns) V.F £95 Contemporary engraving in rather squat and thicker serif capitals. With full account of Kisbie's services which confirms that he served with the 6th Dragoons throughout the Crimea campaign being promoted Trumpeter on 1st October, 1854. He enlisted on 16th June, 1846 at Chelsea, when he was only 14 years of age.

The musters show he was effective from the 1st October to the 31st December. Remarks state from Pte vice McEwan to Trumpet Major at Depot.

1115 KNIGHT, Private David
Born : Unknown
Enlisted :
Medals : Crimea (B.I.S)

Died : Unknown
Status : Probably Rode in the Charge

The musters show he was effective from the 1st October to the 31st December. WO102 L.S.G.C Medal awarded to Farrier Major David Knight recommendation 24.4.1869, issued 7.7.1869 with £10 Gratuity.
Adm1/5631 Saved from the wreck of the "Europa" WO25 Farrier to pension 22nd of April 1873.

1256 LAHEY, Private James
Born : 1834 - Donaghmore Co Cork.
Enlisted : 2nd November 1853
Medals : Crimea (B.I.S), L.S.G.C medal

Died : Unknown
Status : Probably Rode in the Charge

Glendining 19th May 1965. Lot 359. Group of three medals James Lahey as below. Sold with other groups of medals £38. Capital Medals list, summer 1985, item 155. Group of three medals to Pte J.Lahey 6th Dragoons. Crimea Balaklava, Inkermann, Sebastopol. Pte J Lahey 6th Dgns. Contemporary upright engraved capitals.LS & GC Victorian medal Jas Lahey 6th Dragoons. Turkish Crimea British issue. Confirmed WO 100.24. LS & GC confirmed on roll. Recommended 1871-2 by O.C Regt 22nd Feb 1872.Medal sent to Sandhurst 10th August 1872. Born Donaghmore Co Cork. Joined 6th Dragoons at Newcastle upon Tyne 2nd November 1853. Aged 19 years. Domestic Servant. Re-Engaged India for further 12 years on 2nd November 1865, and served until 19th January 1875. Place of residence Cambridge Town, Surrey.
Four pages of service history GVF £345.
The musters show he was effective from the 1st October to the 31st December. WO25 Time Exp. 19/01/1875.

856 LAKIN, Private Charles
Born : Unknown
Enlisted :
Medals : Crimea (B.I.S)

Died : Unknown
Status : Probably Rode in the Charge

The musters show he was effective from the 1st October to the 31st December.

963 LATTIMER, Private Alexander

Born : Date Unknown - Coleraine
Enlisted : 20th October 1846
Medals : Crimea (B.S)

Died : 25th October 1854 - Balaclava
Status : Killed in the Charge

The musters show he was effective from the 1st October to the 25th October. Remarks state killed in action 25th October. Listed on the Casualty Roll as killed at Balaclava. WO100/24 page 234 Remarks: Killed in Action 25th October. WO100/24 page 257 Remarks: Killed in Action - 25th. Oct:54. 9s-3d in credit, effects number 355119, small book lost. Trade on enlistment Farmer.

1171 LAWREY, Private Thomas

Born : Date Unknown - Coleraine
Enlisted :
Medals : Crimea (B.I.S)

Died : Unknown
Status : Probably Rode in the Charge

Spink 21st July 2005, Lot 164, Crimea 1854-56, three clasp, Balaklava, Inkermann, Sebastopol (No.1171 Thomas Lawry 6th D....oons.), depot impressed, one lug removed, unofficial rivets, contact marks, edge bruising, fine, with ornately patterned silver riband buckle. Hammer Price £1000.

The musters show he was effective from the 1st October to the 31st December.

Hunt and Roskill, had the task of fitting the suspension to the medals struck by the mint and manufacturing all the Crimea clasps. Some clasps were attached by them to unnamed medals and many other clasps were sent to the Crimea loose.
Many jewellers sold ornate buckles, as an additional service to the soldier who had his medal privately engraved.
WO25 To 7th Dragoon Guards 14th of September 1857.

1137 LEES, Private Robert

Born : Unknown
Enlisted :
Medals : Crimea (B.I.S)

Died : Unknown
Status : Probably Rode in the Charge

The musters show he was effective from the 1st October to the 31st December.

896 LEMMON, Farrier George

Born : Unknown
Enlisted :
Medals : Crimea (B.I.S)

Died : Unknown
Status : Probably Rode in the Charge

The musters show he was effective from the 1st October to the 31st December.
Adm1/5631 Saved from the wreck of the "Europa"

1024 LEWIS, Private Frederick

Born : Unknown
Enlisted :
Medals : Crimea (B.I.S)

Died : September 1861.
Status : Probably Rode in the Charge

The musters show he was effective from the 1st October to the 31st December. WO25 Died September 1861

1169 LITTLE, Private John

Born : Unknown
Enlisted :
Medals : Crimea (B.I.S)

Died : Unknown
Status : Probably Rode in the Charge

The musters show he was effective from the 1st October to the 31st December.

A member of a group of Crimean War and Indian Mutiny Veterans who paraded for the Queen in Edinburgh, May 1903.

1262 LITTLEWOOD, Private Daniel

Born : Unknown
Enlisted :
Medals : Crimea (B.S)

Died : Unknown
Status : Probably Rode in the Charge

The musters show he was effective from the 1st October to the 27th October.
All three musters endorsed Scutari. Marginal note reads to Scutari 28th October. WO25 Discharged 09/07/1866.

1041 LOWE, Private James

Born : Unknown
Enlisted :
Medals : Crimea (B.I.S)

Died : Unknown
Status : Probably Rode in the Charge

The musters show he was effective from the 1st October to the 31st December.
WO25 Discharged March 1857.

959 LUCAS, Private William

Born : Unknown
Enlisted :
Medals : Crimea (B.I.S)

Died : Unknown
Status : Probably Rode in the Charge

The musters show he was effective from the 1st October to the 31st December. WO25 to 7th Dr Gds 14/09/1857.

1204 LYONS, Private Alexander

Born : Date Unknown - Lambeth
Enlisted : 28th May 1852
Medals : Crimea (B.I.S)

Died : 22nd December 1854 - Malta
Status : Probably Rode in the Charge

The musters show he was effective from the 1st October to the 4th November.
WO12-733 Marginal note reads to Scutari 4th November.
WO100/24 page 249 Remarks: Died at Malta 22 Dec:54.
WO100/24 page 258 Remarks: Died 22 Dec:54-Disease.
Trade on enlistment Baker.

754 LYONS, Private William

Born : Unknown
Enlisted :
Medals : Crimea (B.I.S)

Died : Unknown
Status : Probably Rode in the Charge

The musters show he was effective from the 1st October to the 31st December.
Casualty Roll page 35,. Shows a Pte William Lyons slightly wounded at Balaklava on the 25th October 1854. Could be this soldier or Pte 1161 Lyons.W.

WO12-733 Marginal note written in red reads Laborer Dromara.
WO25 Discharged 11th of May 1869.

1161 LYONS, Private William

Born : Unknown
Enlisted :
Medals : Crimea (B.I.S)

Died : Unknown
Status : Slightly wounded in the Charge

The musters show he was effective from the 1st October to the 31st December.
Casualty Roll page 35,. Shows a Pte William Lyons slightly wounded at Balaklava on the 25th October 1854. Could be this soldier or Pte 754 Lyons.W.
WO12-733 Marginal note written in red reads Carpenter Armagh.
Medal roll WO100-24 Folio 250, entitled to clasp Sebastopol roll endorsed Regt 11th August 1856.
Discharged 26th December 1856.

977 MADGWICK, Private William

Born : January 1826 - Midhurst, Sussex
Enlisted : 24th November 1846
Medals : Crimea (B.I.S)

Died : Unknown
Status : Probably Rode in the Charge

Glendinings Auction 3rd July 1985, Lot 64 Crimea medal with three bars, Balaklava, inkermann, Sebastopol (W.Madgwick, 6th Drgns). Impressed naming "No 977 6th D" has been engraved at the beginning and end of the naming. This appears to have been done on a regimental basis, as it is often seen on medals to the 6th D.Gds Very Fine. VF £340.
Osborne Military Medals September 2008, listed on www. Militarymedals.ca $4,250 Canadian dollars, medal as above.

The musters show he was effective from the 1st October to the 31st December.

Pte William Madgwick 6th Dragoons Heavy Brigade Charger

Born in the town of Midhurst in the county of Sussex in January 1826, 977 Pte William Madgwick attested with the 6th Dragoons on 24 November 1846 at 20 years of age. At the time of his enrolment he was a labourer in Sussex. His service record indicates that he was a private from 24 November 1846 to 27 November 1863. Between 12 November 1857 and 5 May 1858, Pte Madgwick was tried and imprisoned for disgraceful conduct. His record indicates that he has five entries in the Regimental Defaulters book. He is not entitled to the Army Long Service and Good Conduct Medal.
Pte Madgwick served in the Crimea and Turkey. He also served in the East Indies. In the Crimea the 6th Inniskilling Dragoons saw action in the Charge of the Heavy Brigade on 25 October 1854.

Musters for the 6th Inniskilling Dragoons show Madgwick with the unit during the period. It is generally presumed therefore that Madgwick would have charged with the Heavy Brigade.

Pte Madgwick's medal is officially impressed. It has been additionally and unofficially engraved with Madgwick's service number "No. 977" and unit "6th D".

Information supplied by Ken Osborne.
Adm1/5631 Saved from the wreck of the "Europa"

1125 MAGUIRE, Private John

Born : Unknown
Enlisted :
Medals : Crimea (B.I.S)

Died : Unknown
Status : Probably Rode in the Charge

The musters show he was effective from the 1st October to the 31st December.

MANLEY, Brevet Major Robert George

Born : Unknown
Enlisted :
Medals : Crimea (B.I.S), The Turkish Order of the Medjidie (5th Class)

Died:12th March 1889 - Mancetter Lodge, Atherstone
Status : Rode in the Charge

Christie's 17th November 1987, Lot 116, Three: Captain R. G. Manley, 6th Dragoon Guards, Crimea, three clasps, Balaklava, Inkermann, Sebastopol, engraved in serif capitals; Turkey, Order of the Medjidie, Fifth Class, Badge, silver, gold and enamel; Turkish Crimea, Sardinian issue, with claw suspension, nearly very fine (3) £450-550. Hammer price £605.

Fourth son of John Shawe Manley, of Manley Hall, Staffordshire.
Major Robert George Manley entered the army as a Cornet, 1846, Lieutenant, 1847, Captain, 1853 and was a troop leader of his regiment during the charge of the Heavy Brigade at Balaklava, 25th October, 1854 and subsequently at Inkermann, Tchernaya and the siege and fall of Sebastopol (Brevet Major)
Brevet Major 12th December 1854. Retired 1858. [Jackson, Inniskilling Dragoons, p.293.]

The musters show he was effective from the 1st October to the 31st December. Disembarked from the "Tyrone" 7th October. 2 horses lost at sea, 1 horse foraged at public expense.

MARSHALL, Paymaster James

Born : Unknown
Enlisted :
Medals : Crimea (I.S)

Died : Unknown
Status : Effective during the period

The musters show he was effective from the 1st October to the 31st December.

Medal roll WO100-24 Folio 250, entitled to clasp Sebastopol recorded as paymaster J.Marshall. NB Quartermaster on this roll is recorded as J.K.Mountain.
Rank in Regiment Quartermaster on the 14th April 1843 *Harts Army List 1852-53 page 142.*

Paymaster James Marshall 4th May 1855, Quartermaster 14th April 1843. Note 14. Paymaster Marshall E&C served in the Eastern Campaign of 1854-55 including the battles of Balaklava and Inkermann and siege of Sebastopol (Medal and clasps).*Harts Army List 1858 page 140.*

260 remarks: Placed on half pay 24th August 1856.

Photograph courtesy of Glenn Fisher

1206 MAUGHAN, Private George

Born : Unknown
Enlisted :
Medals : Crimea (B.I.S)

Died : August 1922
Status : Probably Rode in the Charge

Liverpool Coin and Medal list Nov/Dec 1988. Item 456. Crimea 3 Bars Balaklava,Inkermann, Sebastopol, Turkish Crimea Sardinian version. Impressed naming with engraved additional details near claw. E Maughan 6th Dragoons NVF £275.

The musters show he was effective from the 1st October to the 31st December.

Heroes of the Crimea by Michael Barthrop p40 - We had picquetted our horses after watering when a shout went up,"the videttes are circling", and they were making the figure eight, showing infantry and cavalry approaching. p41 - Amongst the Inniskillings Sergt Maughan saw how Sergt Bolton had his leg knocked off "The shot hit my horse first, came between us and doubled up my sword like a hook and grazed my leg".

From the Times Thursday 17th August 1922.
Funeral of the late Sergt. Maughan, the Inniskilling Dragoons, a survivor of the Charge of Scarlett's Heavy Brigade at Balaclava, will leave 1 Minford Garden Mansions, Shepherd's Bush Roads at 11:15 tomorrow (Friday) for Hammersmith Cemetery.

1280 MAWSON, Private William

Born : Unknown
Enlisted :
Medals : Crimea (B.S)

Died : Unknown
Status : Probably Rode in the Charge

The musters show he was effective from the 1st October to the 31st December.
WO100/24 page 264 Remarks: Discharged 4 Decr. 1856.

1624 McCANNA, Private John
Born : Unknown
Enlisted :
Medals : Crimea (B.I.S)

Died : Unknown
Status : Slightly wounded in the Charge

The musters show he was effective from the 1st October to the 25th October, 27th December to the 31st December.
WO12-733 First and second musters endorsed Scutari. Marginal note reads to Scutari 26th October.
Casualty Roll: Listed W/Sl at Balaklava.
WO100/24 page 250 Remarks: Invalided-sent home 31st July 1855.

1178 McCARTEN, Private Arthur
Born : Date Unknown - Armagh
Enlisted : 28th May 1852
Medals : Crimea (B.I.S)

Died : 6th April 1855 - Crimea
Status : Probably Rode in the Charge

The musters show he was effective from the 1st October to the 3rd December.
WO12-733 third muster endorsed Scutari. Marginal note reads to Scutari 4th December.
WO100/24 page 250&265 Remark: Died in Crimea 6 April 55.
Trade: on enlistment Baker.

578 McCLEAN, Private Samuel
Born : Unknown
Enlisted :
Medals : Crimea (B.I.S)

Died : Unknown
Status : Probably Rode in the Charge

The musters show he was effective from the 1st October to the 31st December.
WO100/24 page 265 Remarks: Discharged 29 Jany 1856.

1205 McCONVILL, Private Edward
Born : Unknown
Enlisted : 1854
Medals : Crimea (B.I.S), L.S.G.C Medal

Died : Unknown
Status : Probably Rode in the Charge

Sotheby's Auction June 1984. Corporal E. McConville. 6th Dragoons and R.A. Crimea clasps B.I.S officially impressed and further engraving (upside down) L.S & G.C Medal as Corporal 2nd Brigade R.A Surname officially corrected.
The following refers to three Crimean War medals awarded to Edward McConvill.
Crimea Group named to: Edward McConvill. 6th or INNISKILLING Dragoons.
Clasp BALAKLAVA, INKERMAN & SEBASTOPAL.
LONG SERVICE AND GOOD CONDUCT MEDAL NAMED TO: CORPI. E.McConvill. 2nd. BDE. Royal Artillery.
Turkish Crimea medal un-named.
Condition: GVF. Hammer price £275

The musters show he was effective from the 1st October to the 31st December.
Dragoon 1205 Edward McConvill attested for the 6th or Inniskilling Dragoons in 1854 aged 18 years. Served 12 years and 68 days until discharge. The then re-enlisted for a second period on the 26th Aug., 1865 for the Royal Artillery while living in Melbourne Australia and served until again discharged in 1874 aged 39 years. E. McConvill's discharge papers in WO 97/1811 confirm his good conduct Medal his possession of five Good Conduct badges and his entitlement to the Crimea medal with three clasps. All three clasps are also verified on the medal roll WO 100/24 along with his entitlement to a Turkish Medal.
Information supplied by Steven Robb

1102 McKEE, Private William
Born : Unknown
Enlisted :
Medals : Crimea (B.I.S)

Died : Unknown
Status : Probably Rode in the Charge

The musters show he was effective from the 1st October to the 31st December. Remarks state reduced to Private 11th October. WO12-733 1102 Serjeant McKnee William, Paid for 10 days at 2s-2d per diem from 1st Oct to 10th Oct. 9 days on board ship. Marginal note reads Reduced to private 11th October.
WO25 To 5th Lancers November 1858.

1139 McKEOWN, Private John

Born : Unknown
Enlisted :
Medals : Crimea (B.I.S)

Died : Unknown
Status : Probably Rode in the Charge

The musters show he was effective from the 1st October to the 31st December.

670 McKIBBIN, Private William

Born : Unknown
Enlisted :
Medals : Crimea (B.I.S)

Died : 13th May 1856 - Lisburn, Ireland
Status : Probably Rode in the Charge

The musters show he was effective from the 1st October to the 31st December.
WO100/24 page 250 Remarks: Invalided 11 July 55-sent home.
WO100/24 page 265 Remarks: Died 13/5/56, Lisburn, Ireland.

689 McMANUS, Private Patrick

Born : 1823 - County Leitrim, Ireland
Enlisted : 29th March 1841
Medals : Crimea (B.I.S)L.S.G.C Medal

Died : Unknown
Status : Probably Rode in the Charge

Sold on Ebay September 2007 with the following description,
£195
An interesting Turkish Crimea Medal awarded to Private P. McManus,
6th Dragoon Guards, who was present in the charge of the heavy
brigade at Balaklava on 25th October 1854. Turkish Crimea Medal
1855, Sardinian flag to fore issue, with correct period engraved
naming in upright capitals to: (P. McMANUS. 6TH DRAGOONS).
With ornate suspension. Patrick McManus was born in the parish
of Callygallow, County Leitrim, Ireland in 1823. He enlisted as
Private (No.689) into the 6th Dragoon Guards on 29th March 1841
at Longford, aged 18, being described as a Carpenter by trade. He
served as a Private from 29th March 1841 right through to 21st
March 1858, having been granted one instance of Good Conduct
Pay, and he transferred to the 18th Hussars as a Private on 1st April
1858 serving through to 3rd April 1865, earning three more awards
of Good Conduct Pay. He was never promoted.

He had served with the 6th Dragoon Guards in the Crimean War,
and was present at the battle of Balaklava, where he is confirmed as
a member of the Charge of the Heavy Brigade. He also saw action
at Inkermann and during the siege of Sebastopol, receiving the
Crimea Medal with 3 clasps and the Turkish Crimea Medal. He later
received the Long Service and Good Conduct Medal, and he was
discharged at Canterbury on 3rd April 1865 "at his own request".
The 1881 Census shows the same man though shown as 'Patrick
McMonus' as a General Labourer, aged 59, and living at Gateshead,
Durham, married to Ann, aged 41, from Birmingham. They had two
sons, and three daughters, in order of age, Thomas, aged 23, a Glass
Maker; Bessie, aged 16, a General Servant; Mary, aged 14, Servant
at Home; Jane, aged 12, at school, and then Patrick, aged 2. His
nephew, Alexander McMonus, born in Ireland, and aged 17 was also living with him.

The musters show he was effective from the 1st October to the 31st December.

1177 McMANUS, Private Thomas

Born : Unknown
Enlisted :
Medals : Crimea (B.S)

Died : Unknown
Status : Probably Rode in the Charge

The musters show he was effective from the 1st October to the 31st December.
WO100/24 page 265 Remarks: Discharged 26th. Decr. 1856.

The cat of nine tails *Extracts from Leaves from a soldier's note book by Sergt Major Henry Franks pp 6-7.*
The Regiment paraded in the Riding School, the troops formed three sides the fourth side being a wall with some fixings attached. The Guard marched the prisoner, a young fellow of about twenty-three years of age into the centre of the square. He looked around with a contemptuous look, half smile and sneer combined. The Colonel called "Attention" the proceedings of a Court Martial was read out. the Court had sentenced him to receive a hundred lashes for striking a sergeant. He was then tied up to the fixings, two Trumpeters and two Farriers administered 25 lashes each. He took the punishment without moving a muscle.
A period of sixty two years has passed, it has been my ill-fortune to witness many such parades. But 'I have not forgotten', the first parade I attended in the 5th Dragoon Guards in (November 1839).

The harsh conditions, lack of decent food sometimes led to drunkenness and indiscipline, which led to fines, arrest, imprisonment, flogging or both. The death after the punishment of Private Frederick White of the 7th Hussars, made the army take heed of public opinion and in 1847 reduced the maximum number of strokes to fifty.

1027 McNAMARA, Corporal John
Born : Date unknown - Ireland   Died : Unknown
Enlisted : 1st June 1845   Status : Probably Rode in the Charge
Medals : Crimea (B.I.S) 1887 Jubilee (clasp 1897), Coronation Medal 1902, LSGCM, Turkish Crimea.
Group formerly in Brigadier Palmer's collection; sold 1919 for £5-5-0.

The musters show he was effective from the 1st October to the 31st December.

History of the Kings Bodyguard of the Yeoman of the Guard by R. Henwell 1904, page 251. Sgt John McNamara 6th Dragoons, Enlisted 1st June 1845, served 25 1/12 years. 'Discharged July 1873'. Appointed to Yeoman of Guard 9th January, 1878. Still serving in 1904. There is a photograph of McNamara, reproduced in McInnes, *Yeoman of the Guard* p.135, taken from an album presented to the Duke of York (later King George V) to commemorate his marriage in 1893.

1166 McVEIGH, Private Patrick
Born : Unknown   Died : Unknown
Enlisted :   Status : Probably Rode in the Charge
Medals : Crimea (B.I.S)

The musters show he was effective from the 1st October to the 31st December.

1192 MIDDLETON, Private William
Born : Unknown   Died : Unknown
Enlisted :   Status : Probably Rode in the Charge
Medals : Crimea (B.I.S)
1855 British Heavy Brigade French Issue Crimea Medal To W. Middleton 6th Dragoon Guards (Possibly a charger?) For sale in an internet Auction 2nd Feb 2007 Bid US $ 199.99 Gatewest Coin, 1711 Corydon Avenue, Winnipeg, MB, R3N 0J9 CANADA

The musters show he was effective from the 1st October to the 31st December.

WO100-24 Folio 250. Entitled to clasp Sebastopol roll endorsed Regt 11/8/56
WO25 Records 1192 Middleton. W. P to 18th Hussars, 6th of June 1858.

941 MILES, Trumpeter William
Born : Unknown   Died : 3rd of November 1870 - Brighton
Enlisted :   Status : Probably Rode in the Charge
Medals : Crimea (B.I.S), L.S.G.C Medal
James Auction, 33 Timberhill, Norwich. Lot 66. 25th September 1987, est £350. Crimea 3 clasps, B,I,S Tmptr. Wm Miles engraved naming. Capitals, edge bruises otherwise VF.
OMRS Journal. Vol 27, No 3. Auction 1988. Secretarys notes: Stolen Crimea medal at James Auctions on 20th July 1988, discription as above. Information to James of Norwich, 33 Timberhill, Norwich.

The musters show he was effective from the 1st October to the 31st December.
WO 100-24 Folio 245. Entitled to clasp Sebastopol roll as Trumpeter Roll endorsed Regt 11/8/54 endorsed Regt 11/8/56.
WO102 L.S.G.C recommendation 19.7.1869, issued 20.10.1869 with £5 Gratuity.
WO25 Died at Brighton 3rd of November 1870

1053 MILLAR, Private Joseph

Born : Unknown

Enlisted : 5th April 1849

Medals : Crimea (B.I.S)

Died : Unknown

Status : Probably Rode in the Charge

Sotheby 1st March 1984, Lot 47 medal as below Good VF toned £297.

DNW Auction 28th March 2002 Lot No 43, Gordon Everson Collection. Officially impressed.Crimea 1854-56, 3 clasps, Balaklava, Inkermann, Sebastopol (J. Miller, 6th Dragns.) officially impressed naming and additionally engraved 'No. 1053 6th D', as often found to this regiment, minor edge nicks, otherwise very fine £700-900. Hammer price £820

The musters show he was effective from the 1st October to the 31st December.

The musters show he was effective as a Corporal from the 1st October to the 12th November and as a Private from the 13th November. Remarks state reduced to Private.

Joseph Miller enlisted at Liverpool on 5 April 1849, aged 22. He was promoted to Corporal on 13 November 1854, but reduced to Private on 13 November 1854. He served in the Crimea and was present at Balaklava, Inkermann and Sebastopol. He was promoted to Corporal in 1856 and to Sergeant on 12 July 1857, but reduced to Private once more on 9 May 1860. He served in India from 1858 until discharged on 21 July 1860.

704 MILLS, Private Edward

Born : Date unknown - Kidderminster, Worcestershire

Enlisted : June 1841

Medals : Crimea (B.I.S), L.S.G.C Medal

Died : Unknown

Status : Probably Rode in the Charge

Dixons Gazette No 28 Winter 2001/2002, Group of three as below, £2200.

DNW 2nd April 2004, The collection of medals formed by the late John Darwent, Lot 172, Three: Troop Sergeant-Major E. Mills, 6th Dragoons, a witness at the famous Court-Martial of Colonel Crawley. Crimea 1854-56, 3 clasps, Balaklava, Inkermann, Sebastopol (6th Dragoons), officially impressed naming; Army L.S. & G.C., V.R., 3rd issue, small letter reverse (47 Troop Serjt. Major, 6th Dragoons), officially impressed naming; Turkish Crimea 1855, Sardinian issue (47, 6th Dragoons), old engraved naming, contact marks and edge bruising, good fine or better (3) Hammer Price £2000

For sale by Historick Orders May 2008

A scarce combination with a Long Service Medal ,Crimea war medal group named to the same man and regt.Crimea medal named to: E. Mills. 6th. Dragoons Clasps: Balaclava, Inkermann & Sebastopol Original Ribbon Long Service Good Conduct Medal named to: 47 Troop Serjt. Major E.D. Miller. 6th Dragoons Sardinia medal named to 47. E. Miller. 6th Dragoons, service information below. Condition: VF. Cost $7,595.00 or £3750

The musters show he was effective from the 1st October to the 31st December.

Edward Mills was born at Kidderminster, Worcestershire and enlisted in the 6th Dragoons at Birmingham in June 1841, aged 20 years. In the Crimea campaign he is verified as having received the Medal and 'Balaklava', 'Inkermann' and 'Sebastopol' clasps, prior to being discharged at Aldershot in September 1856.

On the 10th October 1857 he re-enlisted in his old regiment at Brighton aged 36, trade stone mason, advanced to Corporal 10th December 1857 and to Sergeant 1st August 1858 . Service in India followed several months later, and while stationed at Mhow he became embroiled in the notorious affair which culminated in the Court-Martial of Lieutenant-Colonel Crawley, C.O. of the 6th Dragoons. When proceedings were convened back in Aldershot in November 1863, Mills was called as a prosecution witness. Sergeant Mills had been a planted witness. When an attempt was made to blacken the character of Sergeant-Major Lilley, his evidence being of far more use to the defence, not least the charge of frequent drunkenness he cast against Regimental Sergeant-Major Lilley, thereby supporting the allegations made by the Colonel.

Mills was asked to specify the occasions when he saw Lilley drunk:-

"In the first place in Parliament Street, Nottingham. I saw him again drunk at Mr Wilkinson's the Victoria at Newcastle-upon-Tyne. I saw him again drunk at Balaclava; he was in the company of S.M.Moreton; he sent me down for three bottles of gin and gave me a sovereign to pay for them. I saw him drunk at Scutari. I pulled off his boots and covered him up in bed that night. I saw him drunk in Durham, when he was on the recruiting service, when the squadron lay there. I found him on his bed drunk.

I saw him in the female hospital which he occupied when we first marched into Mhow; he lived there. The day we marched into Mhow I was Regimental Orderly Sergeant. I went up to my tea at 7 o'clock, and he ordered me away like a dog; he was then drunk, and I went without anything. At Burhampore I saw him drunk in his tent on the line march."

Under cross examination Mills said no one else to his knowledge had seen the events described. The only other person mentioned was S.M.Moreton who was still stationed in India.

Returning to India at the end of the trial, Mills was advanced to Troop Sergeant-Major on the 18th January 1864, an advancement that was nearly curtailed in September of the following year, when, for reasons unknown, he was confined, tried and sentenced to be reduced to the rank of Private, and to receive 28 days imprisonment. Fortuitously, however, his earlier performance back in Aldershot at the Court-Martial had not been forgotten, and Colonel Crawley intervened, the sentence being remitted and Mills re-instated as Troop Sergeant-Major.
The Crawley Affair by A.H.Haley.Bullfinch publications 1972
Discharged to a pension on the 10th October 1867 after 25 years service which included 15 years former service in the 6th Dragoons, in possession of two good conduct badges, he gave his intended place of residence as Cobham Hall, near Gravesend, and he appears with his family in the 1871 census as a resident of Cobham Street, Cobham, Kent - and as being employed as a Sergeant-Major in the Yeomanry Cavalry.
Yeomanry, the name given to the volunteer mounted troops of the home defence army were organised on a county basis, the landed gentry officering the force, the farmers and yeomen serving in its ranks. In March 1793, because of the concern of invasion and domestic unrest, the Government issued , a circular to the Lord-Lieutenants and high Sheriffs, suggesting, the formation of volunteer cavalry units. In 1816 worried by the lack of organisation and training of the Yeomanry regiments the Government required six days paid training per year during peacetime.

938 MITCHELL, Private Michael
Born : Unknown   Died : Unknown
Enlisted :   Status : Probably Rode in the Charge
Medals : Crimea (B.I.S)

The musters show he was effective from the 1st October to the 31st December.
WO100/24 page 264 Remarks: Discharged 26 Decr. 1856.

679 MONAGHAN, Private Patrick
Born : Unknown   Died : Unknown
Enlisted :   Status : Probably Rode in the Charge
Medals : Crimea (B.I.S)

The musters show he was effective from the 1st October to the 31st December. WO25 Discharged 09/03/1867.

1191 MONDAY, Private Henry Charles
Born : Unknown   Died : Unknown
Enlisted :   Status : Probably Rode in the Charge
Medals : Crimea (B.I.S)

The musters show he was effective from the 1st October to the 31st December.
Medal roll Regt. 11-8-56 medal and clasps already issued.
WO25 Discharged 18th of May 1865.

983 MORRIS, Private James
Born : Unknown   Died : Unknown
Enlisted :   Status : Probably Rode in the Charge
Medals : Crimea (B.I.S)

The musters show he was effective from the 1st October to the 31st December.

375 MORRISON Saddler Sergeant Nathaniel
Born : Unknown   Died : Unknown
Enlisted :   Status : Probably Rode in the Charge
Medals : Crimea (B.I.S)

The musters show he was effective as a Private from the 1st October to the 26th November and as a Saddler Sergeant from the 27th November to the 31st December. Remarks state from Private 27th November.

WO100/24 page 244 Remarks: Invalided, sent Home 26/2/55.
WO100/24 page 265 Remarks: Discharged 16 Augt. 1856.
Medal roll Turkish Medal WO 100-24 Folio 265. 375 Saddler Sergt Morrison Nathan. Discharged 18th August 1856

1046 MORTON, Troop Sergeant-Major Andrew

Born : 4th October 1832 - Kinally, near Inniskillen
Enlisted : 4th January 1849
Medals : Crimea (B.I.S), The French Medaille Militaire, L.S.G.C medal

Died : Unknown
Status : Probably Rode in the Charge

The musters show he was effective as a Sergeant from the 1st October to the 31st December.
The French Medaille Militaire. (For) "gallantry in the field in the action of Balaklava on the 25th. of October, 1854, and served with uniform good conduct during the whole of the campaign."

While stationed at Mhow, India he became embroiled in the notorious Crawley affair.

WO102 L.S.G.C Medal awarded to Regimental Sergeant Major Morton recommendation 3.8.1867, issued 6.11.1867 with £15 Gratuity.

SOUTH NOTTS. YEOMANRY CAVALRY.—As Regimental. Sergeant-Major Moreton, who has been connected with the above regiment during the last three years. He is about to leave the county, the following particulars of his career may prove interesting to our readers. He has had many narrow escapes both by flood and field, and his breast is decorated with medals as honourable rewards for his services to his Queen and country. In 1849 he joined the 6th Inniskilliing Dragoons, and with his regiment he remained for move than 20 years.
He served throughout the whole of the Crimean Campaign, and received the French Military War Medal for gallantry and general good conduct, in addition to his other medals .He was with the regiment during the whole of its service in India, and received the medal with gratuity for long service and good conduct. In the year 1854 the Sergeant Major had the misfortune to be on board the Europa troop ship, bound for the Crimea, with the Head Quarters of the " Inniskillings " on board.   Three days after sailing from Southampton the ship was destroyed by fire, and Colonel Moore, the commanding officer, Vet. Surgeon Kelly, together with twenty-one non-commissioned officers and men, two women, and three sailors, the whole of the baggage and horses were lost. The survivors were rescued! about ten hours after taking to the boats, by H.M.S. Tribune.   On this occasion. Sergeant-Major Moreton narrowly escaped becoming food for the fishes. Owing to a violent attack of sea sickness he was in a very weak state of health, and when the ship caught fire the excitement and suspense produced such an effect that he fell into a death-like swoon.   His companions in the boat, thinking him dead, made preparations for throwing him into the sea, but at the earnest intercession of an old soldier, the throwing overboard was postponed till daylight. In the meantime the Sergeant-Major became conscious, and with rough but friendly hands, was lifted on board the Tribune.
He subsequently proceeded to the seat of war, and served with distinction throughout the whole of the campaign, He lost his horse in the Balaklava charge, but fortunately, in the midst of the fight, and when the Inniskilling were reforming to charge a second time, he was enabled to secure a loose horse belonging to a Russian officer, which he instantly mounted, and rode the remainder of the day,.
"When the Indian Mutiny broke out, Sergeant-Major Moreton embarked with his regiment for India, where he remained for nearly nine years, returning to England in 1866.   In March, 1872, he left the Inniskilling Dragoons, having volunteered for duty with the South Notts, Yeomanry Cavalry, and the regimental orders published at the time contain most flattering allusions to his bravery, zeal, and integrity.   His connection with this county has not been very lengthy, but he has nevertheless, earned the esteem and goodwill of the whole of his regiment. Last year he was a candidate for the Governorship of the Borough Gaol, and a short time ago he applied for the post of Master of the Union.   In both cases, we believe, he was second, The testimonials which on these occasions Sergeant-Major Moreton received from the officers of the regiment and others, were of the most flattering .kind, and are the most indisputable evidence of the high Value which was set upon his services.

WO97-1747 Discharge Papers.Regimental Sergeant Major 1046 Andrew Moreton enlisted in the 6th Dragoons at Enniskillin, Fermanagh on the 4th January 1849. Aged 17 yrs 3 months, trade a Labourer. Born Kinally, Nr Enniskillin on the 4th October 1832. Promoted to Corporal 25th August 1853. Sergant 10th May 1854. to TSM 1st April 1855. Tried by Court Martial on the 19th March 1857, reduced but re-instated. re-engaged at Ahmed Nuggur 4th October 1861 for 12 years. Appointed RSM 26th May 1862. Medal entitlement, Crimea 3 clasps, Turkish Crimea, Medaille Militaire and Army L.S.G.C medal, Victorian. Discharged from Cahir on 8th April, 1873 aged 41 years 6 months. 5' 9 1/2" Swarthy complexion. Dark hazel eyes. Dark brown hair, small scar on bridge of nose. Intended place of residence Granby Street, Nottingham. Served Crimea and Turkey 2 years 5 months, India 8 years 5 months, remainder in UK.

472 MORTON, Private Peter

Born : Date unknown - Fakely
Enlisted : 16th November 1836
Medals : Crimea (B.I.S)

Died : 13th June 1855 - Crimea
Status : Probably Rode in the Charge

The musters show he was effective from the 1st October to the 31st December.
WO100/24 page 250 Remarks: Died in Crimea 13/6/55.
Trade on enlistment: Labourer.

MOUAT, Surgeon James

Born : 14th April 1815 - Chatham, Kent
Enlisted :
Medals : Crimea (B.I.S), The Victoria Cross ,The Knight (5th Class) The French Legion of Honour, New Zealand Medal, KCB.

Died : 4 January 1899 - Kensington, W London
Status : Rode in the Charge

The musters show he was effective from the 1st October to the 31st December.
Deputy Inspector of Hospitals James Mouat C.B. (Late 6th. Dragoons).
The Victoria Cross. Presented to him by the Queen, August 7th, 1858, on Portsmouth Common.

(London Gazette 2 June 1858.): "Date of Act of Bravery: 26 Oct. 1854. For having voluntarily proceeded to the assistance of Lieut.-Colonel Morris C.B., 17th Lancers, who was lying dangerously wounded in an exposed position after the retreat of the Light Cavalry at the battle of Balaklava, and having dressed that officer's wounds in the presence and under a heavy fire of the enemy. Thus, by stopping a severe haemonhage, he assisted in saving that officer's life"

James Mouat was born on April 14, 1815, at Chatham, Kent, the son of Surgeon James Mouat MD who was medical officer to the 23rd, 25th, 21st, 16th,13th, F., 4th and 15th Dragoons. His uncle was Dr F.J. Mouat distinguished in the Indian Civil Medical Service. James Mouat, the son, was educated at University College Hospital, London, became MRCS in 1837, and proceeded FRCS in 1852. One year after qualification he joined the 44th Regiment of Foot as Assistant Surgeon. Ten years later he was promoted Surgeon and served throughout the Crimean Campaign with the 6th Dragoons, where he was also in charge of the General Field Hospital of the 3rd Division. He was present at the Fall of Sebastopol, the Battles of Tehernaya and Inkerman, and at the charge of the Light Brigade at Balaklava his gallantry resulted in the award of the Victoria Cross:

Photograph courtesy of Glen Fisher

During the campaign Surgeon Mouat was appointed to the French Legion of Honour, and gained the Crimean Medal with three clasps. In 1855 he was promoted Surgeon Major, and a year later was appointed a Commander of the Order of the Bath. Aged 43 he was given the rank of Deputy Inspector General of Hospitals whilst serving in Turkey.

From 1860 to 1861 and again from 1863 to 1865 he served in New Zealand in the Maori Wars, during the latter campaign as Inspector General of Hospitals, being promoted to Surgeon General in 1864. The New Zealand government voted him "special thanks for his valuable Services to the Colony", he was mentioned in despatches and was awarded the campaign medal.

Surgeon General Mouat retired in 1876, was appointed an honorary Surgeon to the Queen in 1888, and a Knight Commander of the Order of the Bath in 1894. The British Medical Journal obituary of 1899 described this officer's character:

"One who served under Sir James and knew him well, furnishes the following reminiscences of him:
'There never was a more thoroughly soldierly medical officer than Mouat; he was always faultlessly dressed, whether in uniform or in mufti; nothing annoyed him more than slovenly or shabby attire, especially among medical officers. He had a very sharp tongue, and as he usually got hold of the right end of an argument, was formidable in dispute. As he set no small value on himself or his military position, he always kept up considerable style, and was the only senior medical officer the writer can recall who made his camp inspections in a well-appointed carriage and pair.
Sir James Mouat was held in deserved respect by all branches of the service; and in private life was an attached and sincere friend of those who won his esteem'."

Information supplied by Royal Army Medical Corps Historical Museum.

MOUNTAIN, Quarter Master John Kirby
Born : Unknown
Enlisted :
Medals : Crimea (B.I.S)

Died : 12th August 1860 - India
Status : Probably Rode in the Charge

The musters show he was effective as a 838 Regimental Sergeant Major from the 1st October to the 31st December. The India Office records show a John Kirby Mountain, Q.M of the H.M's 6th Inniskilling Dragoons as being buried in Kirkee (old) Cemetery, India, aged 36 years old. He died on the 12th August 1860.

952 MOUNTAIN, Sergeant William
Born : Unknown
Enlisted :
Medals : Crimea (B.I.S)

Died : Unknown
Status : Probably Rode in the Charge

The musters show he was effective from the 1st October to the 31st December. WO25 To 2nd Dr GDS March 1857.

1335 MURUSS, Sergeant Robert
Born : Unknown
Enlisted :
Medals : Crimea (B.I.S)

Died : Unknown
Status : Probably Rode in the Charge

The musters show he was effective as a Corporal from the 16th November to the 31st December.
WO100/24 page 244 Remarks: Invalided, sent home 30 June:55.
WO100/24 page 265 Remarks: Discharged 10th. April 1856.

434 NEEDHAM Corporal Edward
Born : Unknown
Enlisted :
Medals : Crimea (B.I.S) The Distinguished Conduct Medal

Died : Unknown
Status : Probably Rode in the Charge

Glendining's Monday 17th September 1990 Lot 645, A Crimean "Heavy Brigade" D.C.M. group of three to Sergt. Edward Needham, 6th Dragoons: Distinguished Conduct Medal, Vic. (Corpl., 6th Inniskn. Drags.); Crimea 1854 - 56, three bars Balaklava, Inkermann, Sebastopol. Engraved in Serified capitals; Turkish Crimea, Sardinian issue (unnamed). Very fine or slightly better.
The same group also sold at Glendining's Lot 645 18th September 1988.

The musters show he was effective as a Private from the ??? and as a Corporal from the 13th November to the 31st December. Remarks state from Private vice Millar.
The Distinguished Conduct Medal. Recommendation dated 3:1:55.
The following Non-commissioned Officer has been granted medals with gratuity for distinguished conduct in the field under the provisions of the Royal Warrant of 4 December 1854, viz: Corporal Edward Needham £10
Abbot, Recipients of the Distinguished Conduct Medal (2nd edn) p.25.

566 NEVIN, Private Robert
Born : Unknown
Enlisted :
Medals : Crimea (B.I.S)

Died : Unknown
Status : Probably Rode in the Charge

The musters show he was effective from the 1st October to the 31st December.
WO100-24 Discharged 25th December 1856. Adm1/5631 Saved from the wreck of the "Europa"

611 NICOL, Sergeant John
Born : Unknown
Enlisted :
Medals : Crimea (B.I.S)

Died : Unknown
Status : Probably Rode in the Charge

The musters show he was effective from the 1st October to the 31st December. Regimental number shown as 616.

601 NUGENT Private George

Born : 1820 - Cavan
Enlisted : 22nd July 1839
Medals : Crimea (B.I.S)

Died : Unknown
Status : Probably Rode in the Charge

Pair of medals Crimea & Turkish Crimea appeared in a Canadian medal dealers, sales list Eugene Ursual of Ottowa in September 1997. Catalogue 135, No 8602 price £673. (Medals see below)

DNW 30th June 1998, Lot 391, A Heavy Brigade pair awarded to Corporal George Nugent, 6th Dragoons Crimea 1854-56, 3 clasps, Balaklava, Inkermann, Sebastopol (Pve. Geo. Nugent, 6th Dns.) contemporary engraved naming; Turkish Crimea, Sardinian issue (Corpl., 6th Dns.) contact marks, nearly very fine (2) Hammer Price £430

George Nugent was born in Cavan and enlisted for the 6th Dragoons at Dublin on 22 July 1839, aged 19 years. He served in Turkey and the Crimea for 10 months and is confirmed on the muster rolls for the period including the battle of Balaklava. He transferred to the 5th Lancers in March 1858 and was discharged with the rank of Corporal on 18 October 1859.
WO100/24 page 251 Remarks: Invalided-sent home 29/4/55.
From the Times Tuesday June 20th 1854. The following official copies of the depositions, taken at Gibraltar, by the survivors from the Europa:
George Nugent, private 6th Dragoons, said,- I assisted in putting a fire out in one of the seamen's berths at 11 o'clock a.m of the morning of the 31st May. I am not certain whether it was on the morning or the afternoon before the fire. The fire consisted of the burning of a pair of wollen stockings which were ignited by a pipe, but extinguished immediately with two tins of water.
Adm1/5631 Saved from the wreck of the "Europa"
WO25. To 5th Lancers November 1858.

1143 OVENS, Private Francis

Born : Unknown
Enlisted :
Medals : Crimea (B.I.S)

Died : Unknown
Status : Probably Rode in the Charge

The musters show he was effective from the 1st October to the 31st December.

1116 PAINE, Farrier David

Born : Unknown
Enlisted :
Medals : Crimea (B.I.S)

Died : Unknown
Status : Probably Rode in the Charge

The musters show he was effective from the 1st October to the 31st December.

1149 PARKER, Sergeant Charles

Born : Date Unknown - St. Mary's
Enlisted : 15th August 1851
Medals : Crimea (B.I.S)

Died : 19th March 1855 - Scutari
Status : Probably Rode in the Charge

Spink & Son Ltd, Medal Supplement 1988, Crimea Medal, 1854.
2 Bar : Balaklava, Inkermann, (Serjt. Chas. Parker, 6th Drgns.) Impressed good VF £495. Served with the heavy Brigade and roll confirms entitlement to balaklava bar.

The musters show he was effective from the 1st October to the 31st December.
The musters show he was effective as a Corporal from 1st-26th October and as a Sergeant from the 27th October to the 31st December. Remarks state Promoted from Corpl vice Briton deceased.
WO100/24 page 244 Remarks: Died at Scutari 19th. March:55.
Trade on enlistment: Clerk.

831 PARKER, Private William

Born : Unknown
Enlisted :
Medals : Crimea (B.I.S)

Died : Unknown
Status : Probably Rode in the Charge

The musters show he was effective from the 1st October to the 31st December.

660 PATTERSON, Private Walter

Born : 1826 - Laughton
Enlisted : 13th October 1840
Medals : Crimea (B.I) ,The Distinguished Conduct Medal

Died : 21st January 1855 - Scutari
Status : Probably Rode in the Charge

The musters show he was effective from the 1st October to the 31st December.
P.L.: Born: Lorton.
Trade: None.
Enlisted: 13/Oct./40.
Died: 21/Jan./55.
Turkish medal roll WO 100-24 660 Pte Patterson William died 21 January 1855 Scutari.
WO100/24 page 251 Remarks: Died at Scutari 21 Jan:55.
The Distinguished Conduct Medal. Recommendation dated 3:1:55.
The following Non-commissioned Office has been granted medals with gratuity for distinguished conduct in the field under the provisions of the Royal Warrant of 4 December 1854, vis:
Walter Patterson £10
John Patterson fought under Wellington in the Peninsula War.
One of Patterson's sons, Walter, baptised at Laughton on Christmas Eve, 1826, also fought on the battlefield in the Crimea.
'Young Walter will have left Ringmer as a baby when the barracks there closed in 1827, and when he was just eight his father died. Like many fatherless children of service families, Walter and his brother were sent off to the Royal Hibernian School in Dublin, from whence at the age of 14 he enlisted in the 6th Inniskilling Dragoons.
'His enlistment papers show he was just 4ft 6ins tall, and one of two boys in the regiment - presumably mainly employed in caring for the horses. In the following years he served with the Dragoons at stations all over Britain, becoming for a while a regimental bandsman and playing for Queen Victoria.
'In March, 1854, his regiment was sent to the Crimea, and took part in the successful charge of the Heavy Brigade at the battle of Balaklava.
'They were then encamped in the bitter Crimean winter, with too little food, too much work, no winter clothing, constantly wet and freezing cold. The men died in droves and Walter, now 28, was among them.
'On January 10, 1855, he was sent to Florence Nightingale's military hospital at Scutari, but took 11 days to reach it and died on the day he arrived. Three months later his colonel put forward his name as one of four privates in the regiment to be awarded a medal for distinguished conduct in the field.'
A sad end to a resolute Ringmer man.

Transcript of a letter from 660 Pte Walter Patterson, 6th Dragoons:
The letter is addressed to his mother at Cains Cross near Stroud, Gloucestershire. It is countersigned by Lt.Col.HD White, Commanding Officer of the 6th Dragoons.

Camp near Varna
August 2nd 1854

Dear Mother
        Having arrived safe I take the oppertunity of writing to you hoping to find you in good health as thank God this leaves me. I left England on the first of June and arrived at Varna on the 8th July we had a very pleasent voyge we had very little sickness on the passage as for myself I was not sick at all. when we disembarked we encamped close by the sea shore and remained for 14 days then we marched about 6 miles further but not being a healthy place we removed again a few miles and by the time this letter is posted we will have left here as the letters are only posted every fifth day that will be the fifth of the month, this is a very fine country but the people are very dirty this place is very unhealthy at present and i believe this month is the worst in the year we have buryed six men last week with the bowel complaint with not more than 12 hours illness and some I have seen seeing the last of his comrade and the next day buryed himself, we have plenty to eat here such as it is we kill our own meat. I am very sorry to tell you that we lost on the passage out by fire one of the vessels that conveyed part of our Regiment and five Sarjeants and 12 men perished besides our Colonel and Vetenary Surjeon. When you write let me know if you have heard any thing about john and give my love to Phoebe and tell her she would laugh to see the women going about here with their faces covered all you can see is their eyes nose and mouth, the weather here is very unhealty the night is very ... and misty and then the day the sun would almost burn you what we do we have to do before the day sets in and evening sop as not to be in the sun when you write direct. I must now conclude and believe me to remain you loving son. W.P

Private Walter Patterson
6th Iniskilling Dragoons,
Turkey.

Information supplied by: John Saunders (Ringmer History Newsletter)

1121 PATTON, Private John

Born : Unknown
Enlisted :
Medals : Crimea (B.I.S)

Died : Unknown
Status : Probably Rode in the Charge

The musters show he was effective from the 1st October to the 31st December.
Adm1/5631 Saved from the wreck of the "Europa"

905 PAVEY, Sergeant Henry

Born : Unknown
Enlisted :
Medals : Crimea (B.I.S) L.S.G.C Medal

Died : 21st May 1871 - Ellesmere
Status : Probably Rode in the Charge

The musters show he was effective from the 1st October to the 31st December.
WO100/24 page 244 Remarks: Sent home 10th. Nov 55.
WO12-742 Musters 6th Dragoons. 31st July to 30th September 1863. 905 Troop Sergeant Major Pavey, Henry - Present on all three musters (India)

WO102 L.S.G.C Medal recommendation 1.5.1867, issued 24.7.1867 with £15 Gratuity.

21st May 1871 Eddowes Journal ,Shrewsbury Chronicle.
Sgt H Pavey, instructor North Shropshire Yeomanry and pensioner of the 6th Inniskilling Dragoons died 21st May 1871 aged 42 years.
On Saturday last, witnessed a scene which has not occurred in this town (Ellesmere) for many years.
A military funeral of the late Henry Pavey, Sgt Instructor of the Ellesmere troop of the North Shropshire Yeomanry and pensioner of the 6th Inniskilling Dragoons. Sgt Pavey died on the 21st May age 42, he only left his regiment three years since, and became instructor to the above troop. He was at the time unwell, having spent a good deal of his time in India and the Crimean War, his health was very much impared and could not stand the climate. He was not able to go through his duties during the assembling of the troop this year in fact, strange to say, he died the day after the regiment left the town. During his short stay in Ellesmere he was much respected by all who knew him and by the troops whom he taught.
The troop under the command of Captain Cust, assembled in the Bridgewater Arms Yard at 4-o'clock, Major Playne Smith was present. The volunteers under the command of Captain Lloyd also attended. It was arranged that the funeral should be at the cemetery at 5-o'clock, having proceeded to the residence of the late Sergeant. The funeral cortege left the home of the deceased at quarter before five in the following order. Headed by Cpl T.J.Rider of Kenwick, followed by ten of the Yeomanry and a Sgt Major who formed the firing party, they had their carbines reversed and their right arm thrown back. Next the Ellesmere Rifle Corp Band playing the Dead March. The corpse came next and placed on top of the coffin was the helmet and sword and belt belonging to the late Sgt Henry Pavey. Four Pall Bearers, Sgt Parry (Haughton) Sgt J.Thomas (Colemere) Sgt Griffiths (Halston) & Quarter Master Bellis (Croesmere). The two brothers of the late Sergeant, followed by a black horse covered with black cloth and the boots & spurs reversed, across his back and led by two of the Yeomanry, Pte Townsend and Pte Urion, followed by 38 rank and file and two Sgt Majors, Sgt Major Smith of Halston Troop gave command and the usual volley of shots were fired.

Buried on plot 98, Ellesmere Cemetery, originally there was a stone over the grave.

1352 PEPPER, Private Thomas

Born : Unknown
Enlisted :
Medals : Crimea (B.I.S)

Died : Unknown
Status : Probably Rode in the Charge

The musters show he was effective from the 1st October to the 31st December.
WO100/24 page 251 Remarks: Invalided-sent home 15/4/55.

1337 PIGOTT, Paymaster Sergeant Henry

Born : Unknown
Enlisted :
Medals : Crimea (B.S)

Died : Unknown
Status : Probably Rode in the Charge

The musters show he was effective as a Paymaster Clerk from the 1st October to the 31st December.

533 POLKINGHORN, Private Humphrey

Born : 1817, Truro, Conwall
Enlisted : March 1838
Medals : Crimea (B.I.S) The French Medaille Militaire

Died : Unknown
Status : Rode in the Charge

Spinks Numismatic Circular January 1976. H.Polkinghorn. 6th Dragoons.Crimea clasps for Balaklava, Inkermann, Sebastopol. Impressed naming. Turkish Crimea Sardinian type. French Medaille Militaire 2nd Empire with Eagle's wings raised, enamel chipped. Humphrey Polkinghorn was awarded the French Medal for "gallantry and general good conduct in the field"
Spinks Circular No12 June 1999 item 372 as above £1950
Eugene G.Ursual Sales Catalogue No 142. Medals as per Spinks above price £2489.

The musters show he was effective from the 1st October to the 31st December. Paid 92 days on shore at ordinary pay. 58 days at 1d G.C pay. Marginal note restored to 1d Good Conduct pay 4th November.

WO100/24 page 251 Remarks: Invalided 15 April:55-sent home.
WO100/24 page 265 Remarks: Discharged 25 Decr. 1856.

The French Medaille Militaire. (He) "embarked with the first detachment of the regiment for the East, on the 2nd. of June 1854. (He) was present with it in Bulgaria, and during the first winter in the Crimea. (He) received clasps for Balaklava, Inkermann and Sebastopol, and distinguished himself much in the former action".

Born near Truro, Cornwall and attested for the 6th Dragoons in March 1838, aged 21 years. Tried several times by Court-Matial, with time spent in confinement as a result. Discharged in December 1856 owing to the effects of fever contracted in the Crimea.

1239 POOLEY, Private James

Born : Unknown
Enlisted :
Medals : Crimea (B.I.S)

Died : 14th September 1855 - Scutari
Status : Probably Rode in the Charge

The musters show he was effective from the 1st October to the 31st December. WO100/24 page 251 Remarks: Died at Scutari 14 Sept:55.

1028 PORTER, Farrier Henry

Born : Unknown
Enlisted :
Medals : Crimea (B.I.S)

Died : Unknown
Status : Probably Rode in the Charge

The musters show he was effective from the 1st October to the 31st December.

956 PRICE, Private Joshua

Born : Unknown
Enlisted :
Medals : Crimea (B.I.S)

Died : Unknown
Status : Probably Rode in the Charge

The musters show he was effective from the 1st October to the 31st December.
WO100/24 page 251 Remarks: Invalided 15 April:55-sent home.
WO100/24 page 266 Remarks: Died 18 June 1857.

1254 PRYKE, Private William

Born : Unknown
Enlisted :
Medals : Crimea (B.I.S)

Died : Unknown
Status : Probably Rode in the Charge

The musters show he was effective from the 1st October to the 31st December.
WO25 Discharged 18th of November 1856.

951 QUINN, Private Edward

Born : Unknown
Enlisted :
Medals : Crimea (B.S)

Died : Unknown
Status : Probably Rode in the Charge

Glendining 5th April 1956 Lot 246, Group of three to E.Quinn as below. sold with eight other unrelated medals £5.
Wallis and Wallis 13th September 1967, Lot 649. Group of three medals, Crimea three Clasps B,I and S impressed naming.
Turkish Crimea, LS&GC Trophy type to E.Quinn 11th Hussars. VF A scarce heavy brigade group.
Spinks numismatic circular January 1972. E.Quinn 6 D.G Crimea. Clasps for B,I and S impressed naming. L.S & G.C medal 11th hussars, Turkish Crimea (Sardinian version) Engraved naming.
Spinks Auction 12 March 1996. Lot 705. Group of three as above. Estimate £400-£450.

The musters show he was effective from the 1st October to the 31st December.
Private Edward Quinn, a labourer from County Donegal attested for the 6th Dragoons on the 30th October 1846, served with the 6th Dragoons, Heavy Brigade. Transfered to the 11th November 1866, and was discharged after 24 years service on the 15th October 1870.

RAWLINSON, Lieutenant William Sawrey

Born : Unknown
Enlisted :
Medals : Crimea (B.I.S)

Died : Unknown
Status : Probably Rode in the Charge

The musters show he was effective as a Cornet from the 1st-5th October and as a Lieutenant from the 6th October to the 31st December.

Harts Army List 1856 page 140 6th (Inniskilling) Regiment of Dragoons. Lieutenant William Sawrey Rawlinson. Note 5 Cornet 10th June 1853, Lieutenant 6th October 1854. Served in the Eastern Campaign of 1854-55 including the battles of Balaklava, Inkermann and Tchernaya and the siege and fall of Sebastopol. (Medal and clasps)

Bulletins and Other State Intelligence, Published 1859. 6th Dragoons Lieutenant William Sawrey Rawlinson to be Captain, by purchase, vice Augustus Hunt, who retires. Dated 23rd October 1857.

Cumberland post office directory 1873.
Acting Magistrates for the county
William Sawrey RAWLINSON, esq., Duddon Hall.
The Times, Thursday, Jul 03, 1862
On the 26th June 1862 at St George's, Hanover Square, by the Rev.J. P. Sill, rector of Wetheringsett, Suffolk, William Sawrey Rawlinson, Esq, of Dudden Hall, Cumberland. Major 12th Royal Lancers, and late of the Inniskilling Guards, to Elizabeth Mary, only daughter of the late Robert Brooke, Esq, of the Royal Cresent, Bath.
Extracts from the Times Friday 12th 1892 in the case of Rawlinson v Rawlinson. Concerning the cutting of timber at Duddon-Hall. Mr Rawlinson the applicant under his father's will, became, on attaining the age of 25, tenant in fee of the Duddon-Hall estates in Cumberland. This event happened on April 20, 1888. His father had died in 1875. Mrs. Rawlinson, the applicant's mother was entitled to the rents and profits from the estate. Result the applicant was entitled to an inquiry.
Preliminary Advertisement
The Times, Saturday, May 31, 1902.
By order of the Court of the Chancery The valuable Residential and Agricultural estate, known as the Duddon-Hall Estate near Broughton-in-Furness, Lancashire, in the valley of the river Duddon comprising 3,573 acres with the residence, Duddon-hall, will offer for sale by auction....

Photograph courtesy of Glenn Fisher

Duddon Hall is an imposing building that appears in the southwest corner of the Lake District It is now divided into apartments but was once the grand house of the valley, inhabited by the lord of the manor of Dunnerdale with Seathwaite.

The present hall was built in the eighteenth century by Major Leonard Cooper and called at the time Duddon Grove. Gambling away the family fortune he sold the hall to pay his debts.

After litigation the Duddon Hall estates were in 1860 allowed to Major William Sawrey Rawlinson, in right of his maternal ancestor, the Rev. George Millers (St. John's Coll., Camb.; M.A. 1801), and on his death in 1875 they descended to his son William Millers Rawlinson; *Burke, Landed Gentry*.

In its grounds can be seen an elegant Georgian chapel that looks like a pagan temple. The chapel is circular in shape and a handsome stag surmounts its portico. and celebrates his love of hunting. The circular design was made to allow the chapel to double as an arena for cockfights, held on Sunday afternoons.

1238 RENTON, Corporal Robert

Born : Unknown
Enlisted :
Medals : Crimea (B.I.S)

Died : Unknown
Status : Probably Rode in the Charge

The musters show he was effective from the 1st October to the 31st December. WO100/24 page 266 Remarks: Sergeant, Discharged 8 April 1857. Saved from the wreck of the "Europa"

1075 RENWICK, Private George

Born : Unknown
Enlisted :
Medals : Crimea (B.I.S)

Died : Unknown
Status : Probably Rode in the Charge

The musters show he was effective from the 1st October to the 14th December.
Paid 75 days on shore at ordinary pay. 3days on board ship. 3rd muster endorsed Scutari marginal note reads to Scutari 15th Dec. WO25 To England 26th of March 1860.

782 RHODES, Private Samuel

Born : Date Unknown - Southaram
Enlisted : 22nd June 1853
Medals : Crimea (B.I.S)

Died : 23rd February 1855 - Crimea
Status : Probably Rode in the Charge

The musters show he was effective from the 1st October to the 31st December.
WO100/24 page 251 Remarks: Died at Scutari 14 Sept:55.
WO100/24 page 258 Remarks: Died 23 Feb:55 disease.

Trade: on enlistment Mason.

936 RICHARDSON, Private Joseph

Born : Unknown
Enlisted :
Medals : Crimea (B.I.S)

Died : Unknown
Status : Probably Rode in the Charge

The musters show he was effective from the 1st October to the 31st December. WO25 Discharged 31/10/1860.

1201 ROBERTS, Private John

Born : Unknown
Enlisted :
Medals : Crimea (B.I.S)

Died : Unknown
Status : Probably Rode in the Charge

The musters show he was effective from the 1st October to the 31st December.

961 ROBINSON, Private Alexander

Born : Date unknown - Enniskillen
Enlisted : 20th October 1846
Medals : Crimea (B.I.S)

Died : June 1898
Status : Probably Rode in the Charge

Donald Hall Medal list No6 July 1972, item 430. Pair to A. Robinson, Crimea 3 Bars Balaklava, Inkermann, Sebastopol (AR. Robinson 6th or Inniskill D.S) engraved. Turkish Crimea British issue 961 A.Robinson 6th Dragoons. Both medals are fitted with contemporary buckles, ornately engraved. The recipients spurs two sets and regimental badge are included with the medals N.VF £110.

Alexander Robinson born Enniskillen. Joined the regiment 20th October 1846 to 14th August 1861. Served 14 years 295 days. Crimea 2 years, 1 month. East Indies 2 years 3 months. Discharged on his own request with right of registry for deferred pension of 4d a day upon attaining 50 years of age. Conduct Good two good conduct badges. One court martial served in the Crimea and Turkey from June 1854 to July 1856. present at the battles of Balaklava, Inkermann, and at the siege Sebastopol. Description 5' 7 1/2", brown hair, Grey eyes, fair complexion, trade servant.

The musters show he was effective from the 1st October to the 31st December.
"Death of a Balaclava Hero," Inverness Courier, June 24, 1898, p. 5c. Alexander Robinson, an Enniskillen native, Balaclava charge survivor and 21-year veteran, died Wednesday in Glasgow and was buried Saturday. Born Enniskillen, 1828, joined Inniskilling Dragoons in 1846, went to Crimea in 1854 and served entire campaign. "He took part in all the general engagements except the storming of the Alma heights, and he rode in the historic charge of the Heavy Brigade. The warrior and his mare Jenny were presented to the Queen at Aldershot, who clapped both on the shoulder and said they were a clever pair." Served Gen. Laurison and Duke of Cambridge as orderly, served in Indian Mutiny and left service in 1867.

964 ROURKE, Private Michael

Born : February 1826, Stokestown, Ireland
Enlisted : 10th November 1846
Medals : Crimea (B.S)

Died : Unknown
Status : Severely wounded in the Charge

The musters show he was effective from the 1st October to the 25th October.
C.R.: Listed W/D at Balaclava.
WO100/24 page 252 Remarks: Invalided-sent home 2 Jan:55.
WO100/24 page 266 Remarks: Discharged 5 July 55.
He received his medal from the hand of the Queen on 18th May 1855.
An article appeared in
OMRS Journal, Autumn 1975 page 141 by the late Major W.S.Stitt..
Like so many of the Heavy and Light Brigade, Rourke was an Irishman. He was born at Stokestown in Co. Roscommon in February 1826, and worked as a labourer. He was 5ft 9 1/4" , had sandy hair with grey eyes and a "pockpitted" complexion.
On the 10th November 1846 he enlisted into the 6th Dragoon Guards by Private William Fellows, with a bounty of £5-15-6; he also received 2/6d, enlistment payment. On the 19th May 1852 he was awarded a penny daily good conduct pay. On the outbreak of the Crimea War he served in Varna, and he was present at the Charge of the Heavy Brigade at Balaclava. His personal documents record "He was wounded in the upper third of the left forearm by a musket ball at Balaclava". He was medically boarded at Canterbury in March 1855 and was discharged on 3rd July as being unfit for further service.
He received an unusual form of regimental decoration for gallantry and good conduct. He was awarded a minature Crimea Medal with the normal three clasps. It is well made and the rim is engraved in minute block capitals "Pte. Michl. Rourke 6 Dgs. For Gallantry and Good Conduct on the field". This is most unusual especially as there is no mention of the award of a Distinguished Conduct Medal in the P.R.O papers. This miniature is suspended from an ornate scarlet embroidered ribbon and the stitching is contemporary. It is highly probable that this engraved miniature was awarded by the Regiment for some act of gallantry which did not qualify for the Distinguished Conduct Medal.
Saved from the wreck of the "Europa"

1111 ROWE, Troop Sergeant-Major Robert

Born : Unknown
Enlisted :
Medals : Crimea (B.I.S), The Distinguished Conduct Medal

Died : Unknown
Status : Probably Rode in the Charge

The musters show he was effective from the 1st October to the 31st December. The musters show he was effective as a Sergeant from the 1st October to the 31st December. The Distinguished Conduct Medal. Recommendation dated 3:1:55. The following Non-commissioned Officers and men have been granted medals with gratuity for distinguished conduct in the field under the provisions of the Royal Warrant of 4 December 1854, vis: Sergeant Robert Rowe £15.
WO25 Discharged 19th of March 1862.

920 RUSSELL, Private Alexander
Born : Date Unknown - Kirklisten
Enlisted : 24th April 1846
Medals : Crimea (B.I.S)

Died : 24th May 1855 - Crimea
Status : Probably Rode in the Charge

Glendining and Co Auction 28th September 1972, lot 585. Crimea three clasps Balaklava, Inkermann, Sebastopol A.Russell 6th Dragoons impressed naming. VF £70

The musters show he was effective from the 1st October to the 31st December. WO100/24 page 252 Remarks: Died in Crimea 24 May 55.
Trade on enlistment Carpenter. Saved from the wreck of the "Europa"

1224 RYSON, Private James
Born : Unknown
Enlisted :
Medals : Crimea (B.I.S)

Died : Unknown
Status : Probably Rode in the Charge

The musters show he was effective from the 1st October to the 31st December.
WO100/24 page 266 Remarks: Discharged 12 Novr. 1856. Medal rolls show his name spelt "Ryder" and "Ryser".
WO25 Discharged 12th of November 1856.

726 SALT, Farrier James
Born : Unknown
Enlisted :
Medals : Crimea (B.S)

Died : Unknown
Status : Probably Rode in the Charge

The musters show he was effective from the 1st October to the 31st December. WO100/24 page 266 Remarks: Sergeant, Discharged 8 April 1857. Saved from the wreck of the "Europa"

1264 SANDFORD, Corporal George
Born : Unknown
Enlisted :
Medals : Crimea (B.I.S)

Died : 19th March 1863.
Status : Probably Rode in the Charge

The musters show he was effective from the 1st October to the 14th December.3rd muster endorsed Scutari marginal note reads to Scutari 15th December. WO25 Died 19th of March 1863. John Adam Sallabank 376 died at the same time.

882 SAUNDERS, Farrier William
Born : Unknown
Enlisted :
Medals : Crimea (B.I.S)

Died : Unknown
Status : Probably Rode in the Charge

The musters show he was effective from the 1st October to the 31st December. WO25 Discharged 24/09/1857.

980 SCOLLAN, Private John
Born : Unknown
Enlisted :
Medals : Crimea (B.I.S)

Died : Unknown
Status : Probably Rode in the Charge

The musters show he was effective from the 1st October to the 31st December. WO25 To pension 22/10/1872.

1231 SEYMOUR, Private George
Born : Unknown
Enlisted :
Medals : Crimea (B.I.S)

Died : Unknown
Status : Probably Rode in the Charge

The musters show he was effective from the 1st October to the 27th November. Second and third muster endorsed Scutari, marginal note reads to Scutari 28 November. WO100/24 page 252 Remarks: Invalided-sent home 2 June 55. Saved from the wreck of the "Europa"

Royal Horse Artillery

During the Charge of the Heavy Brigade, the Russia cavalry had become tightly packed. To an observant Artillery officer of C Troop, this was an ideal opportunity to pelt the Russians with shot. Captain Brandling, now galloped with C Troop to a location where its fire would clear the Heavy Brigade.

"The Russians, however, halted short of the ridge, and their officers could be seen holding up their swords and endeavouring to rally them, and get them into order, which they very soon would have done, but 'C' troop now came into action, and fired forty-nine shot and shell at them, at a range of between 700 and 800 yards, with admirable results, the 24 pounder howitzers making splendid practice". *Whinyates, Col F. A., From Coruna to Sevastopol, W.H.Allen and Co., London 1884. p134.*

622 SHERRIN, Sergeant James

Born : Unknown
Enlisted :
Medals : Crimea (B.I.S)

Died : Unknown
Status : Probably Rode in the Charge

The musters show he was effective from the 1st October to the 31st December. Paid 92 days at 2s-2d per diem, 9 days on board ship.
The Pay Lists spell his name Sheering. WO25 Discharged 19th of March 1862.

645 SHIELDS, Troop Sergeant-Major Alexander

Born : Unknown
Enlisted : April 1840
Medals : Crimea (B.S) 1887 Jubilee Medal (clasp 1897). [McInnes, Yeoman of the Guard, pp.150-1]

Died : 1st January 1886
Status : Slightly wounded in the Charge

The musters show he was effective from the 1st-25th October. Paid at 2s-0d per diem from 1st to 25th October 25 days. 3 On board ship. All three musters endorsed Scutari. Marginal note reads to Scutari 26th October .
C.R.: Listed W/SI at Balaklava.
WO100/24 page 244 Remarks: Invalided, sent home Feb:55.
WO100/24 page 266 Remarks: Discharged 26 May 55.

Received his medal from the hand of the Queen, May 18th 1855.
A letter dated 3rd September 1855 addressed to 645 Alexander Shields Ref see page 310

History of the Kings Body Guard of the Yeoman of the Guard by Hennell 1904. Page 250. Troop Sergeant Major Alexander Shields 6th Dragoons enlisted April 1840. Served 15 years. Appointed to the Yeoman of the Guard 1855. Died 1st January 1886.

SHUTE, Brevet Lieutenant-Colonel Charles Cameron

Born : 3rd January 1816   Died : 7th May 1895 "Dinsdale" Bournemouth
Enlisted :   Status : Probably Rode in the Charge
Medals : Crimea (B.I.S) ,The Knight (5th Class) The French Legion of Honour, The Turkish Order of the Medjidie (5th Class)

Christie 24th July, 1990 Lot 86. Three. General Sir C.C Shute 6th Iniskilling Dragoons. Turkish Crimea. Sardinian type. Edge inscribed "Colonel C.C.Shute 6th Iniskilling Dragoons". France second empire, Legion of Honour, Fifth class breast badge, silver, gold centres, and enamel. Turkey order of the Medjidie 5th class breast badge silver, gold and enamel. Very Fine. Together with a third class order of the Medjidie silver, gold and enamels, and a 6th dragoons officers waist belt clasp (5) General Sir Charles Cameron Shute K.C.B (1816-1904) Entered the 13th Light Dragoons in 1835 and served in the campaign against the Rajah of Kurnool 1839. Transfered to the 6th Dragoons in 1842. Seved in the Crimea as second in command of the Regiment and took part in the Charge of the Heavy Brigade 25th October 1854, (Mentioned in despatches for Balaklava, recommended for the Victoria Cross) Appointed assistant adjutant General of Cavalry from November until the end of the War, was presernt at Inkermann, Tchernaya, and the siege and fall of Sebastopol. Commanded his Regiment 1875 - 60, and the 4th Dragoon Guards 1861-72. Colonel 16th Lancers 1875 -86 (KCB 1889) Estimate £250-3000 Realised £352.

25 Feb 98 DNW Auction Lot No: 342 Description: 6th (Inniskilling) Dragoons, Officers Waist Belt Clasp, pre-1855 pattern, good condition £100-120 Footnote: Ex Christies 24 July 1990 where it was attributed to General Sir Charles C. Shute, K.C.B. (1816-1904), served in the Crimea as second in command of the regiment and took part in the Charge of the Heavy Brigade, M.I.D. for Balaclava and recommended for the Victoria Cross. Estimate: £100-£120. Hammer Price: £140

General Sir Charles Cameron Shute, K.C.B.
Colonel of the Inniskilling Dragoons
1886-1904.

Son of Thomas Deane Shute, of Burton, and Bramham Hill, Hampshire.
The musters show he was effective from the 1st October to the 31st December. Second and third musters on the staff. 4 horses foraged at public expense.

In 1858 Colonel Shute succeeded Colonel Dalrymple White in command of the Inniskilling Dragoons. His eldest son, Lieutenant-Colonel H.G.D.Shute, D.S.O., Coldstream Guards, became private secretary to Mr Arnold-Forster, the Secretary of State for War.

*Harts Army List 1856 page 140.*Cornet by purchase 19th July 1834, Lieutenent by purchase 13th May 1839. Captain by purchase 5th March 1847. Major 1st June 1854. Brevet Lt. Col. 12th December 1854. Note 3. Lt. Col. Shute served in the 13th Lt Dragoons with the field force of Kurnool, East Indies. Served with the 6th Dragoons the Eastern Campaign of 1854-55 as assistant Adjutant General of the Cavalry Division since 23rd November 1854.

Major & Brevet Lieutenant Colonel Charles Cameron Shute. Knight (5th Class) The French Legion of Honour. Lieut Col. 4th DG 1862. Maj. Gen. 1868. Lieut. Gen. 1877.[Graham, *History of the Sixteenth Lancers,* p 249]

In April 1870 Colonel Cameron Shute, C.B. of the 4th Dragoon Guards, published the following "Suggestions for the Practical Professional Education of Candidates for the Army after passing the Scholastic Examinations, at little expense to themselves and at no cost to the public".

Broad Arrow May 1895
Charles Cameron Shute 6th Dragoons Died Saturday May 7th 1895 at Dinsdale Bournemouth. Buried May 15th Extra-Mural Cemetery Brighton. (Graham records the date of death 30th April 1904).

1339 SINGLE, Corporal William M.

Born : Unknown   Died : Unknown
Enlisted :   Status : Probably Rode in the Charge
Medals : Crimea (B.I.S)

The musters show he was effective from the 1st October to the 3rd October. Paid 3 days on shore at ordinary pay, 3 days on board ship. All three musters endorsed Scutari. Marginal note reads to Scutari 4th Oct.
WO25 Records Private Single William .M regimental number 1333, Discharged 11th of July 1866.

868 SINGLETON, Private John

Born : Date Unknown - Chard
Enlisted : 10th December 1845
Medals : Crimea (B.I.S)

Died : 6th June 1855 - Scutari
Status : Probably Rode in the Charge

The musters show he was effective from the 1st October to the 3rd December.
WO100/24 page 252 Remarks: Died at Scutari 6 June:55. WO100/24 page 259 Remarks: Died 6 Jun:55. Disease.
Trade on enlistment Smith.

1065 SMALLMAN, Corporal Henry

Born : Unknown
Enlisted : June 1849
Medals : Crimea (B.I.S)

Died : Unknown
Status : Probably Rode in the Charge

Glendinings Auction 27th April 1983, Lot 76 Crimea medal with three bars, Balaklava, inkermann, Sebastopol (1065 H.Smallman, 6th Dgns). Impressed naming. The regimental number 1065 is engraved and, in addition, "6 Dgns" has also been engraved after the normal impressed naming. slight edge knock otherwise very fine. Hammer price £300.
Glendinings Auction 27th March 1985, Lot 39 Crimea medal with three bars, Balaklava, Inkermann, Sebastopol (H.Smallman, 6th Dragoons). Impressed naming "No 1065 6th D" has been added to the naming, and this engraved in the same style as is often seen on other medals to this regiment. Very Fine. Hammer price £320.
Spinks Auction 30th November 2000. Lot 84 Crimea 3 clasps as above. with additional comments. Either side of the suspension claw re-fixed, edge bruising. Estimate £400-500.

The musters show he was effective from the 1st October to the 31st December.
Sergeant Henry Smallman enlisted in the 6th Dragoons at Dublin in June 1849 aged 18 years, and was advanced to Corporal in August 1853. Embarked for the Crimea in the Europa in late May 1854. He was aboard her when she caught fire on the last day of the month, when 123 miles west of the Scilly Isles. WO25 Discharged Sergeant 23/01/1860.

1036 SMITH, Private George

Born : Unknown
Enlisted :
Medals : Crimea (B.I.S)

Died : Unknown
Status : Probably Rode in the Charge

The musters show he was effective from the 1st October to the 31st December. Marginal note reads Groom Winchester.
WO100/24 page 252 Remarks: Sent to England 5 July 55. WO25 Discharged March 1857.

1345 SMITH, Private George

Born : Unknown
Enlisted :
Medals : Crimea (B.I.S)

Died : Unknown
Status : Probably Rode in the Charge

The musters show he was effective from the 1st October to the 31st December. WO100/24 page 252 Remarks: Invalided-sent home 29 April 55.
WO100/24 page 266 Remarks: Discharged 31 Jany 57.

974 SMITH, Sergeant William

Born : Unknown
Enlisted :
Medals : Crimea (B.I.S)

Died : Unknown
Status : Probably Rode in the Charge

The musters show he was effective from the 1st October to the 31st December. WO25 To England January 1862.

1212 SNELL, Private Abraham

Born : Date Unknown - Bradfield
Enlisted : 23rd February 1853.
Medals : Crimea (B.I.S)

Died : 23rd December 1854 - Scutari
Status : Probably Rode in the Charge

The musters show he was effective from the 1st October to the 31st December. WO100/24 page 252 Remarks: Died at Scutari 23 Decr:54. The Times of Saturday, 6th January, 1855; page. 8 reported from Scutari on the 25th December 1854 that "Private Abraham Snell, 6th Dragoons" had died at Scutari Hospital on the 23rd December 1854 of dysentery.

1220 SNELLING, Private Henry

Born : Unknown
Enlisted :
Medals : Crimea (B.I.S)

Died : Unknown
Status : Probably Rode in the Charge

The musters show he was effective from the 1st October to the 31st December. Saved from the wreck of the "Europa" WO25 Discharged June 1858.

987 STANNARD, Private John

Born : Date Unknown - Earl Soham
Enlisted : 9th March 1847
Medals : Crimea (B.I.S)

Died : 21st December 1854 - Scutari
Status : Probably Rode in the Charge

The musters show he was effective from the 1st October to the 31st December.
WO100/24 page 252 Remarks: Died at Scutari 21 Dec:54.
Trade at enlistment Labourer.
The Times of Saturday, 6th January, 1855; page. 8 reported from Scutari on the 25th December 1854 that "687, Private J.Stannon, 6th Dragoons" had died on board the Ottawa on the 21st December 1854.

1179 STOCKER, Private William

Born : Unknown
Enlisted :
Medals : Crimea (B.I.S)

Died : Unknown
Status : Probably Rode in the Charge

The musters show he was effective from the 1st October to the 31st December.

1229 STOTHART, Private William

Born : Unknown
Enlisted :
Medals : Crimea (B.I.S)

Died : Unknown
Status : Probably Rode in the Charge

The musters show he was effective from the 13th November - 31st December. Paid* 49 days on shore at ordinary pay. Musters endorsed Scutai. This is then crossed out and a note written below which reads * Omitted, carried to the General total Form 9 page 45.

839 SUGDON, Private Charles

Born : Date Unknown - Beverley
Enlisted : 29th October 1845
Medals : Crimea (B.I.S)

Died : 12th March 1855 - Scutari
Status : Probably Rode in the Charge

The musters show he was effective from the 1st October to the 31st December. WO100/24 page 252 Remarks: Died at Scutari 12 Mar:55. The Pay Lists name him Sugden. Trade: on enlistment Valet.

459 SUTCLIFFE, Hospital Sergeant William

Born : Unknown
Enlisted :
Medals : Crimea (B.I.S), Distinguished Conduct Medal

Died : Unknown
Status : Probably Rode in the Charge

For Sale at Spink 12th March 1996, Lot 692. Three: Hospital Sergeant W. Sutcliffe, 6th Dragoons, Distinguished Conduct Medal (..Serjt. Wm. Sutciffe...); naming very worn. Crimea, three clasps, Balaklava, Inkermann, Sebastopol (Serjt.), officially impressed, suspension loose; Turkish Crimea, Sardinian die, with silver swivel bar suspension, severe edge bruising and contact marks, fine, with copied service papers (3) Ex A.A.Payne Collection, Sotheby's Feb 1970. Estimate £600-700
Hospital Sergeant William Sutcliffe, a shoemaker from Sligo, attested for the 6th Inniskilling Dragoons on 11 June 1836; appointed Hospital Sergeant 13 August 1854, served with the Heavy Brigade in Crimea; recommended for the Distinguished Conduct Medal, with £20 annuity 7 February 1855; Sergeant Sutcliffe was discharged 18 June 1860 after serving 24 years with the Colours. Estimate £600-700
The musters show he was effective from the 1st October to the 31st December.
Her Majesty has been graciously pleased to grant an Annuity of £20 with a silver medal to No 459 Hospital Sergeant William Sutcliffe, for his meritorious conduct, to take effect from 5 November 1854.
Serjeant William Sutcliffe of the 6th was promoted to Hospital Sergeant at Varna in August 1854.

1090 TAAFFE, Private John
Born : Unknown
Enlisted :
Medals : Crimea (B.I.S)

Died : Unknown
Status : Probably Rode in the Charge

The musters show he was effective from the 1st October to the 31st December.
WO100/24 page 252 Remarks: Invalided-sent home 2 June 55.

664 TARLTON, Private William
Born : Unknown
Enlisted :
Medals : Crimea (B.I.S)

Died : Unknown
Status : Probably Rode in the Charge

The musters show he was effective from the 1st October to the 31st December.
WO100/24 page 267 Remarks: Discharged 8 Jany. 1857.

1142 TAYLOR, Orderly Room Clerk George
Born : Unknown
Enlisted :
Medals : Crimea (B.I.S)

Died : Unknown
Status : Probably Rode in the Charge

The musters show he was effective from the 1st October to the 31st December. Remarks state: Date of Appointment as O.R.C 1st June 1854 Regtal. Rank when Appointed Private Present Regtal Rank Sergt.

867 TAYLOR, Private Robert
Born : Unknown
Enlisted :
Medals : Crimea (B.I.S)

Died : Unknown
Status : Probably Rode in the Charge

The musters show he was effective from the 1st October to the 31st December.

596 THOMPSON, Private Archibald
Born : Unknown
Enlisted :
Medals : Crimea (B.I.S)

Died : Unknown
Status : Probably Rode in the Charge

The musters show he was effective from the 1st October to the 31st December.

953 THOMPSON, Private James
Born : Unknown
Enlisted :
Medals : Crimea (B.I.S)

Died : Unknown
Status : Probably Rode in the Charge

The musters show he was effective as a Sergeant from the 1st October to the 15th November and as a Private from the 16th November to the 31st December. Remarks state reduced to Private 16th November.
WO12-742 Musters 6th Dragoons, 31st July to 30th September 1863. 953 Hospital Sgt Thompson, James present on all three musters in India.

380 TOOTH, Corporal John
Born : Unknown
Enlisted :
Medals : Crimea (B.I.S), The Distinguished Conduct Medal

Died : Unknown
Status : Probably Rode in the Charge

The musters show he was effective as a Corporal from the 8th November to the 31st December. Remarks state promoted on augmentation.
The Distinguished Conduct Medal. Recommendation dated 3:1:55.
The following Non-commissioned Officers and men have been granted medals with gratuity for distinguished conduct in the field under the provisions of the Royal Warrant of 4 December 1854, vis: Corporal John Tooth £10

1081 TORRENS, Private John

Born : Date Unknown - Temple Mead
Enlisted : 16th November 1849
Medals : Crimea (B.I.S)

Died : Date Unknown - Aboard Ship
Status : Probably Rode in the Charge

The musters show he was effective from the 1st October to the 31st December. WO100/24 page 267 Remarks: Died on board Ship.
Trade before enlistment Cabinet Maker.

TOWER, Captain Conyers

Born : Unknown
Enlisted :
Medals : Crimea (B.I.S)

Died : March 1903
Status : Probably Rode in the Charge

Donald Hall List 8 April 1974 item 62. Crimea 2 clasps Balaklava & Sebastopol, Captn Conyers Tower 6th Dragoons. Engraved in upright Serif Capitals. Major General Tower served with the 6th Dragoons in the Eastern Campaign of 1854 including the battle of Balaklava and siege of Sebastopol Medal with 2 clasps and Turkish medal. Commanded the 3rd Dragoon Guards during the Abyssinia campaign in 1868 and was present at the assault and capture of Magdala (Mentioned in despatches C.B and medal) Harts Army list 1879 V.F £135.

Second son of Henry Tower, and grandson of Christopher Tower, of Huntsmoor Park, Buckinghamshire.
The musters show he was effective from the 1st October to the 31st December. 3 horses foraged at public expense. To Constantinople 20th September, rejoined October 1854. No of servants not being soldier's 1.

Harts Army List 1856 page 140 Cornet by purchase 7th June 1844, Lieutenant by purchase 6th June 1845, Captain by purchase 18th January 1850, Major 17th May 1861 (3rd Dragoon Guards)
JP for Essex. Lieut. Col. 4th August 1863. Brevet Colonel 4th August 1868. Half pay 11th July 1874. Commandant Cavalry Depot 24th July 1874 to 19th March 1878. Major General 20th March 1878. Retired list (as Lieut. Gen) 20th March 1883. Colonel 3rd Dragoon Guards 5th June 1891 until his death. [Jackson, *Inniskilling Dragoons*, p. 293.]
London Gazette, Tuesday February 10th 1891
3rd Dragoon Guards - Major-Gen. and Honarary Lieut-Gen. Conyers Tower, C.B., to be Colonel, vice Lieut-Gen and Honorary Gen W.H.Seymour, C.B., transferred to the 13th Hussars.

1076 TRIBE, Private John

Born : Date Unknown - Tishington
Enlisted : 22nd October 1849
Medals : Crimea (B.I.S)

Died : 7th February 1855 - Crimea
Status : Probably Rode in the Charge

The musters show he was effective from the 1st October to the 31st December.
WO100/24 page 252 Remarks: Died in Crimea 7 Feb:55.
WO100/24 page 259 Remarks: Died 2 Feb:55. Disease.
Trade on enlistment Groom.

1211 TURNER, Private Robert

Born : Unknown
Enlisted :
Medals : Crimea (B.I.S)

Died : Unknown
Status : Severely wounded in the Charge

The musters show he was effective from the 1st October to the 31st December. Casualty Roll.: Listed W/Sv at Balaklava. All three musters endorsed Scutari. NB Can not be entitled to Inkermann clasp.
WO100/24 page 252 Remarks: Invalided-sent home 16 Feb:55.
WO100/24 page 267 Remarks: Discharged 9 Augt. 55. Saved from the wreck of the "Europa"

659 TUTON, Private George

Born : Unknown
Enlisted :
Medals : Crimea (B.I.S)

Died : Unknown
Status : Probably Rode in the Charge

The musters show he was effective from the 1st October to the 31st December.

722 VERNON, Private Edward

Born : Unknown
Enlisted :
Medals : Crimea (B.I.S)

Died : Unknown
Status : Probably Rode in the Charge

The musters show he was effective from the 1st October to the 31st December.
WO25 Discharged 22nd of September 1856.

1018 WAKEFIELD, Troop Sergeant-Major Thomas Judge

Born : Unknown
Enlisted :
Medals : Crimea (B.I.S), The French Medaille Militaire

Died : Unknown
Status : Rode in the Charge

The musters show he was effective as a Sergeant from the 1st October to the 31st December.

The French Medaille Militaire. (For) "gallantry in the field in the action of Balaklava on the 25th. of October, 1854, and served with uniform good conduct during the whole of the campaign."

WO12-742 Depot musters 6th Dragoons June 1863. On passage home 23rd April 1863. Joined regiment 24th. Discontinued section - Number discontinued or reduced in Regiment since 31st March 1863. Item 2 Sgt Wakefield T.J 1st May discharged.

Involved in the Crawley Affair one of the Sergeant-Majors arrested, and placed in solitary confinement.

The Crawley Affair
In Ahmednugger India in April 1861 Colonel Crawley took over the command of the the 6th Inniskilling Dragoons. A man with fixed ideas and a volatile temper, this was just the ingredient the regiment would need to start a chain reaction that would result in the death of R.S.M Lilley. With the conclusion of the drama being reinacted at Aldershot in November 1863 The event became known as Crawley Affair.
Captain Smales and Dr Turnbull had already been branded as trouble makers, because of their dislike of Captain Renshaw and his wife, whose character had been described as immoral, and whose first husband had divorced her three years earlier under circumstances of the utmost depravity. The Renshaws had been recommended to Crawley by none other than Colonel Shute as a charming couple, and they had become good friends. So it was no surprise that a contrived excuse would be used to show up Smales in an unfavourable light. His refusal to pay money out of hours to Captain Renshaw, even though the demand was sanctioned by Crawley who demanded that the cash was to be issued immediately was to prove his downfall.
He was to consider himself under arrest for refusing to obey an order from his Commanding Officer.
Smales took matters into his own hands and wrote a Memorandum also demanding that the documents be sent on to higher authority. In fact the documentation was to make his situation even more untenable. The recommendations from above was to remove Smales and restore the authority of the Commanding Officer. The only avenue now open was to muster support from within the regiment, and to go on the attack in defence of his good name and honour. A letter was now directed at the War Office informing them that Crawley on various occasions had failed to attend the Muster Parades. All officers on the strength of the regiment were required to attend on the first day of the month. If they were absent then no pay could be drawn for that month. The letter was in fact in breach of army regulations, that all communications to higher authority had to be sent through the Commanding Officer.
The letter was eventually sent on to Sir William Mansfield with a covering letter by Crawly refuting all the accusations. A week letter a reply came that Captain Smales should be brought to a Court Martial.
The case for paymaster Smales could be strengthened by the evidence produced in court by the R.S.M and other Sergeant-Majors.
Sergeant-Major Wakefield had read out the proceedings behind closed doors at R.S.M. Lilley's house, concerning the first three days of the Court-Martial.
This meeting was deemed illegal by the President of the Court. Regimental Sergeant Lilley and Troop Sergeant-Major Wakefield, and Duval had been placed under arrest. R.S.M J. Lilley aged 37 years, a strong and healthy individual died on the 25th May whilst under arrest, the three Sergeant-Majors had been in close arrest for a month. A whitewash to explain the death of Lilley was conceived by Crawley using the argument that he was a drunkard. The Court's verdict to remove Paymaster Smales' from the army. On Smales return to England he campaigned vigorously to clear his name, with newspapers and parliament taking an interest, this resulted in the Court Martial of Lieut-Col Crawley.
The final outcome announced by the Duke of Cambridge, Crawley would resume command of the 6th Dragoons.

A reprint of a pamphlet addressed to members of the House of Commons appeared in the Liverpool Daily Post dated the 14th March 1863. Entitled Military Despotism : or the Inniskilling Dragoons. A tale of Indian Life.

"An extraordinary tale has just been published in the form of a pamphlet, the contents of which appear to be fully authenticated. It has been written by a Colonel at the request of one who tells his story as follows:

"I am a poor man, a working painter by trade, living at Llandudno. My parents are old people residing in Lincolnshire. I had a brother, now dead, who served for nearly 19 years in the Inniskilling Dragoons. He was a kind, good man, an honour to his family and the chief support of our aged father and mother. I subjoin to this pamphlet a certificate given by his late commanding officer, speaking of him in terms that I, as his brother, feel proud and grateful for. After 19 years good and faithful service to his country, my brother suddenly found himself brought up before his commanding officer, not in the orderly room, but in Colonel Crawley's private house. A vague charge was brought against him, the truth of which he to the day of his death strenuously denied. There were no witnesses to prove this charge, but, nevertheless, my brother who had been summoned as a witness on the defence of Captain Smales, against whom Colonel Crawley had preferred charges, was marched to his quarters, a close prisoner.

Thus he was detained in his own room, a sentry duly armed keeping guard over him. His wife was dying at the time, but nevertheless the armed sentry was placed in the dying woman's room. No charge was ever brought against my brother. He died after weeks of close confinement under an Indian sun. His wife died also - his children died - his two comrades who were also made prisoners at the time, and on the same unsubstantial and vague charge, lost one to reason, the other bodily strength. My brother then being dead, they were released after ten days further confinement, without trial, and without any satisfaction being given to them.

I have very great pleasure in testifying the very high opinion I have ever entertained of Sergeant-Major Lilly. I knew him well during his whole service in the Army. He was for a long time in my troop when I was Captain, and was R.S.M. the whole time. I commanded the regiment. I consider him one of the most straightforward, truthful and worthy men I ever knew; thoroughly sober and trustworthy, an excellent soldier, and respected by all who knew him.

C. Shute,   Colonel 4th Dragoon Guards.

The Crawley Affair   A.N Haley Bullfinch Publications 1972

---

457 WALKER, Private William
Born : Unknown   Died : Unknown
Enlisted :   Status : Probably Rode in the Charge
Medals : Crimea (B.I.S)
Medal with 3 bars listed by Heraldene Ltd, London June 1980. Three Bars B.I.S, Naming engraved in the correct style for this regiment (No.457 William Walker, 6th D...) A loose rivet holds on the three bars. N.V.F £350. Medal in the R.Elliott, Widnes collection August 1980.
Large date on obverse, contact marks, unofficial rivets, suspender modified. Balaklava bar crudely re-soldered.

The musters show he was effective from the 1st October to the 31st December. WO25 To England March 1861.

---

857 WALLACE, Private William
Born : Unknown   Died : Unknown
Enlisted :   Status : Probably Rode in the Charge
Medals : Crimea (B.I.S)

The musters show he was effective from the 1st October to the 31st December. WO25 To 7th Dgs 14/09/1857.

---

665 WALSH, Private Patrick
Born : Unknown   Died : Unknown
Enlisted :   Status : Probably Rode in the Charge
Medals : Crimea (B.I.S)

The musters show he was effective from the 1st October to the 31st December. Paid 92 days on shore at ordinary pay. 50 days at 1p G.C pay, 42 days forfeited. 9 days on board ship. Marginal note reads Forfeited 1d GC pay.

1247 WARREN, Private George
Born : Unknown   Died : Unknown
Enlisted :   Status : Probably Rode in the Charge
Medals : Crimea (B.I.S)
His medals are held in the Royal Dragoon Guards Museum at York.

The musters show he was effective from the 1st October to the 31st December. Third muster endorsed Scutari marginal note reads to Scutari 15th Dec.
WO100/24 page 253 Remarks: Invalided-sent home 9/2/55.
WO100/24 page 267 Remarks: Discharged 13 Septr. 1855.

WEIR, Lieutenant & Adjutant Archibald

Born : Unknown
Enlisted :
Medals : Crimea (B.I.S) ,The Turkish Order of the Medjidie (5th Class)

Died : Unknown
Status : Probably Rode in the Charge

The musters show he was effective from the 1st October to the 31st December. No of horses foraged at public expense two, from "Trent".

From the Times Tuesday June 20th 1854. The following official copies of the depositions, taken at Gibraltar, by the survivors from the Europa:

About 10pm on the night of the 31st of May the steward of the Europa came to the cabin which I occupied, and informed me that the ship was on fire. I immediately went to the quarter-deck and asked Colonel Moore if he had any orders to give. His reply was that he had not got any orders to give, except to keep the men quiet and prevent them from getting into the boats. Dr M'Griggor and myself endeavoured to do so, but the boats,I believe, were lowered by some of the crew.This might have been about 20 minutes after I had heard the alarm of fire. I never saw the gig go away, but when the colonel desired me to prevent the men from taking the boats I discovered she had gone. I consider that my men were obedient to orders until they saw the boats lowered and pulling away from the ship, when they endeavoured to get into them. I left the ship, having been pushed into the boat with Lieutenant Black, Dr M'Griggor, Cornet Timson, and the second mate, several soldier's and crew, with a woman,amounting in number to 27.I heard one of the crew cut the boat adrift to prevent her from swamping........

Harts army list 1858, page 140. Captain Archibald Weir. Cornet 21st May 1852, Lieutenant 14th April 1854,Captain 9th October 1857. (Retired 1864).

Adm1/5631 Saved from the wreck of the "Europa"

Colonel Shute referred Weir an ex-ranker to the C.-in-C., the Duke of Cambridge, on a matter of discipline. he wrote "Captain Weir has too well succeeded in sowing a vast amount of dissention amongst the staff of the regiment to which he owes everything, and in which, from being an indifferent R.S.M. and a very moderate adjutant, he has risen from the ranks to be, in only six years, a captain without purchase". Colonel Shute left for home in March 1861. Captain Weir had command of the regiment for a period of six weeks while awaiting the arrival of the new C.O. from England.

Shortly after Shute left, the Brigade Commander Hobson ordered a full dress parade. He found various parts of the barracks dirty, and wrote to Weir expressing dissatisfaction. Weir wrote back disagreeing and was told to withdraw his letter and apologize. He did not and received a severe reprimand. Captain Weir was sucked into The Crawley affair and all his previous skirmishes with authority including his alleged opposition to changes, were all paraded before the Court.

Photograph courtesy of Glenn Fisher

WHEATCROFT, Captain German

Born : Unknown
Enlisted :
Medals : Crimea (B.I.S)

Died : Unknown
Status : Probably Rode in the Charge

The musters show he was effective from the 1st October to the 7th December., promoted Captain 8th December to 31st December.

Fields of War,Warner page 55 mentions Wheatcroft out boar shooting in a letter dated 8th September 1854,Varna.

Harts Army list 1856. Cornet by purchase 19th October 1849, Lieutenant by purchase 22nd August 1851, Captain 8th December 1854.

565 WHELAN, Private Timothy

Born : Unknown
Enlisted :
Medals : Crimea (B.I.S)

Died : Unknown
Status : Probably Rode in the Charge

The musters show he was effective from the 1st October to the 31st December. Paid 92 days on shore, 92 days at 3d GC, 9 days on board ship.

Destruction of the Europa

Accounts were received yesterday, announcing the destruction by fire of the transport Europa, on the night of the 31st of May, and the loss of two officers, four sergeants, 12 men, and one woman of the 6th Dragoons.

The transport ship Europa sailed from Plymouth on Tuesday morning, the 30th of May. She belonged to Messrs. Somes and Wharton, of London, burden per register 841 tons, new measurement, and was commanded by Captain Gardner. The four service troops of the 6th Enniskillen's were embarked at Plymouth in five ships-viz.,the Europa, Escort, Sutlej, Lord Raglan, and Talavera. Each of the last four conveyed a large portion of one troop. The Europa took portions of each of the four troops, viz, five sergeants and 54 rank and file, and the commanding officer and staff, Lieutenant-Colonel Willoughby Moore, Lieutenant and Adjutant Weir, Cornet Henry Timson, Surgeon Macgregor, and Probationary Veterinary Surgeon Kelly. She had in the lower hold 13 officers' horses and 44 troop horses, and carried an extra freight of forage, which may have become overheated and have caused the accident

The Times, Saturday June 17th 1854

Names of officers, men, and one woman, belonging to the 6th Dragoons, who were drowned from the wreck of the ship Europa.

Lieutenant-Colonel Moore
Kelly, veterinary surgeon
A.M'Clelland farrier-Major
Charles Montray, quarter-master sergt.
William Johnson, hospital sergeant.
Thomas W.Gore, hospital sergeant
John Watson, lance-sergeant
Robert Wilson, lance-corporal
John Coleman, private
John Evans, private
James Killender, private
Denis Mahon, private
Patrick Maguire, private
Philip M'Caffrey, private
William Strong private
Abel Walters, private
John Watson, private
Hoult Waning, private
Mrs Parsons.

Names of officers, men, and two women of the 6th Dragoons saved from the ship Europa.

Archibald Weir, Liet. and Adj.
Alexander M'Gregor, surgeon.
Henry Timpson, Cornet
John K.Mountain, R.S.M
Andrew Morton, lance-sergt.
David Gooding, corporal
Robert Cotton, corporal
William Ainsworth, private.
Charles Burnett, private.
*Poter Butter, private.
William Corpe, private.
Charles Clarke, private.
Thomas Caughie, private.
*John Curry, private.
Benjamin de Carle private.
Charles Delany private.
Robert Easy private.
John Elmes private.
Samuel Forsyth, private.
Andrew Ferguson private.
Charles Goble, private.
James Guilleace, private.
Robert Hunter, private.
Thomas Hastler, private.
John Jackson,private.

George Haines, private.
Robert Jennings, private.
David Knight, private.
George Lemmon, private.
Charles Maguire, private
William Madgwick, private.
*Robert Nairn, private.
George Nugent, private.
John Patton, private.
*William Parsons, private.
Alexander Russell, private.
Robert Renton, private.
Michael Rourke, private.
Joseph Ross, private.
Gavin Shephard, private.
Henry Snelling, private.
George Seymour, private.
John Tooth, private.
Robert Turner, private.
William White, private.
John Walsh, private.
Mrs Mahon..
Mrs Currie,
T.Bishop, private servant.
*Unable to locate

WHITE, Lieutenant-Colonel Henry Dalrymple

Born : 5th July 1820   Died : 27th March 1886 - Bournemouth
Enlisted :   Status : Probably Rode in the Charge
Medals : Crimea (B.I.S), The Turkish Order of the Medjidie (4th Class)

The musters show he was effective from the 1st October to the 31st December. Disembarked from the "Trent" 1st October. 5 horses foraged at public expense.

WO100/24 page 260 Remarks: Half Pay 19 Feb 58.

The Inniskillings' 2nd Squadron drove in beside them with a wild Irish yell, their Colonel, Dalrymple White, receiving a sabre stroke which almost bisected his helmet.

Received his medal from the hand of the Queen, May 18th 1855.

The Inniskilling Dragoons, The Records of an Old Heavy Cavalry Regiment by Major E.S. Jackson

RECORD OF THE SERVICES OF GENERAL SIR HENRY DALRYMPLE WHITE, K.C.B.

HENRY DALRYMPLE WHITE, who was born July 5th, 1820, was the eldest son of Vice-Admirai Sir John Chambers White and of Charlotte Elizabeth, his second wife (daughter of Sir Hew Whiteford Dalrymple, Bart., who commanded the army in Portugal at the time of the Convention of Cintra).

With sixteen years' service, all passed in the Inniskilling Dragoons, during which he had at different times been present at manouvres in Russia, Austria, and Germany, he succeeded to the command of the regiment on the death of Colonel Willoughby Moore, at the commencement of the Crimean War. At the battle of Balaklava he had a narrow escape, early in the day, from a shell which burst close to his horse; in the charge he had his helmet cleft with a sword-cut; and afterwards, when the Heavy Brigade moved up the North Valley in support of the Light Cavalry charge, a musket-ball cut his saddle-flap and passed between his leg and his horse without injuring either.

Colonel White came home from the war with the reputation of being one of the best cavalry officers in the Crimea, and, at his levée soon afterwards, H.R.H. the Commander-in-Chief said to him, "I must compliment you in the highest manner about your regiment. There is not a better in the whole army, or one better commanded."

General Sir Henry Dalrymple White, K.C.B.
Colonel of the Inniskilling Dragoons
1874-1886.

In January, 1857, he was selected to accompany General Sir Colin Campbell to Berlin for the investiture of the Prince of Prussia (afterwards first German Emperor) with the Order of the Bath. In May, Lord Cardigan, Inspector-General of Cavalry, reported: "....I have the honour to add that I consider the Inniskilling Dragoons to be one of the finest and most perfect regiments in the Queen's service;" and H.R.H. the Commander-in-Chief assured Colonel White that the report was quite confirmedby his own knowledge of the regiment.

When Her Majesty Queen Victoria held her first distribution of the Victoria Cross in June of this year, the Inniskilling Dragoons were brought up to London from Shorncliffe to be present as a special compliment to their efficiency, H.R.H. the Duke of Cambridge saying he "wished it to be known that they were a model to the British Cavalry."

In 1858, Colonel White retired from the command of the regiment; in 1863 he was appointed Assistant Adjutant-General for Cavalry; in 1866 he was appointed to command the Cavalry brigade in Ireland, and in 1868 the Aldershot Cavalry brigade, with which he combined the office of Inspector-General of Cavalry in Great Britain.

In 1870, his health failing, he retired from the Service with the rank of Major-General. He was gazetted to the Colonelcy of the regiment in 1874. In 1877 he was promoted Lieut.-General, and was made a Knight Commander of the Bath (he had been made a Companion of the Order for his services in the Crimea). He was promoted General in 1879, and died in 1886.

General Sir Henry White was twice married. His second wife, Alice Elizabeth, daughter of Neill Malcolm of Poltalloch, survives him, and recently presented 100l. to the Union Jack Club to endow a bed for the Inniskilling Dragoons in memory of her distinguished husband.

Obituary from the Times Mar 30th 1886.
The Colonel of the Inniskilling Dragoons has fallen vacant by the death, at Bournemouth of General Sir Henry Dalrymple White, K.C.B .,eldest son of the late Vice Admiral Sir John White, K.C.B. Sir Henry White commanded the Inniskilling Dragoons through the whole of the Crimean campaign and from the date of theassembling of the army at Varna to the termination of the war he was never absent from duty. He led his regiment, which was in the first line, most gallantly into action when Sir James Scarlett's Heavy Brigade defeated, at Balaclava, fully five times their number of the cavalry of one of the greatest military Powers in Europe. About the first blow struck in that action cut the helmet from the crest nearly to his skull, but he dashed into and through the masses of the enemy. Colonel White's thoughts were always concentrated on the care of his men and horses, and his zealous performance of his duty during the great hardships of the winter of 1854 laid the first foundation of the disease to which he had fallen a victim. His regiment was in the highest possible order during the period of his command. For his services during the Crimean war he was nominated a Companion of the Bath, received the medal with three clasps, was made a Knight of the Legion of Honour, received the Order of the Medjidie (4th Class), and the Turkish medal. He subsequently commanded the cavalry in Ireland and at Aldershot. He was made a Knight Commander of the Bath in 1877. Sir Henry White was a brilliant cavalry officer, and his death will be deeply felt by the gallant corps with which he has been connected for upwards of 48 years.

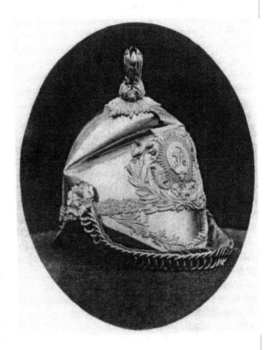

716 WHITE Private William

Born : Date Unknown - Barwell
Enlisted : 9th October 1841
Medals : Crimea (B.I.S)

Died : 12th January 1855 - Passage to Scutari
Status : Probably Rode in the Charge

The musters show he was effective from the 1st October to the 31st December. Paid 92 days on shore, 92 days at 2d GC, 3 days on board ship.
WO100/24 page 253 Remarks: Died passage to Scutari 12/1/55.
WO100/24 page 259 Remarks: Died 12 Jan:55.-Disease.
Trade on enlistment a Butcher.
The Times of Thursday 1st February, 1855; page 8 reported that "Private W.White 6th Dragoons" died on board the Colombo on the 16th January 1855. Saved from the wreck of the "Europa"

1011 WHITTAKER, Private William

Born : Unknown
Enlisted :
Medals : Crimea (B.I.S)

Died : Unknown
Status : Probably Rode in the Charge

The musters show he was effective from the 1st October to the 31st December.

544 WHITTLE, Private James

Born : Unknown
Enlisted :
Medals : Crimea (B.I.S)

Died : Unknown
Status : Probably Rode in the Charge

The musters show he was effective from the 1st October to the 31st December. Paid 92 days on shore, 92 days at 2d GC, "to 3d from 10th Nov" 9 days on board ship.
WO100/24 page 253 Remarks: Invalided-sent home 15/9/55.

1228 WILLIS, Private George
Born : Unknown
Enlisted :
Medals : Crimea (B.I.S)

Died : Unknown
Status : Probably Rode in the Charge

The musters show he was effective from the 1st October to the 31st December.
WO100/24 page 253 Remarks: Sent to England 18 Oct:55.

1216 WILSON, Private William
Born : Unknown
Enlisted : 1853
Medals : Crimea (B.I.S)

Died : Unknown
Status : Probably Rode in the Charge

Glendining and Co. July 1975. W.H.Wilson 6th Dragoons Crimea, clasps for B,I amd S. Impressed naming. (Although this medal has the initials W.H it is authenticated by the Sebastopol roll as only one W.Wilson listed.
Christies 25th July 1989 Lot 18. Crimea 3 clasps B.I.S. W.H Wilson 6th Dragoons officially impressed. Edge bruising VF. together with copy of discharge documents. Cpl William Wilson joined the 6th Dragoons 1853. Served in Crimea where his Regiment took part in the Charge of the Heavy Brigade at Balaklava. Cpl. 1858 Sgt 1858, reduced to Pte 1859. Cpl 1867. Retired after 21 years service 1874. Ex Usher collection 1975. Estimate £300-£400. Hammer price £341.

The musters show he was effective from the 1st October to the 31st December. WO100/24 page 253 Remarks: Invalided, sent home 2/6/56.
WO25 Records Corporal Wilson to pension 2nd of June 1874.

1353 WIRE, Private Thomas
Born : Unknown
Enlisted :
Medals : Crimea (B.I.S)

Died : Unknown
Status : Probably Rode in the Charge

The musters show he was effective from the 1st October to the 31st December.
WO25 Discharged March 1857.

Appendices

Appendix 1 - The Charge Formation

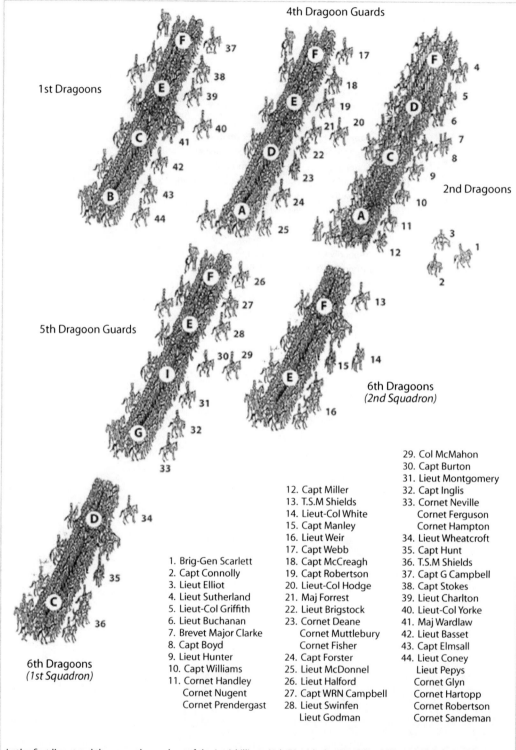

4th Dragoon Guards

1st Dragoons

2nd Dragoons

5th Dragoon Guards

6th Dragoons
(2nd Squadron)

6th Dragoons
(1st Squadron)

1. Brig-Gen Scarlett
2. Capt Connolly
3. Lieut Elliot
4. Lieut Sutherland
5. Lieut-Col Griffith
6. Lieut Buchanan
7. Brevet Major Clarke
8. Capt Boyd
9. Lieut Hunter
10. Capt Williams
11. Cornet Handley
    Cornet Nugent
    Cornet Prendergast
12. Capt Miller
13. T.S.M Shields
14. Lieut-Col White
15. Capt Manley
16. Lieut Weir
17. Capt Webb
18. Capt McCreagh
19. Capt Robertson
20. Lieut-Col Hodge
21. Maj Forrest
22. Lieut Brigstock
23. Cornet Deane
    Cornet Muttlebury
    Cornet Fisher
24. Capt Forster
25. Lieut McDonnel
26. Lieut Halford
27. Capt WRN Campbell
28. Lieut Swinfen
    Lieut Godman
29. Col McMahon
30. Capt Burton
31. Lieut Montgomery
32. Capt Inglis
33. Cornet Neville
    Cornet Ferguson
    Cornet Hampton
34. Lieut Wheatcroft
35. Capt Hunt
36. T.S.M Shields
37. Capt G Campbell
38. Capt Stokes
39. Lieut Charlton
40. Lieut-Col Yorke
41. Maj Wardlaw
42. Lieut Basset
43. Capt Elmsall
44. Lieut Coney
    Lieut Pepys
    Cornet Glyn
    Cornet Hartopp
    Cornet Robertson
    Cornet Sandeman

In the first line stood the second squadron of the Inniskillings (6th D) with the Greys (2nd D) on their left. In the second line stood the first squadron of the Inniskillings (6th D) with the 5th Dragoon Guards and 4th Dragoons Guards to their left. Forming up in the left rear were the 1st Dragoon Guards.

Appendix 2 - Heavy Brigade Casualties

The Charge of Scarlett's *300, by Stanley Berkeley. 1890.*

Table 1. Compiled from the London Gazette 12th November 1854 Officers and 16th December other ranks.

Regiment	Killed	Wounded	Total
1st Dragoons	2	11	13
2nd Dragoons	2	56	58*
4th Dragoon Guards	1	5	6
5th Dragoon Guards	2	11	13
6th Dragoons	2	13	15
Totals	9	96	105

Table 2. From regimental reports. Crimea Doctors Vol 1 John Shepherd p 219/220

Regiment	Killed	Wounded	Notes
1st Dragoons	2	14	
2nd Dragoons	2	58	Note 1
4th Dragoon Guards	1		Note 2
5th Dragoon Guards	2	31	Note 3
6th Dragoons			
Totals			

Notes:

Note 1 No casualties in the Heavy Brigade charge but later, in support of the Light brigade the regiment suffered severe losses from round-shot, shell, grape shot and rifle balls.

Note 2 "many men were wounded by sabres and lancers who did not come into Hospital, their cuts and probes being unimportant"

Note 3 Of the latter 13 were severely injured and were dressed in a regimental hospital and immediately sent on board the transports for passage to Scutari. The Surgeon reported "Some of the wounds were severe, chiefly sabre and lance wounds".

It had been estimated that of all the regiments participating in the Heavy Brigade charge a total of 78 men were killed or wounded.

Children of Deceased Heavy Brigade Troopers who were maintained by the Royal Patriotic Fund 31st Dec 1859

No.	Child's Name.	Father's Name.	Rank in Service, &c.	Father's Death.	Mother's Name.	Mother's Abode.	Child's Age.	Institution, and Date of going to it.
391	HOWARD, Fanny	George	Private, 5th D.G	Crimea, 13th August 1854	Ann	Dublin	16y	B.F.O.A - 20th Aug 1855 - 1
	HOWARD, Harriet						14y	R.V.P.A - 21st Jan 1859 - 2
	HOWARD, Ann Eliza						8y	B.O.A - 20th Aug 1858
1096	FLAMERY, Mary A.	John	Private, 6th D.G	Scutari, Jan 1855	Mary	Exeter	16y	S.D.H - 26th Feb 1856 - 3
1733	WILLIAMS, Lydia Anna	John	Private, 5th D.G	Gibraltar, 7th June 1855	Ann	Dublin	13y	B.F.O.A - 30th Nov 1855
1989	BURY, George	George	Private, 6th D.G	Crimea, 30th Aug 1855	Sarah	London	9y	B.S - Dec 1855
	BURY, Louisa						14y	S.D.H - 1st Oct 1855 - 4
2053	LANGTON, Elizabeth	Daniel	Private, 1st D	Balaclava, 25th Sept 1855	Dead	Leicester	8y	Grandfather, Leicester
2200	GREEN, William	James	T.S.M, 1st D	Crimea, 13th Sept 1855	Ann	Bristol	7y	B.F.I.S - 25th Nov 1859
	GREEN, George						12y	B.F.I.S - 25th Nov 1859

Abreviations of Institutions
B.S - Barnet School
B.F.I.S - Birmingham Free Industrial School
R.V.P.A - Royal Victoria Patriotic Asylum, Wandsworth
B.F.O.A - Bethesda Female Orphan Asylum, Dublin
S.D.H - Soldier's Daughters Home, Hampstead

Remarks
1. In bad health at present, Margate Sea Bathing Infirmary. (Picture below)
2. Removed 3rd April 1859
3 Removed 29th July 1858, Gone to service.
4. Removed 27th Jul 1859, transferred to R.V.P.A 28th July 1859.

Extracts from the return submitted to the House of Commons on the 6th February 1860 showing every child who at any time had been maintained at the charge of the Royal Commissioners of the Patriotic Fund in any orphanage, asylum, school or other institution, or in any family or place under the care of any person other than it's mother. (Chargers shown in bold type)

R.V.P.A - Royal Victoria Patriotic Asylum, Wandsworth

Appendix 4 - The Transport of Sick/Wounded to Scutari

Date	Ship	Sick/Wounded	Died	
22nd Sept	Kangaroo	600	?	Note 1
22nd Sept	Dunbar	500	?	Note 1
23rd Sept	Unknown	300	?	Note 1
24th Sept	Andes	315	7	Note 2
24th Sept	Vulcan	490	22	Note 2
25th Sept	Simoom	?	?	Note 2
12th October (departure)	Cornwall			Note 2
21st December	Golden Fleece	?	3	Note 2
21st December	Victoria	?	6	Note 2
21st December	Sydney	?	5	Note 2
21st December	Tremander	180	20	Note 3
22nd December	Ottawa	151	6	Note 3
22nd December	Gomelza	118	8	Note 3
22nd December	Joseph Shepard	67	7	Note 3
25th December	Brandon	149	1	Note 3
25th December	Tamar	142	3	Note 3
26th December	Joseph Shepard	?	1	Note 3
?	Australia	?	2	Note 3
6th January	Belgravia		43	Note 3
14th January	Thames		19	Note 4
17th January	Colombo	235	23	Note 4
19th January	Arabia	230	7	Note 5
19th January	Kangaroo	93	9	Note 5
19th January	Sydney	151	6	Note 5

The information above is by no means complete , many more wounded and sick were transported to Scutari.
After Alma: 7 transports + 1 War ship took the wounded to Scutari between 14th - 28th Sept.
In October 1854 The Times organised "for the purpose of helping the sick and wounded soldier's a fund". The correspondent for The Times at Scutari was John Cameron McDonald. His main interest was reporting on the Hospitals and transports, working closely with Florence Nightingale. Thomas Shenery was the Times Correspondent at Constantinople, he also contributed reports on Scutari. Information as per Note 3.
Note 1 : 1500 sick and invalids were placed on board the Kangaroo in Kalamitia Bay "the Captain made signals of distress, and remained at anchor from sheer inability to go to sea with his decks encumbered with dead and dying." The Dunbar sailing transport and another ship came to their assistance, the Dunbar being towed back to Scutari by the Kangaroo.
Note 2 : Taken from despatches by William Howard Russell to the Times.
Note 3 : The Times, 6th, 10th, 15th, 29th January 1855. 43 individuals died on the Belgravia from the 22nd December 1854 to January 6th 1855, all of diarrhoea.
Note 4 : The Times, 1st February 1855. 21 died on the board the Colombo between the 10 Jan -17 Jan 1855 Colombo arrived on the 17th with 235 sick, and 23 died on the passage. 19 died on the board the Thames between 5th Jan - 14th Jan. Surgeon William Abbot Anderson died on board ship 3rd January 1855.
Note 5 : The Times, 8th February 1855.

The original scheme of using Chelsea Pensioners to look after the sick and wounded in Scutari Hospital was an ill conceived idea, they themselves requiring nursing assistance. - William Howard Russell, The Times.

Nightingale arrives with Nurses 4th November 1854 - at this time the two hospitals held 8000 sick and wounded, a figure that rode to 14,000 by Feb 1855.
Andes & Cambria made into Hospital ships

The Illustrated London News 6th January 1855

8th Hussars   17th Lancers   Background: Royal Horse Artillery   5th Dragoon Guards   4th Dragoon Guards   1st Dragoons   11th Hussars

On 16 July 1856, the Troops in camp at Aldershot that had returned from the Crimea were reviewed by Her Majesty the Queen.

The Crimean Regiments were found in the Long Valley, the remainder of the Troops present which had been reviewed in a former occasion, or that had not been on Service in the East being formed on Long Hill.

After the Troops had marched past, the Regiments were addressed personally by her Majesty and were then inspected on detail. The Queen walking down each line, the Cavalry having been previously dismounted, and the men formed with reference to the number of Clasps to which entitled.

The following were the Crimean Regiments at Aldershot inspected on this occasion.

2nd Dragoons 'Scots Greys', 6th Dragoons 'Inniskillings'
34th Regiment, 41st Regiment, 49th Regiment
93rd Highlanders
2nd Battalion Rifle Brigade
Detachment Royal Sappers and Miners

The next day (17 July 1856) The Queen visited the huts and stabling of the Regiments during the morning.

In the afternoon, the whole of the Troops were formed on 'Caesar's Camp' and were again reviewed by the Queen, the Troops performing a variety of field movements.

The following Order was issued with reference to Her Majesty's Reviews:

Division Order Camp at Aldershot
18 July 1856

The Queen has been graciously pleased to direct the Lt General Commanding the Camp to express Her Majesty's great satisfaction with the appearance and efficiency of all Arms in the Division at Aldershot.

Her Majesty particularly desires the Lt General to convey to that portion of the Troops lately arrived from the Crimea, her high sense of the Gallantry they displayed before the enemy, as well as her admiration of the fortitude with which they supported the hardships incidental to the late Campaign.

By order
Signed: J S Wood Lt Col   A.A.G.

The following General Order was issued on the return to England of the Crimean Army:
General Order Horse Guards 5 August 1956

The Queen having completed the Review of the Regiments which served in the Army in the East, has commanded his Royal Highness The General Commanding in Chief to welcome their return from that arduous service.

Her Majesty has been graciously pleased to express her admiration of their good order and discipline.

Victorious when opposed to the brave and enterprising enemy with whom it had to contend, the Army has carried the gratitude of the Country.

The patient endurance of evils inseparable from War, and an instinctive determination to overcome them, are characteristic of the British Soldier; and the events of the War, have proved that those national virtues, have not degenerated during a long previous peace.

The Queen deplores the loss of many of her best Officers, and bravest men, but History will consecrate the ground before Sevastopol as the grave of heroes.

By order of His Royal Highness, The General Commanding in Chief, Signed: G A Wetherall Adjutant General.

Her Majesty in her new military costume at the camp, Aldershott.. From The Illustrated London News.

Delivering point using the ringpost. Showing the use
of the sword point against a mounted opponent.

"Picking up heads from the ground" from the 7th
lesson. Showing the method of attacking an enemy
laying on the ground.

Delivering cuts to the head against a mounted opponent, using the dummy post.

The system rests on a few simple principles, shewing
how to attack each point in succession, and thus
enabling the rider at last to reduce his horse to
perfect obedience.

Nolan could prepare horses for duty in 60 days, it
normally took about 10 months. The horses had
to be completely manoeuvrable and be able to be
ridden with one hand. This new system of Equitation
was invented by Monsieur Baucher.

From Captain Nolan's "The Training of Cavalry
Remount Horses: A New System", 1852.

Captain Bernard, 5th Dragoon Guards. Pictured by Fenton 1855

Training Horses

Procurement of horses was on a regimental basis, with a nominated officer (hopefully one with a good 'eye' for horseflesh, and wise in the wicked ways of dealers) being sent to civilian horse fairs and dealers.

Horses were normally bought as three-year-olds (most civilians bought four-year-olds, which gave regiments an advantage in picking promising horses.) The horses were then trained up for about two years before taking their place in the ranks. Horses were normally able to fulfil regimental duties until they were about fifteen, when they were 'cast' – sold back to the civilian market.

Louis Nolan was an acknowledged expert on horses, and wrote a book on the subject – The Training of Cavalry Remount Horses (London, 1852). ('Remount' was a term used for any horse procured for regimental use.) It is difficult to know how widely Nolan's theories and practices were adopted. Some officers at least disliked his methods and thought his book denigrated the British cavalry – hence Lord Paget's sneer that Nolan was 'an officer… who writes books, and was a great man in his own estimation…' [Paget, Light cavalry Brigade.] Nolan described in detail in his book a course of training for horses, lasting a total of 64 days. He advocated that:

When Remount Horses join a regiment, they should be distributed amongst the old horses; they thus become accustomed to the sight of saddles and accoutrements, to the rattling of the swords, etc, etc, and the old horses on each side of them, taking no notice of all these things, inspire the young ones with confidence. [Nolan p. 17.]

To accustom them to battle conditions, they should be trained in the riding school by degrees, by firing pistols near them (and eventually by their riders firing), using drums etc. Their riders should practice the sword exercise first at a walk, until the horse is steady; then at a canter. [Nolan p. 45.]

A well-trained horse became so accustomed to moving in the ranks, that if it lost its rider, it would continue to conform to other horses, often with disastrous consequences for the order of the regiment. Paget describes the behaviour of riderless horses during the Charge of the Light Brigade:

I was of course riding by myself and clear of the line [as CO he was of course leading from the front], and for that reason was a marked object for the poor dumb brutes, who were by this time galloping about in numbers, like mad wild beasts. They consequently made dashes at me, some advancing with me a considerable distance, at one time as many as five on my right and two on my left, cringing on to me, and positively squeezing me… [Paget p. 180.]
From notes by Dr John Rumsby.

Recruits for the cavalry

To expand on the orginal article on page 107 concerning the recruitment of cavalry personnal. I have included the following notes, taken from some orginal research carried out by Dr John Rumsby.

The majority of recruits were recruited in towns. Although many of these may originally have been from rural backgrounds, very few stated agricultural occupations on their enlistment papers. Officers of the time did indeed state that they preferred rural recruits, and did not like artisans, engineers and other industrial urban workers as soldier's, but these are in fact exactly the classes that they drew on for the cavalry.

Again, although the Irish formed a high percentage of the army in general (i.e. a higher proportion than in the population of the British Isles as a whole), they were very much in a minority in the cavalry, even in the two 'Irish' cavalry regiments, the 4th Dragoon Guards and 8th Hussars. The figures vary a little depending whether the regiment concerned had been stationed in Ireland, and the 2nd Dragoons seem to have had a higher proportion of Scots, but normally cavalry were predominantly English, reflecting the practice of their recruiting parties being sent to London and the English manufacturing districts such as Birmingham and West Yorkshire. Some sample figures:

Regiment	Date	English	Irish	Scots
Whole army	1840	46.5	37.2	13.7
4th 'Irish' DG	1856	55	40	5
8th 'Irish' Hussars	1822		40	
9th Lancers	1850	81.1	12.9	6
10th Hussars	1859	84.8%	8.9	5.1
15th Hussars	1830	89	9.5	1.2
16th Lancers	1845	83.2	13.1	3.6

This compares with 68th (Durham) Light Infantry, after several years being stationed in Ireland:

68th LI	1847	64	34	2

Figures for nationality for each regiment can be found in National Archives WO 27 series (Inspection Reports), so it would be possible to get precise proportions for each regiment in the Crimea.

4th Dragoon Guards Averages

The averages of the Regiment calculated to the 31 December 1856, were as follows vis:

Men

Height Ft Inches	Weight St lbs	Age Yrs Mths	Service Yrs Mths
5 - 8 1/4	11 - 4	25 - 7	5 - 10

The regiment consisted of 210 Englishmen, 213 Irishmen, and 30 Scotsmen, of which 279 were Episcopalians (Anglicans), 140 were Roman Catholic, and 34 were Presbyterians.

Wearing Good Conduct Badges:

Badges	1	2	3	4	5	6
Men	44	19	15	2	1	-

Wearing Crimean Medals:

Clasps	1	2	3	4
Men	89	5	169	-

Horses

Height Hds Ins	Age Yrs Mths	Service Yrs Mths
15 - 24	8 - 6	4 - 3

Mares	Geldings	Total
161	191	352

Information supplied by Captain (Retd) W A Henshall, Royal Dragoon Guards Museum at York.

Fearful Scene at Aldermaston. The Times, 25th June 1869.

FEARFUL SCENE AT ALDERSHOT.

On Monday the C, D, and E batteries Royal Horse Artillery, 5th Dragoon Guards, 7th Dragoon Guards, 6th Inniskillings, and 10th Hussars formed up, under the command of Major General H. D. White, C.B., near the Queen's Pavilion, Aldershot, for field movements. The regiments were told off in two brigades. The first, or heavy brigade, consisting of the 5th and 7th Dragoon Guards, and the second, or light brigade, of the 6th Inniskillings and 10th Hussars. The former was commanded by Colonel the Hon. S. G. Calthorpe, and the latter by Colonel Valentine Baker. General White first attacked to the westward, and worked his way to near the waterworks. The General then changed position to the right, and attacked down the Long Valley. In this movement the light brigade formed line and advanced, supported by the heavy brigade, in a parallel line. A dashing charge was made in the advanced line, and when near the north end of the valley Brigadier Baker ordered his brigade to retire by column of troops from the left of the line. As this movement was being executed Brigadier Calthorpe's brigade was coming on at a gallop, and before the rear squadron of the 6th Dragoons had cleared the front, the left squadron of the 7th Dragoon Guards rode upon the flank of the rear squadron of the Iniskillings. A fearful crash was the result, and a number of men and horses were put *hors de combat*. Private Thomas Kateley, 6th Dragoons, had his skull and ribs fractured, and no hopes are entertained of his recovery. The following men were also seriously injured :—Private Thomas Hoy, 6th Dragoons, shoulder dislocated ; Private Charles Marcroft, 6th Dragoons, contusion of shoulder ; Private Chenn, 6th Inniskillings, contusion of ankle ; Private Fitzgerald, 6th Dragoons, contusion of ankle ; Private Galley, 6th Dragoons, sabre cut on the chin ; Privates Flood and Whithy, 6th Dragoons, slightly injured ; Private Ward, 7th Dragoon Guards, also received several severe contusions. Two horses, one belonging to each regiment, had their legs fractured, and were shot on the field ; several other horses were also slightly injured. The men injured belonged to C squadron, 6th Inniskillings, squadron leader, Captain A. F. Stewart ; and to B squadron, 7th Dragoon Guards, squadron leader, Captain D'Olier George.

Trial of O'Reilly, 4th July 1866.

The trial of Private O'Reilly was proceeded with at the Court-martial yesterday. The witness Rorreson was further examined. Private Foley, 5th Dragoon Guards, gave similar testimony as to the conduct of the prisoner in Hoey's publichouse, when Devoy, a civilian, was alleged to have administered the Fenian oath to the soldiers, in company with the prisoner. The Court adjourned to this morning.

A Comrade's Letter from the Aberdeen Weekly Journal August 20th 1897.

THE LATE GENERAL CLARKE
Balaclava Veteran

By the death of General George Calvert Clarke we lose one of the few remaining veterans who fought with the "Heavies" at Balaclava. He was born in London on July 23, 1814, and was the fifth son of the late John Calvert Clarke and Eliza, daughter of the late Richard Astley Sales. He was educated at Eton, and entered the 89th Regiment in 1834. He exchanged as captain into the 2nd Dragoons, Royal Scots Greys, in 1845, and retired on half-pay in 1868. He served throughout the Crimean campaign, being present at the affair of McKenzie's Farm and the battles of Balaclava (charge of the Heavy Brigade, Inkerman, and Tchernaya, and siege and fall of Sebastopol. Our portrait is by W. and A. H. Fry, Brighton.

THE LATE SERGEANT FRASER. OF THE LIGHT BRIGADE.

A COMRADE'S LETTER.

The story of the exploits of the late Sergeant-Major Fraser, of the Light Brigade, who resides in Forres, which appeared in our columns, will be fresh in the readers' memory. We ("Aberdeen Journal") brought the case of the aged veteran for a pension before Sir Robert Finlay, Solicitor-General for England ; Captain Pirie, M.P. ; and Mr John E. Gordon, M.P., but the War Office were inexorable, as this hero of the "Balaclava Charge" was receiving a pension from another Department of the Government. The following letter from an old comrade will be read with interest :—

Garmouth, 14th August, 1897.

Sir,—I have heard from my son-in-law, Sergt.-Major Cochrane, late of the Elgin Volunteers, of the great kindness shown to my late friend and comrade Sergeant Fraser, late of the 13th Light Dragoons, an old Balaclava hero, who died at Forres. I was intimately acquainted with him for some years and served with him in the Crimea, though not in the same regiment or brigade, I being one of the heavy brigade under York Scarlet and he in the light under Lord Cardigan, but we often met together in the Crimea as sergeants. I also served with him for some years in the prison service at Parkhurst. My object in writing to you, sir, is to return my most sincere thanks to the officers, non-commissioned officers, and men of the Forres volunteers for their noble and gallant behaviour to an old and friendless soldier in a time of trouble and death. I am quite sure that I express the feelings of every surviving officer and soldier of the cavalry division in thanking those officers, non-commissioned officers, and men under your command for their kindness to my old friend. —I have the honour to remain, sir, your obedient servant,
J. HARDY,
Late 6th Inniskilling Dragoons.

THE CHARGE AT BALAKLAVA.

Colonel John Shakespear, late of the Royal Artillery, writes as follows:—"The charge of "The Light Brigade" on the 25th of October, 1854, is still a household memory with us, though thirty-five years have slipped by, and I have been urged to give prominence to this anniversary by recording occurrences other than those of mere galloping, cutting, thrusting, and strong language, all of which are very similar on like occasions, and often described in prose and verse. Short and to the point is best suited to what is expected of me. So to begin. Maude's Horse Artillery, with me second in command, opened fire about daylight, and held its ground until the ammunition was exhausted, when it retired a short distance down the hill, where it remained for a time screened from the Russian fire, with the hope of giving confidence to some wavering Turks. Maude was seriously wounded by a Russian shell bursting near his horse, and there were also several casualties amongst the officers, men, horses, and gun-wheels. Some of our field batteries soon arrived and continued the cannonade. In the course of an hour or so our two brigades of cavalry and Horse Artillery formed column under the heights of the Sebastopol plateau, when suddenly about 5,000 Russian cavalry in line, with columns in support, poured down the grass slope, and got a crushing defeat by the gallant charge of our splendid 'Heavy Brigade' of cavalry, under General Scarlett. In the pause that followed I deemed it most desirable to learn what the enemy might be doing, so I mounted a baggage pony, as the horse that had carried me since early morn had been wounded by the splinter of a shell, and rode him to near the crest of the ridge forming our side of the now famed valley, where I tethered him to a tent-peg, and crept through the long grass until my telescope cautioned, 'Beware, the brushwood hills opposite are full of guns, and down the valley troops by the thousand.' Captain Charteris, one of Lord Lucan's aide-de-camps, now rode by, but as he did not see me I hailed him with that information, when he replied, 'The Light Brigade is ordered to attack down the valley,' and while we were speaking it appeared advancing and deploying at the trot and canter. It was then, of course, too late for a warning from us, so at the utmost pace of the pony I got back to the guns, and brought them up at full gallop and placed them over the ridge, where they might most effectively aid 'The Light Brigade' in its inevitable retreat. At that moment Lord Cardigan reined his horse and told me what had happened, while he pointed to a long rent in his cherry-coloured overalls made by a Cossack lancer, who had otherwise missed his aim. Others rode or ran up to us. Amongst the last was Captain Godfrey Morgan, 17th Lancers, now Lord Tredegar, who having had his horse killed and helmet gone, walked sword in hand up to me, and speaking as coolly as on parade, remarked, 'I say, Shakespear, is not this an awful business. What shall I do?' My reply was, 'Quick, jump on a gun limber and go to the rear with us or to the front for action, when you may help to fight a gun.' We must not forget the volley from the 93rd Highlanders that emptied many Russian saddles near the entrance to Balaklava, nor the charge of the French cavalry on the enemy's artillery in the brushwood hills, as they, being mounted on white horses, were very conspicuous. Sights and impressions on a field of battle are rarely forgotten. Even now I fancy I see Nolan and his horse lying dead on the grass, like many others. Of my friend Charteris, Lord Wemyss's brother, I have to relate a remarkable instance of evil foreboding. While out together for a quiet ride on the previous evening we saw signs of the morrow's storm, when he gloomily persisted in saying, 'He wouldn't live through it.' 'Well,' I said, 'we have often been under fire together and we are still here. Why should not the same recur?' However, Fate ordains, and Charteris was killed by a round-shot as I parted from him on the ridge, and my gunners buried him where found."

Birmingham Daily Post 26th October 1889

CAMPS, QUARTERS, AND CASUAL PLACES (Macmillan).

Under the above title Mr. Archibald Forbes republishes 19 articles contributed to various magazines. Reminiscences of the Franco-German war, stories of Indian life, recent impressions of Lucknow and Cawnpur, and fragments of military history make up an eminently readable but necessarily discursive volume. The "Version of Balaclava" drawn from information supplied by an officer of "C" Troop R.H.A. differs in significant details from Kinglake's narrative. This evidence of a cool-headed eye-witness of the charge of the Heavy Brigade, which the troop followed at a short distance, throws light upon several points of importance. Later the troop was halted on the slope of the south valley when the Light Brigade was launched on its career of glory and disaster. Across its front passed the wreck of the splendid squadrons, and its officers gave such aid to the wounded as was possible. Close to the troop came Lord Cardigan, who, seeing the remains of the 8th Hussars retiring, placed himself at their head. Kinglake does not seem to have been aware of the presence of C Troop on the field, or he would doubtless have sought information from its ranks. In "The Warfare of the Future" Mr. Forbes sets himself to combat the idea that campaigns are now more swiftly decisive than before the days of breechloading rifles and field guns.

Books of the week, The Times 23rd Oct 1896

THE ROYAL ARTILLERY.

TO THE EDITOR OF THE TIMES.

Sir,—Having seen in The Times a few days ago a letter signed "Gunner," allow me to tell the public a few things about our Artillery. People have expressed their great surprise at the superiority of the practice of the Russian Artillery over our own. Is this to be wondered at, when men are sent to join the batteries in the Crimea who never fired a shot, either from their wretched carbines, or from a gun of any calibre? I assure you that many men were sent from the company to which I belong who had never fired one single round of service ammunition, excepting only three or four rounds of blank 6-pounder ammunition. With us all goes on as if we were in profound peace; no stir at out-quarters, not a round of ammunition allowed for practice; no wish expressed for officers to be working hard with their men at every sort of artillery work. There are numbers of us pining to be at work in the Crimea, but only little driblets are sent out now and then. Are the public aware that we have a very large force of artillery now in the kingdom that might be sent out, if only to fight as Minié riflemen attached to their own batteries? They can easily be spared from England by calling out militia artillery. A force of foot artillery armed in this way could always fill up vacancies in working the artillery, and would relieve the infantry much in defending the guns. You are always doing much for the army; would that you could purge the Ordnance-office, and see behind the scenes of the Deputy Adjutant-General's office of the Royal Artillery, where they are now concocting more troops of those most unserviceable 6-pounder Horse Artillery, to the detriment and disgust of the rest of the service.

I am, Sir, your most obedient servant,
ANOTHER GUNNER.

Army and Navy Club, Dec. 29, 1854.

The Royal Artillery, The Times 6th Jan 1855

21st October 1876.

THE BALACLAVA COMMEMORATION.

Unfortunately the good advice given by Colonel Trevelyan to those who wish to celebrate the gallant action at Balaclava—namely, that the Light and Heavy Brigade and Royal Artillery survivors should amalgamate and make the anniversary banquet a great success—has not had its desired effect. It appears that after a meeting a day or two since between Mr Aldous, late of the 17th Lancers, and Mr Woodham, late of the 11th Hussars, who was chairman of the committee for the banquet last year, no arrangement for a friendly fusion could be come to, and the result will be that Mr Aldous will bring with him the bulk of the survivors of the Light Brigade, while Mr Woodham, a Light Brigade man himself, will bring to a dinner at the Westminster Palace Hotel the survivors of the Heavy Brigade and of the Royal Horse Artillery, who took part in the charge. Wednesday next is the anniversary of the charge, and while one party will dine at the Westminster Palace Hotel, the Light Brigade will celebrate the day at the Freemasons' Tavern.

The Times, 26th October 1877.

BALACLAVA.—Yesterday being the anniversary (23d) of the battle of Balaclava the usual dinner of the officers who took part in that memorable engagement was held at Willis's Rooms, King-street, St. James's. Lieutenant-General Sir Edward C. Hodge, K.C.B., presided, supported by the following gentlemen :—General Wardlaw, C.B., Lieutenant-General Lord George Paget, Lieutenant-General Sir Thomas McMahon, C.B., Major-General White, Major-General Clarke, Sir George Wombwell, Lieutenant-Colonel Sir William Gordon, Colonel Mussenden, Colonel Trevelyan, Colonel Sandeman, Colonel Portal, Colonel Seagar, Colonel Swinfen, Colonel Godman, Major Wilkin, Major Everard Hutton, Major Jervis, Major Clowes, Major McCreagh, Major Manley, Major Coney, Major Duberley, Lieutenant-Colonel Lenox Prendergast, Deputy Inspector-General Anderson, Surgeon-General Moriat, C.B., V.C., Captain Scott, Captain Harrison, Captain Goad, Captain Clutterbuck, Captain Brigstocke, Captain Hampton Lewis, Mr. Pickworth, and Mr. Kelly. Covers were laid for 34.

Balaclava Dinner 1883.

THE CHARGE OF THE LIGHT BRIGADE.—Yesterday evening a number of officers, who took part in the memorable charge at Balaclava, celebrated the anniversary by dining together at Willis's Rooms. General the Earl of Lucan, G.C.B., presided, supported by General Sir Edward Cooper Hodge, K.C.B., General Clarke, C.B., General Sir Thomas M'Mahon, C.B., General Godman, Lieutenant-General Sir O. P. Beauchamp Walker. K.C.B., Lieutenant-General Shute, Lord Tredegar, Lord Bingham, Surgeon-General Mouat, C.B., V.C., Deputy-Inspector-General Anderson, Colonel Sir W. Gordon, Colonel Duberly, Colonel Ferguson (2d Life Guards), Colonel Swinfen, Colonel Davies, Colonel Lenox Prendergast, Major Manley, Major Coney, Major M'Creagh Thornhill, Major Wilkin, Captain Halford, Captain Teevan, Captain Scott. Fisher Rowe, and Captain Scott. At the Royal Aquarium, Westminster, 60 non-commissioned officers and men, five less than last year, dined together. Sergeant-Major Loy Smith, 11th Hussars, occupied the chair, the vice-chairman being Mr. W. Bird, 8th Hussars. Miss Mellon forwarded a bouquet for each survivor, with the motto " Welcome " attached. The proceedings were strictly private.

Officers Balaclava Dinner 25 Oct 1888.

BALACLAVA DINNER.—The surviving officers present at the battle of Balaclava held their customary anniversary dinner, in commemoration of the day, at Willis's Rooms, King-street, St. James's, yesterday evening. General Sir E. Cooper Hodge, G.C.B., presided, supported by General Sir Thomas McMahon, General W. C. Forrest, C.B., General G. C. Clarke, C.B., General Sir C. P. Beauchamp Walker, K.C.B., General Shute, C.B., General R. Godman, Lieutenant-General Sir Roger Palmer, Surgeon-General Mouat, V.C., C.B., Colonel Mussenden, Colonel L. Prendergast, Colonel Trevelyan, Colonel A. Elliott, Lieutenant-Colonel Sir William Gordon, Major M'Creagh Thornhill, Major G. Clowes, Captain Clutterbuck, and Captain E. R. Fisher-Rowe.

The Graphic October 28th, 1876; Issue 361
The anniversary of the Balaclava charge was celebrated on Wednesday. Lord George Paget presided at the officer's banquet at Willis's Rooms. The men of the Light Brigade dined together at the Westminster Palace Hotel, and those of the Heavy Brigade at Freemason's Tavern

The Balaclava Celibrations Aberdeen Weekly Journal, October 27th 1896

SCOTS GREYS ANNUAL REUNION.

The annual Balaclava dinner of the Royal Scots Greys (Glasgow) Association was held in Aucell's Restaurant on Saturday evening. The chair was taken by Sergeant D. Hunter, supported by Quartermaster-Sergeant Masterson, while Trooper Irvine officiated as croupier. There was a large gathering of old members, amongst the number being four survivors of the charge of the Heavy Brigade at Balaclava—Sergeant Whyte, Troopers W. Swanson, Gray, and Borland. Their physique showed the true types of heavy cavalry. The Chairman gave the toast of " The Queen," after which the Secretary, Trooper M'Kenzie, read a telegram from Colonel Saunderson, M.P., and letters from Lieutenants Hamilton, Houldsworth, and others regretting their inability to be present. The Secretary, in his report, intimated that the funds of the association were in a satisfactory condition, that the membership was steadily increasing, and advised young men leaving the regiment to join this association, which had for its object the assistance of old members during sickness or when out of employment. Quartermaster-Sergeant Masterson said he was more than pleased to see so many old friends who had helped to build up the reputation of "Second to None," and also to meet new friends who had upheld that proud title of their corps. From the reports which he had received he was satisfied that the superstructure was equal to the foundation, that the Scots Greys were able and willing to uphold the prestige of their country in the future as nobly as in the past. The usual toasts were proposed and duly honoured, after which a varied programme of vocal and instrumental music was rendered by members and friends.

Private Walter Fawke, 2nd Dragoons, Scots Greys.

1841 census	John Fawke	50	Baker	
St John St	Sarah	15		
Bromsgrove	Elizabeth	15		
	Joseph	14		
	John	12		
	William	7		
	Walter	5		

1851 census	John Fawke	57	Baker	b. Herefordshire, Ledbury
St John's St	Catherine	54?		Herefordshire, Bolston Court
	John	22	Baker's Son	Worcestershire, Bromsgrove
	William	18	Baker's son	Worcestershire, Bromsgrove
	Walter	15	Brush maker's App.	Worcestershire, Bromsgrove
	1861 census		not found of course	

1871 census	Walter Fawke	33	Professor of Athletics	b. Worcestershire, Bromsgrove
Station Road	Annie	22	wife, no occupation	b. Warwickshire, Birmingham
Bromsgrove	Sarah M.E.	2	daughter	Worcestershire, Birmingham
	Harriet Spittle	45	mother-in-law, no occ.	Warwickshire, Birmingham

1881 census	Walter Fawke	43	Teacher of Callisthenics	Worcestershire, Bromsgrove
High Street	Annie	30	Confectioner	Staffordshire, Wednesbury
Bromsgrove	Alice	2	daughter	Worcestershire, Bromsgrove
	Arthur	4	son	Worcestershire, Bromsgrove
	Kate Duffill	?	general servant (domestic)	Worcestershire, Bromsgrove

1889 Bromsgrove Messenger
'Professor Fawke, an old Scots Grey, gave awesome demonstrations of feats of strength, skill and dexterity, with the broadsword, sabre and scimitar.' '....now 50 years old'

1899   *'A Tribute to Walter Fawke, of Bromsgrove' by John Cotton, Chimes and Rhymes, 1903*
             'Read at a complimentary dinner to Mr. Fawke at the Dog and Pheasant Inn, Bromsgrove, November 29th,
1899, on the   occasion of his leaving the town. Mr Fawke was formerly a Drill Sergeant in the 'Scots
Greys'; a Crimean Soldier, and
             has been for many years a Professor of Physical Training.'

Long years ago, when Raglan sought **To bring the Russian power to nought,** **With him in Crimean regions fought.**	**On Alma's heights his sword flashed bare,** **At Inkerman he bore his share** **At Balaklava he was there.**
With Scarlett - not with Cardigan- **Our hero the red gauntlet ran;** **And valiantly he played the man.**	**If you would hear the stirring tale,** **Of how, amid the guns' hot hail,** **Our cavalry charged down the vale**
He came back wounded ; came to fill **In home-life's less dramatic bill** **A post more honourable still.**	**For he has done good work since then** **Through the past twenty years and ten,** **Building boys into better men.**

1891 census	Walter Fawke	56	Professor of Callisthenics	Worcestershire, Bromsgrove
75/76 High St	Annie	42	Confectioner	Wednesbury
	Harriet A	17	Teacher of Dancing	Worcestershire, Bromsgrove
	Arthur H	14	Scholar	Worcestershire, Bromsgrove
	Edith A	12	Scholar	Worcestershire, Bromsgrove
	3 gentlemen boarders			
	Emily Williams	15	Servant, domestic	Worcestershire, Bromsgrove

Comment from *The Story of Bromsgrove Cottage Hospital, J.T.Banks and C.E.Heydon, 1948*:
'He was a fine, tall man' and very popular. ..... He could cut a sheep in half with one blow of his sword, or cut an apple in two on a man's hand, with the same weapon.' He taught sports at The College school, and was on the Hospital Management Committee, for which he once organised a display by the Gymnastic Club, raising £3 13s 6d.

1901 census   not found
Information supplied by Jennie McGregor-Smith

Index

Index

365

Index

Index

Index

Index

Supplementary Information

Lightning Source UK Ltd.
Milton Keynes UK
22 January 2010

148976UK00001B/10/P

9 780955 655425